Handbook of Biometrics

Handbook of Biometrics

edited by

Anil K. Jain
Michigan State University, USA

Patrick Flynn
University of Notre Dame, USA

Arun A. Ross
West Virginia University, USA

 Springer

Anil K. Jain
Michigan State University
Dept. of Computer Science &
 Engineering
3115 Engineering Building
East Lansing MI 48824 USA
jain@cse.msu.edu

Patrick Flynn
University of Notre Dame
Dept. of Computer Science &
 Engineering
384 Fitzpatrick Hall
Notre Dame IN 46556-5637 USA
flynn@nd.edu

Arun A. Ross
West Virginia University
Dept. of Computer Science &
 Electrical Engineering
Morgantown WV 26506-6109 USA
arun.ross@mail.wvu.edu

ISBN-13: 978-1-4419-4375-0   e-ISBN-13: 978-0-387-71041-9

Printed on acid-free paper.

9 8 7 6 5 4 3 2 1

springer.com

Foreword

Nearly 40 years ago, IBM suggested that a computer user could be recognized at a computer terminal "By something he knows or memorizes.... By something he carries... By a personal physical characteristic". This analysis was done in the context of computer data security - remotely recognizing those authorized to access stored data - and specifically referenced voice recognition as a "personal physical characteristic" useful for human recognition, although automated handwriting, fingerprint, face, and hand geometry systems were, by 1970, also under development. Since that time, automatically recognizing persons by physical and behavioral characteristics has come to be known as "biometric authentication" and applications have broadened far beyond the remote recognition of computer terminal users. Today, biometric technologies are being used in all types of applications not foreseen by the early pioneers and not realizable with "something known" or "something carried", such as in visa and passport issuance, social service administration, and entertainment ticket management systems. There are new technologies available for these tasks: automated iris, hand vein, ear, gait, palm crease and 3-dimensional face recognition systems

This book, edited by Anil K. Jain of Michigan State University and two of his former students, Patrick J. Flynn and Arun Ross - now on the faculties of Notre Dame and West Virginia Universities, respectively- gives us a broad, yet detailed overview of the technologies, applications and implementation challenges of biometric authentication at its current state of development. Chapter authors are some of the best known, and in some cases, the earliest researchers in their fields. With this book, the story is not finished. Rather, it is only beginning. New technologies remain to be discovered. Challenges of incorporating new and existing technologies seamlessly into person-centric systems remain to be resolved. Understanding of the full impact of automated human recognition on both natural rights and social contracts remains to be acquired. In short, this book tells us the very first part of the story of biometric authentication. Future generations will tell us the rest. I fully expect this book to inspire current and future researchers and innovators to think in new ways about the technologies, applications and implications of automated human recognition.

James L. Wayman
San Jose State University

Preface

Biometrics is the science of recognizing the identity of a person based on the physical or behavioral attributes of the individual such as face, fingerprints, voice and iris. With the pronounced need for robust human recognition techniques in critical applications such as secure access control, international border crossing and law enforcement, biometrics has positioned itself as a viable technology that can be integrated into large-scale identity management systems. Biometric systems operate under the premise that many of the physical or behavioral characteristics of humans are distinctive to an individual, and that they can be reliably acquired via appropriately designed sensors and represented in a numerical format that lends itself to automatic decision-making in the context of identity management. Thus, these systems may be viewed as pattern recognition engines that can be incorporated in diverse markets.

While biometric *traits* such as fingerprints have had a long and successful history in forensics, the use of these traits in automated personal recognition systems is a fairly recent accomplishment. But now biometric *technology* is a rapidly evolving field with applications ranging from accessing one's computer to obtaining visa for international travel. The deployment of large-scale biometric systems in both commercial (e.g., grocery stores, Disney World, airports) and government (e.g., US-VISIT) applications has served to increase the public's awareness of this technology. This rapid growth in biometric system deployment has clearly highlighted the challenges associated in designing and integrating these systems. Indeed, the problem of biometric recognition is a "Grand Challenge" in its own right. The past five years has seen a significant growth in biometric research resulting in the development of innovative sensors, novel feature extraction and matching algorithms, enhanced test methodologies and cutting-edge applications. However, there is no single book that succinctly captures the advancements made in biometrics in recent years while presenting the reader with a fundamental understanding of basic concepts in biometrics. The purpose of this book is to address this void by inviting some of the most prominent researchers in biometrics to author individual chapters describing the fundamentals as well as the latest advances in their respective areas of expertise. The result is an edited volume that embodies most of the salient topics in biometric technology thereby giving its readers an understanding of the spectrum of work constituting the field of biometrics.

This book is divided into three logical sections. The first section discusses individual biometric modalities including fingerprints, face, iris, hand geometry, gait, ear, voice, palmprint, signature, teeth and hand vein. The chapters in this section describe some of the proven feature extraction and matching algorithms that have been designed for processing individual biometric modalities. The chapters in the second section discuss the concept of multibiometrics where two or more sources of biometric information are fused in order to enhance the recognition accuracy of these systems. The third section discusses the impact of deploying biometric systems in both civilian and government applications. Topics related to legal and privacy issues as well as forensic science are presented in this section. Finally, there is a discussion on biometric standards and the use of public domain datasets available for performance evaluation and comparison. Each chapter has an elaborate bibliography associated with it, thereby directing the reader to other pertinent literature on specific topics.

This book would not have been possible but for the cooperation and hardwork of the chapter authors. We would like to thank each one of them for their contribution to this project. Several authors also participated in the review process and their extensive comments were useful in refining individual chapters. Thanks are also due to Mohamed Abdel-Mottaleb (University of Miami), Nicolae Duta (Nuance), Max Houck (West Virginia University) and Steve Krawczyk (Michigan State University) for their valuable input during the review process. Special thanks to Julian Fierrez for providing detailed comments on a preliminary draft of the manuscript. Karthik Nandakumar, Abhishek Nagar and Keron Greene (Michigan State University) spent a considerable amount of time editing and typesetting the final manuscript. Their assistance is gratefully acknowledged.

This book has been designed for professionals composed of students, practitioners and researchers in biometrics, pattern recognition and computer security. It can be used as a primary textbook for an undergraduate biometrics class or as a secondary textbook for advanced-level students in computer science and electrical engineering. We hope that the concepts and ideas presented in this book will stimulate further research in this field even as biometric technology becomes an integral part of society in the 21st century.

Anil K. Jain, East Lansing, MI
Patrick J. Flynn, Notre Dame, IN
Arun Ross, Morgantown, WV
July 2007

Contents

1

Introduction to Biometrics

Anil K. Jain[1] and Arun Ross[2]

[1] Department of Computer Science and Engineering, Michigan State University, East Lansing, MI 48824 USA
jain@cse.msu.edu
[2] Lane Department of Computer Science and Electrical Engineering, West Virginia University, Morgantown, WV 26506 USA
arun.ross@mail.wvu.edu

1.1 Introduction

Biometrics is the science of establishing the identity of an individual based on the physical, chemical or behavioral attributes of the person. The relevance of biometrics in modern society has been reinforced by the need for large-scale identity management systems whose functionality relies on the accurate determination of an individual's identity in the context of several different applications. Examples of these applications include sharing networked computer resources, granting access to nuclear facilities, performing remote financial transactions or boarding a commercial flight. The proliferation of web-based services (e.g., online banking) and the deployment of decentralized customer service centers (e.g., credit cards) have further underscored the need for reliable identity management systems that can accommodate a large number of individuals.

The overarching task in an identity management system is the determination (or verification) of an individual's identity (or claimed identity).[3] Such an action may be necessary for a variety of reasons but the primary intention, in most applications, is to prevent impostors from accessing protected resources. Traditional methods of establishing a person's identity include knowledge-based (e.g., passwords) and token-based (e.g., ID cards) mechanisms, but these surrogate representations of identity can easily be lost, shared, manipulated or stolen thereby compromising the intended security. Biometrics[4] offers

---

[3] The *identity* of an individual may be viewed as the information associated with that person in a particular identity management system [15]. For example, a bank issuing credit cards typically associates a customer with her name, password, social security number, address and date of birth. Thus, the identity of the customer in this application will be defined by these personal attributes (i.e., name, address, etc.).

[4] The term *biometric authentication* is perhaps more appropriate than *biometrics* since the latter has been historically used in the field of statistics to refer to the

a natural and reliable solution to certain aspects of identity management by utilizing fully automated or semi-automated schemes to recognize individuals based on their biological characteristics [13]. By using biometrics it is possible to establish an identity based on *who you are*, rather than by *what you possess*, such as an ID card, or *what you remember*, such as a password (Figure 1.1). In some applications, biometrics may be used to supplement ID cards and passwords thereby imparting an additional level of security. Such an arrangement is often called a dual-factor authentication scheme.

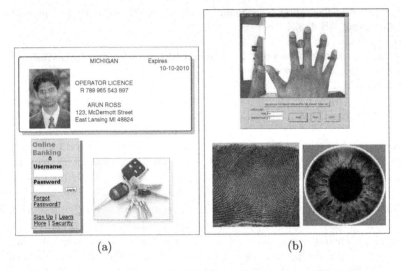

(a)   (b)

Fig. 1.1. Authentication schemes. (a) Traditional schemes use ID cards, passwords and keys to validate individuals and ensure that system resources are accessed by a legitimately enrolled individual. (b) With the advent of biometrics, it is now possible to establish an identity based on "who you are" rather than by "what you possess" or "what you remember".

The effectiveness of an authenticator (biometric or non-biometric) is based on its relevance to a particular application as well as its robustness to various types of malicious attacks. O'Gorman [29] lists a number of attacks that can be launched against authentication systems based on passwords and tokens: (a) client attack (e.g., guessing passwords, stealing tokens); (b) host attack (e.g., accessing plain text file containing passwords); (c) eavesdropping (e.g., "shoulder surfing" for passwords); (d) repudiation (e.g., claiming that token was misplaced); (e) trojan horse attack (e.g., installation of bogus log-in screen to steal passwords); and (f) denial of service (e.g., disabling the system by deliberately supplying an incorrect password several times). While some of these

---

analysis of biological (particularly medical) data [36]. For brevity sake, we adopt the term *biometrics* in this book.

attacks can be deflected by incorporating appropriate defense mechanisms, it is not possible to handle all the problems associated with the use of passwords and tokens.

Biometrics offers certain advantages such as negative recognition and non-repudiation that cannot be provided by tokens and passwords [32]. Negative recognition is the process by which a system determines that a certain individual is indeed enrolled in the system although the individual might deny it. This is especially critical in applications such as welfare disbursement where an impostor may attempt to claim multiple benefits (i.e., double dipping) under different names. Non-repudiation is a way to guarantee that an individual who accesses a certain facility cannot later deny using it (e.g., a person accesses a certain computer resource and later claims that an impostor must have used it under falsified credentials).

Biometric systems use a variety of physical or behavioral characteristics (Figure 1.2), including fingerprint, face, hand/finger geometry, iris, retina, signature, gait, palmprint, voice pattern, ear, hand vein, odor or the DNA information of an individual to establish identity [12, 36]. In the biometric literature, these characteristics are referred to as *traits*, *indicators*, *identifiers* or *modalities*. While biometric systems have their own limitations ([28]) they have an edge over traditional security methods in that they cannot be easily stolen or shared. Besides bolstering security, biometric systems also enhance user convenience by alleviating the need to design and remember passwords.

1.2 Operation of a biometric system

A biometric system is essentially a pattern recognition system that acquires biometric data from an individual, extracts a salient feature set from the data, compares this feature set against the feature set(s) stored in the database, and executes an action based on the result of the comparison. Therefore, a generic biometric system can be viewed as having four main modules: a sensor module; a quality assessment and feature extraction module; a matching module; and a database module. Each of these modules is described below.

1. **Sensor module**: A suitable biometric reader or scanner is required to acquire the raw biometric data of an individual. To obtain fingerprint images, for example, an optical fingerprint sensor may be used to image the friction ridge structure of the fingertip. The sensor module defines the human machine interface and is, therefore, pivotal to the performance of the biometric system. A poorly designed interface can result in a high failure-to-acquire rate (see Section 1.4) and, consequently, low user acceptability. Since most biometric modalities are acquired as images (exceptions include voice which is audio-based and odor which is chemical-based), the quality of the raw data is also impacted by the characteristics of the camera technology that is used.

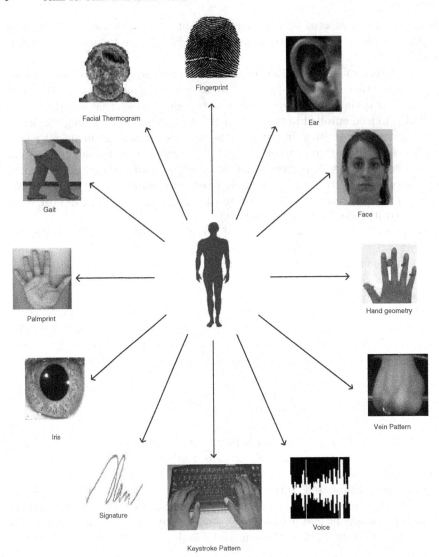

Fig. 1.2. Examples of biometric traits that can be used for authenticating an individual. Physical traits include fingerprint, iris, face and hand geometry while behavioral traits include signature, keystroke dynamics and gait.

2. **Quality assessment and feature extraction module**: The quality of the biometric data acquired by the sensor is first assessed in order to determine its suitability for further processing. Typically, the acquired data is subjected to a signal enhancement algorithm in order to improve its quality. However, in some cases, the quality of the data may be so poor that the user is asked to present the biometric data again. The biometric data is then processed and a set of salient discriminatory features extracted to represent the underlying trait. For example, the position and orientation of minutia points (local ridge and valley anomalies) in a fingerprint image are extracted by the feature extraction module in a fingerprint-based biometric system. During enrollment, this feature set is stored in the database and is commonly referred to as a *template*.

3. **Matching and decision-making module**: The extracted features are compared against the stored templates to generate match scores. In a fingerprint-based biometric system, the number of matching minutiae between the input and the template feature sets is determined and a match score reported. The match score may be moderated by the quality of the presented biometric data. The matcher module also encapsulates a decision making module, in which the match scores are used to either validate a claimed identity or provide a ranking of the enrolled identities in order to identify an individual.

4. **System database module**: The database acts as the repository of biometric information. During the enrollment process, the feature set extracted from the raw biometric sample (i.e., the template) is stored in the database (possibly) along with some biographic information (such as name, Personal Identification Number (PIN), address, etc.) characterizing the user. The data capture during the enrollment process may or may not be supervised by a human depending on the application. For example, a user attempting to create a new computer account in her biometric-enabled workstation may proceed to enroll her biometrics without any supervision; a person desiring to use a biometric-enabled ATM, on the other hand, will have to enroll her biometrics in the presence of a bank officer after presenting her non-biometric credentials.

The template of a user can be extracted from a single biometric sample, or generated by processing multiple samples. Thus, the minutiae template of a finger may be extracted after mosaicing multiple samples of the same finger. Some systems store multiple templates in order to account for the intra-class variations associated with a user. Face recognition systems, for instance, may store multiple templates of an individual, with each template corresponding to a different facial pose with respect to the camera. Depending on the application, the template can be stored in the central database of the biometric system or be recorded on a token (e.g., smart card) issued to the individual.

In the face recognition literature, the raw biometric images stored in the database are often referred to as *gallery images* while those acquired during authentication are known as *probe images*. These are synonymous with the terms *stored images* and *query* or *input images*, respectively.

1.3 Verification versus identification

Depending on the application context, a biometric system may operate either in the verification or identification mode (see Figure 1.3). In the verification mode, the system validates a person's identity by comparing the captured biometric data with her own biometric template(s) stored in the system database. In such a system, an individual who desires to be recognized claims an identity, usually via a PIN, a user name or a smart card, and the system conducts a one-to-one comparison to determine whether the claim is true or not (e.g., "Does this biometric data belong to Bob?"). Verification is typically used for positive recognition, where the aim is to prevent multiple people from using the same identity.

In the identification mode, the system recognizes an individual by searching the templates of all the users in the database for a match. Therefore, the system conducts a one-to-many comparison to establish an individual's identity (or fails if the subject is not enrolled in the system database) without the subject having to claim an identity (e.g., "Whose biometric data is this?"). Identification is a critical component in negative recognition applications where the system establishes whether the person is who she (implicitly or explicitly) denies to be. The purpose of negative recognition is to prevent a single person from using multiple identities. Identification may also be used in positive recognition for convenience (the user is not required to claim an identity). While traditional methods of personal recognition such as passwords, PINs, keys, and tokens may work for positive recognition, negative recognition can only be established through biometrics.

1.4 Performance of a biometric system

Unlike password-based systems, where a *perfect* match between two alphanumeric strings is necessary in order to validate a user's identity, a biometric system seldom encounters two samples of a user's biometric trait that result in exactly the same feature set. This is due to imperfect sensing conditions (e.g., noisy fingerprint due to sensor malfunction), alterations in the user's biometric characteristic (e.g., respiratory ailments impacting speaker recognition), changes in ambient conditions (e.g., inconsistent illumination levels in face recognition) and variations in the user's interaction with the sensor (e.g., occluded iris or partial fingerprints). Thus, seldom do two feature sets originating from the same biometric trait of a user look exactly the same. In

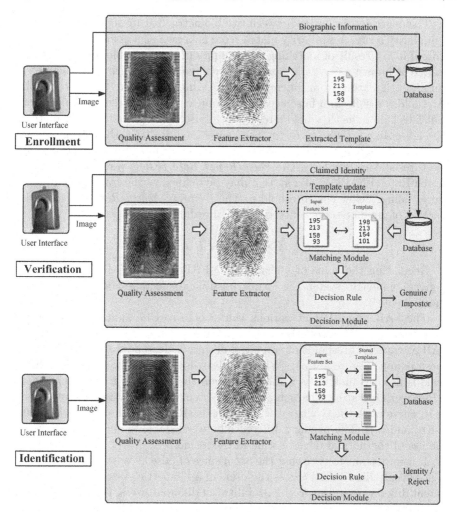

Fig. 1.3. Enrollment and recognition (verification and identification) stages of a biometric system. The quality assessment module determines if the sensed data can be effectively used by the feature extractor. Note that the process of quality assessment in itself may entail the extraction of some features from the sensed data.

fact, a perfect match between two feature sets might indicate the possibility that a replay attack is being launched against the system. The variability observed in the biometric feature set of an individual is referred to as *intra*-class variation, and the variability between feature sets originating from two different individuals is known as *inter*-class variation. A useful feature set exhibits small intra-class variation and large inter-class variation.

The degree of similarity between two biometric feature sets is indicated by a similarity score. A similarity match score is known as a *genuine* or *authentic* score if it is a result of matching two samples of the same biometric trait of a user. It is known as an *impostor* score if it involves comparing two biometric samples originating from different users. An impostor score that exceeds the threshold η results in a false accept (or, a false match), while a genuine score that falls below the threshold η results in a false reject (or, a false non-match). The *False Accept Rate (FAR)* (or, the False Match Rate (FMR)) of a biometric system can therefore be defined as the fraction of impostor scores exceeding the threshold η. Similarly, the *False Reject Rate (FRR)* (or, the False Non-match Rate (FNMR))[5] of a system may be defined as the fraction of genuine scores falling below the threshold η. The *Genuine Accept Rate (GAR)* is the fraction of genuine scores exceeding the threshold η. Therefore,

$$GAR = 1 - FRR. \tag{1.1}$$

Regulating the value of η changes the FRR and the FAR values, but for a given biometric system, it is not possible to decrease both these errors simultaneously.

The FAR and FRR at various values of η can be summarized using a Detection Error Tradeoff (DET) curve [21] that plots the FRR against the FAR at various thresholds on a *normal deviate* scale and interpolates between these points (Figure 1.4(a)). When a linear, logarithmic or semi-logarithmic scale is used to plot these error rates, then the resulting graph is known as a Receiver Operating Characteristic (ROC) curve [7]. In many instances, the ROC curve plots the GAR (rather than the FRR) against the FAR (see Figure 1.4(b) and (c)). The primary difference between the DET and ROC curves is the use of the normal deviate scale in the former.

It is important to note that the occurrence of false accepts and false rejects is not evenly distributed across the users of a biometric system. There are inherent differences in the "recognizability" of different users. Doddington et al. [6] identify four categories of biometric users based on these inherent differences. Although this categorization (more popularly known as "Doddington's zoo") was originally made in the context of speaker recognition, it is applicable to other biometric modalities as well.

1. Sheep represent users whose biometric feature sets are very distinctive and exhibit low intra-class variations. Therefore, these users are expected to have low false accept and false reject errors.
2. Goats refer to users who are prone to false rejects. The biometric feature sets of such users typically exhibit large intra-class variations.

---

[5] It behooves us to point out that, strictly speaking, FMR and FNMR are not always synonymous with FAR and FRR, respectively (see [20] and [19]). However, in this book we treat them as being equivalent.

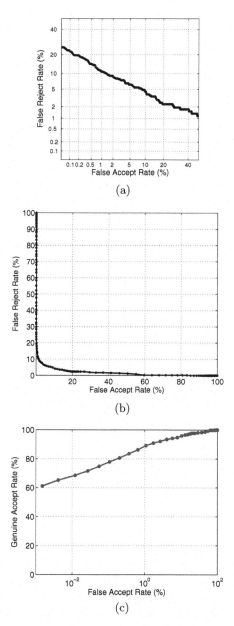

Fig. 1.4. The performance of a biometric system can be summarized using DET and ROC curves. In this example, the performance curves are computed using the match scores of the **Face-G** matcher from the NIST BSSR1 database [25]. The graph in (a) shows a DET curve that plots FRR against FAR in the normal deviate scale. In (b) a ROC curve plots FRR against FAR in the linear scale, while in (c) a ROC curve plots GAR against FAR in a semi-logarithmic scale.

3. Lambs are users whose biometric feature set overlaps extensively with those of other individuals. The biometric feature sets of these users have low inter-class variations. Thus, a randomly chosen user (from the target population) has a high probability of being accepted as a lamb than as a sheep. The false accept rate associated with these users is typically high.
4. Wolves indicate individuals who are successful in manipulating their biometric trait (especially behavioral traits) in order to impersonate legitimately enrolled users of a system. Therefore, these users can increase the false accept rate of the system.

Doddington et al. [6] discuss the use of statistical testing procedures to detect the presence of goats, lambs and wolves in a voice biometric system. A combination of the F-test, Kruskal Wallis test and Durbin test is used to establish the occurrence of these categories of users in the 1998 NIST database of speech segments that was used in the evaluation of speaker recognition algorithms (http://www.nist.gov/speech/tests/spk/1998/current_plan. htm).

Besides the two types of errors (viz., false accept and false reject) indicated above, a biometric system can encounter other types of failures as well. The *Failure to Acquire (FTA)* (also known as Failure to Capture (FTC)) rate denotes the proportion of times the biometric device fails to capture a sample when the biometric characteristic is presented to it. This type of error typically occurs when the device is not able to locate a biometric signal of sufficiently good quality (e.g., an extremely faint fingerprint or an occluded face image). The FTA rate is also impacted by sensor wear and tear. Thus, periodic sensor maintenance is instrumental for the efficient functioning of a biometric system. The *Failure to Enroll (FTE)* rate denotes the proportion of users that cannot be successfully enrolled in a biometric system. User training may be necessary to ensure that an individual interacts with a biometric system appropriately in order to facilitate the acquisition of good quality biometric data. This necessitates the design of robust and efficient user interfaces that can assist an individual both during enrollment and recognition.

There is a tradeoff between the FTE rate and the perceived system accuracy as measured by FAR/FRR. FTE errors typically occur when the system rejects poor quality inputs during enrollment; consequently, if the threshold on quality is high, the system database contains only good quality templates and the perceived system accuracy improves. Because of the interdependence among the failure rates and error rates, all these rates (i.e., FTE, FTC, FAR, FRR) constitute important performance specifications of a biometric system, and should be reported during system evaluation along with the target population using the system.

The performance of a biometric system may also be summarized using other single-valued measures such as the Equal Error Rate (EER) and the d-prime value. The EER refers to that point in a DET curve where the FAR equals the FRR; a lower EER value, therefore, indicates better performance.

The d-prime value (d') measures the separation between the means of the genuine and impostor probability distributions in standard deviation units and is defined as,

$$d' = \frac{\sqrt{2}\,|\,\mu_{genuine} - \mu_{impostor}\,|}{\sqrt{\sigma_{genuine}^2 + \sigma_{impostor}^2}},$$

where the μ's and σ's are the means and standard deviations, respectively, of the genuine and impostor distributions. A higher d-prime value indicates better performance. If the genuine and impostor distributions indeed follow a normal (Gaussian) distribution with equal variance (a very unlikely situation in the practical biometric domain), then d' reduces to the normal deviate value [35]. Poh and Bengio [31] introduce another single-valued measure known as F-Ratio which is defined as,

$$\text{F-ratio} = \frac{\mu_{genuine} - \mu_{impostor}}{\sigma_{genuine} + \sigma_{impostor}}.$$

If the genuine and impostor distributions are Gaussian, then the EER and F-ratio are related according to the following expression:

$$\text{EER} = \frac{1}{2} - \frac{1}{2}\text{erf}\left(\frac{\text{F-ratio}}{\sqrt{2}}\right),$$

where

$$\text{erf}(x) = \frac{2}{\sqrt{\pi}}\int_0^x e^{-t^2}\,dt.$$

In the case of identification, the input feature set is compared against all templates residing in the database in order to determine the top match (i.e, the best match). The top match can be determined by examining the match scores pertaining to all the comparisons and reporting the identity of the template corresponding to the largest similarity score. The *identification rate* indicates the proportion of times a previously enrolled individual is successfully mapped to the correct identity in the system. Here, we assume that the question being asked is, "Does the top match correspond to the correct identity?" An alternate question could be, "Does any one of the top k matches correspond to the correct identity?" (see [23]). The rank-k identification rate, R_k, indicates the proportion of times the correct identity occurs in the top k matches as determined by the match score. Rank-k performance can be summarized using the Cumulative Match Characteristic (CMC) curve ([23]) that plots R_k against k, for $k = 1, 2, \ldots M$ with M being the number of enrolled users. The relationship between CMC and DET/ROC curves has been discussed by Grother and Phillips [9], and Bolle at al. [1].

The biometric of choice for a particular application is primarily dictated by the error rates and failure rates discussed above. Other factors such as the cost of the system, throughput rate, user acceptance, ease of use, robustness of the sensor, etc. also determine the suitability of a biometric system for an application.

1.5 Applications of biometrics

Establishing the identity of a person with high confidence is becoming critical in a number of applications in our vastly interconnected society. Questions like "Is she really who she claims to be?", "Is this person authorized to use this facility?" or "Is he in the watchlist posted by the government?" are routinely being posed in a variety of scenarios ranging from issuing a driver's licence to gaining entry into a country. The need for reliable user authentication techniques has increased in the wake of heightened concerns about security, and rapid advancements in networking, communication and mobility. Thus, biometrics is being increasingly incorporated in several different applications. These applications can be categorized into three main groups (see Table 1.1):

1. Commercial applications such as computer network login, electronic data security, e-commerce, Internet access, ATM or credit card use, physical access control, mobile phone, PDA, medical records management, distance learning, etc.
2. Government applications such as national ID card, managing inmates in a correctional facility, driver's license, social security, welfare-disbursement, border control, passport control, etc.
3. Forensic applications such as corpse identification, criminal investigation, parenthood determination, etc.

Table 1.1. Authentication solutions employing biometrics can be used in a variety of applications which depend on reliable user authentication mechanisms.

FORENSICS	GOVERNMENT	COMMERCIAL
Corpse identification	National ID card	ATM
Criminal investigation	Drivers license; voter registration	Access control; computer login
Parenthood determination	Welfare disbursement	Mobile phone
Missing children	Border crossing	E-commerce; Internet; banking; smart card

Examples of a few applications where biometrics is being used for authenticating individuals are presented below (also see Figure 1.5).

1. The *Schiphol Privium* scheme at Amsterdam's Schipol airport employs iris-scan smart cards to speed up the immigration procedure. Passengers

who are voluntarily enrolled in this scheme insert their smart card at the gate and peek into a camera; the camera acquires the eye image of the traveler and processes it to locate the iris, and computes the Iriscode [3]; the computed Iriscode is compared with the data residing in the smart card to complete user verification. A similar scheme is also being used to verify the identity of Schiphol airport employees working in high-security areas. This is a good example of a biometric system that is being used to enhance user convenience while improving security.

2. The Ben Gurion International Airport at Tel Aviv employs automated hand geometry-based identification kiosks to enable Israeli citizens and frequent international travelers to rapidly go through the passport inspection process. Currently more than 160,000 Israeli citizens are enrolled in this program. The kiosk-based system uses the credit card of the traveler to begin the verification process. The hand geometry information is then used for validating the traveler's identity and ensuring that the individual is not a security hazard. The automated inspection process takes less than 20 seconds and has considerably reduced the waiting time for passengers.

3. Some financial institutions in Japan have installed palm-vein authentication systems in their ATMs to help validate the identity of a customer intending to conduct a transaction. A contactless sensor is used to image the vein pattern pertaining to the customer's palm using a near infrared lighting source. Thus, a person does not have to directly place the palm on the device.

4. Kroger, a US supermarket chain, has deployed fingerprint scanners in some of its stores in order to help customers cash payroll checks or render payment after a purchase. Interested customers can enroll their index finger along with details of their credit/debit card (or electronic check); the customer's driver's licence is used to validate the identity during the time of enrollment.

5. The United States Visitor and Immigration Status Indicator Technology (US-VISIT) is a border security system that has been deployed at 115 airports, 15 seaports and in the secondary inspection areas of the 50 busiest land ports of entry. Foreign visitors entering the United States have their left and right index fingers scanned by a fingerprint sensor. The biometric data acquired is used to validate an individual's travel documents at the port of entry. A biometric exit procedure has also been adopted in some airports and seaports to facilitate a visitor's future trips to the country. Although two-print information is currently being used, the system might employ all ten fingers of a person in the future; this would ensure that the US-VISIT fingerprint database is compatible with the ten-print database maintained by the FBI in its Integrated Automated Fingerprint Identification System (IAFIS - see http://www.fbi.gov/hq/cjisd/iafis.htm).

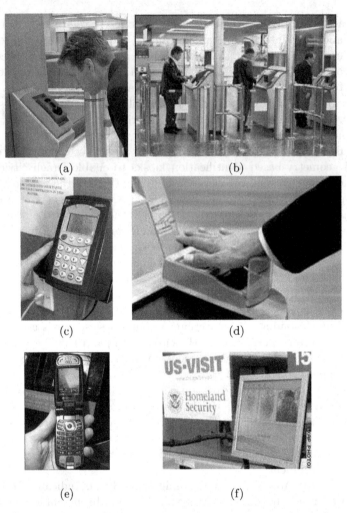

Fig. 1.5. Biometric systems are being deployed in various applications. (a) The Schiphol Privium program at the Amsterdam airport uses iris scans to validate the identity of a traveler (`www.cl.cam.ac.uk`). (b) The Ben Gurion airport in Tel Aviv uses Express Card entry kiosks fitted with hand geometry systems for security and immigration (`www.airportnet.org`). (c) A few Kroger stores in Texas use fingerprint verification systems that enable customers to render payment at the check-out counter. (`www.detnews.com`). (d) Contactless palm-vein systems have been installed in some ATMs in Japan (`www.fujitsu.com`). (e) A cell-phone that validates authorized users using fingerprints and allows them access to functionalities such as mobile-banking (`www.mobileburn.com`). (f) The US-VISIT program currently employs two-print information to validate the travel documents of visitors to the United States (`www.dhs.gov`).

1.6 Biometric characteristics

A number of biometric characteristics are being used in various applications. Each biometric has its pros and cons and, therefore, the choice of a biometric trait for a particular application depends on a variety of issues besides its matching performance (Table 1.2). Jain et al. [12] have identified seven factors that determine the suitability of a physical or a behavioral trait to be used in a biometric application.

1. **Universality**: Every individual accessing the application should possess the trait.
2. **Uniqueness**: The given trait should be sufficiently different across individuals comprising the population.
3. **Permanence**: The biometric trait of an individual should be sufficiently invariant over a period of time with respect to the matching algorithm. A trait that changes significantly over time is not a useful biometric.
4. **Measurability**: It should be possible to acquire and digitize the biometric trait using suitable devices that do not cause undue inconvenience to the individual. Furthermore, the acquired raw data should be amenable to processing in order to extract representative feature sets.
5. **Performance**: The recognition accuracy and the resources required to achieve that accuracy should meet the constraints imposed by the application.
6. **Acceptability**: Individuals in the target population that will utilize the application should be willing to present their biometric trait to the system.
7. **Circumvention**: This refers to the ease with which the trait of an individual can be imitated using artifacts (e.g., fake fingers), in the case of physical traits, and mimicry, in the case of behavioral traits.

No single biometric is expected to effectively meet all the requirements (e.g., accuracy, practicality, cost) imposed by all applications (e.g., Digital Rights Management (DRM), access control, welfare distribution). In other words, no biometric is *ideal* but a number of them are *admissible*. The relevance of a specific biometric to an application is established depending upon the nature and requirements of the application, and the properties of the biometric characteristic. A brief introduction to some of the commonly used biometric characteristics is given below:

1. **Face**: Face recognition is a non-intrusive method, and facial attributes are probably the most common biometric features used by humans to recognize one another. The applications of facial recognition range from a static, controlled "mug-shot" authentication to a dynamic, uncontrolled face identification in a cluttered background. The most popular approaches to face recognition [17] are based on either (i) the location and shape of facial attributes, such as the eyes, eyebrows, nose, lips, and chin and their spatial relationships, or (ii) the overall (global) analysis of the face image

that represents a face as a weighted combination of a number of canonical faces. While the authentication performance of the face recognition systems that are commercially available is reasonable [30], they impose a number of restrictions on how the facial images are obtained, often requiring a fixed and simple background with controlled illumination. These systems also have difficulty in matching face images captured from two different views, under different illumination conditions, and at different times. It is questionable whether the face itself, without any contextual information, is a sufficient basis for recognizing a person from a large number of identities with an extremely high level of confidence. In order for a facial recognition system to work well in practice, it should automatically (i) detect whether a face is present in the acquired image; (ii) locate the face if there is one; and (iii) recognize the face from a general viewpoint (i.e., from any pose) under different ambient conditions.

2. **Fingerprint**: Humans have used fingerprints for personal identification for many decades. The matching (i.e., identification) accuracy using fingerprints has been shown to be very high [37]. A fingerprint is the pattern of ridges and valleys on the surface of a fingertip whose formation is determined during the first seven months of fetal development. It has been empirically determined that the fingerprints of identical twins are different and so are the prints on each finger of the same person [19]. Today, most fingerprint scanners cost less than US $50 when ordered in large quantities and the marginal cost of embedding a fingerprint-based biometric in a system (e.g., laptop computer) has become affordable in a large number of applications. The accuracy of the currently available fingerprint recognition systems is adequate for authentication systems in several applications, particularly forensics. Multiple fingerprints of a person (e.g., ten-prints used in IAFIS) provide additional information to allow for large-scale identification involving millions of identities. One problem with large-scale fingerprint recognition systems is that they require a huge amount of computational resources, especially when operating in the identification mode. Finally, fingerprints of a small fraction of the population may be unsuitable for automatic identification because of genetic factors, aging, environmental or occupational reasons (e.g., manual workers may have a large number of cuts and bruises on their fingerprints that keep changing).

3. **Hand geometry**: Hand geometry recognition systems are based on a number of measurements taken from the human hand, including its shape, size of palm, and the lengths and widths of the fingers [39]. Commercial hand geometry-based authentication systems have been installed in hundreds of locations around the world. The technique is very simple, relatively easy to use, and inexpensive. Environmental factors such as dry weather or individual anomalies such as dry skin do not appear to adversely affect the authentication accuracy of hand geometry-based systems. However, the geometry of the hand is not known to be very distinc-

tive and hand geometry-based recognition systems cannot be scaled up for systems requiring identification of an individual from a large population. Furthermore, hand geometry information may not be invariant during the growth period of children. In addition, an individual's jewelry (e.g., rings) or limitations in dexterity (e.g., from arthritis), may pose challenges in extracting the correct hand geometry information. The physical size of a hand geometry-based system is large, and it cannot be embedded in certain devices like laptops. There are authentication systems available that are based on measurements of only a few fingers (typically, index and middle) instead of the entire hand. These devices are smaller than those used for hand geometry, but still much larger than those used for procuring certain other traits (e.g., fingerprint, face, voice).

4. **Palmprint**: The palms of the human hands contain pattern of ridges and valleys much like the fingerprints. The area of the palm is much larger than the area of a finger and, as a result, palmprints are expected to be even more distinctive than the fingerprints [38]. Since palmprint scanners need to capture a large area, they are bulkier and more expensive than the fingerprint sensors. Human palms also contain additional distinctive features such as principal lines and wrinkles that can be captured even with a lower resolution scanner, which would be cheaper. Finally, when using a high-resolution palmprint scanner, all the features of the hand such as geometry, ridge and valley features (e.g., minutiae and singular points such as deltas), principal lines, and wrinkles may be combined to build a highly accurate biometric system.

5. **Iris**: The iris is the annular region of the eye bounded by the pupil and the sclera (white of the eye) on either side. The visual texture of the iris is formed during fetal development and stabilizes during the first two years of life (the pigmentation, however, continues changing over an extended period of time. The complex iris texture carries very distinctive information useful for personal recognition [4]. The accuracy and speed of currently deployed iris-based recognition systems is promising and support the feasibility of large-scale identification systems based on iris information. Each iris is distinctive and even the irises of identical twins are different. It is possible to detect contact lenses printed with a fake iris (see [3]). The hippus movement of the eye may also be used as a measure of liveness for this biometric. Although early iris-based recognition systems required considerable user participation and were expensive, the newer systems have become more user-friendly and cost-effective [26, 8]. While iris systems have a very low False Accept Rate (FAR) compared to other biometric traits, the False Reject Rate (FRR) of these systems can be rather high [11].

6. **Keystroke**: It is hypothesized that each person types on a keyboard in a characteristic way. This biometric is not expected to be unique to each individual but it may be expected to offer sufficient discriminatory information to permit identity verification [22]. Keystroke dynamics is a be-

havioral biometric; one may expect to observe large intra-class variations in a person's typing patterns due to changes in emotional state, position of the user with respect to the keyboard, type of keyboard used, etc. The keystrokes of a person could be monitored unobtrusively as that person is keying in information. This biometric permits "continuous verification" of an individual's identity over a session after the person logs in using a stronger biometric such as fingerprint or iris.

7. **Signature**: The way a person signs her name is known to be a characteristic of that individual [24, 16]. Although signatures require contact with the writing instrument and an effort on the part of the user, they have been accepted in government, legal, and commercial transactions as a method of authentication. With the proliferation of PDAs and Tablet PCs, on-line signature may emerge as the biometric of choice in these devices. Signature is a behavioral biometric that changes over a period of time and is influenced by the physical and emotional conditions of the signatories. Signatures of some people vary substantially: even successive impressions of their signature are significantly different. Further, professional forgers may be able to reproduce signatures that fool the signature verification system [10].

8. **Voice**: Voice is a combination of physical and behavioral biometric characteristics [2]. The physical features of an individual's voice are based on the shape and size of the appendages (e.g., vocal tracts, mouth, nasal cavities, and lips) that are used in the synthesis of the sound. These physical characteristics of human speech are invariant for an individual, but the behavioral aspect of the speech changes over time due to age, medical conditions (such as common cold), emotional state, etc. Voice is also not very distinctive and may not be appropriate for large-scale identification. A text-dependent voice recognition system is based on the utterance of a fixed predetermined phrase. A text-independent voice recognition system recognizes the speaker independent of what she speaks. A text-independent system is more difficult to design than a text-dependent system but offers more protection against fraud. A disadvantage of voice-based recognition is that speech features are sensitive to a number of factors such as background noise. Speaker recognition is most appropriate in telephone-based applications but the voice signal is typically degraded in quality by the communication channel.

9. **Gait**: Gait refers to the manner in which a person walks, and is one of the few biometric traits that can be used to recognize people at a distance. Therefore, this trait is very appropriate in surveillance scenarios where the identity of an individual can be surreptitiously established. Most gait recognition algorithms attempt to extract the human silhouette in order to derive the spatio-temporal attributes of a moving individual. Hence, the selection of a good model to represent the human body is pivotal to the efficient functioning of a gait recognition system. Some algorithms use the optic flow associated with a set of dynamically extracted moving points

on the human body to describe the gait of an individual [27]. Gait-based systems also offer the possibility of tracking an individual over an extended period of time. However, the gait of an individual is affected by several factors including the choice of footwear, nature of clothing, affliction of the legs, walking surface, etc.

Table 1.2. The false accept and false reject error rates (FAR and FRR) associated with the fingerprint, face, voice and iris modalities. The accuracy estimates of biometric systems depend on a number of test conditions including the sensor employed, acquisition protocol used, subject disposition, number of subjects, number of biometric samples per subject, demographic profile of test subjects, subject habituation, time lapse between data acquisition, etc.

Biometric Trait	Test	Test Conditions	False Reject Rate	False Accept Rate
Fingerprint	FVC 2004 [18]	Exaggerated skin distortion, rotation	2%	2%
Fingerprint	FpVTE 2003 [37]	US Government operational data	0.1%	1%
Face	FRVT 2002 [30]	Varied lighting, outdoor/indoor, time	10%	1%
Voice	NIST 2004 [33]	Text independent, multi-lingual	5-10%	2-5%
Iris	ITIRT 2005 [11]	Indoor environment, multiple visits	0.99%	0.94%

1.7 Summary

Rapid advancements in the field of communications, computer networking and transportation, coupled with heightened concerns about identity fraud and national security, has resulted in a pronounced need for reliable and efficient identity management schemes in a myriad of applications. The process of identity management in the context of a specific application involves the creation, maintenance and obliteration of identities while ensuring that an impostor does not fraudulently gain privileges associated with a legitimately enrolled individual. Traditional authentication techniques based on passwords and tokens are limited in their ability to address issues such as negative recognition and non-repudiation. The advent of biometrics has served to address some of the shortcomings of traditional authentication methods. Biometric systems use the physical and behavioral characteristics of an individual such as fingerprint, face, hand geometry, iris, gait and voice to establish identity.

A broad spectrum of establishments can engage the services of a biometric system including travel and transportation, financial institutions, health care, law enforcement agencies and various government sectors.

The deployment of biometrics in civilian and government applications has raised questions related to the privacy accorded to an enrolled individual [5]. Specifically, questions such as (i) "Will biometric data be used to track people covertly thereby violating their right to privacy?", (ii) "Can the medical condition of a person be surreptitiously elicited from the raw biometric data?", (iii) "Will the acquired biometric data be used only for the intended purpose, or will it be used for previously unexpressed functions, hence resulting in *functionality creep?*", (iv) "Will various biometric databases be linked in order to deduce an individual's social and financial profile?", and (v) "What are the consequences of compromising a user's biometric data?", have advocated societal concerns about the use of biometric solutions in large-scale applications. The promotion of Privacy-Enhancing Technologies (PETs) can assuage some of the legitimate concerns associated with biometric-enabled technology [34, 14]. For example, the use of personal smart cards to store and process the biometric template of an individual can mitigate public concerns related to placing biometric information in a centralized database. Apart from technological solutions to address privacy concerns, government regulations are also required in order to prevent the inappropriate transmission, exchange and processing of biometric data.

References

1. R. Bolle, J. Connell, S. Pankanti, N. Ratha, and A. Senior. The Relationship Between the ROC Curve and the CMC. In *Proceedings of Fourth IEEE Workshop on Automatic Identification Advanced Technologies (AutoID)*, pages 15–20, Buffalo, USA, October 2005.
2. J. P. Campbell. Speaker Recognition: a Tutorial. *Proceedings of the IEEE*, 85(9):1437–1462, September 1997.
3. J. Daugman. Recognizing Persons by their Iris Patterns. In A. K. Jain, R. Bolle, and S. Pankanti, editors, *Biometrics: Personal Identification in Networked Society*, pages 103–122. Kluwer Academic Publishers, London, UK, 1999.
4. J. Daugman. How Iris Recognition Works? *IEEE Transactions on Circuits and Systems for Video Technology*, 14(1):21–30, 2004.
5. S. Davies. Touching Big Brother: How Biometric Technology Will Fuse Flesh and Machine. *Information Technology and People*, 7(4), 1994.
6. G. Doddington, W. Liggett, A. Martin, M. Przybocki, and D. Reynolds. Sheep, Goats, Lambs and Wolves: A Statistical Analysis of Speaker Performance in the NIST 1998 Speaker Recognition Evaluation. In *CD-ROM Proceedings of the Fifth International Conference on Spoken Language Processing (ICSLP)*, Sydney, Australia, November/December 1998.
7. J. Egan. *Signal Detection Theory and ROC Analysis*. Academic Press, New York, 1975.

8. C. L. Fancourt, L. Bogoni, K. J. Hanna, Y. Guo, R. P. Wildes, N. Takahashi, and U. Jain. Iris Recognition at a Distance. In *Fifth International Conference on Audio- and Video-based Biometric Person Authentication (AVBPA)*, pages 1–13, Rye Brook, USA, July 2005.

9. P. Grother and P. J. Phillips. Models of Large Population Recognition Performance. In *Proceedings of the IEEE Computer Society Conference on Computer Vision and Pattern Recognition (CVPR)*, volume 2, pages 68–75, Washington D.C., USA, June/July 2004.

10. W. R. Harrison. *Suspect Documents, their Scientific Examination*. Nelson-Hall Publishers, 1981.

11. International Biometric Group. Independent Testing of Iris Recognition Technology: Final Report. Available at http://www.biometricgroup.com/reports/public/ITIRT.html, May 2005.

12. A. K. Jain, R. Bolle, and S. Pankanti, editors. *Biometrics: Personal Identification in Networked Society*. Kluwer Academic Publishers, 1999.

13. A. K. Jain, A. Ross, and S. Prabhakar. An Introduction to Biometric Recognition. *IEEE Transactions on Circuits and Systems for Video Technology, Special Issue on Image- and Video-Based Biometrics*, 14(1):4–20, January 2004.

14. S. Kenny and J. J. Borking. The Value of Privacy Engineering. *The Journal of Information, Law and Technology (JILT)*, 7(1), 2002.

15. S. Kent and L. Millett. *Who Goes There? Authentication Technologies through the Lens of Privacy*. National Academy Press, 2003.

16. L. Lee, T. Berger, and E. Aviczer. Reliable On-Line Human Signature Verification Systems. *IEEE Transactions on Pattern Analysis and Machine Intelligence*, 18(6):643–647, June 1996.

17. S. Z. Li and Anil K. Jain, editors. *Handbook of Face Recognition*. Springer-Verlag, 2005.

18. D. Maio, D. Maltoni, R. Cappelli, J. L. Wayman, and A. K. Jain. FVC2004: Third Fingerprint Verification Competition. In *Proceedings of International Conference on Biometric Authentication (ICBA)*, pages 1–7, Hong Kong, China, July 2004.

19. D. Maltoni, D. Maio, A. K. Jain, and S. Prabhakar. *Handbook of Fingerprint Recognition*. Springer-Verlag, 2003.

20. A. J. Mansfield and J. L. Wayman. Best Practices in Testing and Reporting Performance of Biometric Devices, Version 2.01. Technical Report NPL Report CMSC 14/02, National Physical Laboratory, August 2002.

21. A. Martin, G. Doddington, T. Kam, M. Ordowski, and M. Przybocki. The DET Curve in Assessment of Detection Task Performance. In *Proceedings of the Fifth European Conference on Speech Communication and Technology*, volume 4, pages 1895–1898, Rhodes, Greece, September 1997.

22. F. Monrose and A. Rubin. Authentication Via Keystroke Dynamics. In *Proceedings of Fourth ACM Conference on Computer and Communications Security*, pages 48–56, Zurich, Switzerland, April 1997.

23. H. Moon and P. J. Phillips. Computational and Performance Aspects of PCA-based Face Recognition Algorithms. *Perception*, 30(5):303–321, 2001.

24. V. S. Nalwa. Automatic On-Line Signature Verification. *Proceedings of the IEEE*, 85(2):215–239, February 1997.

25. National Institute of Standards and Technology. NIST Biometric Scores Set. Available at http://http://www.itl.nist.gov/iad/894.03/biometricscores.

26. M. Negin, T. A. Chmielewski, M. Salganicoff, T. A. Camus, U. M. C. von Seelan, P. L. Venetianer, and G. G. Zhang. An Iris Biometric System for Public and Personal Use. *IEEE Computer*, 33(2):70–75, February 2000.

27. M. S. Nixon, J. N. Carter, D. Cunado, P. S. Huang, and S. V. Stevenage. Automatic Gait Recognition. In A. K. Jain, R. Bolle, and S. Pankanti, editors, *Biometrics: Personal Identification in Networked Society*, pages 231–249. Kluwer Academic Publishers, London, UK, 1999.

28. L. O'Gorman. Seven Issues with Human Authentication Technologies. In *Proc. of Workshop on Automatic Identification Advanced Technologies (AutoID)*, pages 185–186, Tarrytown, USA, March 2002.

29. L. O'Gorman. Comparing Passwords, Tokens, and Biometrics for User Authentication. *Proceedings of the IEEE*, 91(12):2019–2040, December 2003.

30. P. J. Phillips, P. Grother, R. J. Micheals, D. M. Blackburn, E. Tabassi, and J. M. Bone. FRVT2002: Overview and Summary. Available at http://www.frvt.org/FRVT2002, March 2003.

31. N. Poh and S. Bengio. An Investigation of F-ratio Client-Dependent Normalisation on Biometric Authentication Tasks. In *Proceedings of IEEE International Conference on Acoustics, Speech, and Signal Processing (ICASSP)*, volume 1, pages 721–724, Philadelphia, USA, March 2005.

32. S. Prabhakar, S. Pankanti, and A. K. Jain. Biometric Recognition: Security and Privacy Concerns. *IEEE Security and Privacy Magazine*, 1(2):33–42, March-April 2003.

33. M. Przybocki and A. Martin. NIST Speaker Recognition Evaluation Chronicles. In *Odyssey: The Speaker and Language Recognition Workshop*, pages 12–22, Toledo, Spain, May 2004.

34. M. Rejman-Greene. Privacy Issues in the Application of Biometrics: A European Perspective. In J. L. Wayman, A. K. Jain, D. Maltoni, and D. Maio, editors, *Biometric Systems: Technology, Design and Performance Evaluation*, pages 335–359. Springer, 2005.

35. J. A. Swets, W. P. Tanner, and T. G. Birdsall. Decision Processes in Perception. *Psychological Review*, 68(5):301–340, 1961.

36. J. L. Wayman, A. K. Jain, D. Maltoni, and D. Maio, editors. *Biometric Systems: Technology, Design and Performance Evaluation*. Springer, 2005.

37. C. Wilson, A. R. Hicklin, M. Bone, H. Korves, P. Grother, B. Ulery, R. Micheals, M. Zoepfl, S. Otto, and C. Watson. Fingerprint Vendor Technology Evaluation 2003: Summary of Results and Analysis Report. NIST Technical Report NISTIR 7123, National Institute of Standards and Technology, June 2004.

38. D. Zhang, A. W.-K. Kong, J. You, and M. Wong. Online Palmprint Identification. *IEEE Transactions on Pattern Analysis and Machine Intelligence*, 25(9):1041–1050, 2003.

39. R. Zunkel. Hand Geometry Based Authentication. In A. K. Jain, R. Bolle, and S. Pankanti, editors, *Biometrics: Personal Identification in Networked Society*, pages 87–102. Kluwer Academic Publishers, London, UK, 1999.

Fingerprint Recognition

Davide Maltoni and Raffaele Cappelli

Department of Electronics, Informatics and Systems, University of Bologna, Italy
maltoni@csr.unibo.it, cappelli@csr.unibo.it

2.1 Introduction

A *fingerprint* is the representation of the epidermis of a finger: it consists of a pattern of interleaved *ridges* and *valleys* [16]. Fingertip ridges evolved over the years to allow humans to grasp and grip objects. Like everything in the human body, fingerprint ridges form through a combination of genetic and environmental factors. In fact, fingerprint formation is similar to the growth of capillaries and blood vessels in angiogenesis. The genetic code in DNA gives general instructions on the way skin should form in a developing fetus, but the specific way it forms is a result of random events (the exact position of the fetus in the womb at a particular moment, and the exact composition and density of surrounding amniotic fluid). This is the reason why even the fingerprints of identical twins are different [26]. Fingerprints are fully formed (i.e. became stable) at about seven months of fetus development and finger ridge configurations do not change throughout the life of an individual, except in case of accidents such as cuts on the fingertips [3]. This property makes fingerprints a very attractive biometric identifier.

Human fingerprints have been discovered on a large number of archaeological artifacts and historical items [16]. Although these findings provide evidence to show that ancient people were aware of the individuality of fingerprints, it was not until the late sixteenth century that the modern scientific fingerprint technique was first initiated [20, 15, 29]. In 1686, Marcello Malpighi, a professor of anatomy at the university of Bologna, noted in his writings the presence of ridges, spirals and loops in fingerprints. Since then, a large number of researchers have invested huge amounts of effort on fingerprint studies. Henry Fauld, in 1880, was the first to scientifically suggest the individuality of fingerprints based on an empirical observation. At the same time, Herschel asserted that he had practiced fingerprint recognition for about 20 years [29, 34]. These findings established the foundation of modern fingerprint recognition. In the late nineteenth century, Sir Francis Galton conducted an extensive study on fingerprints [20]; he introduced the minutiae features for fingerprint matching in 1888. An important advance in fingerprint recognition was made in 1899 by Edward Henry, who established the well-known "Henry system" of fingerprint classification [29].

In the early twentieth century, fingerprint recognition was formally accepted as a valid personal identification method and became a standard routine in forensics [29]. Fingerprint identification agencies were set up worldwide and criminal fingerprint databases were established [29]. Various fingerprint recognition techniques, including latent fingerprint acquisition, fingerprint classification, and fingerprint matching were developed. For example, the FBI fingerprint identification division was set up, in 1924, with a database of 810,000 fingerprint cards [18, 19].

With the rapid expansion of fingerprint recognition in forensics, operational fingerprint databases grew so large that manual fingerprint identification became infeasible; for instance, the total number of fingerprint cards in the FBI fingerprint database stands well over 200 million and is growing continuously. With thousands of requests being received daily, even a team of more than 1300 fingerprint experts were not able to provide timely responses to these requests [29]. Starting in the early 1960s, the FBI, Home Office in the UK, and Paris Police Department began to invest a large amount of effort in developing Automatic Fingerprint Identification Systems (AFISs) [29]. Based on the observations of how human fingerprint experts perform fingerprint recognition, three major problems in designing AFISs were identified and investigated: digital fingerprint acquisition, local ridge feature extraction, and ridge characteristic pattern matching. Their efforts were so successful that today almost every law enforcement agency worldwide uses an AFIS. These systems have greatly improved the operational productivity of law enforcement agencies and reduced the cost of hiring and training human fingerprint experts.

Automatic fingerprint recognition technology has now rapidly grown beyond forensic applications and into civilian applications. Thanks to good recognition performance and to the growing market of low-cost Personal Computers and acquisition devices, fingerprint-based biometric systems are becoming very popular and are being deployed in a wide range of applications: e.g. PC logon, electronic commerce, ATMs, physical access control [16].

In the following sections, the main components of fingerprint-based biometric systems are introduced: sensing (section 2.2), feature extraction (section 2.3), and matching (section 2.4). Section 2.5 briefly describes recent performance evaluation efforts and introduces synthetic fingerprint generation as a useful tool for easily creating benchmark databases. Finally, section 2.6 draws some conclusions and depicts the main open issues. Due to the extent of this topic, it is not possible to provide here all the details and to cover interesting issues such as classification, indexing and multimodal systems. Interested readers can find in [16] a complete guide to fingerprint recognition.

2.2 Fingerprint Sensing

Historically, in law enforcement applications, the acquisition of fingerprint images was performed by using the so-called "ink-technique": the subject's finger was spread with black ink and pressed against a paper card; the card was then scanned by using a common paper-scanner, producing the final digital image. This kind of process is referred to as off-line fingerprint acquisition or off-line sensing (see Figure 2.1). A particular case of off-line sensing is the acquisition of a latent fingerprint from a crime scene.

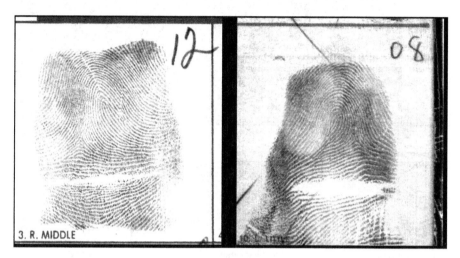

Fig. 2.1. Fingerprint images acquired off-line with the ink technique.

Nowadays, most civil and criminal AFISs accept *live-scan* digital images acquired by directly sensing the finger surface with an electronic fingerprint scanner. No ink is required in this method, and all that a subject has to do is to press his/her finger against the flat surface of a live-scan scanner (see Figure 2.2). The most important part of a fingerprint scanner is the sensor (or sensing element), which is the component where the fingerprint image is formed. Almost all the existing sensors belong to one of the three families: optical, solid-state, and ultrasound [16] [44].

- *Optical sensors.* Frustrated Total Internal Reflection (FTIR) is the oldest and most used live-scan acquisition technique. The finger touches the top side of a glass prism, but while the ridges enter in contact with the prism surface, the valleys remain at a certain distance; the left side of the prism is illuminated through a diffused light. The light entering the prism is reflected at the valleys, and absorbed at the ridges. The lack of reflection allows the ridges to be discriminated from the valleys. The light rays exit from the right side of the prism and are focused through a lens onto a CCD or CMOS image sensor.

Fig. 2.2. The three fingerprint scanners used in FVC2006 [1] and an image collected through each of them.

- *Solid-state sensors.* Solid-state sensors (also known as silicon sensors) became commercially available in the middle 1990s. All silicon-based sensors consist of an array of pixels, each pixel being a tiny sensor itself. The user directly touches the surface of the silicon: neither optical components nor external CCD/CMOS image sensors are needed. Four main effects have been proposed to convert the physical information into electrical signals: capacitive, thermal, electric field, and piezoelectric.
- *Ultrasound sensors.* Ultrasound sensing may be viewed as a kind of echography. A characteristic of sound waves is the ability to penetrate materials, giving a partial echo at each impedance change. This technology is not yet mature enough for large-scale production.

New sensing techniques such as multispectral imaging [35] and 3D touch-less acquisition [13] are being developed to overcome some of the drawbacks of the current fingerprint scanners including: i) the difficulty in working with wet or dry fingers, ii) the skin distortion caused by the pressure of the finger against the scanner surface, and iii) the inability to detect fake fingers.

The quality of a fingerprint scanner, the size of its sensing area and the resolution can heavily influence the performance of a fingerprint recognition algorithm [8]. To maximize compatibility between digital fingerprint images and ensure good quality of the acquired fingerprint impressions, the US Criminal Justice Information Services released a set of specifications that regulate the quality and format of both fingerprint images and FBI-compliant off-line/live-scan scanners (Appendix F and G of CJIS [14]). Unfortunately, the above specifications are targeted to the forensic applications (AFIS sector) and as of today no definitive specifications exist for the evaluation/certification of commercial fingerprint scanners [8].

2.3 Feature extraction

In a fingerprint image, ridges (also called ridge lines) are dark whereas valleys are bright (see Figure 2.3a). Ridges and valleys often run in parallel; sometimes they bifurcate and sometimes they terminate. When analyzed at the global level, the fingerprint pattern exhibits one or more regions where the ridge lines assume distinctive shapes. These regions (called *singularities* or *singular regions*) may be classified into three typologies: *loop*, *delta*, and *whorl* (see Figure 2.3b). Singular regions belonging to loop, delta, and whorl types are typically characterized by ∩, Δ, and O shapes, respectively. The *core* point (used by some algorithms to pre-align fingerprints) corresponds to the center of the north most (uppermost) loop type singularity.

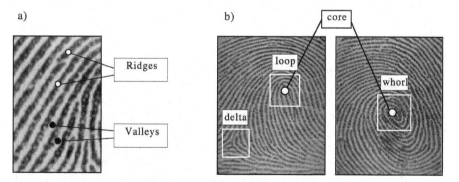

Fig. 2.3. a) Ridges and valleys in a fingerprint image; b) singular regions (white boxes) and core points (circles) in fingerprint images.

At the local level, other important features, called *minutiae* can be found in the fingerprint patterns. Minutia refers to the various ways in which the ridges can be discontinuous. For example, a ridge can abruptly come to an end (termination), or can divide into two ridges (bifurcation) (Figure 2.4). Although several types of minutiae can be considered, usually only a coarse classification (into these two types) is adopted to deal with the practical difficulty in automatically discerning the different types with high accuracy.

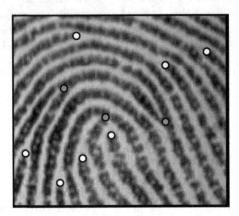

Fig. 2.4. Termination (white) and bifurcation (gray) minutiae in a sample fingerprint.

Figure 2.5 provides a graphical representation of the main feature extraction steps and their interrelations.

2.3.1 Local ridge orientation and frequency

The local ridge orientation at point (x, y) is the angle θ_{xy} that the fingerprint ridges, crossing through an arbitrary small neighborhood centered at (x, y), forms with the horizontal axis. Robust computation methods, based on local averaging of gradient estimates, have been proposed by Donahue and Rokhlin [17], Ratha, Chen and Jain [36], and Bazen and Gerez [5]. The local ridge frequency (or density) f_{xy} at point (x, y) is the the number of ridges per unit length along a hypothetical segment centered at (x, y) and orthogonal to the local ridge orientation θ_{xy}. Hong, Wan, and Jain [24] estimate local ridge frequency by counting the average number of pixels between two consecutive peaks of gray-levels along the direction normal to the local ridge orientation. In the method proposed by Maio and Maltoni [31], the ridge pattern is locally modeled as a sinusoidal-shaped surface, and the variation theorem is exploited to estimate the unknown frequency.

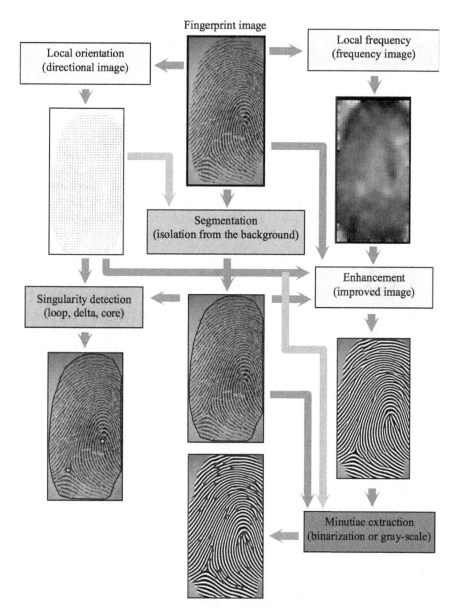

Fig. 2.5. Graphical representation of fingerprint feature extraction steps and their interrelations.

2.3.2 Segmentation

The segmentation task consists in separating the fingerprint area from the background. Because fingerprint images are striated patterns, using a global or local thresholding technique does not allow the fingerprint area to be effectively isolated. Robust segmentation techniques are discussed in [36][30][4].

2.3.3 Singularity detection

Most of the approaches proposed in the literature for singularity detection operate on the fingerprint orientation image. The best-known method is based on Poincaré index (Kawagoe and Tojo [28]). A number of alternative approaches have been proposed for singularity detection; they can be coarsely classified in: 1) methods based on local characteristics of the orientation image, 2) partitioning-based methods, 3) core detection and fingerprint registration approaches [16].

2.3.4 Enhancement and binarization

The performance of minutiae extraction algorithms and fingerprint recognition techniques relies heavily on the quality of the input fingerprint images. In practice, due to skin conditions (e.g., wet or dry, cuts, and bruises), sensor noise, incorrect finger pressure, and inherently low-quality fingers (e.g., elderly people, manual workers), a significant percentage of fingerprint images (approximately 10%) is of poor quality.

The goal of a fingerprint enhancement algorithm is to improve the clarity of the ridge structures in the recoverable regions and mark the unrecoverable regions as too noisy for further processing. The most widely used technique for fingerprint image enhancement is based on *contextual filters*. In contextual filtering, the filter characteristics change according to the local context that is defined by the local ridge orientation and local ridge frequency. An appropriate filter that is tuned to the local ridge frequency and orientation can efficiently remove the undesired noise and preserve the true ridge and valley structure [24].

2.3.5 Minutiae extraction

Most of the proposed methods require the fingerprint gray-scale image to be converted into a binary image. The binary images obtained by the binarization process are submitted to a thinning stage which allows for the ridge line thickness to be reduced to one pixel. Finally, a simple image scan allows the detection of pixels that correspond to minutiae through the pixel-wise computation of crossing number[1] (see Figure 2.6).

---

[1] The crossing number of a pixel in a binary image is defined as half the sum of the differences between pairs of adjacent pixels in the 8-neighborhood; its value

a)   b)   c)   d)

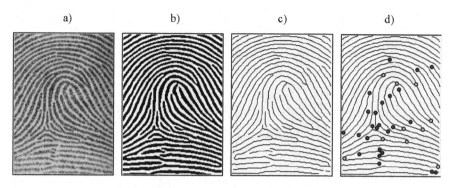

Fig. 2.6. a) A fingerprint gray-scale image; b) the image obtained after enhancement and binarization; c) the image obtained after thinning; d) termination and bifurcation minutiae detected through the pixel-wise computation of the crossing number.

Some authors have proposed minutiae extraction approaches that work directly on the gray-scale images without binarization and thinning. This choice is motivated by the following considerations: i) a significant amount of information may be lost during the binarization process; ii) thinning may introduce a large number of spurious minutiae; iii) most of the binarization techniques do not provide satisfactory results when applied to low-quality images. Maio and Maltoni [30] proposed a direct gray-scale minutiae extraction technique, whose basic idea is to track the ridge lines in the gray-scale image, by 'sailing' according to the local orientation of the ridge pattern.

A post-processing stage (called *minutiae filtering*) is often useful in removing the spurious minutiae detected in highly corrupted regions or introduced by previous processing steps (e.g., thinning) [16].

2.4 Matching

Matching high quality fingerprints with small intra-subject variations is not difficult and every reasonable algorithm can do it with high accuracy. The real challenge is matching samples of poor quality affected by: i) large displacement and/or rotation; ii) non-linear distortion; iii) different pressure and skin condition; iv) feature extraction errors. The two pairs of images in Figure 2.7a visually show high variability (large *intra-subject* variations) that can characterize two different impressions of the same finger. On the other hand, as it is evident from Figure 2.7b, fingerprint images from different fingers may sometimes appear quite similar (small *inter-subject* variations).

---

is 1 for a termination minutia, 2 for an intermediate ridge pixel, and ≥ 3 for a bifurcation or a more complex minutia.

a)   b)

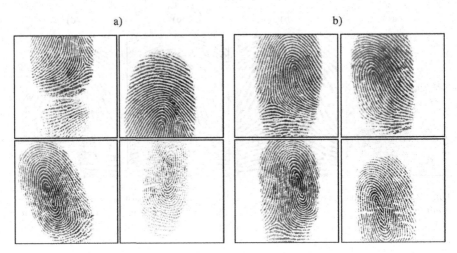

Fig. 2.7. a) Each row shows a pair of impressions of the same finger, taken from the FVC2002 DB1, which were falsely non-matched by most of the algorithms submitted to FVC2002 [32]; b) each row shows a pair of impressions of different fingers, taken from the FVC2002 databases which were falsely matched by some of the algorithms submitted to FVC2002.

The large number of existing approaches to fingerprint matching can be coarsely classified into three families: i) correlation-based matching, ii) minutiae-based matching, and iii) ridge feature-based matching. In the rest of this section, the representation of the fingerprint acquired during enrollment is denoted as the *template* (**T**) and the representation of the fingerprint to be matched is denoted as the *input* (**I**). In case no feature extraction is performed, the fingerprint representation coincides with the grayscale fingerprint image itself.

2.4.1 Correlation-based techniques

Let $\mathbf{I}^{(\Delta x, \Delta y, \theta)}$ represent a rotation of the input image **I** by an angle θ around the origin (usually the image center) and shifted by Δx and Δy pixels in directions x and y, respectively. Then the similarity between the two fingerprint images **T** and **I** can be measured as

$$S(\mathbf{T}, \mathbf{I}) = \max_{\Delta x, \Delta y, \theta} CC(\mathbf{T}, \mathbf{I}^{(\Delta x, \Delta y, \theta)}), \qquad (2.1)$$

where $CC(\mathbf{T}, \mathbf{I}) = \mathbf{T}^T \mathbf{I}$ is the cross-correlation between **T** and **I**. The cross-correlation is a well known measure of image similarity and the maximization in (2.1) allows us to find the optimal registration. The direct application of Equation (2.1) rarely leads to acceptable results, mainly due to the following problems.

- Non-linear distortion makes impressions of the same finger significantly different in terms of global structure; the use of local or block-wise correlation techniques can help to deal with this problem [6].
- Skin condition and finger pressure cause image brightness, contrast, and ridge thickness to vary significantly across different impressions. The use of more sophisticated correlation measures may compensate for these problems.
- A direct application of Equation (1) is computationally very expensive. Local correlation and correlation in the Fourier domain can improve efficiency.

2.4.2 Minutiae-based methods

This is the most popular and widely used technique, being the basis of the fingerprint comparison made by fingerprint examiners. Minutiae are extracted from the two fingerprints and stored as sets of points in the two-dimensional plane. Most common minutiae matching algorithms consider each minutia as a triplet $\mathbf{m} = \{x, y, \theta\}$ that indicates the (x, y) minutia location coordinates and the minutia angle θ. For a mathematical formulation of the minutiae matching problem, see [16]. In the pattern recognition literature the minutiae matching problem has been generally addressed as a *point pattern matching* problem. Hough transform-based approaches are the most commonly used techniques for global minutiae matching [37] [11]; an example is shown in Figure 2.8. The Hough transform technique converts point pattern matching to the problem of detecting peaks in the Hough space of transformation parameters. It discretizes the parameter space $(\Delta x, \Delta y, \theta)$ and accumulates evidence in the discretized space by deriving transformation parameters that relate two sets of points using a substructure of the feature matching technique.

Some authors have proposed *"local minutiae matching"* techniques that consist of comparing two fingerprints according to local minutiae structures [27] [38] [12]; local structures are characterized by attributes that are invariant with respect to global transformation (e.g., translation, rotation, etc.) and therefore are suitable for matching without any a priori global alignment. Matching fingerprints based only on local minutiae arrangements relaxes global spatial relationships which are highly distinctive and therefore reduce the amount of information available for discriminating fingerprints. Global versus local matching is a tradeoff between simplicity, low computational complexity, and high distortion-tolerance (local matching), and high distinctiveness (global matching). Recent matching techniques tend to combine the advantages of both local and global minutiae-matching.

2.4.3 Ridge Feature-based techniques

Three main reasons induce designers of fingerprint recognition techniques to search for other fingerprint distinguishing features, beyond minutiae: 1) reliably extracting minutiae from poor quality fingerprints is very difficult; 2)

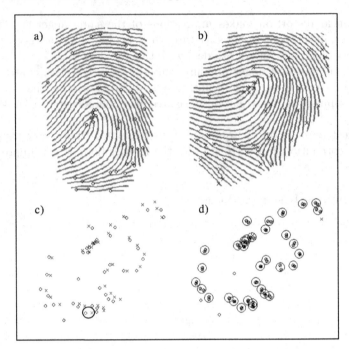

Fig. 2.8. Minutiae matching by the Chang et al. approach [11]. Figures a) and b) show the minutiae extracted from the template and the input fingerprint, respectively; c) the minutiae are coarsely superimposed and the principal pair is marked with an ellipse; d) each circle denotes a pair of minutiae as mated by the algorithm.

minutiae extraction is time consuming; 3) additional features may be used in conjunction with minutiae (and not as an alternative) to increase system accuracy and robustness.

Jain et al. [25] proposed a local texture analysis technique where the fingerprint area of interest is tessellated with respect to the core point (see Figure 2.9). A feature vector (called the *FingerCode*) is composed of an ordered enumeration of the features extracted from the local information contained in each sector specified by the tessellation. Thus the feature elements capture the local texture information and the ordered enumeration of the tessellation captures the global relationship among the local contributions. Matching two fingerprints is then translated into matching their respective FingerCodes, which is simply performed by computing the Euclidean distance between two FingerCodes.

Several approaches have been recently proposed in the literature where non-minutiae features such as spatial relationship of the ridge lines [23], local orientation [39] [22] and local density [41] are used in conjunction with the minutiae to improve the overall system performance.

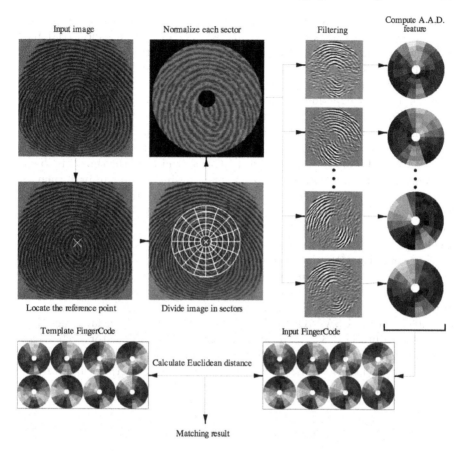

Fig. 2.9. System diagram of Jain et al.'s FingerCode approach [25].

2.5 Performance evaluation

Although the accuracy of fingerprint-based biometric systems can be very high [32], no fingerprint recognition algorithm is perfect. Performance evaluation is important for all biometric systems and particularly so for fingerprint recognition, which is receiving widespread international attention for citizen identity verification and identification. The most-widely known performance evaluation efforts in this field are the Fingerprint Verification Competitions (FVC) and the Fingerprint Vendor Technology Evaluation (FpVTE); other recent initiatives include the NIST SDK Testing [42] and the MINEX campaign aimed at evaluating interoperability [21].

The first Fingerprint Verification Competition (FVC2000 [32]) was organized by the Biometric System Laboratory of the University of Bologna, together with the Biometric Test Center of the San Jose State University and the Pattern Recognition and Image Processing Laboratory of the Michigan

State University. The aim of the initiative was to establish a common benchmark for comparing fingerprint matching algorithms, allowing industrial and academic organizations to compare performance and track improvements of their algorithms. FVC2000 received significant attention from both academic and commercial organizations; several research groups started using FVC2000 datasets for their experimentations and some companies, which initially did not participate in the competition, requested the organizers to certify their performance on the FVC2000 benchmark. The great encouragement received, induced the authors to organize similar initiatives in the year 2002 (FVC2002 [32]), 2004 (FVC2004 [10]), and 2006 (FVC2006, which, at the time this chapter is being written, is still in progress). The growing interest in performance evaluation of fingerprint recognition algorithms is confirmed by the increasing number of participants to FVC (Table 2.1): the number of organizations that registered for the competition grew from 25 (in FVC2000) to 150 (in FVC2006), and the number of algorithms evaluated grew from 11 to 70.

The Fingerprint Vendor Technology Evaluation (FpVTE) 2003 was organized to evaluate the accuracy of fingerprint identification and verification systems [43]. FpVTE2003 was conducted by the U.S. National Institute of Standards & Technology (NIST) as part of its statutory mandate under section 403(c) of the USA PATRIOT Act to certify biometric technologies that may be used in the U.S. Visitor and Immigrant Status Indicator Technology (US-VISIT) Program. Eighteen different companies participated, with 34 systems tested, including the NIST Verification Test Bed fingerprint benchmark system. It is generally believed that FpVTE2003 was the most comprehensive evaluation of fingerprint matching systems ever executed, particularly in terms of the number of fingerprints in the benchmark databases. Table 2.2 summarizes the main differences between FVC2004 and FpVTE2003.

Table 2.1. The four Fingerprint Verification Competitions (FVC): a summary. Beginning with FVC2004, two different sub-competitions (Open Category and Light Category) were organized using the same databases. Each participant was allowed to submit up to one algorithm to each category. The Light category was intended for algorithms characterized by low computational resources, limited memory usage and small template size [10].

Evaluation	Evaluation period	Registered Participants	Algorithms Evaluated
FVC2000	Jul - Aug, 2000	25 (15 withdrew)	11
FVC2002	Apr - Jul, 2002	48 (19 withdrew)	31
FVC2004	Jan - Feb, 2004	110 (64 withdrew)	Open categ.: 41 Light categ.: 26
FVC2006	Nov - Dec, 2006	150 (97 withdrew)	Open categ.: 44 Light categ.: 26

Table 2.2. A comparison between FVC2004 and FpVTE2003, see [10] for more details.

	FVC2004	FpVTE2003
Algorithms Evaluated	*Open Category*: 41 *Light Category*: 26	*Large Scale Test (LST)*: 13 *Medium Scale Test (MST)*: 18 *Small Scale Test (SST)*: 3 (SST only)
Subject population	Students (24 years old on the average)	Operational fingerprint data from a variety of U.S. Government sources including low-quality fingers and low-quality sources
Fingerprint format	Single finger flat impressions acquired through low-cost commercial fingerprint scanners (including small area and sweeping sensors)	Mixed formats (flat, slap, and rolled from different sources; scanned paper cards, and from FBI-compliant fingerprint scanners)
Perturbations	Deliberately exaggerated perturbations (rotation, distortion, dry/wet fingers, ...)	Difficulties mainly due to intrinsic low-quality fingers of some subjects and sometimes due to non-cooperative users
Database availability	Databases are available to the scientific community	Databases are not available due to data protection and privacy issues
Data collection	All the data were acquired for this event	Data coming from existing U.S. Government sources
Database size	4 databases, each containing 800 fingerprints from 100 fingers	48,105 fingerprint sets from 25,309 subjects
Evaluation type	Independent Strongly supervised	Independent Supervised
Anonymous participation	Allowed	Not allowed
Best EER	Best average EER: 2.07% (in the Open Category)	Best EER on MST: 0.2% (MST is the FpVTE2003 test closest to FVC2004 Open Category)

2.5.1 Synthetic Fingerprint Generation

Performance evaluation of fingerprint recognition systems is very data dependent. Therefore, the acquisition conditions and database size must be specified when reporting the results. Typically, to obtain tight confidence intervals at very low error rates, large databases of representative fingerprint images are required. Moreover, once a fingerprint database has been used for testing and optimizing a system, successive testing cycles require new databases previously unseen by the system. Unfortunately, collection of large fingerprint databases is not only expensive in terms of time and money, it is also problematic because of the repetitive monotony of the work (which often leads to collection errors) and of privacy legislation protecting the use of personal data. In several contexts, a synthetic generation of realistic fingerprint images can help to solve the above problems. The most desirable property of such a synthetic fingerprint generator is that it correctly models the various inter-class and intra-class variations in fingerprint images observed in nature. In particular, it should be able to generate realistic "impressions" of the same "virtual finger," by simulating:

- different finger areas touching the sensors;
- non-linear distortions produced by non-orthogonal pressure of the finger against the sensor;
- variations in the ridge line thickness given by pressure intensity or by skin dampness;
- small cuts on the fingertip and other kinds of noise.

The SFinGe approach introduced in [7] is a synthetic fingerprint generator that meets the above requirements and can be used to automatically create large databases of very-realistic fingerprints images (Figure 2.10), thus allowing fingerprint recognition algorithms to be effectively trained, tested, optimized, and compared. The synthetic fingerprints generated emulate images acquired with electronic fingerprint scanners, since almost all applications now require an on-line acquisition. In any case, impressions similar to those acquired by the traditional "ink-technique" may be generated with a few changes to the algorithm.

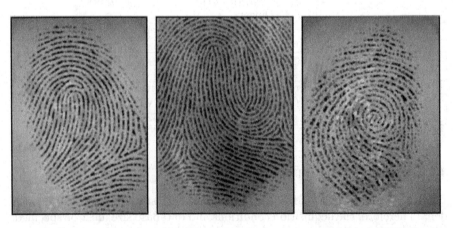

Fig. 2.10. Examples of synthetic fingerprint images generated by the SFinGe approach [7].

2.6 Conclusions

Automatic fingerprint recognition was one of the first applications of machine pattern recognition (it dates back to more than fifty years ago). Because of this, there is a popular misconception that fingerprint recognition is a fully solved problem. On the contrary, fingerprint recognition is still a complex and very challenging pattern recognition task. The most important open issues can be summarized as follows.

Improved feature extraction and matching algorithms. Designing algorithms capable of extracting effective features and matching them in a robust way is very hard, especially in poor quality fingerprint images and when low-cost acquisition devices with a small area are used. Although state-of-the-art fingerprint recognition systems are nowadays effective in matching fingerprints at a very high speed (millions of matches per second) their level of sophistication still cannot rival that of a well-trained fingerprint expert. Further research is necessary to develop feature extraction approaches that can reliably and consistently extract a set of features that provide rich information, comparable to those commonly used by human experts.

Securing fingerprint-based biometric systems. As any other authentication technique, fingerprint recognition is not totally spoof-proof. The main potential threats for fingerprint-based systems are [16]: 1) attacking the communication channels; 2) attacking specific software modules (e.g. replacing the feature extractor or the matcher with a Trojan horse); 3) attacking the database of enrolled templates; 4) presenting fake fingers to the sensor. Recently, the feasibility of the last two types of attacks was reported by some researchers: as far as point 4) is concerned, in [33] it was shown that it is actually possible to spoof fingerprint recognition systems with well-made fake fingertips; as to point 3), in [9], a technique to reverse-engineer minutiae-based fingerprint templates was described. A considerable amount of research on fake-detection approaches (e.g., [2]) and template-protection techniques [40] is definitely needed to address the most critical security threats.

References

1. FVC2006 web site. http://bias.csr.unibo.it/fvc2006.
2. A. Antonelli, R. Cappelli, D. Maio, and D. Maltoni. Fake Finger Detection by Skin Distortion Analysis. *IEEE Transactions on Information Forensics and Security*, 1(3):360–373, September 2006.
3. W. J. Babler. Embryologic development of epidermal ridges and their configuration. *Birth Defects Original Article Series*, 27(2), 1991.
4. A. M. Bazen and S. H. Gerez. Segmentation of Fingerprint Images. In *Proceedings Workshop on Circuits Systems and Signal Processing (ProRISC 2001)*, pages 276–280, 2001.
5. A. M. Bazen and S. H. Gerez. Systematic Methods for the Computation of the Directional Fields and Singular Points of Fingerprints. *IEEE Transactions on Pattern Analysis and Machine Intelligence*, 24(7):905–919, 2002.

6. A. M. Bazen, G. T. B. Verwaaijen, S. H. Gerez, L. P. J. Veelenturf, and B. J. van der Zwaag. A Correlation-Based Fingerprint Verification System. In *Proceedings of Workshop on Circuits Systems and Signal Processing (ProRISC 2000)*, pages 205–213, 2000.

7. R. Cappelli. *Handbook of Fingerprint Recognition*, chapter Synthetic fingerprint generation. Springer, New York, 2003.

8. R. Cappelli, M. Ferrara, and D. Maltoni. The Quality of Fingerprint Scanners and Its Impact on the Accuracy of Fingerprint Recognition Algorithms. In *Proceedings of Multimedia Content Representation, Classification and Security (MRCS2006)*, pages 10–16, 2006.

9. R. Cappelli, A. Lumini, D. Maio, and D. Maltoni. Can Fingerprints be Reconstructed from ISO Templates? In *Proceedings of the International Conference on Control, Automation, Robotics and Vision (ICARCV2006)*, Singapore, December 2006.

10. R. Cappelli, D. Maio, D. Maltoni, J. L. Wayman, and A. K. Jain. Performance Evaluation of Fingerprint Verification Systems. *IEEE Transactions on Pattern Analysis and Machine Intelligence*, 28(1):3–18, January 2006.

11. S. H. Chang, F. H. Cheng, W. H. Hsu, and G. Z. Wu. Fast Algorithm for Point Pattern-Matching: Invariant to Translations, Rotations and Scale Changes. *Pattern Recognition*, 30(2):311–320, 1997.

12. X. Chen, J. Tian, X. Yang, and Y. Zhang. An algorithm for distorted fingerprint matching based on local triangle feature set. *IEEE Transactions on Information Forensics and Security*, 1(2):169–177, 2006.

13. Y. Chen, G. Parziale, E. Diaz-Santana, and A. K. Jain. 3D Touchless Fingerprints: Compatibility with Legacy Rolled Images. In *Proceedings of the Biometric Symposium, Biometric Consortium Conference*, Baltimore, 2006.

14. Criminal Justice Information Services. Electronic Fingerprint Transmission Specification. Int. Report. CJIS-RS-0010 (V7), 1999. http://www.fbi.gov/hq/cjisd/iafis/efts70/cover.htm.

15. H. Cummins and C. Midlo. *Palms and Soles: An Introduction to Dermatoglyphics*. Dover Publications, New York, 1961.

16. A. K. Jain D. Maltoni, D. Maio and S. Prabhakar. *Handbook of Fingerprint Recognition*. Springer, New York, 2003.

17. M. L. Donahue and S. I. Rokhlin. On the use of Level Curves in Image Analysis. *CVGIP: Image Understanding*, 57(2):185–203, 1993.

18. Federal Bureau of Investigation. The Science of Fingerprints: Classification and Uses. Technical Report U.S. Government Publication, Washington, DC, 1984.

19. Federal Bureau of Investigation. The FBI fingerprint identification automation program: issues and options. Technical Report U.S. Government Publication, Washington, DC, Congress of the U.S., Office of Technology Assessment, 1991.

20. F. Galton. *Finger Prints*. Mcmillan, London, 1892.

21. P. Grother, M. McCabe, C. Watson, M. Indovina, W. Salamon, P. Flanagan, E. Tabassi, E. Newton, and C. Wilson. MINEX: Performance and Interoperability of the INCITS 378 Fingerprint Template. Technical Report NISTIR 7296, march 2006.

22. J. Gu, J. Zhou, and C. Yang. Fingerprint recognition by combining global structure and local cues. *IEEE Transactions on Image Processing*, 15(7):1942–1964, 2006.

23. Y. He, J. Tian, L. Li, H. Chen, and X. Yang. Fingerprint matching based on global comprehensive similarity. *IEEE Transactions on Pattern Analysis Machine Intelligence*, 28(6):850–862, 2006.

24. L. Hong, Y. Wan, and A. K. Jain. Fingerprint Image Enhancement: Algorithms and Performance Evaluation. *IEEE Transactions on Pattern Analysis and Machine Intelligence*, 20(8):777–789, 1998.

25. A. K. Jain, S. Prabhakar, L. Hong, and S. Pankanti. Filterbank-Based Fingerprint Matching. *IEEE Transactions on Image Processing*, 9:846–859, 2000.

26. A. K. Jain, S. Prabhakar, and S. Pankanti. On The Similarity of Identical Twin Fingerprints. *Pattern Recognition*, 35(11):2653–2663, 2002.

27. X. Jiang and W. Y. Yau. Fingerprint Minutiae Matching Based on the Local and Global Structures. In *Proceedings of the International Conference on Pattern Recognition (15th)*, volume 2, pages 1042–1045, 2000.

28. M. Kawagoe and A. Tojo. Fingerprint Pattern Classification. *Pattern Recognition*, 17:295–303, 1984.

29. H. C. Lee and R. E. Gaensslen. *Advances in Fingerprint Technology*. Elsevier Publishing, New York, 2nd ed. edition, 2001.

30. D. Maio and D. Maltoni. Direct Gray-Scale Minutiae Detection in Fingerprints. *IEEE Transactions on Pattern Analysis and Machine Intelligence*, 19(1), 1997.

31. D. Maio and D. Maltoni. Ridge-Line Density Estimation in Digital Images. In *Proceedings of the International Conference on Pattern Recognition (14th)*, pages 534–538, 1998.

32. D. Maio, D. Maltoni, R. Cappelli, J. L. Wayman, and A. K. Jain. FVC2000: Fingerprint Verification Competition. *IEEE Transactions on Pattern Analysis Machine Intelligence*, 24(3):402–412, 2002.

33. T. Matsumoto, H. Matsumoto, K. Yamada, and S. Hoshino. Impact of Artificial "Gummy" Fingers on Fingerprint Systems. In *Proceedings of SPIE*, volume 4677, pages 275–289, February 2002.

34. A. Moenssens. *Fingerprint Techniques*. Chilton Book Company, London, 1971.

35. K. A. Nixon and R. K. Rowe. Multispectral Fingerprint Imaging for Spoof Detection. In *Proceedings of the SPIE Conference on Biometric Technology for Human Identification*, volume 5779, pages 214–225, Orlando, 2005.

36. N. K. Ratha, S. Y. Chen, and A. K. Jain. Adaptive Flow Orientation-Based Feature Extraction in Fingerprint Images. *Pattern Recognition*, 28(11):1657–1672, 1995.

37. N. K. Ratha, K. Karu, S. Chen, and A. K. Jain. A Real-Time Matching System for Large Fingerprint Databases. *IEEE Transactions on Pattern Analysis and Machine Intelligence*, 18(8):799–813, 1996.

38. N. K. Ratha, V. D. Pandit, R. M. Bolle, and V. Vaish. Robust Fingerprint Authentication Using Local Structural Similarity. In *Proceedings of Workshop on Applications of Computer Vision*, pages 29–34, 2000.

39. M. Tico and P. Kuosmanen. Fingerprint matching using an orientation-based minutia descriptor. *IEEE Transactions on Pattern Analysis Machine Intelligence*, 25(8):1009–1014, 2003.

40. P. Tuyls and J. Goseling. Capacity and Examples of Template Protecting Biometric Authentication Systems. In *Proceedings of Biometric Authentication Workshop*, pages 158–170, 2004.

41. D. Wan and J. Zhou. Fingerprint recognition using model-based density map. *IEEE Transactions on Image Processing*, 15(6):1690–1696, 2006.

42. C. Watson, C. Wilson, K. Marshall, M. Indovina, and R. Snelick. Studies of One-to-One Fingerprint Matching with Vendor SDK Matchers. Technical Report NISTIR 7221, April 2005.
43. C. Wilson, R. Hicklin, M. Bone, H. Korves, P. Grother, B. Ulery, R. Micheals, M. Zoepfl, S. Otto, and C. Watson. Fingerprint Vendor Technology Evaluation 2003: Summary of Results and Analysis Report. Technical Report NISTIR 7123, june 2004. http://fpvte.nist.gov.
44. X. Xia and L. O'Gorman. Innovations in fingerprint capture devices. *Pattern Recognition*, 36(2):361–369, 2003.

3

Face Recognition

Marios Savvides, Jingu Heo, and Sung Won Park

Department of Electrical and Computer Engineering, Carnegie Mellon University, Pittsburgh, Pennsylvania, USA
Marios.Savvides@ri.cmu.edu, jheo@andrew.cmu.edu, sungwonp@cmu.edu

3.1 Introduction

Robust face recognition systems are in great demand to help fight crime and terrorism. Other applications include providing user authentication for access control to physical and virtual spaces to ensure higher security. However the problem of identifying a person by taking an input face image and matching with the known face images in a database is still a very challenging problem. This is due to the variability of human faces under different operational scenario conditions such as illumination, rotations, expressions, camera view points, aging, makeup, and eyeglasses. Often, these various conditions greatly affect the performance of face recognition systems especially when the systems need to match against large scale databases. This low performance on face recognition prevents systems from being widely deployed in real applications (although many systems have been deployed, their use and accuracy is limited to particular operational scenarios) where errors like the false acceptance rate (FAR) and the false rejection rate (FRR) are considered in advance. FAR is the probability that the systems incorrectly accept an unauthorized person, while FRR is the probability that the systems wrongly reject an authorized person. In order to enhance the overall face recognition algorithm performance, numerous new algorithmic approaches such as Kernel Class-Dependent Feature Analysis (KCFA) [76] [32], Tensorfaces [71], manifold learning methods [58], kernel methods [66], and different Linear Discriminant Analysis (LDA) variants have been proposed [47] showing a great deal of improvement over conventional techniques. Among these, some of the new approaches such as KCFA, emphasize on the generalization to unseen people and Tensorfaces can deal with multiple factor analysis (different pose, illumination). Manifold learning methods can capture the underlying structures in the feature space of facial images. Traditional LDA variants try to find the best separation projection vectors by maximizing the Fisher's criteria [23].

Recently, 3D face recognition has gained attention in the face recognition community due to its inherent capability to overcome some of the traditional problems of 2D imagery such as pose and lighting variation [16] [20] [24]. Commercial 3D acquisition devices can obtain a depth map (3D-shape) of the face. These usually require the user to be in very close proximity to the camera; additionally some devices will require the user to be still for several seconds for a good 3D model acquisition. In contrast 2D face acquisition can work from a distance and not require significant user co-operation. This is the trade-off with desiring to work with 3D shape data. One approach to address this issue is the 3D Morphable Model approach (3DMM) [14] which tries to recover a 3D face model from a 2D face image. 3DMM is an attractive method for handling different poses and illuminations effectively [12] [13] compared to other 3D face recognition approaches. However, this approach still requires significant ground-truth 3D face models for training the system and overall speed of rendering a 3D face takes several seconds. Other approaches to reconstruct the 3D-shape from 2D images of the face include Structure From Motion(SfM) [36]. A more comprehensive survey of recent 3D face recognition algorithms can be found at [63] [19] and the fusion of visual and thermal face recognition can be found at [38] reporting multi-model based face recognition systems lead to improved performance than single modality systems.

In this chapter we mainly focus on 2D-based face recognition approaches with some background on traditional methods in Section 2 and then emphasis on some of the newer approaches that tackle problems with 2D face recognition in the later sections. We briefly touch upon some of the most popularly used face databases by the face recognition community in Section 3. In the following sections, we describe the state-of-the-art techniques for face applications more deeply and show their experimental results. In Section 4, we show that KCFA can be successfully applied to face recognition with large scale challenging databases such as the Face Recognition Grand Challenge (FRGC) database [55] [1]. In section 5, we describe Tensorfaces for face recognition and novel face synthesis under different pose and illumination. Pre-processing approaches that aid 2D face recognition are dealt with in Section 6 detailing how to perform real-time pose correction using Active Appearance Models (AAMs). In Section 7, we show how to deal with very low-resolution, poor quality acquired face images with a novel super-resolution method that utilizes manifold learning techniques to achieve good reconstruction results. We then conclude with a short closing discussion in Section 8.

3.2 Face Recognition Techniques

Face recognition algorithms can be classified into two broad categories according to feature extraction schemes for face representation: feature-based methods and appearance-based methods [81]. Properties and geometric relations such as the areas, distances, and angles between the facial feature points are used as descriptors for face recognition. On the other hand, appearance-based methods consider the global properties of the face image intensity pattern.

Fig. 3.1. The first six basis vectors of Eigenfaces.

Typically appearance-based face recognition algorithms proceed by computing basis vectors to represent the face data efficiently. In the next step, the faces are projected onto these vectors and the projection coefficients can be used for representing the face images. Popular algorithms such as PCA, LDA, ICA, LFA, Correlation Filters, Manifolds and Tensorfaces are based on the appearance of the face. Holistic approaches to face recognition have trouble dealing with pose variations. Building image face mosaics like those in [65] [45] have been introduced to deal with the pose variation problem. We will also discuss in detail an Active Appearance Model approach to pose correction in later section. We review several of the popular face recognition algorithms as well as Elastic Bunch Graph Matching(EBGM) approach [75].

3.2.1 Eigenfaces (PCA)

Eigenfaces [69] also known as Principal Components Analysis (PCA) find the minimum mean squared error linear subspace that maps from the original N-dimensional data space into an M-dimensional feature space. By doing this, Eigenfaces (where typically $M << N$) achieve dimensionality reduction by using the M eigenvectors of the covariance matrix corresponding to the largest eigenvalues. The resulting basis vectors are obtained by finding the optimal basis vectors that maximize the total variance of the projected data(i.e. the set of basis vectors that best describe the data). The optimal basis PCA vectors $\mathbf{W}$ are the ones that maximize the following objective function

$$\mathbf{W}_{PCA} = \arg\max_{\mathbf{W}} |\mathbf{W}^T \mathbf{S}_T \mathbf{W}| = [w_1 \ w_2 \ \cdots \ w_m] \qquad (3.1)$$

where $\mathbf{S}_T$ denotes the total scatter matrix which contains pixel-wise covariances of the face data. Figure 3.1 shows examples of Eigenfaces generated from the generic training images of FRGC dataset [1] after pre-processing the face images such as normalizing faces for rotation, scale and illumination compensation. PCA is good for data representation but not necessarily for class discrimination as we will discuss next.

3.2.2 Linear Discriminant Analysis (LDA) and Fisherfaces

Linear Discriminant Analysis (LDA) [23] is more suited for finding projections that best discriminate different classes. It does this by seeking the optimal projection vectors which maximize the ratio of the between-class scatter and the

Fig. 3.2. The first six basis vectors of Fisherfaces.

within-class scatter (i.e. maximizing class separation in the projected space). The optimal basis vectors of LDA can be denoted as

$$\mathbf{W}_{LDA} = \arg\max_{\mathbf{W}} \frac{|\mathbf{W}^T \mathbf{S}_B \mathbf{W}|}{|\mathbf{W}^T \mathbf{S}_W \mathbf{W}|} \tag{3.2}$$

where $\mathbf{S}_B$ and $\mathbf{S}_W$ indicate between-class scatter matrix and within-class scatter matrix respectively.

Typically when dealing with face images (and most other image based pattern recognition problems) the number of training images is smaller than the number of pixels (or equivalently dimensionality of the data), thus the within-class scatter matrix $\mathbf{S}_W$ is singular causing problems for LDA [23]. To address this issue [10] first performs PCA to reduce the dimensionality of the data in order to overcome this singular-matrix problem and then applies LDA in this lower-dimensional PCA subspace. Improvement in recognition results was shown using this approach over traditional PCA. The projection vectors from Fisherfaces are those that maximize the following objective function:

$$\mathbf{W}_{Fisher} = \arg\max_{\mathbf{W}} \frac{|\mathbf{W}^T \mathbf{W}_{PCA}^T \mathbf{S}_B \mathbf{W}_{PCA} \mathbf{W}|}{|\mathbf{W}^T \mathbf{W}_{PCA}^T \mathbf{S}_W \mathbf{W}_{PCA} \mathbf{W}|} \tag{3.3}$$

Figure 3.2 shows examples of Fisherfaces generated from the generic training images of the FRGC dataset.

3.2.3 LDA variants

Direct LDA (DLDA) [78] derives eigenvectors using simultaneous diagonalization techniques. Unlike other LDA approaches [47], the DLDA simultaneously diagonalizes the between-class scatter matrix first and then diagonalizes the within-class scatter matrix. The eigenvectors with very small (close to zero) eigenvalues in the $\mathbf{S}_B$ can be discarded since they contain no discriminative power, while the eigenvectors with small eigenvalues of the $\mathbf{S}_W$ matrix simultaneously being kept, especially the null-space. Another LDA variant is called the Gram-Schmidt LDA (GSLDA) [82] approach avoids computing the inverse of the within-class scatter matrix or performing the diagonalization step needed in DLDA. These methods assert that the most discriminating power for LDA may lie in the null-space of the within scatter matrix which maximizes the Fisher's ratio.

3.2.4 Independent Component Analysis (ICA)

Independent Components Analysis (ICA) for face recognition has been applied in [8]. ICA seeks a non-orthogonal basis so that the transformed features are statistically independent, while PCA finds an orthogonal basis for face images so that the transformed features are uncorrelated. The basis images developed by PCA depend only on second-order statistics. ICA generalizes the concept of PCA to model higher-order statistical relationships. Original motivation for this decomposition comes from the need to separate audio streams into independent sources without prior knowledge of the mixing process.

3.2.5 Local Feature Analysis (LFA)

LFA [54] constructs a family of locally correlated feature detectors based on eigen-subspace decomposition. A selection or sparsification step produces a minimally correlated and topographically indexed subset of features that define the subspace of interest. Local representations offer robustness against variability due to changes in localized regions of the objects. The features used in the LFA method are less sensitive to illumination changes and are easier for estimating rotations. The LFA algorithm was used as a key component algorithm in FaceIt [56], which is one of the commercial face recognition systems.

3.2.6 Elastic Bunch Graph Matching (EBGM)

EBGM [75] constructs dynamic link architecture using image graphs to represent individual faces. An image graph representing a face image is a geometrical structure consisting of various nodes connected by edges. The nodes are located at facial landmarks such as the pupils and the corners of the mouth as shown in Figure 3.3. A set of training images is represented by the corresponding bunch of image graphs of those images. A set of complex Gabor wavelet coefficients (or Gabor jets) are used as local features at each node. These Gabor jets contain information of multiple orientations and frequencies for each node. When performing face recognition on a new facial image, each graph in the training set is matched to the image and the best match indicates the identity of person.

3.2.7 Neural Networks (NN) and Support Vector Machines (SVM)

Neural Networks and Support Vector Machines (SVMs) are usually used in low dimensional feature spaces due to the computational complexity of the processing involved using high-dimensional face data. Neural network approaches [43] have been widely explored for feature representation and face recognition. However, as the number of people for training increases, NN requires computational burden exponentially. Fusion of multiple neural networks

Fig. 3.3. The face model constructed by EBGM: (a) an image graph, (b) the facial landmarks of a test image detected by EBGM, (c) the image graph of a test image constructed by EBGM.

classifiers improved the overall performance of face recognition [27]. A face recognition system using hybrid neural and dual eigenspace methods has been proposed in [79]. However, in general it is not known what exactly the neural network has learned or how it will behave, and usually a significant amount of training data is required for good generalization which usually requires significant amount of offline training. Support Vector Machines (SVM) [70] [30] have been successfully applied for object recognition, by utilizing the kernel trick which maps data onto higher-dimensional feature spaces. The SVM finds the hyperplane that maximizes the margin of separation in order to minimize the risk of misclassification not only for the training samples, but to enable it to achieve better generalization to the unseen data.

3.2.8 Tensorfaces

Facial images have different appearance due to multiple factors such as variations across people, pose changes, lighting conditions and facial expressions. The Tensorfaces method [71] is proposed to model the variations of these factors by a multilinear framework. Tensors, which are higher-order extensions of matrices, allow us to construct multilinear models so as to analyze multiple factors of these facial variations. Lathauwer et al. [42] proposed Higher-Order Singular Value Decomposition (HOSVD) for tensor decomposition, which is an extension of Singular Value Decomposition (SVD) for matrix decomposition. Vasilescu et al. [71] introduced the idea of tensor decomposition into the area of computer vision and proposed Tensorfaces, a higher-order extension of the Eigenfaces method. By analyzing the tensor consisting of training images, the basis of each facial factor (expression, pose, etc.) in the training images can be obtained.

3.2.9 Manifolds

Learning the similarity among data points is one of the key concepts for the analysis of face images. In the previous work of face image analysis using manifold learning methods, it has been shown that face images lie on a manifold [58] [28] [68] [11]. Also, it has been demonstrated that the variation of a certain facial factor such as various poses or expressions makes a sub-manifold in the manifold structure [29]. So, it is helpful to detect and analyze the underlying manifold structure in the distribution of facial image samples. Traditional methods such as PCA and LDA often see only the Euclidean structure, so they fail to discover the underlying structure if the data lies on a nonlinear manifold. The analysis of manifolds reveals the characteristics of the data distribution and can be applied for dimensionality reduction. Thus, to discover the nonlinear structure of manifolds, manifold learning techniques have been proposed [58] [68] [29]. In many real-world classification problems, the local manifold structure is more important than the global Euclidean structure. Thus, manifold learning techniques often use adjacency information among data samples to preserve the local manifold structure. By manifold learning techniques, neighboring points should still be in close proximity after mapping, and the points far from each other should still be far from each other in the new mapping.

3.2.10 Kernel Methods

Due to the large appearance changes in human face images, the linear subspace methods may not capture the non-linearity in facial image representation. As a result, the PCA and LDA algorithms have been extended to represent nonlinear mappings in a higher-dimensional space [9]. Computing and storing the new features in this higher-dimensional space becomes very expensive. Thus, the kernel trick is used for computational efficiency as it enables us to obtain the necessary inner products in the higher-dimensional feature space without computing the higher-dimensional feature mapping. Examples of kernel methods are Kernel Eigenfaces and Kernel Fisherfaces [77] . Kernel functions can be used without having to form an explicit high-dimensional mapping as long as kernels form an inner product space in this higher dimensional mapping and satisfy Mercer's theorem [51]. A number of papers combining linear subspace methods with the kernel trick including Kernel Direct LDA (KDLDA) [46], Kernel LDA (KDA) [50] or Kernel Fisher's Analysis (KFA), Kernel PCA (KPCA) [37], and Kernel ICA (KICA) [6] have been applied in face recognition showing improved performance over linear approaches.

3.2.11 Correlation Filters

Advanced correlation filter approaches such as those found in [40] [39] process images in the spatial frequency domain using closed form correlation filter solutions designed for specific optimization criteria. One of the most often used correlation filters is the Minimum Average Correlation Energy (MACE) [48] filter. This is designed to minimize the average correlation plane energy resulting from the training images, while constraining the correlation peak value at the origin to pre-specified values. Correlation outputs from MACE filters typically exhibit sharp peaks, making the peak detection and location relatively easy and robust. Developed and applied originally in the field of Automatic Target Recognition (ATR), several different types of correlation filters have been proposed for face recognition in the presence of illumination variations [60], and occlusion [61], including a new hybrid shift-invariant PCA-correlation filter approach called Corefaces [62] that has all the subspace representation power of PCA and the shift-invariant and discrimination properties of advanced correlation filters.

3.3 Databases

There are several publicly available face databases for the research community to use for algorithm development, which provide a standard benchmark when reporting results. Different databases are collected to address a different type of challenge or variations such as illumination, pose, occlusion, etc. A more comprehensive review of available standard databases for developing face recognition algorithms can be found in the face database chapter of this book. In this section, several standard databases including PIE [64], FERET [2], FRGC [55], Yale [3] and AR [4] are briefly introduced to explain the experimental setup of the training and testing that lead to the different results reported in this chapter.

3.3.1 Face Recognition Grand Challenge (FRGC) database

The Face Recognition Grand Challenge (FRGC) conducted by the NIST is aimed at an objective and systematic evaluation of face recognition algorithms under different challenging conditions. Simultaneously, the aim for the FRGC is to push researchers to develop the next generation face recognition algorithms that can reduce the error rate in face recognition systems by an order of magnitude over the Face Recognition Vendor Test (FRVT) 2002 results [15] [56]. Details of the different FRGC experiments can be found at [55]. The FRGC data is partitioned into three datasets: a generic training set which one can use to train the face recognition system (if using PCA, this set is used to generate the PCA subspace), the target set (these are the images acquired under controlled conditions) and the probe set (the test set) captured under un-controlled conditions. The FRGC generic training set contains 12,776 images (from 222 subjects) taken under controlled and uncontrolled illuminations. The gallery set contains 16,028 images (from 466 subjects, with some overlap with subjects in the generic training set) under controlled illumination while the probe set contains 8,014 images (from 466 subjects) under uncontrolled illumination. The similarity matrix of matching scores between the target and probe sets are computed and reported to the NIST in the form of a $16,028 \times 8,014$ similarity matrix. Sample images of the FRGC database are shown in Figure 3.4.

(a) Controlled images   (b) Uncontrolled images

Fig. 3.4. Sample images of the FRGC database.

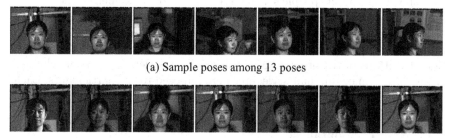

(a) Sample poses among 13 poses

(b) Sample lighting conditions among 43 different lighting conditions

Fig. 3.5. Sample images of the PIE database.

3.3.2 FERET database

Prior to the FRGC, the NIST organized the FERET database and evaluation protocol [57] to facilitate the development of commercial face recognition systems. The FERET database is designed to measure the performance of face recognition algorithms on a large database in practical settings. The FERET program provides a large database of facial images taken from 1,199 individuals and collected between August 1993 and July 1996 to support algorithm development and evaluation. The FERET database consists of 14,126 images of 1,564 sets (1,199 original sets and 365 duplicate sets). For development purposes, 503 sets of images were released to the researchers, and the remaining sets were sequestered for independent evaluation.

3.3.3 Pose Illumination Expression (PIE) database

The CMU Pose, Illumination, and Expression (PIE) database [64] contains 41,368 facial images of 68 people. The images are acquired across different poses, under different illuminations, and with different facial expressions. First, in the CMU 3D Room, each person's images were captured under 13 different poses, 43 different illumination conditions, and 4 kinds of facial expressions. In particular, 43 different illumination conditions were obtained with only 21 flashes, since images were captured both with and without ambient background lighting switched on. Additionally each person has four types of expressions: neutral expression, smiling, blinking, and talking. The CMU PIE database has been extensively used to analyze face images under different illumination and pose and for benchmarking the development of face recognition algorithms to handle such distortions.

3.3.4 AR database

The AR face database [4] was created by the Computer Vision Center (CVC), at Universitat of Autònoma de Barcelona. It contains over 4,000 color images corresponding to 126 people's faces (70 men and 56 women). The images acquired are frontal view pose with different facial expressions, illumination conditions, and occlusions (such as people wearing sun glasses and a scarf) making this database one of the more popular ones for testing face recognition algorithms in the presence of occlusion. No restrictions on wear (clothes, glasses, etc.), make-up, hair style, etc. were imposed to the participants. Each person participated in two sessions, two weeks apart.

3.3.5 Yale Face database

The Yale database [3] contains 165 gray-scale images in GIF format of 15 individuals. There are 11 images per subject, one for each variation such as different facial expression, center-light, with glasses, happy, left-light, with and without glasses, normal, right-light, sad, sleepy, surprised, and wink. The Yale Face Database was extended to the Yale Face Database B, which contains 5760 single light source images of 10 subjects each seen under 576 viewing conditions (9 poses x 64 illumination conditions). For every subject in a particular pose, an image with ambient (background) illumination was also captured.

3.4 Advanced Correlation Filters

Due to their built-in shift invariance and designed distortion tolerance, advanced correlation filters are well suited for biometric verification/identification applications and have been shown to exhibit robustness to illumination variations and other distortions [60]. One of the popular filters called the Minimum Average Correlation Energy filter is designed to minimize the average correlation plane energy E resulting from the N training images defined as

$$E = \sum_{i=1}^{N} \sum_{x=0}^{M-1} \sum_{y=0}^{M-1} c_i(x,y)^2 = \sum_{i=1}^{N} \sum_{u=0}^{M-1} \sum_{v=0}^{M-1} |C_i(u,v)|^2$$

$$= \sum_{i=1}^{N} \sum_{u=0}^{M-1} \sum_{v=0}^{M-1} |H(u,v)|^2 |X_i(u,v)|^2 = \mathbf{h}^+ \sum_{i=1}^{N} \mathbf{D}_i \mathbf{h} = \mathbf{h}^+ \mathbf{D} \mathbf{h}. \quad (3.4)$$

In Eq.(3.4), $c_i(x, y)$ is defined as the ith spatial correlation plane of size $M \times M$ which according to Parseval's theorem preserves the same energy in the Fourier frequency domain $C_i(u, v)$. $H(u, v)$ is the frequency domain filter and $X_i(u, v)$ is the 2D Fourier transform of the ith training image. $\mathbf{D}$ as defined in Eq.(3.4) is a $M^2 \times M^2$ diagonal matrix containing the average power spectrum of the training images along its diagonal. $^+$indicates the complex conjugate transpose. The MACE filter also specifies that correlation peak at the origin to pre-specified values represented below in the following equation:

$$\mathbf{X}^+\mathbf{h} = \mathbf{c} \tag{3.5}$$

where $\mathbf{X}$ is a $M^2 \times N$ complex valued matrix and its ith column contains the lexicographically re-ordered version of the 2D Fourier transform of the ith training image and $\mathbf{c}$ is a $N \times 1$ row vector containing the correlation peaks desired for each of the N training images. Minimizing Eq.(3.4) the while satisfying the linear constraints in Eq.(3.5) yields a closed form solution to the optimization, giving the vectorized MACE filter $\mathbf{h}$ as

$$\mathbf{h} = \mathbf{D}^{-1}\mathbf{X}(\mathbf{X}^+\mathbf{D}^{-1}\mathbf{X})^{-1}\mathbf{u}. \tag{3.6}$$

One of the recent advances in correlation filters is the class-dependent feature analysis (CFA) method which proposes a novel feature extraction method using correlation filters [33] [34] [5] [59]. Since the basis vectors acquired from either PCA or LDA are database dependent, it may be difficult to obtain basis vectors which represent or discriminate faces well on large databases. These approaches also exhibit poor generalization power; they may not discriminate faces well which have not been seen during training. Although kernel approaches such as KPCA, KLDA are attractive because of their ability to effectively use nonlinear mappings of face features, performance of these methods indicates room for improvement. Figure 3.6 shows a brief overview of our proposed work. Normalized face images are effectively mapped onto a high dimensional space using the kernel trick and features are extracted using correlation filters in the CFA framework, and then a kernel support vector machine (SVM) is designed among classes on this reduced feature set. We demonstrate our proposed work on the FRGC database to show the power of the CFA approach and how using this approach as a dimensionality reduction method further improves performance using SVM for classification in this feature space.

3.4.1 Kernel Class Dependent Analysis

In the CFA approach, one filter (e.g., MACE filter) is designed for each class in the generic training set. Then a test image $\mathbf{y}$ is characterized by the correlations of that test image with the n MACE filters, i.e.,

$$\mathbf{c} = \mathbf{H}^T\mathbf{y} = [\mathbf{h}_{\mathbf{MACE}-1} \ \mathbf{h}_{\mathbf{MACE}-2} \ \cdots \ \mathbf{h}_{\mathbf{MACE}-n}]^T\mathbf{y} \tag{3.7}$$

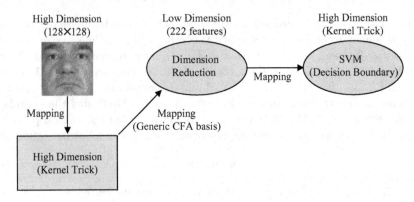

Fig. 3.6. An overview of the KCFA algorithm.

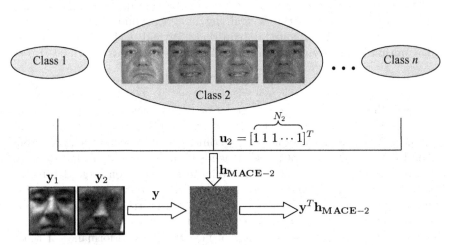

Fig. 3.7. The CFA algorithm; the filter response of $\mathbf{y}_1$ and $\mathbf{h}_{\mathbf{MACE}-2}$ can be distinctive to that of $\mathbf{y}_2$ and $\mathbf{h}_{\mathbf{MACE}-2}$.

where $\mathbf{h}_{\mathbf{MACE}-i}$ is a filter designed for class i which is trained to give a small correlation output (close to 0) for all classes except for class i. For example, the number of filters generated by the FRGC generic training set is 222, since this generic training set contains 222 classes (or subjects). Then each input image $\mathbf{y}$ is projected onto those basis vectors to yield a 222 dimensional feature vector as shown in Figure 3.7 and N indicates the number of images per each class. The similarity of the probe image to the gallery image is computed in this 222 dimensional feature space.

Kernel functions defined by $\mathbf{K}(\mathbf{x}, \mathbf{y}) = \langle \mathbf{\Phi}(x), \mathbf{\Phi}(y) \rangle$ can be used without having to form the mapping explicitly, as long as the chosen kernel functions form an inner product space in this higher dimensional mapping and satisfy Mercer's theorem [70]. Examples of kernel functions are: Polynomial kernel ($\mathbf{K}(x, y) = (\langle \mathbf{x}, \mathbf{y} \rangle + 1)^p$), Radial Basis Function kernel ($\mathbf{K}(\mathbf{x}, \mathbf{y}) = \exp(-\|\mathbf{x} -$

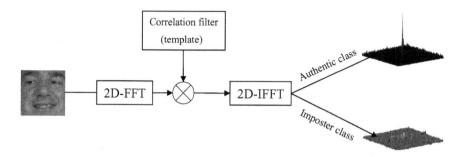

Fig. 3.8. The correlation peaks. The height of the peak indicates confidence of match, so we get a high peak for an authentic class at the origin with low correlation values in the remaining correlation plane. For imposter classes there is no discernible peak detected in the correlation plane.

$\mathbf{y}\|^2/2\sigma^2))$, and Neural-network kernel $(\mathbf{K}(\mathbf{x},\mathbf{y}) = \tanh(k\langle\mathbf{x},\mathbf{y}\rangle - \delta))$. The Kernel Correlation Filters can be extended from the linear correlation filters using the kernel trick. The kernel correlation output of a filter $\mathbf{h}$ and an input $\mathbf{y}$ can be expressed as

$$\Phi(\mathbf{y}) \cdot \Phi(\mathbf{h}) = (\Phi(\mathbf{y}) \cdot \Phi(\mathbf{X}'))(\Phi(\mathbf{X}') \cdot \Phi(\mathbf{X}'))^{-1}\mathbf{u}$$
$$= \mathbf{K}(\mathbf{y},\mathbf{x}_i')\mathbf{K}(\mathbf{x}_i',\mathbf{x}_i')^{-1}\mathbf{u} \qquad (3.8)$$

where $\mathbf{X}'$ and $\mathbf{x}_i'$ indicates the corresponding pre-processed versions of $\mathbf{X}$ and $\mathbf{x}_i$. In the latest KCFA framework using different image representations and image resolutions combined using feature fusion, the pure 1-1 matching performance of KCFA has been improved to 82.4% verification at 0.1% FAR.

3.4.2 Support Vector Machines for Classification

A direct use of the SVM as a classifier on raw pixel data may not be practically feasible (for training) due to the large amount of available training data and large dimensionality of faces. Instead of using the SVM as a direct classifier on image pixels, we use SVMs in KCFA feature space. Since the dimensionality reduction based on KCFA is more efficient and discriminative than other approaches discussed, we use KCFA features (222 dimensional feature space) as an input for training the SVM. We design 466 SVMs (in a one-against all framework) using the gallery set of the FRGC data by changing the labeling information as shown in Figure 3.9. The probe images are then projected on the class-specific SVMs to provide a classification score between all the gallery images and all test images.

As shown in Figure 3.10, the distance measure using the SVM improves the results over the normalized cosine distance in the KCFA feature space and in many practical scenarios we can perform this as we will have access

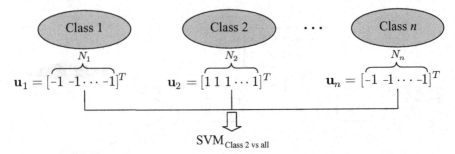

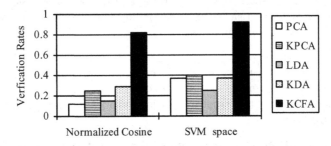

Fig. 3.9. Building decision boundary from class 2 vs. rest of all; **u** indicates the class labeling information vector and N depends on the number of images in each class.

Fig. 3.10. Verification rate (VR) for the FRGC experiment 4 for different methods using the normalized cosine distance and the SVM space (0.1% FAR).

to the Target set. We also compared the different kernel approaches such as KPCA and KDA with different distance measures showing that the KCFA methods based on SVM have superior performance compared to other kernel approaches.

3.5 Tensorfaces

The Tensorfaces method is a novel method to analyze the facial appearance factors such as pose variations, lighting conditions and facial expressions. The traditional Tensorfaces method using multilinear algebra enables us to analyze these facial factors from a particular training set, but it has difficulties analyzing the factors of a new test image when all the factors of the test image are unknown or untrained. Thus, factorization methods for test images have been proposed [73] [52] [53].

3.5.1 Multilinear Analysis of Training Images

A tensor is a multilinear extension of a matrix; while a matrix deals with only two dimensions, a tensor can represent more than two dimensions. Higher-

Order Singular Value Decomposition (HOSVD) [42] is a higher-order extension of Singular Value Decomposition. HOSVD transforms an n-dimensional tensor into the weighted sum of the outer products of n independent vectors. When a training set has three facial factors such as people's identities, lighting conditions, and pose types, one of the general ways to analyze the training set is to construct a $N_{pixel} \times (N_{people} \times N_{light} \times N_{pose})$ matrix $\mathbf{D^{train}}$ which has the vectorized training images as columns. Here, N_{pixel} is defined as the number of pixels in one image, N_{people} is the number of people, N_{light} is the number of lighting conditions, and N_{pose} is the number of pose types in the training set. By using SVD, the matrix representing the training set is decomposed into two orthogonal bases and singular values:

$$\mathbf{D^{train}} = \mathbf{U_{pixel}} \mathbf{S} \mathbf{V}^T \tag{3.9}$$

where $\mathbf{U_{pixel}}$ is the basis of the column space and $\mathbf{V}$ is the basis of the row space of $\mathbf{D^{train}}$. By HOSVD, the same training set can be analyzed in more detail:

$$\mathbf{D^{train}} = \mathbf{U_{pixel}} \mathbf{Z} (\mathbf{U_{people}} \otimes \mathbf{U_{light}} \otimes \mathbf{U_{pose}})^T \tag{3.10}$$

where $\otimes$ represents the Kronecker product. This analysis of face images using HOSVD is called Tensorfaces [71]. The $N_{people} \times N_{people}$ matrix $\mathbf{U_{people}}$ spans the space of people parameters, the $N_{light} \times N_{light}$ matrix $\mathbf{U_{light}}$ spans the space of light parameters, and the $N_{pose} \times N_{pose}$ matrix $\mathbf{U_{pose}}$ spans the space of pose parameters. HOSVD can be represented by two forms; one is using tensors and tensor multiplications while the other is using matrices and the Kroneker products. Eq.(3.10) is the matrix notation of HOSVD. By the analogue of decomposing the training images, one image can be decomposed into the same kinds of factors, no matter whether it is in the training set or not:

$$\mathbf{d} = \mathbf{U_{pixel}} \mathbf{Z} (\mathbf{x_{people}} \otimes \mathbf{x_{light}} \otimes \mathbf{x_{pose}})^T. \tag{3.11}$$

In the case of the training image of the ith person, the jth lighting condition and the kth pose, the person's identity parameter $\mathbf{x_{people}}$ is the ith row of the matrix $\mathbf{U_{people}}$ since the $N_{people} \times 1$ vector $\mathbf{x_{people}}$ is the ith column of $\mathbf{U_{people}}^T$. For the same reason, the lighting parameter $\mathbf{x_{light}}$ of the training image is the jth row of the matrix $\mathbf{U_{light}}$, and $\mathbf{x_{pose}}$ is the kth row of the matrix $\mathbf{U_{pose}}$. The parameters of all the factors for the training image can be easily calculated by the multilinear analysis of the training set [72]. It is also easy to calculate the parameter $\mathbf{x_{people}}$ of a test image when it is the only unknown parameter and all the others are known [72] [74] or estimated by other techniques [67] [73]. However, it has difficulties obtaining the parameters $\mathbf{x_{people}}$, $\mathbf{x_{light}}$, and $\mathbf{x_{pose}}$ when all the parameters are unknown for a test image. In particular, if the test image has untrained pose or lighting conditions, it is more challenging to get the three parameters of the three factors. Consequently, the goal of factorization in the testing process is to solve for all the unknown parameters x_{people}, x_{light}, and x_{pose} of any test image based on the multilinear analysis of the training set.

3.5.2 Multilinear Analysis of Testing Images

To factorize test images which have untrained poses or lighting conditions, a novel factorization method is proposed based on the previous work [52] [53]. By the method, all the factors can be estimated simultaneously without any *a priori* assumption or knowledge of the acquired face image. Moreover, the proposed method is applicable even when a test image has untrained lighting condition or pose. In the proposed method, to obtain factor parameters, first, it is shown that the tensor factorization problem can be formulated as a least squares problem with a quadratic equality constraint.

$$\hat{x} = \arg\min_{x} \|U_{pixel}Zx - d^{test}\|^2 \text{ subject to } \|x\|^2 = 1 \qquad (3.12)$$

where d^{test} is a given test image, and $x = x_{people} \otimes x_{light} \otimes x_{pose}$. The goal is to find $\hat{x}$, the optimal value of x which minimizes the distance between the test image d^{test} and the reconstructed image by the estimated parameters.

Next, $\hat{x}$ is obtained by well-defined numerical optimization techniques which allow us to obtain the facial appearance factors simultaneously. In [52], $\hat{x}$ is estimated by the projection method [80], which is a better optimization scheme than Newton's method to solve the problem. After getting $\hat{x}$, which is the Kronecker product of the mixing factors, it is decomposed into individual factors x_{people}, x_{light}, and x_{pose} by Higher-Order Power Method [41].

Table 3.1. The recognition rates using Tensor Factorization [52].

Methods	People and lightings conditions	People, lighting conditions and poses
EigenFaces	79.3%	69.4%
FisherFaces	89.2%	73.6%
Tensor factorization	95.6%	81.6%

Face recognition and synthesis are the main applications of tensor factorization, and results using the Yale Face Database B [3] can be found in [52]. The database contains 10 people, and each person has 65 different lighting conditions and 9 poses. Two kinds of multilinear models were constructed and tested; one is a bilinear model with two factors consisting of different people and lighting conditions, and the other is a trilinear model with three factors consisting of different people, lighting conditions, and poses. To select lighting variation for training, first, 10 lighting conditions among 65 were discarded since the images under the lighting conditions are so dark that it is

Person & lighting   Pose types

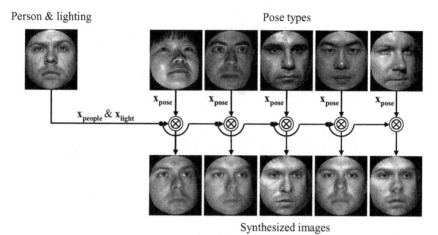

Synthesized images

Fig. 3.11. The results of face synthesis on pose variation using tensor factorization with three factors: people, lighting conditions and poses. The synthesized images still have the person's identity parameter and the lighting parameter of the top left image, but they have different pose types.

hard to extract information from them. Next, every fifth sample was added to the training set. For the bilinear model, 11 lighting conditions of 10 subjects were used for training, while the other 44 lighting conditions were used for testing with no overlap between the two subsets. For the trilinear model, the lighting conditions were the same with the above bilinear model for both training and testing. Additionally, three poses are used for training while the other six poses are used for testing. Here, the three poses for training are the pose 0, 6, and 8 of the Yale Face Database; the pose 0 is the frontal pose, and the pose 6 and 8 are taken from the two largest degrees of the camera optical axis. Table 3.1 shows the results of face recognition, and Figure 3.11 shows the results of face synthesis on pose variation.

3.6 Active Appearance Models for Face Recognition

An Active Appearance Model (AAM) [21] [22] is a statistical model to interpret (in this case) facial images with known parameters. It is comprised of a shape model and an appearance (pixel intensity) model using PCA. The general procedure of an AAM algorithm can be explained as follows. The manually labeled (during training only) shape information (2D vertices) is normalized to deal with global geometric transformations such as scale and rotation using Procrustes Analysis which is a well-known technique for analyzing the statistical distribution of shapes. Then, the normalized shape ($\mathbf{s}$) for an AAM model can be expressed by the mean shape ($\bar{\mathbf{s}}$) and a linear combination of the basis vectors with the amount of projection coefficient vector($\mathbf{p_s}$)

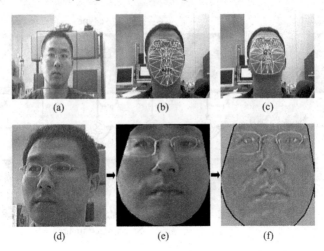

Fig. 3.12. Overview of the integrated face recognition system from video: (a) face detection, (b) AAM fitting, (c) automatic AAM tracking of fiducial facial landmarks, (d) a non-frontal face pose image, (e) face pose correction normalization, and (f) an illumination removal processed image (notice the removal of left cheek specular reflections).

which can be denoted by:

$$\mathbf{s} = \bar{\mathbf{s}} + \mathbf{V_s p_s} \tag{3.13}$$

where $\mathbf{V_s}$ indicates the eigenvector matrix of the shapes. After warping an original image based on the mean shape, the appearance (shape free) model also can be represented by the mean appearance ($\bar{A}(\bar{\mathbf{s}})$) and a linear combination of appearance basis vectors. This can be expressed by:

$$A(\bar{\mathbf{s}}) = \bar{A}(\bar{\mathbf{s}}) + \mathbf{V}_A p_A \tag{3.14}$$

where $A(\bar{\mathbf{s}})$ indicates a vectorized appearance image after warping based on the mean shape, $\mathbf{V}_A$ indicates the eigenvector matrix of the appearances and p_A is the projection coefficient vector. For fitting an AAM into new images, we need to minimize the distance between new images with known model parameters. Then, the objective function can be denoted as

$$E(\mathbf{s}) = \| A(\bar{\mathbf{s}}) - I(\mathbf{s}, \bar{\mathbf{s}}) \|^2 \tag{3.15}$$

where $I(\mathbf{s}, \bar{\mathbf{s}})$ indicates an input image with shape s which is being warped based on the mean shape ($\bar{\mathbf{s}}$). The minimization can be done by assuming a linear relationship between residual errors (δI) and displacement vectors (δc) [21].

By using the current residual errors, the iterative model refinement procedure is applied to find the direction which gives the minimum residual error. To speed this fitting process, the inverse composition algorithm is proposed

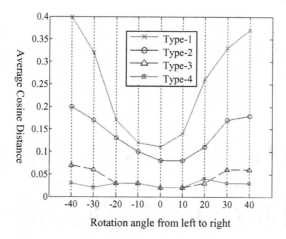

Fig. 3.13. Face matching distance performance across poses.

Table 3.2. Database for performance evaluation

Database (Gallery(G))	Test (Query(Q))
1 frontal image, 10 people, (10 images)	30,40 images, 10 people (376 images)

in [49] [35] [26]. They use the inverse compositional warp update rather than updating $c \leftarrow c + \delta c$, which leads to fast fitting convergence and low computation cost. Typically, for the video-based AAM, the first frame is selected for the shape approximation. Then the estimated shape on the first frame can be the initialization of the shape on the next frame assuming the shape does not change dramatically from frame to frame (high frame rate video capture (>7 fps)). If the first video frame fails to estimate the correct face shape on the image, then the next consecutive frame will also highly likely fail to converge to estimate the correct face shape on the image. In the initialization step in searching for these points, we automatically run a face detector [63] as shown in Figure 3.12 (a) and (b) for providing a good initial region-of-interest search space. Once the AAM fits on the detected face fiducial points and starts tracking, the faces are then warped into neutral frontal pose faces. Finally they are then passed through an illumination-pre-processing step before entering a face recognition matcher system as shown in Figure 12 (e) and (f). By converting non-frontal images into frontal pose and applying illumination compensation, the intra-variations of the same individuals are greatly reduced. Therefore more suitable for inputting these to a face recognition system for robust matching under different pose and illumination conditions [31].

Table 3.2 shows the database for evaluating the face matching performance. From a real video sequence, we captured about 30 images of variyng pose angles per person and measured the matching distance under different preprocessing techniques shown in the paper. Figure 3.13 shows the aver-

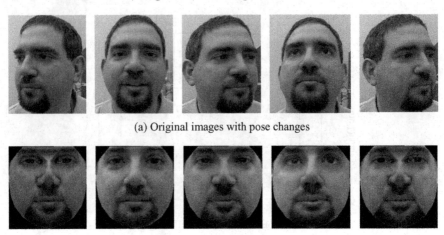

(a) Original images with pose changes

(b) Pose correction into frontal images using symmetry

Fig. 3.14. The results of pose, expression, and illumination normalization using AAM. Each column image in (b) results from the image of the same column in (a).

age matching similarity considering only the pose changes from left to right with different scenario types. Four different types of experiments are evaluated using original raw pose images denoted here (Type-1), AAM pose corrected warped images denoted as (Type-2), and illumination processed images (Type-3), and symmetry imposed images (Type-4) for large pose angles. By converting non-frontal faces into frontal face without expressions, the average distance between same individuals is greatly reduced. These results show that any face recognition algorithm can benefit by applying these approaches as a face-image pre-processing step. More examples of converting non-frontal images into frontal images are shown in Figure 3.14.

3.7 Face Super-resolution using Locality Preserving Projections

Recent work has shown that face images lie on a manifold [58] [28] [68] [11], thus we expected that manifold learning methods in general can improve the analysis of facial images and applications such as face recognition, super-resolution and face synthesis. Based on this idea, Chang et al. [18] developed the Neighbor Embedding algorithm for face super-resolution. They assume that the local distribution structure in sample space is preserved in the down-sampling process, and apply one of the manifold learning methods, Locally Linear Embedding (LLE) [58]. However, most of the manifold learning methods such as LLE have difficulty generating mapping functions for new test images. Thus, manifold analysis so far faced some limitations when applied to face super-resolution problem. Moreover, the objective of super-resolution is to recover a high-dimensional image from a low-dimensional one, where as manifold learning methods are more suited for the opposite,namely dimensionality reduction. LPP tries to find a linear projective mapping for dimensionality reduction. Compared to LPP, other manifold learning techniques such as Isomap Tenenbaum et al.(2003), LLE [58], or Laplacian Eigenmap [11] define the mapping only on the training data. They successfully show the training data are distributed along manifolds, but it is unclear how to evaluate these mappings for new test samples. On the other hand, by using LPP, we can obtain a well-defined transformation matrix which can be applied to a new set of test images which are absent from the training set. In this framework, we apply LPP for every image face patch to model a high-resolution patch $\mathbf{x}_H$ from a down-sampled face patch $\mathbf{x}_L$. Given a high-resolution patch, the corresponding low-resolution patch is computed by down-sampling:

$$\mathbf{x}_L = \mathbf{B}\mathbf{x}_H \qquad (3.16)$$

where $\mathbf{B}$ is the transformation matrix for the mapping from high-resolution to low-resolution. LPP aims to find a low dimensional embedding from a high dimensional patch, so it can be used for dimensionality reduction. LPP performs dimensionality reduction by projecting a high dimensional vector onto a low dimensional subspace. However, LPP can be also applied to the super-resolution problem; which is to map a low-resolution patch onto a high-resolution patch subspace. In this case, we must be able to obtain the coefficients in the high-resolution space from a given low-resolution patch. To do this estimation, various probabilistic approaches such as Belief Propagation have been employed to infer the coefficients of a high-resolution patch from a low-resolution patch [44] [17] [25]. In our case, we employ a Maximum *a posterior* (MAP) estimator to find the LPP coefficients of a high-resolution patch. A MAP approach has also been used to estimate the PCA coefficients of a high-resolution patch from a low-resolution one [44] [25]. Given the patches taken from training images, the LPP coefficients $\mathbf{y}_H$ are calculated by

$$\mathbf{y}_H = \mathbf{A}^T\mathbf{x}_H, \mathbf{x}_H = \mathbf{A}\mathbf{y}_H \qquad (3.17)$$

where $\mathbf{A}$ is the projective matrix of LPP in Eq.(3.17). Maximizing $p(\mathbf{x}_L|\mathbf{x}_H)$ $p(\mathbf{x}_H)$ in Eq.(3.17) is equivalent to maximizing $p(\mathbf{x}_L|\mathbf{y}_H)p(\mathbf{y}_H)$. The prior $p(\mathbf{y}_H)$ is modeled by Gaussian distribution function:

$$p(\mathbf{y}_H) = \frac{1}{Z}\exp\left(-\mathbf{y}_H^T\boldsymbol{\Lambda}^{-1}\mathbf{y}_H\right) \qquad (3.18)$$

where $\boldsymbol{\Lambda} = \text{diag}(\sigma_1^2, \sigma_2^2, \cdots, \sigma_N^2)$ and Z is a normalization constant. The likelihood $p(\mathbf{x}_L|\mathbf{x}_H)$ is denoted by

$$p(\mathbf{x}_L|\mathbf{x}_H) = \frac{1}{Z}\exp\left(-\|\mathbf{B}\mathbf{A}\mathbf{y}_H - \mathbf{x}_L\|^2/\lambda\right). \qquad (3.19)$$

To maximize $p(\mathbf{x}_L|\mathbf{x}_H)p(\mathbf{x}_H)$, the optimal $\mathbf{y}_H$ is given by

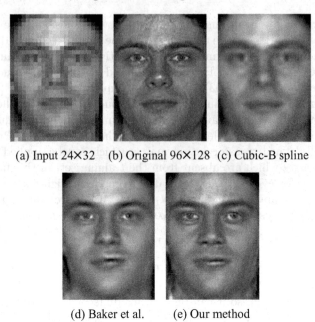

(a) Input 24×32   (b) Original 96×128   (c) Cubic-B spline

(d) Baker et al.   (e) Our method

Fig. 3.15. The results of face super-resolution using LPP and other methods.

$$\mathbf{y}_H^* = (\mathbf{A}^T\mathbf{B}^T\mathbf{B}\mathbf{A} + \lambda\mathbf{\Lambda}^{-1})^{-1}\mathbf{A}^T\mathbf{B}^T\mathbf{x}_L \qquad (3.20)$$

where λ is decided empirically. If λ is too small, $\mathbf{x}_H$ cannot be obtained because $\mathbf{A}^T\mathbf{B}^T\mathbf{B}\mathbf{A}$ is close to singular.

Figure 3.15 shows comparative results using our method and the other competing approaches [7]. Note that our approach results in a more detailed reconstruction, producing a better psychovisual approximation to the original image compared to the other approaches.

3.8 Conclusion

Robust face recognition systems should be able to handle the variations that occur under practical operational scenarios. This means having the ability to handle any and all of face variations under different lighting, pose, expressions, and other variation factors such as low resolution face acquisition from a distance. To improve the performance and address each variation, numerous new algorithms have been proposed aiming at generalization to unseen people, multiple factor analysis and hidden structures of the faces. In case of low resolution faces, pre-processing methods that can enhance the resolution of face images have been detailed. Small pose variations can be handled and trained by different classifiers; however large pose variations can only be modelled by methods such as Tensorfaces and our proposed extensions. Furthermore we show that using computer vision approaches such as Active Appearance Models (AAMs) can be used to model, track facial features to warp back a frontal facial pose as input to traditional classifiers. We have shown that using this and a multi-view AAM approach, we can handle even nearly completely profile views if we assume facial symmetry.

At the core classifier level, many algorithms exist for researchers to choose from. The FRGC database is currently the largest database with the most challenging practical variations which challenge simple algorithms such as PCA by yielding only 12% verification at 0.1% FAR. The new KCFA algorithm approach is promising, performing very efficient dimensionality reduction. Performance has been demonstrated using 222 features only and achieved a maximum verification rate of 82.4% at 0.1% FAR. Having such a low dimensionality allows for faster database searching, with ability to search among millions in a matter of seconds or less. Furthermore, this data is very compact that can easily fit on a smart-card or e-passport for verification.

3.9 Acknowledgments

This research is funded in part by the United States Technical Support Working Group (TSWG) and in part by Carnegie Mellon CyLab.

References

1. http://www.frvt.org/FRVT2006/default.aspx.
2. http://www.itl.nist.gov/iad/humanid/colorferet/home.html.
3. http://cvc.yale.edu/projects/yalefacesB/yalefacesB.html.
4. http://cobweb.ecn.purdue.edu/~aleix/aleix_face_DB.html.
5. R. Abiantun, M. Savvides, and B. V. K Vijayakumar. How Low Can You Go?Low Resolution Face Recognition Study Using Kernel Correlation Feature Analysis on FRGC dataset. In *Proceedings of the IEEE Biometrics Symposium*, September 2006.
6. F. R. Bach and M. I. Jordan. Kernel Independent Component Analysis. *Journal of Machine Learning Research*, 3:1–48, 2002.
7. S. Baker and T. Kanade. Hallucinating Faces. In *Proceedings of the International Conference on Automatic Face and Gesture Recognition*, pages 83–88, 2000.
8. M. S. Bartlett, J. R. Movellan, and T. J. Sejnowski. Face recognition by independent component analysis. *IEEE Transactions on Neural Networks*, 13(6):1450–1464, 2002.
9. G. Baudat and F. Anouar. Generalized Discriminant Analysis Using a Kernel Approach. *Neural Computation*, 12(10):2385–2404, 2000.
10. P. Belhumeur, J. Hespanha, and D. Kriegman. Eigenfaces vs Fisherfaces: Recognition Using Class Specific Linear Projection. *IEEE Transactions on Pattern Analysis and Machine Intelligence*, 19(7):711–720, 1997.
11. M. Belkin and P. Niyogi. Laplacian Eigenmaps and Spectral Techniques for Embedding and Clustering. *Advances in Neural Information Precessing Systems 14, MIT Press, Cambridge*, pages 585–591, 2002.

12. V. Blanz, S. Romdhani, and T. Vetter. Face Identification across Different Poses and Illuminations with a 3D Morphable Model. In *Proceedings of Fifth Int'l Conference Automatic Face and Gesture Recognition*, pages 202–207, 2002.

13. V. Blanz and T. Vetter. A Morphable Model for the Synthesis of 3D Faces. In *Computer Graphics Proceedings of SIGGRAPH*, pages 187–194, 1999.

14. V. Blanz and T. Vetter. Face recognition based on fitting a 3D morphable model. *IEEE Transactions on Pattern Analysis and Machine Intelligence*, 25(9):1063–1074, 2003.

15. M. Bone and D. Blackburn. Face Recognition at a Chokepoint: Scenario Evaluation Results. Evaluation report, Department of Defense, 2002.

16. K. W. Bowyer, K. Chang, and P. Flynn. An Evaluation of Multimodal 2D+3D Face Biometrics. *IEEE Transactions on Pattern Analysis and Machine Intelligence*, 27(4):619–624, April 2005.

17. D. Capel and A. Zisserman. Super-resolution from multiple views using learnt image models. In *Proceedings of the IEEE Computer Society Conference on Computer Vision and Pattern Recognition*, volume 2, pages 627–634, 2001.

18. H. Chang, D. Y. Yeung, and Y. Xiong. Super-resolution through Neighbor Embedding. In *Proceedings of the IEEE Computer Society Conference on Computer Vision and Pattern Recognition*, volume 1, pages 275–282, 2004.

19. K. Chang, K. Bowyer, and P. Flynn. A Survey of Approaches and Challenges in 3D and Multi-Modal 2D+3D Face Recognition. *Computer Vision and Image Understanding*, 101(1):1–15, 2006.

20. X. Chen, P. Flynn, and K. Bowyer. IR and Visible Light Face Recognition. *Computer Vision and Image Understanding*, 99(3):332–358, September 2005.

21. T. Cootes, G. Edwards, and C. Taylor. Active appearance models. In *Proceedings of the European Conference on Computer Vision*, volume 2, pages 484–498, 1998.

22. T. F. Cootes, K. Walker, and C. J. Taylor. View-Based Active Appearance Models. In *Proceedings of the IEEE Conference on Automatic Face and Gesture Recognition*, pages 227–232, March 2000.

23. R. O. Duda, P. E. Hart, and D. G. Stork. *Pattern Classification*. Wiley-Interscience Publication, 2000.

24. P. Flynn and A. Jain. BONSAI: 3D Object Recognition Using Constrained Search. *Computer Vision and Image Understanding*, 13(10):1066–1075, October 1991.

25. W. T. Freeman and E. C. Pasztor. Learning low-level vision. In *Proceedings of the IEEE Computer Society Conference on Computer Vision and Pattern Recognition*, volume 2, pages 1182–1189, 1999.

26. R. Gross, S. Baker, I. Matthews, and T. Kanade. Face Recognition Across Pose and Illumination. In Stan Z. Li and Anil K. Jain, editors, *Handbook of Face Recognition*. Springer, New York, 2004.

27. S. Gutta, J. R. J. Huang, P. Jonathon, and H. Wechsler. Mixture of experts for classification of gender, ethnic origin, and pose of human faces. *IEEE Transactions on Neural Networks*, 11(4):948–960, 2000.

28. X. He and O. Niyogi. Locality preserving projections. *Advances in Neural Information Processing Systems*, 16, 2003.

29. X. He, S. Yan, Y. Hu, P. Niyogi, and H. Zhang. Face Recognition Using Laplacianfaces. *IEEE Transactions on Pattern Analysis and Machine Intelligence*, 27(3), March 2005.

30. B. Heisele, P. Ho, and T. Poggio. Face Recognition with Support Vector Machines: Global versus Component-based Approach. In *Proceedings of the IEEE International Conference on Computer Vision*, volume 2, pages 688–694, 2001.

31. J. Heo and M. Savvides. Real-time Face Tracking and Pose Correction for Face Recognition using Active Appearance Models. *The International Society of Optical Engineering(SPIE) (to appear)*, 2007.

32. J. Heo, M. Savvides, R. Abiantun, C. Xie, and B. V. K. Vijaya Kumar. Face Recognition with Kernel Correlation Filters on a Large Scale Database. In *Proceedings of the International Conference on Acoustics, Speech, and Signal Processing*, 2006.

33. J. Heo, M. Savvides, and B. V. K. Vijaya Kumar. Large scale face recognition with distance measure in support vector machine spaces. In *Proceedings of the International conference on Enterprise Information systems*, 2006.

34. J. Heo, M. Savvides, C. Xie, and B. V. K. Vijaya Kumar. Which Facial Regions are Discriminative? Partial Face Recognition of FRGC data using Support Vector Machine Kernel Correlation Feature Analysis. In *Proceedings of the IEEE Computer Society Conference on Computer Vision and Pattern Recognition*, 2006.

35. C. Hu, J. Xiao, I. Matthews, S. Baker, J. Cohn, and T. Kanade. Fitting a Single Active Appearance Model Simultaneously to Multiple Images. In *Proceedings of the British Machine Vision Conference*, September 2004.

36. T. Kanade and D. D. Morris. Factorization Methods for Structure From Motion. *Philosophical Transactions of the Royal Society of London, Series A*, 356(1740):1153–1173, 1998.

37. K. I. Kim, K. Jung, and H. J. Kim. Face recognition using kernel principal component analysis. *IEEE Signal Processing Letters*, 9(2):40–42, 2002.

38. S. G. Kong, J. Heo, F. Boughorbel, Y. Zheng, B. R. Abidi, A. Koschan, M. Yi, and M. A. Abidi. Adaptive Fusion of Visual and Thermal IR Images for Illumination-Invariant Face Recognition. *International Journal of Computer Vision, Special Issue on Object Tracking and Classification Beyond the Visible Spectrum*, 71(2):215–233, February 2007.

39. B. V. K. Vijaya Kumar. Tutorial survey of composite filter designs for optical correlators. *Applied Optics*, 31(2):4773–4801, 1992.

40. B. V. K. Vijaya Kumar, Abhijit Mahalanobis, and Richard D. Juday. *Correlation Pattern Recognition*. Cambridge University Press, UK, November 2005.

41. L. D. Lathauwer, P. Common, B. D. Moor, and J. Vandewalle. Higher-order power method - application in independent component analysis. In *Proceedings of the International Symposium on Nonlinear Theory and its Applications (NOLTA'95)*, pages 91–96, 1995.

42. L. D. Lathauwer, B. D. Moor, and J. Vandewalle. A multilinear singular value decomposition. *SIAM Journal of Matrix Analysis and Applications*, 21(4):1253–1278, 2000.

43. S. Lawrence, C. L. Giles, A. C. Tsoi, and A. D. Back. Face Recognition: A Convolutional Neural-Network Approach. *IEEE Transactions on Neural Networks*, 8(1):98–113, 1997.

44. C. Liu, H. Shum, and C. Zhang. A Two-Step Approach to Hallucinating Faces: Global Parametric Model and Local Nonparametric Model. In *Proceedings of the IEEE Computer Society Conference on Computer Vision and Pattern Recognition*, volume 1, pages 192–198, 2001.

45. X. Liu and T. Chen. Pose Robust Face Recognition Based on Mosaicing –An Example Usage of Face In Action (FIA) Database. In *Demo session of the IEEE International Conference on Computer Vision and Pattern Recognition*, 2004.
46. J. Lu, K. N. Plataniotis, and A. N. Venetsanopoulos. Face recognition using kernel direct discriminant analysis algorithms. *IEEE Transactions on Neural Networks*, 14(1):117–126, 2003.
47. J. Lu, K. N. Plataniotis, and A. N. Venetsanopoulos. Face recognition using LDA-based algorithms. *IEEE Transactions on Neural Networks*, 14(1):195–200, 2003.
48. A. Mahalanobis, B. V. K. Vijaya Kumar, and D. Casasent. Minimum average correlation energy filters. *Applied Optics*, 26:3633–3630, 1987.
49. I. Matthews and S. Baker. Active Appearance Models Revisited. *International Journal of Computer Vision*, 60(2):135–164, 2004.
50. S. Mika, G. Ratsch, J. Weston, B. Scholkopf, and K. R. Muller. Fisher Discriminant Analysis with Kernels. In *Proceedings of IEEE Neural Networks for Signal Processing Workshop*, 1999.
51. K. R. Muller, K. Tsuda S. Mika, G. Ratsch, and B. Scholkopf. Introduction to Kernel-Based Learning Algorithms. *IEEE Transactions on Neural Network*, 12(2):181–202, 2001.
52. S. W. Park and M. Savvides. Estimating mixing factors simultaneously in multilinear tensor decomposition for robust face recognition and synthesis. In *Proceedings of the IEEE Computer Society Conference on Computer Vision and Pattern Recognition Workshop*, 2006.
53. S. W. Park and M. Savvides. Individual TensorFace Subspaces For Efficient and Robust Face Recognition That Do Not Require Factorization. In *Proceedings of the Biometrics Symposium 2006*, September 2006.
54. P. S. Penev and J. J. Atick. Local Feature Analysis: A General Statistical Theory for Object Representation. *Network: Computation in Neural Systems*, 7(3):477–500, 1996.
55. P. J. Phillips, P. J. Flynn, T. Scruggs, K. W. Bowyer, J. Chang, K. Hoffman, J. Marques, J. Min, and W. Worek. Fisher Discriminant Analysis with Kernels. In *Proceedings of the IEEE Computer Society Conference on Computer Vision and Pattern Recognition*, pages 947–954, 2005.
56. P. J. Phillips, P. Grother, R. J. Micheals, D. M. Blackburn, E. Tabassi, and M. Bone. Face Recognition Vendor Test 2002. Evaluation report, National Institute of Standards and Technology, 2003.
57. P. J. Phillips, H. Moon, S. A. Rizvi, and P. J. Rauss. The FERET Evaluation Methodology for Face-Recognition Algorithms. *IEEE Transactions on Pattern Analysis and Machine Intelligence*, 22(10):1090–1104, 2000.
58. S. Roweis and L. K. Saul. Nonlinear Dimensionality Reduction by Locally Linear Embedding. *Science*, 290(5500):2323–2326, 2000.
59. M. Savvides, J. Heo, R. Abiantun, C. Xie, and B. V. K. Vijaya Kumar. Class Dependent Kernel Discrete Cosine Transform Features for Enhanced Holistic Face Recognition in FRGC-II. In *IEEE Conference on Acoustic, Speech, and Signal Processing*, 2006.
60. M. Savvides, B. V. K. Vijaya Kumar, and P. Khosla. Face verification using correlation filters. In *Proceedings of Third IEEE Automatic Identification Advanced Technologies*, pages 56–61, Tarrytown, NY, 2002.

61. M. Savvides, B. V. K. Vijaya Kumar, and P. Khosla. Robust, Shift-Invariant Biometric Identification from Partial Face Images. In *Biometric Technologies for Human Identification, SPIE Defense and Security Symposium*, volume 5404, pages 124–135, 2004.
62. M. Savvides, B. V. K. Vijaya Kumar, and P. Khosla. Corefaces: A Shift-Invariant Principal Component Analysis (PCA) Correlation Filter bank for Illumination-Tolerant Face Recognition. *Face Biometrics for Personal Identification Multi-Sensory Multi-Modal Systems*, 2007.
63. A. Scheenstra, A. Ruifrok, and R. C. Veltkamp. A Survey of 3D Face Recognition Methods. *Lecture Notes in Computer Science, Springer*, 3546:891–899, 2005.
64. T. Sim, S. Baker, and M. Bsat. The CMU Pose, Illumination, and Expression (PIE) Database. In *Proceedings Fifth Intl Conference Automatic Face and Gesture Recognition*, 2002.
65. R. Singh, M. Vatsa, A. Ross, and A. Noore. Performance Enhancement of 2D Face Recognition via Mosaicing. In *Proceedings of 4th IEEE Workshop on Automatic Identification Advanced Technologies (AutoID)*, pages 63–68, 2005.
66. J. S. Taylor and N. Cristianni. *Kernel Methods for Pattern Analysis*. Cambridge University Press, 2004.
67. J. B. Tenenbaum and W. T. Freeman. Separating style and content with bilinear models. *Neural Computation*, 12:1246–1283, 2000.
68. J. B. Tenenbaum, V. Silva, and J. C. Langford. A global geometric framework for nonlinear dimensionality reduction. *Science*, 290(12):2319–2323, 2003.
69. M. Turk and A. Pentland. Eigenfaces for Recognition. *Journal of Cognitive Neuroscience*, 3(1):71–86, 1991.
70. V. N. Vapnik. *The Nature of Statistical Learning Theory*. Springer-Verlag, New York, 1995.
71. M. A. O. Vasilescu and D. Terzopoulos. Multilinear analysis of image ensembles: TensorFaces. In *Proceedings European Conference on Computer Vision*, pages 447–460, 2002.
72. M. A. O. Vasilescu and D. Terzopoulos. Multilinear subspace analysis of image ensembles. In *Proceedings of the IEEE Computer Society Conference on Computer Vision and Pattern Recognition*, volume 2, pages 93–99, June 2002.
73. M. A. O. Vasilescu and D. Terzopoulos. Multilinear independent components analysis. In *Proceedings of the IEEE Computer Society Conference on Computer Vision and Pattern Recognition*, volume 1, pages 547–553, June 2005.
74. H. Wang and N. Ahuja. Facial expression decomposition. In *Proceedings of the IEEE International Conference on Computer Vision*, volume 2, pages 958–965, 2003.
75. L. Wiskott, J. M. Fellous, N. Krüger, and C. von der Malsburg. Face Recognition by Elastic Bunch Graph Matching. *IEEE Transactions on Pattern Analysis and Machine Intelligence*, 19(7):775–779, 1997.
76. C. Xie, M. Savvides, and B. V. K. Vijaya Kumar. Kernel Correlation Filter Based Redundant Class-Dependence Feature Analysis (KCFA) on FRGC2.0 Data. In *IEEE Workshop on Analysis and Modeling of Faces and Gestures (AMFG)*, pages 32–43, 2005.
77. M. H. Yang. Kernel Eigenfaces vs. Kernel Fisherfaces: Face Recognition using Kernel Methods. In *IEEE Conference on Automatic Face and Gesture Recognition*, pages 215–220, 2002.
78. H. Yu and J. Yang. A direct LDA algorithm for high-dimensional data with application to face recognition. *Pattern Recognition*, 34(10):2067–2070, 2001.

79. D. Zhang, H. Peng, J. Zhou, and S. K. Pal. A novel face recognition system using hybrid neural and dual eigenspaces methods. *IEEE Transactions on Systems, Man and Cybernetics - Part A*, 32(6):787–793, 2002.

80. Z. Zhang and Y. Huang. A Projection Method for Least Squares Problems with a Quadratic Equality Constraint. *Journal of Matrix Analysis and Applications*, 25(1):188–212, 2003.

81. W. Zhao, R. Chellappa, A. Rosenfeld, and P. J. Phillips. Face Recognition: A Literature Survey. *ACM Computing Surveys*, pages 399–458, 2003.

82. W. Zheng, C. Zou, and L. Zhao. Real-Time Face Recognition Using Gram-Schmidt Orthgonalization for LDA. In *IEEE Conference of Pattern Recognition*, pages 403–406, 2004.

4

Iris Recognition

John Daugman

University of Cambridge, The Computer Laboratory
J.J. Thomson Avenue, Cambridge CB3 0FD, United Kingdom
john.daugman@CL.cam.ac.uk

4.1 Introduction

Over the past 15 years, iris recognition has developed rapidly from its first live demonstration and first actual method patent [1], to a mainstream field of biometric development with a large number of active researchers in both academia and industry. To date, some 50 million persons worldwide have been enrolled in iris recognition systems that use the author's algorithms. But other systems are also being developed, demonstrated, and tested in Government-sponsored competitions with good results; and there is no doubt that in the future there will exist a lively equilibrium of diverse methods and viable products available for deployment, maybe even interoperably.

Because iris recognition is designed for use in identification mode ("one-to-many" exhaustive search, at least with the author's algorithms) so that a user is not even asked to claim or assert an identity, as opposed to simple verification (a "one-to-one" test of some claimed identity), the number of iris comparisons done so far is staggering. In one particular deployment linking all 27 air, land, and sea-ports of entry into the United Arab Emirates, that compares the irises of arriving travellers to all stored in a central database, some 5 trillion (5×10^{12}) iris comparisons have been performed since 2001. About 10 million arriving travellers have used that system, with 12 billion iris comparisons now being performed daily [2] at a speed of about 1 million comparisons per second per search engine. Data from 200 billion such iris comparisons will be plotted in this chapter, a number that is larger than the estimated number of neurons in the human brain, or the estimated number of stars in our galaxy. Closer to home, the UK has recently launched Project IRIS (Iris Recognition Immigration System) which allows travellers to enter the UK from abroad without passport presentation or any other assertion of identity, but just by looking at an iris camera at an automatic gate. If they have been enrolled in the system and are recognized, then their border-control formalities are finished and the gate opens. About 200,000 travellers to the UK in recent months have benefitted from this convenience [3].

Notwithstanding such existing public deployments at many airports in several countries, basic research into alternative methods continues. The anticipated large-scale applications of biometric technologies such as iris recognition are driving innovations at all levels, ranging from sensors, to user interfaces, to algorithms and decision theory. At the same time as these good innovations, possibly even outpacing them, the demands on the technology are becoming greater. In addition to the requirement to function on a national scale to detect any multiple identities upon issuance of biometric ID cards, expectations are also being raised for development of more tolerant and fluid user interfaces that aim to replace the "stop and stare" camera interface with iris recognition "on the move, off-axis, and at a distance" [4].

Scientific and engineering literature about iris recognition grows monthly, with contributions from several dozen university and industrial laboratories around the world. Many databases of iris images are available for download, further stimulating research; some are summarized in Chapter 25 of this book. An excellent and comprehensive review of the expanding literature about iris recognition, with 141 references, has recently appeared [5]. I will not attempt to duplicate such a literature survey here. Instead, I will briefly review the historical development of iris recognition, from its inception as a speculative idea to early efforts at commercialization, and its current drivers; and then I will present a number of new methods that I have developed and found beneficial, which I will illustrate here with publicly available iris images.

4.2 A Short History of Iris Recognition

4.2.1 Early Speculation about its Possibility

Divination of all sorts of things based on iris patterns goes back to ancient Egypt, to Chaldea in Babylonia, and to ancient Greece, as documented in stone inscriptions, painted ceramic artefacts, and the writings of Hippocrates. Clinical divination persists today as "iridology." The idea of using the iris as a distinguishing human identifier was suggested in 1885 by French physician Alphonse Bertillon [6], describing both color and pattern type. In 1949 British ophthalmologist James Doggart [7] commented specifically (p. 27) on the complexity of iris patterns and suggested that they might be sufficiently unique to serve in the same way as fingerprints. In 1987 American ophthalmologists Flom and Safir [8] managed to patent Doggart's concept, but they had no algorithm or specific method to make it possible. They acknowledged that they had encountered the idea in Doggart's book, yet their patent asserted claim over any method for iris recognition, if any could actually be developed. (Ironically, the only specific method disclosed in this patent was a conceptual flow chart for controlling an illuminator to drive the pupil to a pre-determined size; in fact this proves unnecessary and is not a feature of any actual iris recognition system.) Although the Flom-Safir patent has now expired worldwide, its broad if unimplemented claim over any use of the iris for human identification inhibited developers from trying to create actual methods. In 1989 when I was teaching at Harvard University, Flom and Safir (who by coincidence was my neighbor in Cambridge MA) asked me to try to create actual methods for iris recognition, which I did and patented [1]. After live demonstrations, we formed a company to exploit these algorithms.

4.2.2 Commercialization Efforts, 1993–2006

The company that we founded licensed my algorithms to a number of camera developers and security-related systems integrators. Those algorithms used methods that persist widely today in this technology, such as multi-scale Gabor wavelet encoding, binarization based on zero-crossings, Exclusive-OR bit vector comparison logic, and Hamming Distance similarity metrics. Unfortunately, a new management installed by new investors focused on re-branding and media positioning tactics more than on technology considerations. During the period 2001–2006 a crucial mistake was advocacy of clearly inferior cameras when superior ones were available and well proven, only because of their comparative royalty streams. For example, one camera widely recognized (even internally) as the "gold standard," featuring autofocus, autozoom, and superb resolution, was de-licensed and banned from use by partners, while inferior cameras lacking such features were promoted and even mandated by an ostensible "certification" program. Consequently, a number of high-profile test deployments generated unnecessarily poor results, and the inherent powers and potential of iris recognition were generally clouded if not contradicted by apparently high rates of Failures-to-Enroll or False Rejections.

Disputes over licensing terms with several of the company's own partners, especially the more successful partners, escalated into a series of lawsuits. Finally, having expended its funding resources both on aggressive litigation and on re-branding exercises that tried to portray the algorithms as having been developed in-house, the company had made enemies of those it most needed as friends, and collapsed. Never having become profitable, it was acquired in 2006 solely for its IP assets (patents and my core algorithms) by a multi-biometric holding company. Meanwhile a number of other start-ups offering iris recognition have appeared; but they too, with the exception of one systems integrator, are all struggling to survive. None have any public deployments using their own proprietary algorithms. For nearly all investors in this sector up until the present time, iris recognition has proved an enticing but perilous seduction, like the song of the Sirens (irresistible sea nymphs in Greek mythology) who drowned many passing sailors.

4.2.3 Current Stimulants

Iris recognition technology research and development today is expanding rapidly, at several dozen universities and industrial research venues. Enthusiasm for the technology and its potential is strong, as is the level of innovation in response to its undeniable challenges, particularly regarding image capture. Among the stimulants that seem to be driving this creative energy are:

- Evidence emerging in tests that iris recognition seems the biometric with best performance, in terms of large database accuracy and search speed.
- Legislation in several countries for national programs involving biometric ID cards, or biometrics replacing passports in automated border-crossing.
- NIST Iris Challenge Evaluation [9] ("large-scale") based on images from 240 Subjects; its training database was downloaded by 42 research groups.
- Biometric Data Interchange Format Standards [10], and databases of iris images for algorithm development and testing.
- Numerous international conferences and books that include the topic.
- Popular futurism and movies, from *James Bond* to *Minority Report*.
- Cultural iconography associated with the eye (the "Window to the Soul;" affective significance of eye contact, and communication through gaze).
- The intellectual pleasure of solving multi-disciplinary problems combining mathematics, information theory, computer vision, statistics, biology, ergonomics, decision theory, and naturally occurring human randomness.

4.3 Active Contours, Flexible Generalized Embedded Coordinates

Iris recognition begins with finding an iris in an image, demarcating its inner and outer boundaries at pupil and sclera, detecting the upper and lower eyelid boundaries if they occlude, and detecting and excluding any superimposed eyelashes, or reflections from the cornea or eyeglasses. These processes may collectively be called segmentation. Precision in assigning the true inner and outer iris boundaries, even if they are partly invisible, is important because the mapping of the iris in a dimensionless (size-invariant and pupil dilation-invariant) coordinate system is critically dependent on this. Inaccuracy in the detection, modelling, and representation of these boundaries can cause different mappings of the iris pattern in its extracted description, and such differences could cause failures to match.

It is natural to start by thinking of the iris as an annulus. Soon one discovers that the inner and outer boundaries are usually not concentric. A simple solution is then to create a non-concentric pseudo-polar coordinate system for mapping the iris, relaxing the assumption that the iris and pupil share a common center, and requiring only that the pupil is fully contained within the iris. This "doubly-dimensionless pseudo-polar coordinate system" was the basis of my original paper on iris recognition [11] and Patent [1], and this iris coordinate system was incorporated into ISO Standard 19794-6 for iris data [10]. But soon one discovers also that often the pupil boundary is non-circular, and usually the iris outer boundary is non-circular. Performance in iris recognition is significantly improved by relaxing both of those assumptions, replacing them with more disciplined methods for faithfully detecting and modelling those boundaries whatever their shapes, and defining a more flexible and generalized coordinate system on their basis.

Because the iris outer boundary is often partly occluded by eyelids, and the iris inner boundary may be partly occluded by reflections from illumination, and sometimes both boundaries also by reflections from eyeglasses, it is necessary to fit flexible contours that can tolerate interruptions and continue their trajectory under them on a principled basis, driven somehow by the data that exists elsewhere. A further constraint is that both the inner and outer boundary models must form closed curves. A final goal is that we would like to impose a constraint on smoothness, based on the credibility of any evidence for non-smooth curvature.

An excellent way to achieve all of these goals is to describe the iris inner and outer boundaries in terms of "Active Contours" based on discrete Fourier series expansions of the contour data. By employing Fourier components whose frequencies are integer multiples of $1/(2\pi)$, closure, orthogonality, and completeness are ensured. Selecting the number of frequency components allows control over the degree of smoothness that is imposed, and over the fidelity of the approximation. In essence, truncating the discrete Fourier series after a certain number of terms amounts to low-pass filtering the boundary curvature data in the active contour model.

These methods are illustrated in Figures 4.1 and 4.2. In the lower left-hand corner of each Figure are shown two "snakes," each consisting of a fuzzy ribbon-like data distribution and a dotted curve which is a discrete Fourier series approximation to the data, including continuation across gap interruptions. The lower snake in each snake box is the curvature map for the pupil boundary, and the upper snake is the curvature map for the iris outer boundary, with the endpoints joining up at the 6-o'clock position. The interruptions correspond to detected occlusions by eyelids (indicated by separate splines in both images), or by specular reflections. The data plotted as the grey level for each snake is the image gradient in the radial direction. Thus the relative thickness of each snake represents roughly the sharpness of the corresponding radial edge. If an iris boundary were well-described as a circular edge, then the corresponding snake in its box should be flat and straight. In general this is not the case.

The dotted curve that is plotted within each snake, and also superimposed on the corresponding loci of points in the iris image, is a discrete Fourier series approximation to the data. (In both Figures detected eyelid occlusions are also demarcated by white splines, and they interrupt the corresponding outer boundary data snake, although the estimated contour continues through such interruptions.) The estimation procedure is to compute a Fourier expansion of the N regularly-spaced angular samples of radial gradient edge data $\{r_\theta\}$ for $\theta = 0$ to $\theta = N - 1$. A set of M discrete Fourier coefficients $\{C_k\}$, for $k = 0$ to $k = M - 1$, are computed from the data sequence $\{r_\theta\}$ as follows:

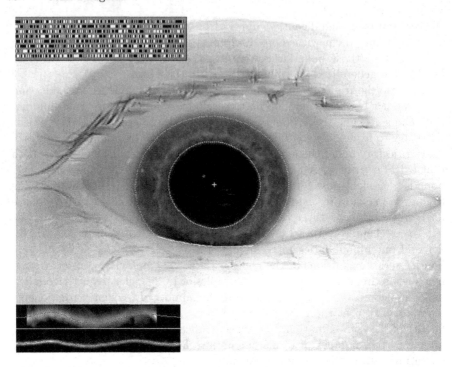

Fig. 4.1. Active contours enhance iris segmentation, because they allow for non-circular boundaries and enable flexible coordinate systems. The box in the lower-left shows curvature maps for the inner and outer iris boundaries, which would be flat and straight if they were circles. Here the outer boundary (upper plot) is particularly non-circular. Dotted curves in the box and on the iris are Fourier series approximations. This iris is NIST ICE-1 file 239261.

$$C_k = \sum_{\theta=0}^{N-1} r_\theta e^{-2\pi i k\theta/N} \qquad (4.1)$$

Note that the zeroth-order coefficient or "DC term" C_0 extracts information about the average curvature of the (pupil or outer iris) boundary, in other words, about its radius when it is approximated just as a simple circle.

From these M discrete Fourier coefficients, an approximation to the corresponding iris boundary (now without interruptions, and at a resolution determined by M) is obtained as the new sequence $\{R_\theta\}$ for $\theta = 0$ to $\theta = N - 1$:

$$R_\theta = \frac{1}{N} \sum_{k=0}^{M-1} C_k e^{2\pi i k\theta/N} \qquad (4.2)$$

As is generally true of active contour methods [12, 13], there is a trade-off between how precisely one wants the model to fit all the data (improved

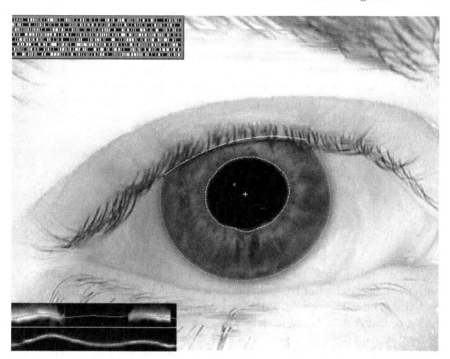

Fig. 4.2. Active contours enhance iris segmentation, because they allow for non-circular boundaries and enable flexible coordinate systems. The box in the lower-left shows curvature maps for the inner and outer iris boundaries, which would be flat and straight if they were circles. Here the pupil boundary (lower plot) is particularly non-circular. Dotted curves in the box and on the iris are Fourier series approximations. This iris is NIST ICE-1 file 240461.

by increasing M), versus how much one wishes to impose constraints such as keeping the model simple and of low-dimensional curvature (achieved by reducing M, for example $M = 1$ enforces a circular model). Thus the number M of activated Fourier coefficients is a specification for the number of degrees-of-freedom in the shape model. I have found that a good choice of M for capturing the true pupil boundary with appropriate fidelity is $M = 17$, whereas a good choice for the iris outer boundary where the data is often much weaker is $M = 5$. It is also useful to impose monotonically decreasing weights on the computed Fourier coefficients $\{C_k\}$ as a further control on the resolution of the approximation $\{R_\theta\} \approx \{r_\theta\}$, which amounts to low-pass filtering the curvature map in its Fourier representation. Altogether these manipulations, particularly the two different choices for M, implement the computer vision principle that strong data (the pupil boundary) may be modelled with only weak constraints, whereas weak data (the outer boundary) should be modelled with strong constraints, i.e. allowing fewer degrees-of-freedom.

The active contour models for the inner and outer iris boundaries support an isometric mapping of the iris tissue between them, regardless of the actual shapes of the contours. Suppose the contour model for the pupillary boundary consists of cartesian coordinates $(x_p(\theta), y_p(\theta))$ with arc parameter $\theta \in [0, 2\pi]$, while the outer boundary of the iris at the sclera is described by contour model $(x_s(\theta), y_s(\theta))$. Then a shape-flexible, size-invariant, and pupil dilation-invariant, dimensionless coordinate system for the iris portion of the image $I(x, y)$ can be represented by the normalized mapping

$$I(x(r, \theta), y(r, \theta)) \rightarrow I(r, \theta) \tag{4.3}$$

where the dimensionless parameter $r \in [0, 1]$ spans the unit interval, and

$$\begin{bmatrix} x(r, \theta) \\ y(r, \theta) \end{bmatrix} = \begin{bmatrix} x_p(\theta) \; x_s(\theta) \\ y_p(\theta) \; y_s(\theta) \end{bmatrix} \begin{bmatrix} 1 - r \\ r \end{bmatrix} \tag{4.4}$$

The execution time for the entire subroutine that fits active contours to both the inner and outer iris boundaries is just 3.5 msec on a 3 GHz PC with optimized code. The benefit of the new adaptive coordinate system based on active contours may be gauged by the improvement it offers in recognition performance on difficult image databases. The NIST ICE-1 iris database contains many difficult images, producing a high False Reject Rate (FRR) which degrades the Equal Error Rate (EER). Algorithms that yielded an EER of 1% (EER = 0.01) when using enforced circular models improved 10-fold to an EER of 0.1% (EER = 0.0011) on the same database by adopting this active contours approach instead.

4.4 Fourier-based Trigonometry and Correction for Off-Axis Gaze

A limitation of current iris recognition cameras is that they require an on-axis image of an eye, usually achieved through what may be called a "stop and stare" interface in which a user must align her optical axis with the camera's optical axis. This is not as flexible or fluid as it might be. Moreover, sometimes the standard cameras acquire images for which the on-axis assumption is not true. For example, the NIST iris images that were made available and used for training in ICE-1 contained several with very deviated gaze, probably because the user's gaze was distracted by an adjacent monitor.

The on-axis requirement can be relaxed by correcting the projective deformation of the iris when it is imaged off-axis, provided that one can reliably estimate the actual parameters of gaze. Dorairaj et al. [14] approached this by seeking the gaze parameters that optimize the value of an integro-differential operator [11, 15] which detects circular boundaries. The gaze parameters that we seek include two spherical angles for eye pose, but the projective geometry depends also on the distance between eye and camera which may be unknown, and it depends on the surface curvature of the iris which is generally not zero. If simplifying assumptions and approximations are made about the latter factors, then a simple affine projective transformation may suffice to make the iris recognizable against itself as imaged in other poses, orthographic or not.

The essence of the problem is then estimating the two angles of gaze relative to the camera. Eye morphology is so variable in terms of visible sclera and eyelid occlusion that it is unlikely that such factors could support robust estimation, at least when only one eye is imaged; although it must be noted that humans are very impressively skilled somehow at monitoring each other's gaze direction. In the absence of solving that mystery, an obvious alternative approach would be to assume that an orthographic image of the iris should reveal a circular pupil; therefore detecting ellipticity of the pupil indicates off-axis image acquisition, and so estimating the elongation and orientation of that ellipse would yield the two parameters of gaze deviation, modulo π in direction. We present here a somewhat more robust variant of this idea, which does not assume that the true pupil shape is circular when viewed orthographically. This method of estimating gaze (and thus correcting for off-axis imaging) uses a new approach that may be called "Fourier-based trigonometry."

The method arises from the observation that Fourier series expansions of the X- and Y-coordinates of the detected pupil boundary contain shape distortion information related to deviated gaze, in the relationships among the real and imaginary coefficients of the lowest frequency term of each of those series expansions. In the special case that the true pupil boundary when viewed orthographically is really a circle, then this method reduces to the simpler "ellipticity" method outlined above.

We begin by considering that simple special case of a circular pupil. Let $X(t)$ and $Y(t)$ be the parameterized coordinate vectors of the pupil boundary, so the range of t is from 0 to 2π in one cycle around this closed curve. Clearly in the case of a circular pupil with radius A, origin-centered for simplicity, these functions are just $X(t) = A\cos(t)$ and $Y(t) = A\sin(t)$. In the case of deviated gaze along a cardinal axis, and assuming the camera distance is large compared with the iris diameter so there is simple foreshortening along the cardinal axis, these functions become: $X(t) = A\cos(t)$ and $Y(t) = B\sin(t)$, with $A \neq B$. Finally, if the gaze deviation is not along a cardinal axis but rather in direction θ, then these functions take the more general conic form for an oriented ellipse:

$$X(t) = [A\cos^2\theta + B\sin^2\theta]\cos(t) + [(B - A)\cos\theta\sin\theta]\sin(t) \qquad (4.5)$$

$$Y(t) = [(B - A)\cos\theta\sin\theta]\cos(t) + [B\cos^2\theta + A\sin^2\theta]\sin(t) \qquad (4.6)$$

It is noteworthy that the information we seek about gaze deviation, namely the direction and magnitude of deviation, are contained in the form of Fourier coefficients on the harmonic functions $\cos(t)$ and $\sin(t)$ that represent in their

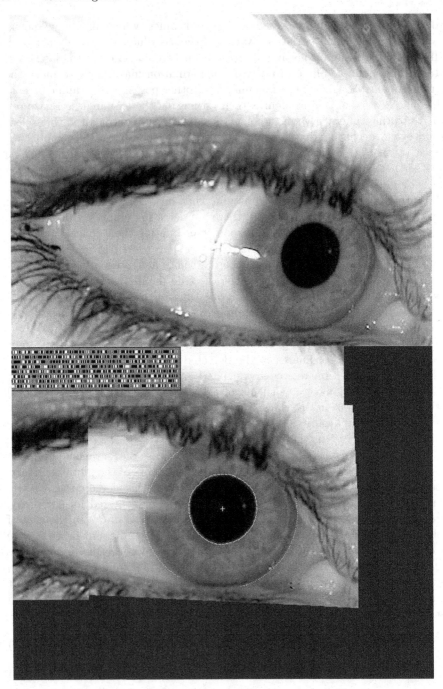

Fig. 4.3. Gaze estimation enables transformation of an eye image with deviated gaze, into one apparently looking directly at the camera. Without this transformation, such images would fail to be matched. This iris is NIST ICE-1 file 244858.

linear combination the contour data $X(t)$ and $Y(t)$. Specifically, the lowest complex-valued coefficient in a Fourier series expansion of the empirical function $X(t)$ contains as its real and imaginary parts, a and b, respectively:

$$a = A\cos^2\theta + B\sin^2\theta \tag{4.7}$$

$$b = (B - A)\cos\theta\sin\theta \tag{4.8}$$

Likewise the first complex-valued coefficient in a Fourier series expansion of the empirical function $Y(t)$ contains as its real and imaginary parts, c and d, respectively:

$$c = (B - A)\cos\theta\sin\theta \tag{4.9}$$

$$d = B\cos^2\theta + A\sin^2\theta \tag{4.10}$$

Thus, we can infer the gaze deviation parameters we seek just by computing the relevant Fourier coefficients of empirical contour functions $X(t)$ and $Y(t)$. This estimation process is independent of the higher-order Fourier coefficients which will exist when the pupil has some more complex and irregular shape than a circle. The method is not restricted to such an assumption about circular shape.

Algebraic manipulation extracts from the four empirical Fourier coefficients a, b, c, d the gaze deviation parameters we need. It should be noted that although the right-hand sides of (4.8) and (4.9) above appear to be identical functions of the desired parameters, these equations express constraints based on different empirical data. Quantities a and b are obtained from $X(t)$, whereas c and d are obtained from $Y(t)$. The computed direction of gaze deviation (modulo π) has essentially the form of Fourier phase information, and is:

$$\theta = 0.5\arctan\left(\frac{-b - c}{a - d}\right) \tag{4.11}$$

while the magnitude of gaze deviation in direction θ is expressed not as an angle but as the projective aspect ratio $\gamma = B/A$ which will be the affine transformation parameter:

$$\gamma = \frac{(a + d)\cos(2\theta) + a - d}{(a + d)\cos(2\theta) - a + d} \tag{4.12}$$

By estimating these parameters, the "Fourier-based trigonometry" allows the projective geometric deformation caused by gaze deviation to be reversed by an affine transformation of the off-axis image. This is illustrated in Figure 4.3, showing in its upper panel image 244858 from the NIST ICE-1 database, and in the lower panel the same eye image after "correcting" the gaze deviation by an affine transformation with extracted parameters (θ, γ). The result of the transformation is to convert such images into apparent orthographic form, seeming to rotate the eyes in their sockets, making them recognizable against other images of the same eye. A limitation of this method is that the affine transformation assumes the iris is planar, whereas in fact it is a surface with some curvature.

4.5 Detecting and Excluding Eyelashes by Statistical Inference

One of the ways in which iris image data may be corrupted, besides reflections, camera noise, and eyelid occlusion, is occlusion by eyelashes (usually from the upper eyelid). These often have random and complex shapes, combining with each other to form masses of intersecting elements rather than just simple hair-like strands that might be amenable to detection by elementary shape models. They can be the strongest signals in the iris image, in terms of contrast or energy, and they could dominate the IrisCode with spurious information if not detected and excluded from the encoded data.

The inference of eyelashes and their exclusion from the IrisCode can be handled by statistical estimation methods that depend essentially on determining whether the distribution of iris pixels is multi-modal. If the lower tail of the iris pixel histogram supports an hypothesis of multi-modal mixing, then an appropriate threshold can be computed and pixels outside it can be excluded from influencing the IrisCode.

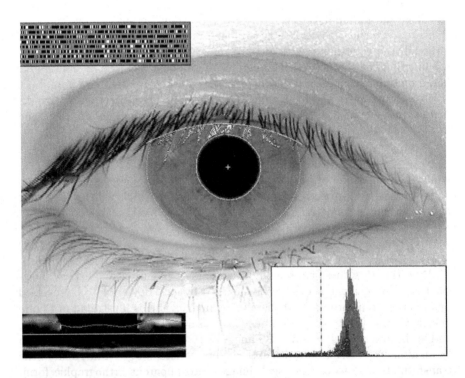

Fig. 4.4. Statistical inference of eyelashes from the iris pixel histogram, and determination of a threshold for excluding the lashes (labelled in white) from influencing the IrisCode. This iris is NIST ICE-1 file 239766.

Figure 4.4 illustrates this method. The panel in lower-right corner super-imposes four histograms, all computed from just the pixels in the segmented iris portion of the image, between the detected eyelids. The solid grey distribution is a histogram of all the iris pixels (ranging from 0 to 255). The two dotted outline histograms break this up into two components, one for just the lower part of the iris (white dotted curve), and the other for just the upper part of the iris (black dotted curve). The solid black histogram is the difference between these two histograms. We are interested in whether the cumulatives from the left of this difference histogram pass a test of being statistically separable from the mother (solid grey) distribution. If so, based on significant Z-score deviations between their respective quartiles, then an hypothesis may be accepted that the iris contains superimposed eyelashes.

The vertical dashed line in the histogram panel indicates the computed threshold where such an hypothesis in this case (for this image) is supported. If that hypothesis also passes a further test on the deviation between the threshold quartile and the median of the mother distribution, thus confirming that not only are there two populations but also that they are sufficiently different from each, then the threshold is accepted and pixels below it are deemed to arise from superimposed eyelashes.

In the iris image itself in Figure 4.4, these detected eyelashes within the iris have been marked now as white pixels. Their positions are recorded in a mask array that prevents them from influencing any data that encodes the iris texture. This eyelash detection subroutine executes in less than 1 msec.

4.6 Alternative Score Normalization Rules

Iris recognition works by performing a test of statistical independence between two IrisCodes, in order to decide whether they arise from the same or from different irises [1, 2, 11]. This test of statistical independence is equivalent to tossing a coin many times (each toss representing a comparison between two bits in the two IrisCodes), in order to decide whether or not the coin is fair by delivering roughly 50-50 outcomes. If such a result is obtained then the irises can be judged independent; but if there is a great preponderance of (say) "heads," meaning that a large majority of corresponding bit pairs agreed, then that is strong evidence that the IrisCodes came from the same iris. But what is the effect of greatly varying numbers of such "coin tosses" in these correlated Bernoulli trials, due to varying amounts of iris data being visible between eyelids or reflections and available for comparison?

Areas of the iris that are obscured by eyelids, or by eyelashes, or by reflections from eyeglasses, or that have low contrast or poor signal-to-noise ratio, are detected by the image processing algorithms and prevented from influencing the iris comparisons, through bit-wise mask functions. Whereas the IrisCode bits themselves contain phase data [1, 2, 11] that is ExclusiveOR'ed ($\otimes$) to detect disagreement and thereby determine similarity between two irises, the bits to be considered are first selected by ANDing ($\cap$) each pair with the associated mask functions of both irises to ensure their validity and their significance. The norms ($\|\quad\|$) of the resultant bit vector and of the AND'ed mask vectors are then measured in order to compute a raw Hamming Distance HD_{raw}, as the fraction of meaningful bits that disagree between two irises whose two phase code bit vectors are denoted $\{codeA,\ codeB\}$ and whose mask bit vectors are denoted $\{maskA,\ maskB\}$:

$$HD_{\mathrm{raw}} = \frac{\|(codeA \otimes codeB) \cap maskA \cap maskB\|}{\|maskA \cap maskB\|} \tag{4.13}$$

The number of bits pairings available for comparison, $\|maskA \cap maskB\|$, is usually nearly a thousand. But if one of the irises has (say) almost complete occlusion of its upper half by a drooping upper eyelid, and if the other iris being compared with it has almost complete occlusion of its lower half, then the common area available for comparison may be almost nil. In such cases, returning to the coin-tossing analogy, our test for the "fairness" of the coin (i.e. statistical independence of the two IrisCodes by finding a nearly 50-50 result) will be based upon a very small number of Bernoulli trials indeed. So, the interpretation of any given deviation from the 50-50 outcome expected for independence must take into account the total amount of comparison data that was available. This is the role of score normalization.

A natural choice for the score normalization rule is to re-scale all deviations from 0.5 raw Hamming Distance in proportion to the square-root of the number of bits that were compared when obtaining that score. The reason for such a rule is that the expected standard deviation in the distribution of Bernoulli trial outcomes (expressed as a fraction of the n Bernoulli trials having a given outcome), is $\sigma = \sqrt{pq/n}$ where p and q are the respective outcome probabilities (both nominally 0.5 in this case). Thus, decision confidence levels can be maintained irrespective of how many bits n were actually compared, by mapping each raw Hamming Distance HD_{raw} into a normalized score HD_{norm} using a re-scaling rule such as:

$$HD_{\mathrm{norm}} = 0.5 - (0.5 - HD_{\mathrm{raw}})\sqrt{\frac{n}{911}} \tag{4.14}$$

This normalization should transform all samples of scores obtained when comparing different eyes into samples drawn from the same binomial distribution, whereas the raw scores HD_{raw} might be samples from many different binomial distributions having standard deviations σ dependent on the number of bits n that were actually available for comparison. This normalization maintains constant confidence levels for decisions using a given Hamming Distance threshold, regardless of the value of n. The scaling parameter 911 is the typical number of bits compared (unmasked) between two different irises, as estimated from one particular (early) database.

The benefit of score normalization is to prevent False Matches arising by chance due to few bits being compared (just as few coin tosses may well yield

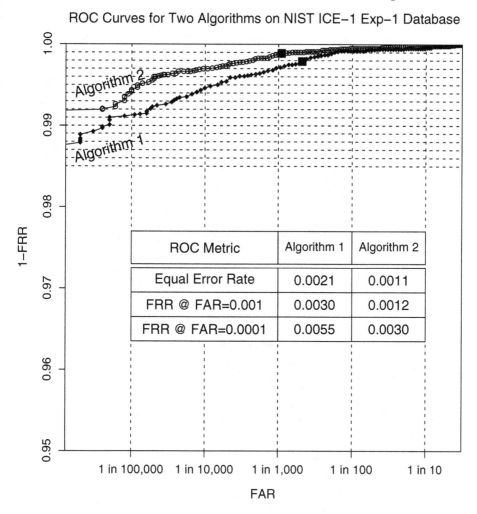

Fig. 4.5. Comparison of two algorithms on the NIST ICE-1 database, with (**1**) and without (**2**) score normalization. Solid squares mark their EER points. In this region of the ROC curve near Equal Error Rates, where the required False Match Rates are not very demanding, best performance is achieved without score normalization.

all "heads"). But the cost of this normalization for n is to penalize same-eye matches when few bits are available for comparison; even if they all agreed, so that $HD_{\mathrm{raw}} = 0$, the resulting HD_{norm} may be above the acceptance threshold and the match would be rejected. This penalty is apparent by comparing False Reject performance with and without score normalization on the NIST ICE-1 iris database, consisting of a few thousand iris images that NIST released together with "ground truth" information. This image database contained many very difficult and corrupted images, often in poor focus and with much eyelid occlusion, and sometimes with the iris partly outside of the image frame. In the region of the ROC curve (trade-off between False Reject and False Accept Rates, FRR vs FAR) where one tolerates rather high FAR such as 1 in 1,000 or 1 in 10,000, as shown in Figure 4.5, the cost of score normalization (Algorithm 1) on FRR is clear. The Equal Error Rate (where FRR = FAR) is about 0.001 without score normalization, but 0.002 with normalization. Similarly at other nominal points of interest in this region of the ROC curve, as tabulated within Figure 4.5, the cost of score normalization is roughly a doubling in FRR. But in much more aggressive regions of the ROC, where one demands an FAR of perhaps 1 in a billion for applications such as national database search or "all-against-all" cross-comparisons to discover any multiple identities, we will see that score normalization is paramount.

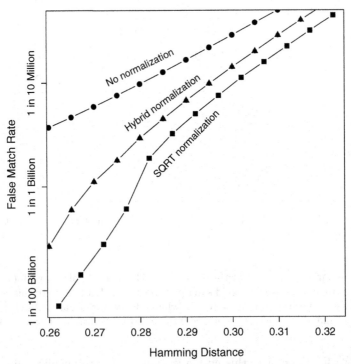

Fig. 4.6. Comparison of three methods of score normalization, based on 200 billion iris cross-comparisons using the UAE database of 632,500 IrisCodes. False Match Rates are plotted in semi-logarithmic coordinates, versus decision criterion. The range of the ordinate in this plot spans a factor of 300,000 to 1.

For the UAE database, Figure 4.6 compares False Match Rates for three approaches to normalizing scores based on the number of bits compared. The upper plot takes no account of the number of bits, so it has the highest False Match Rates. The bottom curve in Figure 4.6 shows the benefit of score normalization using the rule given in (4.14), causing the observed False Match Rate to plummet to 1 in 200 billion at a criterion around $HD_{\text{norm}} = 0.262$. This performance is about 2,000 times better than without the normalization (note the semi-logarithmic coordinates). The middle curve represents a hybrid normalization rule that is a linear combination of the other two, taking into account the number of bits compared only when in a certain range.

We learn from these comparisons of alternative normalization rules that performance in different regions of the ROC curve is optimized by different rules. In the relatively undemanding domain highlighted in Figure 4.5, near the Equal Error Rate point of either ROC curve and involving a relatively small database, best performance was achieved without score normalization because that amounts to a penalty on good matches when few bits were compared. But in the vastly more demanding domain of national-scale databases involving possibly astronomic numbers of cross-comparisons, as shown in Figure 4.6 with 200 billion iris comparisons, normalizing scores by the number of bits on which they were based is a critical necessity.

4.7 Adapting for Large-Scale Applications

Figure 4.7 presents a histogram of all 200 billion cross-comparison similarity scores among the 632,500 different irises in the UAE database, using the score normalization rule. The vast majority of IrisCodes from different eyes disagreed in roughly 50% of their bits, as expected since the bits are equiprobable and uncorrelated between different eyes [11, 15]. Very few pairings of IrisCodes could disagree in fewer than 35% or more than 65% of their bits, as is evident from the distribution.

The solid curve fitting the data very closely in Figure 4.7 is a binomial probability density function. This theoretical form was chosen because comparisons between bits from different IrisCodes are Bernoulli trials, or conceptually "coin tosses," and Bernoulli trials generate binomial distributions. If one tossed a coin whose probability of "heads" is p in a series of N independent tosses and counted the number m of "heads" outcomes, and if one tallied this fraction $x = m/N$ in a large number of such repeated runs of N tosses, then the expected distribution of x would be as per the curve in Figure 4.7:

$$f(x) = \frac{N!}{m!(N-m)!}\, p^m (1-p)^{(N-m)} \tag{4.15}$$

The analogy between tossing coins and comparing bits between different IrisCodes is deep but imperfect, because any given IrisCode has internal correlations arising from iris features, especially in the radial direction [11]. Further correlations are introduced because the patterns are encoded using 2D Gabor wavelet filters [15], whose lowpass aspect introduces correlations in amplitude,

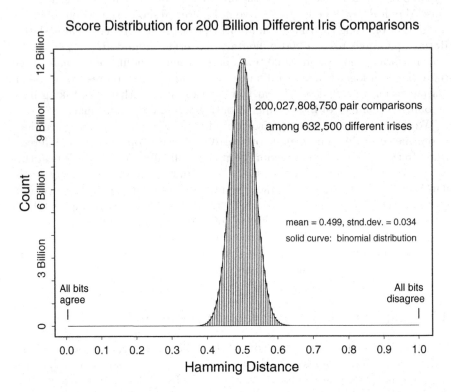

Fig. 4.7. Distribution of HD_{norm} normalized similarity scores (4.14) for 200 billion different pairings of iris patterns, without relative rotations. The solid curve fitting the histogram is a binomial density (4.15).

and whose bandpass aspect introduces correlations in phase, both of which linger to an extent that is inversely proportional to the filter bandwidth. The effect of these correlations is to reduce the value of the distribution parameter N to a number significantly smaller than the number of bits that are actually compared between two IrisCodes; N becomes the number of effectively independent bit comparisons. The value of p is very close to 0.5 (empirically 0.499 for the UAE database), because the states of each bit are equiprobable *a priori*, and so IrisCode bit pairings are equally likely to agree or disagree.

The binomial functional form that describes so well the distribution of normalized similarity scores for comparisons between different iris patterns is key to the robustness of these algorithms in large-scale search applications. The tails of the binomial attenuate extremely rapidly, because of the dominating central tendency caused by the factorial terms in (4.15). Rapidly attenuating tails are critical for a biometric to survive the vast numbers of opportunities to make False Matches without actually making any, when applied in an "all-against-all" mode of searching for matching or multiple identities, as is contemplated in some national ID card projects in the UK and in Europe.

Table 4.1. False Match Rates with HD_{norm} Score Normalization: Dependence on Decision Threshold Criterion (based on 200 Billion Comparisons, UAE Database)

HD Criterion	Observed False Match Rate
0.220	0 (theor: 1 in 5 $\times 10^{15}$)
0.225	0 (theor: 1 in 1 $\times 10^{15}$)
0.230	0 (theor: 1 in 3 $\times 10^{14}$)
0.235	0 (theor: 1 in 9 $\times 10^{13}$)
0.240	0 (theor: 1 in 3 $\times 10^{13}$)
0.245	0 (theor: 1 in 8 $\times 10^{12}$)
0.250	0 (theor: 1 in 2 $\times 10^{12}$)
0.255	0 (theor: 1 in 7 $\times 10^{11}$)
0.262	1 in 200 billion
0.267	1 in 50 billion
0.272	1 in 13 billion
0.277	1 in 2.7 billion
0.282	1 in 284 million
0.287	1 in 96 million
0.292	1 in 40 million
0.297	1 in 18 million
0.302	1 in 8 million
0.307	1 in 4 million
0.312	1 in 2 million
0.317	1 in 1 million

The cumulatives (up to various thresholds) under the left tail of the distribution of normalized similarity scores for different irises compared at multiple relative tilts, reveal the False Match Rates among the 200 billion iris comparisons if the identification decision policy used those thresholds. These rates are provided in Table 4.1. Although the smallest observed match was near 0.26, the Table has been extended down to 0.22 using the theoretical cumulative of the extreme value distribution of multiple samples from the binomial (4.15) plotted as the solid curve in Figure 4.7, in order to extrapolate theoretically expected False Match Rates for such decision policies. These False Match Rates, whether observed or theoretical, also serve as confidence levels that can be associated with a given quality of match using the score normalization rule (4.14). In this analysis, only a single eye is presumed to be presented.

Under the assumption of independence between left and right eye IrisCodes, which is strongly supported by available data (see Figure 6 of [15]), the confidence levels in Table 4.1 could be multiplied together for matches obtained with both eyes. A method allowing IrisCodes to be *indexed* by their collisions with substrings, thereby replacing exhaustive search by almost instantaneous direct addressing with IrisCodes, is the subject of a separate paper [16].

Acknowledgment: Figures and material in Sections 4.3–4.7 are ©IEEE and reproduced with permission.

References

1. J. G. Daugman. US Patent 5,291,560. *Biometric Personal Identification System Based on Iris Analysis*, 1994.
2. J. G. Daugman. Probing the uniqueness and randomness of iriscodes: Results from 200 billion iris pair comparisons. *Proc. IEEE*, 94(11):1927–1935, 2006.
3. UK Government Home Office, Project IRIS website. http://iris.gov.uk.
4. J. Matey, K. Hanna, R. Kolcyznski, D. LoIacono, S. Mangru, O. Naroditsky, M. Tinker, T. Zappia, and W-Y. Zhao. Iris on the Move: Acquisition of images for iris recognition in less constrained environments. *Proc. IEEE*, 94(11):1936–1947, 2006.
5. K. Bowyer and K. Hollingsworth and P. Flynn. Image understanding for iris biometrics: a survey. Technical Report CSE, Univ. Notre Dame, 2007.
6. A. Bertillon. La couleur de l'iris. *Revue Scientifique*, 1885.
7. J. H. Doggart. *Ocular Signs in Slit-lamp Microscopy*. Kimpton, London, 1949.
8. L. Flom and A. Safir. US Patent 4,641,349. *Iris Recognition System*, 1987.
9. National Institute of Standards and Technology. Iris Challenge Evaluation. http://iris.nist.gov/ice/.
10. ISO/IEC Standard 19794-6. Information Technology – Biometric Data Interchange Formats, Part 6: Iris Image Data, 2005.
11. J. G. Daugman. High confidence visual recognition of persons by a test of statistical independence. *IEEE Trans. Pattern Analysis and Machine Intelligence*, 15(11):1148–1161, 1993.
12. A. Blake and M. Isard. *Active Contours*. Springer, Heidelberg, Germany, 1998.
13. M. Kass, A. Witkin, and D. Terzopoulos. Snakes: active contour models. *International Journal of Computer Vision*, 1:321–331, 1988.
14. V. Dorairaj, N. Schmid, and G. Fahmy. Performance evaluation of non-ideal iris based recognition system implementing global ICA encoding. In *Proc. IEEE Int'l Conference on Image Processing (ICIP)*, volume 3, pages 285–288, 2005.
15. J. G. Daugman. How iris recognition works. *IEEE Trans. Circuits and Systems for Video Technology*, 14(1):21–30, 2004.
16. F. Hao, J. G. Daugman, and P. Zielinski. A fast search algorithm for a large fuzzy database. *Submitted: IEEE Trans. Information Forensics & Security*, 2007.

Hand Geometry Recognition

David P. Sidlauskas[1] and Samir Tamer[2]

[1] Consultant `dsidlauskas@att.net`
[2] Ingersoll Rand Recognition Systems, California, USA `samir_tamer@irco.com`

5.1 Hand Geometry: A historical perspective

Hand Geometry is an authentication technology with a long history of use. Ancient paintings in Chauvet Cavern have been carbon dated to be 31,000 years old. Some say that the handprints left with these paintings are the artist's unique signature. This is, perhaps, the first use of Hand Geometry for identification, but surely not the last [15].

More recently, in July of 1858, Sir William Herschel had Rajyadhar Konai, a local businessman, impress his hand print on the back of a contract in order to uniquely tie Konai to the contract. Thus began the first recorded systematic capture of hand and finger images for identification purposes [1].

The first commercial Hand Geometry scanner was the Identimat introduced by Identimation in the early 1970's. This device used a 1,000 watt light bulb to activate mechanically scanned photocells for measuring the hand shape. Identimation was bought by a new company, Identimat, in 1976, and in 1979 was sold to the Wackenhut Corporation and placed in their Stellar Systems subsidiary. The Identimat was in continuous production until 1987.

Members of Stellar Systems went on to form Recognition Systems in 1986 to develop advanced methods of Hand Geometry utilizing the low cost digital imaging and image processing technology then becoming available. Recognition Systems, now a division of Ingersoll Rand, is the leading hand geometry manufacturer, producing hundreds of thousands of Hand Geometry terminals for the Security and Time and Attendance markets.

Biomet Partners, Inc., founded in 1992, has developed a two finger identification device that applies the principles of hand geometry to the index and middle finger. The two-finger geometry readers from Biomet Partners have been in commercial use since 1995, starting with the Digi-2 cameras. Many thousands of units are installed throughout the world, in a wide variety of applications. While not strictly a hand geometry product, it is sometimes included in that class.

5.2 History of Development

In the mid 1960's Robert Miller of New Jersey was studying an army clothing procurement report where he came upon the observation that hand sizes were so varied that they could be used to identify people. This led this avid inventor to develop the first automatic Hand Geometry identification device (Figure 5.1). The pattern recognition function of this device was accomplished using purely mechanical means. Four spring loaded rods were arranged so that when the users hand was properly placed, the tips of the fingers moved the rods such that their opposite end took on a pattern reflecting the relative lengths of the user's finger. If this pattern matched the pattern of holes punched into the user's identity card, a simple switch, which could be used to operate an electrified lock, was activated.

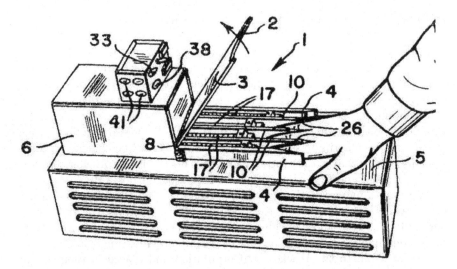

Fig. 5.1. Patent drawing of Mechanical Hand Reader.

In the commercial version of this device, the Identimat (Figure 5.2), the simple rods were replaced by a mechanism that scanned photocells underneath the grooves into which the fingers were placed. A 1,000 watt overhead lamp provided the illumination source. Attached to the same scanning mechanism was a magnetic stripe read head, so that as the hand was scanned so was the user's magnetic stripe card. If pulses read from the card matched in time the signals from the scanning photocells, within a threshold, the user's identity was verified. This product was used successfully in a variety of application including Nuclear Weapons Security, employee Time and Attendance recording, and general access control. Production was discontinued in 1987.

In 1986 Recognition Systems was incorporated to develop and market modern Hand Geometry readers that exploited the low cost digital imaging and

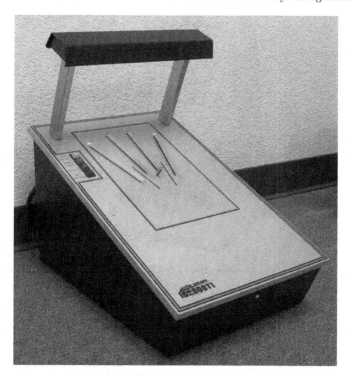

Fig. 5.2. The Identimat: the first commercial hand reader.

image processing technology then becoming available (Figure 5.3). Their ID3D line of hand readers used a solid state digital image sensor to capture a 3 dimensional image of the hand. The optical system of the hand reader was optimized to capture a simple binary image of the hand, much like a shadow silhouette. This binary image yields detailed information about the shape of the hand, but is unaffected by surface features such as skin color, dirt, and ambient light. A low cost microprocessor was used to process this information using proprietary pattern recognition algorithms to produce the very small 9 byte hand identification template that Hand Geometry became noted for.

The ID3D was revolutionary in a number of ways beyond the technological advancements that it brought to Hand Geometry. Its developers recognized that not only did they have to keep the bad guys out, but they also had to let the good guys in... every time. While rest of the biometrics industry at that time focused on the highest possible level of security, the ID3D was designed to ensure a low False Reject rate in real world applications. This technology consistently provided access to authorized users and provided a significant deterrent for unauthorized access. This reliability made it the first biometric product appropriate for large markets such as employee time and attendance recording where its biometric capabilities made it cost effective

Fig. 5.3. A modern hand reader: the GT-400 from Recognition Systems LLC.

and its user friendly performance made it practical. At the same time, security was not compromised as is evidenced by the widespread use of this device in high security applications such as the national nuclear weapons laboratories and nuclear power plants. Every operating nuclear power plant in the United States has installed Hand Geometry for access control.

Most biometric terminals of that time were simple devices that might provide a set of relay contacts that closed on identity verification, or an RS-232 port for signaling the event. The ID3D was radically different in that it was designed not simply as a hand scanner, but as a complete solution for Access Control or Time and Attendance applications. It could be used alone to control access to a door, providing timed door unlock, door alarm contact monitoring, printer data logging, control of access by time and location, and all of the other functions of a modern access control system. A significant innovation was the use of Wiegand and magnetic stripe card reader emulation which enabled the ID3D to be connected into existing access control systems as easily as a standard card reader, thus providing a simple biometric upgrade path for existing systems.

Finally, and perhaps most importantly, the ID3D was designed to be commercially successful as a cost effective solution for the customer and a profit generating product for its manufacturer. The ID3D drove Recognition Systems to profitability early, and continues to generate handsome profits to this day. It can be fairly said that from the beginning of the commercialization of biometrics with the introduction of the Identimat in 1972 until the present time, the great bulk of the biometric terminal industry's profits for biometric terminals has been earned by the ID3D and its offspring.

In 1992 Biomet Partners was formed to develop a two finger version of a hand reader. The Digi-2 was introduced to the marketplace in 1995 and is in use throughout the world. This device uses a CCD camera to acquire a digital image of the fingers. Images are acquired from 2 viewpoints so that the 3-dimensional properties of the fingers are captured. A microprocessor is used to extract identity discriminating features from the image and compare them with features obtained during enrollment. The enrollment template is 20 bytes long. The VeryFast Access Control Terminal shown in Figure 5.4 is based upon the Digi-2 camera.

Fig. 5.4. Biomet Partner's VeryFast Access Control Terminal.

5.3 Interesting Applications

Commercial advancements for biometric devices began in earnest in the 1970s when the Identimat was installed as part of an employee attendance time clock at system Shearson Hamill, a Wall Street investment firm. This was most likely the first installation of a commercial biometric device. Subsequently, hundreds of Identimat devices were used for physical access at secure facilities run by Western Electric, the Department of Energy, U.S. Naval Intelligence, and like organizations [13].

The oldest ongoing general application of biometrics belongs to the University of Georgia which, in 1973, installed the Identimat from Identimation to restrict entry into its all-you-can-eat dining halls. This system is still in daily operation having been upgraded several times as Hand Geometry technology advanced.

A significant number of Identimat scanners were also installed at the Savannah River Nuclear Weapons Laboratory, attesting to its high level of performance even at that early phase of the technologies development. These were later replaced by early models of the ID3D, signaling the commercial transition from the early electro-mechanical hand scanners to the modern all digital devices.

Other applications of hand geometry systems include:

- The 1996 Olympic Games where access to and from the Olympic Village was controlled
- Colombian legislature where hand readers were used to secure voting
- San Francisco International Airport
- Child day care centers use hand geometry systems to verify the identity of parents. Lotus Development and New Mexico Elementary schools are examples of this
- The INSPASS pilot program employs hand geometry systems to track border crossings for frequent travelers
- The University of Georgia has used hand geometry systems since 1973 for their student meal programs
- All operating United States nuclear power plants

5.3.1 Application Guidelines

Characteristics of suitable applications:

- There are a large number of users.
- Harsh environments, especially outdoors.
- A habituated user group who use the device frequently.
- Ease of use is important.
- Very low failure to enroll and failure to acquire are important.
- Speed of operation is important.
- Simple integration with existing systems is required.

Characteristics of unsuitable applications:

- Where identification of one out of many is required.
- Where small size is required.
- Uncooperative users.

Factors that influence performance:

- Poorly trained users.
- Improperly located reader, too high or to low.
- Direct sunlight or other very bright lights.
- Rings if stones are not turned up.
- Large bandages or casts on fingers.
- Significant deformity of the hand, missing fingers.

In general, hand geometry has found successful application in physical Access Control and employee time and attendance data collection. It is less suitable for applications such as border control, national ID, PC security and others in which the characteristics of unsuitable application listed above are all present.

5.4 Technology

When a user presents a biometric sample, hand geometry systems follow the same basic steps as other biometric devices: capturing the sample, processing the raw sample into a biometric template, and comparing the observed template to a reference template in the enrollment database. Most hand geometry systems also incorporate the optional step of updating the reference template in the enrollment database after a successful verification. These processes are illustrated in Figure 5.5.

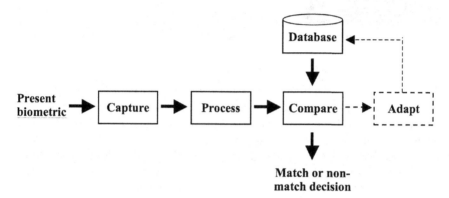

Fig. 5.5. Processing steps in a biometric system using hand geometry.

5.4.1 Hand Capture

Capturing the biometric sample is often achieved by a standard optical camera or a flat-bed scanner. Some units rely only on ambient light, but most provide their own illumination, generally in the near infrared. Because hand geometry is based on analyzing the contours of the hand, these systems binarize the captured grayscale image into a black-and-white silhouette (Figure 5.6). Because of this, hand geometry systems are insensitive to changes in surface features such as tattoos, hair, cuts, scrapes, burns, dirt, or other contaminants that may affect other biometric modalities.

Many hand geometry systems image the hand from directly above the back of the hand or directly below the palm, resulting in a standard 2D image. Some gain 3D information from the same camera by introducing a mirror into the system [10, 19]. Depending on mirror positioning, this can yield an orthogonal view or an off-axis view of the hand. The resolution of existing commercial hand geometry readers is generally much lower than that used for fingerprint recognition; on the order of 100-200 dpi for research systems [10, 7]. Such low resolution images result in insensitivity to variations in hand placement or

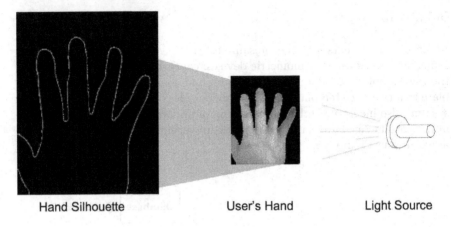

Hand Silhouette   **User's Hand**   **Light Source**

Fig. 5.6. Depiction of hand casting a shadow/silhouette.

physiology. They also minimize the influence of band aids, gauze, etc. Recently, some systems have begun to capture a full 3D model of the hand [5]. Such systems use multiple cameras, structured light, or rangefinder cameras. While these systems hold the promise of increased performance, none of them has yet been commercialized.

The overall size of an optical-camera hand geometry unit can be minimized by "folding" the optical path. This is accomplished by adding a second mirror to the system, directly above the hand, as shown in Figure 5.7. The same system increases the contrast in the image by placing a highly reflective surface under the hand, reducing the binarization process to a simple thresholding operation. To ensure that the orthogonal view across the hand is equally high-contrast, a similar reflective material is also placed on the side-wall of the capture area.

5.4.2 Processing

Some hand geometry units rely on finger-positioning guides to aid in repeatable placement of the hand. For these systems, a pre-processing step is required to remove the positioning pins from the image. While this increases processing at the image level, it may decrease the overall computational power required for the algorithm, as the algorithm is no longer required to account for hand rotation or hand deformation due to varying hand placement [2]. As will be discussed in a following section, a significant number of researchers are investigating pin-free hand geometry systems, as they are seen as more user friendly than systems with pins. Others feel that the tactile feedback provided by the pins is a positive feature that enhances ease of use as well as performance.

Processing the captured image varies greatly for different types of hand geometry systems. Commercial systems and most academic systems begin

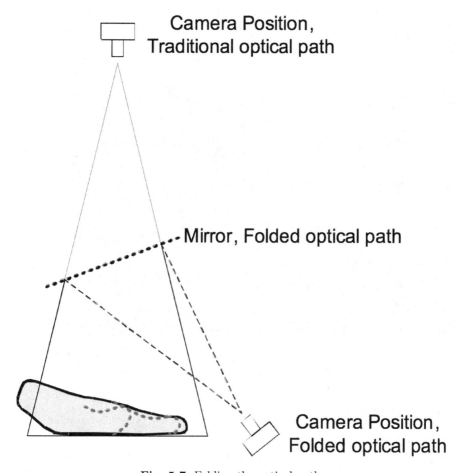

Fig. 5.7. Folding the optical path.

by measuring geometric features in the binarized hand-image [22]. Measurements typically include finger lengths, widths, surface areas, angles between landmarks, and ratios of those quantities [10, 7, 22, 17]. See Figure 5.8. Research has also included systems that operate directly on the hand contour, using the points on the silhouette as landmarks or feeding the entire contour into a comparison engine [19, 2, 20]. Thus there are two distinct classes of hand geometry feature sets based on binary hand images.

The geometric features so derived most often show a great deal of correlation with each other, making classification difficult. Methods such as Principal Component Analysis are often use to transform the raw features into a non-correlated feature set, thus simplifying classification.

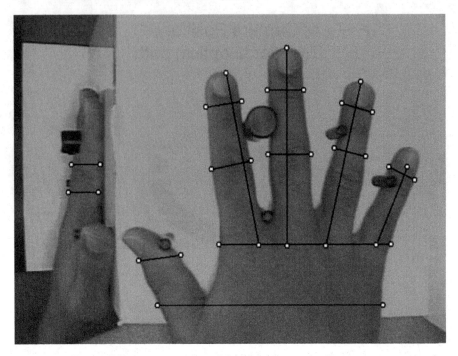

Fig. 5.8. Example top-view image with side-mirror, showing measurements for length, width, and thickness [10].

5.4.3 Classification

The classification step quantifies the level of similarity between two hand templates. The classification method is matched to the feature extraction and feature transform methods utilized in the processing step. The most common approach is to utilize Euclidean distance metrics as in [10], but many other approaches have been documented. These include correlation methods [5, 11], principal component analysis [2], and calculating the mean alignment error of corresponding points along the hand contour. Reference [17] implements several classification/comparison methods, including Gaussian mixture models.

5.4.4 Template Adaptation

The optional step of Template Adaptation improves the biometric performance of hand geometry systems by adapting to changes in the users' physiology over time. Such changes can originate, for example, from weight gain, weight loss, swelling of the hand, or the onset of degenerative diseases such as arthritis. The timescale of these processes is generally slow, on the order of weeks or months. Template adaptation cannot accommodate extreme changes in hand geometry that occur quickly, such as the loss of a digit in an accident.

5.5 Performance

Reported performance of hand geometry systems varies widely, making the classification of Hand Geometry as a modality quite difficult. Even ranking the efficacy of each algorithm within the modality is difficult, because each reported result is based on a different dataset. Some of the factors that influence an algorithm's error rates when calculated using a particular dataset include:

- Capture device : each researcher uses a different type of camera or flatbed scanner, resulting in varying image resolution, contrast, and parallax (caused by the camera-to-hand distance)
- Dataset size : some datasets utilize such a small number of users or hand placements that the uncertainty in the measurements is on the same order of magnitude as the reported results
- Demographics : most datasets are based on college students (since most research is performed at colleges and universities) but some are based on other demographic segments such as office workers, construction workers, children, the elderly, or particular ethnic groups. Each demographic group may have different physiological or behavioral traits that aid or hinder hand placement
- Low-quality images : no public reports address low-quality hand placements. For example, people with arthritis (or similar conditions) may be unable to lay their hand flat against a platen or may have non-repeatable hand placements. Hands with missing or mangled fingers may confuse algorithms looking for "normal" fingers. Rings with the stone turned sideways can bridge adjacent fingers, changing their apparent length. Bandages sometimes change the apparent size/shape of fingers, creating local distortions that must be accommodated
- Habituation: users who interact with a biometric system may adjust their behavior over time, lowering the measured error rates
- Laboratory vs. operational testing : most datasets are captured in a laboratory environment, but some are collected in operational environments that can be indoors or outdoors, and can include a mixture of trained and untrained users
- Hand constraints : constraining the hand (i.e., via finger-alignment pins) reduces the variation presented to the algorithm, thus presenting an easier problem to solve
- Metrics : For example, some published results do not indicate whether they were calculated as 1-try or 3-try attempt
- Timescale : since the hand can change over time, it is a much harder problem to compare enrollment and verification images that were collected months apart than it is to compare images captured in the same session (seconds apart)

Until free datasets are publicly available to researchers, it will be difficult to compare the efficacy of hand geometry algorithms head-to-head. Performance data from a selection of publications are shown in Table 5.1.

Table 5.1. Select performance values recorded in the literature.

Reference	Year	Users	Pins	Feature basis	FAR	FRR	EER
[10]	1999	50	Yes	Geometric	2%	14%	
[9]	1999	53	Yes	Contours	2%	3.5%	
[16]	2000	20	Yes	Geometric			4.9%
[14]	2001	28	No	Contours	1%	1%	1%
[11]	2003	100	No	Geometric	2%	22%	
[19]	2004	51	Yes	Contours			0%
[4]	2004	70	No	Geometric	1%	3%	
[3]	2005	80	No	Contours	0.8%	3.8%	
[2]	2006	40	No	Contours	1%	2.42%	2%
[20]	2006	458	No	Contours	0.1%	3.9%	

The performance numbers recorded in the literature are generally self-reported results from the algorithm developer. Only a few independent third-party tests of hand geometry systems are freely available. One is the 1991 report on biometric devices from Sandia National Labs in the United States [8]. In that test, 80-100 users participated in a laboratory test of the ID-3D from Recognition Systems. Participants in the study used the system over a period of 3 months. In an attempt to measure performance on a habituated user population, the test administrators chose to remove the first few weeks of data from their calculations.

The Sandia test was more statistically significant than other tests of hand geometry at that time, registering more than 5000 genuine placements and more than 5000 imposter attempts. The 1-try EER was calculated as 0.2% and the 3-try EER was calculated as 0.1% based on data taken during the 3-month test. Average verification time was reported as 5 seconds, including the time it took users to type in a PIN on the ID-3D keypad. Figure 5.9 depicts the 1-try and 2-try false reject rate vs. security threshold, as well as the 3-try false accept rate.

An independent test of the HandKey II is freely available from the National Physical Lab (NPL) in the United Kingdom [18]. That test, published in 2001, took place in a normal office environment. Users in the test were non-habituated, implying that they had not adjusted their behavior or acclimated to the operation of the handreaders. Enrollments were typically separated from verifications by 1-2 months. These two facts set the NPL test apart from the Sandia test.

Performance metrics in the NPL test included the failure to acquire rate (FTA) and the failure to enroll rate (FTE), further setting it apart from the

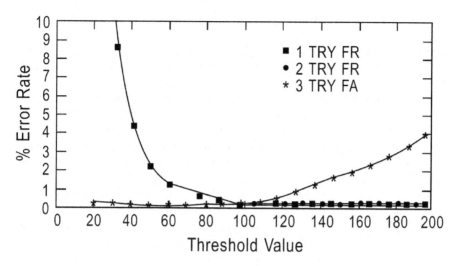

Fig. 5.9. Hand geometry performance measured at Sandia.

Sandia test. All 200 users were able to enroll in the HandKey II, resulting in a 0.0% FTE. During the 3-month test, the FTA was also 0.0%. Transaction times were slower than in the Sandia test, with a mean transaction time of 10 seconds, including the time it took users to type in a PIN on the keypad. A 3-try EER of 0.5% may be read from the published graph, recreated here as Figure 5.10.

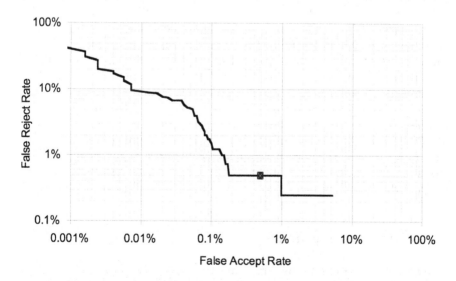

Fig. 5.10. Three-Try FAR/FRR measured at the NPL.

5.6 Standardization

As the biometrics industry continues to mature, it will move away from a constellation of disconnected, proprietary products, and towards a continuum of biometric modules connected by national and international standards. Such standards not only allow a biometric product to work with access control panels and card readers, but also enable enrollment templates from one product to be matched against observation templates from another product or even another vendor. To ensure that the data blocks are correctly identified and parsed, they are often combined with other standards such as BioAPI or CBEFF.

Biometric data interchange standards have existed for several years. The widest-reaching standard today is ANSI/NIST-ITL 1-2000, which describes the data interchange format for transmitting fingerprints, face images, and other information between many law enforcement agencies around the world (e.g., police agencies, the FBI, CIA and Interpol) [12]. Similar biometric data interchange standards have been published to facilitate the exchange of other biometric modalities such as the iris, face, and hand.

The US national standard for hand geometry is ANSI INCITS 396-2005, which details a biometric data block containing one or more hand silhouettes. Each silhouette is accompanied by metadata including (if known) which hand was imaged, whether it was imaged from above or below, details about the camera used to capture the image. To minimize the size of the data block, the silhouette is encoded using a Freeman Chain Code. This method can be used to trace the contours of any closed curve, using as little as two binary bits of data for each point along the curve. For example, a curve with 960 points could be described with 960*2=1920 binary bits, or 240 bytes.

International biometric standards are managed under the auspices of a Joint Technical Committee formed between the International Standards Organization (ISO) and the International Electrotechnical Commission (IEC). One of the biometric standards, ISO/IEC 19794, describes biometric data blocks. Part 10 of that standard details a data format for encoding hand silhouettes using a Freeman Chain Code. ISO/IEC 19794-10 is very similar to ANSI INCITS 396-2005, though the two are not binary compatible. The ISO/IEC document is considered by some to be a refinement of the US standard. In addition to the normative requirements of the biometric data block, both standards include "best practices" sections for hand placement and for design of the optical system.

5.7 Future developments

Current research in hand geometry seems to focus on two areas:

- Lowering the false match rate, and

- Eliminating the need for hand-placement guides on the platen.

In late 2006, Recognition Systems announced a new hand geometry product based on a larger 20-byte template, which provides increased performance over the 9-byte template used in that company's earlier models. The company also claims that using higher-resolution optics results in lower false match rates in the new product.

Academic researchers have offered many hand geometry algorithms allowing unconstrained hand placement on a scanning surface (see Table 5.1). At least one researcher has gone the extra step of removing the scanning surface completely, requiring the user to simply wave his or her hand at the camera from a distance [21] as shown in Figure 5.11. That system locates the creases of the finger joints in a grayscale image, then combines that information with face recognition data captured in the same image. All of these approaches show promise, and may be incorporated into commercial products.

Fig. 5.11. Sample presentation of a dual biometric system with face recognition and unconstrained hand recognition [21].

It is not clear where the performance limits lie for hand geometry. The timeline of research shown in Table 5.1 indicates that algorithms are extracting more and more performance from hand silhouettes; this implies that performance is not limited by the biometric content of the hand, but rather by the algorithms that extract that content.

Combining the two major classes of hand geometry algorithm, based on contours or on geometric features, may result in even higher-performance algorithms than those published in the literature. Also, algorithms developed for unconstrained hand placement may provide higher performance when coupled with the more repeatable hand presentations of a constrained system (one utilizing a platen with finger-positioning pins).

In addition to evolutionary hand geometry algorithms, the future holds the promise of better hand recognition by combining hand geometry into multi-biometric systems. Several researchers have improved the performance of geometry-only approaches by adding texture data from a palmprint taken from the same image (before binarization) that generated the hand silhouette [11]. Hand geometry has also been combined with face recognition on a border-crossing project along the Israeli - Palestinian border [6]. Other multi-biometric implementations including hand geometry can be imagined, including hand/finger and hand/vein.

References

1. www.correctionhistory.org/html/chronicl/dcjs/html/nyidbur2.html.
2. G. Amayeh, G. Bebis, A. Erol, and M. Nicolescu. Peg-Free Hand Shape Verification Using High Order Zernike Moments. In *Proceedings of the IEEE Computer Society Workshop on Biometrics (in conjunction with the IEEE Conference on Computer Vision and Pattern Recognition)*, volume 2, pages 40–47, New York, June 2006.
3. G. Boreki and A. Zimmer. Hand geometry feature extraction through curvature profile analysis. http://w3.impa.br/~lvelho/sibgrapi2005/html/p13063/p13063.pdf.
4. Y. Bulatov, S. Jambawalikar, P. Kumar, and S. Sethia. Hand recognition using geometric classifiers. In *Proceedings of the International Conference on Biometric Authentication (ICBA'04)*, pages 753–759, Hong Kong, China, July 2004.
5. D. L. Woodard P. J. Flynn. Personal identification utilizing finger surface features. In *Proceedings of the IEEE Computer Society Conference on Computer Vision and Pattern Recognition (CVPR 2005)*, volume 2, pages 1030–1036, June 2005.
6. GAO-03-174. Technology assessment: Using biometrics for border security, November 2002.
7. S. Gonzalez, C. M. Travieso, J. B. Alonso, and M. A. Ferrer. Automatic biometric identification system by hand geometry. In *Proceedings of the 37th Annual International Carnahan Conference on Security Technology*, pages 281– 284, October 2003.
8. J. P. Holmes, L. J. Wright, and R. L. Maxwell. A performance evaluation of biometric identification devices, June 1991. http://infoserve.sandia.gov/cgi-bin/techlib/access-control.pl/1991/910276.pdf.
9. A. K. Jain and N. Duta. Deformable matching of hand shapes for verification. In *International Conference on Image Processing*, October 1999.

10. A. K. Jain, A. Ross, and S. Pankanti. A prototype hand geometry based verification system. In *Proceedings of the 2nd International Conference on Audio Video based Biometric Personal Authentication (AVBPA)*, pages 166–171, Washington D. C., March 1999.

11. A. Kumar, D. C. M. Wong, H. C. Shen, and A. K. Jain. Personal Verification Using Palmprint and Hand Geometry Biometric. In *Proceedings of the 4th International Conference on Audio- and Video-Based Biometric Person Authentication (AVBPA))*, pages 668–678, Guildford, UK, June 2003.

12. M. McCabe. ANSI/NIST fingerprint standard update, September 2005.

13. B. Miller. Vital Signs of Identity. *IEEE Spectrum*, page 22, February 1994.

14. C. Oden, A. Ercil, V. Yildiz, H. Kirmizitas, and B. Buke. Hand recognition using implicit polynomials and geometric features. In *Proceedings of the Third International Conference on Audio- and Video-Based Biometric Person Authentication, Lecture Notes in Computer Science*, volume 2091, pages 336–341, June 2001.

15. J. Renaghan. Etched in stone. *Zoogoer*, August 1997.

16. R. Sanchez-Reillo. Hand geometry pattern recognition through Gaussian mixture modeling. In *15th International Conference on Pattern Recognition (ICPR'00)*, volume 2, pages 937–940, 2000.

17. R. Sanchez-Reillo, C. Sanchez-Avila, and A. Gonzales-Marcos. Biometric identification through hand geometry measurements. *IEEE Transactions on Pattern Analysis and Machine Intelligence*, (10):22, February 2000.

18. T. Mansfield and G. Kelly and D. Chandler and J. Kan. Biometric Product Testing Final Report. Technical report, National Physical Laboratory of UK, March 2001.

19. R. N. J. Veldhuis, A. M. Bazen, W. Booij, and A. J. Hendrikse. A Comparison of Hand-Geometry Recognition Methods Based on Low and High-Level Features. In *Proceedings of the 15th Annual Workshop on Circuits, Systems and Signal Processing (ProRISC)*, pages 326–330, Veldhoven, Netherlands, 2004.

20. E. Yoruk, E. Konukoglu, B. Sankur, and J. Darbon. Shape-based hand recognition. *IEEE Transactions on Image Processing*, (7):15, July 2006.

21. G. Zheng, T. E. Boult, and C. J. Wang. Personal Identification by Projective Invariant Hand Geometry. In *Proceedings of Biometrics Symposium 2005*, September 2005.

22. R. Zunkel. *Biometrics: Personal Identification in Networked Society*, chapter Hand Geometry Based Authentication. Kluwer Academic Publishers, 1999.

6

Gait Recognition

Sudeep Sarkar and Zongyi Liu

Computer Science and Engineering, University of South Florida, Tampa, Florida, USA
{sarkar,zliu4}@cse.usf.edu

6.1 Introduction

Consider the task of recognizing someone from 300m away. Such scenarios arise in wide-area monitoring and asset protection. What sources of biometrics could one use? Of course, the collection of fingerprint or iris scans at such distances is implausible. It is probable that face data can be captured, but resolution and outdoor sources of variations, such as sunlight and shadows, would be hard issues to overcome. So instead of physical biometrics that are direct signatures of the physiology of the person, we turn to behavioral biometrics. One such behavioral biometrics is gait, or more precisely, in our context, the pattern of shape and motion in video of a walking person. The gait of a person is determined by their underlying musculo-skeletal structure, so it is plausible that it has some ability to discriminate between persons. Indeed there were human perception experiments done in the 1970's by Cutting and Kozlowski [5] based on light point displays that showed it is possible to identify a person from the manner of walking, i.e. gait. More recently, Stevenage *et al.* [30] showed that humans can identify individuals on the basis of their gait signature, without reliance on shape, in the presence of lighting variations and under brief exposures.

The first effort toward *recognition from gait* in computer vision was probably by Niyogi and Adelson in the early 1990s [26]. Over the past five years or so, significant progress has been made in terms of the diversity of gait recognition algorithms. This chapter is not meant to be an extensive review of gait recognition research. For that, one should consider the excellent reviews in [2, 25]. Instead, this chapter will focus on three aspects. First is a gait recognition research resource framework, namely the HumanID Gait Challenge problem, which has been recently constructed to study and to evaluate progress. It has been used quite extensively. Second is a discussion of the basic approaches to gait recognition. Third is a discussion of the lessons learnt and some of our ideas about how to move gait recognition research forward.

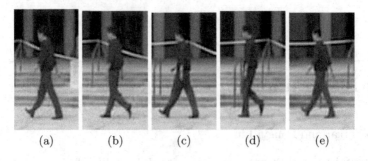

(a)   (b)   (c)   (d)   (e)

Fig. 6.1. A gait cycle can be partitioned into four periods: (i) right stance period when the right foot is in contact with the floor, beginning from "right heel-strike" (photo a) and ending at "right toe-off" (photo d) (ii) left swing period when the left foot is not in contact with the floor, beginning from "left toe-off" (photo b) and ending at "left heel-strike" (photo c) (iii) left stance period when the left foot is in contact with the floor, beginning from "left heel-strike" (photo c) and ending at "left toe-off" (photo e) and (iv) right swing period when the right foot is not in contact with the floor, beginning from "right toe-off" (photo d) and ending at "right heel-strike" (photo e). Moreover, the time between these periods, i.e., when both feet are in contact with the floor, is called "double limb support".

The gait of a person is a periodic activity with each gait cycle covering two strides – the left foot forward and right foot forward strides. Each stride spans the double-support stance to the legs-together stance as the legs swings past each other and back to the double-support stance (see Fig. 6.1). Potential sources for gait biometrics can be seen to derive from two aspects: *shape and dynamics*. Shape refers to the configuration or shape of the persons as they perform different gait phases. Dynamics refers to the *rate* of transition between these phases and is usually the aspect one refers to when one talks about gait in traditional problem contexts, such as bio-mechanics or human motion recognition. In this respect, research for the development for gait biometrics has to synthesize both shape and human motion research. Designing well performing gait recognition algorithms does not appear to be a straightforward application of existing methods developed in shape research or those in human motion research, independently of each other. The challenge is to overcome gait motion variations due to various conditions such as footwear, clothing, walking surface, carrying objects, over elapsed time, walking speed, indoor vs. outdoors, and so on. Given the lack of theoretical understanding or modeling of how these factors effect gait shape and dynamics, gait recognition research, like most biometrics research, is reliant on datasets. It is the dataset that will expose issues, and move the area forward.

A meta analysis of the identification rates reported in the recent literature on different kinds of datasets reveal consistent patterns of influence. We considered the publicly available experimental protocols and datasets (> 25 persons) such as the CMU-Mobo dataset [7] (indoor, 25 subjects), the UMD dataset [13] (outdoor, 55 subjects), the Southampton Large dataset [36] (indoor and outdoor, 115 subjects), the CASIA Gait Dataset [39] (indoor, 124 subjects), and the HumanID Gait Challenge dataset [28] (outdoor, 122 subjects). Of course, the caveat is that the conclusions are conditioned on the kinds of variations of each covariate in the respective dataset. A definitive conclusion is hard to make. However, this kind of meta-analysis has some conclusive weight since it encompasses the findings of multiple research groups. It should provide some directions for focusing future research. In Table 6.1 we list the average identification rates for matching across different conditions, i.e. the probe and the gallery differed with respect to the indicated covariate. From the table we can see that outdoor gait recognition, recognition across walking surface-type change, and recognition across months are all hard problems. Clothing, footwear, carrying condition, and walking speed does not seem to be hard covariates to overcome. We also see that performance drops with dataset size, which suggests that it is imperative to demonstrate the efficacy of an idea on as large a dataset as possible.

Table 6.1. Meta analysis of gait identification rates as reported in the literature for different conditions. The average of the rates reported in [28, 38, 24, 36, 16, 13, 3, 34, 10, 33, 8, 2, 22, 31, 39] are listed for different conditions.

(a)

Data Set Condition	Average Rate
Indoor data	69
Outdoor data	**59**
No. of Subjects < 50	72
No. of Subjects > 50	**60**

(b)

Comparing Across	Average Rate
Elapsed Time (days)	73
Elapsed Time (6 months)	**16**
Views (30°)	78
Shoe types	77
Surface types	**37**
Carrying condition	71
Different speeds	69
Clothing types	73

6.2 The HumanID Gait Challenge Problem

The HumanID gait challenge problem was formulated in the DARPA HumanID At a Distance program to facilitate objective, quantitative measurement of gait research progress on a large dataset [28]. The problem definition has three components: a dataset, challenge experiments of different difficulty levels, and a simple gait recognition approach that is intended to set a baseline performance level to improve upon.

(a)   (b)

Fig. 6.2. Samples from the HumanID gait challenge dataset: subject walking on grass (a) along the frontal half of the elliptical path, (b) along the back half of the elliptical path.

Fig. 6.3. Examples of manual silhouettes that are available for a subset of the HumanID gait challenge dataset.

6.2.1 The Dataset

Fig. 6.2 shows some sample frames from this dataset. It was collected outdoors and each person in the data set was studied under combination of as many as five conditions or covariates. The conditions are: (i) two camera angles (L and R), (ii) two shoe types (A and B), (iii) two surfaces (Grass and Concrete), (iv) with and without carrying a brief case (B or NB), and (v) two different dates six months apart, May and November. Attempt was made to acquire a person's gait in all possible combinations, and there are up to 32 sequences for some persons. Hence, the full dataset can be partitioned into 32 subsets, one for each combination of the 5 covariates. Comparisons between these subsets are used to set up challenge experiments; more on this later. The full data set consists of 1870 sequences from 122 individuals. This dataset is unique in the number of covariates exercised. It is the only data set to include walking on a grass surface.

In addition to the raw data sequence, there is ancillary information associated with the data. First, for each sequence, there is meta-data information about the subject's age, sex, reported height, self reported weight, foot dominance, and shoe information. Second, for a subset of this dataset, we have

Table 6.2. The gallery and probe set specifications for each of gait challenge experiments. The covariates are coded as follows: C–concrete surface, G–grass surface, A–first shoe type, B–second shoe type, BF–carrying a briefcase, NB–no briefcase, M–data collected in May, N_1–new subjects in November data, and N_2–repeat subjects in November. The gallery for all of the experiments is (G, A, R, NB, M + N_1) and consists of 122 individuals.

Exp.	Probe (Surface, Shoe, View, Carry, Elapsed Time) (C/G, A/B, L/R, NB/BF, time)	Number of Subjects	Difference
A*	(G, A, L, NB, M + N_1)	122	V[1]
B*	(G, B, R, NB, M + N_1)	54	S[2]
C	(G, B, L, NB, M + N_1)	54	S+V
D*	(C, A, R, NB, M + N_1)	121	F[3]
E	(C, B, R, NB, M + N_1)	60	F+S
F	(C, A, L, NB, M + N_1)	121	F+V
G	(C, B, L, NB, M + N_1)	60	F+S+V
H*	(G, A, R, BF, M + N_1)	120	B[4]
I	(G, B, R, BF, M + N_1)	60	S+B
J	(G, A, L, BF, M + N_1)	120	V+B
K*	(G, A/B, R, NB, N_2)	33	T[5]+S+C[6]
L	(C, A/B, R, NB, N_2)	33	F+T+S+C

[1] view, [2] shoe, [3] surface, [4] carry, [5] elapsed time, [6] clothing, [*] key experiments

created manual silhouettes (see Fig. 6.3). One should not use the silhouettes to be the final test set of any recognition algorithm, but they should be used to build models or to study segmentation errors. More details about the process of creating these manual silhouettes and the quality checks performed can be found in [19]; here we highlight some salient aspects. Up to 71 subjects from one of the two collection periods (May collection) were chosen for manual silhouette specification. The sequences corresponding to these subjects were chosen from the (i) gallery set (sequences taken on grass, with shoe type A, right camera view), (ii) probe B (on grass, with shoe type B, right camera view), (iii) probe D (on concrete, with shoe type A, right camera view), (iv) probe H (on grass, with shoe A, right camera view, carrying briefcase), and probe K (on grass, elapsed time). We manually specified the silhouette in each frame over one walking cycle, of approximately 30 to 40 image frames. This cycle was chosen to begin at the right heel strike phase of the walking cycle through to the next right heel strike. Whenever possible, we attempted to pick this gait cycle from the same 3D location in each sequence. In addition to marking a pixel as being from the background or subject, we also provided more detailed specifications in terms of body parts. We explicitly labeled the head, torso, left arm, right arm, left upper leg, left lower leg, right upper leg, and right lower leg using different colors.

6.2.2 The Challenge Experiments

Along with the dataset, the gait challenge problem includes a definition of a set of twelve challenge experiments (A through L), spanning different levels of difficulty. This provides a common benchmark to compare performance with other algorithms. The experiments are designed to investigate the effect on performance of the five factors, i.e. change in viewing angle, change in shoe type, change in walking surfaces (concrete and grass), carrying or not carrying a briefcase, and temporal differences. The results from the twelve experiments provide an ordering of the difficulty of the experiments. The signatures are the video sequences of gait. To allow for a comparison among a set of experiments and limit the total number of experiments, the gallery set was fixed as the control. Then, twelve probe sets were created to examine the effects of different covariates on performance. The gallery consists of sequences with the following covariates: Grass, Shoe Type A, Right Camera, No Briefcase, and collected in May along with those from the *new* subjects from November. This set was selected as the gallery because it was one of the largest for a given set of covariates. The structure of the twelve probe sets is listed in Table 6.2. The last two experiments study the impact of elapsed time. The elapsed time covariate implicitly includes a change of shoe and clothing because we did not require subjects to wear the same clothes or shoes in both data collections. Because of the implicit change of shoe, we assume that a different set of shoes were used in the May and November data collections. This is noted in Table 6.2 by A/B for shoe type in experiments K and L. The key experiments are those that involve controlled change in just one covariate and are marked with an asterisk in the table.

6.2.3 Baseline Gait Algorithm

The third aspect of the gait challenge problem is a simple but effective baseline algorithm to provide performance benchmarks for the experiments. Ideally, this should be a combination of "standard" vision modules that accomplishes the task. Drawing from the recent success of template based recognition strategies in computer vision, we developed a four-part algorithm that relies on silhouette template matching. The first part semi-automatically defines bounding boxes around the moving person in each frame of a sequence. The second part extracts silhouettes from the bounding boxes using expectation maximization based on Mahalanobis distance between foreground and background color model at each pixel. Each silhouette is scaled to a height of 128 pixels and centered (automatically) in each frame along the horizontal direction so that the centerline of the torso is at the middle of the frame. The third part computes the gait period from the silhouettes. The gait period is used to partition the sequences for spatial-temporal correlation. The fourth part performs spatial-temporal correlation to compute the similarity between two gait sequences.

Let the probe and the gallery silhouette sequences be denoted by $\mathbf{S_P} = \{\mathbf{S_P}(1), \cdots, \mathbf{S_P}(M)\}$ and $\mathbf{S_G} = \{\mathbf{S_G}(1), \cdots, \mathbf{S_G}(N)\}$, respectively. First, the probe (input) sequence is partitioned into subsequences, each roughly over one gait period, N_{Gait}. Gait periodicity is estimated based on periodic variation of the count the number of foreground pixels in the lower part of the silhouette in each frame over time. This number will reach a maximum when the two legs are farthest apart (full stride stance) and drop to a minimum when the legs overlap (heels together stance).

Second, each of these probe subsequences, $\mathbf{S_{Pk}} = \{\mathbf{S_P}(k), \cdots, \mathbf{S_P}(k + N_{Gait})\}$, is cross correlated with the given gallery sequence, $\mathbf{S_G}$.

$$\text{Corr}(\mathbf{S_{Pk}}, \mathbf{S_G})(l) = \sum_{j=1}^{N_{Gait}} S\left(\mathbf{S_P}(k + j), \mathbf{S_G}(l + j)\right) \qquad (6.1)$$

where, the similarity between two image frames, $S(\mathbf{S_P}(i), \mathbf{S_G}(j))$, is defined to be the Tanimoto similarity between the silhouettes, i.e. the ratio of the number of common pixels to the number of pixels in their union. The overall similarity measure is chosen to be the median value of the maximum correlation of the gallery sequence with each of these probe subsequences. The strategy for breaking up the probe sequence into subsequences allows us to address the case when we have segmentation errors in some contiguous sets of frames due to some background subtraction artifact or due to localized motion in the background.

$$\text{Sim}(\mathbf{S_P}, \mathbf{S_G}) = \text{Median}_k \left(\max_l \text{Corr}(\mathbf{S_{Pk}}, \mathbf{S_G})(l) \right) \qquad (6.2)$$

The baseline algorithm is parameter free. We find that the algorithm, although straightforward, performs quite well on some of the experiments and is quite competitive with the first generation of gait recognition algorithms.

6.2.4 Reported Performance

The results reported for the Gait Challenge problem are of two types, ones that report results on the first version of the dataset that was released with 71 subjects and the second set of results are those reported for the full dataset with 122 subjects. The smaller dataset allow us to conducts the first 8 experiments listed in Table 6.2, but with reduced gallery set sizes. In Fig. 6.4(a) we have tracked the baseline performance and the best performance reported in the literature. To date, we can identify 18 papers that reported results on the smaller version of the problem. In 2002, when the Gait Challenge Problem was released, the performance of the baseline algorithm was better than the best reported performance. By 2004, while the baseline algorithm performance improved as the algorithm was fine-tuned, the performance of the best performance improved significantly and continued to improve through 2006.

We see this trend also for the results reported in 6 papers on the full dataset in Fig. 6.4(b).

As is evident, the Gait Challenge Problem has already spurred the development of gait recognition algorithms with improving performance. What is particularly interesting to notice is that the performance on hard experiments such those across surface (Experiment D) and elapsed time (Experiment K) has improved. Of course, there is still room for further improvement. Another interesting aspect is that the improvement of performance from 2004 to 2006 was not due to "continued engineering" of existing approaches, but involved the redesign of the recognition approaches. For instance, the greatest gains came from approaches that analyzed the silhouette shapes rather than the dynamics. Dynamics is important, but by itself is not sufficient.

6.3 Recognition Approaches

Almost all approaches to gait recognition are based, either directly or indirectly, on the silhouettes of the person, which seems to be the low-level feature representation of choice. This is partly due to its ease of extraction by simple background subtraction; all approaches assume static cameras. Other reasons include the robustness of the silhouettes with respect to clothing color and texture (it is, however, sensitive to the shape of clothing). The silhouette representation can also be extracted from low-resolution images of persons taken at a distance, when edge based representation becomes unreliable.

Gait recognition approaches, especially those that have been shown to work for more than 20 persons, are basically of three types: (i) temporal alignment based, (ii) silhouette shape based, and (iii) static parameter based approaches. Here we outline some of the approaches. The interested reader is advised to track new publications as new and exciting approaches appear almost every month.

6.3.1 Temporal Alignment Based Approaches

The temporal alignment based approach emphasizes both shape and dynamics and is the most common one. It treats the sequence as a time series and involves a classic three stage processing framework. The first stage is the extraction of features such as whole silhouettes [28, 2], or principal components of silhouette boundary vector variations [38], or silhouette width vectors [13], or pre-shape representation [35], or silhouette parts [17, 36], or Fourier descriptors [24]. The gait research group at the University of Southampton (Nixon *et al.*) has probably experimented with the largest number of possible feature types for recognition. This step also involves some normalization of size to impart some invariance with respect to distance from camera. The second step involves the alignment of sequences of these features, corresponding to the given two sequences to be matched. The alignment process can be

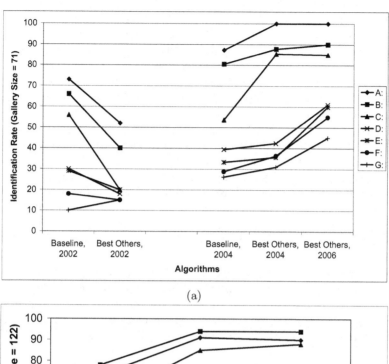

(a)

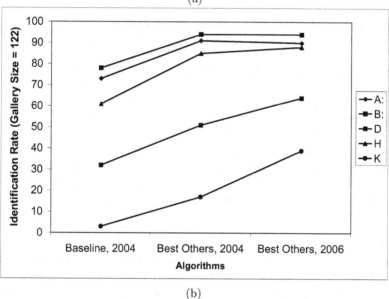

(b)

Fig. 6.4. Improvement in gait recognition algorithms over time with respect to the baseline performance. (a) We have tracked results presented on the first release of the gait dataset with 71 subjects in the gallery. We show the snap of the baseline performance and the best results reported on the dataset in 2002 for the first 8 experiments listed in Table 6.2. (b) Tracking results on the full dataset with 122 subjects for the key experiments listed in Table 6.2. From 2004 to 2006, the best reported performances are better on all the experiments.

based on simple temporal correlation [28, 38], or dynamic time warping [35], or hidden Markov models [13, 35, 16] or phase locked-loops [2], or Fourier analysis [17, 24]. The third aspect is the distance measure used, which can be Euclidean [38], or simple dot product based [28, 13], or based on prob-abilistic models, or Procrustes distance [35], or derived based on manifold analysis [15, 14]. Some examples of this class of approaches to gait recognition are the following.

Robledo and Sarkar [27] proposed an approach of relational distributions and space of probability functions (SoPF). This method includes four stages: (i) segment person from a motion sequence, using the binary silhouette rep-resentation, (ii) extract low level features and build relational distributions – accumulated occurrences of each relationship between paired image features, (iii) build a space of probability functions (SoPF) from the relational distribu-tions of a training dataset, and use PCA to reduce dimensions, and (iv) project relational distributions of test data into SoPF, and compute similarities based on their coordinates.

Nixon and Carter [25] have performed extensive analyses on indoor gait data that allow for study of gait under low segmentation error conditions. One of their approaches is based on body shape area [6]. They first mask selected body parts in a sequence of silhouettes, then consider its area as the time varying signal for recognition. On an indoor gait database consisting of 114 subjects filmed under laboratory condition, a 75% recognition rate has been reported. Another feature is Fourier descriptors [24], where subject's boundary and spatio-temporal deformations is modeled with Fourier descriptors. This resulted in a somewhat increased recognition rate of over 85% for the 115 person dataset.

Tan et al. [38] considered the body length vector as the feature, which they compute from the vector of distances to the silhouette boundary from the silhouette center. The distance vector is then normalized with respect to the magnitude and size. These one-dimensional vectors are then represented in a smaller dimensional space using PCA. Two sequences of body length vector are aligned by simple correlation and normalized Euclidean distances are computed.

The UMD group used the silhouette width vector as the feature [11, 13]. The width vector was defined to be the vector of silhouette widths at each row. The silhouettes were height normalized to arrive at vector of fixed lengths. They exhaustively experimented with different variations of this feature. Se-quence alignment was achieved based on *person specific* Hidden Markov mod-els. The gait of *each* person was represented as sequence of state transitions. The states correspond to the different gait stances and the observation model for each state was represented as distances from the average stance shape for that person. Each HMM was built using the Baum-Welch algorithm and recognition was performed by matching any given sequence to the HMMs using the Viterbi algorithm. The identity of the HMM that results in the maximum probability match was selected. In a more recent version of this basic approach [35], they used better shape representation, with much improved performance. First, they extracted pre-shape vector by subtracting the centroid and normalizing for scale. Then, correlation with these shape vectors was performed using dynamic time-warping in shape space, or using HMM with shape cues based on Procrustes distance.

Lee and Grimson [17] opted for more high level features. They partitioned a silhouette into 7 elongated regions, corresponding to the different body parts. Each region was represented using four features: centroid coordinate pair, aspect ratio, and orientation. Gait similarity was computed from either the average of the features in all the frames of a sequence, or the magnitudes and phases of each region feature related to the dominant walking frequency. In a more recent work [16], they experimented with HMM based alignment of two sequences, with improved results.

A nice head to head study of this class of approaches was recently done by Boulgouris *et al.* [1]. They compared silhouette features such as width vectors, vertical and horizontal projections, angular representations, and plain silhouettes. Plain silhouettes seem to perform the best. In terms of matching, they experimented with frequency domain, dynamic time warping, linear time normalization, and HMM. Time warping methods seemed to result in better performance when matching across surface changes. A variation of the HMM approach, where the overall distance was the accumulation of the observation probability, ignoring the transition probabilities, resulted in almost similar performance as the full HMM. This point to the importance of silhouette shape information for recognition and leads us to a second class of approaches to gait recognition, which is discussed next.

6.3.2 Shape Based Approaches

This class of approaches emphasizes the silhouette shape similarity and underplays the temporal information. So far, they have demonstrated high performance. One direction involves the transformation of the silhouette sequence into a single image representation. The simplest such transformation is the averaged silhouette, computed by simply summing the silhouettes over one gait cycle [20]. Similarity is based on just the Euclidean distance between the average silhouettes from two silhouette sequences. The performance is as good as the baseline algorithm, discussed earlier. A sophisticated version of this idea, with enhanced performance, was also proposed by Han and Bhanu [8]. Instead of just over one gait cycle, they summed all the silhouettes in the sequence, followed by a reduced dimensional representation built using the PCA or Linear Discriminant Analysis (LDA). The training process was enhanced by synthesizing training data based on expected errors of the silhouettes. Similarity was computed in this linear subspace.

Other single image representations include the use an image representation derived from the width vectors in each frame (Frieze patterns) [18] and the use of the amplitude of the Discrete Fourier transform of the raw silhouette sequence [40]. However, these representations do tend to implicitly encode dynamics.

Another way of using shape information preserves individual silhouettes but disregards the sequence ordering, and treats the sequences as just a collection of silhouette shapes [3, 34] (CMU). In this approach, the silhouettes were first vertically normalized and horizontally centered, based on the first and second order moments. Then, silhouettes with similar shapes were clustered using the spectral partitioning framework, based on graph weights built out of the correlation of high variance areas in the shape, representing parts such as arms and legs. The power of this representation partly derives from the ability to identify and disregard low-quality silhouettes in a sequence; bad silhouettes form a separate cluster. A probe was identified by comparing the collection of its silhouette shapes to the gallery shape clusters.

To date the best reported performance on the HumanID Gait Challenge problem (and on other datasets such as Maryland and CMU) is by Liu and Sarkar's gait recognition approach that normalizes the gait of each person to a standard gait model [22]. This standard gait model was a population-HMM model built using silhouette sequences from all persons in the gallery. Note that this is unlike the UMD approach where per-person HMMs are used. One p-HMM represented the average gait over the population and was used to normalize any given gait sequence. The dynamics for any given gait sequence, $\mathbf{F} = \{\mathbf{f_1}, \cdots, \mathbf{f_N}\}$, was normalized by first estimating the stance state for each frame and then averaging the frames mapped to each state to produce one, dynamics-normalized, gait cycle over N_s frames, denoted by $\mathbf{F_{DN}} = \{\mathbf{g_1}, \cdots, \mathbf{g_{N_s}}\}$. The dynamics normalized gait cycle was computed by averaging frames mapped to the same state. This was referred to as the *stance-frame*, $\mathbf{g_i}$. Fig. 6.5 shows some stance-frames for one subject under different conditions. Notice that the stance-frames for the same stance are similar across different sequences, which indicates that silhouette-to-stance matching is correctly estimated. Also note the differences in the "width" of the silhouettes for the same stance, but across different conditions. This has to do with the silhouette detection algorithm that used the same set of parameters across conditions, some with different backgrounds, resulting in over-segmentation in some cases. Thus, a dynamics normalized gait cycle consists of a fixed number of stance frames, which simplifies the similarity computation between two given sequences. A separate alignment process was not needed. They simply considered the distances between the corresponding stance-frames. Instead of simple Euclidean distances between stance-frames, distances in the Linear Discriminant Analysis (LDA) Space were computed. The LDA was designed to maximize the differences between frames from different subjects and to minimize the distances between frames from the same subject under different conditions.

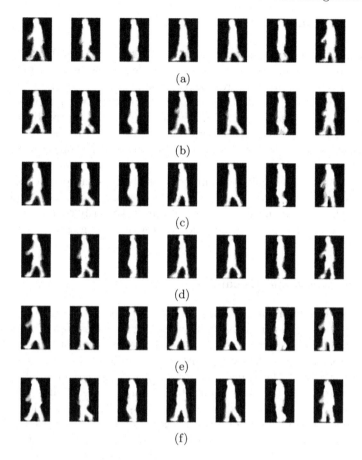

Fig. 6.5. Example of dynamics-normalized stance-frames from a single subject based on the sequence in (a) gallery, and the corresponding probe sequences with changes in (b) view, (c) shoe-type, (d) surface, (e) carrying condition, and (f) elasped time.

6.3.3 Static Parameters

The third class of approaches opts for parameters that can be used to characterize gait dynamics, such as stride length, cadence, and stride speed along with static body parameters such as the ratio of sizes of various body parts [10, 32]. However, these approaches have not reported high performances on common databases, partly due to their need for 3D calibration information.

6.4 Discussion and Future Areas

Study of gait recognition has made notable progress since 2001. Results have been reported on common datasets by multiple groups. It is natural to ask that apart from recognition scores, what fundamental understanding has been gained by this effort? Do we have an understanding of what aspects of gait are important for recognition? What vision aspects of the problem should one concentrate upon to improve performance? Is quality of the segmentation of the person the bottleneck to improved performance? Can performance be improved by a better matching method? How does gait compare to face for outdoor scenarios? Can gait be combined with face to improve performance? We consider these questions and discuss some preliminary findings. Since most of these findings are empirically based they are necessarily constrained by the dataset. However, the observations should provide some guidance for productive future work.

6.4.1 Gait Shape and Dynamics

At least three different approaches [22, 35, 34] that analyzed stance shape differences resulted in better recognition, especially across the difficult covariates. Recently, Boulgouris *et al.* [1] found that a variation of the per-subject HMM approach, where the overall distance is based on just the observation probability, ignoring the transition probabilities, resulted in similar performance as the full HMM. This points to the importance of silhouette shape information for recognition. It does appear that gait dynamics, which has been the core focus of most study of human gait in computer vision, is susceptible to change. However, the evidence of this is not conclusive. Perhaps a better understanding of the change in dynamics for the same person under various conditions is needed.

6.4.2 Silhouette Quality and Gait Recognition

The quality of the silhouettes is dependent on the discrimination between the background and foreground (subject). Segmentation of silhouettes in outdoor sequences is difficult primarily because of existence of shadow artifacts, changing illumination due to shifting cloud cover, and inevitable movements in the background. When comparing sequences taken months apart, differences in clothing and even background would lead to different silhouette qualities. This drop in quality of extracted silhouettes can also be offered as an explanation for the drop in gait-recognition when comparing templates across surfaces (Experiment D in the Gait Challenge Problem) because the corresponding gallery and probe sequences also differ with respect to the background. Is the poor performance across these conditions due to fundamental changes in gait under these conditions? Or are they due to vagaries of low-level processing?

It is reasonable to suggest that the quality of the low-level representation is probably at fault.

In [21, 19] we have demonstrated, based on both manual (clean) silhouettes and automatically "cleaned" silhouettes, that the poor performance cannot be explained by the silhouette quality. We have established that the low performance under the impact of surface and time variation can not be explained by poor silhouette quality. We based our conclusions on two gait recognition algorithms, one exploits both shape and dynamics, while the other exploits shape alone. The drop in performance due to surface and time condition that we observe in the gait challenge problem is *not* due to differences in background or silhouette errors. This observation is also corroborated by the performances reported by Lee *et al.* [16]. This observation has implication for future work direction in gait recognition. Instead of searching for better methods for silhouette detection to improve recognition, it would be more productive to study and isolate components of gait that do not change under shoe, surface, or time.

6.4.3 Covariates to Conquer

Focused analysis of the study of the impact of a covariate on match-score distribution, suggest that shoe type has the least effect on performance, but the effect is nevertheless statistically significant [28]. This is followed by either a change in camera view or carrying a brief case. Carrying a brief case does not affect performance as much as one might expect. This effect is marginally larger than changing shoe type but is substantially smaller than a change in surface type. In future experiments, it may be interesting to investigate the effect of carrying a backpack rather than a briefcase, or to vary the object that is carried.

One of the factors that has large impact is elapsed time between probe and gallery sequence acquisition, resulting in lower recognition rates for changes when matching sequences over time. This dependence on time has been reported by others too, but for indoor sequences and for less than six months' elapsed time. When the difference in time between gallery (the pre-stored template) and probe (the input data) is in the order of minutes, the identification performance ranges from 91% to 95% [37, 9, 3], whereas the performances drop to 30% to 54% when the differences are in the order of months and days [17, 4, 3] for similar sized datasets. Our speculation is that other changes that naturally occur between video acquisition sessions are very important. These include change in clothing worn by the subject, change in the outdoor lighting conditions, and inherent variation in gait over elapsed time. Of these, it is not likely that clothing is the key factor given the high recognition performance for matching across clothing changes that has been in reported in [39]. For applications that require matching across days or months, this elapsed time variation issue needs to be studied in more detail. However, there are many applications, such as short term tracking across many surveillance cameras, for which these long term related variations would not be important.

The other factor with large impact on gait recognition is walking surface. With the subject walking on grass in the gallery sequence and on concrete in the probe sequence, highest reported rank-one recognition is only 57%[22]. Performance degradation might be even larger if we considered other surface types, such as sand or gravel that might reasonably be encountered in some applications. The large effect of surface type on performance suggests that an important future research topic might be to investigate whether the change in gait with surface type is predictable. For example, given a description of gait from walking on concrete, is it possible to predict the gait description that would be obtained from walking on grass or sand? Alternatively, is there some other description of gait that is not as sensitive to change in surface type?

6.4.4 Future Datasets

It is to be expected that each gait research group would collect their own data set to develop ideas. This is an important process. For instance one new dataset is the CASIA infrared night gait dataset [31]. It consists of gait data from 153 subjects collected outdoors, at night, with and without carrying condition, and at two different speeds. This dataset nicely complements existing datasets that are collected during the day. Given the data-driven nature of biometrics research, the key to future progress are such data sets collected to explore issues not considered or raised by existing ones. One idea for a future data is the following. As of today there is a need for the better understanding of the variation of gait due to surface conditions and across elapsed time. Ideally, the dataset to support this would consist of gait data from around 1000 subjects, which is an order of magnitude larger than current large datasets. It should include gait data repeated at regular time intervals of weeks spanning about a year. The dataset should be collected in outdoor conditions, preferably collected at a distance of 300m to reflect real world conditions. The dataset should come with a set of well defined experiments in terms of gallery and probe sets. These experiments influence the types of algorithms that will be developed. For the experiments to be effective at influencing the direction of gait research the design of the experiments needs to solve the *three bears problem*; the experiments must be neither too hard nor too easy, but just right. If performance on the experiments is easily saturated, then the gait recognition community will not be challenged. If experiments are too hard, then it will not be possible to make progress on gait recognition. Ideally, the set of experiments should vary in difficulty, characterize where the gait recognition problem is solvable, and explore the factors that affect performance. A set of experiments cannot meet this ideal unless the appropriate set of data is collected.

(a)　　　　　(b)　　　　　(c)　　　　　(d)

Fig. 6.6. The face samples under different conditions. The candidates for the gallery sets are (a) Regular expression with mugshot lighting, and (b) Regular expression, overhead lighting images. The probes are taken outdoors with (c) regular expression, far view and (d) regular expression, near view.

6.4.5 Face and Gait

One way to improve recognition performance for outdoors, at-a-distance scenario, is to fuse gait with face information. Several studies have started to consider this [29, 12, 23]. In [29] it was shown, based on 26 subjects, that the best performance of gait+face as around 89%, whereas the individually gait was 68% and face was 73%. In [12] it was shown that identification rate maxed out upon fusion of gait and face using outdoors data from 30 subjects. On a somewhat larger dataset of 46 subjects, it is shown in [41] that performance of gait+face improves to 91% from 87% and 85% for gait and *profile* face, respectively. In [23] we considered a larger subject pool. We studied recognition improvement in the HumanID Gait Challenge experiments based on gait data along with the corresponding face data that was collected for each subject, both indoors and outdoors. Fig. 6.6 shows some examples of the face data. We considered if the performance on the key experiments in the gait challenge problem could be improved upon by fusing gait with face. Fig. 6.7 shows the performances of all 5 covariates in gait challenge dataset: view, shoe-type, surface, briefcase, and time, in terms of verification rate at 5% false alarm rate. The results demonstrate that combination substantially improves upon recognition from single modality alone. We also found that the inter-modal combination, i.e. face+gait, is better than the combinations of the same modality, i.e. face+face and gait+gait. In fact, we observed that intra-modal combination does not seem to improve performance by a significant amount.

6.5 Conclusion

In this chapter we have provided a snapshot of the state of gait recognition research and some directions for future research. Over the past 5 or so years,

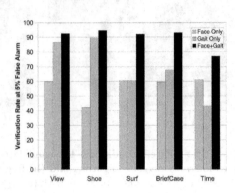

Fig. 6.7. Verification rate at a false alarm rate of 5% for the five key experiments HumanID gait challenge dataset: view, shoe-type, surface, briefcase and time.

tremendous progress has been made on this problem and we are seeing a continued increase in interest in this problem. The use of common datasets has helped focus the research community on the hard problems in gait recognition in a short time span, instead of designing yet-another-gait recognition algorithm on proprietary data sets. We hope that this trend will continue and new, larger, datasets will replace existing ones. In addition to biometrics, the problem of gait recognition is a rich source for investigating computer vision problems in both static and dynamic shape analysis. It also provides an excellent context to study 3D issues, such as automatic calibration, reconstruction, etc. in outdoor settings from multiple viewpoints.

References

1. N.V. Boulgouris, D. Hatzinakos, and K.N. Plataniotis. Gait recognition: a challenging signal processing technology for biometric identification. *IEEE Signal Processing Magazine*, 22(6):78–90, Nov. 2005.
2. Jeffrey E. Boyd. Synchronization of oscillations for machine perception of gaits. *Computer Vision and Image Understanding*, 96(1):35–59, Oct. 2004.
3. R. Collins, R. Gross, and J. Shi. Silhouette-based human identification from body shape and gait. In *Proc. of International Conference on Automatic Face and Gesture Recognition*, pages 366–371, 2002.
4. N. Cuntoor, A. Kale, and R. Chellappa. Combining multiple evidences for gait recognition. In *Prof. of International Conference on Acoustics, Speech and Signal Processing*, volume 3, pages 113–116, 2003.
5. J. E. Cutting and L. T. Kozlowski. Recognition of friends by their walk. *Bulletin of the Psychonomic Society*, 9:353–356, 1977.
6. J. P. Foster, Nixon M. S., and Prugel-Bennett A. Automatic gait recognition using area-based metrics. *Pattern Recognition Letters*, 24:2489–2497, 2003.

7. R. Gross and J. Shi. The CMU motion of body (MoBo) database. Tech. report CMU-RI-TR-01-18, Robotics Institute, Carnegie Mellon University, June 2001.

8. J. Han and B. Bhanu. Statistical feature fusion for gait-based human recognition. In *Proc. of IEEE Conference on Computer Vision and Pattern Recognition*, volume II, pages 842–847, June 2004.

9. J. Hayfron-Acquah, M. Nixon, and J. Carter. Automatic gait recognition by symmetry analysis. *Pattern Recognition Letters*, 24(13):2175–2183, Sept. 2003.

10. A. Johnson and A. Bobick. A multi-view method for gait recognition using static body parameters. In *International Conference on Audio- and Video-Based Biometric Person Authentication*, pages 301–311, 2001.

11. A. Kale, A.N. Rajagopalan, N. Cuntoor, and V. Kruger. Gait-based recognition of humans using continuous HMMs. In *Proc. of International Conference on Automatic Face and Gesture Recognition*, pages 336–341, 2002.

12. A. Kale, A. Roy Chowdhury, and R. Chellappa. Fusion of gait and face for human recognition. In *Proc. of International Conference on Acoustics, Speech, and Signal Processing*, pages V–901–904, 2004.

13. Amit Kale, Aravind Sundaresan, A. N. Rajagopalan, Naresh P. Cuntoor, Amit K. Roy-Chowdhury, Volker Krger, and Rama Chellappa. Identification of humans using gait. *IEEE Transactions on Image Processing*, 13(9):1163–1173, Sept. 2004.

14. D. Kaziska and A. Srivastava. Cyclostationary Processes on Shape Spaces for Gait-Based Recognition. In *Proc. of European Conference on Computer Vision*, pages 442–453, 2006.

15. C. Lee and A. Elgammal. Gait style and gait content: Bilinear models for gait recognition using gait re-sampling. In *Proc. of International Conference on Automatic Face and Gesture Recognition*, pages 147–152, May 2004.

16. L. Lee, G. Dalley, and K. Tieu. Learning pedestrian models for silhouette refinement. In *Proc. of International Conference on Computer Vision*, pages 663 – 670, 2003.

17. L. Lee and W.E.L. Grimson. Gait analysis for recognition and classification. In *Proc. of International Conference on Automatic Face and Gesture Recognition*, pages 155–162, 2002.

18. Y. Liu, R. Collins, and Y. Tsin. Gait sequence analysis using frieze patterns. In *Proc. of European Conference on Computer Vision*, pages 657–671, May 2002.

19. Z. Liu, L. Malave, A. Osuntogun, P. Sudhakar, and S. Sarkar. Toward understanding the limits of gait recognition. In *Proc. of SPIE Defense and Security Symposium: Biometric Technology for Human Identification*, pages 195–205, 2004.

20. Z. Liu and S. Sarkar. Simplest representation yet for gait recognition: Averaged silhouette. In *Proc. of International Conference on Pattern Recognition*, volume 4, pages 211–214, 2004.

21. Z. Liu and S. Sarkar. Effect of silhouette quality on hard problems in gait recognition. *IEEE Transactions on Systems, Man, and Cybernetics (PartB)*, 35(2):170–183, April 2005.

22. Z. Liu and S. Sarkar. Improved Gait Recognition by Gait Dynamics Normalization. *IEEE Transactions on Pattern Analysis and Machine Intelligence*, 28(6):863–876, 2006.

23. Z. Liu and S. Sarkar. Outdoor recognition at a distance by fusing gait and face. *Image and Vision Computing*, Oct. 2006. In press.

24. S. D. Mowbry and M. S. Nixon. Automatic gait recognition via fourier descriptors of deformable objects. In *Proc. of Audio Visual Biometric Person Authentication*, pages 566–573, 2003.
25. Mark S. Nixon and John N. Carter. Advances in automatic gait recognition. In *Proc. of International Conference on Automatic Face and Gesture Recognition*, pages 139–146, 2004.
26. S.A. Niyogi and E.H. Adelson. Analyzing gait with spatiotemporal surfaces. In *Proc. of IEEE Workshop on Non-Rigid Motion*, pages 24–29, 1994.
27. I. Robledo Vega and S. Sarkar. Representation of the evolution of feature relationship statistics: Human gait-based recognition. *IEEE Transactions on Pattern Analysis and Machine Intelligence*, 25(10):1323–1328, Oct 2003.
28. S. Sarkar, P. Jonathon Phillips, Z. Liu, I. Robledo-Vega, P. Grother, and K. W. Bowyer. The Human ID gait challenge problem: Data sets, performance, and analysis. *IEEE Transactions on Pattern Analysis and Machine Intelligence*, II:162–177, Feb 2005.
29. G. Shakhnarovich and T. Darrell. On probabilistic combination of face and gait cues for identification. *Proceedings of the Fifth IEEE International Conference on Automatic Face and Gesture Recognition*, 2002.
30. S. V. Stevenage, M. S. Nixon, and Vince K. Visual analysis of gait as a cue to identity. *Applied Cognitive Psychology*, 13(6):513–526, Dec. 1999.
31. D. Tan, K. Huang, S. Yu, and T. Tan. Efficient night gait recognition based on template matching. In *Proc. of International Conference on Pattern Recognition*, volume 3, pages 1000–1003, 2006.
32. R. Tanawongsuwan and A. Bobick. Gait recognition from time-normalized joint-angle trajectories in the walking plane. In *Proc. of IEEE Conference on Computer Vision and Pattern Recognition*, pages II:726–731, 2001.
33. R. Tanawongsuwan and A. Bobick. Performance analysis of time-distance gait parameters under different speeds. In *International Conference on Audio- and Video-Based Biometric Person Authentication*, pages 715–724, 2003.
34. D. Tolliver and R. Collins. Gait shape estimation for identification. In *International Conference on Audio- and Video-Based Biometric Person Authentication*, pages 734–742, 2003.
35. A. Veeraraghavan, A. Roy Chowdhury, and R. Chellappa. Role of shape and kinematics in human movement analysis. In *Proc. of IEEE Conference on Computer Vision and Pattern Recognition*, Washington D.C., USA, June 2004.
36. D. K. Wagg and M. S. Nixon. On automated model-based extraction and analysis of gait. In *International Conference on Automatic Face and Gesture Recognition*, pages 11–16, 2004.
37. L. Wang, W. Hu, and T. Tan. A new attempt to gait-based human identification. In *Proc. of International Conference on Pattern Recognition*, volume 1, pages 115–118, 2002.
38. L. Wang, T. Tan, H. Ning, and W. Hu. Silhouette analysis-based gait recognition for human identification. *IEEE Transactions on Pattern Analysis and Machine Intelligence*, 25:1505–1518, Dec. 2003.
39. Shiqi Yu, Daoliang Tan, and Tieniu Tan. A framework for evaluating the effect of view angle, clothing and carrying condition on gait recognition. In *Proc. of International Conference on Pattern Recognition*, volume 4, pages 441–444, 2006.
40. G. Zhao, R. Chen, G. Liu, and H. Li. Amplitude spectrum-based gait recognition. In *Proc. of International Conference on Automatic Face and Gesture Recognition*, pages 23–28, 2004.

41. X. Zhou and B. Bhanu. Feature fusion of face and gait for human recognition at a distance in video. In *Proc. of International Conference on Pattern Recognition*, volume 4, pages 529–532, Aug. 2006.

The Ear as a Biometric

D. J. Hurley, B. Arbab-Zavar, and M. S. Nixon

University of Southampton, UK
djh@analyticalengines.co.uk, baz05r@ecs.soton.ac.uk,
msn@ecs.soton.ac.uk

7.1 Introduction

The potential of the human ear for personal identification was recognized and advocated as long ago as 1890 by the French criminologist Alphonse Bertillon. In his seminal work on biometrics he writes [4],

> "The ear, thanks to these multiple small valleys and hills which furrow across it, is the most significant factor from the point of view of identification. Immutable in its form since birth, resistant to the influences of environment and education, this organ remains, during the entire life, like the intangible legacy of heredity and of the intra-uterine life".

Ear biometrics has received scant attention compared to the more popular techniques of face, eye, or fingerprint recognition. However, ears have played a significant role in forensic science for many years, especially in the United States, where an ear classification system based on manual measurements was developed by Iannarelli, and has been in use for more than 40 years [21], although the reliability of ear-print evidence has recently been challenged [24, 14]. Rutty et al. have considered how Iannarelli's manual techniques might be automated [32] and a European initiative has looked at the value of ear prints in forensics [25].

Ears have certain advantages over the more established biometrics; as Bertillon pointed out, they have a rich and stable structure that changes little with age. The ear does not suffer from changes in facial expression, and is firmly fixed in the middle of the side of the head so that the immediate background is more predictable than is the case for face recognition which usually requires the face to be captured against a controlled background. Collection does not have an associated hygiene issue, as may be the case with contact biometrics, and is unlikely to cause anxiety as may happen with iris and retina measurements. The ear is large compared with the iris, retina, and fingerprint and therefore is more easily captured at a distance.

Burge et al. [7, 8] were amongst the first to describe the ear's potential as a biometric using graph matching techniques on a Voronoi diagram of curves extracted from the Canny edge map. Moreno et al. [27] tackled the problem with some success using neural networks and reported a recognition rate of 93% on a dataset of 168 images using a two-stage neural network technique. Hurley et al. used force field feature extraction [17, 16, 20] to map the ear to an energy field which highlights "potential wells" and "potential channels" as features. By achieving a recognition rate of 99.2% on a dataset of 252 images, [20] this method proved to yield a much better performance than PCA when the images were poorly registered. The approach is also robust to noise; adding 19dB of Gaussian noise actually improved the performance to 99.6% [19]. Abdel-Mottaleb et al. [1] used the force field transform to obtain a smooth surface representation for the ear and then applied different surface curvature extractors to gather the features.

Statistical holistic analysis, especially Principal Components Analysis (PCA), has proved to be one of the most popular approaches to ear recognition. Victor et al. [34] applied PCA to both face and ear recognition and concluded that the face yields a better performance than the ear. However, Chang et al. [9] conducted a similar experiment and reached a different conclusion: no significant difference was observed between face and ear biometrics when using PCA. The image dataset in [34] had less control over earrings, hair, lighting etc. and as suggested by Chang et al., this may account for the discrepancy between the two experiments. Chang et al. also reported a recognition rate of 90.9% using an ear and face multimodal approach. Zhang et al. [42] developed a system combining Independent Components Analysis (ICA) with a Radial Basis Function (RBF) network and showed that better performance can be achieved using ICA instead of PCA. However both PCA and ICA offer almost no invariance and therefore require very accurate registration in order to achieve consistently good results.

Yuizono et al. [41] treated the recognition task as an optimisation problem, proposing a system using a specially developed genetic local search targeting the ear images. Given that their work does not include any feature extraction process, it has no invariant properties. Some studies have focused on geometrical approaches [28, 13]; Mu et al. [28] reported an 85% recognition rate using such an approach. Alvarez et al. [3] proposed an ovoid model for segmentation and normalization of the ear.

Yan et al. [37, 40] captured 3D ear images using a range scanner and used Iterative Closest Point (ICP) registration for recognition to achieve a 97.8% recognition rate. Chen et al. proposed a 3D ear detection and recognition system using a model ear for detection, and using ICP and a local surface descriptor for recognition, reporting a recognition rate of 90.4% [12, 11, 10, 6].

A number of multimodal approaches to ear recognition have also been considered [9, 36, 22, 31]. Iwano et al. [22] combined ear images and speech using a composite posterior probability, and showed that the performance improves using ear images in addition to speech in the presence of noise. In this study,

PCA was applied to extract the ear features. Chang et al. [9] and Rahman et al. [31] proposed multimodal biometric systems using PCA on both face and ear. Both studies reported an increase in performance when using multimodal biometrics instead of individual biometrics, achieving multi-modal recognition rates of 90.9% and 94.4% respectively. Yan et al. [36] conducted multi-modal experiments on a dataset of 203 images to test the efficacy of various combinations of 2D-PCA, 3D-PCA, and 3D-Edges with the recognition results shown in Table 7.1. For further details of multi-modal ear and face biometrics see the chapter by Bowyer. An introductory survey of ear biometrics has been

Table 7.1. Yan et al. multi-modal results on a dataset of 203 images.

2d-pca,	3d-pca,	3d-edge,	3d-pca+3d-edge,	2d-pca+3d-edge,	2d-pca+3d-pca,	all 3
71.9%	64.8%	71.9%	80.2%	89.7%	89.1%	90.6%

provided by Pun et al. [30].

In related studies Akkermans et al. [2] developed an ear biomeric system based on the acoustic properties of the ear. They measure the acoustic transfer function of the ear by projecting a sound wave at the ear and observing the change in the reflected signal.

We will start this chapter with a review of the anatomy and physiology of the ear and how this is likely to affect its biometric properties. The ear biometrics field is still so small that we will be able to touch on most of the main techniques. In particular, we will describe PCA in some detail as this has proved to be one of the most popular techniques. Despite its intricate mathematical nature, it is quite easy to implement and even easier to use, and should allow the reader to do some simple experiments with ear biometrics in order to confirm their biometric potential. Finally, we will consider the future of ear biometrics and related issues.

7.2 Evidence and Support for Ears as a Biometric

The structure of the ear is not quite so random as Bertillon seems to suggest; it has a definite structure just like the face. Most people when asked could easily draw the outline of the ear but only the experienced artist would be able to reproduce from memory its detailed intricate structure. As shown in Figure 7.1, the shape of the ear tends to be dominated by the outer rim or helix, and also by the shape of the lobe. There is also an inner helix or antihelix which runs roughly parallel to the outer helix but forks into two branches at the upper extremity. The inner helix and the lower of these two branches forms the top and left side of the concha, named for its shell-like appearance. The bottom of the concha merges into the very distinctive intertragic notch, which due to its very sharp bend at the bottom can form a useful reference point for biometric purposes. Note also the crus of helix where the helix intersects with the lower branch of the antihelix. This is one of the points used by Iannarelli as a reference point for his measurement system, the other point being the antitragus or the little bump on the left of the intertragic notch [21]. The front of the concha opens into the external ear canal or acoustic or auditory meatus, more commonly referred to as the ear hole, although this is usually somewhat concealed by the flesh around and above the tragus. It is interesting to note [29] that the embryonic ear has a small number of about 6 individual growth nodules which eventually develop along with the foetus to become the fully formed auricle in the newborn infant, striking a note with Bertillon's earlier observation.

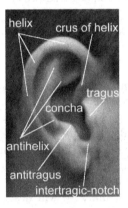

Fig. 7.1. Anatomy of the ear. In addition to the familiar rim or helix and ear lobe, the ear also has other prominent features such as the anti-helix which runs parallel to the helix, and a distinctive hairpin-bend shape just above the lobe called the intertragic notch. The central area or concha is named for its shell-like appearance.

Figure 7.2 shows a small sample of human ears indicating the rich variety of different shapes. Notice that some ears have well formed lobes, whereas others have almost none. These latter are called "attached lobes" and make measurement of the length of the ear difficult.

Because of the tendency of the inner and outer helices to run parallel, there is quite a degree of correlation between them which detracts somewhat from the biometric value of the ear; indeed it could also be argued that the concha is simply the space that remains when the other parts have been accounted for, so that it is also highly correlated to its neighbouring parts and therefore contributes less independent information than might appear to be the case at first.

The outer ear called the auricula or pinna forms only part of the total ear organ which has evolved to locate, collect, and process sound waves. Many

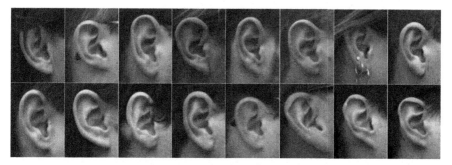

Fig. 7.2. Examples of the human ear shape. Notice that helices, concha, intertragic notch, etc. are present in all the examples, but that some ears have so called attached lobes, where the lobes are poorly formed or are almost non-existent.

other mammals like horses, dogs, and cats can articulate their ears to better locate particular sound sources. Fortunately for the purpose of biometrics we humans can hardly articulate our ears; our ears are held rigidly in position by cartilaginous tissue which is firmly attached to the bone at the side of the head. The ear owes its semi-rigid shape due to this stiff tissue which underlies its soft flesh.

The face has roughly the same visual complexity as the ear; quite simple changes in the parameters which define the size and shape of the eyes, nose, mouth, and cheek-bones can lead to a wide range of facial appearances. In this, we regard perfect symmetry as a mark of beauty, but we should note that the ear lacks all symmetry. It is also worth noting that since the face is symmetrical about its centre-line, therefore its structure really only represents half-a-face from a biometrics perspective because the information on the left side reflects that on the right. The ear has no symmetry and therefore does not suffer from this drawback giving it an advantage over the face, and of course the face is contorted during speech and when expressing emotions, and its appearance is often altered by make-up, spectacles, and beards and moustaches, whereas the ear does not move and only has to support earrings, spectacle frames, and sometimes hearing aids, although of course it is often occluded by hair. As such, the ear is much less susceptible to covariate interference than many other biometrics, with particular invariance to age.

7.3 Approaches to Ear Biometrics

7.3.1 The early work of Iannarelli and Forensic Ears

Alfred Iannarelli developed a system of ear classification used by American law enforcement agencies. In late 1949 he became interested in the ear as a means of personal identification in the context of forensic science. He subsequently developed the Iannarelli System of Ear Identification [21]. As shown

Fig. 7.3. Iannarelli's manual ear measurement system.

in Figure 7.3 his system essentially consists of taking a number measurements around the ear by placing a transparent compass with 8 spokes at equal 45° intervals over an enlarged photograph of the ear. The first part of registration is achieved by ensuring that a reference line touches the crus of helix at the top and touches the innermost point on the tragus at the bottom. Normalisation and the second step of registration are accomplished by adjusting the enlargement mechanism until a second reference line exactly spans the concha from top to bottom. Iannarelli has appeared personally as an expert witness in many court cases involving ear evidence, or is often cited as an ear identification expert by other expert witnesses [24]. In the preface to his book Iannarelli states,

> "Through 38 years of research and application in earology, the author has found that in literally thousands of ears that were examined by visual means, photographs, ear prints, and latent ear print impressions, no two ears were found to be identical - not even the ears of any one individual. This uniqueness held true in cases of identical and fraternal twins, triplets, and quadruplets"

When Iannarelli suggests that "not even the ears of any one individual are unique" he has unwittingly touched on the nub of the biometrics problem. It is not an advantage, as he seems to suggest, that the ear samples from the same individual over time are not unique. On the contrary the less these samples are unique, then the less are we entitled to claim that an individual's biometric is unique. If we think of individuals' samples as forming points in a feature space, then these points will form clusters for each individual. It is the extent to which these different clusters are separated from one and other and the extent to which the individual clusters are closely grouped around their own averages, that determines how well a particular biometric system performs. In recent times attempts have been made to automate Iannarelli's system [32].

7.3.2 Burge and Burger Proof of Concept

Burge and Burger [7, 8] were the first to investigate the human ear as a biometric in the context of machine vision. Inspired by the earlier work of

Iannarelli [21], they conducted a proof of concept study where the viability of the ear as a biometric was shown both theoretically in terms of the uniqueness and measurability over time, and in practice through the implementation of a computer vision based system. Each subject's ear was modeled as an adjacency graph built from the Voronoi diagram of its Canny extracted curve segments. They devised a novel graph matching algorithm for authentication which takes into account the erroneous curve segments which can occur in the ear image due to changes such as lighting, shadowing, and occlusion. They found that the features are robust and could be reliably extracted from a distance. Figure 7.4 shows the extracted curves, Voronoi diagram, and a neighbourhood graph for a typical ear. They identified the problem of occlusion by hair as a major

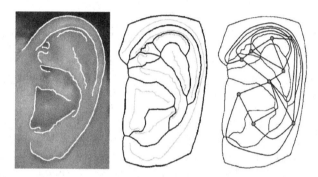

Fig. 7.4. Graph model: Stages in building the ear biometric graph model. A generalized Voronoi diagram (centre) of the Canny extracted edge curves (left) is built and a neighborhood graph (right) is extracted.

obstacle and proposed the use of thermal imagery to overcome this obstacle.

7.3.3 Principal Components Analysis

Principal Components Analysis, closely related to Singular Value Decomposition, has been one of the most popular approaches to ear recognition [34, 9, 20, 22, 35, 31]. It is an elegant, easy to implement and easy to use technique, so we will attempt to describe it in sufficient detail for the reader to be able to understand and implement it readily with a view to being able to set up a simple ear recognition experiment to confirm the basic biometric potential of the ear. The underlying mathematics can be found in [33, 23].

We will first show how images can be looked upon as vectors, and how any picture can be constructed as a summation of elementary picture-vectors. We will then show how PCA can process these vectors to achieve image compression, and how this in turn can be used for biometrics.

We are familiar with the real coordinate space R^3 where any point can be represented as a linear combination of 3 unit value basis vectors mutually at right angles to each other. For example, the point (3,4,5) can be expressed as,

$$3(1,0,0) + 4(0,1,0) + 5(0,0,1) = (3,0,0) + (0,4,0) + (0,0,5) = (3,4,5).$$

We could also express any point as the sum of non-standard basis vectors, providing that none of the chosen basis vectors is a linear combination of the other two. For example, we can also write,

$$(3,4,5) = 1.333(1,2,3) + 0.333(2,3,1) + 0.333(3,1,2).$$

Now if we admit the possibility of negative value pixels, then pictures can also be treated as vectors so that any picture can be expressed as a linear combination of unit value basis picture-vectors. For example, a trivial four element picture can be expressed as,

$$\begin{bmatrix} 1 & 2 \\ 3 & 4 \end{bmatrix} = 1 \begin{bmatrix} 1 & 0 \\ 0 & 0 \end{bmatrix} + 2 \begin{bmatrix} 0 & 1 \\ 0 & 0 \end{bmatrix} + 3 \begin{bmatrix} 0 & 0 \\ 1 & 0 \end{bmatrix} + 4 \begin{bmatrix} 0 & 0 \\ 0 & 1 \end{bmatrix}$$

In the example which follows taken from [20] we will be dealing with 111x73 -pixel images. This would require 111x73 = 8103 sparse elementary picture-vectors, each with only one pixel set to 1 and the remaining pixels set to 0, and a set of 8103 weights to specify a particular picture, obviously not resulting in any compression advantage.

In this real example we use a subset of the XM2VTS face profiles database [26], consisting of 4 ear images for each of 63 subjects giving us a total of 252 images. Now here is how the "magic" of PCA works; by taking one of the four samples from each of the 63 subjects we produce a special *projection matrix* **P** which enables us to compute a set of 63 weights for each of the 252 images which when used to scale a set of 63 special picture-vectors already encoded in **P** produces a reasonable facsimile of the original image. Instead of requiring 8103 weights we can make do with only 63 which is a very high degree of compression of well over 100:1, albeit lossy compression. These weights form convenient 63 element feature vectors representing each picture and are perfect for biometric comparison as they allow us to calculate the *distance* between pictures by doing a simple vector subtraction.

We will now give the details of the calculations involved. In order to carry out matrix multiplication of the 111x73 picture-vectors we first have to encode them as 8103x1 column vectors by stacking the 73 columns on top of each other. Any results can be recoded as rectangular matrices for display purposes.

The projection matrix is calculated as follows

Let **p** be any of the 63 first of four picture samples
Let **m** be the average over the 63 pictures i.e.$(\sum \mathbf{p})/63$
Let $\mathbf{d} = \mathbf{p} - \mathbf{m}$ be the difference between each picture and the average
Let **D** be the array formed by the 63 columns of difference pictures **d**
Then the projection matrix is given by,

$$\mathbf{P} = \mathbf{D}S(\mathbf{D^T D}), \tag{7.1}$$

where $S(\mathbf{M})$ is a function that returns a matrix whose columns are the normalised eigenvectors of matrix $\mathbf{M}$.

The basis-pictures or *eigenvectors* are simply the columns of $\mathbf{P}$.
The weights for picture $\mathbf{p}$ are given by

$$\mathbf{w} = \mathbf{d}^{\mathbf{T}}\mathbf{P}. \tag{7.2}$$

The compressed image for a given picture $\mathbf{p}$ is given by

$$\mathbf{c} = \mathbf{P}\mathbf{w}^{\mathbf{T}} + \mathbf{m}. \tag{7.3}$$

Figure 7.5 shows the first 36 of the 63 eigenvctors, whereas Figure 7.6 shows the projections and eigenvector spectra for 3 subjects. Notice that the leftmost projections are the best facsimiles because they have been used in forming the projection matrix. Notice also that the eigenvector spectra, consisting of the 63 weights, do not rapidly diminish to zero, in fact all of these 63 weights are used for comparison. Each set of 63 weights is treated as a vector and the Manhattan distances between these vectors are used as a suitable metric,

$$distance = \sum_{n=0}^{62} |\mathbf{w}_i(n) - \mathbf{w}_j(n)|. \tag{7.4}$$

The means and standard deviations of the inter-class and intra-class distributions can then be calculated to gauge the efficacy of the technique. The spreads or standard deviations of the two distributions should be small compared to the separation of their means for a good biometric. Since 63 of the samples are used in forming $\mathbf{P}$, we do not include them in the biometric comparison so that only $252 - 63 = 189$ ear images are used for performance evaluation. In this experiment a recognition rate of $186/189$ or 98.4% was achieved [20].

7.3.4 Force Field Transform

Hurley et al. [17, 18, 16, 20] have developed an invertible linear transform which transforms an ear image into a force field by pretending that pixels have a mutual attraction proportional to their intensities and inversely to the square of the distance between them rather like Newton's Universal Law of Gravitation (Figure 7.7). Underlying this force field there is an associated energy field which in the case of an ear takes the form of a smooth surface with a number of peaks joined by ridges as shown in Figure 7.8. The peaks correspond to potential energy wells and to extend the analogy the ridges correspond to potential energy channels. Since the transform also turns out to be invertible, all of the original information is preserved and since the otherwise smooth surface is modulated by these peaks and ridges, it is argued that much of the information is transferred to these features and that therefore they should make good features.

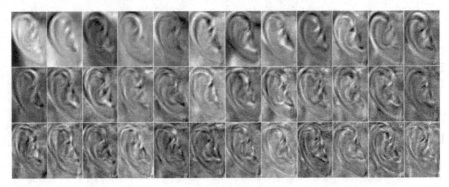

Fig. 7.5. The first 36 of the set of 63 eigenvectors computed from the subset of 63 ear images selected from the 252 image database. The first of the four samples from each of the 63 subjects was used in forming the projection matrix. These are the basis picture-vectors which will be scaled by the computed weights to produce the compressed or projected images.

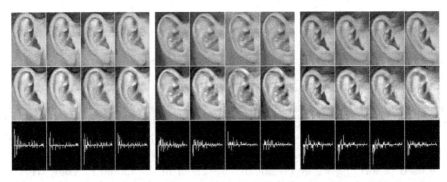

Fig. 7.6. PCA projections and eigenvector spectra for 3 subjects. The top rows show the original images whilst the middle rows are their corresponding projections into the eigenvector subspace. The bottom row depicts the eigenvector spectrum for each image consisting of the 63 weights used to render its projection.

Gravitation

$$\mathbf{F} = Gm_e m_m \frac{\mathbf{r}}{|\mathbf{r}|^3}$$

Fig. 7.7. Newton's Universal Law of Gravitation. The earth and moon are mutually attracted according to the product of their masses m_e and m_m respectively, and inversely proportional to the square of the distance between them. G is the gravitational constant of proportionality.

$$\mathbf{F}(\mathbf{r}_j) = \sum_i \left\{ P(\mathbf{r}_i) \frac{\mathbf{r}_i - \mathbf{r}_j}{|\mathbf{r}_i - \mathbf{r}_j|^3} \right\} \forall i \neq j, \ 0 \ \forall i = j \qquad (7.5)$$

$$E(\mathbf{r}_j) = \sum_i \frac{P(\mathbf{r}_i)}{|\mathbf{r}_i - \mathbf{r}_j|} \forall i \neq j, \ 0 \ \forall i = j \qquad (7.6)$$

Two distinct methods of extracting these features are offered. The first

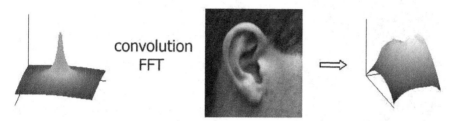

Fig. 7.8. Generating an ear energy surface by convolution. The energy field for an ear (right) is obtained by locating a unit value potential function (left) at each pixel location and scaling it by the value of the pixel and then finding the sum of all the resulting functions. For efficiency this is actually calculated in the frequency domain.

method depicted in Figure 7.9 (left) is algorithmic, where test pixels seeded around the perimeter of the force field are allowed to follow the force direction joining together here and there to form channels which terminate in potential wells. The second method depicted in Figure 7.9 (centre) is analytical, and results from an analysis of the mechanism of the first method leading to a scalar function based on the divergence of the force direction. The second method was used to obtain a recognition rate of over 99% on a dataset of 252 ear images consisting of 4 time lapsed samples from each of 63 subjects, extracted from the XM2VTS face profiles database [26].

Equations 7.5 and 7.6 show how the force and energy fields are calculated at any point $\mathbf{r}_j$. These equations must be applied at every pixel position to generate the complete fields. In practice this computation would be done in the frequency domain using Equation 7.7 where $\Im$ stands for FFT.

$$Energy = \sqrt{MN} \left\{ \Im^{-1} \left[\Im \left(potential \right) \times \Im \left(image \right) \right] \right\} \qquad (7.7)$$

Convergence provides a more general description of channels and wells in the form of a mathematical function in which wells and channels are revealed to be peaks and ridges, respectively in the function value. This function maps the force field $\mathbf{F}(\mathbf{r})$ to a scalar field $C(\mathbf{r})$, taking the force as input, and returning the additive inverse of the divergence of the force direction, and is defined by,

$$C(\mathbf{r}) = -\text{div}\mathbf{f}(\mathbf{r}) = -\lim_{\Delta A \to 0} \frac{\oint \mathbf{f}(\mathbf{r}) \cdot d\mathbf{l}}{\Delta A} = -\nabla \cdot \mathbf{f}(\mathbf{r}) = -\left(\frac{\partial f_x}{\partial x} + \frac{\partial f_y}{\partial y} \right) \qquad (7.8)$$

where $\mathbf{f}(\mathbf{r}) = \frac{\mathbf{F}(\mathbf{r})}{|\mathbf{F}(\mathbf{r})|}$ is the force direction, ΔA is incremental area, and dl is its boundary outward normal. This function is real valued and takes negative values as well as positive ones where negative values correspond to force direction divergence. Note that the function is non-linear because it is based on force direction and therefore must be calculated in the given order.

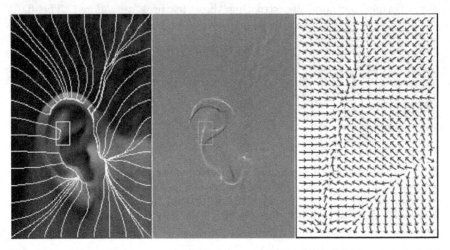

Fig. 7.9. Force and convergence fields for an ear. The force field for an ear (left) and its corresponding convergence field (centre). The force direction field (right) corresponds to the small rectangular inserts surrounding a potential well on the inner helix.

7.3.5 Three Dimensional Ear Biometrics

The auricle has a rich and deep three dimensional structure, so it is not surprising that a number of research groups have focused their attention in this direction.

Yan and Bowyer ICP Approach

Yan et al. [38, 36, 39, 37, 40] use a Minolta VIVID 910 range scanner to capture both depth and colour information. The device uses a laser to scan the ear, and depth is automatically calculated using triangulation. They have developed a fully automatic ear biometric system using ICP based 3D shape matching for recognition, and using both 2D appearance and 3D depth data for automatic ear extraction which not only extracts the ear image but also separates it from hair and earrings. They achieve almost 98% recognition on a time-lapse dataset of 1,386 images over 415 subjects, with an equal error rate of 1.2%. The 2D and 3D image datasets used in this work are available to other research groups. For further details, see Chapter 25.

Ear extraction uses a multistage process which uses both 2D and 3D data and curvature estimation to detect the ear pit which is then used to initialize an elliptical active contour to locate the ear outline and crop the 3D ear data.

Ear pit detection includes: (i) geometric prepossessing to locate the nose tip to act as the hub of a sector which includes the ear with a high degree of confidence; (ii) skin detection to isolate the face and ear region from the hair and clothes; (iii) surface curvature estimation to detect the pit regions depicted in black in the image; (iv) surface segmentation and classification, and curvature information to select amongst possible multiple pit regions using a voting scheme to select the most likely candidate. The detected ear pit is then used to initialize an active contour algorithm to find the ear outlines. Both 2D colour and 3D depth are used to drive the contour, as using either alone is inadequate since there are cases in which there is no clear colour or depth change around the ear contour.

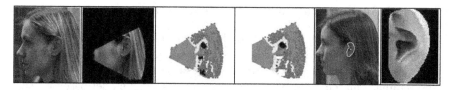

Fig. 7.10. 3D ear extraction. From left to right, skin detection and most likely sector generation, pit detection and selection, ear outline location, 3D ear extraction

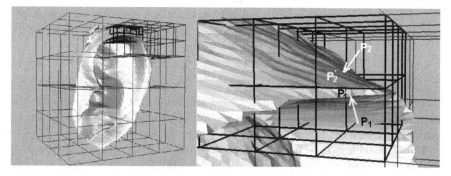

Fig. 7.11. Voxelization: Left: 3D image space is partitioned into voxels. Right: Two voxel centres P_1 and P_2 and their closest points on the gallery surface P_1' and P_2'.

3D shape matching: ICP [5] has been widely used for 3D shape matching due to its simplicity and accuracy, however it is computationally expensive.

Given a probe point set P and a gallery point set G, ICP iteratively calculates the rigid transform T that best aligns P and G. At the ith iteration, the transform T_i is the transform that minimizes the mean square differences between the corresponding points of P_i and G. The corresponding points are the closest points between the two point-sets. P_i is then updated using T_i.

Yan et al. [38] have developed an efficient ICP registration method called "Pre-computed Voxel Closest Neighbours" which exploits the fact that subjects have to be enrolled beforehand for biometrics. Since the most time consuming part of the ICP algorithm is finding the closest points between the probe and the gallery (of order $N_P \log N_G$) the main idea of this method is to approximate each point of the probe with a nearby point whose nearest point in the gallery point set is pre-computed. They proposed a quantised 3D volume using voxels, as shown in Figure 7.11. Placing the 3D probe image into this volume, each point of the probe falls into a voxel. Each probe point is then approximated by the voxel centre wherein it is placed. For each voxel the closest point in 3D space on the gallery surface is computed ahead of time. Figure 7.11 shows the closest points to the two voxel centres P_1 and P_2.

Chen and Bhanu Local Surface Patch Approach

Chen et al. [12, 11, 10, 6] have also tackled 3D ear biometrics using a Minolta range scanner as the basis of a complete 3D recognition system on a dataset of 52 subjects consisting of two images per subject. The ears are detected using template matching of edge clusters against an ear model based on the helix and antihelix, and then a number of feature points are extracted based on local surface shape. A signature called a "Local Surface Patch" based on local curvature is computed for each feature point and is used in combination with ICP to achieve a recognition rate of 90.4%

Feature points extraction: Shape index S_i is a quantitative measure of surface shape [15] based on principal curvatures which classifies surface shape as one of 9 basic types represented by values in the interval $[0,1]$,

$$S_i(p) = \frac{1}{2} - \frac{1}{\pi} \tan^{-1} \frac{k_1(p) + k_2(p)}{k_1(p) - k_2(p)}, \qquad (7.9)$$

where k_1 and k_2 are the maximum and minimum principal curvatures respectively. Chen et al. then choose as feature points those where the index is locally maximum or minimum.

Local Surface Patch: A local surface patch (LSP) [12] comprises the neighbourhood of points N around a feature point P which are close enough to the feature point in Euclidean distance and surface normal.

$$N = \{N_i : N_i \ pixel, \|N_i - P\| \le \varepsilon_1, \cos^{-1}(n_p \bullet n_{n_i}) < A\}. \qquad (7.10)$$

For each feature point, shape index values of its LSP points and the dot product of surface normal vectors of the feature point and its LSP points are computed, and accumulated in a 2D histogram. The 2D histogram accumulates this information in bins along two axes. These two axes are the shape index with range [0,1] and the dot product of surface normal vectors which is in the range [-1,1]. A surface type of "concave", "convex", or "saddle" is also allocated to each LSP. Taken together the 2D histogram, the surface type and the centroid of the local surface patch make up a distinctive signature for each patch.

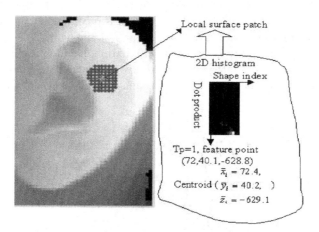

Fig. 7.12. Local Surface Patch. The LSP constitutes a characteristic signature consisting of a 2D histogram, a surface type, and a centroid.

Recognition: This is a two stage process based on LSP for coarse alignment and ICP for fine alignment of probe and gallery images. Probe images are compared against all images in the gallery; each comparison is started by identifying the best match for each probe LSP in the gallery. Assuming that the true set of matches which pairs the patches that depict similar features in both probe and gallery is a subset of the total matches, a geometric constraint is applied to divide the matches into groups where each pair of matches in a group must satisfy the following condition,

$$d_{C_1,C_2} = |d_{P_1,P_2} - d_{G_1,G_2}| < \varepsilon_2 \qquad (7.11)$$

where $C_1 = \{P_1, G_1\}$ and $C_2 = \{P_2, G_2\}$ are the matches for probe and gallery patches P and G respectively, and d_{P_1,P_2} and d_{G_1,G_2} are the Euclidean distances between patch centroids. The above constraint guarantees that a group of matches preserves the mutual position of the patches. In other words d_{P_1,P_2} should be consistent with d_{G_1,G_2}. Note that with this definition a match can be placed in more than one group. The biggest group is then declared as the true match subset.

Starting with an initial rigid transform based on the true match subset, ICP is applied to find the refined alignment between the probe and the gallery image. Having compared all the gallery images to the probe, the gallery image with least root mean square (RMS) error is classified as the correct match.

7.3.6 Acoustic Ear Recognition

Akkermans et al. [2] have exploited the acoustic properties of the ear for recognition. It turns out that the ear by virtue of its special shape behaves like a filter so that a sound signal played into the ear is returned in a modified form. This acoustic transfer function forms the basis of the acoustic ear signature. An obvious commercial use is that a small microphone might be incorporated into the earpiece of a mobile phone to receive the reflected sound signal and the existing loudspeaker could be used to generate the test signal.

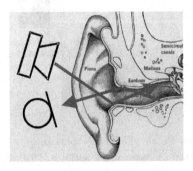

Fig. 7.13. An ear signature is generated by probing the ear with a sound signal which is reflected and picked up by a small microphone. The shape of the pinna and the ear canal determine the acoustic transfer function which forms the basis of the signature.

Akkermans et al. measure the impulse response of the ear by sending a noise signal $n(t)$ with a spectrum $N(\omega)$ into the pinna and ear canal and measuring the response $r(t)$. Next, the response is transformed into the frequency domain by using an FFT to calculate the output frequency spectrum $R(\omega)$. Finally, an estimate is obtained of the transfer function $H(\omega) = R(\omega)/N(\omega)$, where $H(\omega)$ is the cascade of the transfer functions of the loudspeaker, pinna and ear canal, and microphone as shown in Figure 7.14.

The test dataset consists of 8 ear signatures collected from each of 31 subjects using headphones and a separate set of 8 signatures from 17 subjects using a modified mobile phone with a small microphone incorporated into the earpiece. The correlation metric,

$$C = \frac{\mathbf{x} \cdot \mathbf{y}}{\|\mathbf{x}\| \, \|\mathbf{y}\|} \tag{7.12}$$

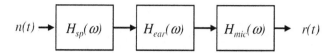

Fig. 7.14. Calculating the impulse response of the ear

was used for comparison where **x** and **y** are the feature vectors taken relative to the mean of the population. Using Fisher LDA analysis equal error rates of 1.5% - 7% were obtained depending on whether headphones were used or mobile phones.

7.4 Conclusions and Outlook

The ear as a biometric is no longer in its infancy and it has shown encouraging progress so far - which is improving, especially with the interest created by the recent research into its 3D potential. It enjoys forensics support, it's structure appears individual, and it appears to have less variance with age than other biometrics.

It is also most unusual, even unique, in that it supports not only visual recognition but also acoustic recognition at the same time. This, together with its deep 3-dimensional structure will make it very difficult to fake thus ensuring that the ear will occupy a special place in situations requiring a high degree of protection against impersonation.

The all important question of "just how good is the ear as a biometric" has only begun to be answered. The initial test results, even with quite small datasets, were disappointing, but now we have regular reports of recognition rates in the high 90's on more sizeable datasets. But there is clearly a need for much better intra-class testing, both in terms of the number of samples per subject and of variability over time. However we will not dwell on this topic as it is treated in depth in Chapter 25.

Most of the recent work has focused on the overall appearance or on the shape of the ear, whether it be PCA, force field, or ICP, but it may prove profitable to further investigate if different and particular parts of the ear are more important than others from a recognition perspective. There is also a need to develop techniques with better invariance, perhaps more model based, and to seek out high speed recognition techniques to cope with the very large datasets that are likely to be encountered in practice.

We must not forget that the inherent disadvantage of the occlusion of the ear by hair will always be a problem, but even this might be ameliorated by the development of thermal imaging schemes. But one thing is for certain, and that is that there are many questions to be answered, so we can look forward to many interesting research studies addressing these issues.

Acknowledgements

The authors would like to thank Mark Burge and Wilhelm Burger for supplying figure 4, Kevin Bowyer and Ping Yan for figures 10 and 11, Bir Bhanu and Hui Chen for figure 12, and Ton Akkermans, Daniel Schobben and Tom Kevenaar for figure 13 and 14. We would also like to thank our editors, Pat Flynn, Anil Jain, and Arun Ross, for their relentless endeavours in bringing this project to fruition.

References

1. M. Abdel-Mottaleb and J. Zhou. Human ear recognition from face profile images. In *Proc. 1st International Conference on Biometrics (ICB)*, pages 786–792, 2006.
2. A. H. M. Akkermans, T. A. M. Kevenaar, and D. W. E. Schobben. Acoustic ear recognition for person identification. In *Fourth IEEE Workshop on Automatic Identification Advanced Technologies (AutoID'05)*, pages 219–223, 2005.
3. L. Alvarez, E. Gonzalez, and L. Mazorra. Fitting ear contour using an ovoid model. In *Proc. of 39 IEEE International Carnahan Conference on Security Technology*, pages 145–148, 2005.
4. A. Bertillon. *La photographie judiciaire, avec un appendice sur la classification et l'identification anthropometriques*. Gauthier-Villars, Paris, 1890.
5. P. J. Besl and N. D. McKay. A method for registration of 3-d shapes. *IEEE Trans. Pattern Analysis and Machine Intelligence*, pages 239–256, 1992.
6. B. Bhanu and H. Chen. Human ear recognition in 3-d. In *Proc. Workshop on Multimodal User Authentication*, pages 91–98, Santa Barbara, CA, 2003.
7. M. Burge and W. Burger. Ear biometrics. In A. Jain, R. Bolle, and S. Pankanti, editors, *BIOMETRICS: Personal Identification in a Networked Society*, pages 273–286. Kluwer Academic, 1998.
8. M. Burge and W. Burger. Ear biometrics in computer vision. In *Proc. of ICPR 2000*, pages 822–826, 2002.
9. K. Chang, K.W. Bowyer, S. Sarkar, and B. Victor. Comparison and combination of ear and face images in appearance-based biometrics. *IEEE Trans. Pattern Analysis and Machine Intelligence*, 25(9):1160–1165, 2003.
10. H. Chen and B. Bhanu. Contour matching for 3-d ear recognition. In *Proc. IEEE Workshop on Applications of Computer Vision*, pages 123–128, Colorado, 2005.
11. H. Chen and B. Bhanu. Shape model-based ear detection from side face range images. In *Proc. of the 2005 IEEE Computer Society Conference on Computer Vision and Pattern Recognition (CVPR'05) - Workshops*, volume 3, page 122, 2005.
12. H. Chen, B. Bhanu, and R. Wang. Performance evaluation and prediction for 3-d ear recognition. In *Proc. of International Conference on Audio and Video based Biometric Person Authentication*, pages 748–757, NY, 2005.
13. M. Choras. Ear biometrics based on geometrical feature extraction. *Electronic Letters on Computer Vision and Image Analysis (Journal ELCVIA)*, 5(3):84–95, 2005.

14. Man convicted of murder by earprint is freed, January 22 2004. www.timesonline.co.uk/article/0,1-973291,00.html.
15. C. Dorai and A. Jain. Cosmos-a representation scheme for free-form surfaces. In *Proc. IEEE Conf. Computer Vision*, pages 1024–1029, 1995.
16. D. J. Hurley. *Force Field Feature Extraction for Ear Biometrics*. PhD thesis, Electronics and Computer Science, University of Southampton, 2001.
17. D. J. Hurley, M. S. Nixon, and J. N. Carter. Force field energy functionals for image feature extraction. In *Proc. 10th British Machine Vision Conference*, pages 604–613, 1999.
18. D. J. Hurley, M. S. Nixon, and J. N. Carter. Force field energy functionals for image feature extraction. *Image and Vision Computing, Special Issue on BMVC 99*, 20(5-6):311–317, 2002.
19. D. J. Hurley, M. S. Nixon, and J. N. Carter. Ear biometrics by force field convergence. In *Proc. AVBPA*, pages 386–394, 2005.
20. D. J. Hurley, M. S. Nixon, and J. N. Carter. Force field feature extraction for ear biometrics. *Computer Vision and Image Understanding*, 98:491–512, 2005.
21. A. Iannarelli. *Ear Identification*. Paramount Publishing Company, Freemont, California, 1989.
22. K. Iwano, T. Hirose, E. Kamibayashi, and S. Furui. Audio-visual person authentication using speech and ear images. In *Proc. of Workshop on Multimodal User Authentication*, pages 85–90, 2003.
23. I. T. Jolliffe. *Principal Component Analysis*. Springer, New York, 1986.
24. State v. david wayne kunze, 1999. Court of Appeals of Washington, Division 2, 97 Wash. App. 832, 988 P.2d 977.
25. L. Meijermana, S. Shollb, F. De Contic, M. Giaconc, C. van der Lugtd, A. Drusinic, P. Vanezis, and G. Maata. Exploratory study on classification and individualisation of earprints. *Forensic Science International*, 140:91–99, 2004.
26. K. Messer, J. Matas, J. Kittler, J. Luettin, and G. Maitre. Xm2vtsdb: The extended m2vts database. In *Proc. AVBPA*, Washington D.C., 1999.
27. B. Moreno and A. Sanchez. On the use of outer ear images for personal identification in security applications. In *Proc. IEEE 33rd Annual Intl. Conf. on Security Technology*, pages 469–476, 1999.
28. Z. Mu, L. Yuan, Z. Xu, D. Xi, and S. Qi. Shape and structural feature based ear recognition. In *Advances in Biometric Person Authentication*, volume LNCS 3338, pages 663–670. Springer, Berlin / Heidelberg, 2004.
29. J. L. Northern and M. P. Downs. *Hearing in Children*. Lippincott Williams & Wilkins, 5 edition, 2002.
30. K. Pun and Y. Moon. Recent advances in ear biometrics. In *Proc. of the Sixth International Conference on Automatic Face and Gesture Recognition*, pages 164–169, 2004.
31. M. M. Rahman and S. Ishikawa. Proposing a passive biometric system for robotic vision. In *Proc. of the Tenth International Symposium on Artificial Life and Robotics*, Oita, Japan, 2005.
32. G.N. Rutty, A. Abbas, and D. Crossling. Could earprint identification be computerised? an illustrated proof of concept paper. *International Journal of Legal Medicine*, 119(6):335–343, 2005.
33. M. Turk and A. Pentland. Eigenfaces for recognition. *Journal of Cognitive Neuroscience*, 3(1):71–86, 1991.

34. B. Victor, K. W. Bowyer, and S. Sarkar. An evaluation of face and ear biometrics. In *Proc. ICPR*, pages 429–432, 2002.

35. Y. Wang, H. Turusawa, K. Sato, and S. Nakayama. Study on human recognition with ear. In *Image, Information Processing Society of Japan (IPSJ) Kyushu Chapter Symposium*, 2003.

36. P. Yan and K. W. Bowyer. 2D and 3D ear recognition. In *Biometric Consortium Conference*, 2004.

37. P. Yan and K. W. Bowyer. Empirical evaluation of advanced ear biometrics. In *IEEE Computer Society Conference on Computer Vision and Pattern Recognition (CVPR'05) - Workshops*, page 41, 2005.

38. P. Yan and K. W. Bowyer. A fast algorithm for icp-based 3d shape biometrics. In *Fourth IEEE Workshop on Automatic Identification Advanced Technologies (AutoID)*, pages 213–218, NY, 2005.

39. P. Yan and K. W. Bowyer. Icp-based approaches for 3D ear recognition. In *Biometric Technology for Human Identification II, Proc. of SPIE*, volume 5779, pages 282–291, 2005.

40. P. Yan and K. W. Bowyer. Biometric recognition using three-dimensional ear shape. *IEEE Trans. Pattern Analysis and Machine Intelligence*, 29(8):1–12, August 2007.

41. T. Yuizono, Y. Wang, K. Satoh, and S. Nakayama. Study on individual recognition for ear images by using genetic local search. In *Proc. of the 2002 Congress on Evolutionary Computation*, pages 237–242, 2002.

42. H. Zhang, Z. Mu, W. Qu, L. Liu, and C. Zhang. A novel approach for ear recognition based on ica and rbf network. In *Proc. of the Fourth International Conference on Machine Learning and Cybernetics*, pages 4511–4515, 2005.

8

Voice Biometrics

Joaquín González-Rodríguez, Doroteo Torre Toledano, and Javier
Ortega-García

ATVS – UAM, Escuela Politécnica Superior, Universidad Autónoma de Madrid,
Madrid, Spain
{joaquin.gonzalez,doroteo.torre,javier.ortega}@uam.es

8.1 Introduction

Recent data on mobile phone users all over the world, the number of telephone
landlines in operation, and recent VoIP (Voice over IP networks) deployments,
confirm that voice is the most accessible biometric trait as no extra acquisition
device or transmission system is needed. This fact gives voice an overwhelming
advantage over other biometric traits, especially when remote users or systems
are taken into account. However, the voice trait is not only related with personal characteristics, but also with many environmental and sociolinguistic
variables, as voice generation is the result of an extremely complex process.
Thus, the transmitted voice will embed a degraded version of speaker specificities and will be influenced by many contextual variables that are difficult
to deal with. Fortunately, state-of-the-art technologies and applications are
presently able to compensate for all those sources of variability allowing for
efficient and reliable value-added applications that enable remote authentication or voice detection based just in telephone-transmitted voice signals [39],
[16].

8.1.1 Applications

Due to the pervasiveness of voice signals, the range of possible applications
of voice biometrics is wider than for other usual biometric traits. We can
distinguish three major types of applications which take advantage of the
biometric information present in the speech signal:

- Voice authentication (access control, typically remote by phone) and background recognition (natural voice checking) [11].
- Speaker detection (e.g. blacklisting detection in call centers or wiretapping
  and surveillance), also known as speaker spotting.
- Forensic speaker recognition (use of the voice as evidence in courts of law
  or as intelligence in police investigations) [42].

These applications will be addressed in section 8.6.

8.1.2 Technology

The main source of information encoded in the voice signal is undoubtedly the linguistic content. For that reason it is not surprising that depending on how the linguistic content is used or controlled, we can distinguish two very different types of speaker recognition technologies with different potential applications.

Firstly, *text-dependent* technologies, where the user is required to utter a specific key-phrase (e.g., "Open, Sesame") or sequence (e.g., "12-34-56"), have been the major subject of biometric access control and voice authentication applications [38], [16]. The security level of password based systems can then be enhanced by requiring knowledge of the password, and also requiring the true owner of the password to utter it. In order to avoid possible theft recordings of true passwords, text-dependent systems can be enhanced to ask for random prompts, unexpected to the caller, which cannot be easily fabricated by an impostor. All the technological details related with text-dependent speaker recognition and applications are addressed in section 8.4.

The second type of speaker recognition technologies are those known as *text-independent*. They are the driving factor of the remaining two types of applications, namely speaker detection and forensic speaker recognition. Since the linguistic content is the main source of information encoded in the speech, text-independency has been a major challenge and the main subject of research of the speaker recognition community in the last two decades. The NIST SRE (Speaker Recognition Evaluations) conducted yearly since 1996 [35], [39] have fostered excellence in research in this area, with extraordinary progress obtained year by year based in blind evaluation with common databases and protocols, and very specially the sharing of information among participants in the follow-up workshop after each evaluation. Text-independent systems, including technological details and applications, will be addressed in detail in section 8.5.

8.2 Identity information in the speech signal

In this section, we will deal with how the speaker specificities are embedded into the speech signal. Speech production is a extremely complex process whose result depends on many variables at different levels, including from sociolinguistic factors (e.g. level of education, linguistic context and dialectal differences) to physiological issues (e.g. vocal tract length, shape and tissues and the dynamic configuration of the articulatory organs). These multiple influences will be simultaneously present in each speech act, and some or all of them will contain specificities of the speaker. For that reason, we need to clarify and clearly distinguish the different levels and sources of speaker information that we should be able to extract in order to model speaker individualities.

8.2.1 Language generation and speech production

The process by which humans are able to construct a language-coded message has been the subject of study for years in the area of psycholinguistics. But once the message has been coded in the human brain, a complex physiological and articulatory process is still needed to finally produce a speech waveform (the voice) that contains the linguistic message (as well as many other sources of information, one of which is the speaker identity) encoded as a combination of temporal-spectral characteristics. This process is the subject of study of phoneticians and some other speech analysis related areas (engineers, physicians, etc.). Details on language generation and speech production can be found in [50], [27], [41]. The speech production process is very complex and would deserve several book chapters by itself, but we are here interested in those aspects related with the encoding of some kind of individual information in the final speech signal that is transmitted out of the speaker mouth. In both stages of voice production (language generation and speech production), speaker specificities are introduced. In the field of voice biometrics –also known as speaker recognition– these two components correspond with which is usually known as high-level (linguistic) and low-level (acoustic) characteristics.

8.2.2 Multiple information levels

Experiments with human listeners have shown, as our own experience tells us, that humans recognize speakers by a combination of different information levels, and what is specially important, with different weights for different speakers (e.g. one speaker can show very characteristic pitch contours, and another one can have a strong nasalization which make them "sound" different). Automatic systems will intend to take advantage of the different sources of information available, combining them in the best possible way for every speaker [15].

Idiolectal characteristics of a speaker [12] are at the highest level that is usually taken into account by the technology to date, and describe how a speaker use a specific linguistic system. This "use" is determined by a multitude of factors, some of them quite stable in adults such as level of education, sociological and family conditions and town of origin. But there are also some high-level factors which are highly dependent on the environment, as e.g., a male doctor does not use language in the same way when talking with his colleagues at the hospital (sociolects), with his family at home, or with his friends playing cards. We will describe idiolectal recognition of speakers in more detail in section 8.5.2, taking advantage of frequency of use of different linguistic patterns, which will be extracted as shown in section 8.3.3.

As second major group of characteristics going down towards lower information levels in the speech signal we find *phonotactics* [10], which describe the use by each speaker of the phone units and possible realizations available. Phonotactics are essential for the correct use of a language, and a key in foreign language learning, but when we look into phonotactic speaker specificities we can find certain usage patterns distinctive from other users. The use of phonotactics for automatic speaker recognition is fully described in section 8.5.3, from the same set of tokens as idiolects described in section 8.3.3.

In a third group we find *prosody*, which is the combination of instantaneous energy, intonation, speech rate and unit durations that provides speech with naturalness, full sense, and emotional tone. Prosody determines prosodic objectives at the phrase and discourse level, and define instantaneous actions to comply with those objectives. It helps to clarify the message ("nine hundred twenty seven" can be distinguished as "927" or "900 27" by means of prosody), the type of message (declarative, interrogative, imperative), or the state of mind of the speaker. But in the way each speaker uses the different prosodic elements, many speaker specificities are included, such as, for example, characteristic pitch contours in start and end of phrase or accent group. The automatic extraction of pitch and energy information is described in section 8.3.4, while the use of prosodic features to automatically recognize speakers is described in section 8.5.4.

Finally, at the lower level, we find the short-term *spectral* characteristics of the speech signals, directly related to the individual articulatory actions related with each phone being produced and also to the individual physiological configuration of the speech production apparatus. This spectral information has been the main source of individuality in speech used in actual applications, and the main focus of the research for almost twenty years [43], [54], [8]. Spectral information intends to extract the peculiarities of speaker's vocal tracts and their respective articulation dynamics. Two types of low level information has been typically used, *static* information related to each analysis frame and *dynamic* information related to how this information evolves in adjacent frames, taking into account the strongly speaker-dependent phenomenon of co-articulation, the process by which an individual dynamically moves from one articulation position to the next one. Details on short term analysis and parameterization will be given in sections 8.3.1 and 8.3.2, while short-term spectral systems will be described in section 8.5.1.

8.3 Feature Extraction and Tokenization

The first step in the construction of automatic speaker recognition systems is the reliable extraction of features and tokens that contain identifying information of interest. In this section, we will briefly show the procedures used to extract both short-term feature vectors (spectral information, energy, pitch) and mid-term and long-term tokens as phones, syllables and words.

8.3.1 Short-term analysis

In order to perform reliable spectral analysis, signals must show stationary properties that are not easy to observe in constantly-changing speech signals. However, if we restrict our analysis window to short lengths between 20 and 40 ms., our articulatory system is not able to significantly change in such a short time frame, obtaining what is usually called pseudo-stationary signals per frame. This process is depicted in figure 8.1. Those windowed signals can be assumed, due to pseudo-stationarity, to come from a specific LTI (linear time-invariant) system for that frame, and then we can perform, usually after using some kind of cosine-like windowing as hamming or hanning, spectral analysis over this short-term window, obtaining spectral envelopes that change frame by frame [41], [27].

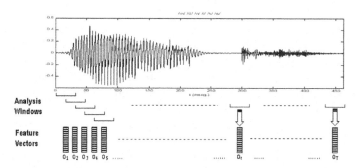

Fig. 8.1. Short-term analysis and parameterization of a speech signal.

8.3.2 Parameterization

This short-time hamming/hanning windowed signals have all of the desired temporal/spectral information, albeit at a high bit rate (e.g. telephone speech digitized with sampling frequency 8 kHz in a 32 ms. window means 256 samples x 16 bits/sample = 4096 bits = 512 bytes per frame). Linear Predictive Coding (LPC) of speech has proved to be a valid way to compress the spectral envelope in an all-pole model (valid for all non-nasal sounds, and still a good approximation for nasal sounds) with just 10 to 16 coefficients, which means that the spectral information in a frame can be represented in about 50 bytes, which is 10% of the original bit rate. Instead of LPC coefficients, highly correlated among them (covariance matrix far from diagonal), pseudo-orthogonal cepstral coefficients are usually used, either directly derived as in LPCC (LPC-derived Cepstral vectors) from LPC coefficients, or directly obtained from a perceptually-based mel-filter spectral analysis as in MFCC (Mel-Frequency based Cepstral Coefficients). Some other related forms are described in the literature, as PLP (Perceptually based Linear Prediction)

[25], LSF (Line Spectral Frequencies) [28] and many others, not detailed here for simplicity. By far, one of the main factors of speech variability comes from the use of different transmission channels (e.g. testing telephone speech with microphone-recorded speaker models). Cepstral representation has also the advantage that invariant channels add a constant cepstral offset that can be easily subtracted (CMS.- Cepstral Mean Subtraction), and non-speech cepstral components can also be eliminated as done in RASTA filtering of cepstral instantaneous vectors [26]. In order to take coarticulation into account, delta (velocity) and delta-delta (acceleration) coefficients are obtained from the static window-based information, computing an estimate of how each frame coefficient varies across adjacent windows (typically between ± 3, no more than ± 5).

8.3.3 Phonetic and word tokenization

Hidden Markov Models (HMM) [40] are the most succesful and widely used tool (with the exception of some ANN architectures [37]) for phonetic, syllable and word tokenization, that is, the translation from sampled speech into a time-aligned sequence of linguistic units. Left-to-RightHMMs are state-machines which statistically model pseudostationary pieces of speech (states) and the transitions (left-to-right forced, keeping a temporal sense) between states, trying to imitate somehow the movements of our articulatory organs, which tend to rest (in all non-plosive sounds) in articulatory positions (assumed as pseudostationary states) and continuously move (transition) from one state to the following. Presently, most HMMs model the information in each state with continuous probability density functions, typically mixtures of gaussians. This particular kind of models are usually known as CDHMM (Continuous Density HMM, as opposite to the former VQ-based Discrete Density HMMs). HMM training is usually done through Baum-Welch estimation, while decoding and time alignment is usually performed through Viterbi decoding. The performance of those spectral-only HMMs is improved by the use of language models, which impose some linguistic or grammatical constraints on the almost infinite combination of all possible units. To allow for increased efficiency, pruning of the beam search is also a generalized mechanism to significantly accelerate the recognition process with no or little degradation on the performance.

8.3.4 Prosodic tokenization

Basic prosodic features as pitch and energy are also obtained at a frame level. The window energy is very easily obtained through Parseval's theorem, either in temporal or spectral form, and the instantaneous pitch can be determined by, e.g., autocorrelation or cepstral-decomposition based methods, usually smoothed with some time filtering [41]. Other important prosodic features are those related with linguistic units duration, speech rate, and all those related with accent. In all those cases, precise segmentation is required, marking the syllable positions and the energy and pitch contours to detect accent positions and phrase or speech turn markers. Phonetic and syllabic segmentation of speech is a complex issue that is far from solved [53] and although it can be useful for speaker recognition [1], prosodic systems do not always require such a detailed segmentation [13].

8.4 Text-dependent speaker recognition

Speaker recognition systems can be classified into two broad subtypes: text-dependent and text-independent. The former use the lexical content of the speech for speaker recognition, while the latter try to minimize the influence of the lexical content, which is considered unknown for the recognition of the speaker. This distinction makes these two subtypes of speaker recognition systems very different in terms both of techniques used and of potential applications. This section is devoted to text-dependent speaker recognition systems, which find their main application in interactive systems where collaboration from the users is required in order to authenticate their identities. The typical example of these applications is voice authentication over the telephone for interactive voice response systems that require some level of security like banking applications or password reset. The use of a text-dependent speaker recognition system requires, similarly to other biometric modalities, an enrollment phase in which the user provides several templates to build a user model and a recognition phase in which a new voice sample is matched against the user model.

8.4.1 Classification of systems and techniques

We can classify text-dependent speaker recognition systems from an application point of view into two types: fixed-text and variable-text systems. In fixed-text systems, the lexical content in the enrollment and the recognition samples is always the same. In variable-text systems, the lexical content in the recognition sample is different in every access trial from the lexical content of the enrollment samples. Variable-text systems are more flexible and more robust against attacks that use recordings from an user or imitations after hearing of the true speaker uttering the correct password. An interesting possibility is the generation of a randomly generated password prompt that is different each time the user is verified (text-prompted system), thus making it almost impossible to use a recording. With respect to the techniques used for text-dependent speaker recognition, it has been demonstrated [14] that information present at different levels of the speech signal (glottal excitation, spectral and suprasegmental features) can be used effectively to detect the user's identity. However, the most widely used information is the spectral content of the speech signal, determined by the physical configuration and dynamics of the vocal tract. This information is typically summarized as a temporal sequence of MFCC vectors, each of which represents a window of 20-40 ms of speech. In this way, the problem of text-dependent speaker recognition is reduced to a problem of comparing a sequence of MFCC vectors to a model of the user. For this comparison there are two methods that have been widely used: template-based methods and statistical methods. In template-based methods [20], [17] the model of the speaker consists of several sequences of vectors corresponding to the enrollment utterances, and recognition is performed by comparing the verification utterance against the enrollment utterances. This comparison is performed using Dynamic Time Warping (DTW) as an effective way to compensate for time misalignments between the different utterances. While these methods are still used, particularly for embedded systems with very limited resources, statistical methods, and in particular Hidden Markov Models (HMMs) [40], tend to be used more often than template based models. HMMs provide more flexibility, allow to choose speech units from sub-phoneme units to words and enable the design of text-prompted systems [38], [6].

8.4.2 Databases and benchmarks

The first databases used for text-dependent speaker verification were databases not specifically designed for this task like the TI-DIGITS [33] and TIMIT [21] databases. One of the first databases specifically designed for text-dependent speaker recognition research is YOHO [5]. It consists of 96 utterances for enrollment collected in 4 different sessions and 40 utterances for test collected on 10 sessions for each of a total of 138 speakers. Each utterance consists in different sets of three digit pairs (e.g., "12-34-56"). This is probably the most extended and well known benchmark for comparison and is frequently used to assess text-dependent systems. However, the YOHO database has several limitations. For instance, it only contains speech recorded on a single microphone in a quiet environment and was not designed to simulate informed forgeries (i.e. impostors uttering the password of an user). More recently the MIT Mobile Device Speaker Verification Corpus [55] has been designed to allow research on text-dependent speaker verification on realistic noisy conditions, while the BIOSEC Baseline Corpus [19] has been designed to simulate informed forgeries (including also bilingual material and several biometric modalities besides voice). One of the main difficulties of the comparison of different text-dependent speaker verification systems is that these systems tend to be language dependent, and therefore many researchers tend to present their results in their custom database, making it impossible to make direct comparisons. The comparison of different commercial systems is even more difficult. Fortunately, a recent publication [16] compares the technical performance of a few commercial systems. However, as with other biometric modalities, technical performance is not the only dimension to evaluate and other measures related to the usability of the systems should be evaluated as well [51].

8.4.3 Case study: Text-dependent speaker recognition with HMM speaker adaptation and HMM reestimation

As an example of text-dependent system tested on the YOHO benchmark database, we present the results obtained with two text-dependent speaker recognition systems developed by the authors. The systems simulate a text-prompted system based on a set of speaker-independent and context-independent phonetic HMMs trained on TIMIT. Enrollment consists in using several sentences of a speaker to adapt the HMMs to the speaker. We compare two ways of performing this adaptation: with a single pass of Baum-Welch reestimation and with Maximum Likelihood Linear Regression (MLLR) [32]. The former is the most conventional approach but requires using very simple HMMs (just one or a few Gaussians per state). The later is more novel and allows using more complex HMMs. Speaker verification consists in computing the acoustic score produced during the forced alignment of an utterance with its phonetic transcription using both the speaker adapted HMMs and the speaker-independent HMMs. The final score in this experiment is simply the ratio between those scores (no score normalization is included in the results presented).

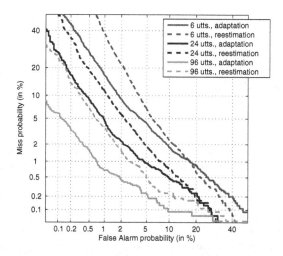

Fig. 8.2. Example results on YOHO of two text-dependent speaker recognition systems based on speaker-independent phonetic HMMs and MLLR speaker-adaptation and Baum-Welch re-estimation for different amounts of enrollment speech.

An important issue in developing text-dependent speaker recognition systems is the amount of training material required for enrollment. YOHO contains 4 sessions with 24 utterances each. This is a very large amount of enrollment material that could rarely be obtained in a realistic application. For this reason figure 8.2 shows results for the two systems training with the four sessions (96 utterances), one session (24 utterances) or only 6 utterances from one session. As could be expected, performance is greatly improved with more training material, but practical systems need to find a compromise between performance and ease and convenience of use. Figure 8.2 also compares the system based on Baum-Welch re-estimation and the one based MLLR adaptation, showing better performance for the MLLR-based systems for all enrollment conditions.

8.5 Text-independent speaker recognition

Text-independent speaker recognition have been largely dominated, since 1970s to the end of 20th century, by short term spectral-based systems. Since 2000, higher level systems started to be developed with good enough results in the same highly challenging tasks (NIST SR evaluations). However, spectral systems have continued to outperform high-level systems (NIST 2006 SRE was the latest benchmark by the time of writing), with the best detection results due to recent advanced channel compensation mechanisms.

8.5.1 Short-term spectral systems

When short-time spectral analysis is used to model the speaker specificities, we are modeling the different "sounds" a person can produce, specially due to his/her own vocal tract and articulatory organs. As humans need multiple sounds (or acoustically different symbols) to speak in any common language, we are clearly facing a multiclass space of characteristics. Vector Quantization techniques are efficient in such multiclass problems, and have been used for speaker identification [4], typically obtaining a specific VQ model per speaker, and computing the distance from any utterance to any model as the weighted sum of the minimum per frame distances to the closest codevector of the codebook. The use of boundaries and centroids instead of probability densities yields poorer performance for VQ than for fully-connected Continuous Density HMMs, known as ergodic HMMs (E-HMM) [34]. However, the critical performance factor in E-HMM is the product number of states times number of Gaussians per state, which strongly cancels the influence of transitions in those fully-connected models. Then, a 5-state 4-Gaussian per state E-HMM system will perform similarly than a 4-state 5-Gaussian/state, a 2-state 10-Gaussian/state, or even, what is specially interesting, a 1-state 20 Gaussian/state system, which is generally known as GMM or Gaussian Mixture Model. Those one-state E-HMMs, or GMMs, have the large advantage that avoids both Baum-Welch estimation for training, as no alignment between speech and states is necessary (all speech is aligned with the same single state), and Viterbi decoding for testing (again no need for time alignment), which accelerates computation times with no degradation of performance.

GMM is a generative technique where a mixture of multidimensional gaussians tries to model the underlying unknown statistical distribution of the speaker data. GMM became the state-of-the-art technique in the 1990's, both when maximum likelihood (through Expectation-Maximization, EM) or discriminative training (Maximum Mutual Information, MMI) was used. However, it was the use of MAP adaptation of the means from a Universal Background Model (UBM) which gave GMMs a major advantage over other techniques [43], specially when used with compensation techniques as Z-norm (impostor score normalization), T-norm (utterance compensation), H-norm (handset dependent Z-norm), HT-norm (H+T-norm) or Feature Mapping (channel identification and compensation) [44].

Discriminative techniques such as Artificial Neural Networks have been used for years [18], but their performance never approached that of GMMs. However, the availability in the late 90's of Support Vector Machines (SVM) [47] as an efficient discriminatively trained classifier, has given GMM its major competitor as equivalent performance is obtained using SVM in a much higher dimensional space when appropriate kernels such as GLDS (Generalized Linear Discriminant Sequence Kernel) [8] are used.

Recently, the use of SuperVectors [30], a mixed GMM-SVM [9] technique that considers the means of the GMM for every utterance (both in training and testing) as points in a very high dimensional space (dimension equals the number of mixtures of the GMM times the dimension of the parameterized vectors) using an SVM per speaker to classify unknown utterances from the trained speaker hyperplane.

A main advantage of SuperVectors is that they fit perfectly into new channel compensation methods [31] based on detecting those directions with maximum variability between different recordings from the same speaker, trying to cancel or minimize their effect. Several related techniques of this family have emerged, as Factor Analysis (channel and speaker factors), Nuisance Attribute Projection (NAP) or Within Class Covariance Normalization (WCCN), all of them showing significant enhancements over their respective baseline systems.

8.5.2 Idiolectal systems

Most text-independent speaker recognition systems were based on short-term spectral features until the work of Doddington [12] opened a new world of possibilities for improving text-independent speaker recognition systems. Doddington realized and proved that speech from different speakers differ not only on the acoustics, but also on other characteristics like the word usage. In particular, in his work he modeled the word usage of each particular speaker using an n-gram that modeled word sequences and their probabilities and demonstrated that using those models could improve the performance of a baseline acoustic/spectral GMM system. More important than this particular result is the fact that this work boosted research in the use of higher levels of information (idiolectal, phonotactic, prosodic, etc.) for text-independent speaker recognition. After the publication of this work a number of researchers met at the summer workshop SuperSID [15] where these ideas were further developed and tested on a common testbed. Next sections describe two of the most successful systems exploiting higher levels of information: phonotactic systems, which try to model pronunciation idiosyncrasies, and prosodic systems, which model speaker-specific prosodic patterns.

8.5.3 Phonotactic systems

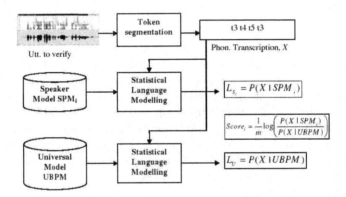

Fig. 8.3. Verification of an utterance against a speaker model in phonotactic speaker recognition

A typical phonotactic speaker recognition system consists of two main building blocks: the phonetic decoders, which transform speech into a sequence of phonetic labels and the n-gram statistical language modeling stage, which models the frequencies of phones and phone sequences for each particular speaker. The phonetic decoders –typically based on Hidden Markov Models (HMMs)– can either be taken from a preexisting speech recognizer or trained *ad hoc*. For the purpose of speaker recognition, it is not very important to have very accurate phonetic decoders and it is not even important to have a phonetic decoder in the language of the speakers to be recognized. This somewhat surprising fact has been analyzed in [52] showing that speaker-dependent phonetic errors made by the decoder seem to be speaker specific, and therefore useful information for speaker recognition as long as these errors are consistent for each particular speaker.

Once a phonetic decoder is available, the phonetic decodings of many sentences from many different speakers can be used to train a Universal Background Phone Model (UBPM) representing all the possible speakers. Speaker Phone Models (SPM_i) are trained using several phonetic decoders of each particular speaker. Since the speech available to train a speaker model is often limited, speaker models are interpolated with the UBPM to increase robustness in parameter estimation. Once the statistical language models are trained, the procedure to verify a test utterance against a speaker model SPM_i is represented in Figure 8.3. The first step is to produce its phonetic decoding, X, in the same way as the decodings used to train SPM_i and UBPM. Then, the phonetic decoding of the test utterance, X, and the statistical models (SPM_i, UBPM) are used to compute the likelihoods of the phonetic decoding, X, given the speaker model SPM_i and the background model UBPM. The recognition score is the log of the ratio of both likelihoods. This process, which is usually described as Phone Recognition followed by Language Modeling (PRLM) may be repeated for different phonetic decoders (e.g., different languages or complexities) and the different recognition scores simply added or fused for better performance, yielding a method known as Parallel PRLM or PPRLM. Recently, several improvements have been proposed on the baseline PPRLM systems. One of the most important in terms of performance improvement is the use of the whole phone recognition lattice [24] instead of the one-best decoding hypothesis. The recognition lattice is a directed acyclic graph containing the most likely hypotheses along with their probabilities. This much richer information allows for a better estimation of the n-grams on limited speech materials, and therefore for much better results. Other important improvement is the use of SVMs for classifying the whole n-grams trained with either the one-best hypotheses or with lattices [7], [24] instead of using them in a statistical classification framework.

8.5.4 Prosodic systems

One of the pioneering and most successful prosodic systems in text-independent speaker recognition is the work of Adami [13]. The system consists of two main building blocks: the prosodic tokenizer, which analyzes the prosody, and represents it as a sequence of prosodic labels or tokens and the n-gram statistical language modeling stage, which models the frequencies of prosodic tokens and their sequences for each particular speaker. Some other possibilities for modeling the prosodic information that have also proved to be quite successful are the use of Non-uniform Extraction Region Features (NERFs) delimited by long-enough pauses [29] or NERFs defined by the syllabic structure of the sentence (SNERFs) [48].

The authors have implemented a prosodic system based on Adami's work in which the second block is exactly the same for phonotactic and prosodic speaker recognition with only minor adjustments to improve performance. The tokenization process consists of two stages. Firstly, for each speech utterance, temporal trajectories of the prosodic features, (fundamental frequency -or pitch- and energy) are extracted. Secondly, both contours are segmented and labelled by means of a slope quantification process. Figure 8.4 shows a table containing 17 prosodic tokens. One token represents unvoiced segments, while 16 are used for representing voiced segments depending on the slope (fast-rising, slow-rising, fast-falling, slow-falling) of the energy and pitch. Figure 8.4 shows also an example utterance segmented and labelled using these prosodic tokens.

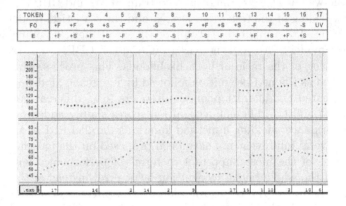

TOKEN	1	2	3	4	5	6	7	8	9	10	11	12	13	14	15	16	17
FO	+F	+F	+S	+S	-F	-F	-S	-S	+F	+F	+S	+S	-F	-F	-S	-S	UV
E	+F	+S	+F	+S	-F	-S	-F	-S	-F	-S	-F	-F	+F	+S	+F	+S	·

Fig. 8.4. Prosodic token alphabet (top table) and sample tokenization of pitch and energy contours (bottom figure).

8.5.5 Databases and Benchmarks

In the early 1990s, text-independent speaker recognition was a major challenge, with a future difficult to foresee. By that time, modest research initiatives were developed with very limited databases, resulting in non-homogenous publications with no way to compare and improve systems in similar tasks. Fortunately, in 1996 NIST started the yearly Speaker Recognition Evaluations, which have been undoubtedly the driving force of significant advances. Present state-of-the-art performance was totally unexpected just 10 years ago. This success has been driven by two factors. Firstly, the use of common databases and protocols in blind evaluation of systems has permitted fair comparison between systems on exactly the same task. Secondly, the post-evaluation workshops have allowed participants to share their experiences, improvements, failures, etc. in a highly cooperative environment. The role of the LDC (Linguistic Data Consortium) providing new challenging speech material is also noticeable, as the needs have been continuously increasing (both in amount of speech and requirements in recording). From the different phases of Switchboard to the latest Fisher-style databases, much progress has been made. Past evaluation sets (development, train and test audio and keys -solutions-) are available through LDC for new researchers to evaluate their systems without competitive pressures. Even though "official" results have been restricted to participants, it is extremely easy to follow the progress of the technology as participants often present their new developments in Speaker ID sessions in international conferences as ICASSP or InterSpeech (formerly EuroSpeech), or the series of ISCA/IEEE Odyssey workshops.

8.5.6 Case study: the ATVS multilevel text-independent system

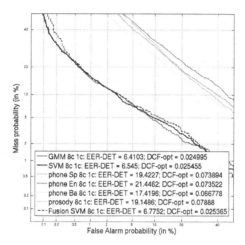

Fig. 8.5. Performance of ATVS subsystems in NIST'06 Speaker Recognition Evaluation comparing spectral (GMM and SVM), phonotactic and prosodic systems.

The authors have participated in NIST SRE yearly tests since 2001, and have developed different spectral (generative and discriminative) and higher level systems. A detailed description of our multilevel approach is found in [23], and here we present our results in NIST SRE06 in the 8c1c task (8 training conversations and 1 conversation for testing), in order to see the performance of different subsystems on the same task. The main differences of 2006 ATVS systems compared to the 2005 systems described in [23] are the use of Feature Mapping in both GMM and SVM, the use of 3rd order polynomial expansion (instead of 2nd order) in the GLDS kernel, and the use of one PRLM trained with SpeechDat (the best from the three PRLM systems shown).

As shown in figure 8.5, the spectral systems (GMM and SVM) perform similarly, while our higher level systems obtain enough individualization information ($\sim 20\%$ EER) but still far from the performance of spectral systems.

After the evaluation, SuperVector-GMM and NAP channel compensation have been included in our system, providing significant enhancements over the best spectral systems, as shown in figure 8.6 for the NIST SRE06 1c1c-male subtask.

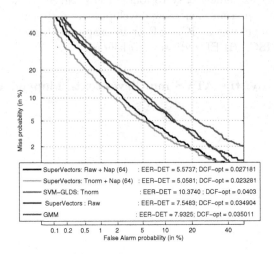

Fig. 8.6. Post-eval performance improvements over NIST'06 SRE ATVS system based on NAP channel compensation and SuperVector-GMMs (1c-1c male sub-task).

8.6 Applications

Voice authentication is a classical biometric application where a speaker tries to be verified either as a cooperative speaker (e.g., to be given access to a specific system as his/her bank account) or as a non-cooperative user (e.g., confirming his/her presence at home in an automatic home parole control application). Some specific forms of voice authentication are growing presently as those related with Digital Rights Management (DRM) [36], as described in the MPEG-21 standard or other proprietary rights management architectures, where the voice can be used to give access to secured media contents from media authors and producers to distributors and final users. Another interesting application is voice bio-encryption, where the voice is used to generate user encryption keys which can be securely used as are neither stored nor accesible as are dynamically generated from voice [49].

However, other forms of exploiting the biometric information present in the voice signal are emerging. One of those systems is known as voice surveillance, blacklisting detection or speaker spotting, where multiple simultaneous input lines (hundreds or thousands in massive call centers or wiretapping systems) can be supervised in real-time to detect speakers from a list.

Finally, the use of automatic speaker recognition systems in forensics allows for transparency and testability [46] on the use of voice as evidence in courts of law [45], [42], as anticipated in modern forensic science [2]. Automatic systems can be adapted to provide Likelihood Ratios at their output [22], following the well-established methodology of DNA, in what is known as the golden standard in forensic science. Moreover, calibration of LR [3] values provide the unifying approach to use LR in different conditions and with different types of evidence, enabling the combination of different sources of knowledge in forensic science.

8.7 Conclusions

From an analysis of the different sources of individualization information present in the speech signal, we have summarized the procedures for signal processing and parameterization with the objective of obtaining highly reliable low-dimension parametric vectors. Text-dependent systems have presently obtained a prevalent position for remote authentication, as realistic objective evaluations have recently shown. With respect to text-independent, recent developments (supervectors, channel factors/NAP compensation) have provided major advances assessed in NIST SRE evals that enable different applications that, far from classical biometric authentication techniques, use the biometric information present in the speech signal with objectives different than remote authentication but sometimes even more interesting and useful. In this sense we have shown that state-of-the-art speaker recognition systems are ready to face real and critical (specially remote) applications where the easily accessible speech signal is used as a highly reliable biometric trait.

References

1. A. G. Adami and H. Hermansky. Segmentation of speech for speaker and language recognition. In *Proceedings of Interspeech*, pages 841–844, 2003.
2. C.G.G. Aitken and F. Taroni. *Statistics and the Evaluation of Evidence for Forensic Scientists*. John Wiley and Sons, 2 edition, 2004.
3. N. Brummer and J. Preez. Application-independent evaluation of speaker detection. *Computer, Speech and Language*, 20:230–275, 2006.
4. D. K. Burton. Text-dependent speaker verification using vector quantization source coding. *IEEE Transactions on Acoustics, Speech and Signal Processing*, 35:133–143, 1987.
5. J. Campbell and A. Higgins. Yoho speaker verification (ldc94s16). http://www.ldc.upenn.edu.
6. J. P. Campbell. Testing with the yoho cd-rom voice verification corpus. In *Proceedings of the IEEE International Conference on Acoustics, Speech, and Signal Processing*, pages 341–344, 1995.

7. W. M. Campbell, J. P. Campbell, D. A. Reynolds, D. A. Jones, and T. R. Leek. High-level speaker verification with support vector machines. In *Proceedings of the IEEE International Conference on Acoustics, Speech and Signal Processing*, pages 73–76, 2004.

8. W.M. Campbell. Generalized linear discriminant sequence kernels for speaker recognition. In *Proceedings of the International Conference on Acoustics, Speech and Signal Processing*, pages 161–164, 2002.

9. W.M. Campbell, D.E. Sturim, and D.A. Reynolds. Support vector machines using gmm supervectors for speaker verification. *IEEE Signal Processing Letters*, 13:308–311, 2006.

10. P. Carr. *English Phonetics and Phonology: An Introduction*. Blackwell Publishing, Incorporated, 1999.

11. Voice Biometrics Conference. http://www.voicebiocon.com.

12. G. Doddington. Speaker recognition based on idiolectal differences between speakers. In *Proceedings of Interspeech*, volume 4, pages 2517–2520, 2001.

13. A. G. Adami et al. Modeling prosodic dynamics for speaker recognition. In *Proceedings of the IEEE International Conference on Acoustics, Speech and Signal Processing*, volume IV, pages 788–791, 2003.

14. B. Yegnanarayana et. al. Combining evidence from source, suprasegmental and spectral features for a fixed-text speaker verification system. *IEEE Transactions on Speech and Audio Processing*, 13:575–582, 2005.

15. D. Reynolds et al. Supersid project: Exploiting high-level information for high-accuracy speaker recognition. In *Proceedings of the IEEE International Conference on Acoustics, Speech and Signal Processing*, volume IV, pages 784–787, April 2003.

16. M. Wagner et al. An evaluation of 'commercial off-the-shelf' speaker verification systems. In *Proceedings of IEEE Odyssey*, 2006.

17. V. Ramasubramanian et. al. Text-dependent speaker-recognition systems based on one-pass dynamic programming algorithm. In *Proceedings of the IEEE International Conference on Acoustics, Speech and Signal Processing*, pages 901–904, 2006.

18. K. R. Farrell, R. J. Mammone, and K. T. Assaleh. Speaker recognition using neural networks and conventional classifiers. *IEEE Transactions on Speech and Audio Processing*, 2:194–205, 1994.

19. J. Fierrez-Aguilar, J. Ortega-Garcia, D. T. Toledano, and J. Gonzalez-Rodriguez. Biosec baseline corpus: A multimodal biometric database. *Pattern Recognition*, 40:1389–1392, 2007.

20. S. Furui. Cepstral analysis technique for automatic speaker verification. *IEEE Transactions on Acoustics, Speech and Signal Processing*, 29:254–272, 1981.

21. J. S. Garofolo, L. F. Lamel, W. M. Fisher, J. G. Fiscus, D. S. Pallet, N. L. Dahlgren, and V. Zue. Timit acoustic-phonetic continuous speech corpus (ldc93s1). http://www.ldc.upenn.edu.

22. J. Gonzalez-Rodriguez, A. Drygajlo, D. Ramos-Castro, M. Garcia-Gomar, and J. Ortega-Garcia. Robust estimation, interpretation and assessment of likelihood ratios in forensic speaker recognition. *Computer, Speech and Language*, 20:331–335, 2006.

23. J. Gonzalez-Rodriguez, D. Ramos-Castro, D. T. Toledano, A. Montero-Asenjo, J. Gonzalez-Dominguez, I. Lopez-Moreno, J. Fierrez-Aguilar, D. Garcia-Romero, and J. Ortega-Garcia. Speaker recognition: the atvs-uam system at nist sre 05. *IEEE AES Magazine*, 22:15–21, 2007.

24. A. O. Hatch, B. Peskin, and A. Stolcke. Improved phonetic speaker recognition using lattice decoding. In *Proceedings of the IEEE International Conference on Acoustics, Speech and Signal Processing*, pages 165–168, 2005.
25. H. Hermansky, B. Hanson, and H. Wakita. Perceptually based linear predictive analysis of speech. In *Proceedings of the IEEE International Conference on Acoustics, Speech and Signal Processing*, volume 10, pages 509–512, 1985.
26. H. Hermansky and N. Morgan. Rasta processing of speech. *IEEE Transactions on Speech and Audio Processing*, 2(4):578–589, October 1984.
27. X. Huang, A. Acero, and H.-W. Hon. *Spoken Language Processing: A Guide to Theory, Algorithm and System Development*. Prentice Hall PTR, 2001.
28. F. Itakura. Line spectrum representation of linear predictive coefficients of speech signals. *Journal of the Acoustical Society of America*, 57:S35, 1975.
29. Sachin Kajarekar, Luciana Ferrer, Kemal Sonmez, Jing Zheng, Elizabeth Shriberg, and Andreas Stolcke. Modeling NERFs for speaker recognition. In *Proceedings of IEEE Odyssey*, pages 51–56, Toledo, Spain, June 2004.
30. P. Kenny, G. Boulianne, and P. Dumouchel. Eigenvoice modeling with sparse training data. *IEEE Transactions on Speech and Audio Processing*, 13:345–354, 2005.
31. P. Kenny and P. Dumouchel. Disentangling speaker and channel effects in speaker verification. In *Proceedings of the IEEE International Conference on Acoustics, Speech, and Signal Processing*, pages 37–40, 2004.
32. C. J. Leggetter and P. C. Woodland. Maximum likelihood linear regression for speaker adaptation of continuous density hidden markov models. *Computer, Speech and Language*, 9:171–185, 1995.
33. R. G. Leonard and G. Doddington. Tidigits (ldc93s10). http://www.ldc.upenn.edu.
34. T. Matsui and S. Furui. Comparison of text-independent speaker recognition methods using vq-distortion and discrete/continuous hmms. In *Proceedings of the IEEE International Conference on Acoustics, Speech, and Signal Processing*, pages 157–160, 1992.
35. Nist speaker recognition evaluation. http://www.nist.gov/speech/tests/spk/.
36. J. Ortega-Garcia, J. Bigun, D. Reynolds, and J. Gonzalez-Rodriguez. Authentication gets personal with biometrics. *IEEE Signal Processing Magazine*, 21:50–62, 2004.
37. Matejka Pavel, Schwarz Petr, Cernock Jan, and Chytil Pavel. Phonotactic language identification using high quality phoneme recognition. In *Proceedings of InterSpeech*, pages 2237–2240, 2005.
38. CAVE Project. Cave - the european caller verification project. http://www.ptt-telecom.nl/cave/.
39. M. A. Przybocki, A. F. Martin, and A. N. Le. Nist speaker recognition evaluation chronicles part 2. In *Proceedings of IEEE Odyssey*, 2006.
40. L. R. Rabiner. A tutorial on hidden markov models and selected applications in speech recognition. *Proceedings of the IEEE*, 77:257–286, 1989.
41. L. R. Rabiner and R. W. Schafer. *Digital Processing of Speech Signals*. Prentice Hall, 1978.
42. D. Ramos-Castro, J. Gonzalez-Rodriguez, and J. Ortega-Garcia. Likelihood ratio calibration in a transparent and testable forensic speaker recognition framework. In *Proceedings of IEEE Odyssey*, 2006.
43. D. Reynolds, T. Quatieri, and R. Dunn. Speaker verification using adapted gaussian mixture models. *Digital Signal Processing*, 10:19–41, 2000.

44. D. A. Reynolds. Channel robust speaker verification via feature mapping. In *Proceedings of the IEEE International Conference on Acoustics, Speech and Signal Processing*, volume 2, pages 53–56, 2003.

45. P. Rose. *Forensic Speaker Identification*. CRC, 1 edition, 2002.

46. M. J. Saks and J. J. Koehler. The coming paradigm shift in forensic identification science. *Science*, 309:892–895, 2005.

47. B. Scholkopf, S. Kah-Kay, C.J.C. Burges, F. Girosi, P. Niyogi, T. Poggio, and V. Vapnik. Comparing support vector machines with gaussian kernels to radial basis function classifiers. *IEEE Transactions on Signal Processing*, 45:2758–2765, 1997.

48. Elizabeth Shriberg, Luciana Ferrer, Anand Venkataraman, and Sachin Kajarekar. SVM modeling of "SNERF-Grams" for speaker recognition. In *Proc. Intl. Conf. Spoken Language Systems*, pages 1409–1412, Jeju, Korea, October 2004.

49. C. Soutar, D. Roberge, A. Stoianov, R. Gilroy, and B.V.K. Vijaya Kumar. Biometric encryption. (Online) http://www.bio-scrypt.com.

50. K. N. Stevens. *Acoustic Phonetics (Current Studies in Linguistics)*. The MIT Press, 2000.

51. D. T. Toledano, R. Fernandez-Pozo, A. Hernandez-Trapote, and L. Hernandez-Gomez. Usability evaluation of multi-modal biometric verification systems. *Interacting With Computers*, 18:1101–1122, 2006.

52. D. T. Toledano, C. Fombella, J. Gonzalez-Rodriguez, and L. Hernandez-Gomez. On the relationship between phonetic modeling precision and phonetic speaker recognition accuracy. In *Proceedings of InterSpeech*, pages 1993–1996, 2005.

53. D. T. Toledano, L. Hernandez-Gomez, and L. Villarrubia-Grande. Automatic phonetic segmentation. *IEEE Transactions on Speech and Audio Processing*, 11:617–625, 2003.

54. V. Wan and W. Campbell. Support vector machines for speaker verification and identification. In *Proceedings of the IEEE Workshop on Neural Networks for Signal Processing*, volume 2, pages 775–784, 2000.

55. R. Woo, A. Park, and T. J. Hazen. The mit mobile device speaker verification corpus: data collection and preliminary experiments. In *Proceedings of IEEE Odyssey*, 2006.

A Palmprint Authentication System

Guangming Lu[1,3], David Zhang[2], Wai Kin Kong[2], and Michael Wong[2]

[1] Graduate School at Shenzhen, Tsinghua University, China
luguangm@hit.edu.cn
[2] Biometrics Research Centre (UGC/CRC), Department of Computing The Hong Kong Polytechnic University, Kowloon, Hong Kong
{csdzhang, cswkkong, csmkwong}comp.polyu.edu.hk
[3] Biocomputing Research Lab School of Computer Science and Engineering Harbin Institute of Technology, Harbin, China

9.1 Introduction

Biometrics lies in the heart of today's society. There has been an ever-growing need to automatically authenticate individuals for various applications, such as information confidentiality, homeland security, and computer security. Traditional knowledge-based or token-based personal identification or verification is unreliable, inconvenient, and inefficient. Knowledge-based approaches use "something that you know" to make a personal identification, such as password and personal identity number. Token-based approaches use "something that you have" to make a personal identification, such as passport or ID card. Since those approaches are not based on any inherent attributes of an individual to make the identification, they cannot differentiate between an authorized person and an impostor who fraudulently acquires the "token" or "knowledge" of the authorized person. This is why biometric systems have become prevalent in recent years.

Biometrics involves identifying an individual based on his/her physiological or behavioral characteristics. Many parts of our body and various behaviors are embedded with information for personal identification. In fact, using biometrics for person authentication is not new, it has been implemented for thousands of years. Numerous research efforts have been aimed at this subject resulting in the development of various techniques related to signal acquisition, feature extraction, matching and classification. Most importantly, various biometric systems including fingerprint, iris, hand geometry, voice and face recognition systems have been deployed for various applications [7]. According to the International Biometric Group (IBG, New York), the market for biometric technologies will nearly double in size this year alone. Among all biometrics, hand-based biometrics, including hand geometry and fingerprint, are the most popular biometrics gaining 60% market share in 2003 [5].

The palmprint system is a hand-based biometric technology. Palmprint is concerned with the inner surface of a hand. A palm is covered with the same kind of skin as the fingertips and it is larger than a fingertip in size. Many features of a palmprint can be used to uniquely identify a person, including (a) *Geometry Features*: According to the palm's shape, we can easily get the corresponding geometry features, such as width, length and area. (b) *Principal Line Features*: Both location and form of principal lines in a palmprint are very important physiological characteristics for identifying individuals because they vary little over time. (c) *Wrinkle Features*: In a palmprint, there are many wrinkles which are different from the principal lines in that they are thinner and more irregular. (d) *Delta Point Features*: The delta point is defined as the center of a delta-like region in the palmprint. Usually, there are delta points located in the finger-root region. (e) *Minutiae Features*: A palmprint is basically composed of the ridges, allowing the minutiae features to be used as another significant measurement. Figure 9.1 illustrates some major features that can be observed on a palm. Therefore, it is quite natural to think of using palmprint to recognize a person, similar to fingerprint, hand geometry and hand vein [6, 4, 9, 14].

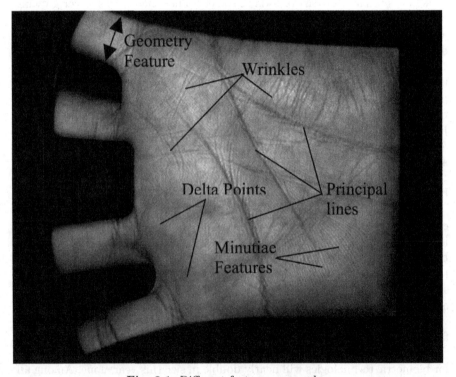

Fig. 9.1. Different features on a palm.

Research on this topic focuses on features and methods to represent the palmprints. Generally, methods can be classified into five categories: line-based, subspace-based, local statistical-based, global statistical-based, and coding-based approaches. The line-based approaches either develop edge detectors or employ the exiting edge detection methods to extract palm lines [17, 18]. The palm lines are either matched directly or represented in other formats for matching. Subspace-based methods, also called appearance-based approaches in the face recognition literature, generally involve principal component analysis (PCA), linear discriminant analysis (LDA) and independent component analysis (ICA) [12, 19, 10, 15]. The subspace coefficients are considered as features. In addition to applying PCA, LDA and ICA directly to palmprint images, researchers also employ wavelets, discrete cosine transform (DCT) and kernels in their methods [13, 3]. Local statistical approaches transform images into another domain and then divide the transformed images into several small regions [20]. Local statistics such as means and variances of each small region are calculated and regarded as features. Gabor, wavelets and Fourier transforms have been applied. Researchers compute global statistical features like moments, center of gravity, and density directly from the whole transformed images [22]. Coding approaches encode the filtered coefficients as features [21] using gabor filters. Phase [21, 11] and orientation [16] features have been encoded for palmprint representation. Most of these techniques focus on the algorithm research of feature extraction, classification, and matching.

Some companies, including NEC and PRINTRAK, have developed several palmprint systems for criminal applications [1, 2]. On the basis of fingerprint technology, their systems exploit high resolution palmprint images to extract detailed features like minutiae for matching the latent prints. Such an approach is not suitable for developing a palmprint authentication system for civil applications, which requires a fast, accurate and reliable method for personal identification. Based on our previous research [21], we developed a novel palmprint authentication system to fulfill such requirements.

The rest of this chapter is organized as follows: The system framework is shown in Section 9.2, the recognition engine is described in Section 9.3, experimental results of verification, identification, robustness, and computation time are provided in Section 9.4, and finally, the conclusion is given in Section 9.5.

9.2 System Framework

The proposed palmprint authentication system has four major components: *User Interface Module, Acquisition Module, Recognition Module* and *External Module*. Fig. 9.2 shows the breakdown of each module of the palmprint authentication system. Fig. 9.3(a) shows the palmprint authentication system installed at Biometric Research Center (BRC), Department of Computing,

The Hong Kong Polytechnic University. The functions of each component are listed below:

1. *User Interface Module* provides an interface between the system and users for the smooth authentication operation. We designed a flat platen surface for the palm acquisition (Fig. 9.3(b)). It is crucial to develop a good user interface such that users are happy to use the device.
2. *Acquisition Module* is the channel for the palmprints to be acquired for the further processing.
3. *Recognition Module* is the key part of our system, which will determine whether a user is authenticated. It consists of image pre-processing, feature extraction, template creation, database updating, and matching.
4. *External Module* receives the signal from the recognition module, to allow some operations to be performed or deny the operations requested. This module is actually an interfacing component, which may be connected to other hardware or software components. Our system presents an external interface for physical door access control or an employee attendance system.

Since the design philosophy and implementation of the user interface and acquisition modules have been described in [21], and the external interface is an application dependent component, we do not intend to discuss them further, and will concentrate on the discussion about the recognition module in detail.

9.3 Recognition Engine

After the palmprint images are captured by the Acquisition Module, they are fed into the recognition engine for palmprint authentication. The recognition engine is the key part of the palmprint authentication system, consisting of: image preprocessing, feature extraction, and matching.

9.3.1 Image Preprocessing

When capturing a palmprint, the position, direction and stretching degree may vary from time to time. As a result, even the palmprints from the same palm could have a little rotation and translation. Also, the sizes of palms are different from one another, so the preprocessing algorithm is used to align different palmprints and extract the corresponding central part for feature extraction. In our palmprint system, both rotation and translation are constrained to some extent by the capture device panel, which positions the palms with several pegs. The preprocessing algorithm can then locate the coordination system of the palmprints quickly by the following five steps:

1. Use a threshold to convert the original grayscale image into a binary image, then use a low-pass filter to smooth the binary image.

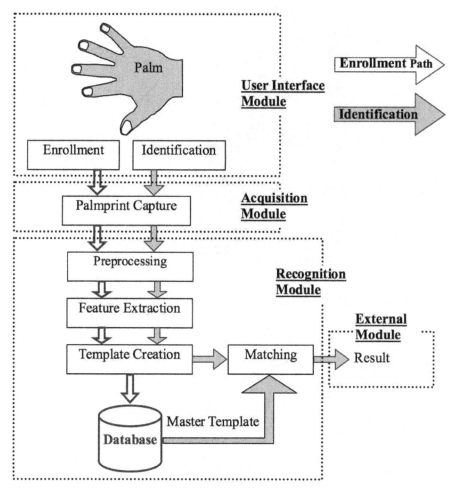

Fig. 9.2. The breakdown of each module of the palmprint authentication system.

2. Trace the boundary of the gaps between fingers (H1 and H2).
3. Compute the common tangent of the boundaries of the gaps $H1$ and $H2$. $T1$ and $T2$ are the tangent points of $H1$ and $H2$, respectively.
4. Align $T1$ and $T2$ to determine the Y-axis of the palmprint coordination system and make a line passing through the midpoint of the two points ($T1$ and $T2$), which is perpendicular to this Y-axis to determine the origin of the system.
5. Extract the central part of the image as shown in Figure 9.4 to be used for feature extraction.

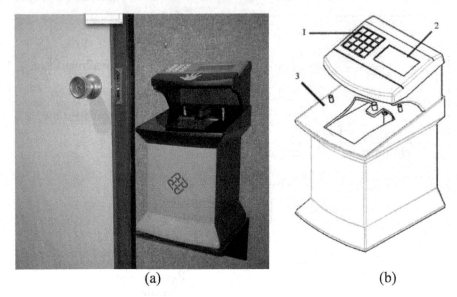

Fig. 9.3. (a) The palmprint authentication system installed at BRC. (b) The interface of palmprint acquisition device: 1-the key pad, 2-LCD display, 3-palm putting and location flat surface.

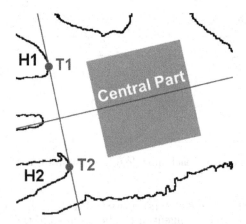

Fig. 9.4. Localizing the salient region of the palm. H1 and H2 are the boundary of the gaps between the two fingers, and T1 and T2 are the tangent points of H1 and H2, respectively. The central part is extracted at a desired distance from line joining T1 and T2 symmetrically positioned about a perpendicual line passing through the mid point of T1 and T2.

9.3.2 Feature extraction

The feature extraction technique implemented on the proposed palmprint system is modified from Zhang et al. [21], where a single circular zero DC (direct current) Gabor filter is applied to the preprocessed palmprint images and the phase information is coded as a feature vector called PalmCode. The modified technique exploited four circular zero DC Gabor filters with the following general formula:

$$G_D = \frac{1}{2\pi\sigma^2} \exp\left\{-\frac{(x' - x_0)^2 + (y' - y_0)^2}{2\sigma^2}\right\} \left\{\exp(i2\pi\omega x') - \exp(-2(\pi\omega\sigma)^2)\right\}$$

(9.1)

where $x' = x\cos\theta + y\sin\theta$ and $y' = -x\sin\theta + y\cos\theta$; (x_0, y_0) is the center of the function in the spatial domain of the function; ω is the frequency of the sinusoidal plane wave along the orientation θ; σ is the standard deviation of the circular Gaussian function; θ is the direction of the filter. The four Gabor filters share the same parameters, σ and ω, only differing in θ. The corresponding values of θ are 0, $\pi/4$, $\pi/2$ and $3\pi/4$.

In the previous approach, only the phase information is exploited but the magnitude information is neglected. The proposed method is to use the magnitude to be a fusion condition combining different PalmCodes generated by the four Gabor filters. Mathematically, the implementation has the following steps:

1. The four Gabor filters are applied to the preprocessed palmprint image, I, described as $G_j * I$, where G_j (j=1, 2, 3, 4) is the circular zero DC Gabor filter and "*" represents an operator of convolution.
2. The square of the magnitudes of the sample point is obtained by $M_j(x, y) = G_j(x, y) * I \times \overline{G_j(x, y) * I}$, where "–" represents complex conjugate.
3. According to the fusion rule, $k = \arg\max_j (M_j(x, y))$, the phase information at point (x, y) is coded as the following:

$$h_r = 1 \quad \text{if} \quad Re[G_k * I] \geq 0,$$

(9.2)

$$h_r = 0 \quad \text{if} \quad Re[G_k * I] < 0,$$

(9.3)

$$h_i = 1 \quad \text{if} \quad Im[G_k * I] \geq 0,$$

(9.4)

$$h_i = 1 \quad \text{if} \quad Im[G_k * I] < 0.$$

(9.5)

This coding method is named as Fusion Code, which is represented by a set of bits. Our experiments show that the Fusion Code is more stable and efficient for palmprint authentication.

9.3.3 Feature Matching

Feature matching determines the degree of similarity between the identification template and the master template. In this work, the normalized Hamming distance is implemented for comparing two Fusion Codes. The normalized Hamming distance is represented by

$$D_0 = \frac{\sum_{i=1}^{N} \sum_{j=1}^{N} P_M(i,j) \cap Q_M(i,j) \cap (P_R(i,j) \otimes Q_R(i,j) + P_I(i,j) \otimes Q_I(i,j))}{2 \sum_{i=1}^{N} \sum_{j=1}^{N} P_M(i,j) \cap Q_M(i,j)},$$

(9.6)

where $P_R(Q_R)$, $P_I(Q_I)$ and $P_M(Q_M)$ are the real part, imaginary part and mask of the Fusion Code $P(Q)$, respectively; $\otimes$ and $\cap$ are Boolean operators, XOR and AND, respectively [21]. The range of normalized Hamming distances is between zero and one where zero represents perfect matching. Because of imperfect preprocessing, one Fusion Code is vertically and horizontal translated to match the other. The ranges of the vertical and the horizontal translations are defined from -2 to 2. The minimum D_0 value obtained from the translated matching is considered to be the final matching score.

9.4 Performance Evaluation

9.4.1 Testing Database

We collected palmprint images from 200 individuals using the palmprint capture device described previously [21]. The subjects are mainly students and staff volunteers from The Hong Kong Polytechnic University. In this dataset, 134 people are male, about 86% are younger than 30 years, about 11% are aged between 30 and 50, and about 3% are older than 50. In addition, we collected the palmprint images on two separate occasions. On each occasion, the subject was asked to provide about 10 images each of the left and right palm. Therefore, each person provided around 40 images, resulting in a total number of 8,025 images from 400 different palms. In addition, we changed the light source and adjusted the focus of the CCD camera so that the images collected on the first and second occasions could be regarded as being captured by two different palmprint devices. The average time interval between the first and second occasions was 70 days. The size of all the testing images used in the following experiments is 384 × 284 with 75dpi, in 256 gray levels.

9.4.2 Experimental Results of Verification

Verification refers to the problem of confirming or denying a claim of identity, also considered one to one matching. We performed two separate group tests of verification. In the first experiment, we used one image of each palm for registration, while 3 images of each palm were used for registration in the second experiment. In the first experiment, each palmprint is matched with all registered images. A correct matching occurs if two matched images are from the same palm, incorrect matching otherwise. The total number of matchings performed are 32,119,735, among these 76,565 correspond to genuine matches and the rest are incorrect matchings. Fig. 9.5(a) shows the probability of genuine and imposter distributions estimated by the correct and incorrect matchings. Some thresholds and corresponding false acceptance rates (FARs) and false rejection rates (FRRs) are listed in Table 9.1. According to Table 9.1, using one palmprint image for registration, the proposed system can be operated at a false acceptance rate at 0.096% and a false rejection rate at 1.05%.

Threshold	Registered image = 1		Registered images = 3	
	FAR(%)	FRR(%)	FAR(%)	FRR(%)
0.32	0.000027	8.15	0.000012	5.12
0.34	0.00094	4.02	0.0016	2.18
0.36	0.011	1.94	0.017	0.86
0.38	0.096	1.05	0.15	0.43
0.40	0.68	0.59	1.03	0.19

Table 9.1. False acceptance rates (FARs) and false rejection rates (FRRs) associated with different threshold values for the palmprints verification results.

In the second experiment, the testing database is divided into two sets, 1) registration and 2) testing. Three palmprint images of each palm collected in the first occasion are selected for registration. The registration database contains 1,200 palmprint images and the rest are used for testing. In this verification test, each palmprint image is matched with all the palmprint images in the testing database. Therefore, each testing image produces three Hamming distances for one registered palm. We take the minimum of them as the final Hamming distance. For achieving statistically reliable results, this test is repeated for three times by selecting other palmprint images for the registration database. Total number of Hamming distances from correct matchings and incorrect matchings are 20,475 and 8,169,525, respectively. Fig. 9.5(b) shows the probability of genuine and imposter distributions estimated by the correct and incorrect matchings, respectively. Some threshold values along with its corresponding false acceptance and false rejection rates are also listed in Table 9.1. According to Table 9.1 and Fig. 9.5, we can conclude that using three templates can provide better verification accuracy. In fact, using more palmprint images of the same palm during registration can provide more information to the system so that it can recognize the noise or deformed features.

9.4.3 Experimental Results of Identification

Identification test is a one-against-many, N comparison process. In this experiment, N is set to 400, which is the total number of different palms in our database. As in the previous verification experiment, the palmprint database is divided into two sets, 1) registration and 2) testing. Registration contains

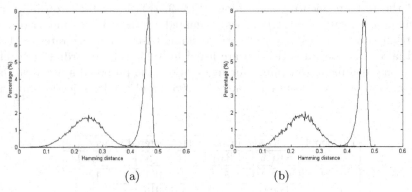

Fig. 9.5. Verification test results. (a) and (b) show the Genuine and imposter distributions for verification tests with one and three registered images per palm, respectively.

1200 palmprint images, three images per palm, while the testing database has 6,825 palmprint images. Each palmprint image for testing is matched to all of the images for registration, therefore each testing image generates 3 correct and 1197 incorrect matchings. The minimum Hamming distances of correct matchings and incorrect matchings are regarded as the identification Hamming distances of genuine and impostor, respectively. This experiment is also called a one-trial test since the user only provides one palmprint image in the test to make one decision. A practical biometric system collects several biometric signals to make one decision. Therefore, in this experiment, we implement one, two, and three-trial tests. In the two-trial test, a pair of images in testing belonging to the same palm is matched to all of the images in registration. Each pair of the palmprint images in the two-trial test generates 6 correct and 2,394 incorrect matchings. The minimum Hamming distances of correct matchings and incorrect matchings are considered the identification Hamming distances of genuine and imposter, respectively. Similarly, in the three-trial test, the identification Hamming distances of genuine and imposter are obtained from 9 correct and 3,591 incorrect matchings, respectively. Each test is repeated three times by selecting other palmprints from the registration database. In each test, the number of identification Hamming distances of both genuine and imposter matchings are 20,475. Fig. 9.6 shows ROC curves of the three tests and Table 9.2 lists threshold values along with its corresponding FAR and FRR. According to Fig. 9.6 and Table 9.2, more input palmprints can provide more accurate results.

9.4.4 Computation time

Another key issue for a civilian personal identification system is whether the system can run in real time. The proposed method is implemented using C

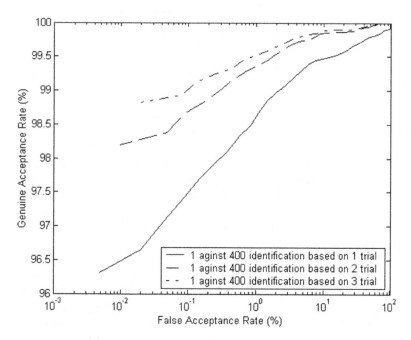

Fig. 9.6. The ROC curves for a 1-against-400 identification testing with different number of trials.

Threshold	Trial=1		Trial=2		Trial=3	
	FAR (%)	FRR (%)	FAR (%)	FRR (%)	FAR (%)	FRR (%)
0.320	0.0049	3.69	0.0098	1.80	0.020	1.17
0.325	0.0439	2.93	0.088	1.34	0.131	1.06
0.330	0.15	2.29	0.28	1.02	0.42	0.68
0.335	0.37	1.90	0.68	0.72	0.96	0.48
0.340	0.84	1.51	1.43	0.57	1.93	0.37
0.345	1.45	1.16	2.32	0.42	3.02	0.26

Table 9.2. FARs and FRRs with different threshold values for the 1-to-400 palmprints identification results.

language and Assembly language on an Intel Pentium IV processor (1.4GHz) with 128M memory. The execution times for image collection, image preprocessing, feature extraction and matching are listed in Table 9.3. The total execution time for a 1-against-400 identification, each palm with 3 templates, is less than 1 second. Users will not feel any delay when using our system.

Operations	Execution Time
Image collection	340ms
Preprocessing	250ms
Feature extraction	180ms
Matching	1.3μs

Table 9.3. Execution time of the palmprint authentication system.

9.4.5 Robustness

As a practical biometric system, in addition to accuracy and speed, robustness of the system is important. Here, we present three experiments to illustrate the robustness of our system. The first tests the effects of jewelry such as rings, on the accuracy of some preprocessing algorithms. The second tests noise on the palmprints, which directly affects the performance of the system. The third experiment tests the ability of the system to identify palmprints of identical twins.

Fig. 9.7 shows three palmprint images with and without rings on the fingers and their corresponding preprocessed sub-images. It shows that the preprocessing algorithm described in Section 9.3 is not affected by jewelry.

To verify the robustness due to image noise, Fig. 9.8(a) provides a clear palmprint image and Figs. 9.8(b)-(f) show five palmprint images, each covered with writing. Their Hamming distances are given in Table 9.3; all of them smaller than 0.29. Compared to the Hamming distances of imposters in Tables 9.1 and 9.2, all the Hamming distances in Table 9.4 are relatively small. Fig. 9.8 and Table 9.4 illustrates that the proposed palmprint authentication system is very robust to noise on the palmprint.

A test of identical twins is regarded as an important test for biometric authentication that not all biometrics, including face and DNA, can pass. However, the palmprints of identical twins have enough distinctive information to distinguish them. We collected 590 palmprint images from 30 pairs of identical twins ranging in age between 6 and 45 years. Each provided around 10 images of their left palms and 10 images of their right palms. Some samples of identical twin palmprints are shown in Fig. 9.9. Based on this database, we match a palmprint in the twin database with his/her identical twin sibling to produce imposter matching scores, and match against the samples of their own to get the genuine scores. The genuine and imposter distributions are given in Fig. 9.10. From the figure, we find that identical twin palmprints can easily be separated, just like twins' fingerprints [8].

9.5 Conclusions

In this chapter, we have presented a novel biometric system based on the palmprint. The proposed system can accurately identify a person in real time,

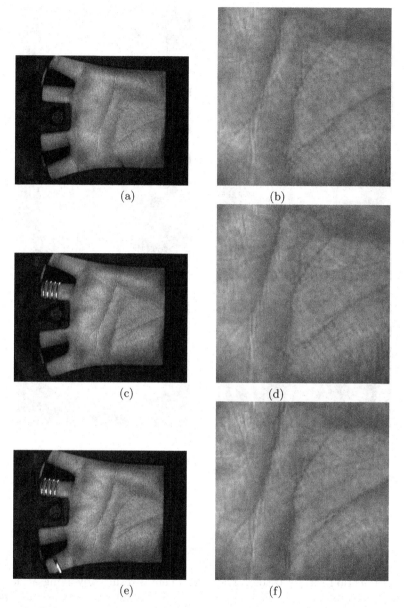

Fig. 9.7. Palmprint images with ring on the fingers for testing the robustness of the system.

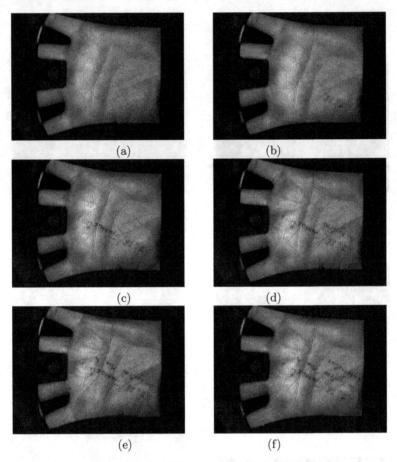

Fig. 9.8. Palmprint images with different texts for testing the robustness of the system.

which is suitable for various civil applications such as access control. Experimental results show that the proposed system can identify 400 palms with a false acceptance rate at 0.02%, and a genuine acceptance rate at 98.83%. For verification, the system can operate at a false acceptance rate of 0.017% and a false rejection rate of 0.86%. The experimental results involving accuracy, speed, and robustness demonstrate that the palmprint authentication system is comparable with other hand-based biometrics systems, such as hand geometry and fingerprint [6, 4, 9, 14], and is practical for real-world applications. The system has been successfully operating in the Biometric Research Center, Department of Computing, The Hong Kong Polytechnic University since March 2003 for access control.

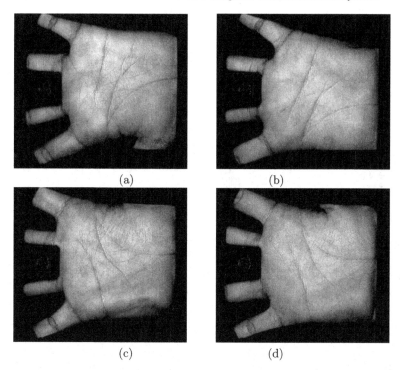

Fig. 9.9. Identical twins palmprints. (a), (b) are their left hands, and (c), (d) are their right hands, respectively.

Acknowledgements

This research is partially supported by the UGC/CRC fund from the Hong Kong SAR Government and the central fund from The Hong Kong Polytechnic University.

References

1. NEC automatic palmprint identification system. `http://www.nectech.com/afis/download/PalmprintDtsht.q.pdf`.
2. Printrak palmprint identification system. `http://www.printrakinternational.com/omnitrak.htm`.
3. T. Connie, A. T. B. Jin, M. G. K. Ong, and D. N. C. Ling. An automated palmprint recognition system. *Image and Vision Computing*, 23(5):501–515, 2005.
4. S. K. Im, H. M. Park, Y. W. Kim, S. C. Han, S. W. Kim, and C. H. Kang. An biometric identification system by extracting hand vein patterns. *Journal of the Korean Physical Society*, 38(3):268–272, 2001.
5. International Biometric Group. Biometric market report 2003-2007. `http://www.biometricgroup.com/reports/public/market\_report.html`.

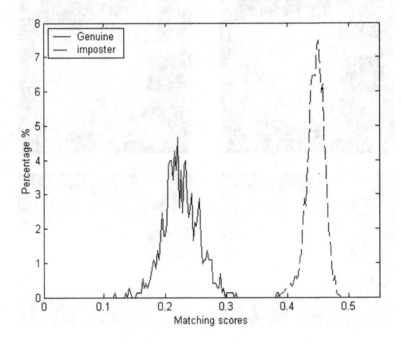

Fig. 9.10. The genuine and imposter distributions for measuring the similarity of identical twins palmprints.

6. A. Jain, L. Hong, and R. Bolle. On-line fingerprint verification. *IEEE Transactions on Pattern Analysis and Machine Intelligence*, 19(4):302–314, 1997.
7. A. K. Jain, R. Bolle, and S. Pankanti, editors. *Biometrics: Personal Identification in Networked Society*. Kluwer Academic Publishers, 1999.
8. A. K. Jain, S. Prabhakar, and S. Pankanti. On the similarity of identical twin fingerprints. *Pattern Recognition*, 35(11):2653–2662, 2002.
9. A. K. Jain, A. Ross, and S. Prabhakar. An introduction to biometric recognition. *IEEE Transactions on Circuits and Systems for Video Technology, Special Issue on Image- and Video- Based Biometrics*, 14(1), 2004.
10. X. Y. Jing and D. Zhang. A face and palmprint recognition approach based on discriminant DCT feature extraction. *IEEE Transactions on Systems, Man, and Cybernetics - Part B: Cybernetics*, 34(6):2405–2415, 2004.
11. A. Kong and D. Zhang. Palmprint identification using feature-level fusion. *Pattern Recognition*, 39(3):478–487, 2006.
12. G. Lu, D. Zhang, and K. Wang. Palmprint Recognition Using Eigenpalms Features. *Pattern Recognition Letters*, 24:1473–1477, 2003.
13. G. M. Lu, K. Q. Wang, and D. Zhang. Wavelet based independent component analysis for palmprint identification. In *Proceedings of International Conference on Machine Learning and Cybernetics*, volume 6, pages 3547–3550, 2004.
14. R. Sanchez-Reillo, C. Sanchez-Avilla, and A. Gonzalez-Marcos. Biometric identification through hand geometry measurements. *IEEE Transactions on Pattern Analysis and Machine Intelligence*, 22(10):1168–1171, 2000.

15. L. Shang, D. S. Huang, J. X. Du, and C. H. Zheng. Palmprint recognition using FastICA algorithm and radial basis probabilistic neural network. *Neurocomputing (on-line available)*, 2006.
16. Z. Sun, T. Tan, Y. Wang, and S. Z. Li. Ordinal palmprint representation for personal identification. volume 1, pages 279–284, 2005.
17. X. Wu, K. Wang, and D. Zhang. Fuzzy direction element energy feature (FDEEF) based palmprint identification. In *Proceedings of International Conference on Pattern Recognition*, volume 1, pages 95–98, 2002.
18. X. Wu, K. Wang, and D. Zhang. A novel approach of palm-line extraction. In *Proceeding of the Third International Conference on Image and Graphics*, pages 230–233, 2004.
19. X. Wu, D. Zhang, and K. Wang. Fisherpalms based palmprint recognition. *Pattern Recognition Letters*, 24:2829–2838, 2003.
20. J. You, W. K. Kong, D. Zhang, and K. H. Cheung. On hierarchical palmprint coding with multiple features for personal identification in large databases. *IEEE Transactions on Circuits and Systems for Video Technology*, 14(2):234–243, 2004.
21. D. Zhang, W. K. Kong, J. You, and M. Wong. On-line palmprint identification. *IEEE Transactions on Pattern Analysis and Machine Intelligence*, 25(9):1041–1050, 2003.
22. L. Zhang and D. Zhang. Characterization of palmprints by wavelet signatures via directional context modeling. *IEEE Transactions on Systems, Man and Cybernetics, Part B*, 34(3):1335–1347, 2004.

On-Line Signature Verification

Julian Fierrez and Javier Ortega-Garcia

ATVS-UAM, Escuela Politecnica Superior, Universidad Autonoma de Madrid, Madrid, Spain
{julian.fierrez,javier.ortega}@uam.es

10.1 Introduction

Automatic signature verification is an important research area because of the social and legal acceptance and widespread use of the handwritten signature as a personal authentication method [66, 45, 67]. Another advantage of the handwritten signature as a biometric modality is that it is easily acquired either with an inking pen over a sheet of paper or by electronic means with a number of existing pointer-based devices (e.g., pen tablets, PDAs, Tablet PCs, touch screens, etc.)

In spite of the advantages of the handwritten signature modality, the practical deployment of this technology is very slow and signature biometrics still remains a challenging research problem. This is mainly due to the large intra-class variations and, when considering forgeries, small inter-class variations as well. Figs. 10.5 and 10.6 show some examples of Chinese and European signatures where this effect is evident. Other challenges of signature biometrics include low universality, as not everyone may be able to sign, low permanence, as the handwritten signature tends to vary along time, and vulnerability to direct attacks using forgeries.

Similar to some other biometric modalities (e.g., PIN-based voice biometrics), impostors may know some information about the client that degrades signature verification performance when it is exploited, for example, signature shape. As a result, two kinds of impostors are usually considered in signature verification, namely: *casual impostors* (producing *random forgeries*), when no information about the target signature is known, and *real impostors* (producing *skilled forgeries*), when some information regarding the signature being forged is used. Different kinds of information available to the impostors produce different types of forgeries (e.g., statically skilled forgeries, over-the-shoulder forgeries, professional forgeries, etc.)

Signature verification methods can be classified according to the input signature information into two classes: *on-line* and *off-line*. On-line refers to the use of the time functions of the dynamic signing process (e.g., position trajectories, or pressure versus time), which are obtained using acquisition devices like touch screens or digitizing tablets. Off-line refers to the use of the static image of the signature. This chapter deals with on-line signature verification. Signature verification based on the static image of the signature can be found in [67, 21, 76]. Note also that some off-line problems can be solved using on-line methods [36], as some dynamic information can be estimated from the static images [55], and viceversa, as static images can be easily generated from the dynamic information.

The chapter is organized as follows: The introduction is completed with an overview of the history of signature recognition, some practical applications and commercial systems, and standardization efforts related to on-line signature biometrics. Sect. 10.2 outlines the system architecture of on-line signature verification systems, and presents some of the key concepts related to each of the modules. In Sect. 10.3 we summarize the existing reference systems and publicly available on-line signature databases. Sect. 10.4 describes a case study of signature verification combining feature- and function-based approaches on a widely available signature corpus. Sect. 10.5 summarizes the chapter and outlines some open problems in on-line signature verification.

10.1.1 History

Osborn [62] was one of the first published works studying the problem of signature verification. In this pioneer work the problem of signature verification was studied from the forensic examiner point of view, including recommendations for practitioners and some real-world case studies. Fig. 10.1 shows two sets of signatures from a celebrated case of a contested will in New York in the year 1900, involving an estate worth more than six million dollars. The court accepted that the five signatures on the left were genuine and the five on the right were forgeries, which led to the establishment of Rice University in Houston. Modern approaches for the forensic examination of signatures are summarized in Hilton [31].

The first published work on automatic signature verification seems to be Mauceri [50]. This work was followed by the popular development of Herbst and Liu in 1977 [30], which also summarized the state-of-the-art up to that date. This was followed by an increasing number of approaches, summarized in the state-of-the-art survey in 1989 by Plamondon and Lorette [66]. This survey of existing methods was updated in 1994 [45] and subsequently in 2000 [67]. In the meantime, the popular methods of Dynamic Time Warping [53], and Hidden Markov Models [80] were successfully applied to on-line signature verification, and the search for good global features was significantly advanced [47].

Some recent milestones in the history of signature verification are the availability of benchmark databases [60], and the organization of the First International Signature Verification Competition (SVC) in 2004 [81].

Fig. 10.1. Genuine (left) and forged signatures (right) in a celebrated court case [62].

10.1.2 Applications

The most important applications of on-line signature biometrics are in the legal (document authentication), medical (record protection), and banking sectors (cheque and credit card processing). The main applications include:

- Signature forensics. This is the oldest application of the handwritten signature [31], commonly applied to the off-line image of the written signature. Forensic approaches for the evaluation of on-line signature evidence are now under development [28].
- Signature authentication. This type of application includes system login based on signature, document encryption, web access, etc. One example for Tablet PC can be found in [2].
- Signature surveillance. The automatic comparison of on-line signatures can be used to track and detect signers (e.g., blacklists of individuals), or can be used to warn the human operator at points of sales or other credit card-based services.
- Digital Rights Management based on signature [59].
- Biometric cryptosystems based on signature. New developments have demonstrated the feasibility of generating cryptographic keys based on the time functions of the on-line signatures [25].

10.1.3 Commercial Systems

From the IBG's Biometrics Market and Industry Report 2006-2010 [37], it can be observed that the signature modality is the second behavioral trait in commercial importance just after voice biometrics, with approximately 1.7% of the current market share. Although the market for signature systems is growing at a faster rate than other biometric modalities, especially due to the advent of touch-screen portable devices, signature biometrics is only a small

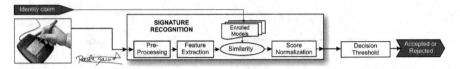

Fig. 10.2. Architecture adopted by most on-line signature verification systems.

fraction of the biometrics market, which is mainly dominated by modalities like fingerprint (43.6% of the market share) and face (19.0%).

A number of companies are currently distributing handwritten signature verification products on different platforms. Some examples are included in the following list, which is not exhaustive:

- Communication Intelligence Corporation has a number of signature verification products [9], including SignatureOne®and Sign-it®, which enable signature-based system login using dynamic signature information.
- SOFTPRO distributes a number of signature verification modules enabling both static and on-line signature verification [73].
- Cyber-SIGN sells various plug-ins and applications for on-line signature verification [10].

10.1.4 Standardization

The ISO/IEC JTC1 SC37 committee is addressing the interoperability issues in various biometric systems [72]. One point of particular importance subject to standardization, in order to enable the interoperability of signature systems, is the interchange formats for storage and transfer of signature data. The signature modality is represented by two parts of the standard ISO/IEC 19795.

Part 7 of the standard defines a time series format that allows the transmission and storage of a series of time-stamped pen-based standard channels (e.g., x position, y position, time, velocity, etc.). Along with these channels, the storage of proprietary data is also permitted. A set of recommendations and best practices are also given with the standard. Part 11, now in consideration, defines a set of common statistical features extracted from the raw data, which can be extended by another set of proprietary features. The whole feature set must allow interoperability at a feature level between samples collected on different types of devices.

10.2 On-Line Signature Verification Systems

The common architecture of on-line signature verification systems is depicted in Fig. 10.2. In the following sections we will summarize the main techniques and related issues for each of the system modules.

One major research trend in biometric verification is the successful exploitation of the different information levels embodied in the biometric signal at hand. This is usually done by combining the confidences provided by a number of different machine experts [5, 44], each one working at a specific information level. Multilevel approaches for on-line signature verification are described in [41, 23].

10.2.1 Data Acquisition and Preprocessing

The on-line acquisition of the time functions of the handwritten signature is usually carried out by using devices such as digitizing tablets [79, 34] or touch screens, such as those included in Tablet PCs and PDAs. These acquisition devices provide coordinate information (e.g., horizontal x and vertical y pen position) and, in some cases, pen pressure and pen angle versus time [71]. Other on-line signature acquisition devices are dedicated pens with specialized hardware attached to provide some on-line signature data such as coordinate or velocity information [33].

On-line signature capture devices usually operate at between 100 and 200 samples per second. Taking into account the Nyquist sampling criterion and the fact that the maximum frequencies of the related biomechanical sequences are always under 20-30 Hz [4], this sampling frequency leads to a precise discrete-time signature representation.

Some preprocessing steps before feature extraction are noise filtering (for example with Gaussian windows [38]) and resampling. Resampling is carried out in some systems in order to obtain a shape-based representation consisting of equidistant points [38]. Other systems avoid the resampling step as some discriminative speed characteristics are lost in the process [43].

10.2.2 Feature Extraction

Many different approaches have been considered in order to extract discriminative information from on-line signature data [66]. The existing methods can broadly be divided into two classes: *feature-based*, in which a holistic vector representation consisting of a set of global features is derived from the signature trajectories [47, 42], and *function-based*, in which time sequences describing local properties of the signature are used for recognition [53, 15, 38, 49], e.g., position trajectory, velocity, acceleration, force, or pressure [48]. A case study of feature- and function-based approaches is given in Sect. 10.4. Although recent works show that feature-based approaches are competitive with respect to function-based methods in some situations [23], the latter approach has traditionally yielded better results.

The set of features used can be a result of a feature selection process [40] during a development phase [47, 48, 23], or can be adapted during the enrollment phase to the specificities of the user at hand. The latter approach is believed to be better suited to the problem of signature verification [46, 13], mainly because of the large differences in information content and complexity between signers [7, 14]. However, the user-specific approach encounters challenges of training data scarcity.

10.2.3 Enrollment

Depending on the matching strategy, enrollment can be divided into two classes: *reference-based*, and *model-based*.

In reference-based enrollment [38, 43], the features extracted from the set of training signatures are stored as a set of template signatures, each one in the template set corresponding to one training signature. The matching process is then performed by comparing the input signature to each one of the reference templates and then combining the resulting matching scores with a score-level fusion technique [20, 70].

In model-based enrollment [41, 23], the set of training signatures of a given subject is used to estimate a statistical model which describes the behavior of that particular signer. As in the feature extraction process, the model complexity can also be adjusted to be user-dependent [78, 64].

Reference-based enrollment is more appropriate than model-based enrollment when the set of training signatures is small. This is because the statistical models used for signature verification (typically HMMs [80]) require at least 4 to 6 training signatures to perform reasonably well [19]. An experimental comparison of reference- versus training-based enrollment for different training set sizes can be found in [22]. As a rule of thumb, although reference-based enrollment can provide satisfactory performance results with fewer than 5 training signatures in some scenarios (e.g., 3 training signatures in [38]), it is generally accepted that a training set of around 5 signatures is the best cost-performance operating point for automatic on-line signature verification [29, 53, 22, 19]. The same observation was noticed as early as 80 years ago when considering static signatures for human verification [62].

A big challenge related to the enrollment stage is the time variation of signatures [24]. This problem can be alleviated by using training signatures from different sessions [19]. An alternative approach is template or model adaptation [77], which may be more appropriate for practical deployments.

10.2.4 Similarity Computation

Pre-Alignment

The matching stage is generally preceded by a *pre-alignment* between the input signature and the enrolled template/model. In the case of reference-based enrollment, the pre-alignment is usually conducted before feature extraction based only on the signature shape. Techniques following this approach include basic position and rotation alignment, or more sophisticated approaches based

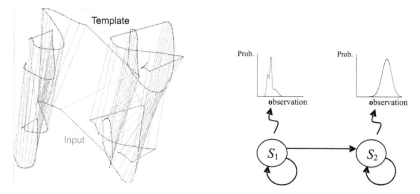

Fig. 10.3. Example of local elastic matching of signatures based on DTW (left, Chinese signature from SVC 2004) and regional modeling based on HMM (right).

on boundary warping [65]. In the case of model-based enrollment, the pre-alignment usually consists in the application of a common reference system [35], for example: position trajectories with respect to the initial point or to the center of mass, scaling to a fixed size frame, etc.

When no pre-alignment is used, the alignment is either embedded in the matching procedure [43] or a fixed frame is used during acquisition in order to have pre-aligned signatures [23].

Matching

In feature-based approaches with reference-based enrollment, the matching scores are usually obtained by using some kind of distance measure between the feature vectors of input and template signatures [57, 47], or a trained classifier. Distance measures used for signature verification include Euclidean distance, weighted Euclidean distance, and Mahalanobis distance. Trained classifiers include approaches like Neural Networks [63]. In the case of feature-based approaches with model-based enrollment, statistical models such as non-parametric density estimation based on Parzen Windows have been used [23]. This latter case is discussed in Sect. 10.4.

Function-based approaches can be classified into *local* and *regional* depending on the matching strategy.

In local approaches, the time functions of the different signatures (or some elaboration of the signatures, based on extended features of the time functions at each sampling point) are directly matched by using elastic distance measures such as Dynamic Time Warping [51, 43, 16]. An example of this elastic matching process is shown in the left part of Fig. 10.3, which is obtained by using the DTW approach described by Fierrez-Aguilar et al. [22].

In regional methods, the time functions are converted into a sequence of vectors, each one describing regional properties of a segment of the signature

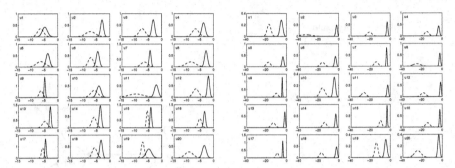

Fig. 10.4. Gaussian fit of client (solid) and impostor (dashed) score distributions of SVC 2004 development corpus for a HMM-based system for skilled (4 left columns) and random forgeries (4 right columns).

[11]. One of the most popular regional approaches is the method based on Hidden Markov Models [80, 41, 11]. In most of the cases, the HMMs model stroke-based sequences. Direct modeling of the time functions with HMMs has also been studied [19]. This latter case is developed as a case study in Sect. 10.4 by using the topology shown in the right part of Fig. 10.3.

10.2.5 Score Normalization

The matching scores obtained by comparing the input signature with the template or the enrolled model are usually normalized to a common range such as $[0, 1]$ before comparing them to a decision threshold, using different mapping functions [39]. This score normalization step is crucial when combining different matchers in a multibiometric approach [70].

As in the other modules of the system, the score normalization step can be also user-dependent. A simple experiment helps to visualize the rationale behind user-dependent score normalization. In Fig. 10.4 we show Gaussian fits of the user-dependent matching scores obtained with the function-based system described in Sect. 10.4, on different users in the development set of the Signature Verification Competition (SVC) described in Sect. 10.3.2. We can observe large differences both in the individual verification performance, and in the client-impostor scoring regions. The main objective of user-dependent score normalization techniques [24] is to prevent such misalignments, which are also compensated with user-dependent thresholds [13, 38].

The substantial differences across subjects of the user-dependent score distributions observed in signature verification are related to the complexity of signatures [7, 14] and their robustness against forgery attacks, but this relationship is not fully understood.

10.3 Resources for On-Line Signature Verification

10.3.1 Reference Systems

The availability of open source reference systems in biometrics research is an important milestone, as they provide a baseline to which results obtained with the new systems can be compared. This is the case, for example, of the NIST Fingerprint Image Software [58], which is used as a reference system in many studies [1].

Although there is no widely available reference system for signature verification to date, new efforts are being directed to the development of an open source framework within the Biosecure Network of Excellence [27]. The proposed framework will enable the efficient implementation and evaluation of various techniques (including feature-based and function-based approaches) and system components (including data parsing, pre-processing, feature extraction/selection, and reference template/model storage) related to on-line signature verification [8].

10.3.2 On-Line Signature Databases

One key element for performance evaluation of biometric systems is the availability of biometric databases. The availability of on-line signature databases corresponding to a large population of individuals, together with the desirable presence of biometric variability (i.e., multi-session, multiple acquisition sensors, different signal quality, etc.), and the availability of different kinds of forgeries, make signature database collection a time-consuming and complicated process. Additionally, the legal issues regarding data protection are controversial [68]. For these reasons, the number of available on-line signature biometric databases is quite limited.

The available on-line signature databases are normally obtained as a result of collaborative efforts in joint research projects (e.g., BIOMET [26], MCYT [60], or MYIDEA [12]; all of them are multimodal databases that include the signature modality [17]), or international benchmarks such as SVC 2004 [81]. In a few cases, on-line signature databases are available through the authors of research publications [11, 51].

In the following list we outline some public domain signature databases.

BIOMET. Five different modalities are present in the BIOMET database [26]: audio, face, hand, fingerprint and signature. Three different sessions were realized, with three and five months spacing between them. The number of persons participating in the collection of the database was 130 for the first campaign, 106 for the second, and 91 for the last, with 15 genuine and 17 impostor signatures per user. The signature acquisition device was a WACOM Intuos2 set at 200 Hz. The first session was acquired by using a Grip Pen (without visual feedback) and the remaining sessions were captured with an Ink Pen over a sheet of paper.

MCYT. The MCYT bimodal biometric database consists of fingerprint and on-line signature modalities [60]. In order to acquire the dynamic signature sequences, a WACOM Intuos pen tablet was employed. The sampling frequency was set to 100 Hz. The capture area was further divided into 37.5 mm (width) × 17.5 mm (height) blocks which were used as frames for acquisition [21]. Signature corpus comprises genuine (25 per user in groups of 5) and shape-based skilled forgeries (25 per user from 5 different impostors). The forgeries were generated by contributors to the database imitating other contributors. For this task they were given the printed signature to imitate and were asked not only to imitate the shape but also to generate the imitation without artifacts such as time breaks or slowdowns. Fig. 10.6 shows some example signatures. The MCYT signature corpus was released in 2003 by the Biometric Recognition Group–ATVS [3] and it has been used in more than 30 research groups worldwide [69, 32, 36, 54, 52]. Paper templates of 75 signers (and their associated skilled forgeries) were also selected and digitized with a scanner at 600 dpi [21]. The resulting subcorpus is comprised of 2250 signature images, with 15 genuine signatures and 15 forgeries per user (contributed by 3 different user-specific forgers). This subcorpus is also available [3].

SVC. The First International Signature Verification Competition (SVC) was organized in 2004 providing a common reference for system comparison on the same data and evaluation protocol [81]. The development corpus of the extended task (including coordinate and timing information, pen orientation and pressure) is available through the competition website [74]. This corpus consists of 40 sets of signatures. Each set contains 20 genuine signatures from one contributor (acquired in two separate sessions) and 20 skilled forgeries from five other contributors. The SVC database is especially challenging due to several factors, including: *i*) no visual feedback when writing (acquisition was conducted by using a WACOM tablet with a Grip Pen), *ii*) subjects used invented signatures different to the ones used in daily life in order to protect their personal data, *iii*) skilled forgers imitated not only the shape but also the dynamics, and *iv*) time span between training and testing signatures was at least one week. The signatures are in either English or Chinese (see Fig. 10.5).

Other ongoing efforts in on-line signature database collection include the Biosecure multimodal database [6], which will include the signature modality acquired with different devices (WACOM Intuos3 digitizing tablet, Samsung Q1 Tablet PC, and HP iPAQ hx2790 PDA) for the same subjects (around 1000) in order to enable interoperability experiments [18].

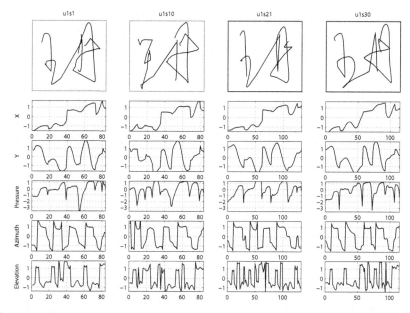

Fig. 10.5. Signature examples from SVC 2004 corpus. For a particular subject, two genuine signatures (left columns) and two skilled forgeries (right columns) are given. Plots of the coordinate trajectories, pressure signal and pen orientation functions are also given.

10.4 Case Study: Combining Feature- and Function-Based Approaches

Feature-Based Approach

This subsystem is based on previous approaches [56, 57, 47] and is further detailed by Fierrez-Aguilar et al. [23].

Feature extraction and selection. The complete set of global features is given in Table 10.1. Note that an on-line signature acquisition process capturing position trajectories and pressure signals both at pen-down and pen-up intervals is assumed. Otherwise, the feature set should be reduced, discarding features based on trajectory signals during pen-ups (e.g., features 32 and 41). Even though the given set has been demonstrated to be robust to the common distortions encountered in the handwritten scenario, not all the parameters are fully rotation/scale invariant, so either a controlled signature acquisition is assumed (as in MCYT database) or some kind of pre-alignment should be performed before computing them. Although pen inclination signals (i.e., azimuth and altitude) have shown discriminative power in some studies [71], no features based on them are introduced in the proposed set. The features in Table 10.1 are sorted by individual

Table 10.1. Set of global features sorted by individual discriminative power (T denotes time interval, t denotes time instant, N denotes number of events, θ denotes angle, **bold** denotes novel feature, *italic* denotes adapted from [56, 57, 47], roman denotes extracted from [56, 57, 47]).

Ranking	Feature Description	Ranking	Feature Description
1	signature total duration T_s	2	N(pen-ups)
3	N(sign changes of dx/dt and dy/dt)	4	average jerk $\bar{j}$ [56]
5	standard deviation of a_y	6	standard deviation of v_y
7	(standard deviation of y)/Δ_y	8	N(local maxima in x)
9	standard deviation of a_x	10	standard deviation of v_x
11	j_{rms}	12	N(local maxima in y)
13	t(2nd pen-down)/T_s	14	(average velocity $\bar{v}$)/$v_{x,max}$
15	$\dfrac{A_{min}=(y_{max}-y_{min})(x_{max}-x_{min})}{(\Delta_x=\sum_{i=1}^{pen\text{-}downs}(x_{max\,|i}-x_{min\,|i}))\Delta_y}$	16	$(x_{last\ pen\text{-}up}-x_{max})/\Delta_x$
17	$(x_{1st\ pen\text{-}down}-x_{min})/\Delta_x$	18	$(y_{last\ pen\text{-}up}-y_{min})/\Delta_y$
19	$(y_{1st\ pen\text{-}down}-y_{min})/\Delta_y$	20	$(T_w\bar{v})/(y_{max}-y_{min})$
21	$(T_w\bar{v})/(x_{max}-x_{min})$	22	(pen-down duration T_w)/T_s
23	$\bar{v}/v_{y,max}$	24	$(y_{last\ pen\text{-}up}-y_{max})/\Delta_y$
25	$\dfrac{T((dy/dt)/(dx/dt)>0)}{T((dy/dt)/(dx/dt)<0)}$	26	$\bar{v}/v_{max}$
27	$(y_{1st\ pen\text{-}down}-y_{max})/\Delta_y$	28	$(x_{last\ pen\text{-}up}-x_{min})/\Delta_x$
29	(velocity rms v)/v_{max}	30	$\dfrac{(x_{max}-x_{min})\Delta_y}{(y_{max}-y_{min})\Delta_x}$
31	(velocity correlation $v_{x,y}$)/v_{max}^2 [57]	32	$T(v_y > 0|pen\text{-}up)/T_w$
33	$N(v_x = 0)$	34	direction histogram s_1 [57]
35	$(y_{2nd\ local\ max}-y_{1st\ pen\text{-}down})/\Delta_y$	36	$(x_{max}-x_{min})/x_{acquisition\ range}$
37	$(x_{1st\ pen\text{-}down}-x_{max})/\Delta_x$	38	T(curvature > Threshold$_{curv}$)/T_w
39	(integrated abs. centr. acc. a_{Ic})/a_{max} [57]	40	$T(v_x > 0)/T_w$
41	$T(v_x < 0|pen\text{-}up)/T_w$	42	$T(v_x > 0|pen\text{-}up)/T_w$
43	$(x_{3rd\ local\ max}-x_{1st\ pen\text{-}down})/\Delta_x$	44	$N(v_y = 0)$
45	(acceleration rms a)/a_{max}	46	(standard deviation of x)/Δ_x
47	$\dfrac{T((dx/dt)(dy/dt)>0)}{T((dx/dt)(dy/dt)<0)}$	48	(tangential acceleration rms a_t)/a_{max}
49	$(x_{2nd\ local\ max}-x_{1st\ pen\text{-}down})/\Delta_x$	50	$T(v_y < 0|pen\text{-}up)/T_w$
51	direction histogram s_2	52	t(3rd pen-down)/T_s
53	(max distance between points)/A_{min}	54	$(y_{3rd\ local\ max}-y_{1st\ pen\text{-}down})/\Delta_y$
55	$(\bar{x}-x_{min})/\bar{x}$	56	direction histogram s_5
57	direction histogram s_3	58	$T(v_x < 0)/T_w$
59	$T(v_y > 0)/T_w$	60	$T(v_y < 0)/T_w$
61	direction histogram s_8	62	(1st $t(v_{x,min})$)/T_w
63	direction histogram s_6	64	T(1st pen-up)/T_w
65	spatial histogram t_4	66	direction histogram s_4
67	$(y_{max}-y_{min})/y_{acquisition\ range}$	68	(1st $t(v_{x,max})$)/T_w
69	(centripetal acceleration rms a_c)/a_{max}	70	spatial histogram t_1
71	θ(1st to 2nd pen-down)	72	θ(1st pen-down to 2nd pen-up)
73	direction histogram s_7	74	$t(j_{x,max})/T_w$
75	spatial histogram t_2	76	$j_{x,max}$
77	θ(1st pen-down to last pen-up)	78	θ(1st pen-down to 1st pen-up)
79	(1st $t(x_{max})$)/T_w	80	$\bar{j}_x$
81	T(2nd pen-up)/T_w	82	(1st $t(v_{max})$)/T_w
83	$j_{y,max}$	84	θ(2nd pen-down to 2nd pen-up)
85	j_{max}	86	spatial histogram t_3
87	(1st $t(v_{y,min})$)/T_w	88	(2nd $t(x_{max})$)/T_w
89	(3rd $t(x_{max})$)/T_w	90	(1st $t(v_{y,max})$)/T_w
91	$t(j_{max})/T_w$	92	$t(j_{y,max})/T_w$
93	direction change histogram c_2	94	(3rd $t(y_{max})$)/T_w
95	direction change histogram c_4	96	$\bar{j}_y$
97	direction change histogram c_3	98	θ(initial direction)
99	θ(before last pen-up)	100	(2nd $t(y_{max})$)/T_w

inter-user discriminative power. For each feature F_k, $k = 1,\ldots,100$, we compute the scalar Mahalanobis distance [75] d_{i,F_k}^{M} between the mean of the F_k-parameterized training signatures of client i, $i = 1,\ldots,330$, and the F_k-parameterized set of all training signatures from all users. Features are then ranked according to the following inter-user class separability measure $S(F_k)$

$$S(F_k) = \sum_{i=1}^{330} \sum_{j=1}^{330} |d_{i,F_k}^{\mathrm{M}} - d_{j,F_k}^{\mathrm{M}}| \tag{10.1}$$

Similarity computation. Given the feature vectors of the training set of signatures of a client $\mathcal{C}$, a non-parametric estimation $\lambda_{\mathcal{C}}^{\mathrm{PWC}}$ of their multivariate probability density function is obtained by using Parzen Gaussian Windows [75]. On the other hand, given the feature vector $\mathbf{o}_T$ of an input signature and a claimed identity $\mathcal{C}$ modeled as $\lambda_{\mathcal{C}}^{\mathrm{PWC}}$, the following similarity matching score is used

$$s_{\mathrm{PWC}} = p\left(\mathbf{o}_T | \lambda_{\mathcal{C}}^{\mathrm{PWC}}\right) \tag{10.2}$$

Function-Based Approach

This subsystem is based on earlier approaches [80, 61] and is further detailed in Fierrez and Ortega-Gracia [19].

Feature extraction. Signature trajectories are first preprocessed by subtracting the center of mass followed by a rotation alignment based on the average path tangent angle. The signature is then parameterized as the following set of 7 discrete-time functions $\{x[n], y[n], p[n], \theta[n], v[n], \rho[n], a[n]\}$, $n = 1, \ldots, N_s$, and the first-order time derivatives of all of them, totalling 14 discrete functions. The functions p, θ, v, ρ, and a denote, respectively, pressure, path tangent angle, path velocity magnitude, log curvature radius and total acceleration magnitude. A claim-dependent linear transformation is finally applied to each function so as to obtain zero mean and unit standard deviation values.

Similarity computation. Given the parameterized enrollment set of signatures of a client $\mathcal{C}$, a left-to-right Hidden Markov Model $\lambda_{\mathcal{C}}^{\mathrm{HMM}}$ is estimated [75]. No transition skips between states are allowed and multivariate Gaussian Mixture density observations are used. On the other hand, given the function-based representation $\mathbf{O}_T$ of a test signature (with a duration of N_s time samples) and a claimed identity $\mathcal{C}$ modeled as $\lambda_{\mathcal{C}}^{\mathrm{HMM}}$, the following similarity matching score is used

$$s_{\mathrm{HMM}} = \frac{1}{N_s} \log p\left(\mathbf{O}_T | \lambda_{\mathcal{C}}^{\mathrm{HMM}}\right) \tag{10.3}$$

The HMM system described above was submitted by the Biometric Recognition Group–ATVS to the First International Signature Verification Competition 2004 with very good results [81]. Considering not only position trajectories but also pressure signals, the proposed system was ranked first for random forgeries and second for skilled forgeries. The proposed system was only outperformed by the winner of the competition, which was based on a DTW approach [43]. Interestingly, it has been recently shown that the HMM approach outperforms an implementation of the DTW approach used by the winner when enough training signatures are available [22], which is also the case when comparing the HMM method to the feature-based approach described before. More comparative experiments with the function-based system can be found in Garcia-Salicetti et al. [27].

Database and Experimental Protocol

All the signatures of the MCYT database [60] are used for the experiments (330 signers with 25 genuine signatures and 25 skilled forgeries per signer). Two examples of genuine signatures (left and central columns) and one forgery (right column) are given in Fig. 10.6.

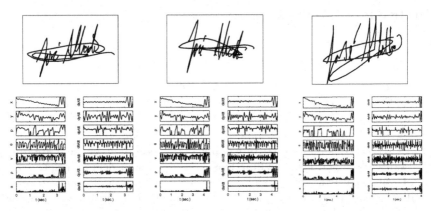

Two genuine signatures (left and central columns) and one skilled forgery (right column). A function-based representation is depicted below each signature.

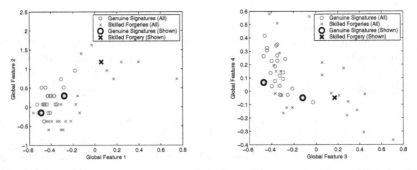

Best individually performing global features, i.e., 1st versus 2nd (left), and 3rd versus 4th (right), are depicted for all the signatures of the above user. Features from the genuine signatures and forgery shown above are highlighted.

Fig. 10.6. Signatures from MCYT corpus with extracted functions and features.

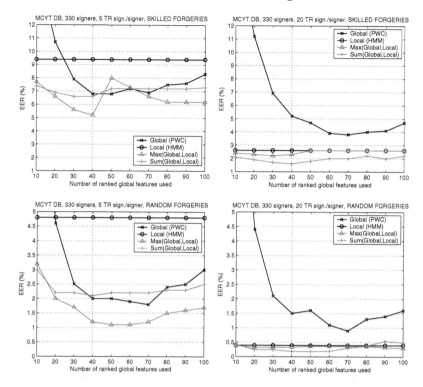

Fig. 10.7. Verification performance with user-independent decision thresholds for an increasing number of ranked global features.

The signature corpus is divided into training and test sets. In case of skilled forgeries, the training set comprises either 5 or 20 genuine signatures and the test set consist of the remaining samples (i.e., 330×20 or 330×5 client, respectively, and 330×25 impostor similarity test scores). In case of random forgeries (i.e., impostors are claiming someone else's identity using their own signatures), client similarity scores are as above and we use one signature of each of the remaining users as impostor data so the number of impostor similarity scores is 330×329.

Results

In Fig. 10.7, verification performance results in four common conditions (few/many training signatures and skilled/random forgeries) are given for: *i*) the feature-based system with an increasing number of ranked global features, *ii*) the function-based system, and *iii*) their combination through max and sum fusion rules [44].

The feature-based system outperforms the function-based approach when training with 5 signatures, and the opposite occurs when training with 20 signatures. The two systems are also shown to provide complementary information for the verification task, which is well exploited in the cases of small and large training set sizes using the max and sum rules respectively. Also interestingly, we have found a good working point of the combined system in the four conditions depicted in Fig. 10.7 when using the first 40 ranked features for the global approach. This is highlighted with a vertical dashed line.

10.5 Summary

This chapter started with some historical events related to signature verification, potential applications of this technology, examples of commercial systems, and some notes on the progress of standardization in on-line signature verification.

We then provided a brief review of the state-of-the-art in on-line signature verification, by outlining the main approaches to the following modules: data acquisition and preprocessing, feature extraction (feature- or function-based), enrollment (reference- or model-based), matching with or without pre-alignment, and score normalization. Based on this review, we conclude that the dominant approaches are based on global features with distance measures, or time functions either with statistical modeling (HMM) or elastic matching (DTW). We have also summarized some on-line signature databases such as MCYT or SVC, and we have provided a case study combining feature- and function-based approaches.

Alongside the review of the state-of-the-art, we have also pointed out some open problems in signature verification, such as the large behavioral differences between signers (which make especially appropriate the use of signer-specific features, models, or score mappings), or the signature variations in time (which may be overcome with multi-session training or template adaptation techniques). Other research directions include: multilevel recognition approaches, better understanding of the discriminative features against forgers and between different signers, understanding of the variability and complexity factors in signature, and their relation to verification performance.

Acknowledgements

This work has been supported by the Spanish projects TIC2003-08382-C05-01 and TEC2006-13141-C03-03, and by the European NoE Biosecure. The postdoctoral research of J. F. is supported by a Marie Curie Outgoing International Fellowship.

References

1. F. Alonso-Fernandez, J. Fierrez-Aguilar, H. Fronthaler, K. Kollreider, J. Ortega-Garcia, J. Gonzalez-Rodriguez, and J. Bigun. Combining multiple matchers for fingerprint verification: A case study in Biosecure Network of Excellence. *Annals of Telecommunications*, 62(1-2):62–82, 2007.

2. F. Alonso-Fernandez, J. Fierrez-Aguilar, J. Ortega-Garcia, and J. Gonzalez-Rodriguez. A web-based secure access system using signature verification over Tablet PC. *IEEE Aerospace and Electronic Systems Mag.*, 22:3–8, 2007.

3. ATVS. Biometric Recognition Group, 2006. (http://atvs.ii.uam.es/).

4. R. Baron and R. Plamondon. Acceleration measurement with an instrumented pen for signature verification and handwriting analysis. *IEEE Trans. on Instrum. Measurement*, 38(6):1132–1138, 1989.

5. E. S. Bigun, J. Bigun, B. Duc, and S. Fischer. Expert conciliation for multi modal person authentication systems by Bayesian statistics. In *Proc. of AVBPA*, pages 291–300. Springer LNCS-1206, 1997.

6. Biosecure, 2007. Biometrics for Secure Authentication, FP6 NoE IST-2002-507634. (http://www.biosecure.info/).

7. J. Brault and R. Plamondon. A complexity measure of handwritten curves: Modeling of dynamic signature forgery. *IEEE Trans. on SMC*, 23(2):400–413, 1993.

8. G. Chollet, G. Aversano, B. Dorizzi, and D. Petrovska-Delacretaz. The 1st Biosecure residential workshop. In *Proc. of ISPA*, pages 251–256. IEEE, 2005.

9. CIC. (http://www.cic.com/).

10. CYBERSIGN. (http://www.cybersign.com/).

11. J. G. A. Dolfing, E. H. L. Aarts, and J. J. G. M. van Oosterhout. On-line signature verification with Hidden Markov Models. In *Proc. of ICPR*, pages 1309–1312. IEEE CS Press, 1998.

12. B. Dumas, J. Hennebert, et al. MyIdea - Sensors specifications and acquisition protocol. Computer Science Department Research Report DIUF-RR 2005.01, University de Fribourg, Switzerland, January 2005.

13. M. Fairhurst and P. Brittan. An evaluation of parallel strategies for feature vector construction in automatic signature verification systems. *Intl. J. of Pattern Recog. and Art. Intell.*, 8(3):661–678, 1994.

14. M. Fairhurst, E. Kaplani, and R. Guest. Complexity measures in handwritten signature verification. In *Proc. 1st Int. Conf. on Universal Access in Human-Computer Interaction*, pages 305–309, 2001.

15. M. C. Fairhurst. Signature verification revisited: Promoting practical exploitation of biometric technology. *IEE Electronics and Communication Engineering Journal*, 9(6):273–280, 1997.

16. M. Faundez-Zanuy. On-line signature recognition based on VQ-DTW. *Pattern Recognition*, 40:981–992, 2007.

17. M. Faundez-Zanuy, J. Fierrez-Aguilar, J. Ortega-Garcia, and J. Gonzalez-Rodriguez. Multimodal biometric databases: An overview. *IEEE Aerospace and Electronic Systems Magazine*, 21(8):29–37, 2006.

18. J. Fierrez. The Biosecure multimodal biometric database. In *Biosecure Research Project Workshop*, Vigo, Spain, September 2005. (http://www.gts.tsc.uvigo.es/BioSecureWorkshop/).

19. J. Fierrez, J. Ortega-Garcia, D. Ramos, and J. Gonzalez-Rodriguez. Hmm-based on-line signature verification: Feature extraction and signature modeling. *Pattern Recognition Letters*, 2007. (to appear).

20. J. Fierrez-Aguilar. *Adapted Fusion Schemes for Multimodal Biometric Authentication*. PhD thesis, Universidad Politecnica de Madrid, 2006.

21. J. Fierrez-Aguilar, N. Alonso-Hermira, G. Moreno-Marquez, and J. Ortega-Garcia. An off-line signature verification system based on fusion of local and global information. In *Proc. BIOAW*, pages 295–306. Springer LNCS-3087, 2004.

22. J. Fierrez-Aguilar, S. Krawczyk, J. Ortega-Garcia, and A. K. Jain. Fusion of local and regional approaches for on-line signature verification. In *Proc. of IWBRS*, pages 188–196. Springer LNCS-3781, 2005.

23. J. Fierrez-Aguilar, L. Nanni, J. Lopez-Penalba, J. Ortega-Garcia, and D. Maltoni. An on-line signature verification system based on fusion of local and global information. In *Proc. of AVBPA*, pages 523–532. Springer LNCS-3546, 2005.

24. J. Fierrez-Aguilar, J. Ortega-Garcia, and J. Gonzalez-Rodriguez. Target dependent score normalization techniques and their application to signature verification. *IEEE Trans. on SMC-C*, 35(3):418–425, 2005.

25. M. Freire-Santos, J. Fierrez-Aguilar, and J. Ortega-Garcia. Cryptographic key generation using handwritten signature. In *Proc. of SPIE*, volume 6202, pages 225–231, 2006.

26. S. Garcia-Salicetti et al. BIOMET: A multimodal person authentication database including face, voice, fingerprint, hand and signature modalities. In *Proc. of AVBPA*, pages 845–853. Springer LNCS-2688, 2003.

27. S. Garcia-Salicetti, J. Fierrez-Aguilar, F. Alonso-Fernandez, C. Vielhauer, R. Guest, L. Allano, T. Doan Trung, T. Scheidat, B. Ly Van, J. Dittmann, B. Dorizzi, J. Ortega-Garcia, J. Gonzalez-Rodriguez, and M. Bacile di Castiglione. Biosecure reference systems for on-line signature verification: A study of complementarity. *Annals of Telecommunications*, 62(1-2):36–61, 2007.

28. J. Gonzalez-Rodriguez, J. Fierrez-Aguilar, D. Ramos-Castro, and J. Ortega-Garcia. Bayesian analysis of fingerprint, face and signature evidences with automatic biometric systems. *Forensic Science Intl.*, 155(2-3):126–140, 2005.

29. G. Gupta and R. Joyce. A study of some pen motion features in dynamic handritten signature verification. Technical report, Dept. of Computer Science, James Cook University, Townsville, Australia, 1997.

30. N. Herbst and C. Liu. Automatic signature verification based on accelerometry. *IBM J. Res. Dev.*, pages 245–253, 1977.

31. O. Hilton. Signatures - review and a new view. *J. of Forensic Sciences*, 37(1):125–129, 1992.

32. Y. Hongo, D. Muramatsu, and T. Matsumoto. Adaboost-based on-line signature verifier. In *Proc. of SPIE*, volume 5779, pages 373–380, 2005.

33. C. Hook, J. Kempf, and G. Scharfenberg. A novel digitizing pen for the analysis of pen pressure and inclination in handwriting biometrics. In *Proc. of BIOAW*, pages 283–294. Springer LNCS-3087, 2004.

34. ID-House. (http://www.idhouse.com/mmperiph.htm).

35. J. Igarza, L. Gomez, I. Hernaez, and I. Goirizelaia. Searching for an optimal reference system for on-line signature verification based on (x,y) alignment. In *Proc. of ICBA*, pages 519–525. Springer LNCS-3072, 2004.

36. J. J. Igarza, I. Hernaez, I. Goirizelaia, K. Espinosa, and J. Escolar. Off-line signature recognition based on dynamic methods. In *Proc. of SPIE*, volume 5779, pages 336–343, 2005.

37. International Biometric Group. Biometrics market and industry report 2006-2010. (http://www.biometricgroup.com/).
38. A. K. Jain, F. D. Griess, and S. D. Connell. On-line signature verification. *Pattern Recognition*, 35(12):2963–2972, 2002.
39. A. K. Jain, K. Nandakumar, and A. Ross. Score normalization in multimodal biometric systems. *Pattern Recognition*, 38:2270–2285, 2005.
40. A. K. Jain and D. Zongker. Feature selection: Evaluation, application, and small sample performance. *IEEE Trans. on PAMI*, 19(2):153–158, 1997.
41. R. S. Kashi, J. Hu, W. L. Nelson, and W. Turin. On-line handwritten signature verification using Hidden Markov Model features. In *Proc. of ICDAR*, volume 1, pages 253–257. IEEE CS Press, 1997.
42. H. Ketabdar, J. Richiardi, and A. Drygajlo. Global feature selection for on-line signature verification. In *Proc. of 12th International Graphonomics Society Conference*, 2005.
43. A. Kholmatov and B. Yanikoglu. Identity authentication using improved online signature verification method. *Pattern Recog. Letters*, 26(15):2400–2408, 2005.
44. J. Kittler, M. Hatef, R. Duin, and J. Matas. On combining classifiers. *IEEE Trans. on PAMI*, 20(3):226–239, 1998.
45. F. Leclerc and R. Plamondon. Automatic signature verification: The state of the art, 1989–1993. *Intl. Jour. of Pattern Rec. and Artificial Intell.*, 8(3):643–660, 1994.
46. L. Lee. *On-Line Systems for Human Signature Verification*. PhD thesis, Cornell University, 1992.
47. L. L. Lee, T. Berger, and E. Aviczer. Reliable on-line human signature verification systems. *IEEE Trans. on PAMI*, 18(6):643–647, 1996.
48. H. Lei and V. Govindaraju. A comparative study on the consistency of features in on-line signature verification. *Pattern Recog. Letters*, 26(15):2483–2489, 2005.
49. B. Li, D. Zhang, and K. Wang. On-line signature verification based on NCA (Null Component Analysis) and PCA (Principal Component Analysis). *Pattern Analysis and Application*, 8:345–356, 2006.
50. A. Mauceri. Feasibility studies of personal identification by signature verification. Technical Report SID 65 24 RADC TR 65 33, Space and Information System Division, American Aviation Co, Anaheim, California, 1965.
51. M. E. Munich and P. Perona. Visual identification by signature tracking. *IEEE Trans. on PAMI*, 25(2):200–217, 2003.
52. D. Muramatsu, M. Kondo, M. Sasaki, S. Tachibana, and T. Matsumoto. A Markov chain Monte Carlo algorithm for Bayesian dynamic signature verification. *IEEE Trans. on IFS*, 1(1):22–34, 2006.
53. V. S. Nalwa. Automatic on-line signature verification. *Proc. of the IEEE*, 85(2):215–239, 1997.
54. L. Nanni and A. Lumini. Advanced methods for two-class problem formulation for on-line signature verification. *Neurocomputing*, 69:854–857, 2006.
55. E.-M. Nel, J. A. du Preez, and B. M. Herbst. Estimating the pen trajectories of static signatures using hidden markov models. *IEEE Trans. on PAMI*, 27(11):1733–1743, 2005.
56. W. Nelson and E. Kishon. Use of dynamic features for signature verification. In *Proc. of the IEEE Intl. Conf. on Systems, Man, and Cybernetics*, volume 1, pages 201–205, 1991.
57. W. Nelson, W. Turin, and T. Hastie. Statistical methods for on-line signature verification. *Intl. J. of Pattern Recog. and Artif. Intell.*, 8(3):749–770, 1994.

58. NIST. (http://www.itl.nist.gov/iad/894.03/fing/fing.html).
59. J. Ortega-Garcia, J. Bigun, D. Reynolds, and J. Gonzalez-Rodriguez. Authentication gets personal with biometrics. *IEEE Signal Processing Magazine*, 21(2):50–62, 2004.
60. J. Ortega-Garcia, J. Fierrez-Aguilar, et al. MCYT baseline corpus: a bimodal biometric database. *IEE Proc. Vision, Image and Signal Processing*, 150(6):391–401, 2003.
61. J. Ortega-Garcia, J. Fierrez-Aguilar, J. Martin-Rello, and J. Gonzalez-Rodriguez. Complete signal modeling and score normalization for function-based dynamic signature verification. In *Proc. of AVBPA*, pages 658–667. Springer LNCS-2688, 2003.
62. A. Osborn. *Questioned Documents*. Boyd Printing Co, Albany, NY, 1929.
63. A. Pacut and A. Czajka. Recognition of human signatures. In *Proc. of IJCNN*, volume 2, pages 1560–1564, 2001.
64. J. M. Pascual and V. Cardenoso. Automatic on-line signature verification based on HMMs with user dependent structure. Technical Report IT-DI-2006-1, Dept. of Computer Science, Universidad de Valladolid, Valladolid, Spain, 2006.
65. R. Phelps. A holistic approach to signature verification. In *Proc. of ICPR*, page 1187, 1982.
66. R. Plamondon and G. Lorette. Automatic signature verification and writer identification: The state of the art. *Pattern Recognition*, 22(2):107–131, 1989.
67. R. Plamondon and S. N. Srihari. On-line and off-line handwriting recognition: A comprehensive survey. *IEEE Trans. PAMI*, 22(1):63–84, 2000.
68. M. Rejman-Greene. *Biometric Systems: Technology, Design and Performance Evaluation*, chapter Privacy Issues in the Application of Biometrics: A European Perspective, pages 335–359. Springer, 2005.
69. J. Richiardi and A. Drygajlo. Gaussian Mixture Models for on-line signature verification. In *Proc. of ACM SIGMM Workshop on Biometric Methods and Applications*, pages 115–122, 2003.
70. A. Ross, K. Nandakumar, and A. K. Jain. *Handbook of Multibiometrics*. Springer, 2006.
71. D. Sakamoto, H. Morita, T. Ohishi, Y. Komiya, and T. Matsumoto. On-line signature verification algorithm incorporating pen position, pen pressure and pen inclination. In *Proc. of ICASSP*, volume 2, pages 993–996, 2001.
72. SC37, 2005. ISO/IEC JTC 1/SC 37. (http://www.jtc1.org/sc37/).
73. SOFTPRO. (http://www.signplus.com/).
74. SVC. (http://www.cs.ust.hk/svc2004/).
75. S. Theodoridis and K. Koutroumbas. *Pattern Recognition*. Academic Press, 2003.
76. C. M. Travieso, J. B. Alonso, and M. A. Ferrer. Off-line geometric parameters for automatic signature verification using fixed point arithmetic. *IEEE Trans. on PAMI*, 27(8):993–997, 2005.
77. U. Uludag, A. Ross, and A. K. Jain. Biometric template selection and update: A case study in fingerprints. *Pattern Recognition*, 37(7):1533–1542, 2004.
78. B. Ly Van, S. Garcia-Salicetti, and B. Dorizzi. Fusion of HMM's likelihood and Viterbi path for on-line signature verification. In *Proc. of BIOAW*, pages 318–331. Springer LNCS-3087, 2004.
79. WACOM. (http://www.wacom.com/).
80. L. Yang, B. K. Widjaja, and R. Prasad. Application of Hidden Markov Models for signature verification. *Pattern Recognition*, 28(2):161–170, 1995.

81. D. Y. Yeung, H. Chang, Y. Xiong, S. George, R. Kashi, T. Matsumoto, and G. Rigoll. SVC2004: First International Signature Verification Competition. In *Proc. of ICBA*, pages 16–22. Springer LNCS-3072, 2004.

3D Face Recognition

Patrick J. Flynn, Timothy Faltemier, and Kevin W. Bowyer

Department of Computer Science and Engineering, University of Notre Dame, Notre Dame, Indiana, USA
flynn@nd.edu, tfaltemi@cse.nd.edu, kwb@cse.nd.edu

11.1 Introduction

The use of face appearance (photometry) for biometric recognition has been popular with researchers for many years. Some systems have successfully made the transition from the research laboratory to the commercial sector. However, it is possible to degrade the performance of such 2D face recognition systems through environmental changes such as lighting variations (*e.g.*, high contrast shadows on the face), nonfrontal face pose, and other contaminating actions. Moreover, a 2D face image is a measurement of both the face geometry (shape), the albedo and pigmentation of the skin, and its embedding in the sensing environment with illuminator positions as well as spatial and spectral characteristics.

It can be argued that biometric recognition should employ measurements that are purely subject-intrinsic, avoiding incorporation of other contaminating inputs and the effects of imaging system transformations as much as possible. This argument has motivated the use of 3D images of the face (as well as other body sites such as the ear) for biometric matching. However, 3D images of objects differ from their 2D counterparts. The units of measurement are different, being physical positions rather than photometric measurements (the physical measurements may be calculated from photometric measurements, however). The sources of noise and other contamination are different and also sensor-dependent. One must employ different low-level image processing operators to improve image quality and extract meaningful features for matching.

The amount of research on 3D face recognition has been sufficient to yield prior survey papers [18], and the emergence of commercial systems (sensors plus matchers) for 3D face recognition has prompted interest in government-sponsored evaluations of these methods for assessment of technology prior to procurement [25]. Many research groups are continuing to focus their efforts on 3D face recognition, which should yield additional novel techniques and opportunities for principled comparison in the future.

This chapter describes technologies for 3D sensing that are or may be applicable for face image acquisition, discusses some typical low-level processing necessary for images produced by current sensors, and surveys the work of many research groups in the area as well as results from a recent US Government evaluation of 3D face recognition technology. We conclude the chapter by noting some key issues that should be addressed prior to wider deployment of 3D face recognition technology in applications.

11.2 3D Sensors and Data for Face Recognition

The researcher interested in 3D face recognition has a variety of potential data sources available. While 3D sensors have been in existence for decades, they are often more expensive, slower to produce images, or their outputs have greater contamination than typical 2D (photometric) sensors. A broad understanding of the issues involved in 3D sensing should guide the choice of a sensing technology. A comprehensive survey and comparison of 3D sensing is beyond the scope of this chapter (such surveys and comparisons do exist, *e.g.,* [17, 9]). We will simply note some of the key classes of 3D sensors that have been developed for or applied to face sensing for biometric matching.

- **Active structured lighting** – This class of sensor obtains 3D data by processing one or more images, typically acquired from a single camera, of the 3D object of interest as illuminated by a light pattern such as a stripe, grid, or coded field. Calibration of the sensor involves determination of the transformation relating coordinates in the light pattern with coordinates in the camera's field of view. A simple example, employed in several sensors, is point ranging, where a laser projector emits a fixed beam, which intersects the object to be sensed, and the intersection point is imaged in a camera. Knowledge of the angles between the laser beam axis and the camera's optical axis, along with the baseline distance between camera and laser, allows the range to be determined. Extension of this to the problem of extracting range along a stripe produced by a line projector is straightforward. Accurate determination of the angles involved can be difficult but fixturing and calibration are typically used.

  Point and stripe ranging are the simplest examples of structured light sensors since solution of the correspondence problem is trivial (the position of a point is unique, and position along a stripe can be controlled by fixturing). However, assembly of an image from individual point measurements or profiles requires the processing of multiple frames, which can be time-consuming. More complex structured light (*e.g.,* grid-structured patterns, multi-point patterns, or multi-stripe patterns) allow range to be determined at more positions in a single image, but the correspondence problem is more difficult. The ranging technique must know which point in a multi-point pattern or which stripe in a multi-stripe image is being used in triangulation. An incorrect decision distorts the estimated measurement, often significantly. Solutions to the correspondence problem have employed coded patterns of various sorts, including color coding and Gray coding across multiple frames [6, 28].

Application of structured light to 3D imaging of the face introduces some constraints on sensors. The active illumination must be eye-safe in terms of power, and ideally would be invisible to avoid discomfort for subjects. Acquisition should be rapid to minimize contamination due to subject motion; ideally, it should be a snapshot. Figure 11.1 shows an image taken by the Minolta Vivid 910 scanner[1] when the subject moves during scanning.

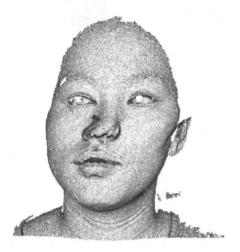

Fig. 11.1. A face image containing distortion due to subject movement during acquisition.

Figure 11.2 contains a photograph of a Minolta 910 structured light range scanner (which has been used in extensive data collection projects at several universities) and an example of the 3D imagery produced by the sensor.

The FRGC 2.0 database [24], discussed in detail in another chapter in this volume, is a large database of 2D and 3D face images used in the US Government's Face Recognition Grand Challenge program. 4,960 of the images in the FRGC 2.0 corpus are 3D face scans captured by a Minolta 910 scanner. This database has been distributed to over 100 research groups worldwide and a large fraction of the published work in 3D face recognition employs this database.

- **Passive and Assisted Stereo imaging** – Stereo imaging is the task of obtaining three-dimensional measurements from a multiple camera rig.

---

[1] http://www.minolta3d.com

 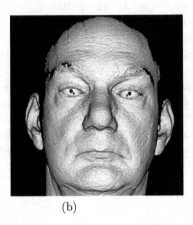

(a)   (b)

Fig. 11.2. Structured light range scanner. (a): Minolta 910 scanner. (b) 3D image of the third author from the Minolta scanner. The 3D data is rendered as a shaded mesh.

Different assumptions about the type of reconstruction desired (*e.g.*, metric reconstruction, reconstruction up to a projective factor, *etc.*), the number and types of cameras available, and the type of calibration performed can yield different imaging techniques. The key task for a stereo reconstruction algorithm is solving the correspondence problem; that is, finding pixels in each camera's raster that are images of the same point in 3D. Epipolar constraints limit the search for correspondences to a line in a 2-camera rig (see, *e.g.*, [14]). The search should have a reject option since some points seen by one camera cannot be seen by the other camera(s). Since sensed reflectance is a function of view angle as well as surface material and incident illumination, it is common to base the correspondence search on a local match of intensity variation using measures akin to correlation; this implies that matches cannot be determined for "featureless" surfaces. However, "assisted" stereo imaging, in which a texture pattern is projected onto the surface during stereo sensing, can accelerate the matching process. Application of passive stereo imaging to 3D face image acquisition is straightforward, provided the correspondence problem can be addressed. The typical human face has a reasonable amount of visual texture, providing a basis for local matching in correspondence search. There are commercial sensors that employ texture projectors to allow assisted stereo sensing of the face [1]. Figure 11.3 contains a picture of a texture-assisted stereo face imaging system sold by 3DMD, along with a shaded mesh rendering of an image of the third author acquired with that sensor.

The format of data produced by a 3D face sensor may depend on the technology used to obtain an image. Structured light sensors that employ a linear pattern generally assemble the profiles into a raster-plus-flag structure,

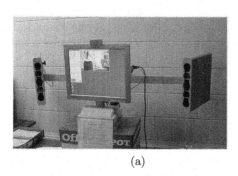
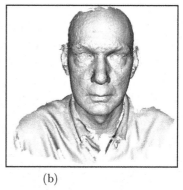

(a)   (b)

Fig. 11.3. Texture-assisted stereo camera developed by 3DMD. (a): the sensor (each of the two arms ends in a stereo rig with a texture projector; software registers the two partial face images along the midline). (b) an image of the third author from the 3DMD sensor.

where each pixel in the raster has a Boolean flag that denotes validity of the measurement and, if the flag is true, the 3D coordinates of the scene point. Thus:

$$\mathcal{R} = \{p_{ij}, i = 1, \dots N_r, j = 1, \dots N_c\},$$

where N_r and N_c are the number of rows and columns, respectively,

$$p_{ij} = (f_{ij}; x_{ij}, y_{ij}, z_{ij}[; r_{ij}, g_{ij}, b_{ij}]),$$

f_{ij} is TRUE if the range data (x_{ij}, y_{ij}, z_{ij}) is valid, and FALSE otherwise. It is not uncommon for raster-structured range scanners to measure color (r_{ij}, g_{ij}, b_{ij}) at each pixel also.

There are structured-light profilers that allow the line orientation to be modified between scans (*e.g.*, the FastSCAN sensor from Polhemus [26]); such scanners may not produce a raster-structured image output. Such scanners, as well as stereo cameras, would typically produce a cloud of 3D points, perhaps with an accompanying texture map and perhaps including a 3D mesh connecting the points, as their output:

$$\mathcal{R} = \{p_i, i = 1, \dots N_p\}, \text{ where}$$

$$p_i = (x_i, y_i, z_i[; r_i, g_i, b_i]),$$

$$\mathcal{M} = \{e_j, j = 1, \dots N_e\}$$

denotes the mesh in terms of an edge list, and

$$e_j = (i_{j_1}, i_{j_2})$$

denotes an edge existing between points p_{i_1} and p_{i_2}. Meshes can be constructed on point cloud data through a variety of procedures.

Figure 11.4 shows close-ups of the nose area of the images in Figures 11.2 and 11.3. The sampling resolution of the assisted stereo sensor is somewhat coarser than that of the structured light sensor. This is due to the resolution of the optical pattern projected on the object to assist the stereo correspondence search.

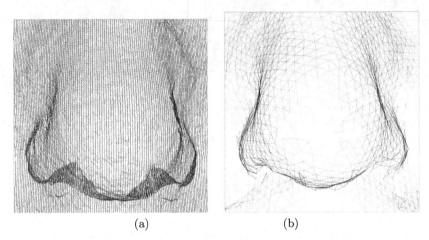

(a)   (b)

Fig. 11.4. Sampling and resolution of structured light and assisted-stereo cameras. (a): Close-up of the nose region in Figure 11.2(a). (b): Close-up of the nose region in Figure 11.3.

11.3 3D Face Image Processing

Regardless of the approach to face matching (global, local, or 'hybrid'), many of the 3D face recognition systems employed in the literature employ some *ad hoc* post-acquisition image processing to reduce noise, remove holes, and improve the quality of the data produced by the range imaging sensor. While the techniques vary widely from system to system, it is common to see some of the following general processing operations:

- **Mesh repair** – Any structured-light range scanner that generates a raster structured output will generate images with "missing" pixels from time to time. These invalid pixels should be ignored and treated as holes if the data is interpreted as a polygonal mesh interpolating the valid range data. Small holes in the mesh are relatively easy to fill; local averaging can produce (x, y, z) estimates at the missing location. Larger holes can be filled by 'nibbling' away the invalid pixels one at a time by averaging, or through fitting a surface to the hole area using available data as constraints, followed by resampling within the hole.

- **Smoothing** – The smoothing operation is designed to suppress random noise arising from the sensor. Different sensors can exhibit different types of noise. It is usually an oversimplification to assume that the noise contamination is zero-mean, normally distributed, and affecting the z coordinate (the gaze direction) exclusively. Hence, smoothers such as mean filters designed to match that sort of noise may not achieve the desired results. For example, range scanners that employ lasers can generate data contaminated by laser speckle. Imaging of concavities can generate significant range excursions due to complex light reflections (including multipath effects) within those concavities. This frequently happens at the eyes in 3D face imaging with laser scanners, as the incident illumination is reflected into the eyeball through the lens, emerges again, and is detected. Stereo scanners and those projected-light sensors that employ patterns can also suffer miscorrespondences, wherein two scene points in a stereo pair are mistakenly corresponded, or the coordinates of a position on the projected pattern are poorly estimated. Such correspondence errors also yield gross errors in position estimates. Median filtering of the local neighborhood can often suppress the worst of these errors, provided that these errors do not affect several neighboring pixels. Linear smoothing of the result can help to suppress the contouring produced by median operator.
- **Local feature extraction** – Local shape descriptors can be useful in the detection of face features that can be used subsequently in matching or registration. For example, Chang et al. [8] computed curvature on the face range image to detect candidate points for the nose tip and the saddle formed by the nose bridge and the interocular curve. Surface curvature can be calculated in range data using a variety of techniques; one simple method fits a small curved patch $f(x,y)$ (bi-quadratic or bi-cubic) to the range data in the neighborhood of each point of interest, and computes the mean and Gaussian curvatures (denoted $H(x,y)$ and $K(x,y)$, respectively) by analytic differentiation of the fitted surface f:

$$H(x,y) = \frac{(1+f_y^2)f_{xx} - 2f_xf_yf_{xy} + (1+f_x^2)f_{yy}}{1(1+f_x^2+f_y^2)^{\frac{3}{2}}}$$

$$K(x,y) = \frac{f_{xx}f_{yy} - f_{xy}^2}{(1+f_x^2+f_y^2)^2}.$$

As noted by Besl[4] and others, the signs of $H(x,y)$ and $K(x,y)$ allow the surface type to be classified; a nose is typically classified as a peak, the nose bridge/interocular curve intersection as a saddle point, and the eye areas near the tear ducts as pits. Figure 11.5 shows the labeled face regions obtained from curvature signs for a range image of the third author. Red areas were classified as peaks, black areas were classified as pits, and light blue areas were classified as saddles.

Surface normals can also be calculated at range pixels by fitting a local planar patch $f(x,y)$ to the neighborhood of a pixel of interest and returning

Fig. 11.5. Curvature-sign based labeling of pixels in a 3D image of a face.

its normal vector $n(x, y)$:

$$f(x, y) = z = ax + by + c$$

$$n(x, y) = \frac{(-a, -b, 1)}{(1 + a^2 + b^2)^{1/2}}$$

As noted above, many 3D sensors provide a color image along with the 3D shape data if they employ color cameras in the depth extraction process. This has led to a number of techniques for *multimodal* recognition of faces using 2D (color) and 3D information gathered from the camera. While a detailed discussion of such techniques is outside the scope of this chapter, we note that intensity face recognition techniques may also require preprocessing of the input color image using techniques such as normalization, smoothing, and resampling.

11.4 Representations and Features for 3D Face Recognition

Techniques for 3D face recognition in the literature employ a broad range of face descriptors to use in the matching step. Some descriptors amount to a *complete* representation, in that the original face shape can be recovered (perhaps approximately) from the representation (*e.g.*, a principal components representation). Others are *incomplete* since they cannot yield such a reconstruction, but these can offer other benefits (*e.g.*, robustness to occlusion). This section provides an overview of some selected techniques.

11.4.1 Subspace and other transform models

Principal Component Analysis (PCA) and Linear Discriminant Analysis (LDA) are two members of a family of *subspace representations* for arbitrary multivariate data. Such techniques work by computing a set of basis vectors for the observation space defined by 'unraveling' geometrically normalized training image data into multidimensional points (one point per training image). The various techniques differ in the way the new basis vectors are extracted. In PCA, the basis vectors are eigenvectors of the sample covariance matrix of the training data. If 're-raveled' into an image form, they can be displayed as face-like images commonly called 'eigenfaces'. Since they are all orthogonal and unit length, they can be assembled into a linear transformation that operationally imposes a rotation (called the *varimax rotation* in statistical literature) on the original data. The sample covariance matrix of the rotated training data is diagonal. Thus, the PCA basis, viewed as a transform, describes the image as a linear combination of eigenfaces. Each basis image has an associated eigenvalue that measures the sample variance of the training data along the corresponding coordinate in the face space. It is common to discard face space coordinates associated with eigenfaces that are arbitrary due to rank-deficiency of the covariance matrix as well as those with small eigenvalues. This yields an effective data compression technique that maximizes variance retained.

By contrast, LDA's basis vector set is the set of eigenvectors of $S_w^{-1}S_b$, where S_w is the within-class scatter matrix and S_b is the between-class scatter matrix. Thus, LDA requires labeled training data and defines a linear transform that attempts to minimize within-class spread and maximize between-class spread. A practical problem in LDA computations is the inversion of S_w, which is usually not full rank.

While popularized in the context of 2D face recognition, the depth coordinate of a 3D face scan can be interpreted as a brightness value and used as the basis for matching using PCA and/or LDA. This idea has been used and evaluated by Hesher *et al.* [16], Tsalakanidou *et al.* [12], Chang *et al.* [7, 8] and Gokberk [3].

Nonlinear face transformations have also been employed in 3D face recognition. Bronstein *et al.* [2] developed a face representation designed to be robust to isometric transformations of the face, assumed to include facial expression variations. An input face image is transformed to a canonical form using an iterative approximate multidimensional scaling technique employing a geodesic distance map computed from facial feature points.

11.4.2 Global and Local Point set models

The Iterative Closest Point (ICP) algorithm, originally published by Besl and McKay [5], is a well-known closely examined technique for data set registration that can be applied to any data dimensionality. It processes two data sets: the *data shape* to which a transform is applied, and the *model shape* to which the transformed data shape is progressively aligned. A key assumption of ICP (not always valid in some uses) is that the data shape is a "subset" of the model shape, in that it will, if successfully transformed, be aligned with a portion of the model shape. The ICP concept is easily applied to face recognition using 3D data; systems that employ this technique are noted below. All such systems employ a sampling of 3D points from the input range data and a sampling from each model face as the basis for matching.

Some recent work [30, 8] has employed multiple local point set models as the basis for matching. Robustness to facial expression variation motivates this idea. If a region of the face is both distinctive in shape and invariant to facial expression change, it can be used in matching.

11.4.3 Deformation models

Lu and Jain [20] developed a deformation-modeling technique that is used in conjunction with ICP-based alignment to match 3D faces in the presence of expression variation. This method expresses a face configuration (possibly including expression-based deformation) using a subject-specific 3D face mesh captured with a neutral expression plus the locations of control points whose positions are sensitive to expression. Control points are matched between different images and used to deform the neutral mesh to match. In addition, control point locations are used to estimate a rigid head pose transform.

Passalis *et al.* [23] developed a deformable model for face representation. The model architecture is based on a 2D parametrization of the face surface. A particular point on the face is indexed through a particular pair of parametric coordinates (u, v). At specified locations on the face, 3D geometry as well as other surface attributes are associated, forming 'control points'. Subdivision algorithms can then be applied to obtain the attribute values at locations not corresponding to control points; this yields an effective multiresolution representation of the shape. Once the 2D domain is established and key data corresponded to the domain, a wavelet transform is used to generate a signature for the encoded data and used in matching.

11.4.4 Feature Detectors

It is sometimes useful to automatically detect key points on the face for registration. Sometimes, these points correspond to anatomical features and can be described using anthropometric labels (*e.g.*, [11]); often, the term 'landmark' is used for such points. In the 3D context, landmarks that are distinctive in terms of local shape (as opposed to photometry) are most useful for registration or matching. The automatic detection of landmarks in 3D face images has received focused attention in recent years (*e.g.*, [29, 10, 27]). Generally, feature detectors employ local analysis (*e.g.*, curvature estimation and surface patch classification or shape index thresholding). An alternative method not dependent on global processing (and subject to its noise sensitivity) might involve critical point analysis of an approximating surface fit to the face data. To the authors' knowledge, a comparison between such methods has not been performed as of the time of this writing.

It is easily shown that three non-collinear 3D landmarks determine the pose of the face if it is assumed to be rigid; hence, a viable alignment technique would involve detection of three landmarks and estimating a rigid transformation to correspond them to a canonical face model containing compatible landmark points. In general, the pose transformation would need to include an affine component to account for distortions in the corresponding triangular configurations arising from face size, individual face feature positions, and the accuracy of landmark localization. The degree of nonrigidity might in itself be useful as a matching score for 3D face recognition.

Lu and Jain [19] propose a method of feature extraction based on a directional maximum in a 3D image. A nose profile is represented by different subspaces and a nearest neighbor approach is used to select the best candidates for the nose tip. Of the nose candidates, the point that best fits the statistical feature location model (i.e. the nose should be below the eyes and above the mouth) is selected as the final nose tip. This information is used to bootstrap the location of additional feature points (eyes and mouth corners) and is then used to align each image to a standard model for automatic 3D face recognition in images with large pose variation. Faltemier *et al.* [30] identify a candidate nose region using curvature estimation (the nose tip is robustly classified as a 'cap' shape), and refine the nose tip position using a generic nose model which is aligned to the data using ICP.

11.5 Recognition

A recent broad survey of face recognition research is given by Zhao et al. [32] and a survey focusing specifically on face recognition using 3D data is given in Bowyer et al. [18]. This section identifies several recent works which are representative of current and emerging themes in this research area.

11.5.1 Indexing: Rapid Rejection of Candidates

The issue of scalability is assuming greater importance as face recognition systems begin to be used in application domains. Indexing is a commonly used term for a 'pre-recognition screening' step that rapidly discards gallery models which (based on simple tests) cannot match the probe model. In the area of 3D face recognition, indexing has been addressed in a small number of papers.

Mian *et al.* [21] developed a 3D face recognition system intended to handle expression variations. This system employs an indexing step intended to efficiently reject face models that are poor matches to the probe image. This 'rejection classifier' employs a spherical face representation, which is a radially indexed histogram containing range pixel counts as a function of distance from an automatically detected nose tip. This histogram is precomputed for each model face and can be easily computed for a probe face to be classified.

Design parameters include the number of bins and the corresponding radius quantization values. The technique would seem to depend strongly on very accurate location of the nose tip.

11.5.2 Matching via Alignment

As noted earlier, a number of works in 3D face recognition employ ICP or one of its many variants for matching. The inputs to a typical one-to-one ICP implementation for 3D face matching include a data shape (typically a point set obtained from the probe image, usually by sampling and a model shape (fixed in position), to which the data shape is registered by application of a rigid transform. This transform typically includes three rotational degrees of freedom and three translational degrees of freedom. It is common for the gallery and probe sets to be translated so that their centroids are at the origin before ICP iterations commence. At each iteration, two major steps are executed.

1. The first step is the nearest-neighbor search, wherein the closest model shape point to each data shape point is determined. This step's time complexity is $O(mn)$ for an m-point model shape and an n-point data shape, if linear search is used; special data structures (e.g., the k-D tree [13] or a volumetric index storage [15, 34]), can reduce the complexity of the search at the cost of additional up-front computation and/or memory storage.
2. The second step is the estimation of a rigid transform for the data shape to best align it with the model shape, based on the correspondences found in step 1. Assuming a large number of point correspondences is present, a least-squares estimate is easily computed.

After step 2 is calculated, a suitable distance value (e.g., RMS distance) is computed over the corresponding points. This is usually interpreted as the quality of the match, where smaller is better. These two steps are repeated until a termination criterion (generally involving an upper limit on the number of iteration steps, a low threshold on the distance value, or a low threshold on the change in distance between subsequent iterations) is met. ICP can become trapped in local minima. To reduce this likelihood, multiple ICP runs can be performed. Alternatively, a high-quality initial estimate of the rotation (i.e., pre-alignment of the data shape) can reduce the likelihood of convergence to nonglobal optima of the distance function.

Lu et al. [33] used the iterative closest point (ICP) algorithm to align 3D meshes containing face geometry, as a component of a 2D/3D face recognition system. Their surface matching algorithm computes an initial coarse registration transform based on facial feature point locations. Iterative adjustment employs a variant of ICP that employs both point set alignment and surface mesh alignment at each iteration. Once this process is run, the ICP algorithm reports an average root-mean-square distance that represents the separation between the gallery and probe meshes. The performance of the overall system included performance figures for the 3D module alone, the 2D module alone, and the combination of these modules. A database containing about 600 range scans was used in testing, and the 3D module's rank-1-correct recognition rate was 86%. Fusion of the 3D system's output with that of the 2D module yielded a rank-1 accuracy of 90%. In a verification scenario at a fixed false accept rate of 0.001, the correct identification rate was 0.85 for an image database containing only neutral expressions and 0.6 for the entire database. The authors report that nearly all of the errors in recognition with the full database were caused by a change in expression between the probe and the gallery images.

Maurer et al. [31] created an algorithm that uses fusion of 2D and 3D face data for multimodal face recognition. Their algorithm first cleans each mesh, extracts relevant face data, and then performs ICP on the 3D set to generate a distance map between the two aligned meshes which allows a score to be generated from the results. The 2D component of their algorithm uses the recognition system created by Neven Vision and fuses the results with those of the 3D matcher based on the quality of each match. If the 3D match was very good, then the match is considered correct and the 2D score is not used. If this is not the case, then the results are fused together to return a combined score. They report results on their 3D algorithm, as well as reporting the 2D component's contribution to the 3D performance. They achieved an 87.0% verification rate at a false accept rate of 0.1% using 3D face information and matching all 4007 images in the FRGC v2.0 data set [22] vs. all 4007 images regardless of expression.

Chang et al. [8] use multiple overlapping nose regions and obtain increased performance relative to using one whole-frontal-face region. These nose regions include a nose circle, nose ellipse, and a region composed of just the nose itself. This method uses the ICP algorithm to perform image matching and reports results on a superset of the FRGC v2 data set containing 4,485 3D face images. 2D skin detection is performed for automated removal of hair and other non-skin based artifacts on the 3D scan. They report results of 97.1% rank one recognition on a neutral gallery matched to neutral probes and 87.1% rank one recognition on nonneutral probes matched to a neutral gallery. The product fusion metric was used to process the results from multiple regions. When the neutral gallery was matched to the neutral probe set, maximum performance was reported when only two of the three regions were combined. The authors mention that increased performance may be gained by using additional regions, but did not explore anything beyond three overlapping nose regions.

11.5.3 Matching Deformable Models

Lu et al. [20] present an algorithm for matching 2.5D scans in the presence of expressions and pose variation using deformable face models. A small control set is used to synthesize a unique deformation template for a desired expression class (smile, surprise, etc.). A thin-plate-spline (TPS) mapping technique drives the deformation process. The deformation template is then applied to a neutral gallery image to generate a subject specific 3D deformation model. The model is then matched to a given test scan using the ICP algorithm. The authors report results on three different types of experiments. The first data set contains 10 subjects with 3 different poses and seven different expressions. Rank one results of 92.1% are reported when deformation modeling is used compared to 87.6% when it is not. The second data set consists of 90 subjects in the gallery and 533 2.5D test scans and similar results are reported. Data for the first two experiments was gathered at the authors' institution. The data for the final experiment was taken from the FRGC v2 [22] data set and consisted of 50 randomly chosen subjects in the gallery and 150 2.5D test scans. When deformation modeling is employed, a rank one recognition rate of 97% is reported (81% was achieved without deformation modeling).

Passalis *et al.* [23] used an annotated face model (AFM) discussed above to represent a face. The processing yielded a wavelet-based face signature. The signature is matched to other signatures by taking the sum of the distances between each annotated point in the probe template and its corresponding point in the gallery template. They reported a 89.5% rank one recognition rate using the FRGC2.0 data set's 3D imagery, with the earliest image of each subject as a gallery image and all subsequent images considered probes.

11.5.4 Subspace Methods for Matching

The application of PCA to 3D image data is straightforward if one retains the depth (z) component of the 3D face image and treats it as a pseudo-intensity value. As with intensity images, the 3D data must be geometrically normalized, often using automatically detected face features such as the nose tip or eye corners. The use of geometric information in PCA offers intriguing possibilities not available to 2D imagery. Normally, illumination artifacts are not present (although extreme lighting situations can badly corrupt the data). In addition, the depth component likely contains more low-frequency and less high-frequency content than an intensity image, which would typically mean that fewer principal components are needed for a representation of fixed fidelity. However, these potential advantages may be offset by traditional criticisms of PCA, namely its global character and thus its sensitivity to expression variation.

Hesher *et al.* [16] used multiple range images per subject to allow a greater possibility of matching using a PCA technique. Once the sensor acquires the range images and they are normalized, principal component analysis (PCA) is used to reduce the dimensions of the image representation and facilitate matching. Noise and background information were documented as factors that degraded performance. Performance figures ranked from the mid-80% to mid-90% range on a 222 image database. Tsalakanidou *et al.* [12] extend the PCA approach to include the use of color images. Multiple tests using the XM2VTS multimodal database, with matchers that employed color images alone, 3D shape alone, and 3D + color were compared. Using color in addition to 3D images caused the recognition rate to increase. While the rank-1 performance of the various modules of this technique are not competitive by today's standards, the work demonstrates a principled way to combine independent matchers' outputs.

Bronstein *et al.* [2] described a technique to transform the facial surface to a space where the representation is invariant to isometric transformations (i.e. expressions or manipulations of the face). They obtain geometric invariants in the images that allow multi-modal 2D+3D recognition using 2D face texture images mapped onto a 3D face. Once this combined image is generated, they use eigendecomposition of canonical and flattened texture images. Experiments on an image database of 200 images showed that the proposed technique outperforms a 2D PCA (eigenfaces) approach.

11.5.5 Matching Local Surface Features

Mian *et al.* [21] developed a 3D face recognition system intended to handle expression variations. This system employs a coarse model for indexing, as discussed in Section 11.5.1. The primary representation of the face, used to represent faces in the gallery that survived the indexing step, is a global face subset identified, through a segmentation procedure, to be expression-invariant. This segmentation is performed by thresholding the variance in the z-coordinate of a registered set of training images whose members are diverse in subjects and expressions. This expression-invariant representation is matched against probe images using ICP. Two matchers were demonstrated. One employed the entire face image and yielded a rank-1 correct recognition rate of 76.5%. The other employed an automatically located mask to segment the probe image prior to matching and yielded a rank-1 correct rate of 88%-96% depending on the presence of variant facial expressions in the probe set.

Faltemier *et al.* [30] describe a region committee voting procedure for 3D face recognition. This matching architecture was designed to be robust to face expression variations. The technique automatically detects a nose tip using curvature information and then extracts several regions around the nose as the basis for matching. Each of these local regions is matched against a gallery of compatible features using ICP, yielding an RMS error interpreted as a match score. These matching scores are combined using voting, and the model with the highest vote count is accepted (there is a reject option for situations that yield too few votes). Experiments with the FRGC2.0 data set [22] yielded 95% correct rank-1 identification.

11.5.6 Comparisons

Gökberk *et al.* [3] perform a comparative evaluation of five face shape representations, (point clouds, surface normals, facial profiles, PCA, and LDA) using the well known 3D-RMA data set [8] of 571 images from 106 subjects. They find that the ICP and LDA approaches offer the best average performance. They also perform various fusion techniques for combining the results from different shape representations to achieve a rank-one recognition rate of 99.0%.

11.6 Comments and Emerging Themes

This chapter has presented background material relating to the acquisition of 3D data, the representation of faces using such data, and techniques for face identification based on these representations. The literature demonstrates that the level of interest in 3D face recognition is high among biometric techniques. The recent FRVT2006 evaluation [25] demonstrated that 3D face recognition has potential to be a strong biometric. However, the use of 3D data for face recognition is not without challenges and drawbacks, and some of these have contributed to the relatively small market position of 3D face recognizers. One key drawback is the complexity of the sensor. Although a variety of techniques exist for acquisition of 3D data, as a rule they are more expensive and slower to produce output data than commodity 2D sensors. These sensors can also be delicate and can also require recalibration periodically. In order for 3D face recognition systems to assume a greater role in deployment, better and less expensive sensors will need to emerge.

Looking forward, a few themes in research and development for this technology area are apparent and are worth mentioning.

1. Sensing – At present, 3D sensors for face recognition tend to be expensive and (depending on the technology) can be slow to produce data, produce data with artifacts and other noise contaminants, or produce low-resolution data. New technologies and improvements in processing speed may make video-rate range imaging a reality if appropriate research effort is devoted to the task.

2. Scaling – Increasing attention is being paid to the problems of large subject databases for face recognition. Although the sizes of databases are increasing rapidly (*e.g.* [22]), all such databases are too small to do more than scratch the surface of the scaling problem. Synthesis of artificial imagery may offer benefits, but there is no substitute for a large database of real imagery from a good sensor. The systems issues surrounding large-scale matching (*i.e.*, keeping response time reasonable when the number of matches performed increases by an order of magnitude) also need attention.

3. Variability – Robustness of matchers to facial expression variation has been a popular research topic recently. It is encouraging to see so many different types of approach to this problem, including both isolated local features (data driven) and global deformation models (anatomically

driven). The relative scarcity of data that captures expression variation is a factor here.

4. The time dimension – We see an opportunity for 3D 'range video' processing for face recognition in the near future, as sensors improve. This issue has received relatively little attention to date. Active research groups looking at color video in face recognition may yield valuable lessons that can engender a critical examination of range video analysis.

References

1. 3DMD Corp. 3dMDface system. URL: http://www.3dmd.com/Products/ 3DSystems.asp (accessed March 2007), 2007.
2. M. M. B. Alexander M. Bronstein and R. Kimmel. Three-dimensional face recognition. *Int. J. of Computer Vision*, 64(1):5–30, August 2005.
3. B. Gökberk and L. Akarun. Comparative Analysis of Decision-level Fusion Algorithms for 3D Face Recognition. In *Proc. 18th International Conference on Pattern Recognition (ICPR 2006)*, pages 1018–1021, August 2006.
4. P. J. Besl and R. C. Jain. Invariant Surface Characteristics for 3D Object Recognition in Range Images. *Computer Vision, Graphics, and Image Processing*, 33:33–80, 1986.
5. P. J. Besl and N. D. McKay. A Method for Registration of 3-D Shapes. *IEEE Trans. on Pattern Analysis and Machine Intelligence*, 14(2):239–256, 1992.
6. K. Boyer and A. Kak. Color-encoded structured light for rapid active ranging. *IEEE Transactions on Pattern Analysis and Machine Intelligence*, 9(1):14–28, January 1987.
7. K. I. Chang, K. W. Bowyer, and P. J. Flynn. An evaluation of multi-modal 2D+3D face biometrics. *IEEE Transactions on Pattern Analysis and Machine Intelligence*, 27(4):619–624, 2005.
8. K. I. Chang, K. W. Bowyer, and P. J. Flynn. Multiple nose region matching for 3D face recognition under varying facial expression. *IEEE Transactions on Pattern Analysis and Machine Intelligence*, 28(10):1695–1700, October 2006.
9. Christopher Boehnen and Patrick Flynn. Accuracy of 3D Scanning Technologies in a Face Scanning Context. In *Proc. 5th Int. Conf. on 3-D Digital Imaging and Modeling (3DIM 2005)*, pages 310–317, June 2005.
10. D. Colbry, G. Stockman, and A. Jain. Detection of Anchor Points for 3D Face Verification. In *Proc. IEEE Workshop on Advanced 3D Imaging for Safety and Security (A3DISS)*, June 2005.
11. D. DeCarlo, D. Metaxas, and M. Stone. An Anthropometric Face Model using Variational Techniques. In *Proc. SIGGRAPH 1998*, pages 67–74, 1998.
12. F. Tsalakanidou and D. Tzovaras and M. G. Strintzis. Use of depth and colour eigenfaces for face recognition. *Pattern Recognition Letters*, 24(9-10):1427–1435, June 2003.
13. J. H. Friedman, J. L. Bentley, and R. A. Finkel. An Algorithm for Finding Best Matches in Logarithmic Expected Time. *ACM Trans. Math. Softw.*, 3(3):209–226, September 1977.
14. A. Fusiello. Elements of geometric computer vision. CVOnline compendium of computer vision. URL: http://homepages.inf.ed.ac.uk/rbf/

CVonline/LOCAL_COPIES/FUSIELLO4/tutorial.html (accessed March 2007), 2007.

15. M. Greenspan and G. Godin. A nearest neighbor method for efficient ICP. In *Proc.3rd International Conference on 3-D Digital Imaging and Modeling (3DIM01)*, pages 161–170, 2001.

16. C. Hesher, A. Srivastava, and G. Erlebacher. A novel technique for face recognition using range images. In *Proc. Seventh Int. Symp. on Signal Processing and Its Applications*, pages 201–204, 2003.

17. R. Jarvis. *Range Sensing for Computer Vision*, pages 17–56. Elsevier, 1993.

18. K. W. Bowyer and K. Chang and P. J. Flynn. A survey of approaches and challenges in 3D and multi-modal 3D+2D face recognition. *Computer Vision and Image Understanding*, 101(1):1–15, January 2006.

19. X. Lu and A. K. Jain. Automatic Feature Extraction for Multiview 3D Face Recognition. In *Proc. Int. Conf. on Automatic Face and Gesture Recognition (FG2006)*, pages 585–590, April 2006.

20. X. Lu and A. K. Jain. Deformation Modeling for Robust 3D Face Matching. In *Proc. IEEE Computer Society Conference on Computer Vision and Pattern Recognition (CVPR2006)*, pages 1377 – 1383, June 2006.

21. A. Mian, M. Bennamoun, and R. Owens. Automatic 3d face detection, normalization and recognition. In *Proc. 3rd Int. Symp. on 3D Data Processing, Visualization, and Transmission*, pages 735–742, June 2006.

22. National Institute of Standards and Technology. FRGC 2.0 data. URL: http://face.nist.gov, 2006.

23. G. Passalis, I. Kakadiaris, and T. Theoharis. Intra-class retrieval of non-rigid 3D objects: Application to Face Recognition. *IEEE Trans. on Pattern Analysis and Machine Intelligence*, 29(2), 2007.

24. P. J. Phillips, P. J. Flynn, T. Scruggs, K. W. Bowyer, J. Chang, K. Hoffman, J. Marques, J. Min, and W. Worek. Overview of the face recognition grand challenge. In *Proc. CVPR*, pages I:947–954, 2005.

25. P. J. Phillips, W. T. Scruggs, A. J. O'Toole, P. J. Flynn, K. Bowyer, C. L. Schott, and M. Sharpe. FRVT 2006 and ICE 2006 Large-Scale Results. Technical Report NISTIR 7408 (http://face.nist.gov, accessed April 2007), National Institute of Standards and Technology, 2007.

26. Polhemus Corp. FASTScan Handheld Laser Scanner. URL: http://www.polhemus.com/?page=Scanning_Fastscan (accessed May 2007), 2007.

27. A. Salah, H. Çınar, L. Akarun, and B. Sankur. Exact 2D-3D Facial Landmarking for Registration and Recognition. *Annals of Telecommunications*, 62(1–2):83–108, 2007.

28. K. Sato and S. Inokuchi. Range-Imaging System Utilizing Nematic Liquid Crystal Mask. In *Proc. Int. Conf. on Computer Vision (ICCV 1987)*, 1987.

29. Y. Sun and L. Yin. Evaluation of 3D Facial Feature Selection for Individual Facial Model Identification. In *Proc. 18th Int. Conf. on Pattern Recognition*, pages 562 – 565, 2006.

30. T. Faltemier and K. Bowyer and P. Flynn. 3D Face Recognition with Region Committee Voting. In *Proc. 3rd. Int. Symp. on 3D Data Processing, Visualization, and Transmission (3DPVT 2006)*, 2006.

31. T. Maurer and D. Guigonis and I. Maslov and B. Pesenti and A. Tsaregorodtsev and D. West and G. Medioni. Performance of Geometrix ActiveID(TM) 3D Face

Recognition Engine on the FRGC Data. In *Proc. IEEE Conf. on Computer Vision and Pattern Recognition*, pages 154–161, June 2005.

32. W. Zhao and R. Chellappa and P. J. Phillips and A. Rosenfeld. Face recognition: A literature survey. *ACM Computing Surveys*, 35(4), December 2003.

33. X. Lu and A. K. Jain and D. Colbry. Matching 2.5D Face Scans to 3D Models. *IEEE Trans. on Pattern Analysis and Machine Intelligence*, 28(1), January 2006.

34. P. Yan and K. Bowyer. A Fast Algorithm for ICP-based 3D Shape Biometrics. *Computer Vision and Image Understanding*, to appear.

Automatic Forensic Dental Identification

Hong Chen and Anil K. Jain

Department of Computer Science and Engineering,
Michigan State University, East Lansing, MI 48824, USA
{chenhon2,jain}@cse.msu.edu

12.1 Forensic Identification

There are two main purposes for forensic identification of humans: *suspect identification* and *victim identification.* For suspect identification, evidence such as fingerprints, bite marks, and blood samples are collected at crime scenes. Based on this evidence, the guilt or innocence of the suspects can be confirmed. The goal of victim identification is to determine the identity of victims based on characteristics of the human remains. Based on the number of victims involved, victim identification is categorized into two types: *individual victim identification* and *disaster victim identification.*

Victim identification can be achieved by matching antemortem (AM) and postmortem (PM) *circumstantial* evidence and *physical* evidence [2]. The circumstantial evidence includes a victim's clothing, jewelry, and pocket contents. If the antemortem description of the same circumstantial evidence can be provided, it may assist in the victim's correct identification. However, circumstantial evidence can easily be attributed to the wrong person, particularly when there are many disaster victims to be identified. Physical evidence is more reliable, and includes *external evidence, internal evidence, dental evidence,* and *genetic evidence* [2]. External evidence includes gender, estimated age, height, build, color of skin, etc. Specific features, such as scars, moles, tattoos, and abnormalities, are especially useful if they can be matched with antemortem records, and fingerprints are valuable external evidences as well. Internal examination (autopsy) is often necessary for determining the cause of death. An autopsy may also find medical evidence that can assist in identification, such as previous fractures or surgery, missing organs (e.g., appendix, kidney), or implants. Genetic identification involves comparing DNA samples from an individual with antemortem DNA, or with DNA samples from the suspected victim's ancestors or descendants. Genetic identification is especially useful when the bodies of the victims are severely mutilated. Dental evidence (such as fillings or missing teeth) is particularly important, since it can offer sufficient evidence to positively identify a victim without the need for additional information. The use of dental evidence for human identification is discussed in the remainder of this chapter. Table 12.1 compares the various methods of identifying victims in terms of *accuracy, time needed for identification, antemortem record availability* (the possibility of obtaining antemortem evidence), *robustness to decomposition (of the body)* and *instrument requirement* (number of instruments needed for matching).

Table 12.1. A Comparison of Evidence Types Used in Victim Identification

Evidence type	Circumstantial	Physical			
		External	Internal	Genetic	Dental
Accuracy	Med.	High	Low	High	High
Time for Identification	Short	Short	Long	Long	Short
Antemortem Record Availability	High	Med.	Low	High	Med.
Robustness to Decomposition	Med.	Low	Low	Med.	High
Instrument Requirement	Low	Med.	High	High	Med.

This chapter begins with a brief survey of the procedure of manual forensic dental identification, and introduces the dental radiograph-based approach for forensic identification. We also discuss some challenges to automatic identification based on dental records, and briefly introduce a prototype system for identifying humans based on dental radiographs.

12.2 Manual Forensic Dental Identification

First of all, unidentified human remains are reported to the police who then initiate a request for dental identification. A presumptive identification is often available (e.g., wallet or driver's license found on the body), which will enable antemortem records to be located. In other instances, using the database of missing persons, the location where the body is found, or other physical characteristics and circumstantial evidence may enable a putative identification. Antemortem records are then obtained from the dentist of the suspected missing person.

The forensic dentist produces a postmortem record by carefully charting and writing descriptions of the dental structures and radiographs. An example of dental chart is shown in Figure 12.1. If the antemortem records are available, postmortem radiographs should be taken which replicate the type and angle of the antemortem records [15]. Radiographs are marked with a rubber-dam punch to indicate antemortem and postmortem to prevent confusion - one hole for antemortem films and two holes for postmortem films [1].

Once the postmortem record is complete, a comparison between the two records can be carried out. A methodical and systematic comparison is required to examine each tooth and surrounding structures. While dental restorations play a significant role in the identification process, many other

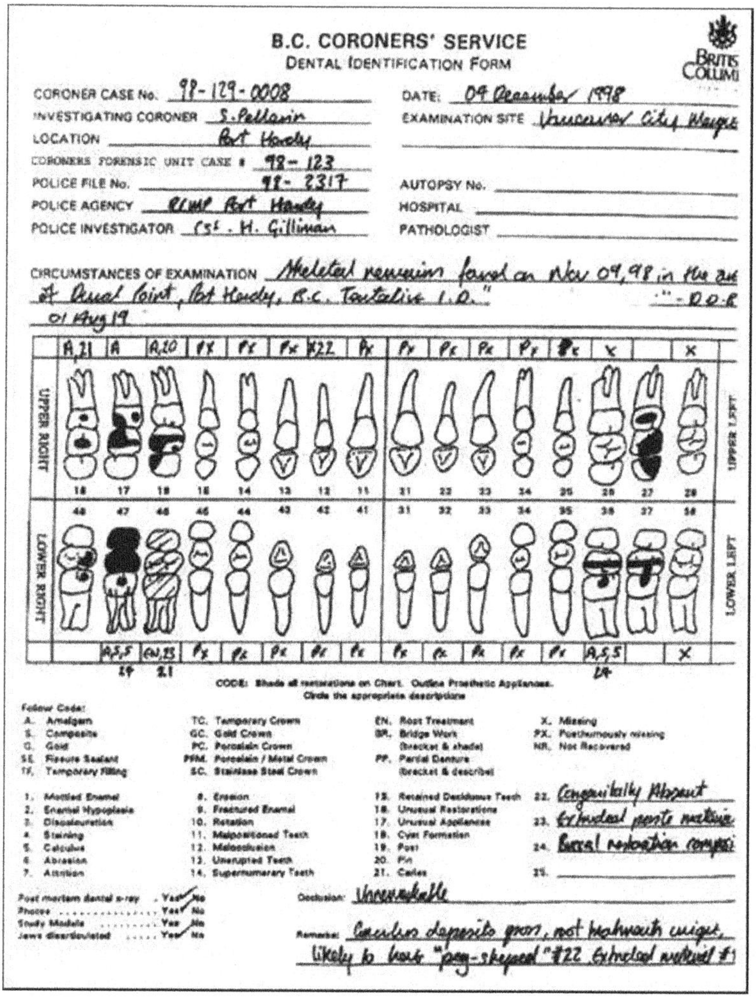

Fig. 12.1. An example of postmortem dental chart [24].

oral features such as pathological and morphological characteristics are assessed [1]. Such additional features play a particularly important role in those individuals with minimal restorations. Because of the progressive decrease in dental cavities, so-called non-restorative cases are likely to become more common [22].

Similarities and discrepancies are noted during the comparison process [26]. There are two types of discrepancies, explainable and unexplainable. Explainable discrepancies normally relate to the time elapsed between the antemortem and postmortem records, e.g., teeth extracted or restorations placed or enlarged. If a discrepancy is unexplainable, for example a tooth is not present on the antemortem record but is present on the postmortem record, then an exclusion must be made [1].

The American Board of Forensic Odontology recommends that dental identification conclusions be limited to the following four conclusions [1]:

- Positive identification: the antemortem and postmortem data match in sufficient detail, with no unexplainable discrepancies, to establish that they are from the same individual.
- Possible identification: the antemortem and postmortem data have consistent features but, because of the quality of either the postmortem remains or the antemortem evidence, it is not possible to establish identity positively.
- Insufficient evidence: the available information is insufficient to form the basis for a conclusion.
- Exclusion: the antemortem and postmortem data are clearly inconsistent.

It is important to note that there is no minimum number of concordant points or features that are required for a positive identification. In many cases a single tooth can be used for identification if it contains sufficiently unique features. On the other hand, a full-mouth series of radiographs may not reveal sufficient detail to render a positive conclusion [1]. The discretion of identification lies with the odontologist who must be prepared to justify the conclusions in court [24].

Recent disasters have brought the significance of dental identification to the public's attention. For example, in the terrorist attack on Sept. 11, 2001, many victims were identifiable only from pieces of jaw bones. Dentists were asked to help in identifying the victims using dental records and about 20% of the 973 victims identified in the first year after the 9/11 attack were identified using dental records [23]. Victims of the 2004 Asian tsunami were also identified based on dental information [27, 3]: 75% of the tsunami victims in Thailand were identified using dental records, 10% by fingerprints, and just 0.5% using DNA profiling. The remaining victims were identified using a combination of techniques.

12.3 Identification of Humans Using Dental Radiographs

Dental radiographs are one of the most valuable pieces of evidence for dental identification. This section begins with an overview of dental radiographs (also known as dental X-rays) and then describes how dental radiographs can be used to identify victims.

12.3.1 Dental Radiographs

There are three common types of dental radiographs (dental X-rays): *peri-apical*, *bitewing*, and *panoramic*. Periapical X-rays (all radiographs in Figure

12.2(a) except the two between the rows) show the entire tooth, including the crown, root, and the bone surrounding the root. Bitewing X-rays (the two radiographs between the rows in Figure 12.2(a) and all the radiographs in Figure 12.2(b)) are taken during most routine dental check-ups and are useful for revealing cavities in the teeth. One difference between periapical and bitewing radiographs is the imaging setup. For bitewing radiographs, the film is parallel to the teeth and the X-ray beam is perpendicular to both the teeth and the film. In contrast, periapical radiographs do not require that the film be parallel to the teeth. In some cases, the film and the teeth are deliberately set not to be parallel so that the whole tooth can be imaged on a small radiograph film. Periapical X-rays are useful for diagnosing abscessed teeth and periodontal disease. The third type of X-ray is the panoramic X-ray. As its name suggests, panoramic X-rays give a broad overview of the entire dentition (the development of teeth and their arrangement in the mouth). Panoramic X-rays provide information not only about the teeth, but also about upper and lower jawbones, sinuses, and other hard and soft tissues in the head and neck (Figure 12.2(c)). Panoramic films are entirely extraoral, which means that the film remains outside of the mouth while the X-ray machine shoots the beam through other tissues from the outside. Since it is entirely extraoral, panoramic radiographs work quite well for people who cannot tolerate the placement of films inside their mouths. Another advantage of panoramic film is that it takes very little radiation to expose it. The amount of radiation needed to expose a panoramic X-ray film is about the same as the radiation needed to expose two intraoral films (periapical or bitewing). The disadvantage of panoramic radiographs is that the resolution is lower than that of intraoral images, which means the edges and structures in the panoramic images are fuzzy.

For diagnosis and documentation purposes, dentists usually collect three types of dental radiograph series: the *initial full mouth series*, the *yearly bitewing series*, and the *panoramic X-ray film*. Figure 12.2(a) is an example of the initial full mouth series, which combines bitewing and periapical X-rays to show a complete survey of the teeth and bones. It consists of 2 or 4 bitewing films taken at an angle in order to look for decay, and 14 periapical films taken from other angles to show the tips of the roots and the supporting bone. In the full mouth series, each tooth is seen in multiple films. This redundancy helps dentists create a mental image of the teeth in three dimensional (3D) space. A yearly bitewing series (Figure 12.2(b)) consists of either 2 or 4 bitewing films. A bitewing series is the minimum set of X-rays that most dental offices take to document the internal structure of the teeth and gums. The third type of radiograph series consists of a single panoramic radiograph.

With the development of digital imaging technology, digital X-ray machines are becoming popular in dental clinics. Digital dental radiographs have several advantages [7]: i) compared to traditional radiographs, only half the dosage of radiation is needed for obtaining a dental radiograph of comparable quality; ii) digital dental radiographs do not require time for film development,

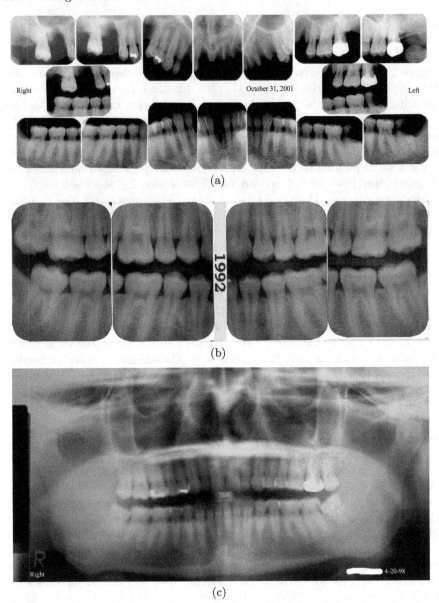

Fig. 12.2. Three types of dental radiograph series. (a) Full mouth series; (b) bitewing series; (c) panoramic series.

so dentists need to wait for only a few seconds before the acquired image is displayed; iii) dentists can take another image instantly if the acquired image is not good enough, so in general digital dental radiographs in a patient's record have better image quality than conventional dental radiographs; iv) digital radiographs are easier to store and process, while conventional radiographs need to be digitized for image processing; v) digital dental radiographs are environmentally friendly since they do not generate chemical wastes used in film processing; vi) digital radiographs also have been shown to have some diagnostic advantages for several diseases. Mainly due to their advantages in speed, storage, and image quality, digital dental radiographs will be routinely used for victim identification in the future.

12.3.2 Dental Radiographs for Identification

An individual's dental record includes information about the number of teeth present, the orientation of those teeth, and dental restorations. Each dental restoration is unique because it is designed specifically for that particular tooth. An individual's dentition is defined by a combination of all these characteristics, and can be used to distinguish one individual from another. The major challenge in the field of forensic dentistry is to determine how unique the features of an individual's dentition are, and whether this information is useful for identification purposes. The information about dentition is represented in the form of dental codes and dental radiographs. The dental codes are symbol strings for description of the type of dental restorations, the presence/absence of the teeth, and the number of cusps in the teeth, etc. Many studies have been done to define this characteristic of "uniqueness" in dental codes for identification purposes. Adams concluded from his analysis [5, 6] that when adequate antemortem dental codes are available for comparison, the inherent variability of the human dentition could accurately establish identity with a high degree of confidence, especially when unique dental restorations are encountered. One challenge to future efforts in forensic identification based on dental codes is the decline in the number of dental restorations, which is attributed to increased awareness of healthy dental habits. While general descriptions of dentition can be quite useful for excluding possible identities in cases where a limited number of identities are possible, large scale efforts to identify victims based on dentition are hindered when only dental codes are available. The availability of antemortem dental radiographs in addition to dental codes allows individuals with common dental characteristics to be distinguished from one another based on visual features in the images.

Forensic identification of humans based on dental information requires the availability of antemortem dental records, including dental radiographs, written records, tooth molds and photographs. Antemortem radiographs should be obtained if possible. The antemortem dental radiographs may have been acquired in several situations. Taking dental radiographs is very routine during the dental clinical visits in the United States and Britain. Also in the United

States and some other countries, newly recruited soldiers are required to have
dental examinations that include taking their dental radiographs. The discovery and collection of antemortem records is ordinarily the responsibility of
investigative agencies. These agencies might locate records from sources such
as hospitals, dental schools, health care providers, dental insurance carriers,
public aid insurance administrators, and the FBI National Crime Information
Center (NCIC). Other resources include military service, judicial detention,
oral surgeons, orthodontists, etc.

12.4 Automatic Dental Identification

Identifying the 2,749 victims of 9/11 disaster took around 40 months [4], and
the number of Asian tsunami victims identified during the first 9 months was
only 2,200 (out of an estimated total of 190,000) [3]. The low efficiency rate of
current manual dental identification methods makes it imperative that we develop algorithms to automatically identify disaster victims. There have been
a number of attempts to utilize machine intelligence to facilitate the identification of victims, e.g., the winID system [21] (*http://www.WinID.com*) and
the Odontosearch system (*http://www.jpac.pacom.mil/CIL/entry.htm*). However, these systems are based on dental description codes entered by human
experts. The reduced prevalence of dental restorations limits the usefulness
of matching methods based on dental descriptions and encourages continued
research on the use of dental radiographs for identification. This section discusses some of the challenges for dental radiographs based identification and
introduces a system for automating the use of dental radiographs for victim
identification [19, 14, 8, 9, 17, 18, 10, 20, 11].

12.4.1 Challenges

One major challenge in automatic identification based on dental X-rays is the
poor image quality of dental radiographs. Whether due to incorrect operation
of the X-ray equipment during image acquisition or digitization, to irregular
arrangement of teeth, or to degradation of the radiograph films, the contours
of teeth often appear to be blurred and the different tissues contrast poorly
in many radiographs. These factors make it difficult to automatically extract
edge features and tooth boundaries from the radiographs.

A second challenge is changes in the dentition over time, such as tooth
eruption and loss, the emergence, abrasion, falling and replacement of dental restorations, the sliding of neighboring teeth after a tooth is extracted,
orthodontic operations, etc. These changes cause inconsistent appearances of
teeth in AM and PM radiographs from the same individual and are difficult
to model.

A third challenge is the changes in the imaging angle. Since dental radiographs are 2D projections of 3D structures, changes in the imaging angle

result in complex deformations. Figure 12.3 shows an AM-PM image pair in which the changes in the imaging angle result in significant deformations in the periapical radiograph images.

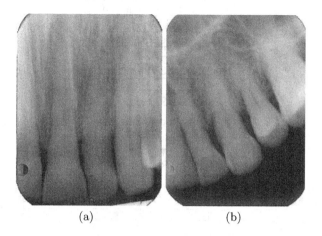

(a)   (b)

Fig. 12.3. Changes in the imaging angle result in significant deformations in the appearances of corresponding teeth in AM (a) and PM (b) periapical radiograph images.

12.4.2 Automatic Dental Radiograph-based Identification System

In order to automate the identification procedure, we need to explore new features other than dental restorations and abnormalities. Figure 12.4 shows the architecture of an automatic system. Figure 12.5 shows the process of matching two pairs of AM and PM images. The details of each stage are given below.

Feature Extraction

The first step in processing dental radiographs is to extract features from them. An image quality evaluation function assesses the quality of the image in terms of image type (panoramic or non-panoramic), exposure imbalance, and image blurring before it is processed. A warning message is issued to request user interaction during the following steps if the image is assessed as a panoramic image or the image has imbalanced exposure or blurring. Figure 12.6 shows images that are assessed to be of poor quality.

The features extracted for matching purposes are the contours of teeth and the contours of dental work. Before extracting these features, the radiographs are segmented into regions using Fast Marching algorithm [25], so that each

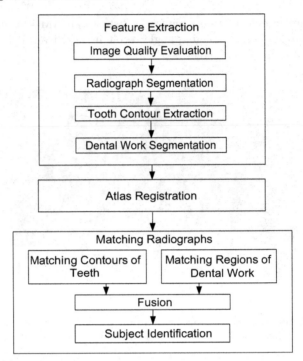

Fig. 12.4. Block diagram of automatic dental identification system.

region contains only one tooth. Figure 12.7 shows examples of radiograph segmentation.

Boundary extraction methods are then applied to each region of the image to extract contours of each tooth and dental restoration. An active shape model (ASM) [12] is used to extract eigen-shapes from aligned training tooth contours, which include tooth contours, and their scaled and rotated variations [11]. Figure 12.8 shows five most principal deformations of teeth, which, respectively, represent scaling, rotation, and variations in tooth width, tooth root and crown shapes. The ASM combined with splines are used to extract tooth contours. Figure 12.9 shows some extracted contours. Anisotropic diffusion [9] is used to enhance radiograph images and segment regions of dental work (including crowns, fillings, and root canal treatment). Results are shown in Figure 12.10.

Atlas Registration

The second step is to register the input radiographs to the human dental atlas, which is a descriptive model of the shape and relative positions of teeth (Figure 12.11). This registration step is important because the matching algorithm cannot properly align two sequences of teeth if they do not contain the

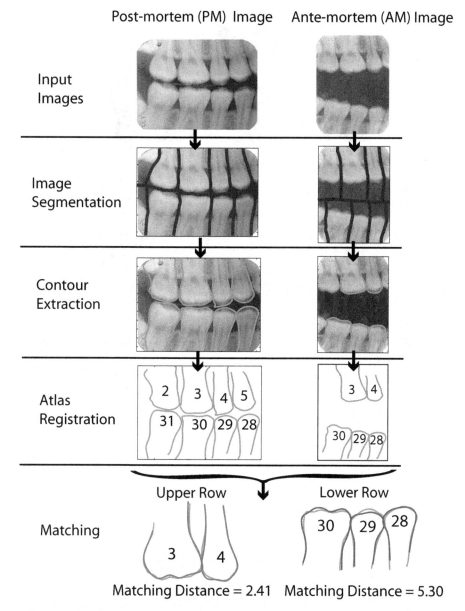

Fig. 12.5. Fully automatic process of matching one pair of PM and AM images.

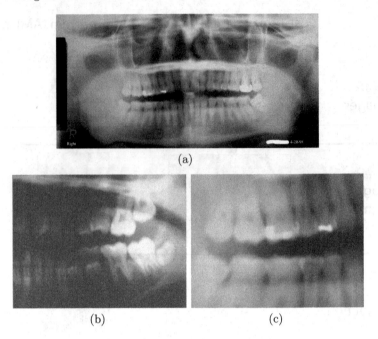

(a)

(b)   (c)

Fig. 12.6. Images assessed as poor quality. (a) A panoramic image; (b) an unequally exposed image; (c) a blurred image.

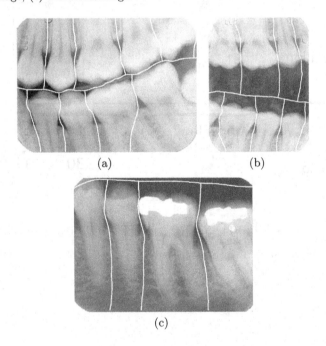

(a)   (b)

(c)

Fig. 12.7. Some examples of correct segmentation.

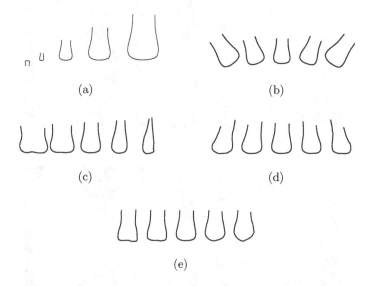

Fig. 12.8. First five modes of the shape model of teeth. The middle shape in each row is the mean shape, while the other four shapes are, from left to right, mean shape plus four eigenvectors multiplied by -2, -1, 1, and 2 times the square root of the corresponding eigenvalues.

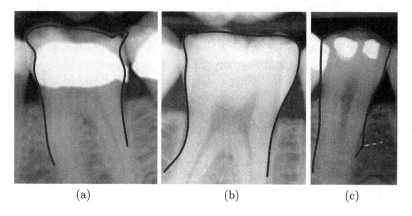

Fig. 12.9. Tooth shapes extracted using Active Shape Models.

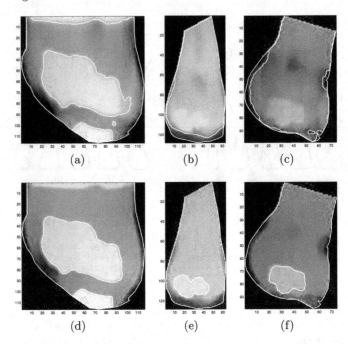

Fig. 12.10. Extracted dental work contours with and without image enhancement. (a), (b) and (c) Without enhancement. (d), (e) and (f) After enhancement.

same number of teeth. Missing teeth can be detected by labeling the existing teeth based on known dental anatomy. The anatomy-based tooth labeling can also accelerate the image matching stage, since a pair of PM-AM images need not be matched if they do not share the same label. A hybrid model involving Support Vector Machines (SVMs) and a Hidden Markov Model (HMM) (Figure 12.12) is used for representation of the dental atlas and estimation of the tooth indices in dental radiograph images. The HMM serves as an underlying representation of the dental atlas by representing various teeth and the distances between the neighboring teeth as HMM states. The SVM classifies the teeth into 3 classes based on their contours. Missing teeth in a radiograph can be detected by registering the observed tooth shapes and the distances between adjacent teeth to the dental atlas. Furthermore, instead of simply assigning a class label to each tooth, the posterior class probability associated with each tooth is extracted from the SVM and passed to the HMM. This approach reduces the impact of classification errors during registration. The hybrid model yields the probability of registering the teeth sequence in a radiograph to its possible positions in the atlas. The top-m ($m = 3$) possible registrations are explored further in the radiograph matching stage. Figure 12.13 shows some examples of tooth index estimation.

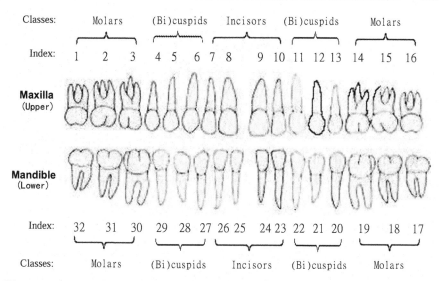

Fig. 12.11. Dental Atlas of a complete set of adult teeth containing indices and classification labels of the teeth.

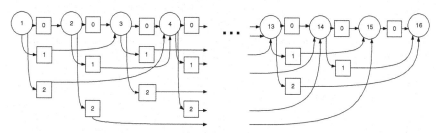

Fig. 12.12. SVM/HMM model for the upper row of 16 teeth. The circles represent teeth, and the number inside each circle is the tooth index. The squares represent missing teeth, and the number inside each square is the number of missing teeth.

Matching

For matching corresponding teeth from PM and AM radiographs, the tooth contours are registered, and corresponding contour points are located for calculating the distance between the contours. The distance between two tooth contours A and B is given as

$$D_{tc}(A, B) = \min_{\forall T} \frac{1}{|TAP|} \sum_{\text{all } a \in TAP} \|T(a) - Cor(a)\|, \tag{12.1}$$

where T is a rigid transformation (combined with scaling), $T(a)$ is the vector of coordinates of point a after transformation T, TAP is the set of corresponding points on A, and $Cor(a)$ is the vector of coordinates of point a's corresponding

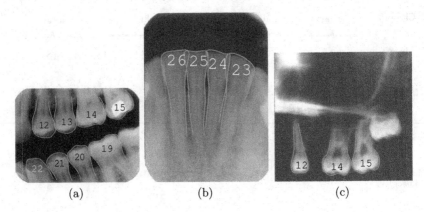

(a)   (b)   (c)

Fig. 12.13. Examples of successful registration of the dental atlas to (a) a bitewing image, (b) a periapical image, and (c) an image with a missing tooth. In (c), teeth numbered as 12, 14, and 15 are correctly registered. The missing tooth (number 13) is detected.

point in contour B. The distance $D_{tc}(A, B)$ is minimized by searching for the optimal transformation T using Sequential Quadratic Programming [16].

If dental work is present in both teeth, the regions of dental work are also matched to calculate the distance between dental work. Given two images F and G, the ratio of Misaligned Pixels (R_{mp}) between them is defined as:

$$R_{mp}(F, G) = \frac{\sum_{(x,y)\in A} F'(x, y) \oplus G'(x, y)}{\sum_{(x,y)\in A} F'(x, y) + G'(x, y)}, \qquad (12.2)$$

where A is the overlapped region of tooth pixels and dental work pixels in images F and G, $\oplus$ is the 'Exclusive-OR' operator, and F' and G' are the results of preprocessing on F and G, i.e.,

$$F'(x, y) = \begin{cases} 0, & \text{if } F(x, y) \text{ is a tooth pixel;} \\ 1, & \text{if } F(x, y) \text{ is a dental work pixel.} \end{cases} \qquad (12.3)$$

Image G' is defined in a similar way. The metric R_{mp} is used to measure the alignment of the dental work. The distance between the dental work in images F and G is defined as:

$$D_{dw}(F, G) = \min_{\text{for all } T} R_{mp}(T(F), G), \qquad (12.4)$$

where T is a rigid transformation (combined with scaling) and optimized using Sequential Quadratic Programming [16].

The matching distance D_{tc} is combined with D_{dw} to generate the fused distance D_f between the two teeth, A and B, as follows

$$D_f(A, B) = D_{tc}(A, B) \cdot (1 + \cdot(T(D_{dw}))), \qquad (12.5)$$

where

$$T(D_{dw}) = \begin{cases} P(\omega_i|D_{dw}) - P(\omega_g|D_{dw}), & \text{if } D_{dw} \text{ is available} \\ 0, & \text{otherwise,} \end{cases} \quad (12.6)$$

and $p(\omega_i|D_{dw})$ and $p(\omega_g|D_{dw})$ are probabilities estimated using a Parzen window approach with a Gaussian kernel [13].

Given two tooth sequences R and S, suppose ζ is one of the top-m estimated tooth indices (based on atlas registration) for teeth in sequence R, and η is one of the top-m estimated tooth indices for teeth in sequence S. In our experiments, we use $m = 3$. Despite the fact that the numbers of teeth in R and S may be different, as long as there are corresponding teeth, denote them as $(R_1, S_1), (R_2, S_2), ..., (R_n, S_n)$, where $n \geq 1$. We denote the distance between sequences R and S based on indices ζ and η as $D_{\zeta,\eta}(R, S)$, given by

$$D_{\zeta,\eta}(R, S) = \begin{cases} \frac{1}{n}\sum_{i=1}^{n} D_f(R_i, S_i), & \text{if } n \geq 1, \\ \infty, & \text{otherwise,} \end{cases} \quad (12.7)$$

where $D_f(R_i, S_i)$ is the distance between teeth R_i and S_i, defined in Eqn. (12.5). The minimum value of $D_{\zeta,\eta}$ among all the combinations of top-m indices for R and S is the distance between sequences R and S,

$$D(R, S) = \min_{\forall \zeta, \eta} D_{\zeta,\eta}(R, S). \quad (12.8)$$

To estimate the similarity between radiographs of two subjects Φ and Ψ, assume that tooth sequence R belongs to Φ and tooth sequence S belongs to Ψ. Denote the distance measure between subjects Φ and Ψ as $Ds(\Phi, \Psi)$, given by:

$$D_s(\Phi, \Psi) = \frac{D_{ss}(R, \Psi)}{\#\{R|R \in \Phi, \sum_{S \in \Psi} n(R, S) > 0\}}, \quad (12.9)$$

where Φ means all tooth sequences of subject Φ, Ψ means all tooth sequences of subject Ψ, and

$$D_{ss}(R, \Psi) = \sum_{R \in \Phi} \min_{S \in \Psi} \kappa(R, S), \quad (12.10)$$

$$\kappa(R, S) = \begin{cases} D(R, S), & \text{if } n(R, S) > 0, \\ \infty, & \text{if } n(R, S) = 0, \end{cases} \quad (12.11)$$

where $n(R, S)$ is the number of corresponding teeth used for the computation of $D(R, S)$. The denominator in Eqn. (12.9) is the number of sequences of Φ that have corresponding teeth in any sequence of Ψ. According to Eqns. (12.9), (12.10), and (12.11), first, the distance between the sequence R (of subject Φ) and the subject Ψ, $D_{ss}(R, \Psi)$, is calculated as the minimum distance between sequence R and all the sequences of subject Ψ. Then we calculate the distance between subject Φ and subject Ψ, $D_s(\Phi, \Psi)$, as the average distances between all subject Φ's sequences and subject Ψ.

12.5 Experimental Results

Insufficiency of data in dental radiograph databases is a challenge to this re-search. We obtained dental radiographs from three sources. The first source is the FBI's Criminal Justice Information Service (CJIS) division, which is interested in utilizing dental radiographs for identifying Missing and Uniden-tified Persons (MUPs). The second source is the Washington State Police Department, and the third source is Dr. Robert Howell, a professor in the Department of Oral and Maxillofacial Pathology at West Virginia University. The database includes 33 AM and PM matched subjects, with a total of 360 PM and 316 AM dental sequences, containing a total of 810 PM teeth and 892 AM teeth. Images of 4 of the subjects could not be used for following reasons: i) tooth contours cannot be extracted due to poor image quality, ii) there are variations in dental structure due to tooth development or orthodontic treat-ment. So, we tested the retrieval for 29 subjects but included the AM images of these 4 subjects as the imposter identities in the database. Figure 12.14 shows the Cumulative Match Characteristics (CMC) curve for retrieving the 29 subjects from the database consisting of 33 subjects. Using top-2 retrievals, the retrieval accuracy is 27/29 (=93%). The accuracy reaches 100% when the top-7 retrievals are used. Figure 12.15 shows PM and AM radiographs of a successfully retrieved subject. Figure 12.16 shows radiographs of a subject that was not successfully retrieved from the database in top-1 retrieval.

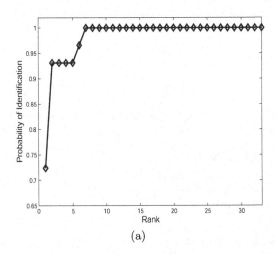

(a)

Fig. 12.14. Cumulative matching characteristics (CMC) curve for subject retrieval.

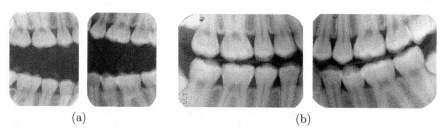

(a)   (b)

Fig. 12.15. A successfully retrieved subject. (a) PM radiographs; (b) AM radiographs

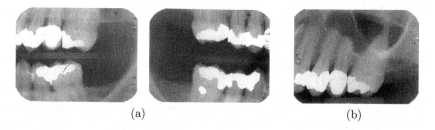

(a)   (b)

Fig. 12.16. A subject not correctly retrieved from the database due to insufficient number of teeth in the AM image. (a) PM radiographs; (b) AM radiograph.

12.6 Summary and Future Work

Dental radiographs contain valuable information to identify victims when other biometric traits are not available. This chapter introduced the forensic identification of humans based on dental radiographs. Challenges to automatic processing and matching of dental information are discussed, and each stage in the proposed automatic identification system was described. Experimental results on a small database are presented. Future work should include detection of dental abnormality, such as tumors and periodontal disease, and incorporate this information in matching. Non-tooth features, such as the trabecular pattern of mandible bones and the shapes of the sinus and the canals in the mandibular and maxilla bones, can also be used for improving matching accuracy. A large database needs to be collected and made available to researchers to evaluate the performance of automatic systems.

Acknowledgements

This work was supported by the National Science Foundation grant EIA-0131079.

References

1. ABFO body identification guidelines. http://www.abfo.org/ID.htm.
2. Disaster victim identification. http://www.interpol.int/Public/DisasterVictim/Guide.
3. Dental records beat DNA in tsunami IDs. *New Scientists*, 2516:12, Sept. 2005. http://www.newscientist.com/article.ns?id=mg18725163.900.
4. Forensic identification of 9/11 victims ends, February 2005. http://abcnews.go.com/WNT/story?id=525937\&page=1.
5. B. Adams. The diversity of adult dental patterns in the United States and the implications for personal identification. *Journal of Forensic Science*, 48(3):497–503, 2003.
6. B. Adams. Establishing personal identification based on specific patterns of missing, filled and unrestored teeth. *Journal of Forensic Science*, 48(3):487–496, 2003.
7. E. Arana and L. Marti-Bonmati. Digital dental radiology. http://www.priory.com/den/dentrvg1.htm.
8. Hong Chen and Anil Jain. Tooth contour extraction for matching dental radiographs. In *Proc. ICPR (International Conference on Pattern Recognition)*, volume III, pages 522–525, Cambridge, U.K., 2004.
9. Hong Chen and Anil Jain. Dental biometrics: Alignment and matching of dental radiographs. *IEEE Trans. on Pattern Analysis and Machine Intelligence*, 27(8):1319–1326, 2005.
10. Hong Chen and Anil Jain. Dental biometrics: alignment and matching of dental radiographs. In *Proc. WACV (Workshop on Applications of Computer Vision)*, pages 316–321, Breckenridge, Colorado, January 2005.
11. Hong Chen and Anil K. Jain. Active shape model-based tooth contour extraction. Technical Report MSU-CSE-07-17, Department of Computer Science and Engineering, Michigan State University, 2007.
12. T. F. Cootes and C. J. Taylor. Active shape models - 'smart snakes'. In *Proc. British Machine Vision Conf.*, pages 266–275, 1992.
13. Richard O. Duda, Peter E. Hart, and David G. Stork. *Pattern Classification*, chapter 10, pages 164–174. Wiley Interscience, 2nd edition, 2001.
14. G. Fahmy, D. Nassar, E. Haj-Said, H. Chen, O. Nomir, J. Zhou, R. Howell, H. H. Ammar, M. Abdel-Mottaleb, and A. K. Jain. Towards an automated dental identification system (ADIS). In *Proc. ICBA (International Conference on Biometric Authentication)*, volume LNCS 3072, pages 789–796, Hong Kong, July 2004.
15. M. Goldstein, Sweet D. J., and Wood R. E. A specimen positioning device for dental radiographic identification. *Journal of Forensic Science*, 43:185–189, 1998.
16. S. P. Han. A globally convergent method for nonlinear programming. *Journal of Optimization Theory and Applications*, 22:297, 1977.
17. Anil Jain and Hong Chen. Matching of dental X-ray images for human identification. *Pattern Recognition*, 37(7):1519–1532, 2004.
18. Anil Jain and Hong Chen. Registration of dental atlas to radiographs for human identification. In *Proc. of SPIE Conference on Biometric Technology for Human Identification II*, volume 5779, pages 292–298, Orlando, Florida, 2005.

19. Anil Jain, Hong Chen, and Silviu Minut. Dental biometrics: human identification using dental radiographs. In *Proc. 4th International Conference on AVBPA (Audio- and Video-based Biometric Person Authentication)*, pages 429–437, Guildford, U.K., 2003.

20. Mohammad H. Mahoor and Mohamed Abdel-Mottaleb. Classification and numbering of teeth in dental bitewing images. *Pattern Recognition*, 38(4):577–586, 2005.

21. J. McGarvey. WinID: Dental identification system, 2005. `http://www.winid.com`.

22. J. Murray. *Prevention of Oral Disease*. Oxford: Oxford University Press, 1986.

23. Patrice O'Shaughnessy. More than half of victims IDd. *New York Daily News*, 11 Sep. 2002.

24. I. A. Pretty and D. Sweet. A look at forensic dentistry - part 1: The role of teeth in the determination of human identity. *British Dental Journal*, 190(7):359–366, April 2001.

25. James Sethian. *Level Set Methods and Fast Marching Methods*. Cambridge University Press, Cambridge, UK, 2nd edition, 1999.

26. H. Silverstein. *Comparison of antemortem and postmortem findings. In: Manual of forensic odontology*. Ontario: Manticore, 3rd edition edition, 1995.

27. Panarat Thepgumpanat. Thai tsunami forensic centre produces first IDs. *Reuters*, `http://www.alertnet.org/`, 18 Jan. 2005.

13

Hand Vascular Pattern Technology

Alex Hwansoo Choi[1] and Chung Nguyen Tran[2]

[1] Department of Information Engineering, Myongji University, San 38-2 Namdong, Yongin, Kyunggido, Korea
alexchoi@tech-sphere.com
[2] Techsphere, Co. Ltd., 980-54, Bangbae, Seocho, Seoul, Korea
tnchung@tech-sphere.com

13.1 Introduction

The field of hand vascular pattern technology or vein pattern technology uses the subcutaneous vascular network on the back of the hand to verify the identity of individuals in biometric applications. The principle of this technology is based on the fact that the pattern of blood vessels is unique to each individual, even between identical twins. Therefore, the pattern of the hand blood vessels is a highly distinctive feature that can be used for verifying the identity of the individual. Hand vascular pattern biometric technology is relatively new and is in the process of being continuously refined and developed.

The hand vascular pattern was first considered as a potential technology in the biometric security field in the early 1990s. In 1992, Shimizu brought into focus the potential for use of the hand vascular technology in his published paper on trans-body imaging [1]. In 1995, Cross and Smith introduced thermographic imaging technology for acquiring the subcutaneous vascular network on the back of the hand for biometric applications [2]. Since then, a large number of research efforts have continuously contributed to hand vascular pattern technology. It was not until 1997 that the first practical application was developed. The introduction of BK-100 in 1997 by Alex Hwansoo Choi, the co-founder of BK systems, was one of the first commercial products based on hand vascular pattern technology. Using near-infrared light, images of blood vessels on the back of the hand were acquired by a camera sensitive to the near-infrared light range. The deoxidized hemoglobin in blood vessels absorbs infrared rays and causes the blood vessels to appear as black patterns in captured images. The vascular patterns were pre-processed and used for verification. Several improved versions of this device were developed until the end of 1998.

In 2000, Techsphere Co. Ltd., founded by members of BK Systems, continued to research and develop the technology. During this period, they published their first research paper on the use of hand vascular pattern technology for personal identification [3], and other investigations were conducted to further improve the technology [4-7]. Based on the results of these efforts, a new commercial product under the name VP-II was released. In this new product, Techsphere completely redesigned the BK Systems products and applied many advanced digital processing technologies to make highly reliable and cost-effective devices. These important design changes have made hand vascular pattern technology popular in a variety of civilian applications such as airport security, hospital, or finance and banking.

Since the introduction of hand vascular pattern technology, a number of efforts have been made to develop other vascular pattern technologies utilizing different parts of the hand such as finger veins and palm veins. In 2003, Fujitsu announced its first commercial product using the vascular pattern technology into the general market. Fujitsu Palm Vein products employ vascular patterns on the palm as a means of extracting biometric features [8]. At the same time, Hitachi developed another identification system that utilizes vascular pattern in the fingers [9]. Its first commercial product, finger-vein identification, was also first released into the market in 2003.

Although hand vascular pattern technology is still an ongoing area of biometric research, a large number of units have been deployed in many applications such as access control, time and attendance, security, and hospitals. The market for hand vascular pattern technology has been rapidly growing. Compared to other biometric modalities this technology provides advantages such as higher authentication accuracy and better usability. Moreover, since vascular patterns lie under the skin, it is not affected by adverse sensing environments encountered in applications such as factories or construction sites where other biometric technologies show limitations. Because of these desirable features, vascular pattern technology is being incorporated into various authentication solutions for use in public places.

The remainder of this chapter is organized as follows: In Section 13.2, the history of development of hand vascular pattern technology is presented. Section 13.3 introduces some typical applications of hand vascular pattern recognition systems. The detailed technology and technical problems are presented in Section 13.4. Section 13.5 presents the performance evaluation of most of the available vascular pattern recognition systems. Our conclusions and remarks are given in Section 13.6.

13.2 Development of Hand Vascular Pattern Technology

The history of development of hand vascular pattern technology goes back to early 1997 when BK Systems announced its first commercial product, BK-100. This product has been mainly sold in Korean and Japanese markets. In the early stages, the product was limited to physical access control applications. Fig. 13.1 shows a prototype of the BK-100 hand vascular pattern recognition system. In 1998, the first patent on hand vascular pattern technology was assigned to BK systems. This invention described and claimed an apparatus and method for identifying individuals through their subcutaneous vascular patterns [10]. Based on this invention, new commercial versions, BK-200 and BK-300, were released to the market. Unfortunately, the development of these products was discontinued at the end of 1998.

Fig. 13.1. Prototype of the first hand vascular commercial product BK-100.

In 2000, Techsphere was founded by several former employees of BK Systems and made significant improvements to the BK-100 system [3-7] including utilizing advanced digital imaging technologies and low cost digital circuits to manufacture more reliable and cost-effective products. This resulted in the commercial product VP-II in 2001, which was more compact and therefore more suitable for certain applications. The VP-II included a new guidance handle so that users could easily align their hand in a proper location under the scanner and it also provided better user interface to make the system highly configurable. Fig. 13.2 shows a prototype of the VP-II product. In order to gain wider acceptance in various applications, VP-II was continuously improved to adapt for large-scale identification applications. As the number of users enrolled in the system grew to thousands, faster processing ability and larger storage were required. New commercial versions, VP-II S and VP-II M, were released to satisfy these requirements.

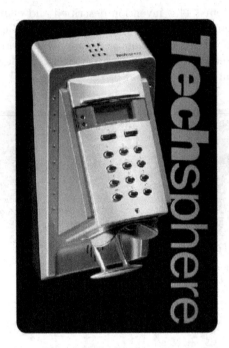

Fig. 13.2. VP-II Stand alone system for personal identification.

In spite of many successful deployments, the system cost was still too high to expand into a broader segment of the market. A new design based on an application-specific processor was developed for efficient realization of hardware [4]. This reduced the hardware and firmware complexity. Although many of the VP-II units were installed throughout the world, these were still stand-alone units that were only used for a single location. In the ubiquitous network society, the requirement that users can be easily identified anytime and anywhere needs to be met. The introduction of the integrated solution using a new Network Control Unit (NCU) made the product capable of being used in a TCP/IP network over the Internet. The VP-II NCU allows all users to access all the systems in the network by registering once since it transmits the vascular data template of enrolled users to all connected devices in real time. Fig. 13.3 shows an example of VP-II used in TCP/IP network.

As biometric technology matures, there will be an increasing interaction among different technologies and applications. Hand vascular pattern technology should become an open solution through which other systems or applications can easily access resources or information. In addition, it should allow other security vendors with their own proprietary solutions to integrate with it in a standard protocol. In order to satisfy this requirement, new protocols have been developed to allow other systems access to all the functionalities

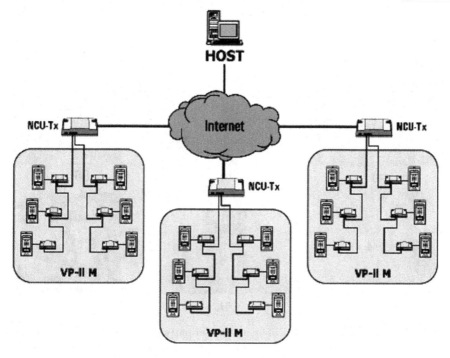

Fig. 13.3. Configuration of VP-II used in TCP/IP network.

of VP-II. It means that hand vascular pattern technology can be used in large-scale security solutions such as database server solutions or smart card solutions. To make the product more adaptive to other products from different vendors, hand vascular pattern technology is being adapted to national and international standards. In January, 2007, hand vascular pattern technology was finally adopted by the International Standard Organization (ISO) [11].

13.3 General Applications

Typical application of vascular pattern technology can be classified as follows:

- **Physical access control and Time attendance** – Physical access control and time attendance may be the most widely used application of hand vascular pattern technology. Utilizing hand vascular pattern technology, solutions have been developed to help manage employee attendance and overtime work at large organizations in an effective and efficient manner. The time and attendance solution employing hand vascular technology has enabled many local governments to enhance work productivity through automation, establish a sound attendance pattern through personal identification, and boost morale through transparent and precise budget allocation.

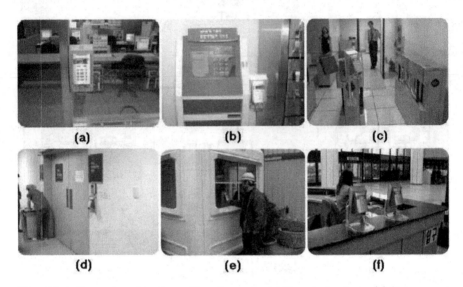

Fig. 13.4. General applications of hand vascular pattern technology; (a) Door access control, (b) Banking solutions, (c) Transportation (airport security), (d) Hospitals, (e) Construction sites, and (f) Schools

- **Finance and Banking** – With the rapid growth of ATM services and credit cards, fraudulent withdrawal of money by using fake or stolen bankcards has become a serious problem. Hand vascular pattern technology can be integrated into banking solutions by two different methods. In the first method, vascular patterns of customers are stored in the bank's database server. The authentication is carried out by comparing a customer's hand vascular pattern with their enrolled pattern in the database server. In the second method, hand vascular patterns of customers are stored in biometric ID cards which are kept by customers. During authentication, the customer's hand vascular pattern is compared with the pattern stored in the card for verification. Based on various requirements such as timely response or level of security, banks will decide the appropriate method for their solutions.
- **Travel and Transportation** – Since the 9/11 terrorist attack, national security problems are of great concern in almost every country. Many security fences have been established in order to avoid the infiltration of terrorists. Access to many sensitive areas such as airports, train stations, and other public places are being closely monitored. Hand vascular pattern technology has been chosen to provide a secure physical access control in many of these areas. Due to its superior authentication performance, ease

of use, and user satisfaction, the hand vascular system was adopted by Incheon International Airport, the largest airport in Korea, and by several major international airports in Japan for physical access control.

- **Hospitals** – Many areas of a hospital require tight security, including medicine cabinets and storage rooms, operating rooms, and data centers where patient records are managed and stored. Some sensitive data such as those related to research studies on dangerous virus may be used with dire consequences if it falls into terrorist hands. Consequently, biometric security methods should be used to protect such sensitive data. Many hospitals have installed hand vascular systems as means for physical access control.

- **Construction Sites** – Unlike other biometric traits which can be adversely affected by external factors such as dirt or oil, the hand vascular pattern is robust to these sources of noise because it lies under the skin of human body. Therefore, the hand vascular pattern technology is appropriate for use in environments such as factories or construction sites.

- **Schools** – The commonly used RF ID cards do not offer high levels of security because people tend to lose them or fail to return their cards. As a result, many universities have adopted hand vascular pattern recognition systems to enhance security for valuable equipment in research laboratories and private belongings in dormitories. It is not only more cost-effective in the long term but also provides an enhanced level of security through individual identification and managerial convenience.

In recent years, many hand vascular pattern recognition systems have been deployed in civilian applications in hospitals, schools, banks, or airports. However, the widest use of hand vascular pattern recognition is for security management in highly secure places like airports. The typical deployment of hand vascular pattern recognition systems can be found at Incheon International Airport, Korea.

Incheon International Airport opened for business in early 2001 and became the largest international airport for international civilian air transportation and cargo traffic in Korea. After September 11 of 2001 when the terrorist hijackings occurred, the airport's security system was upgraded to advanced and state-of-the-art security facilities in response to terrorist threats and various epidemics in southern Asia.

The primary goal in selecting hand vascular pattern recognition systems was to establish a high security access management system and ensure a robust and stringent employee identification process throughout their IT system.

The configuration of hand vascular pattern recognition systems at Incheon Airport is divided into 3 major areas: enrollment center, server room and entry gates between air and land sides. The control tower is also access controlled by vascular biometrics. Fig. 13.5 shows the general configuration for security management system at Incheon Airport using hand vascular pattern technology.

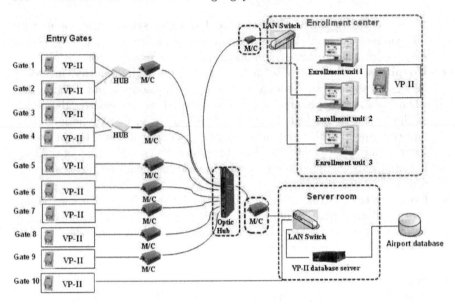

Fig. 13.5. General configuration of security management system at Incheon International Airport using hand vascular technology. M/C is Optical Media Converter.

Each VP-II unit is integrated with HID proximity card readers to enhance the security measure and all VP-II units are connected via TCP/IP network to be available for use for all gates and offices in the airport.

The enrollment process is executed in the enrollment center which is connected with a VP-II database server and managed by the IT department staff. The main IT server room is used for storing the VP-II database. The VP-II scanners at this airport now are being used by more than 30,000 users including all staff members of Incheon International Airport and contractors. "Using the VP-II system for accessing office rooms and presenting attendance is very simple and easy. You never need to worry about remembering your PIN number or bringing the ID card with you", said staff members at Incheon Airport. According to the security manager of Incheon Airport, the adoption of hand vascular pattern recognition systems provides a highly reliable method for controlling the access of their staff and an efficient method for managing their employee attendance.

13.4 Technology

Hand vascular patterns are the representation of blood vessel networks inside the back of hand. The hand vascular pattern recognition system operates by comparing the hand vascular pattern of a user being authenticated against a pre-registered pattern already stored in the database. Fig. 13.6 shows a typical operation of the hand vascular pattern recognition system.

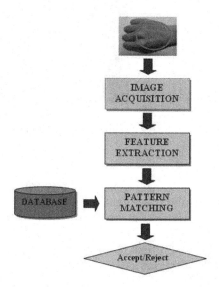

Fig. 13.6. Operation of a typical vascular biometric identification system.

The system uses an infrared (IR) camera that can acquire the pattern of hand blood vessels from the back of the hand. The near-infrared rays of the camera illuminate the back of the hand. The deoxidized hemoglobin in blood vessels absorbs the infrared rays and causes the vascular patterns to appear as black patterns in resulting images. The vascular patterns are then extracted by various digital signal processing algorithms. The extracted vascular pattern is then compared against pre-registered patterns in smart storage devices or database servers to authenticate the individual. Major steps in a typical hand vascular pattern recognition system are image acquisition, feature extraction, and pattern matching.

13.4.1 Image Acquisition

Since the hand vascular pattern lies under the skin, it can not be seen by the human eye. Therefore, we can not use visible light, which occupies a very narrow band (approx. 400 - 700nm wavelength), for photographing. Hand vascular patterns can only be captured under the near-infrared light (approx. 800 - 1000nm wavelength), which can penetrate into the tissues. Blood vessels absorb more infrared radiation than the surrounding tissue [12], which causes the blood vessels to appear as black patterns in the resulting image captured by a charge-couple device (CCD) camera. Fig. 13.7 shows an example of hand images obtained by visible light and near-infrared light.

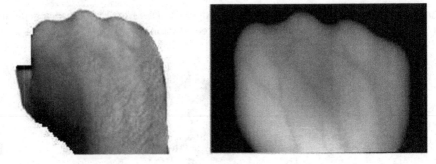

Fig. 13.7. The hand image obtained by visible light (left) and infrared light (right). Images are from [13].

To capture the image of blood vessels under near-infrared light, the scanner uses an LED array to emit the light and illuminate the hand. A CCD camera sensitive to near-infrared light is used to photograph the image. A near-infrared filter attached in front of the CCD camera is used to block all undesired visible light emitted by external sources. The image of blood vessels can be acquired by either reflection or transmission.

- Transmission method: The hand is illuminated by an LED array and the CCD camera captures the light that passes through the hand. To use this method, the LED array is above the hand and the CCD camera is placed on the opposite side of the LED array with respect to the hand. Fig. 13.8 shows the configuration for the LED array and the CCD camera.
- Reflection method: Here the hand is illuminated by an LED array and the CCD camera captures the light that is reflected back from the hand. So, the illumination LED array and the CCD camera are positioned in the same location. Fig. 13.9 shows the configuration for the illumination LED array and the CCD camera.

The reflection method is preferred since the transmission method is often sensitive to changes in the hand's light transmittance, which is easily affected by temperature or weather. If the hand's light transmittance is relatively high, the blood vessels are not very clear in captured images. In contrast, the light transmittance does not significantly affect the level or contrast of the reflected light. Another reason why the reflection method is preferred is due to its easy configuration. Since the illumination LED array and the CCD camera can be located in the same place, the system is easy to embed into small devices.

13.4.2 Feature Extraction

The hand vascular images captured from the acquisition devices contain not only the vascular patterns but also undesired noise and irregular effects such as shadow of the hand and hairs on the skin surface. The captured images

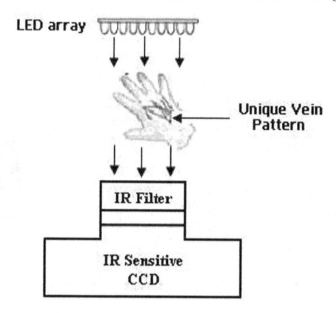

Fig. 13.8. Configuration of transmission-based acquisition method.

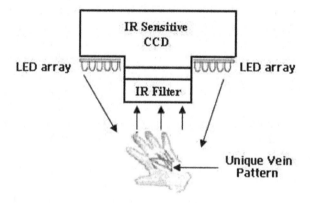

Fig. 13.9. Configuration of reflection-based acquisition method.

should be pre-processed before being used for verification. The aim of a feature extraction algorithm is to accurately extract the vascular patterns from raw images. A typical feature extraction algorithm commonly consists of various image processing steps to remove the noise and irregular effects, enhance the clarity of vascular patterns, and separate the vascular patterns from the background. The final vascular patterns obtained by the feature extraction algorithm are represented as binary images. Fig. 13.10 shows the procedure of a typical feature extraction algorithm for extracting hand vascular patterns from raw images.

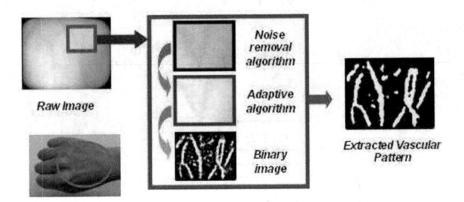

Fig. 13.10. The flow chart of a typical feature extraction algorithm.

The noise removal algorithm is based on a low-pass filter. To improve the clarity of vascular patterns in captured images, an enhancement algorithm is commonly used. A number of algorithms based on filtering techniques have been proposed for enhancing the clarity of vascular patterns in captured images [3,5]. However, these algorithms often enhance the vascular patterns without considering the directional information that is often present. As a result, there could be some loss of connectivity of vascular patterns which lead to the degradation of verification performance. Consequently, one should use an appropriate filter that is adaptive to vascular pattern orientations to efficiently remove undesired noise and preserve the true vascular patterns. To meet this requirement, Im et al. [6] proposed a direction-based vascular pattern extraction algorithm.

The algorithm proposed in [6] utilized two different preprocessing filters: Row Vascular Pattern Extraction Filter (RVPEF) for effective extraction of the horizontal vascular patterns and Column Vascular Pattern Extraction Filter (CVPEF) for effective extraction of the vertical vascular patterns. The final vascular patterns are obtained by combining the outputs from both the filters. Fig. 13.11 shows the flow chart of the direction-based vascular pattern extraction algorithm. Fig. 13.12 shows an example of the final patterns obtained by the direction based extraction algorithm [6]. Fig 13.12(a) is the input image, while Figs. 13.12(b) and 13.12(c) show the loss of connectivity of vascular patterns due to the lack of directional information of vascular patterns. Figs. 13.12(d) and 13.12(e) show the results of the enhancement filters along horizontal and vertical directions. Fig. 13.12(f) shows the final vascular patterns obtained by the direction-based extraction algorithm. This algorithm can efficiently preserve the true vascular patterns and significantly reduce the loss of connectivity.

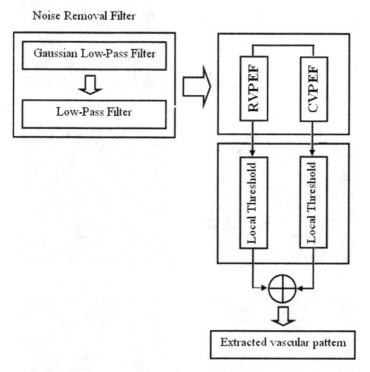

Fig. 13.11. Flow chart of the direction-based vascular pattern extraction algorithm. Image is from [6].

13.4.3 Pattern Matching

In the matching step, the extracted vascular pattern from the feature extraction step is compared against the pre-registered pattern in the database to obtain a matching score. The matching score is then used to compare with the pre-defined system threshold value to decide whether the user can be authenticated or not. Typical methods that are commonly used for pattern matching are structural matching [14] and template matching [15].

Structural matching is based on comparing locations of feature points such as line endings and bifurcations extracted from two patterns being compared to obtain the matching score. This method has been used widely in fingerprint matching. However, unlike the fingerprint patterns, the hand vascular patterns have fewer minutiae-like feature points. Therefore, it is not appropriate to apply only this method for good vascular pattern matching results.

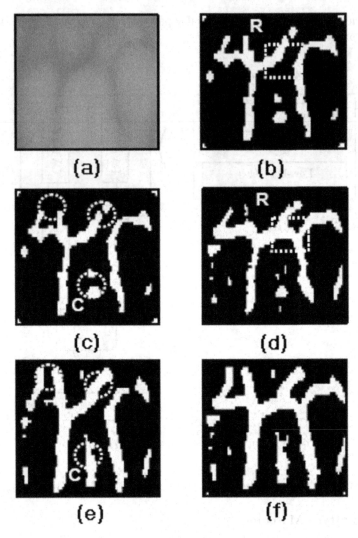

Fig. 13.12. Example of hand vascular pattern obtained by direction-based vascular pattern extraction algorithm. Image is from [6].

Template matching is the most popular and widely used method for matching the vascular patterns. It is based on the comparison of pixel values of two vascular pattern images and has been commonly used for matching line-shaped patterns. Moreover, use of template matching does not require any additional steps to calculate the feature points such as line endings and bifurcations and is robust for vascular pattern matching.

13.5 Performance Evaluation

Hand vascular pattern technology and other vein pattern technologies are relatively new and unlike other biometric modalities, they have not been formally and thoroughly tested by independent third party organizations. The testing results have been typically reported individually by vendors using their own testing databases. Therefore, the reported performance of hand vascular pattern technology and other vein pattern technologies is often quite varied among different vendors. Moreover, there is no standard evaluation method or public benchmark database for testing, which makes it difficult to compare hand vascular pattern technologies across systems from different vendors.

Although various vascular pattern technology developers use different methods and databases for evaluating their systems, the performance of any hand vascular recognition system is usually reported as follows:

- At specific operating points: show the genuine error rate at a fixed impostor error rates.
- Equal Error Rate (EER): is the error rate at which the False Acceptance Rate (FAR) equals to the False Rejection Rate (FRR).
- Detection Error Trade-off (DET) curve: shows performance across a range of decision thresholds.

The DET curves are seen as the most useful method for reporting accuracy results in which the operating point of the system can be easily determined to satisfy the application requirements. A number of studies have reported their results based on their proprietary databases [4,5,9,12,16-21]. Some results in these publications report EER as low as 0% [12,16,21]. However, the databases utilized in many of these tests were often collected in laboratory environment which does not reflect the real world conditions where the systems are deployed. Moreover, the number of participants in these reports was not large enough to obtain accurate results with sufficient confidence.

To obtain more comprehensive results, many studies [4,5,9,13,17,19] have tried to increase the number of participants in their tests. However, this is a time-consuming and expensive process. Therefore, increasing the number of testing participants is often associated with increasing the number of trials for each participant to reduce the cost and obtain more realistic results. Most of the databases in these reports were collected from external environments. The range of testing participants also varied from young people to old people, from men to women. The testing environment was also established outdoors to reflect the near-real world operation. The testing results reported in terms of the EER from these publications are shown on Table 13.1.

To assess the verification speed of the hand vascular pattern recognition system and to evaluate whether the system can be used in reality, the response time of the system is usually measured. In some places such as airports or schools, the system has to be fast enough to be utilized by large number of

Publication	Number of users	Images per user	EER
[9]	687	10	0.145%
[17]	-	20	2.300%
[4,5]	490	10	0.010%
[19]	400	8	0.128%
[13]	500	10	0.695%

Table 13.1. Performance of selected vascular/vein identification systems.

users. In some serious place such as a hospital, if the system operates slowly, it could lead to many dangerous problems in some emergency cases.

The response time is the time for the system to acquire the vascular pattern, pre-process and compare it with the pre-registered pattern stored in the database for verification. Table 13.2 shows the verification speed of some selected commercial biometric systems.

Biometric System	Company	Verification Time [sec]
Hand Vascular Pattern	Techsphere	0.133
Finger Vein Pattern	Hitachi	0.5
Fingerprint	Identix	0.5
Fingerprint	Biometric Identification	1
Hand Shape	RSI	1
Finger Shape	Biomet Partners	1

Table 13.2. Verification speed of typical biometric identification systems.

13.6 Conclusions

Hand vascular pattern technology is relatively new, but it has already gained considerable attention in the biometric community. This is supported by the fact that a large number of research attempts have been conducted to improve the technology in recent years.

Since the release of the first commercial product in 1997, thousands of units have been installed in various applications including access control and time and attendance, banking solutions, transportation, hospital, construction sites, and schools. In addition, because the technology uses features inside the human body, it is less susceptible to surface defects (as in fingerprints) and ambient illumination (as in face). The rapidly increasing number of installed units in various applications within a short time implies that hand vascular pattern technology will be a promising technology in the security field. Although the hand vascular pattern has provided high accuracy and good usability, its performance may degrade under some adverse conditions such as cold weather, undesired noise or external sources.

Future research should attempt to deal with the following issues:

- Acquisition devices: the acquisition device should be improved to make it possible to work in various environments with high tolerance from irregular effects such as illumination, extreme temperature, and sunlight. The acquisition devices should also be more compact to make it suitable to install in many different places.
- Feature extraction algorithm: a more efficient and robust feature extraction algorithm should be developed to deal with undesired noise, shadow, hair, and irregular effects caused by external sources.
- Matching algorithm: the matching algorithm should be improved to reduce the matching score for unauthorized users and increase the matching score for authorized users. Moreover, it should also be capable of reducing the effects from the translations, orientation or non-rigid deformations of the hand.

References

1. K. Shimizu, "Optical Trans-body Imaging Feasibility of Optical CT and Functional Imaging of Living Body," Medicina Philosophica, vol. 11, pp. 620-629, 1992.
2. J. M. Cross and C. L. Smith, "Thermographic Imaging of the Subcutaneous Vascular Network of the Back of the Hand for Biometric Identification," International Carnahan Conference on Security Technology, pp. 20 - 35, October 1995.
3. S. K. Im, H. M. Park, Y. W. Kim, S. C. Han, S.W. Kim, and C. H. Kang, "Biometric Identification System by Extracting Hand Vein Patterns," Journal of the Korean Physical Society, vol. 38, no. 3, pp. 268-272, March 2001.
4. S. K. Im, H. S. Choi, and S. W. Kim, "Design for an Application Specific Processor to Implement a Filter Bank Algorithm for Hand Vascular Pattern Verification," Journal of Korean Physics Society, vol. 41, pp. 461-467, 2002.
5. S. K. Im and H. S. Choi, "A Filter Bank Algorithm for Hand Vascular Pattern Biometrics," Proceedings of ICCARV'02, pp. 776-781, 2002.
6. S. K. Im, H. S. Choi, and S. W. Kim, "A Direction-based Vascular Pattern Extraction Algorithm for Hand Vascular Pattern Verification," ETRI J., vol. 25-2, pp. 101-108, 2003.
7. S. K. Im, H. M. Park, S. W. Kim, C. K. Chung; H. S. Choi, "Improved Vein Pattern Extracting Algorithm and Its Implementation," ICCE 2000, pp. 2-3, June 2000.

8. M. Watanabe, T. Endoh, M. Shiohara, and S. Sasaki, "Palm Vein Authentication Technology and Its Applications," Proceedings of Biometric Consortium Conference, September 2005.

9. N. Miura, A. Nagasaka, and T. Miyatake, "Feature Extraction of Finger-Vein Patterns Based on Repeated Line Tracking and Its Application to Personal Identification," Machine Vision and Applications, vol. 15, pp. 194-203, 2004.

10. H. S. Choi and BK Systems, "Apparatus and Method for Identifying Individuals Through Their Subcutaneous Vein Patterns and Integrated System using Said Apparatus and Method," US Patent, no. US6302375B1, 1998.

11. ISO/IEC 19794-9 Information Technology: Biometric Data Interchange Format Part 9: Vascular image data.

12. L. Wang and G. Leedham, "Near- and Far- Infrared Imaging for Vein Pattern Biometrics," Proceedings of the IEEE International Conference on Video and Signal, pp. 52-59, 2006.

13. A. M. Badawi, "Hand Vein Biometric Verification Prototype: A Testing Performance and Patterns Similarity," IPCV, pp. 3-9, 2006.

14. W. Zhang and Y. Wang, "Core-based Structure Matching Algorithm of Fingerprint Verification," Proceedings of IEEE International Conference on Pattern Recognition, vol. 1, pp. 70-74, 2002.

15. A. K. Jain, R. P. W. Duin, and J. Mao, "Statistical Pattern Recognition: A Review," IEEE Trans. on Pattern Analysis and Machine Intelligence, vol. 22, pp. 4 - 37, 2000.

16. Y. Ding, D. Zhuang and K. Wang, "A Study of Hand Vein Recognition Method," Proceedings of the IEEE International conference on Mechatronics & Automation, pp. 2106-2110, July 2005.

17. C. L. Lin and K. C. Fan, "Biometric Verification using Thermal Images of Palm-Dorsa Vein Patterns," IEEE Trans. On Circuits and Systems, vol. 14, pp. 199-213, 2004

18. L. Wang and G. Leedham, "A Thermal Hand Vein Pattern Verification System," ICAPR'05, pp. 58-65, 2005.

19. Z. Zhang, S. Ma, and X. Han, "Multiscale Feature Extraction of Finger-Vein Patterns Based on Curvelets and Local Interconnection Structure Neural Network," ICPR 2006, pp. 145-148, August 2006.

20. Z. B. Zhang, D. Y. Wu, S. L. Ma, and J. Ma, "Multiscale Feature Extraction of Finger-Vein Patterns Based on Wavelet and Local Interconnection Structure Neural Network," ICNN&B, vol. 2, pp. 1081-1084, 2005.

21. T. Tanaka and N. Kubo, "Biometric Authentication by Hand Vein Patterns," SICE 2004, vol. 1, pp. 249-253, August 2004.

22. A. K. Jain, A. Ross and S. Prabhakar, "An Introduction to Biometrics," IEEE Trans. on Circuits and Systems for Video Technology, vol. 14, no. 1, pp. 4-20, 2004.

Introduction to Multibiometrics

Arun Ross[1], Karthik Nandakumar[2], and Anil K. Jain[2]

[1] Lane Department of Computer Science and Electrical Engineering, West
Virginia University, Morgantown, WV 26506, USA
`arun.ross@mail.wvu.edu`

[2] Department of Computer Science and Engineering, Michigan State University,
East Lansing, MI 48824
`nandakum@cse.msu.edu,jain@cse.msu.edu`

14.1 Introduction

Most biometric systems that are presently in use, typically use a single biometric trait to establish identity (i.e., they are unibiometric systems). With
the proliferation of biometric-based solutions in civilian and law enforcement
applications, it is important that the vulnerabilities and limitations of these
systems are clearly understood. Some of the challenges commonly encountered
by biometric systems are listed below.

1. Noise in sensed data: The biometric data being presented to the system may be contaminated by noise due to imperfect acquisition conditions or
subtle variations in the biometric itself. For example, a scar can change a subject's fingerprint while the common cold can alter the voice characteristics of a
speaker. Similarly, unfavorable illumination conditions may significantly affect
the face and iris images acquired from an individual. Noisy data can result in
an individual being incorrectly labeled as an impostor thereby increasing the
False Reject Rate (FRR) of the system.

2. Non-universality: The biometric system may not be able to acquire
meaningful biometric data from a subset of individuals resulting in a failure-
to-enroll (FTE) error. For example, a fingerprint system may fail to image the
friction ridge structure of some individuals due to the poor quality of their
fingerprints. Similarly, an iris recognition system may be unable to obtain the
iris information of a subject with long eyelashes, drooping eyelids or certain
pathological conditions of the eye. Exception processing will be necessary in
order to accommodate such users into the authentication system.

3. Upper bound on identification accuracy: The matching performance of
a unibiometric system cannot be continuously improved by tuning the feature extraction and matching modules. There is an implicit upper bound on
the number of distinguishable patterns (i.e., the number of distinct biometric feature sets) that can be represented using a template. The capacity of

a template is constrained by the variations observed in the feature set of each subject (i.e., *intra*-class variations) and the variations between feature sets of different subjects (i.e., *inter*-class variations). Table 1.2 lists the error rates associated with four biometric modalities - fingerprints, face, voice, iris - as suggested by recent public tests. These statistics suggest that there is a tremendous scope for performance improvement especially in the context of large-scale authentication systems.

4. Spoof attacks: Behavioral traits such as voice [15] and signature [16] are vulnerable to spoof attacks by an impostor attempting to mimic the traits corresponding to legitimately enrolled subjects. Physical traits such as fingerprints can also be spoofed by inscribing ridge-like structures on synthetic material such as gelatine and play-doh [38, 47]. Targeted spoof attacks can undermine the security afforded by the biometric system and, consequently, mitigate its benefits [48].

Some of the limitations of a unibiometric system can be addressed by designing a system that consolidates *multiple* sources of biometric information. This can be accomplished by fusing, for example, multiple traits of an individual, or multiple feature extraction and matching algorithms operating on the same biometric. Such systems, known as multibiometric systems [53, 25, 19], can improve the matching accuracy of a biometric system while increasing population coverage and deterring spoof attacks. In this chapter, the various sources of biometric information that can be fused as well as the different levels of fusion that are possible are discussed.

14.2 Taxonomy of Multibiometric Systems

In the realm of biometrics, the consolidation of evidence presented by multiple biometric sources is an effective way of enhancing the recognition accuracy of an authentication system. For example, the Integrated Automated Fingerprint Identification System (IAFIS) maintained by the FBI integrates the information presented by multiple fingers to determine a match in the master file. Some of the earliest *multimodal* biometric systems reported in the literature combined the face (image/video) and voice (audio) traits of individuals [9, 4].

A multibiometric system relies on the evidence presented by multiple sources of biometric information. Based on the nature of these sources, a multibiometric system can be classified into one of the following six categories [53]: multi-sensor, multi-algorithm, multi-instance, multi-sample, multimodal and hybrid.

1. Multi-sensor systems: Multi-sensor systems employ multiple sensors to capture a single biometric trait of an individual. For example, a face recognition system may deploy multiple 2D cameras to acquire the face image of a subject [35]; an infrared sensor may be used in conjunction with a visible-light sensor to acquire the subsurface information of a person's face [29, 7, 57]; a multispectral camera may be used to acquire images of the iris, face or finger

[54, 43]; or an optical as well as a capacitive sensor may be used to image the fingerprint of a subject [37]. The use of multiple sensors, in some instances, can result in the acquisition of complementary information that can enhance the recognition ability of the system. For example, based on the nature of illumination due to ambient lighting, the infrared and visible-light images of a person's face can present different levels of information resulting in enhanced matching accuracy. Similarly, the performance of a 2D face matching system can be improved by utilizing the shape information presented by 3D range images.

2. Multi-algorithm systems: In some cases, invoking multiple feature extraction and/or matching algorithms on the same biometric data can result in improved matching performance. Multi-algorithm systems consolidate the output of multiple feature extraction algorithms, or that of multiple matchers operating on the same feature set. These systems do not necessitate the deployment of new sensors and, hence, are cost-effective compared to other types of multibiometric systems. But on the other hand, the introduction of new feature extraction and matching modules can increase the computational complexity of these systems. Ross et al. [52] describe a fingerprint recognition system that utilizes minutiae as well as texture information to represent and match fingerprint images. The inclusion of the texture-based algorithm introduces additional processing time associated with the application of Gabor filters on the input fingerprint image. However, the performance of the hybrid matcher is shown to exceed that of the individual matchers. Lu et al. [36] discuss a face recognition system that combines three different feature extraction schemes (Principal Component Analysis (PCA), Independent Component Analysis (ICA) and Linear Discriminant Analysis (LDA)). The authors postulate that the use of different feature sets makes the system robust to a variety of intra-class variations normally associated with the face biometric. Experimental results indicate that combining multiple face classifiers can enhance the identification rate of the biometric system.

3. Multi-instance systems: These systems use multiple instances of the same body trait and have also been referred to as multi-unit systems in the literature. For example, the left and right index fingers, or the left and right irises of an individual, may be used to verify an individual's identity [45, 27]. The US-VISIT border security program presently uses the left- and right-index fingers of visitors to validate their travel documents at the port of entry. FBI's IAFIS combines the evidence of all ten fingers to determine a matching identity in the database. These systems can be cost-effective if a single sensor is used to acquire the multi-unit data in a sequential fashion (e.g., US-VISIT). However, in some instances, it may be desirable to obtain the multi-unit data simultaneously (e.g., IAFIS) thereby demanding the design of an effective (and possibly more expensive) acquisition device.

4. Multi-sample systems: A single sensor may be used to acquire multiple samples of the same biometric trait in order to account for the variations that can occur in the trait, or to obtain a more complete representation of

the underlying trait. A face system, for example, may capture (and store) the frontal profile of a person's face along with the left and right profiles in order to account for variations in the facial pose. Similarly, a fingerprint system equipped with a small size sensor may acquire multiple dab prints of an individual's finger in order to obtain images of various regions of the fingerprint. A mosaicing scheme may then be used to stitch the multiple impressions and create a composite image. One of the key issues in a multi-sample system is determining the *number* of samples that have to be acquired from an individual. It is important that the procured samples represent the *variability* as well as the *typicality* of the individual's biometric data. To this end, the desired relationship between the samples has to be established before-hand in order to optimize the benefits of the integration strategy. For example, a face recognition system utilizing both the frontal- and side-profile images of an individual may stipulate that the side-profile image should be a three-quarter view of the face [17, 42]. Alternately, given a set of biometric samples, the system should be able to automatically select the "optimal" subset that would best represent the individual's variability. Uludag et al. [58] discuss two such schemes in the context of fingerprint recognition. The first method, called DEND, employs a clustering strategy to choose a template set that best represents the intra-class variations, while the second method, called MDIST, selects templates that exhibit maximum similarity with the rest of the impressions.

5. Multimodal systems: Multimodal systems establish identity based on the evidence of multiple biometric traits. For example, some of the earliest multimodal biometric systems utilized face and voice features to establish the identity of an individual [4, 10, 3]. Physically uncorrelated traits (e.g., fingerprint and iris) are expected to result in better *improvement* in performance than correlated traits (e.g., voice and lip movement). The cost of deploying these systems is substantially more due to the requirement of new sensors and, consequently, the development of appropriate user interfaces. The identification accuracy can be significantly improved by utilizing an increasing number of traits although the *curse-of-dimensionality* phenomenon would impose a bound on this number. The curse-of-dimensionality limits the number of attributes (or features) used in a pattern classification system when only a small number of training samples is available [14]. The number of traits used in a specific application will also be restricted by practical considerations such as the cost of deployment, enrollment time, throughput time, expected error rate, user habituation issues, etc.

6. Hybrid systems: Chang et al. [5] use the term *hybrid* to describe systems that integrate a subset of the five scenarios discussed above. For example, Brunelli et al. [4] discuss an arrangement in which two speaker recognition algorithms are combined with three face recognition algorithms at the match score and rank levels via a HyperBF network. Thus, the system is multi-algorithmic as well as multimodal in its design. Similarly, the NIST BSSR1 dataset [40] has match scores pertaining to two different face matchers operating on the frontal face image of an individual (multi-algorithm), and a

fingerprint matcher operating on the left- and right-index fingers of the same individual (multi-instance).

Another category of multibiometric systems combine primary biometric identifiers (such as face and fingerprint) with soft biometric attributes (such as gender, height, weight, eye color, etc.). Soft biometric traits cannot be used to distinguish individuals reliably since the same attribute is likely to be shared by several different people in the target population. However, when used in conjunction with primary biometric traits, the performance of the authentication system can be significantly enhanced [23]. Soft biometric attributes also help in filtering (or indexing) large biometric databases by limiting the number of entries to be searched in the database. For example, if it is determined (automatically or manually) that the subject is an "Asian Male", then the system can constrain its search to only those identities in the database labeled with these attributes. Alternately, soft biometric traits can be used in surveillance applications to decide if at all primary biometric information has to be acquired from a certain individual. Automated techniques to estimate soft biometric characteristics is an ongoing area of research and is likely to benefit law enforcement and border control biometric applications.

14.3 Levels of fusion

Based on the type of information available in a certain module, different levels of fusion can be defined. Sanderson and Paliwal [55] categorize the various levels of fusion into two broad categories: pre-classification or fusion *before* matching and post-classification or fusion *after* matching (see Figure 14.1). Such a categorization is necessary since the amount of information available for fusion reduces drastically once the matcher has been invoked. Pre-classification fusion schemes typically require the development of new matching techniques (since the matchers used by the individual sources may no longer be relevant) thereby introducing additional challenges. Pre-classification schemes include fusion at the sensor (or raw data) and the feature levels while post-classification schemes include fusion at the match score, rank and decision levels. A brief description of each of these fusion levels is presented in this section.

14.3.1 Sensor-level fusion

The raw biometric data (e.g., a face image) acquired from an individual represents the richest source of information although it is expected to be contaminated by noise (e.g., non-uniform illumination, background clutter, etc.). Sensor-level fusion refers to the consolidation of (a) raw data obtained using multiple sensors or (b) multiple snapshots of a biometric using a single sensor. Mosaicing multiple impressions of the same finger is a good example of fusion

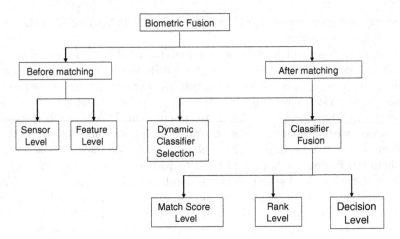

Fig. 14.1. Fusion can be accomplished at various levels in a biometric system. Most multibiometric systems fuse information at the match score level or the decision level. More recently researchers have begun to fuse information at the sensor and feature levels. In biometric systems operating in the identification mode, fusion can be done at the rank level.

at this level. Jain and Ross [24] discuss a mosaicing scheme that creates a composite fingerprint image from the evidence presented by multiple dab prints. The algorithm uses the minutiae points to first approximately register the two images using a simple affine transformation. The Iterative Closest Point (ICP) algorithm is then used to register the ridge information corresponding to the two images after applying a low-pass filter to the individual images and normalizing their histograms. The normalization ensures that the pixel intensities of the individual dab prints are comparable. Blending is accomplished by merely concatenating the two registered images. The performance using the mosaiced image templates was shown to exceed that of the individual dab print templates.

14.3.2 Feature-level fusion

In feature-level fusion, the feature sets originating from multiple biometric algorithms are consolidated into a single feature set by the application of appropriate feature normalization, transformation and reduction schemes. The primary benefit of feature-level fusion is the detection of correlated feature values generated by different biometric algorithms and, in the process, identifying a salient set of features that can improve recognition accuracy. Eliciting this feature set typically requires the use of dimensionality reduction methods [22, 46] and, therefore, feature-level fusion assumes the availability of a large number of training data. Also, the feature sets being fused are typically expected to reside in commensurate vector space in order to permit the application of a suitable matching technique upon consolidating the feature sets.

Feature-level fusion is challenging for the following reasons:

1. The relationship between the feature spaces of different biometric systems may not be known.
2. The feature sets of multiple modalities may be incompatible. For example, the minutiae set of fingerprints and the eigen-coefficients of face are irreconcilable. One is a variable length feature set (i.e., it varies across images) whose individual values parameterize a minutia point; the other is a fixed length feature set (i.e., all images are represented by a fixed number of eigen-coefficients) whose individual values are scalar entities.
3. If the two feature sets are fixed length feature vectors, then one could consider concatenating them to generate a new feature set. However, concatenating two feature vectors might lead to the curse-of-dimensionality problem ([21]) where increasing the number of features might actually degrade the system performance especially in the presence of small number of training samples. Although the curse-of-dimensionality is a well known problem in pattern recognition, it is particularly pronounced in biometric applications because of the time, effort and cost required to collect large amounts of biometric (training) data.
4. Most commercial biometric systems do not provide access to the feature sets used in their products. Hence, very few biometric researchers have focused on integration at the feature level and most of them generally prefer fusion schemes that use match scores or decision labels.

If the length of each of the two feature vectors to be consolidated is fixed across all users, then a feature concatenation scheme followed by a dimensionality reduction procedure may be adopted. Let $\mathbf{X} = \{x_1, x_2, \ldots, x_m\}$ and $\mathbf{Y} = \{y_1, y_2, \ldots, y_n\}$ denote two feature vectors ($\mathbf{X} \in R^m$ and $\mathbf{Y} \in R^n$) representing the information extracted from two different biometric sources. The objective is to fuse these two feature sets in order to yield a new feature vector, $\mathbf{Z}$, that would better represent an individual. The vector $\mathbf{Z}$ of dimensionality k, $k < (m+n)$, can be generated by first concatenating vectors $\mathbf{X}$ and $\mathbf{Y}$, and then performing feature selection or feature transformation on the resultant feature vector in order to reduce its dimensionality. The key stages of such an approach are described below.

Feature Normalization

The individual feature values of vectors $\mathbf{X} = \{x_1, x_2, \ldots, x_m\}$ and $\mathbf{Y} = \{y_1, y_2, \ldots, y_n\}$ may exhibit significant differences in their range as well as form (i.e., distribution). Concatenating such diverse feature values will not be appropriate in many cases. For example, if the x_i's are in the range $[0, 100]$ while the y_i's are in the range $[0, 1]$, then the distance between two concatenated feature vectors will be more sensitive to the x_i's than the y_i's. The goal of feature normalization is to modify the location (mean) and scale (variance) of the features values via a transformation function in order to map them into a common domain. Adopting an appropriate normalization scheme also helps address the problem of outliers in feature values. While a variety of normalization schemes can be used, two simple schemes are discussed here: the min-max and median normalization schemes.

Let x and x' denote a feature value before and after normalization, respectively. The min-max technique computes x' as

$$x' = \frac{x - \min(F_x)}{\max(F_x) - \min(F_x)}, \tag{14.1}$$

where F_x is the function which generates x, and $\min(F_x)$ and $\max(F_x)$ represent the minimum and maximum of all possible x values that will be observed, respectively. The min-max technique is effective when the minimum and the maximum values of the component feature values are known beforehand. In cases where such information is not available, an estimate of these parameters has to be obtained from the available set of training data. The estimate may be affected by the presence of outliers in the training data and this makes min-max normalization sensitive to outliers. The median normalization scheme, on the other hand, is relatively robust to the presence of noise in the training data. In this case, x' is computed as

$$x' = \frac{x - median(F_x)}{median(|\, (x - median(F_x))\, |)}. \tag{14.2}$$

The denominator is known as the Median Absolute Deviation (MAD) and is an estimate of the scale parameter of the feature value. Although, this normalization scheme is relatively insensitive to outliers, it has a low efficiency compared to the mean and standard deviation estimators. Normalizing the feature values via any of these techniques results in modified feature vectors $\mathbf{X}' = \{x'_1, x'_2, \ldots x'_m\}$ and $\mathbf{Y}' = \{y'_1, y'_2, \ldots y'_n\}$. Feature normalization may not be necessary in cases where the feature values pertaining to multiple sources are already comparable.

Feature Selection or Transformation

Concatenating the two feature vectors, $\mathbf{X}'$ and $\mathbf{Y}'$, results in a new feature vector, $\mathbf{Z}' = \{x'_1, x'_2, \ldots x'_m, y'_1, y'_2, \ldots y'_n\}$, $\mathbf{Z}' \in R^{m+n}$. The curse-of-dimensionality dictates that the new vector of dimensionality $(m + n)$ need not necessarily result in an improved matching performance compared to that obtained by $\mathbf{X}'$ and $\mathbf{Y}'$ alone. The feature selection process is a dimensionality reduction scheme that entails choosing a minimal feature set of size k, $k < (m + n)$, such that a criterion (objective) function applied to the training set of feature vectors is optimized. There are several feature selection algorithms in the literature, and any one of these could be used to reduce the dimensionality of the feature set $\mathbf{Z}'$. Examples include sequential forward selection (SFS), sequential backward selection (SBS), sequential forward floating search (SFFS), sequential backward floating search (SBFS), "plus l take away r" and branch-and-bound search (see [46] and [26] for details). Feature selection techniques rely on an appropriately formulated criterion function to elicit the optimal subset of features from a larger feature set. In the case of a biometric system, this criterion function could be the Equal Error Rate (EER); the d-prime measure; the area of overlap between genuine and impostor training scores; the average GAR at pre-determined FAR values in the ROC/DET curves corresponding to the training set; or the area under the ROC curve (AUC).

Dimensionality reduction may also be accomplished using feature *transformation* methods where the vector $\mathbf{Z}'$ is subjected to a linear or a non-linear mapping that projects it to a lower dimensional subspace. Examples of such transformations include the use of principal component analysis (PCA), independent component analysis (ICA), multidimensional scaling (MDS), Kohonen Maps and neural networks ([22]). The application of a feature selection or feature transformation procedure results in a new feature vector $\mathbf{Z} = \{z_1, z_2, \ldots z_k\}$ which can now be used to represent the identity of an individual.

Ross and Govindarajan [50] apply feature-level fusion to three different scenarios: (a) multi-algorithm, where two different face recognition algorithms based on Principal Component Analysis (PCA) and Linear Discriminant Analysis (LDA) are combined; (b) multi-sensor, where three different color channels of a face image are independently subjected to LDA and then combined; and (c) multimodal, where the face and hand geometry feature vectors are combined.

14.3.3 Score-level fusion

A match score represents the result of comparing two feature sets extracted using the same feature extractor. A *similarity* score denotes how "similar" the two feature sets are, while a *distance* score denotes how "different" they are[3].

In score-level fusion the match scores output by multiple biometric matchers are combined to generate a new match score (a scalar) that can be subsequently used by the verification or identification modules for rendering an identity decision. Fusion at this level is the most commonly discussed approach in the biometric literature primarily due to the ease of accessing and processing match scores (compared to the raw biometric data or the feature set extracted from the data). Fusion methods at this level can be broadly classified into three categories [53]: density-based schemes, transformation-based schemes and classifier-based schemes.

---

[3] Consequently, a high similarity score between a pair of feature sets indicates a good match whereas a high distance score indicates a poor match.

Density-based fusion schemes

Let $\mathbf{s} = [s_1, s_2, \ldots, s_R]$ denote the scores emitted by multiple matchers, with s_j representing the match score of the jth matcher, $j = 1, \ldots, R$. Further, let the labels ω_0 and ω_1 denote the genuine and impostor classes, respectively. Then, by Bayes decision theory [14], the probability of error can be minimized by adopting the following decision rule[4].

$$\text{Assign } \mathbf{s} \rightarrow \omega_i \text{ if}$$

$$P(\omega_i|\mathbf{s}) > P(\omega_j|\mathbf{s}), i \neq j, \quad and \quad i, j = 0, 1. \tag{14.3}$$

Here, the *a posteriori* probability $P(\omega_i|\mathbf{s})$, $i = 0, 1$, can be derived from the class-conditional density function $p(\mathbf{s}|\omega_i)$ using the Bayes formula, i.e.,

$$P(\omega_i|\mathbf{s}) = \frac{p(\mathbf{s}|\omega_i)P(\omega_i)}{p(\mathbf{s})}, \tag{14.4}$$

where $P(\omega_i)$ is the *a priori* probability of observing class ω_i and $p(\mathbf{s})$ denotes the probability of encountering $\mathbf{s}$. Thus, equation (14.3) can be re-written as

$$\text{Assign } \mathbf{s} \rightarrow \omega_i \text{ if}$$

$$\frac{p(\mathbf{s}|\omega_i)}{p(\mathbf{s}|\omega_j)} > \tau, i \neq j, \quad and \quad i, j = 0, 1 \tag{14.5}$$

where $\frac{p(\mathbf{s}|\omega_i)}{p(\mathbf{s}|\omega_j)}$ is known as the *likelihood ratio* and $\tau = \frac{P(\omega_j)}{P(\omega_i)}$ is a pre-determined threshold. The density $p(\mathbf{s}|\omega_i)$ is typically estimated from a training set of match score vectors, using parametric or non-parametric techniques [56]. However, a large number of training samples is necessary to reliably estimate the joint-density function $p(\mathbf{s}|\omega_i)$ especially if the dimensionality of the feature vector $\mathbf{s}$ is large. In the absence of sufficient number of training samples (which is typically the case when the multibiometric system is first deployed or if its parameters are subsequently adjusted), it is commonly assumed that the scalar scores $s_i, s_2, \ldots s_R$ are generated by R independent random processes. This assumption permits the density function to be expressed as

$$p(\mathbf{s}|\omega_i) = \prod_{j=1}^{R} p(s_j|\omega_i), \tag{14.6}$$

where the joint-density function is now replaced by the product of its marginals. The marginal densities, $p(s_j|\omega_i)$, $j = 1, 2, \ldots R$, $i = 0, 1$, are estimated from a

---

[4] This is known as the Bayes decision rule or the minimum-error-rate classification rule under the 0-1 loss function [14]

training set of genuine and impostor scores corresponding to each of the R biometric matchers. Equation (14.6) results in the *product rule* which combines the scores generated by the R matchers as,

$$s_{prod} = \prod_{j=1}^{R} \frac{p(s_j|\omega_0)}{p(s_j|\omega_1)}. \tag{14.7}$$

Kittler et al. [28] modify the product rule by further assuming that the *a posteriori* probability $P(\omega_i|\mathbf{s})$ of class ω_i does not deviate much from its *a priori* probability $P(\omega_i)$ resulting in the *sum rule*:

$$s_{sum} = \frac{\sum_{j=1}^{R} p(s_j|\omega_0)}{\sum_{j=1}^{R} p(s_j|\omega_1)}. \tag{14.8}$$

Similar expressions can be derived for combining the match scores using the max, min and median rules [53, 28]. All the aforementioned rules implicitly assume that the match scores are *continuous* random variables. Dass et al. [11] relax this assumption and represent the univariate density functions (i.e., the marginals in Equation (14.6)) as a mixture of discrete as well as continuous components. The resulting density functions are referred to as generalized densities. The authors demonstrate that the use of generalized density estimates (as opposed to continuous density estimates) significantly enhances the matching performance of the fusion algorithm. Furthermore, they use copula functions [41, 8] to model the correlation structure between the match scores $s_1, s_2, \ldots, s_R$ and, subsequently, define a novel fusion rule known as the *copula fusion rule*.

Transformation-based fusion schemes

Density-based schemes, as stated earlier, require a large number of training samples (i.e., genuine and impostor match scores) in order to accurately estimate the density functions. This may not be possible in most multibiometric systems due to the time, effort and cost involved in acquiring labeled multibiometric data in an operational environment. In such situations, it may be necessary to *directly* combine the match scores generated by multiple matchers using simple fusion operators (such as the simple sum of scores or order statistics) without first interpreting them in a probabilistic framework. However, such an approach is meaningful only when the scores output by the matchers are comparable. To facilitate this, a score normalization process is essential to transform the multiple match scores into a common domain. The process of score normalization entails changing the location and the scale parameters of the underlying match score distributions in order to ensure compatibility between multiple score variables.

Once the match scores output by multiple matchers are transformed into a common domain they can be combined using simple fusion operators

Table 14.1. Summary of score normalization techniques.

Normalization Technique	Robustness	Efficiency
Min-max	No	High
Decimal scaling	No	High
Z-score	No	High
Median and MAD	Yes	Moderate
Double sigmoid	Yes	High
Tanh-estimators	Yes	High

such as the sum of scores, product of scores or order statistics (e.g., maximum/minimum of scores or median score).

Classifier-based fusion schemes

In the verification mode of operation, the match scores generated by the multiple matchers may be input to a trained pattern classifier, such as a neural network, in order to determine the class label (genuine or impostor). In this approach, the goal is to directly estimate the class rather than to compute an intermediate scalar value. Classifier-based fusion schemes assume the availability of a large representative number of genuine and impostor scores during the training phase of the classifier when its parameters are computed. The component scores do not have to be transformed into a common domain prior to invoking the classifier.

In the biometric literature several classifiers have been used to consolidate the match scores of multiple matchers. Brunelli and Falavigna [4] use a HyperBF network to combine matchers based on voice and face features. Verlinde and Cholet [59] compare the relative performance of three different classifiers, namely, the k-Nearest Neighbor classifier using vector quantization, the decision tree classifier, and a classifier based on the logistic regression model when fusing the match scores originating from three biometric matchers. Experiments on the M2VTS database ([44]) show that the total error rate (sum of the false accept and false reject rates) of the multimodal system is an order of magnitude less than that of the individual matchers. Chatzis et al. [6] use classical k-means clustering, fuzzy clustering and median radial basis function (MRBF) algorithms for fusion at the match score level. The proposed system combines the output of five different face and voice matchers. Each matcher provides a match score and a quality metric indicating the reliability of the match score. These values are concatenated to form a ten-dimensional vector that is input to the classifiers. Ben-Yacoub et al. [2] evaluate a number of classification schemes for fusion including support vector machine (SVM) with polynomial kernels, SVM with Gaussian kernels, C4.5 decision trees, multilayer perceptron, Fisher linear discriminant, and Bayesian classifier. Experimental evaluations on the XM2VTS database ([39]) consisting of 295 subjects suggest the benefit of score level fusion. Bigun et al. [3]

propose a novel algorithm based on the Bayesian classifier that takes into account the estimated accuracy of the individual classifiers (i.e., matchers) during the fusion process. Sanderson and Paliwal [55] use a support vector machine (SVM) to combine the scores of face and speech experts. In order to address noisy input, they design structurally noise-resistant classifiers based on a piece-wise linear classifier and a modified Bayesian classifier. Wang et al. [60] view the match scores obtained from face and iris recognition modules as a two-dimensional feature vector and use Fisher's discriminant analysis and a neural network classifier to classify this match score vector. Ross and Jain [51] use decision tree and linear discriminant classifiers for classifying the match scores pertaining to the face, fingerprint and hand geometry modalities.

14.3.4 Rank-level fusion

When a biometric system operates in the identification mode, the output of the system can be viewed as a ranking of the enrolled identities. In this case, the output indicates the set of possible matching identities sorted in decreasing order of confidence. The goal of rank level fusion schemes is to consolidate the ranks output by the individual biometric subsystems in order to derive a consensus rank for each identity. Ranks provide more insight into the decision-making process of the matcher compared to just the identity of the best match, but they reveal less information than match scores. However, unlike match scores, the rankings output by multiple biometric systems are comparable. As a result, no normalization is needed and this makes rank level fusion schemes simpler to implement compared to the score level fusion techniques.

Let us assume that there are M users enrolled in the database and let the number of matchers be R. Let $r_{j,k}$ be the rank assigned to user k by the jth matcher, $j = 1, \ldots, R$ and $k = 1, \ldots, M$. Let s_k be a statistic computed for user k such that the user with the lowest value of s is assigned the highest consensus (or reordered) rank. Ho et al. [18] describe the following three methods to compute the statistic s.

1. Highest Rank Method: In the highest rank method, each user is assigned the highest rank (minimum r value) as computed by different matchers, i.e., the statistic for user k is

$$s_k = \min_{j=1}^{R} r_{j,k}. \tag{14.9}$$

Ties are broken randomly to arrive at a strict ranking order. This method is useful only when the number of users is large compared to the number of matchers, which is typically the case in large-scale authentication systems. If this condition is not satisfied, the system will encounter several ties thereby rendering the final ranking uninformative. An advantage of the highest rank method is that it can utilize the strength of each matcher effectively. Even if only one matcher assigns a high rank to the correct identity, it is still very likely that this user will receive a high rank after reordering.

2. Borda Count Method: The Borda count method uses the sum of the ranks assigned by the individual matchers to calculate the value of s, i.e., the statistic for user k is

$$s_k = \sum_{j=1}^{R} r_{j,k}.$$ (14.10)

The magnitude of the Borda count for each user is a measure of the degree of agreement among the different matchers on whether the input belongs to that user. The Borda count method assumes that the ranks assigned to the users by the matchers are statistically independent and that all the matchers perform equally well.

3. Logistic Regression Method: The logistic regression method is a generalization of the Borda count method where a weighted sum of the individual ranks is calculated, i.e., the statistic for user k is

$$s_k = \sum_{j=1}^{R} w_j r_{j,k}.$$ (14.11)

The weight, w_j, to be assigned to the jth matcher, $j = 1, \ldots, R$, is determined by logistic regression [1]. The logistic regression method is useful when the different biometric matchers have significant differences in their accuracies. However, this method requires a training phase to determine the weights.

14.3.5 Decision-level fusion

Many commercial off-the-shelf (COTS) biometric matchers provide access only to the final recognition decision. When such COTS matchers are used to build a multibiometric system, only decision level fusion is feasible. Methods proposed in the literature for decision level fusion include "AND" and "OR" rules [12], majority voting [34], weighted majority voting [30], Bayesian decision fusion [61], the Dempster-Shafer theory of evidence [61] and behavior knowledge space [20].

Let M denote the number of possible decisions (also known as *class labels* or simply *classes* in the pattern recognition literature; these three terms are used interchangeably in the following discussion) in a biometric system. Also, let $\omega_1, \omega_2, \ldots \omega_M$ indicate the classes associated with each of these decisions.

1. "AND" and "OR" Rules: In a multibiometric verification system, the simplest method of combining decisions output by the different matchers is to use the "AND" and "OR" rules. The output of the "AND" rule is a "match" only when all the biometric matchers agree that the input sample matches

with the template. On the contrary, the "OR" rule outputs a "match" decision as long as at least one matcher decides that the input sample matches with the template. The limitation of these two rules is their tendency to result in extreme operating points. When the "AND" rule is applied, the False Accept Rate (FAR) of the multibiometric system is extremely low (lower than the FAR of the individual matchers) while the False Reject Rate (FRR) is high (greater than the FRR of the individual matchers). Similarly, the "OR" rule leads to higher FAR and lower FRR than the individual matchers. When one biometric matcher has a substantially higher equal error rate compared to the other matcher, the combination of the two matchers using "AND" and "OR" rules may actually degrade the overall performance [12]. Due to this phenomenon, the "AND" and "OR" rules are rarely used in practical multibiometric systems.

2. Majority Voting: The most common approach for decision level fusion is majority voting where the input biometric sample is assigned to that identity on which a majority of the matchers agree. If there are R biometric matchers, the input sample is assigned an identity when at least k of the matchers agree on that identity, where

$$k = \begin{cases} \frac{R}{2} + 1 & \text{if } R \text{ is even,} \\ \frac{R+1}{2} & \text{otherwise.} \end{cases} \qquad (14.12)$$

When none of the identities is supported by k matchers, a reject decision is output by the system. Majority voting assumes that all the matchers perform equally well. The advantages of majority voting are: (i) no apriori knowledge about the matchers is needed, and (ii) no training is required to come up with the final decision. A theoretical analysis of the majority voting fusion scheme was done by [33] who established limits on the accuracy of the majority vote rule based on the number of matchers, the individual accuracy of each matcher and the pairwise dependence between the matchers.

3. Weighted Majority Voting: When the matchers used in a multibiometric system are not of similar recognition accuracy (i.e, imbalanced matchers/classifiers), it is reasonable to assign higher weights to the decisions made by the more accurate matchers. In order to facilitate this weighting, the labels output by the individual matchers are converted into degrees of support for the M classes as follows.

$$s_{j,k} = \begin{cases} 1, & \text{if output of the } j^{th} \text{ matcher is class } \omega_k, \\ 0, & \text{otherwise,} \end{cases} \qquad (14.13)$$

where $j = 1, \ldots, R$ and $k = 1, \ldots, M$. The discriminant function[5] for class ω_k computed using weighted voting is

---

[5] The discriminant function is used to classify an input pattern. Typically, a discriminant function is defined for each pattern class and the input pattern is assigned to the class whose discriminant function gives the maximum response.

$$g_k = \sum_{j=1}^{R} w_j s_{j,k}, \tag{14.14}$$

where w_j is the weight assigned to the jth matcher. A test sample is assigned to the class with the highest score (value of discriminant function).

4. Bayesian Decision Fusion: The Bayesian decision fusion scheme relies on transforming the discrete decision labels output by the individual matchers into continuous probability values. The first step in the transformation is the generation of the confusion matrix for each matcher by applying the matcher to a training set $\mathbf{D}$. Let CM^j be the $M \times M$ confusion matrix for the jth matcher. The (k, r)th element of the matrix CM^j (denoted as $cm_{k,r}^j$) is the number of instances in the training data set where a pattern whose true class label is ω_k is assigned to the class ω_r by the jth matcher. Let the total number of data instances in $\mathbf{D}$ be N and the number of elements that belong to class ω_k be N_k. Let c_j be the class label assigned to the test sample by the jth matcher. The value $cm_{k,c_j}^j / N_k$ can be considered as an estimate of the conditional probability $P(c_j | \omega_k)$ and N_k / N can be treated as an estimate of the prior probability of class ω_k. Given the vector of decisions made by R matchers $\mathbf{c} = [c_1, \ldots, c_R]$, we are interested in calculating the posterior probability of class ω_k, i.e., $P(\omega_k | \mathbf{c})$. According to the Bayes rule,

$$P(\omega_k | \mathbf{c}) = \frac{P(\mathbf{c} | \omega_k) P(\omega_k)}{P(\mathbf{x})}, \tag{14.15}$$

where $k = 1, \ldots, M$. The denominator in Equation 14.15 is independent of the class ω_k and can be ignored for the decision making purpose. Therefore, the discriminant function for class ω_k is

$$g_k = P(\mathbf{c} | \omega_k) P(\omega_k). \tag{14.16}$$

The Bayes decision fusion technique chooses that class which has the largest value of discriminant function calculated using equation 14.16. To simplify the computation of $P(\mathbf{c} | \omega_k)$, one can assume conditional independence between the different matchers. Under this assumption, the decision rule is known as naive Bayes rule and $P(\mathbf{c} | \omega_k)$ is computed as

$$P(\mathbf{c} | \omega_k) = P(c_1, \ldots, c_R | \omega_k) = \prod_{j=1}^{R} P(c_j | \omega_k). \tag{14.17}$$

The accuracy of the naive Bayes decision fusion rule has been found to be fairly robust even when the matchers are not independent [13].

5. Dempster-Shafer Theory of Evidence: The Dempster-Shafer theory of evidence is based on the concept of assigning degrees of belief for uncertain events. Note that the degree of belief for an event is different from the probability of the event. This subtle difference is explained in the following example.

Suppose we know that a biometric matcher has a reliability of 0.95, i.e., the output of the matcher is reliable 95% of the time and unreliable 5% of the time. Suppose that the matcher outputs a "match" decision. We can assign a 0.95 degree of belief to the "match" decision and a zero degree of belief to the "non-match" decision. The zero belief does not rule out the "non-match" decision completely, unlike a zero probability. Instead, the zero belief indicates that there is no reason to believe that the input does not match successfully against the template. Hence, we can view belief theory as a generalization of probability theory. Indeed, belief functions are more flexible than probabilities when our knowledge about the problem is incomplete.

Rogova [49] and Kuncheva et al. [31] propose the following methodology to compute the belief functions and to accumulate the belief functions according to the Dempster's rule. For a given input pattern, the decisions made by R classifiers for a M-class problem is represented using a $R \times M$ matrix known as a decision profile (DP) [31] which is given by,

$$DP = \begin{bmatrix} s_{1,1} & \cdots & s_{1,k} & \cdots & s_{1,M} \\ \cdots & & & & \\ s_{j,1} & \cdots & s_{j,k} & \cdots & s_{j,M} \\ \cdots & & & & \\ s_{R,1} & \cdots & s_{R,k} & \cdots & s_{R,M} \end{bmatrix},$$

where $s_{j,k}$ is the degree of support provided by the jth matcher to the kth class. At the decision level, the degree of support is expressed as

$$s_{j,k} = \begin{cases} 1, & \text{if output of the } j^{th} \text{ matcher is class } \omega_k, \\ 0, & \text{otherwise,} \end{cases} \quad (14.18)$$

where $j = 1, \ldots, R$ and $k = 1, \ldots, M$. The decision template (DT^k) of each class ω_k is the average decision profile for all the training instances that belong to the class ω_k. When the degrees of support defined in Equation 14.18 are used, one can easily see that the elements of the decision template DT^k are related to the elements of the confusion matrices of the R matchers in the following manner.

$$DT_{j,r}^k = \frac{CM_{k,r}^j}{N_k}, \quad (14.19)$$

where N_k is the number of instances in the training set $\mathbf{D}$ that belong to class ω_k, $j = 1, \ldots, R$ and $k, r = 1, \ldots, M$. For a given test pattern X^t, the decision profile DP^t is computed after the decisions of the R matchers are obtained. The similarity between DP^t and the decision templates for the various classes is calculated as follows.

$$\Phi_{j,k} = \frac{\left(1 + (\|DT_j^k - DP_j^t\|)^2\right)^{-1}}{\sum_{r=1}^{M} \left(\left(1 + (\|DT_j^r - DP_j^t\|)^2\right)^{-1}\right)}, \quad (14.20)$$

where DT_j^k represents the jth row of DT^k belonging to class ω_k, DP_j^t represents the jth row of DP^t belonging to the test pattern X^t, and $||.||$ denotes the matrix norm. For every class $k = 1, \ldots, M$ and for every matcher $j = 1, \ldots, R$, we can compute the degree of belief as

$$b_{j,k} = \frac{\Phi_{j,k}\left[\prod_{r=1,r \neq k}^{M}(1 - \Phi_{j,r})\right]}{1 - \Phi_{j,k}\left[\prod_{r=1,r \neq k}^{M}(1 - \Phi_{j,r})\right]}. \tag{14.21}$$

The accumulated degree of belief for each class $k = 1, \ldots, M$ based on the outputs of R matchers is then obtained using the Dempster's rule as

$$g_k = \prod_{j=1}^{R} b_{j,k}. \tag{14.22}$$

The test pattern X^t is assigned to the class having the highest degree of belief g_k.

14.4 Summary

Multibiometric systems are expected to enhance the recognition accuracy of a personal authentication system by reconciling the evidence presented by multiple sources of information. In this chapter, the different sources of biometric information as well as the type of information that can be consolidated was presented. Different fusion strategies were also discussed. Typically, early integration strategies (e.g., feature-level) are expected to result in better performance than late integration (e.g., score-level) strategies. However, it is difficult to predict the performance gain due to each of these strategies prior to invoking the fusion methodology. While the *availability* of multiple sources of biometric information (pertaining either to a single trait or to multiple traits) may present a compelling case for fusion, the *correlation* between the sources has to be examined before determining their suitability for fusion. Combining uncorrelated or negatively correlated sources is expected to result in a better improvement in matching performance than combining positively correlated sources. This has been demonstrated by Kuncheva et al. [32] for fusion at the decision level using the majority vote scheme. Combining sources that make complementary errors is assumed to be beneficial. However, defining an appropriate diversity measure to predict fusion performance has been elusive thus far.

References

1. A. Agresti. *An Introduction to Categorical Data Analysis*. Wiley, 1996.

2. S. Ben-Yacoub, Y. Abdeljaoued, and E. Mayoraz. Fusion of Face and Speech data for Person Identity Verification. *IEEE Transactions on Neural Networks*, 10(5):1065–1075, September 1999.
3. E. S. Bigun, J. Bigun, B. Duc, and S. Fischer. Expert Conciliation for Multi-modal Person Authentication Systems using Bayesian Statistics. In *First International Conference on Audio- and Video-based Biometric Person Authentication (AVBPA)*, pages 291–300, Crans-Montana, Switzerland, March 1997.
4. R. Brunelli and D. Falavigna. Person Identification Using Multiple Cues. *IEEE Transactions on Pattern Analysis and Machine Intelligence*, 17(10):955–966, October 1995.
5. K. I. Chang, K. W. Bowyer, and P. J. Flynn. An Evaluation of Multimodal 2D+3D Face Biometrics. *IEEE Transactions on Pattern Analysis and Machine Intelligence*, 27(4):619–624, April 2005.
6. V. Chatzis, A. G. Bors, and I. Pitas. Multimodal Decision-level Fusion for Person Authentication. *IEEE Transactions on Systems, Man, and Cybernetics, Part A: Systems and Humans*, 29(6):674–681, November 1999.
7. X. Chen, P. J. Flynn, and K. W. Bowyer. IR and Visible Light Face Recognition. *Computer Vision and Image Understanding*, 99(3):332–358, September 2005.
8. U. Cherubini, E. Luciano, and W. Vecchiato. *Copula Methods in Finance*. Wiley, 2004.
9. C. C. Chibelushi, F. Deravi, and J. S. Mason. Voice and Facial Image Integration for Speaker Recognition. In R. I. Damper, W. Hall, and J. W. Richards, editors, *Multimedia Technologies and Future Applications*, pages 155–161. Pentech Press, London, 1994.
10. C. C. Chibelushi, J. S. D. Mason, and F. Deravi. Feature-level Data Fusion for Bimodal Person Recognition. In *Proceedings of the Sixth International Conference on Image Processing and Its Applications*, volume 1, pages 399–403, Dublin, Ireland, July 1997.
11. S. C. Dass, K. Nandakumar, and A. K. Jain. A Principled Approach to Score Level Fusion in Multimodal Biometric Systems. In *Proceedings of Fifth International Conference on Audio- and Video-based Biometric Person Authentication (AVBPA)*, pages 1049–1058, Rye Brook, USA, July 2005.
12. J. Daugman. Combining Multiple Biometrics. Available at http://www.cl.cam.ac.uk/users/jgd1000/combine/combine.html, 2000.
13. P. Domingos and M. Pazzani. On the Optimality of the Simple Bayesian Classifier under Zero-One Loss. *Machine Learning*, 29(2-3):103–130, November/December 1997.
14. R. O. Duda, P. E. Hart, and D. G. Stork. *Pattern Classification*. John Wiley & Sons, 2001.
15. A. Eriksson and P. Wretling. How Flexible is the Human Voice? A Case Study of Mimicry. In *Proceedings of the European Conference on Speech Technology*, pages 1043–1046, Rhodes, 1997.
16. W. R. Harrison. *Suspect Documents, their Scientific Examination*. Nelson-Hall Publishers, 1981.
17. H. Hill, P. G. Schyns, and S. Akamatsu. Information and Viewpoint Dependence in Face Recognition. *Cognition*, 62(2):201–222, February 1997.
18. T. K. Ho, J. J. Hull, and S. N. Srihari. Decision Combination in Multiple Classifier Systems. *IEEE Transactions on Pattern Analysis and Machine Intelligence*, 16(1):66–75, January 1994.

19. L. Hong, A. K. Jain, and S. Pankanti. Can Multibiometrics Improve Performance? In *Proceedings of IEEE Workshop on Automatic Identification Advanced Technologies (AutoID)*, pages 59–64, New Jersey, USA, October 1999.
20. Y. S. Huang and C. Y. Suen. Method of Combining Multiple Experts for the Recognition of Unconstrained Handwritten Numerals. *IEEE Transactions on Pattern Analysis and Machine Intelligence*, 17(1):90–94, January 1995.
21. A. K. Jain and B. Chandrasekaran. Dimensionality and Sample Size Considerations in Pattern Recognition Practice. In P.R. Krishnaiah and L. N. Kanal, editors, *Handbook of Statistics*, volume 2, pages 835–855. North-Holland, Amsterdam, 1982.
22. A. K. Jain, R. P. W. Duin, and J. Mao. Statistical Pattern Recognition: A Review. *IEEE Transactions on Pattern Analysis and Machine Intelligence*, 22(1):4–37, January 2000.
23. A. K. Jain, K. Nandakumar, X. Lu, and U. Park. Integrating Faces, Fingerprints and Soft Biometric Traits for User Recognition. In *Proceedings of ECCV International Workshop on Biometric Authentication (BioAW)*, volume LNCS 3087, pages 259–269, Prague, Czech Republic, May 2004. Springer.
24. A. K. Jain and A. Ross. Fingerprint Mosaicking. In *IEEE International Conference on Acoustics, Speech, and Signal Processing (ICASSP)*, volume 4, pages 4064–4067, Orlando, USA, May 2002.
25. A. K. Jain and A. Ross. Multibiometric Systems. *Communications of the ACM, Special Issue on Multimodal Interfaces*, 47(1):34–40, January 2004.
26. A. K. Jain and D. Zongker. Feature Selection: Evaluation, Application, and Small Sample Performance. *IEEE Transactions on Pattern Analysis and Machine Intelligence*, 19(2):153–158, February 1997.
27. J. Jang, K. R. Park, J. Son, and Y. Lee. Multi-unit Iris Recognition System by Image Check Algorithm. In *Proceedings of International Conference on Biometric Authentication (ICBA)*, pages 450–457, Hong Kong, July 2004.
28. J. Kittler, M. Hatef, R. P. Duin, and J. G. Matas. On Combining Classifiers. *IEEE Transactions on Pattern Analysis and Machine Intelligence*, 20(3):226–239, March 1998.
29. A. Kong, J. Heo, B. Abidi, J. Paik, and M. Abidi. Recent Advances in Visual and Infrared Face Recognition - A Review. *Computer Vision and Image Understanding*, 97(1):103–135, January 2005.
30. L. I. Kuncheva. *Combining Pattern Classifiers - Methods and Algorithms*. Wiley, 2004.
31. L. I. Kuncheva, J. C. Bezdek, and R. P. W. Duin. Decision Templates for Multiple Classifier Fusion: An Experimental Comparison. *Pattern Recognition*, 34(2):299–314, 2001.
32. L. I. Kuncheva, C. J. Whitaker, C. A. Shipp, and R. P. W. Duin. Is Independence Good for Combining Classifiers? In *Proceedings of International Conference on Pattern Recognition (ICPR)*, volume 2, pages 168–171, Barcelona, Spain, 2000.
33. L. I. Kuncheva, C. J. Whitaker, C. A. Shipp, and R. P. W. Duin. Limits on the Majority Vote Accuracy in Classifier Fusion. *Pattern Analysis and Applications*, 6(1):22–31, 2003.
34. L. Lam and C. Y. Suen. Application of Majority Voting to Pattern Recognition: An Analysis of its Behavior and Performance. *IEEE Transactions on Systems, Man, and Cybernetics, Part A: Systems and Humans*, 27(5):553–568, 1997.

35. J. Lee, B. Moghaddam, H. Pfister, and R. Machiraju. Finding Optimal Views for 3D Face Shape Modeling. In *Proceedings of the IEEE International Conference on Automatic Face and Gesture Recognition (FG)*, pages 31–36, Seoul, Korea, May 2004.
36. X. Lu, Y. Wang, and A. K. Jain. Combining Classifiers for Face Recognition. In *IEEE International Conference on Multimedia and Expo (ICME)*, volume 3, pages 13–16, Baltimore, USA, July 2003.
37. G. L. Marcialis and F. Roli. Fingerprint Verification by Fusion of Optical and Capacitive Sensors. *Pattern Recognition Letters*, 25(11):1315–1322, August 2004.
38. T. Matsumoto, H. Matsumoto, K. Yamada, and S. Hoshino. Impact of Artificial Gummy Fingers on Fingerprint Systems. In *Optical Security and Counterfeit Deterrence Techniques IV, Proceedings of SPIE*, volume 4677, pages 275–289, San Jose, USA, January 2002.
39. K. Messer, J. Matas, J. Kittler, J. Luettin, and G. Maitre. XM2VTSDB: The Extended M2VTS Database. In *Proceedings of Second International Conference on Audio- and Video-Based Biometric Person Authentication (AVBPA)*, pages 72–77, Washington D.C., USA, March 1999.
40. National Institute of Standards and Technology. NIST Biometric Scores Set. Available at http://http://www.itl.nist.gov/iad/894.03/biometricscores, 2004.
41. R. B. Nelsen. *An Introduction to Copulas*. Springer, 1999.
42. A. O'Toole, H. Bulthoff, N. Troje, and T. Vetter. Face Recognition across Large Viewpoint Changes. In *Proceedings of the International Workshop on Automatic Face- and Gesture-Recognition (IWAFGR)*, pages 326–331, Zurich, Switzerland, June 1995.
43. Z. Pan, G. Healey, M. Prasad, and B. Tromberg. Face Recognition in Hyperspectral Images. *IEEE Transactions on Pattern Analysis and Machine Intelligence*, 25(12):1552–1560, December 2003.
44. S. Pigeon and L. Vandendrope. M2VTS Multimodal Face Database Release 1.00. Available at http://www.tele.ucl.ac.be/PROJECTS/M2VTS/m2fdb.html, 1996.
45. S. Prabhakar and A. K. Jain. Decision-level Fusion in Fingerprint Verification. Technical Report MSU-CSE-00-24, Michigan State University, October 2000.
46. P. Pudil, J. Novovicova, and J. Kittler. Floating Search Methods in Feature Selection. *Pattern Recognition Letters*, 15(11):1119–1124, November 1994.
47. T. Putte and J. Keuning. Biometrical Fingerprint Recognition: Don't Get Your Fingers Burned. In *Proceedings of IFIP TC8/WG8.8 Fourth Working Conference on Smart Card Research and Advanced Applications*, pages 289–303, 2000.
48. N. K. Ratha, J. H. Connell, and R. M. Bolle. An Analysis of Minutiae Matching Strength. In *Proceedings of Third International Conference on Audio- and Video-Based Biometric Person Authentication (AVBPA)*, pages 223–228, Halmstad, Sweden, June 2001.
49. G. Rogova. Combining the Results of Several Neural Network Classifiers. *Neural Networks*, 7(5):777–781, 1994.
50. A. Ross and R. Govindarajan. Feature Level Fusion Using Hand and Face Biometrics. In *Proceedings of SPIE Conference on Biometric Technology for Human Identification II*, volume 5779, pages 196–204, Orlando, USA, March 2005.

51. A. Ross and A. K. Jain. Information Fusion in Biometrics. *Pattern Recognition Letters*, 24(13):2115–2125, September 2003.

52. A. Ross, A. K. Jain, and J. Reisman. A Hybrid Fingerprint Matcher. *Pattern Recognition*, 36(7):1661–1673, July 2003.

53. A. Ross, K. Nandakumar, and A. K. Jain. *Handbook of Multibiometrics*. Springer, New York, USA, 1st edition, 2006.

54. R. K. Rowe and K. A. Nixon. Fingerprint Enhancement Using a Multispectral Sensor. In *Proceedings of SPIE Conference on Biometric Technology for Human Identification II*, volume 5779, pages 81–93, March 2005.

55. C. Sanderson and K. K. Paliwal. Information Fusion and Person Verification Using Speech and Face Information. Research Paper IDIAP-RR 02-33, IDIAP, September 2002.

56. D. W. Scott. *Multivariate Density Estimation: Theory, Practice and Visualization*. Wiley Series in Probability and Statistics. Wiley-Interscience, August 1992.

57. D. A. Socolinsky, A. Selinger, and J. D. Neuheisel. Face Recognition with Visible and Thermal Infrared Imagery. *Computer Vision and Image Understanding*, 91(1-2):72–114, July-August 2003.

58. U. Uludag, A. Ross, and A. K. Jain. Biometric Template Selection and Update: A Case Study in Fingerprints. *Pattern Recognition*, 37(7):1533–1542, July 2004.

59. P. Verlinde and G. Cholet. Comparing Decision Fusion Paradigms using k-NN based Classifiers, Decision Trees and Logistic Regression in a Multi-modal Identity Verification Application. In *Proceedings of Second International Conference on Audio- and Video-Based Biometric Person Authentication (AVBPA)*, pages 188–193, Washington D.C., USA, March 1999.

60. Y. Wang, T. Tan, and A. K. Jain. Combining Face and Iris Biometrics for Identity Verification. In *Fourth International Conference on Audio- and Video-based Biometric Person Authentication (AVBPA)*, pages 805–813, Guildford, UK, June 2003.

61. L. Xu, A. Krzyzak, and C. Y. Suen. Methods for Combining Multiple Classifiers and their Applications to Handwriting Recognition. *IEEE Transactions on Systems, Man, and Cybernetics*, 22(3):418–435, 1992.

15

Multispectral Face Recognition

Diego A. Socolinsky

Equinox Corporation, Baltimore, MD 21202, USA
diego@equinoxsensors.com

15.1 Introduction

Face recognition technology has steadily progressed from adequately handling only well-controlled imagery to tackling increasingly more realistic conditions. This progression has seen the introduction of nuisance factors such as pose, illumination, occlusion and facial expression as integral components of the standard face recognition problem. A large body of research has accrued, aimed at coping with increased levels of image variability while maintaining high recognition performance. Variation in level and nature of illumination is among the most insidious problems for recognition algorithms, and thus a considerable portion of that research centers around it. Among other techniques, the use of thermal infrared imagery, by itself or in combination with other modalities, has been proposed as an alternative means of handling the problem of variable illumination conditions.

Variation in illumination conditions between enrollment and testing is one of the major problems for visible-spectrum-based face recognition [2, 26]. Since the radiance sensed by a visible camera at a given image location is proportional to the product of object albedo and incident light, changes in illumination can have dramatic effects on object appearance. In terms of faces, this makes modeling the distribution of appearances of a single person under multiple lighting conditions very difficult. Cast shadows, specularities and other non-Lambertian phenomena make the problem even harder. Multiple techniques have been developed to handle this issue [3, 31, 16, 26, 11], all of which improve recognition performance by explicitly taking into account the effect of illumination on facial appearance. An alternative route taken by some researchers is to explore the potential of thermal infrared imagery for face recognition. The primary advantage of this imaging modality is that changes in ambient illumination have little or no influence on facial appearance. Thus, instead of incorporating the large variability in appearance caused by lighting variation into a model, a new imaging modality is chosen so that such variability is simply not present.

Another critical shortcoming of visible cameras is that as the level of illumination decreases, the signal to noise ratio rises quickly, and recognition becomes impossible. Compared to the human eye, standard visible cameras are not very sensitive, which means that even at illumination levels for which a human can easily discern and recognize faces, automatic recognition is not feasible. Of course, as the light level decreases further into darkness, automatic processing remains impossible. This issue has been addressed recently by using both thermal infrared and intensified near-infrared (NIR) imagery, alone or in combination.

While thermal imagery provides us with the advantages of illumination invariance and no-light operation, it is not without shortcomings. Of particular importance is the fact that thermal emissions from the face are dependent on ambient temperature and wind conditions, as well as on metabolic activity of the subject. Additionally, the fact that the lenses of most glasses are opaque in the thermal infrared means that a large portion of the population have partial occlusions in the infrared images of their face. This is an important issue that must be addressed by any deployable thermal face recognition system. Fortunately, most of the situations that hamper recognition performance with thermal imagery are not a problem for visible imagery, and vice-versa. For this reason, systems using a combination of both modalities have proved time and again to be superior to those using either modality separately.

In Section 15.2, we review the nature of thermal infrared imagery of the human face. This provides motivation for the use of such imagery in biometric applications, and also indicates some of the strengths and weaknesses of the modality. The rest of the chapter is structured to reflect the nature of the recognition task, and the historical development of the field. We progress through same-session recognition experiments (training and testing face images acquired in the same session), where we mention the earliest and simplest experimental setups used to validate the use of thermal imagery for biometrics, to more complex and realistic scenarios where we explore the effect of time passage, unconstrained outdoor illumination and low light levels. Most of the research highlighted in this chapter is due to work at Equinox Corporation, although we mention the efforts of other groups.

15.2 Imaging Modalities

Before discussing specifics of multispectral face recognition, we should briefly review the nature of the imagery in each band of the spectrum. Figure 15.1 shows wavelengths from just below 0.4 microns up to 14 microns. The human eye is sensitive to radiation roughly in the range between 0.4 and 0.7 microns, depending on individual variation. Blue colors are perceived toward the low end of that range, while reds are near the top. Imagery captured in this range is purely reflective, meaning that the photons sensed by the focal plane array originate at a light source, bounce off the target object and into the

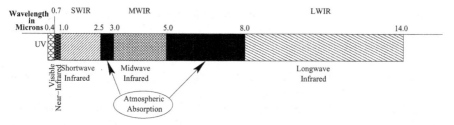

Fig. 15.1. Nomenclature for various portions of the electromagnetic spectrum.

camera. This is also true of imaging in the next two slices of the spectrum: near-infrared (NIR), which ranges from 0.7 to about 1 micron, and shortwave infrared (SWIR), which comprises the range from 1 to 2.5 microns. Moisture suspended in the atmosphere is mostly responsible for the absorption bands 2.5–3 microns, and 5–8 microns, which is why we normally do not image in those wavelengths. Between 5 and 8 microns lies the midwave infrared (MWIR) spectrum. This is an interesting modality, as it has both reflective and emissive properties. That is, photons impinging on the focal plane array fall into two categories: reflected ones, much as in the lower wavelengths, and emitted ones, which are radiated by the target object by virtue of its temperature, and are independent of external illuminants. Finally, the range between 8 and 14 microns is known as longwave infrared (LWIR), and consists primarily of emitted radiation. Note that regardless of wavelength, smooth objects such as a mirror will reflect radiation, and thus no imaging modality is completely invariant to illumination effects.

Figure 15.2 shows a face simultaneously imaged in the visible, SWIR, MWIR and LWIR spectra. Even though both visible and SWIR imagery are strictly reflective, it is interesting to note the fairly pronounced difference in the appearance of the subject between the two modalities. For most people, hair has a much higher albedo in the SWIR, resulting in light hair colored images. Likewise, most clothing dyes have higher albedo in the NIR and SWIR than in the visible spectrum, thus clothing often appears much brighter in those modalities. The change in appearance when we move to longer wavelengths is quite dramatic, as we start to see the emissive component taking over. The images in Figure 15.2 were acquired indoors, and thus the reflective aspects of MWIR are not emphasized, resulting in rather similar MWIR and LWIR images. An interesting fact, well known to anyone familiar with thermal imagery, is that glass is completely opaque in the MWIR and LWIR, as can be seen by looking at the eyeglasses in Figures 15.2(c) and 15.2(d). Glass also has very low emissivity in the MWIR and LWIR (compared to skin), which combined with the fact that room temperature is normally lower than skin temperature, explains why it appears darker than skin. This has obvious consequences for any biometric application that exploits the appearance of the human face.

The emissivity of a material, as the name indicates, measures the aptitude of that material for radiating energy at a given wavelength, and is standardized on a scale from 0 to 1. It has a meaning analogous to the albedo for reflective imagery. It follows from conservation of energy (Kirchoff's Law) that the higher the emissivity, the higher the absorption and therefore the lower the reflectivity. This is relevant for thermal imaging biometrics because the emissivity of human skin is relatively high in the MWIR and almost unity in the LWIR [30]. Consequently, incident LWIR illumination has almost no effect on radiance measured by a LWIR camera. This is the fundamental basis for the illumination invariance of thermal infrared face recognition.

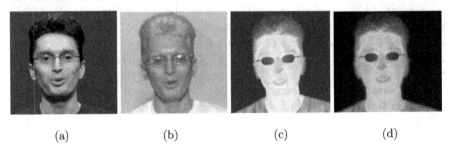

(a)　　　　　(b)　　　　　(c)　　　　　(d)

Fig. 15.2. A face simultaneously imaged in the (a) visible spectrum 0.4-0.7 microns, (b) shortwave infared 0.9-1.7 microns, (c) midwave infrared 3.0-5.0 microns, and (d) longwave infrared 8.0-14.0 microns.

Both MWIR and LWIR imagery can be acquired without the need for any external illumination, since all objects above absolute zero temperature radiate considerable energy in those wavelengths. For regions in the SWIR and below, an external light source is necessary, and therefore darkness becomes a limiting factor for imaging. Image intensification in the NIR is one approach to acquiring reflective imagery near the visible spectrum with low light levels. The most common technology for image intensification is through the use of a microchannel plate (MCP). MCPs are made of several million tightly packed channels about 10 microns in diameter. Each channel functions as an independent photomultiplier, and since the channels are arranged in a spatially coherent fashion, any light pattern impinging on the input end of the MCP results in the same (intensified) pattern being emitted out the output end. When a photon enters the input end of an individual channel, it releases an electron within the tube. A strong potential difference of several thousand volts is applied between input and output ends of the microchannel, thus accelerating the electrons. As the accelerated electrons travel down the channel, they release more electrons from the tube material as they collide with the inside walls. This effect is called an electron cascade, and is the crux of the intensification process, as one original electron, through the application of a strong potential difference, generates a much larger number of electrons.

Gain factors of 10^6 or more are achievable through this process. Accelerated electrons exit the microchannel, and collide against a phosphor screen. Upon collision, electrons release photons from the phosphor, and these photons constitute the final intensified image. Optics in front and behind the MCP allow light to be focused on the front end and the intensified output to be viewed on the back. Modern image intensifiers are lightweight and operate on very low power.

Typical military grade devices will operate for dozens of hours on standard AA batteries and provide enough photomultiplication to allow for navigation and basic tasks under moonless overcast night conditions. Even though it greatly increases the signal strength, photomultiplication also creates a characteristic noise pattern. While a detailed analysis of intensifier noise is beyond the scope of this chapter, Figure 15.3 shows decreasing intensified image quality as a function of decreasing light level. Strong noise at low light levels is a problem for face recognition systems, severely compromising performance.

Fig. 15.3. Intensified NIR images of the same subject under decreasing light levels.

15.3 Feasibility of LWIR Imagery as a Biometric

The first studies in thermal infrared face recognition were aimed at determining whether the imaging modality held any promise for human identification. In this context, simple experiments were designed, where enrollment and testing images of multiple subjects were acquired during a short period of time. This type of scenario is often referred to as same-session recognition, since it tests the ability to recognize as such images of the same subject acquired during the same data collection session. While same-session studies are easier to organize, their results do not directly reflect the viability of the biometric for real-world use, since under operational conditions biometric enrollment and verification would occur at different times. Nonetheless, these studies provide a reasonable idea of viability, and can be used as a stepping stone toward more accurate performance estimates.

Wilder et al. [29] use a low-quality LWIR pyrolectric sensor to collect indoor and outdoor imagery during a single session. They show that recognition performance is roughly comparable between visible and thermal modalities, and that using a simple fusion strategy to combine both modalities greatly increases performance. Cutler's work [7] uses a low-sensitivity MWIR sensor and the PCA-based eigenfaces algorithm, and concludes that recognition performance is equivalent to that attainable in the visible spectrum. Socolinsky et al. [18] used a database of approximately 90 subjects, collected during a single session and containing controlled variations in illumination to show that recognition in the LWIR spectrum outperforms visible-based recognition with two different algorithms. More recently, Freidrich and Yeshurun [10] show that recognition rates achieved with thermal imagery on a pose and expression variant same-session database are higher than those achieved with comparable visible imagery. As part of a time-lapse study, Chen et al. [6] find that same-session recognition in the LWIR spectrum outperforms visible recognition, when both of them use a PCA-based algorithm.

The most comprehensive study to date on same-session thermal infrared recognition is Socolinsky and Selinger [25]. The database used comprises ninety ethnically and gender diverse subjects imaged during a single day. All images were collected with a custom sensor capable of simultaneously imaging visible and LWIR images through a common aperture. This provides a unique opportunity to compare performance on imagery which differs only in modality, but is alike in all other respects, such as pose, illumination and expression. In order to gauge the effect of illumination variation on recognition performance, the authors collected imagery under three controlled lighting conditions, and for a variety of facial expressions. We should note (see [25] for more details) that all eye coordinates were manually located on the visible images and transferred to the LWIR ones via their coregistered nature.

Socolinsky and Selinger [25] compares recognition performance for visible and thermal imagery across multiple data representation algorithms, including PCA, LDA, ICA and LFA. Each of these representations was coupled with a number of distance measures including L^1, L^2 and angle. Figure 15.4 shows cumulative match curves for LDA-based recognition for visible and thermal imagery under a variety of distance measures. The general conclusion to be drawn from these performance graphs is that in a same-session recognition scenario, thermal imagery is superior to visible imagery, at least if the illumination is not carefully controlled. In fact, even if the illumination is kept under strict control, thermal recognition performance is higher than its visible counterpart (this is not shown in the graphs), although the difference is not so pronounced. This clearly indicates that the pattern of thermal emission from a person's face is distinct, and bears strict correlation with his or her identity. A second definitive conclusion of the study is that using a combination of visible and thermal imagery greatly outperforms the use of visible (or LWIR) imagery alone. This is supported by further studies by other researchers [6, 5]. Fusion results were obtained by simply adding individual modality scores (distances), and using the composite number as a new distance.

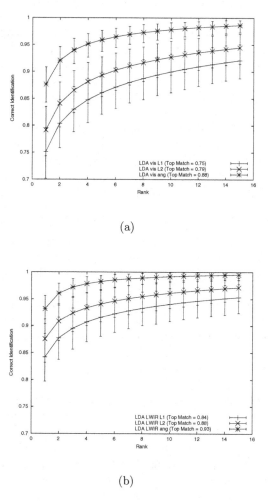

(a)

(b)

Fig. 15.4. Cumulative recognition rates for LDA-based identification algorithms on (a) visible and (b) LWIR imagery.

15.4 Stability of Thermal Biometrics

Results from same-session experiments serve only to provide initial evidence that thermal imaging of the face may be a valid biometric signature. They are not sufficient to assert that conclusion, since any biometric face identification system must operate on imagery acquired later than the original enrollment session. In order for the system to be useful, it must be able to match imagery of a subject to the enrollment imagery for a long period of time after enrollment. It is well-known that performance of visible face recognition algorithms degrades as time elapsed between training and testing images increases [15]. Facial appearance changes with weight fluctuations, facial hair, makeup, aging, exposure to sunlight and many other factors. The task of a face recognition system is to ignore as many of these exogenous factors as possible, and still home in on the underlying identity variable, which is unchanged. To the extent that an imaging modality is able to provide a more stable and discriminating signature over time, it can be considered better for facial recognition. The only way to evaluate this stability is through the time-consuming process of collecting data over an extended period at regular intervals.

Studies by two research groups on the same dataset shed complementary light on the issue of stability of thermal face biometrics. Chen et al. [5, 6] collected a database of visible and LWIR images of 240 distinct subjects, acquired under controlled conditions over a period of ten weeks. During each weekly session, each subject was imaged under two different illumination conditions, and with two different expressions. Visible images were acquired in color and with a 1200 × 1600 pixel resolution. Thermal images were acquired at 320 × 240 resolution and 12 bit per pixel depth. Eye coordinates used for geometric normalization of all images, both visible and thermal, were manually located independently in each modality.

In their studies [6, 5], the authors find that a PCA-based recognition algorithm using LWIR imagery outperformed the same algorithm using visible images, in a same-session scenario, yet underperformed it when the test imagery was acquired a week or more after the enrollment imagery. Furthermore, the loss in performance suffered when using LWIR imagery was more severe than the corresponding loss when using visible imagery. They attribute these results to the noticeable variability in thermal appearance of subjects' faces imaged at different times. The conclusion is that thermal infrared imagery is less suitable than visible imagery for face recognition applications, due to its instability over time. However, the study also notes that when used in concert with visible imagery as part of a fused system, overall performance is superior to even state-of-the-art commercial (visible only) systems.

Using the same data, we conducted a new study [22]. In order to evaluate recognition performance with time-lapse data, we performed the following experiments. The first-week frontal illumination images of each subject with neutral expression were used as the gallery. Thus the gallery contains a single image of each subject. For all weeks, the probe set contains neutral expression images of each subject, with mugshot lighting. The number of subjects in each week ranges from 44 to 68, while the number of overlapping subjects with respect to the first week ranges from 31 to 56. In addition to the PCA algorithm used previously [6, 5], we also tested the proprietary Equinox algorithm. This algorithm works natively on visible-thermal image pairs, and is capable of using either or both modalities as its input. Experimental results are shown in Figure 15.5.

Focusing for a moment on the performance curves, we do not see a clearly decreasing performance trend for either modality. This appears to indicate that whatever time-lapse effects are responsible for performance degradation versus same-session results remain roughly constant over the ten week trial period. Other studies have shown that over a period of years, face recognition performance degrades linearly with time [15]. Following that observation, we assume that weekly recognition performances for both algorithms and modalities are drawn independently and distributed according to a (locally) constant distribution, which we may assume to be Gaussian. Using this assumption, we estimate the standard deviation of that distribution, and plot error bars at two standard deviations. We see that, consistently with prior results [6, 5], thermal performance is lower than visible performance when using PCA as a the recognition algorithm. When using the Equinox algorithm, we note that overall recognition performance is markedly improved in both modalities. More importantly, we see that weekly performance curves for both modalities cross each other multiple times, while remaining within each other's error bars. This indicates that the performance difference between modalities using this algorithm is not statistically significant. In fact, the difference between mean performances for the modalities is only 0.21 standard deviations, hardly a significant difference. We should also note that the mean visible time-lapse performance with this algorithm is 88.65%, compared to approximately 86.5% for the FaceIt algorithm [6]. This shows that the Equinox algorithm is competitive with the commercial state-of-the-art face recognition systems on this data set, and therefore provides a fair means of evaluating thermal recognition performance, as using a poor visible algorithm for comparison would make thermal recognition appear better. As many previous studies have shown [19, 25, 6], fusion greatly increases performance, which is also illustrated in Figure 15.5.

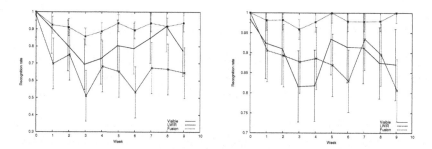

Fig. 15.5. Left: top-rank recognition results for visible, LWIR and fusion as a function of weeks elapsed between enrollment and testing, using PCA. Right: top-rank recognition results for visible, LWIR and fusion as a function of weeks elapsed between enrollment and testing, using the Equinox algorithm. Note that the x-coordinate of each curve is slightly offset in order to better present the error bars.

When this study is taken in context with Chen et al. [6], it shows that care must be exercised when evaluating imaging modalities based solely on the outcome of classification experiments. Specifically referring to face recognition with visible and thermal imagery, the study shows that there is no significant difference in recognition performance when a state-of-the-art algorithm is used for both modalities. Thus thermal face imagery provides a stable biometric signature suitable for recognition, with relative advantages and disadvantages with respect to visible imagery, which are dependent on the situation.

15.5 Face Recognition in Very Low Light

One primary disadvantage of face recognition with visible cameras is that it requires relatively high levels of illumination. Recognition in dim or dark conditions is simply not possible with standard imaging technology. This limits deployment opportunities to those scenarios where daylight or artificial illumination is available, and eliminates many covert uses. The main imaging modalities capable of functioning in dark environments without additional illumination are thermal infrared and intensified near infrared (I2). While thermal imaging can operate in complete darkness, such as subterranean environments, intensified NIR sensors require some ambient illumination. Latest generation intensifiers can yield useful imagery at light levels which the naked eye perceives as pitch black, so for all but the darkest situations, intensified imagery can be used instead of or in conjunction with thermal imagery. This section provides a brief overview of both approaches to face recognition in low light.

15.5.1 Thermal-Only Recognition

The first step in any automated face recognition task is the detection and localization of the subject's face. There is a large literature on the subject of face detection in the visible spectrum (see for example [28] and the references therein). Face detection and tracking using a combination of visible and thermal imagery is addressed by Eveland [9], who develops a system capable of detecting and tracking faces using either one or both modalities together. The second major step after face localization, is geometric normalization. This normally entails the detection of two or more points on the face, and the subsequent affine mapping of the acquired image onto a canonical geometry. In the visible spectrum, geometric normalization is often achieved by locating the centers of both eyes, and affinely mapping them to standard locations. Automated location of eyes (and pupils) in visible imagery is a well-studied problem [8, 32], both passively and with active methods.

It is easy to see that thermal images of human faces have fewer readily localizable landmarks, even by a human operator. The eyes themselves are completely uniform, with no distinction whatsoever between pupil, iris and sclera. Chen et al. [6] performed experiments with manual localization of eye centers in LWIR imagery, and they report that due to the lack of detail in such imagery around the eyes, it was difficult to obtain precise measurements.

Furthermore, they note that recognition performance with thermal imagery decays more rapidly as a function of incorrect eye localization than does recognition with visible images. Freidrich and Yeshurun [10] use a combination of filtering and thresholding to detect the center point of the eyebrows as landmarks. They do not provide experimental results as to the accuracy of the procedure, but they claim that a recognition system using those landmarks performed well. We undertook a study [20] to determine the feasibility of a fully automated face recognition system operating exclusively in the thermal domain. That is, without the aid of a coregistered visible sensor. As we pointed out above, face detection has already been tackled in this context, we focused our efforts on detection of eyes and comparative performance analysis versus the equivalent process with visible imagery.

In order to detect eyes in thermal images, we rely on the face location detected using the face detection and tracking algorithm described by Eveland [9] and Socolinsky et al. [24]. We then look for the eye locations in the upper half of the face area using a slightly modified version of the object detector provided in the Intel Open Computer Vision Library [1]. The detection algorithm is based on the rapid object detection scheme using a boosted cascade of simple feature classifiers introduced by Viola and Jones [27] and extended by Lienhart and Maudt [13]. The OpenCV version of the algorithm extends the Haar-like features by an efficient set of 45 degree rotated features and uses small decision trees instead of stumps as weak classifiers. Since we know that there is only one eye on the left and right halves of the face, we force the algorithm to return the best guess regarding its location. Figure 15.6 shows an example of face and eyes automatically detected in a thermal infrared image.

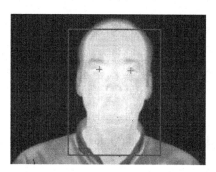

Fig. 15.6. Automatic detection of the face and eyes in a thermal infrared image

The drawback of the algorithm, and of eye detection in thermal infrared in general, is that it fails to detect the eye center locations for subjects wearing glasses. Glasses are opaque in the thermal infrared spectrum and therefore show up black in thermal images, blocking the view of the eyes. In these images the glasses can be easily segmented and the eye center location can be inferred from the shape of the lens. Unfortunately, the errors incurred by such inference are rather large. For the experiments outlined below, only images of subjects without glasses were used. Proper normalization of thermal images of subjects wearing glasses is an area of active research. A recent paper [12] introduces a method for detecting and segmenting glasses on infrared facial imagery. Additionally, they report recognition results after applying a method for filling in the area obscured by eyeglasses with an average eye-region image. Using the FaceIt commercial face recognition system, they observe marked improvement after removal of eyeglasses. Our own experiments on the subject (which predate [12]) show that when using an algorithm capable of handling occlusion, removal of eyeglasses does not provide a statistically significant performance boost.

In order to evaluate the viability of thermal-only face recognition, we compare its performance against a similar visible-only system, even though that system would not function in the dark. In the visible spectrum, we search for the center of the pupil of the open eye. The initial search area relies on the position of the face as returned by a face detector [9]. Within this region, we look for a dark circle surrounded by lighter background using an operator similar to the Hough transform widely used for detection in the iris recognition community [8]. We performed localization and recognition experiments using a large database of over 3700 images of 207 subjects not wearing glasses. Images were collected during several sessions, both indoors and outdoors. All thermal imagery was collected with an uncooled LWIR sensor at 320×240 resolution, and coregistered visible imagery was acquired for all frames. Recognition performance was evaluated both using a PCA-based algorithm, and the proprietary Equinox algorithm. For more details, see Socolinsky and Selinger [20].

	Visible		LWIR	
	Mean	Std deviation	Mean	Std deviation
Left x	0.57	1.10	1.95	2.03
Left y	0.55	0.84	1.57	1.68
Right x	0.60	1.14	2.81	2.07
Right y	0.57	0.84	1.53	1.68

Table 15.1. Means and standard deviations of eye detection errors

Table 15.1 shows the mean absolute error and the standard deviation of the error in the x and y coordinates for the left and right eye, for detection in both modalities. The means and standard deviations of the visible errors stay below 1 pixel, while the LWIR errors go up to 2.8 pixels, and the standard deviations reach 1.75. At the resolution of our images the average size of an eye is 20 pixels wide by 15 pixels high, so although the error increase from visible to LWIR is large, LWIR values still stay within 15% of the eye size.

	Visible detection		LWIR detection	
Gallery/Probe	Visible	LWIR	Visible	LWIR
Indoor/Indoor	99.47	95.79	95.80 (96)	87.90 (92)
Outdoor/Outdoor	88.74	96.03	82.78 (93)	92.72 (97)
Indoor/Outdoor	87.90	90.45	73.25 (83)	78.34 (87)
Average	92.03	94.09	83.94 (91)	86.32 (92)

Table 15.2. Match recognition performance of the Equinox algorithm with eyes detected in the visible and LWIR domains. Figures in parentheses show percentage of corresponding performance with eyes detected in the visible domain

Top match recognition performances for the Equinox algorithm are shown in Table 15.2. Recognition performance with LWIR eye detection is followed in parentheses by the percentage of the corresponding performance with visible eye locations that this represents. The decrease in performance incurred by locating eyes in the LWIR is about the same in both modalities (performance with LWIR eye locations is about 90% of the performance with visible eye locations). This is in contrast with the observation by Chen et al. [6], but is probably due to the difficulty of the data set as well as a lower error in the eye center location. In practical terms, this indicates that while LWIR face recognition can be performed exclusive of any additional sensors, and in complete darkness, more work is needed to improve face normalization. More robust localization of eyes or other facial landmarks is needed to close the performance gap with visible-based normalization.

15.5.2 Fusion of Intensified NIR and Thermal Imagery

Image intensification provides an alternative technology to thermal imaging for face recognition in low light levels. Intensified near infrared imagery (I2) is the most prevalent technology in night vision systems, both civilian and military [1]. It is a relatively low cost technology compared to thermal imaging, and can function with very little ambient light. Since I2 imagery is reflective in nature, it shares many properties with standard visible imagery, and indeed a comparison of visible and I2 images of the same scene under high light conditions shows them to be very similar. This suggests the possibility that an automated system could recognize faces acquired with an I2 system based on visible enrollment imagery. We summarize some results on I2 to visible matching under decreasing light levels. More details can be found in Socolinsky et al. [23].

We performed a data collection and a series of experiments aimed at elucidating the role of I2 imagery in low-light face recognition. Data was collected

---

[1] Technically, this imagery spans the range from 600 to 900 nanometers, which overlaps the visible spectrum. However, night-time luminance favors the near-infrared portion of this range, and thus we will refer to it as intensified near infrared.

from a set of 96 volunteers over two sessions separated by one week, in order to avoid over-estimating performance due to same-session artifacts. Imagery was collected with a scientific-grade Dalsa 1M15 visible sensor with 1024×1024 pixel resolution binned into 512×512, an Indigo Merlin LWIR sensor with 320×240 pixels, and another Dalsa 1M15 visible sensor outfitted with an ITT PVS-14 image intensifier. Peak sensitivity for the Dalsa sensor occurs at 820 nanometers, which is comparable to the peak sensitivity of the PVS-14. Figure 15.7 shows the arrangement of cameras and lights used. The intensified and LWIR sensors were coregistered through the use of a dichroic beamsplitter, and the visible sensor was placed above the previous two, in a boresighted configuration.

Fig. 15.7. Camera and lighting setup for image collection

Imagery was collected in an interior basement room, with no windows and two sets of consecutive doors, ensuring no light penetration from the adjacent hallway. During data collection, all room lighting, both in the inner and outer rooms was kept off, and the only source of illumination was provided by sources controlled as part of the experiment. Lighting was controlled with the use of two custom made fixtures. These fixtures consist of rectangular boxes closed on five sides and sealed against light leaks at all joints. Each box contains a 20 watt low-power compact fluorescent bulb, selected for its low heat output, with a color temperature of $2700K$. The front side of each fixture features a slotted channel, also sealed against light leaks, which fits a series of perforated panels with different levels of light transmission. Each panel is made of an opaque material, and has a hole centered over the bulb, allowing an amount of light proportional to the area of the hole to exit the light fixture. Five different light levels were selected by varying the size of the exit aperture in each panel. This lighting system has two key advantages over the obvious alternative of a rheostat-based system. First, it allows for repeatable light levels, which is hard to achieve with a variable resistor. Second, it ensures that the color temperature of the light is constant throughout the different light levels, whereas a dimmer induces a red shift as the light level decreases.

By using two light sources symmetrically located in front of the subject, we insure even illumination across the face.

At the brightest light level, the illuminance at the subject's face was 9 lux, as measured by a Spectra P-2000EL-A light meter. For reference, full moonlight is about 1 lux, and a standard office environment is illuminated to an average of about 300 lux. Second, third and fourth light levels each decreased by a factor of sixteen, while the fifth light level was about half of the fourth. At the lowest light level, illuminance at the subject's face was about 0.001 lux, which is consistent with starlight conditions. The estimates at the lowest light levels may be optimistic, with the actual light level being lower than the estimate. Note that the Dalsa 1M15 camera is very sensitive, so whereas other cameras may have trouble imaging noiselessly at 9 lux illuminance, this is plenty of light for this sensor.

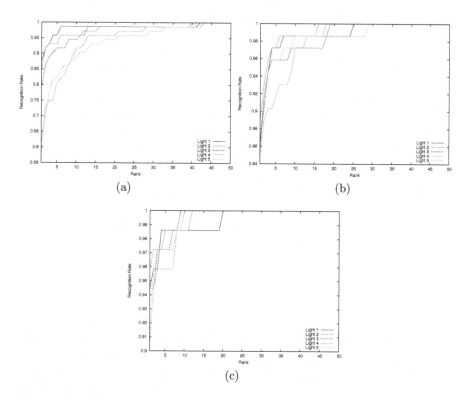

Fig. 15.8. Performance of Equinox algorithm for (a) I2, (b) LWIR and (c) fused images as a function of decreasing light level. Each curve corresponds to a different light level, with Light 1 being the brightest and Light 5 the dimmest.

Figure 15.8 shows some of the results of this study in the form of cumulative match curves. Using the Equinox recognition algorithm, we tested matching I2 probes under varying levels of illumination to well-illuminated visible gallery images. This simulates the scenario where a subject is to be identified in low-light conditions against a good enrollment image, such as a passport or driver's license photo. As we can see, performance decreases rather gracefully with illumination level. By contrast, the same experiment performed with visible probes shows chance performance for all but the two brightest light levels. Note that at the darkest light levels, top match I2 performance is about 60%, but the unaided human eye can barely discern the presence of a head six feet away. For the two brightest light levels, performance with visible probes is slightly higher than with I2 probes, but the difference is small and perhaps not statistically significant with a set of under 100 test subjects. For comparison, we include in Figure 15.8 recognition results for LWIR probes (with eye locations from the I2 images) and for fusion of I2 and LWIR. Performance with LWIR images is independent of light level, and fusion between modalities clearly improves performance across all light levels, to the low to mid ninety percent range, depending on illumination.

While Socolinsky et al. [23] includes further analysis and conclusion, we see from the results above that I2 imagery can be used successfully for face recognition under certain circumstances. Much lower levels of ambient illumination become acceptable if we use I2 instead of visible imagery. Unfortunately, at truly low light levels, the amount of noise in I2 imagery becomes untenable, and performance is reduced below a useful level for most applications. On the other hand, when using I2 and LWIR imagery in combination, we obtain very good performance for a broad range of light levels. Further research in face recognition with I2 imagery should concentrate on improved noise reduction strategies in order to increase performance at the lowest light levels. In all fairness, however, we should point out that at the lowest light levels used in this study, recognition of unfamiliar faces is hard even for humans using a direct-view I2 device.

15.6 Face Recognition Outdoors

Face recognition in outdoor conditions is known to be a very difficult task [15]. This is primarily due to the dramatic illumination effects caused by unconstrained outdoor lighting. Thermal imaging has a unique advantage in this context, given the very high emissivity of human skin, and the resulting near complete illumination invariance of face imagery in the LWIR spectrum. This section outlines the results of a study of outdoor face recognition performance using visible and LWIR imagery [21].

The majority of the imagery used in this study was collected during eight separate day-long sessions spanning a two week period. A total of 385 subjects participated in the collection. Four of the sessions were held indoors in a room with no windows and carefully controlled illumination. Subjects were imaged against a plain background some seven feet from the cameras, and illuminated by a combination of overhead fluorescent lighting and two photographic lights with umbrella-type diffusers positioned symmetrically on both sides of the cameras and about six feet up from the floor. The remaining four sessions were held outdoors at two different locations. During the four outdoor sessions, the weather included sun, partial clouds and moderate rain. All illumination was natural; no lights or reflectors were added. Subjects were always shaded by the side of a building, but were imaged against an unconstrained natural background which included moving vehicles, trees and pedestrians. Even during periods of rain, subjects were imaged outside and uncovered, in an earnest attempt to simulate true operational conditions. For each individual, the earliest available video sequence in each modality is used for gallery images and all subsequent sequences in future sessions are used for probe images. For all sessions, subjects were cooperative, standing about seven feet from the cameras, and looking directly at them when so requested. We used a sensor capable of acquiring coregistered visible and LWIR video. The visible component has a spatial resolution of 640×480 pixels, and 8 bits of spectral resolution. The thermal sensor is uncooled, and has 12 bits of depth, sensing between 8μ and 12μ at a resolution of 320×240 pixels.

Faces were automatically detected in all acquired indoor and outdoor frames, using a system based on the algorithm described in Socolinsky et al. [17]. No operator intervention was required for this step. Recall that since visible and thermal images are coregistered, eye locations in one modality give us those in the other. Thermal images were appropriately calibrated, and visible images were pre-processed through a simple yet effective illumination compensation method to boost performance (for details see [21]). We should emphasize the fact that all data used for the experiments below was processed in a completely automatic fashion in an attempt to simulate true operational conditions.

	Vis	LWIR	Fusion
Indoor	97.05	93.93	98.40
Outdoor	67.06	83.02	89.02

Table 15.3. Top-match recognition results for indoor and outdoor probes with indoor gallery

Table 15.3 shows a summary of the top-match results obtained with the Equinox algorithm. In this case, gallery images for each subject came from indoor collections, while probes came from either indoor or outdoor collections, depending on the experiment. For indoor probes, performance is probably saturated for the visible recognizer, and not far behind in the LWIR. As usual, fusion of both modalities yields the best results. Comparing indoor versus outdoor performance shows that the latter is considerably lower with visible imagery, and significantly so even with thermal imagery. Fusion of both modalities improves the situation, but performance outdoors is statistically significantly lower than indoors, even for fusion. As a reference, note that a PCA-based recognizer yields only 22% top-match recognition for the outdoor probes.

It is clear from this experiment, as from those in Phillips et al. [15] that face recognition outdoors with visible imagery is far less accurate than when performed under fairly controlled indoor conditions. For outdoor use, thermal imaging provides a considerable performance boost. Fusion of both imaging modalities improves performance under all tests and algorithms. The value of thermal imagery for outdoor face recognition is undoubtable. When used in combination with visible imagery, even though the latter is a poor performer, combined accuracy is high enough to make a system useful for a number of realistic applications that could not be accomplished with visible imagery alone. The ability to handle large unconstrained variations in lighting is a key requisite of any realistically deployable system, and the addition of thermal imaging puts us several steps closer to that goal.

15.7 Other Multispectral Approaches

Researchers have proposed other multispectral face recognition approaches besides the ones reviewed above. Most notable is the use of many narrow band sensors within the visible or NIR spectrum. This work was pioneered by Pan et al. [14]. The authors used a hyperspectral camera capable of sampling in 31 spectral bands between 0.7 and 1 microns. Images are acquired under controlled illumination and require ten seconds for a complete set of 31 bands. The uniqueness of the authors' approach lies in the fact that they do not exploit the geometric structure of the face at all. Rather, they use the sampled spectral signature of the skin at a few points on the face as their biometric, thus essentially attempting to recognize people by their 'color'. A valuable feature of this approach is that is has a high degree of pose invariance built in.[2]

The Pan et al. [14] study is based on a database of 200 subjects, collected over five weeks, with various illumination, pose and expression conditions. Using a combination of facial tissue types (forehead, cheeks, lip, etc) the authors achieve top-match recognition rates slightly above 90% for frontal probes acquired in the same session as the gallery images. If frontal probes are taken from a different date than the gallery images, top-match performance drops to about 65%. When out-of-plane face rotation is taken into account, top-match recognition rates drop to about 75% for 45 degree rotation and 50% for full profile, all for same-session comparisons. While these performances

---

[2] Pose invariance in this method is not complete, however. There is a fair amount of dependence on face orientation due to the fact that bidirectional reflectance effects are not taken into account in the author's model.

may lag behind those of more traditional 'full-face' recognition methods, it is important to note that they rely on completely different underlying features, and thus should be largely uncorrelated with traditional methods. A related approach to multispectral recognition in the visible domain can be found in Chang et al. [4].

15.8 Conclusion

Multispectral face recognition is still a nascent field. There is enough evidence to show that the use of different imaging modalities, either alone or in combination can enhance recognition performance under a broad range of circumstances. However, the added expense and complication of using specialized sensors has kept these approaches on the outskirts of mainstream face recognition research. As the current requirements for biometrics systems increasingly demand low cost devices, it is hard to see multispectral approaches becoming widespread. Rather, they will likely evolve to fill niches where traditional approaches cannot operate successfully due to environmental restrictions; face recognition at nighttime is possibly one such area. Barring a drastic reduction in the cost of non-visible camera sensors, the future of multispectral face recognition is likely split between the laboratory and the highly specialized real-world application.

References

1. Open computer vision library. http://sourceforge.net/projects/opencvlibrary/.
2. Yael Adini, Yael Moses, and Shimon Ullman. Face Recognition: The Problem of Compensating for Changes in Illumination Direction. *IEEE Transactions on Pattern Analysis and Machine Intelligence*, 19(7):721–732, July 1997.
3. P. N. Belhumeur and D. J. Kriegman. What is the set of images of an object under all possible illumination conditions. *IJCV*, 28(3):245–260, July 1998.
4. Hong Chang, Andreas Koschan, Besma Abidi, and Mongi Abidi. Physics-based fusion of multispectral data for improved face recognition. In *ICPR '06: Proceedings of the 18th International Conference on Pattern Recognition (ICPR'06)*, pages 1083–1086. IEEE Computer Society, 2006.
5. X. Chen, P. Flynn, and K. Bowyer. PCA-based face recognition in infrared imagery: Baseline and comparative studies. In *International Workshop on Analysis and Modeling of Faces and Gestures*, Nice, France, October 2003.
6. X. Chen, P. Flynn, and K. Bowyer. Visible-light and infrared face recognition. In *Proceedings of the Workshop on Multimodal User Authentication*, Santa Barbara, CA, December 2003.
7. R. Cutler. Face recognition using infrared images and eigenfaces. Technical report, University of Maryland, April 1996. Available at http://www.cs.umd.edu/ rgc/pub/ireigenface.pdf.
8. J. Daugman. How iris recognition works. *IEEE Transactions on Circuits and Systems for Video Technology*, 14(1), January 2004.

9. C.K. Eveland. *Utilizing Visible and Thermal Infrared Video for the Fast Detection and Tracking of Faces*. PhD thesis, University of Rochester, Rochester, NY, December 2002.

10. G. Friedrich and Y. Yeshurun. Seeing people in the dark: Face recognition in infrared images. In *BMCV02*, 2002.

11. Ralph Gross, Iain Matthews, and Simon Baker. Fisher light-fields for face recognition across pose and illumination. In *Proceedings of the German Symposium on Pattern Recognition (DAGM)*, September 2002.

12. J. Heo, S. G. Kong, B. R. Abidi, and M. A. Abidi. Fusion of visual and thermal signatures with eyeglass removal for robust face recognition. In *Proceedings of CVPR Workshop on Object Tracking and Classification Beyond the Visible Spectrum (OTCBVS) 2004*, Washington, DC, June 2004.

13. R. Lienhart and J. Maudt. An extended set of haar-like features for rapid object detection. In *Proceedings ICIP 2002*, volume 1, pages 900–903, 2002.

14. Zhihong Pan, Glenn Healey, Manish Prasad, and Bruce Tromberg. Face recognition in hyperspectral images. *IEEE Trans. Pattern Anal. Mach. Intell.*, 25(12):1552–1560, 2003.

15. P. J. Phillips, D. Blackburn, M. Bone, P. Grother, R. Micheals, and E. Tabassi. Face recognition vendor test 2002 (FRVT 2002). Available at http://www.frvt.org/FRVT2002/default.htm, 2002.

16. A. Shashua and T. R. Raviv. The quotient image: Class based re-rendering and recognition with varying illuminations. *IEEE TPAMI*, 23(2):129–139, 2001.

17. D. Socolinsky, J. Neuheisel, C. Priebe, and J. DeVinney. A boosted cccd classifier for fast face detection. In *35th Symposium on the Interface*, Salt Lake City, UT, March 2003.

18. D. Socolinsky, L. Wolff, J. Neuheisel, and C. Eveland. Illumination Invariant Face Recognition Using Thermal Infrared Imagery. In *Proceedings CVPR*, Kauai, December 2001.

19. D. A. Socolinsky and A. Selinger. A comparative analysis of face recognition performance with visible and thermal infrared imagery. In *Proceedings ICPR*, Quebec, Canada, August 2002.

20. D. A. Socolinsky and A. Selinger. Face recognition in the dark. In *Proceedings of CVPR Workshop on Object Tracking and Classification Beyond the Visible Spectrum (OTCBVS) 2004*, Washington, DC, June 2004.

21. D. A. Socolinsky and A. Selinger. Thermal face recognition in an operational scenario. In *CVPR04*, pages II: 1012–1019, 2004.

22. D. A. Socolinsky and A. Selinger. Thermal face recognition over time. In *Proceedings of ICPR 2004*, Cambridge, UK, August 2004.

23. D. A. Socolinsky, L. B. Wolff, and Andrew J. Lundberg. Image intensification for low-light face recognition. In *CVPR Workshop on Biometrics 06*, New York, 2006.

24. D.A. Socolinsky, J.D. Neuheisel, C.E. Priebe, D. Marchette, and J.G. DeVinney. A boosted cccd classifier for fast face detection. *Computing Science and Statistics*, 35, 2003.

25. D.A. Socolinsky and A. Selinger. Face recognition with visible and thermal infrared imagery. *Computer Vision and Image Understanding*, July - August 2003.

26. S. Romdhani V. Blanz and T. Vetter. Face identification across different poses and illuminations with a 3D morphable model. In *AFGR02*, pages 192–197, 2002.

27. P. Viola and M. Jones. Rapid object detection using a boosted cascade of simple features. In *CVPR01*, pages I:511–518, 2001.

28. P. Viola and M. Jones. Robust real-time face detection. In *ICCV01*, page II: 747, 2001.

29. Joseph Wilder, P. Jonathon Phillips, Cunhong Jiang, and Stephen Wiener. Comparison of Visible and Infra-Red Imagery for Face Recognition. In *Proceedings of 2nd International Conference on Automatic Face & Gesture Recognition*, pages 182–187, Killington, VT, 1996.

30. L. Wolff, D. Socolinsky, and C. Eveland. Quantitative Measurement of Illumination Invariance for Face Recognition Using Thermal Infrared Imagery. In *Proceedings CVBVS*, Kauai, December 2001.

31. W. Zhao and R. Chellappa. Robust face recognition using symmetric shape-from-shading. Technical report, Center for Automation Research, University of Maryland, College Park, 1999. Available at http://citeseer.nj.nec.com/zhao99robust.html".

32. Zhiwei Zhu, Kikuo Fujimura, and Qiang Ji. Real-time eye detection and tracking under various light conditions. In *Proceedings of the symposium on Eye tracking research & applications*, pages 139–144. ACM Press, 2002.

16

Multibiometrics Using Face and Ear

Christopher Middendorff and Kevin W. Bowyer

University of Notre Dame, Notre Dame, Indiana, USA
{cmidden1,kwb}@cse.nd.edu

16.1 Introduction

In this chapter, we consider and evaluate several techniques for multibiometric processing of ear and face images. Common terminology for multibiometric systems appears in an earlier chapter, and is mentioned here in abbreviated form.

- *Site*: the body part being sensed (*e.g., the ear*).
- *Sensor*: the mechanism for acquiring raw biometric information (*e.g.*, a color camera).
- *Algorithm*: a computer procedure for computing the quality of match between processed biometric signatures.
- *Mode*: a combination of site, sensor, and algorithm.
- *Multi-instance*: The use of several sets of raw data acquired from the same site and sensor and the same algorithm.
- *Multi-sensor*: The use of multiple sensors (and perhaps algorithms) to capture data from the same site.
- *Multi-algorithm*: The use of multiple matching algorithms on the same data.

Figure 16.1 depicts four examples of multibiometric systems. Figure16.2 shows examples of images captured by two sensors (2D and 3D) and the two sites relevant to this chapter (face and ear).

Incorporating a concept of time allows for another subcategory: *multi-presentation*. In this method, a single feature is captured multiple times by a single sensor with some delay between acquisitions, and these images are submitted to a single algorithm.

16.1.1 Images

In order to combine biometrics, they must be *fused* at some level, and the method of combination will affect the recognition rate of the system. The

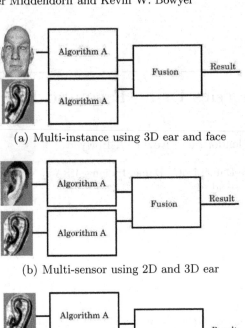

(a) Multi-instance using 3D ear and face

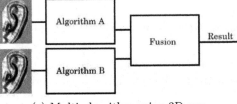

(b) Multi-sensor using 2D and 3D ear

(c) Multi-algorithm using 3D ear

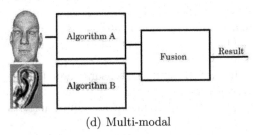

(d) Multi-modal

Fig. 16.1. Examples of multi-biometrics systems.

levels of fusion have been discussed in an earlier chapter, and include the following:

- *Sensor level* fusion combines the multiple raw data sets (typically images) produced by the sensor. Chang et al. [6] concatenated ear and face images before applying a Principal Components Analysis-based system for recognition.

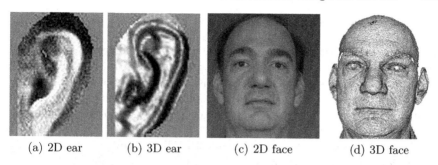

(a) 2D ear   (b) 3D ear   (c) 2D face   (d) 3D face

Fig. 16.2. Examples of multiple features using different capture methods.

- *Feature level* fusion combines multiple extracted feature sets arising from the low-level processing of the outputs of multiple sensors into a single composite set used in subsequent processing.
- *Score level* fusion combines the recognition (matching) scores from each recognition algorithm. Examples of score level fusion include using the sum of matching scores, or their minimum, as the overall matching score for recognition decisions. Care must be taken to make matching scores commensurate if arithmetic fusion is performed. This is typically done by normalization to a standardized interval or distribution, or by weighting; however, the result of *ad hoc* normalization or weighting schemes must be carefully validated before they can be used with confidence.
- *Decision level* (or *rank level*) fusion makes a final decision based on the hypothesis rankings produced by the individual matching algorithms. A simple example of this is the Borda count: adding the rank-match of the face and ear, and taking the lowest sum as the rank-one match.

In this chapter, we review popular methods of individual face and ear biometrics and results of combining them. Updated results are presented with a detailed explanation of how they were acquired. The following sections describe benefits and challenges to multi-biometrics, followed by a discussion of multi-biometrics.

16.2 Review of Mono-modal Face and Ear Biometrics

Before performing multi-biometrics on face and ear, it is important to understand the background for mono-modal biometrics involving these sites. Various studies have shown how the face [28] and ear [6, 27] are viable biometric features. Due to the different features, different methods of evaluation, and different methods of combining the evaluations, we will review common methods of biometrics and their evaluation, and describe how they can be combined.

16.2.1 2D Face Recognition

Intuitively, the face is a reasonable feature to use as a biometric. Recognizing each other by facial appearance is something humans do regularly. Automating the process in computer vision, however, is an active field of study. Locating *any* face in an image automatically is challenging, let alone determining the identity of the person it belongs to. Various classifications of face recognition systems are covered by Zhao et al. [28].

The Face Recognition Vendor Test [2] (FRVT) is a government-sponsored recognition technology evaluation used to determine the quality and scalability of face recognition systems. It also provides the face recognition community with potential research directions. The FRVT 2002 [20] consisted of main two tests: high computational intensity and medium computational intensity. Systems in either category had to be fully automatic. The high computational intensity test requires a system to perform recognition across 121,000 frontal images in 1 day and 2 hours. The medium computational intensity task had two subclasses: still and video. The still portion was used to measure performance changes under effects such as time between images, lighting change and pose. The video portion was designed to test whether video clips help recognition performance.

The Face Recognition Grand Challenge [1] (FRGC) provides 50,000 recordings divided into training and validation sets. The FRGC consists of six experiments: one controlled probe and one controlled gallery, four controlled probe and four controlled gallery, controlled 3D probe and gallery, uncontrolled probe and uncontrolled gallery, 3D gallery and controlled 2D probe, 3D gallery and uncontrolled 3D probe.

Eigenfaces – Principal Components Analysis

The eigenface technique introduced by Sirovich and Kirby [23] for representation and developed for recognition by Turk and Pentland [24] has remained a popular method of face recognition, and has been extended to the ear and other biometric sources as well. This method uses Principal Components Analysis (PCA) to create a space where faces can be compared against each other for matching.

Landmark points are determined on the feature. These points are structural components of the feature, such as the centers of the eyes, so they can be determined on all subjects. The landmark points are then used to normalize the feature in position and size, enforcing a concept of a standard pose.

Once the feature is normalized, a mask is then applied around the feature, labeling which pixels are part of the feature and which are not, determining the data to use for PCA. Ideally, the mask will leave only the sought biometric feature and remove everything else from the image. The shape and size can directly affect the quality of the recognition. A mask that is too small can crop out important structures of the biometric feature (as in Figure 16.3(b));

one that is too large can allow meaningless background features (e.g. hair) to be included in the analysis. In the experiments presented in this chapter, an elliptical mask was used, tuned experimentally over the course of several single biometric experiments.

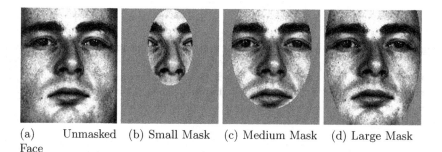

(a)   Unmasked   (b) Small Mask   (c) Medium Mask   (d) Large Mask
Face

Fig. 16.3. A normalized feature, and three potential masks used to crop out the face.

After the images in the training set have been normalized and masked, Principal Components Analysis determines eigenvectors $F_1, F_2, ...F_m$. The number of eigenvectors m has a maximum value of $min(R, C)$, where R is the number of training images and C the number of pixels in a training image.

The space is tuned to reduce the number of vectors used. Ideally, all possible combinations of the eigenvectors would be explored, using the set which yielded the maximum recognition rate for some validation case. However, this would require the test to be run 2^m times. Dimension reduction is traditionally performed by dropping vectors from the front (the eigenvector representing the highest variance in the data, usually associated with intensity changes in the images) and from the back (in the direction of the least variance, considered to be negligible).

After PCA is performed, the vectors define a "face space" into which a face I can be projected as a point I' in this space. The image I' is defined as $I' = \alpha_1 F_1 + \alpha_2 F_2 + ... + \alpha_m F_m$. The vector $\alpha = \{\alpha_1, ...\alpha_m\}$ is the location of the face in the eigenface space, and is the result of the projection.

Recognition is performed by projecting the gallery into this space, and comparing a projected probe point against these gallery points. The distance between a probe point and a gallery point is used as a matching metric for those two points. Different distance metrics are considered by Yambor et al. [13], which advocates the use of the Mahalanobis Cosine in face space for intensity images.

To use PCA for identification, the feature to be used for identification must be *segmented*, or isolated from the rest of the image. This is usually accomplished by manually finding *landmark points* on the image, and trans-

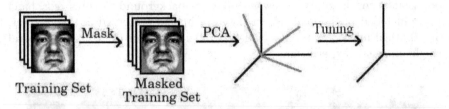

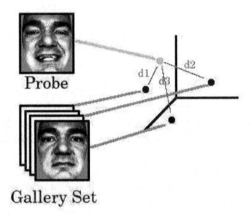

Fig. 16.4. An example of the creation of the face space. The input images are taken, normalized in position and size, and masked. This mask gives us a constant number of feature pixels from each image, as well as removing non-essential components from the image. Principal Components Analysis is then performed to generate the face space. Dimensions are then dropped to reduce the size of this space, resulting in the final face space.

Fig. 16.5. An example of how this face space is used for recognition. The probe image and the gallery images are normalized and masked, then projected into the space that was previously generated. The distances from the probe to each gallery point are calculated, and the gallery image closest to the probe is the rank-one match.

forming these landmark points to standard *landmark destination points*, thus normalizing the feature in rotation, scale and translation. On a portrait face these are typically the centers of the eyes.

An important component of the transformation is the scaling; because the features are normalized in size, the same size mask can be applied to each feature, resulting in a constant-sized feature. This is desirable because the use of PCA demands that each extracted feature be the same size. From a biometric standpoint, normalization in position and size enforces a concept of a standard image frame for each sample.

Using a mask in conjunction with landmark points for segmentation provides many benefits: the mask provides a uniform number of image pixels, and the transformation to align the landmark points with the landmark destination points provides uniformity in rotation, translation and scale. However, in these experiments operator intervention was required to design the mask and label the landmark points. For practical implementation, automatic segmentation and automatic landmark point detection would be ideal. While automatic segmentation of features is an active field of research, the resulting algorithms are not yet as good as we would like. Commercial face recognition systems may sometimes fail to correctly detect the face in what appears to be a subjectively simple image.

In addition to segmentation quality, performance using the eigenface method will also vary due to the quality of the images used to generate the space. When comparing a probe image to the gallery, the images are projected into the space and the distance from the probe to each of the gallery images is calculated. If the set used to generate the space does not have much variance, then probe-gallery distances will be affected by the inability to accurately approximate them.

Similarly, the number of eigenvectors retained for the space will affect the ability to accurately approximate a projected feature. Consider a trivial example where the eigenvectors of a plane lay along the x- and y-axes of a Cartesian plane, and for this data set, $(x, y) = (x', y')$. Any point in that plane can be approximated perfectly. If we reduce this to one dimension by removing the y-axis, the mapping looks something like $(x, y) = (x', 0)$, and the error increases the further a point actually is from the line $y = 0$. For these reasons, the error $I - I'$ must be kept within some acceptable range.

16.2.2 2D Ear Recognition

One of the first to use ear biometrics was Iannarelli [17], who developed a manual system of recognition using the ear. The image was adjusted to a standard pose, and the measurements of the ear feature were taken by hand. This system used twelve features of the ear, as well as race and gender information, to uniquely identify 10,000 subjects.

Pun and Moon [21] gave an overview of ear biometrics. They cite the ear's smaller size and more uniform color as desirable traits for pattern recognition. Other characteristics are that it is less invasive than iris or fingerprint recognition, and more reliable than voice. They state that the principal methods of ear biometrics are PCA, force field transformation, local surface patch comparisons using range data, Voronoi diagram matching, neural networks and genetic algorithms.

Performance with PCA is dependent on the location of the landmark points. While the eye centers provide objective landmark points for the profile face, the variable ear shape makes selecting landmark points more subjective and challenging, as some features may be more obscure on some subjects. Chang [6] used the triangular fossa and incisure intertragica (Figure 16.6(a)), and Yan [26] used triangular fossa and antitragus (Figure 16.6(b)).

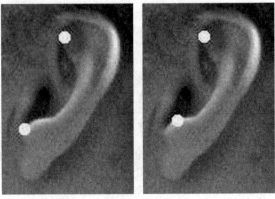

(a) Using the Incisure In-   (b) Using the Antitragus
tertragica

Fig. 16.6. Two different landmark points. In 16.6(a), the Triangular Fossa (top point) and Incisure Intertragica (bottom point) are used as landmarks. In 16.6(b), the Triangular Fossa and Antitragus are used.

The following experiment demonstrates the importance of mask quality. Original landmark points were annotated by hand in a dataset of 415 subjects (one gallery, one probe for each subject). The dataset was studied in four subsets: "small" and "small2" had 88 images each, "med" had 202 images (the 176 images from "small" and "small2", with 28 more) and "all" used the full 415-subject dataset. The landmarks are shifted to the left and right by 2, 4, 6, 8 and 10 pixels, modifying the part of the ear visible through the mask.

Datasets "small" and "small2" are person-disjoint sets, chosen to illustrate the effect of the gallery on performance; two sets of the same size can have differing recognition rates. The sets "small," "medium" and "large", where "small" is a subset of "medium", which is a subset of "large", demonstrate the negative effect that gallery size has on recognition.

The performance of each data set varied with the position of the landmark points. As the landmark points shift, the sections of the ear which are occluded by the mask and those that are revealed by it will change. By shifting away parts of the ear and shifting in undistinguishing features (i.e. hair or cheeks), performance suffered. As Figure 16.7 demonstrates, the maximum performance of each data set peaks at a particular point (not necessarily the points we chose, meaning that our results could be higher). Each point represents the best possible performance of any number of vectors used, for each horizontal shift of our landmarks. This maximum point over all vectors was determined by exhaustively calculating the performance when dropping vectors from the front and back. Determining the parameters which provide the best performance would normally be done when first designing a biometric system, to select the best landmark points and mask.

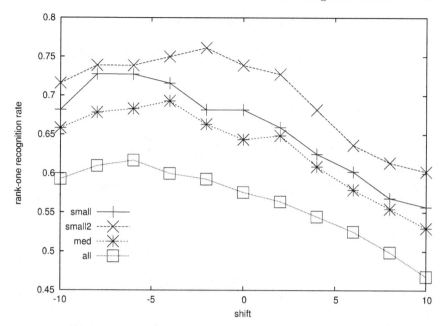

Fig. 16.7. The effects of shift on four data sets of varying sizes. The negative shift shifts landmark points to the left; the positive shift moves them to the right.

Geometric methods such as Choraś [11, 12] use automatically-extracted properties of the ear (width and length, for example) as the elements of the feature vector. Comparison is done by determining the difference between the measurements of the probe feature and the measurements of each gallery feature.

Hurley et al. [16] approach ear biometrics by modeling the image as a Gaussian force field, where the pixels exert "forces" on each other modeled after a magnetic field. The field lines created by the force field generate channels, which can be used for identification. They compare this method to PCA using manual registration of the ear images. The force field method gave a 99.2% recognition rate, using 4 samples of each of 63 subjects, taken over a period of 5 months. The PCA method gave a recognition rate of 98.4%.

16.2.3 3D Face Methods

A survey by Bowyer et al. [5] categorized 3D face methods into two categories: one which performed recognition based solely on 3D shape, and multibiometrics which used both the 2D and 3D information. Lao et al. [19] perform fusion at the feature-extraction level, using isoluminance contours to perform stereo matching. Recognition rates of 87-96% are reported using a dataset of 10 subjects, with four images at each of nine poses for each subject. Chang et al. [7] use PCA for both the intensity and range images, with 99% rank-one recognition using 200 subjects for the fused methods. Individually, PCA achieved 94% rank-one recognition for the range images and 89% for the intensity images.

16.2.4 3D Ear Methods

Iterative Closest Point (ICP) is a method of calculating a rigid transformation, aligning two sets of points as closely as possible and minimizing the distance between them. In a biometric application, these "point clouds" are 3D gallery images being aligned to a probe image. The difference (a distance measured in millimeters) between gallery and probe points can be used for comparison. The gallery image of the probe-gallery pair with the least difference is the rank-one match of the probe.

Chen and Bhanu [10] utilized ICP in a three-step process to recognize an ear by its 3D shape. The first step was to use the 3D data to determine the location of the outer edge of the ear (the "helix"), using the strong depth difference between the ear helix and the head to determine the edge voxels. These helix voxels were located for the probe ear and the gallery ears. ICP was then used to align the helix of the probe to each of the gallery images. Once this "coarse alignment" was performed, the transformation was applied to each gallery image. ICP was then used again on the entire image, and the error was used as the matching criterion. For testing, a set of 60 manually-extracted ear images (a probe and a gallery for each of 30 subjects) was used. Rank-one recognition on this data set was 93.3%.

Yan and Bowyer [27] used ICP on the entire ear image, with the ear automatically segmented. First, the nose tip is located using the depth image. Then, skin detection [15] is used to locate the skin region. Curvature information [3, 14] for this area is calculated and used to locate the ear pit. This point is used as the starting point of an active contour model [18] used on both the 2D and 3D images to determine the final ear candidate. ICP was used with various subsamplings of probe and gallery, as well as different variants of ICP: point-to-point (minimizing the distance between two sets of points), point-to-surface (minimizing the distance between a point and a calculated surface), and a combination. The non-subsampled probe and gallery gave the best performance (97.6% rank-one recognition). Each recognition took 15-18 seconds to perform. Subsampling reduced recognition performance by about 1% but also reduced the time required to 2-3 seconds per match. Experiments were performed on a 415-subject data set with 1386 probes and 415 gallery.

Using 3D images clearly demonstrates an advantage over 2D images for ear biometrics. The rank-one recognition for the ICP method of ear recognition was 97.6%, while the best performance for the 2D method was 61.7% rank-one recognition on the same subjects.

Bowyer et al. [5] report that one of the challenges of 3D is sensor difficulties. One of these is "the myth of illumination invariance," because while the 3D shape is illumination-independent as a physical property, it cannot be *sensed* independently of illumination. If part of the object is saturated in light, then any light projected by the sensor will not be detected because the sensor is already saturated by the existing light conditions. Another challenge is that algorithms need to be improved, so features that are elastic (such as the face) are not treated as though they are rigid (as they are with eigenfaces or ICP).

16.2.5 Multi-biometric Recognition Using Face and Ear

Chang et al. [6] demonstrated the utility of a multi-instance biometric, using PCA to evaluate 2D portrait face and ear. This method used manually land-marked faces and ears. The probes differed from the gallery in one of three categories: day (88 subjects), lighting (111 subjects) and pose (101 subjects). Fusion was performed at the extraction level, concatenating the ear image onto the face image before performing recognition. Face and ear had compa-rable rank-one recognition rates in the day-variation experiment, 70.5% and 71.6%, respectively. In the lighting variation experiment, rank-one recognition was 64.9% for the face and 68.5% for the ear. In the pose variation experi-ment, rank-one recognition for the face and ear were just over 20% and 10%, respectively, when trained on the gallery set. When combined, performance improved significantly for the day variation experiment, increasing to 90% when the two metrics were combined. A statistically significant difference is also achieved in the lighting-variant experiment, with a combined rank-one score of 87.4%.

Rahman and Ishikawa [22] used a multi-instance approach and com-bined 2D PCA methods of ear and face, using profile images with manually-extracted features. Instead of the usual portrait face, the profile was used. Combining profile face with ear using 18 subjects had up to a 94.44% recogni-tion rate. One advantage to this method is that the profile face and ear inputs are captured in the same image, reducing the amount of subject participation necessary (capturing a portrait face and asking them to turn to the side) or the amount of hardware (multiple cameras to capture images of the face and ear simultaneously).

Yan [25] explored 3D face and ear for a combined biometric on a dataset of 174 probe and gallery subjects. In this experiment, features were extracted automatically. Using ICP, rank-one recognition for face was 93.1%, and rank-one recognition for ear was 97.7%. The fused biometrics achieved 100% rank-one recognition.

16.2.6 Face + Ear vs. Ear + Ear vs. Face + Face

Multi-biometrics combining face and ear are inherently multi-instance sys-tems. From a technical standpoint, this means that while the same type of sensor is used for each biometric feature, a different method will have to be applied to segment each feature. Additionally, multiple sensors may be necessary to capture the features (for example, a system of cameras set up around a subject to simultaneously capture face and ear). Using the same sensor to capture the *same* feature (multi-presentation) is simpler since more sensors aren't necessary, and the same segmentation algorithm can be applied to each input.

Chang et al. [8] compares multimodal and multi-presentation methods, using the face as the biometric feature. The authors state that although it widely demonstrated that multi-biometrics can outperform individual biometric features, the exact conclusions are muddled: how much improvement comes from simply having a variety of images, and how much is from having *different* data? This paper contrasts the use of 2D + 3D to using multi-presentation 2D. Using a 198-subject gallery, the multi-sensor (2D + 3D) method had rank-one recognition of 97.5%, outperforming the multi-presentation (multiple 2D) method which had rank-one recognition of 94.4%. However, using more probe images for the multi-presentation experiment further improved peformance, reportedly reaching a plateau of 96% rank-one recognition in the range of using four images to represent a person in the gallery and probe set, making the performance comparable to the multi-sensor biometric.

16.3 Examples

We will illustrate the concepts from this chapter by walking through experiments similar to those discussed in the previous section. When designing a multi-biometric, four things must be considered: the biometric feature or features to use, the method or methods of evaluation, the level of fusion and how it will be performed, and the final evaluation. In each experiment here, biometrics are fused at the score level, using one of four different fusions: simple sum, weighted-sum (70% face, 30% ear), the reverse weighted-sum (30% face, 70% ear), and min fusion.

16.3.1 An example using multi-instance biometrics

The experiment is similar to one performed by Chang et al. in [6], which performed recognition using PCA on the intensity images of the profile ear and portrait face. In that study, fusion was performed at the extraction level. Here, the multi-biometric is *multi-instance* and fusion is performed at the score level.

Step 1: Feature Extraction

The features in this experiment were extracted using a two-step process: image normalization and masking. Feature landmarks were first annotated by an operator. For the face, the eye centers were used. The triangular fossa and antitragus (shown in Figure 16.6(b)) were used for the ear.

The image is transformed to align the landmarks with the landmark destination points, normalizing the images in size and location. A custom mask is then applied around the feature in the transformed image to crop out the non-feature pixels. The result is a set of extracted features of a normalized size.

Step 2: Individual Evaluation

Principal Components Analysis is performed individually for the ear and face, using the implementation by Beveridge [4]. For each feature, the 411-subject gallery is used to generate the PCA space. Each probe generates a distance file, giving the distance to each gallery image (samples from a file shown in Table 16.1). The Mahalanobis Cosine angle was used, so the distance range is from $[-1, 1]$, where -1 is the best possible score and 1 is the worst.

gallery subject	distance
02463	-0.426
04201	-0.197
04202	-0.024
04203	0.106
04213	0.008
04217	0.020
04221	0.034

Table 16.1. An example of distances from the probe subject (02463) to the gallery points in eigenface space, using the Mahalanobis Cosine as the distance metric. In this experiment there were 411 total subjects.

Using these scores, individual recognition rates can be calculated (though they are useful for comparative purposes, these rankings are not used in score-level fusion). Ear had a rank-one recognition rate of 62.2% and the face had a rank-one recognition rate of 88.1%. In Chang's original experiment, the face and ear had comparable performance of approximately 71% recognition and when fused yielded 90.4% rank-one recognition. In Chang's experiments, unlike this one, images were selected for quality. Ears which had structural changes (e.g. earrings), were obscured (e.g. hair) or had lighting variation, were removed from Chang's data set. A lower-quality dataset can account for this difference in performance.

Step 3: Score Fusion

Each probe now has a distance to every gallery image, for both the face and ear. To perform sum fusion, the distance from the probe ear to the ear of a

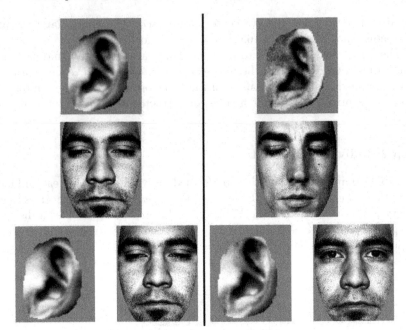

Fig. 16.8. An example of a fusion metric performing where both individual metrics failed. The left column is the probe set, the right column is the gallery set.

gallery subject is added to the score from the probe face to the face of the same gallery subject. The rank-one match is the gallery whose sum is the least.

We also perform two weighted-sum fusions and a min fusion. The weighted-sum fusions use weights of 70% ear and 30% face, and 30% ear and 70% face. The min fusion rule ranks matches in the order of the minimum of the ear and face matching scores.

Step 4: Fused Recognition Rate

After collecting the rank-one matches for all probes, the recognition rate is the number of correct matches divided by the number of probes. In this experiment, the rank-one recognition rates using all combination methods was 100%.

Figure 16.8 shows a subject where the individual PCA methods *both* failed to identify the individual, but together succeeded.

16.3.2 An example using multi-modal biometrics

The fusion of 2D face with 3D ear as in Yan and Bowyer [26] was also performed with the 411-subject gallery. This method is multi-modal, as it is *multi-instance* (face and ear), *multi-sensor* (2D and 3D), and *multi-algorithm* (PCA and ICP). This section will focus specifically on what was done for ICP to avoid redundancy with the previous section.

Step 1: Feature Extraction

Yan and Bowyer [26] used the method outlined in Section 16.2.4 for ear feature extraction. The 3D information was used to localize the head, color information was used to determine the skin region. Curvature analysis was performed within this region to locate the ear pit, which was used as a starting point for the active contours used to extract the ear.

Step 2: Individual Evaluation

The probe and gallery images are aligned using the Iterative Closest Point algorithm, yielding a rigid transformation for each (probe, gallery) pair. The RMS distance between closest points in the aligned images is the matching score (lower scores reflect better alignment). Table 16.2 shows examples of these distances for a fixed probe ear image from subject 02463.

gallery subject	distance
02463	0.38
04201	1.05
04202	1.05
04203	1.28
04213	1.28
04217	1.14
04221	0.94

Table 16.2. An example of RMS distances between a single probe ear image from subject 02463 and gallery ear images from several subjects.

Rank-one recognition with the PCA face component is 88.1%, and rank-one recognition with the ICP ear component (using RMS distance as the matching score) is 91.6%.

Step 3: Score Fusion

The score range for ICP is from $[0, \inf)$, where lower scores mean closer matches. The range using the Mahalanobis cosine with PCA is $[-1, 1]$, where lower is better. Because the ranges don't match, the scores need to be normalized to the same range before they can be compared. We accomplish this using *min-max* normalization for each data set. For each score s in dataset i, $s'_i = (s_i - min_i)/(min_i - max_i)$, where min_i and max_i are the minimum and maximum value for each data set. This scales the scores in each dataset to the range $[0, 1]$, allowing them to be fused. In this case, the sets $i = 1$ and $i = 2$ are the PCA and ICP distances.

The four fusion approaches from the previous section are tested again here. The effect of weighting here will be especially interesting, since the individual biometrics perform equally well.

Step 4: Fused Recognition Rate

Using a simple sum-of-normalized-scores fusion rule, the combined recognition rate is 97.6%. Weighted sums of normalized scores using 70% face and 30% ear gave a recognition rate of 95.6%. When using 70% of the ear score and 30% of the face score, a recognition rate of 97.8% was achieved. Using the min score gave a recognition rate of 81.5%. Figure 16.9 shows rank vs. recognition.

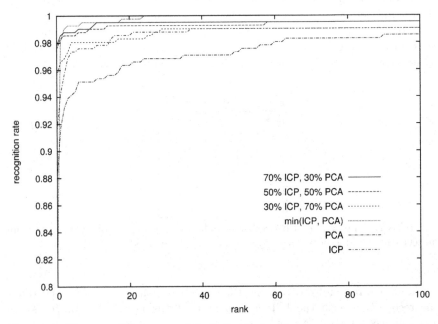

Fig. 16.9. The recognition rates of the individual metrics, and the combined rates.

Using the minimum distance caused the system to perform worse than either metric alone, where combining provided improvement in each case. Weighting the ear heavier provided the best fusion of the methods demonstrated, though all sum fusions improved the recognition rate.

16.4 Discussion

As stated in the literature, combining ear and face biometrics can improve performance over using either metric alone. The face is larger, but changes easily with expression (e.g. Chang et al. [9]) and over time. The ear is smaller, changes less over time, and is rigid to expression changes. However, it is also more easily occluded.

The advantage of using 2D methods is that capturing the sample is simple: "regular" images can be captured in a fraction of a second, from a wide range. These types of images, however, lose the notion of depth.

An advantage to using both ear and face is that of increased coverage. Even if one of the features is occluded (e.g. hair covering the ear), some recognition is possible if one of the biometric features can be captured (if, for example, the face is still available). However, more equipment is required to acquire the additional data. In the case of combining 2D and 3D images, for example, a system needs both types of sensor. Another limitation is that of subject cooperation. For combined biometrics requiring features that cannot be acquired simultaneously (such as a multi-instance system requiring the face and ear), the subject will have to assist the system. In instances where cooperation cannot be guaranteed, a multi-biometric may not be feasible.

The preprocessing stage of a biometric system is a step which is often left to manual methods. Feature location, segmentation, and normalization are all important for biometric evaluation, and performing this step manually over thousands of images can create a bottleneck in the deployment of the system. Automation is made difficult by occlusion, lighting, and structural changes which make it difficult to write definitive rules for defining a feature. Automatic detection and segmentation of the ear is still an active research topic.

Evaluation methods are constantly being refined, with new results being published on larger datasets. Lab testing allows more processing time, which can in turn give higher results. In the field, however, system speed is important. In a security scenario, for example, identifying a person is not useful if they walked away from the sensor an hour ago.

In this chapter we focused on multi-biometrics in the context of the ear and face as features to be used for identification. These techniques are already multi-instance (same sensor for the ear and face) but can also be multi-modal (different sensors or algorithms for the ear and face). The multiple features will provide two comparison points instead of a single one for identification.

References

1. Face Recognition Grand Challenge. http://www.frvt.org/FRGC.
2. Face Recognition Vendor Test. http://www.frvt.org.

3. Paul J. Besl and Ramesh C. Jain. Invariant surface characteristics for 3D object recognition in range images. In *Computer Vision Graphics Image Processing*, volume 33, pages 30–80, 1986.
4. R. Beveridge, K. She, B. Draper, and G. Givens. Evaluation of face recognition algorithm (release version 5.0). In *URL: www.cs.colostate.edu/evalfacerec/index.html.*
5. Kevin W. Bowyer, Kyong I. Chang, and Patrick J. Flynn. A survey of approaches and challenges in 3D and multi-modal 3D+2D face recognition. *Computer Vision and Image Understanding*, 101:1 – 15, 2006.
6. K. Chang, K. Bowyer, and V. Barnabas. Comparison and combination of ear and face images in appearance-based biometrics. *IEEE Transaction on Pattern Analysis and Machine Intelligence*, 25:1160–1165, 2003.
7. K. Chang, K. Bowyer, and P. Flynn. Face recognition using 2D and 3D facial data. In *Workshop on Multimodal User Authentication*, pages 25–32, 2003.
8. K. Chang, K. Bowyer, and P. Flynn. An evaluation of multi-modal 2D+3D face biometrics. *IEEE Transaction on Pattern Analysis and Machine Intelligence*, 27:619–624, 2005.
9. Kyong Chang, Kevin W. Bowyer, and Patrick J. Flynn. Effects of facial expression in 3D face recognition. In *Biometric Technology for Human Identification II, Proceedings of SPIE*, volume 5779, pages 132–143, March 2005.
10. Hui Chen and Bir Bhanu. Contour matching for 3D ear recognition. In *Seventh IEEE Workshop on Application of Computer Vision*, pages 123–128, 2005.
11. Michal Choraś. Ear biometrics based on geometrical feature extraction. *Electronic Letters on Computer Vision and Image Analysis*, 5(3):84–95, 2005.
12. Michal Choraś. Further developments in geometrical algorithms for ear biometrics. In *4th International Conference on Articulated Motion and Deformable Objects, AMDO 2006*, pages 58–67, 2006.
13. Bruce A. Draper, Wendy S. Yambor, and J. Ross Beveridge. Analyzing PCA-based face recognition algorithms: Eigenvector selection and distance measures. In *Second Workshop on Empirical Evaluation in Computer Vision*, pages 39 – 60, 2000.
14. P. Flynn and A. Jain. Surface classification: Hypothesis testing and parameter estimation. In *IEEE Conference on Computer Vision Pattern Recognition*, pages 261–267, 1988.
15. R.-L. Hsu, M. Abdel-Mottaleb, and A. Jain. Face detection in color images. *IEEE Transaction on Pattern Analysis and Machine Intelligence*, 24:696–706, 2002.
16. David Hurley, Mark S. Nixon, and John Carter. Force field feature extraction for ear biometrics. *Computer Vision and Image Understanding*, 98:491–512, 2005.
17. A. Iannarelli. *Ear Identification*. Paramont Publishing Company, 1989.
18. Michael Kass, Andrew Witkin, and Demetri Terzopoulos. Snakes: Active contour models. *International Journal of Computer Vision*, 1:321–331, 1987.
19. S. Lao, Y. Sumi, M. Kawade, and F. Tomita. 3D template matching for pose invariant face recognition using 3D facial model built with isoluminance line based stereo vision. In *Proceedings of 15th International Conference on Pattern Recognition*, volume 2, pages 911–916, 2000.
20. P.J. Phillips, P. Grother, R.J Micheals, D.M. Blackburn, E Tabassi, and J.M. Bone. FRVT 2002: Overview and summary. In *http://www.frvt.org/FRVT2002/default.htm*, 2003.

21. K.H. Pun and Y.S. Moon. Recent advances in ear biometrics. In *Proceedings of the Sixth International Conference on Automatic Face and Gesture Recognition*, pages 164–169, May, 2004.
22. M. Masudur Rahman and Seiji Ishikawa. Proposing a passive biometric system for robotic vision. In *Proceedings of the Tenth International Symposium on Artifical Life and Robotics*, 2005.
23. L. Sirovich and M. Kirby. Low dimensional procedure for characterization of human faces. *Journal of the Optical Society of America*, 4:519–524, March 1987.
24. Matthew Turk and Alex Pentland. Eigenfaces for recognition. *Journal of Cognitive Neuroscience*, 3(1):71–86, 1991.
25. Ping Yan. *Ear Biometrics in Human Identification*. PhD thesis, University of Notre Dame, 2006.
26. Ping Yan and Kevin W. Bowyer. Multi-Biometrics 2D and 3D ear recognition. In *Audio- and Video-based Biometric Person Authentication*, pages 503–512, 2005.
27. Ping Yan and Kevin W. Bowyer. Biometric recognition using 3D ear shape. *IEEE Transaction on Pattern Analysis and Machine Intelligence*, to appear.
28. W. Zhao, R. Chellappa, P.J. Phillips, and A. Rosenfeld. Face recognition: A literature survey. *ACM Computing Surveys*, 35(4):399–458, 2003.

Incorporating Ancillary Information in Multibiometric Systems

Karthik Nandakumar[1], Arun Ross[2], and Anil K. Jain[1]

[1] Department of Computer Science and Engineering, Michigan State University, East Lansing, MI 48824, USA {nandakum,jain}@cse.msu.edu

[2] Lane Department of Computer Science and Electrical Engineering, West Virginia University, Morgantown, WV 26506, USA arun.ross@mail.wvu.edu

17.1 Introduction

Information fusion in a multibiometric system can be accomplished at the sensor, feature, match score, rank, or decision levels. Depending on the level of fusion, inputs to the fusion module may consist of raw images, features, match scores, ranks or identity decisions generated by the individual biometric sources. Apart from these inputs, a multibiometric system may have access to ancillary information that may be beneficial in the decision generation process. *Intrinsic* ancillary information is derived from the same biometric sample that is used for verifying or establishing the identity of the user. An example of intrinsic information is the quality of the acquired biometric sample (e.g., fingerprint image quality). *Extrinsic* information is derived from sources other than the acquired biometric sample. For instance, characteristics such as gender, ethnicity, height or weight of the user (collectively known as soft biometric traits) can be obtained as the user approaches a fingerprint recognition system. Though the ancillary information may not be directly related to the identity of the user, it is still useful for recognition in many ways, especially in a multibiometric system. The main difficulty in incorporating ancillary information in a multibiometric system lies in (i) designing techniques that can automatically extract the required ancillary information from the individual, and (ii) designing fusion mechanisms that can effectively utilize this additional information to improve recognition accuracy. This chapter presents some techniques that have been proposed in the literature to address these challenges in the context of quality-based fusion and soft biometrics.

17.2 Quality-based fusion

The quality of the acquired biometric data directly affects the ability of the biometric matcher to perform the matching process accurately and effectively.

Noise can be present in the biometric data due to defective or improperly maintained sensors, incorrect user interaction or adverse ambient conditions. For example, accumulation of dirt on a fingerprint sensor can result in the acquisition of a noisy fingerprint image. When noisy fingerprint images are processed by a minutiae-based fingerprint recognition algorithm, a number of false (spurious) minutia points may be detected. Figures 17.1(c) and 17.1(d) show the minutiae extracted from good quality (Figure 17.1(a)) and noisy fingerprint (Figure 17.1(b)) images, respectively, using the minutiae extraction algorithm proposed in [16]. We observe that no false minutia is detected in the good quality fingerprint image shown in Figure 17.1(c). On the other hand, Figure 17.1(d) indicates that several spurious minutiae are detected in the noisy image. In practice, some true minutiae may not be detected in poor quality images. These spurious and missing minutiae will eventually lead to errors in fingerprint matching [6].

Estimating the quality of a biometric sample and predicting the performance of a biometric matcher based on the estimated quality can be very useful in building robust multibiometric systems. This will allow us to dynamically assign weights to the individual biometric matchers based on the quality of the input biometric sample. For example, consider a bimodal biometric system utilizing iris and fingerprint for personal recognition. Assume that during a particular access attempt by the user, the iris image is of poor quality while the fingerprint image quality is sufficiently good. In this case, it would be instructive for the biometric system to automatically assign a higher weight to the fingerprint matcher and a lower weight to the iris matcher. With this motivation in mind, we now describe methods for automatically determining the quality of iris and fingerprint images, and incorporating them into a fusion framework.

17.2.1 Fingerprint image quality

A good quality assessment algorithm must be able to accurately determine the quality of local regions in the biometric sample and also provide a metric to describe the overall (global) quality of the sample. Several methods have been proposed for estimating the quality of a fingerprint image. Within a small region of a fingerprint image, the orientation of ridges is almost constant. Hence, spatially adjacent regions in a fingerprint image usually exhibit a primary dominant direction (exceptions include regions associated with singular points). Bolle et al. [5] use the directional histogram to classify local regions of a fingerprint image as being either directional or non-directional. They tessellate a fingerprint image into blocks and compute the histogram of intensities in each block based on the ridge direction. If the maximum value of the histogram is greater than a threshold, the block is labeled as directional. Further, a relative weight is assigned to each block based on its distance from the centroid of the fingerprint area. Since the regions near the centroid of the fingerprint area are likely to provide more discriminatory information than

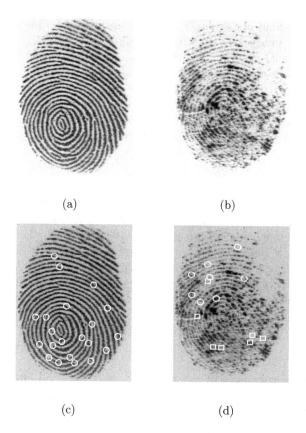

(a)   (b)

(c)   (d)

Fig. 17.1. Minutiae extraction results for fingerprint images of varying quality. (a) A good quality fingerprint image. (b) A noisy fingerprint image. (c) Minutia points detected in the good quality fingerprint image by an automatic minutiae extraction algorithm. (d) Minutia points detected in the noisy fingerprint image. The circles represent true minutia points while the squares represent false (spurious) minutiae. While no spurious minutia is detected in the good quality fingerprint image, several false minutia points are detected when the fingerprint image quality is poor.

the peripheral regions, higher weights are assigned to the blocks near the centroid. The weight, w_i, of the ith block centered at $l_i = [x_i, y_i]$ is computed as

$$w_i = \exp\left(\frac{-||l_i - l_c||^2}{2r^2}\right),\qquad(17.1)$$

where $l_c = [x_c, y_c]$ is the location of the centroid of the fingerprint area and r is a normalization constant. The ratio of the total weight of the directional blocks to the total weight of all the blocks in the fingerprint image is used as a measure of the global fingerprint image quality. In the same way, Gabor filters can be used instead of the directional histogram to determine if the regions of a fingerprint image have a clear ridge-valley structure [15].

The directional nature of the ridges in a local fingerprint region can also be measured in terms of its coherence value, which is a good measure of the local quality in that region [6]. The fingerprint image is divided into small blocks and the gradient vector at each pixel in a block B is computed. Let Σ be the covariance of the gradient vectors in B. Let the two eigenvalues of Σ be λ_1 and λ_2 such that $\lambda_1 \geq \lambda_2$. The coherence, γ, of the block is defined as

$$\gamma = \frac{(\lambda_1 - \lambda_2)^2}{(\lambda_1 + \lambda_2)^2}, \tag{17.2}$$

with $0 \leq \gamma \leq 1$. When the value of γ of a block B is close to 1 ($\lambda_1 \gg \lambda_2$), it indicates that the ridges in the fingerprint region are strongly oriented in a specific direction, indicating a good quality region. On the other hand, a value of γ that is close to 0 ($\lambda_1 \approx \lambda_2$) indicates the ridges do not have a clear direction which is mostly due to poor quality. We can also compute a global quality index for the fingerprint image as a weighted average of the block-wise coherence measures. The global quality index can be estimated as

$$Q_{finger} = \sum_{j=1}^{N} w_j \gamma_j, \tag{17.3}$$

where γ_j is the coherence of the jth block, N is the total number of blocks and w_j is the weight assigned to a block (see equation (17.1)). Figure 17.2 shows the local quality maps of two fingerprint images and their global quality indices.

The coherence-based fingerprint image quality measure described above quantifies the quality of an individual fingerprint image. When both the template and query fingerprint images are available during matching, it is also possible to compute a single quality index to represent the quality of the match between the two images. Such a measure is known as *pairwise* fingerprint quality [25] and it can be obtained as follows. Let T_f and I_f represent the template and query fingerprint images, respectively. We can partition T_f and I_f into blocks and estimate the coherence γ and γ' for each block in T_f and I_f, respectively. Let $M_1, \ldots, M_m$ be the m minutiae in T_f, where $M_i = \{x_i, y_i, \theta_i\}$, $i = 1, \ldots, m$, (x_i, y_i) represents the location of the ith minutia point in T_f and θ_i is the direction of the ith minutia. Let $M'_1, \ldots, M'_n$ be the n minutiae in I_f, where $M'_j = \{x'_j, y'_j, \theta'_j\}$, $j = 1, \ldots, n$. Let $\gamma(x, y)$ and $\gamma'(x, y)$ be the quality (coherence) of the block which contains the location (x, y) in T_f and I_f, respectively. Let $\Delta = [\Delta x, \Delta y, \Delta \theta]$ represent the translation and rotation parameters that transform a point (x, y) in T_f to a point (x', y') in I_f and let t be the transformation function. Let A and A' denote the areas of the fingerprint regions in the template and the query. The area of overlap, A_o, between the fingerprint regions of T_f and I_f can be computed using Δ. The

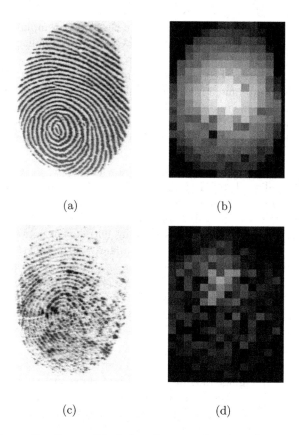

(a)   (b)

(c)   (d)

Fig. 17.2. Computing the quality index Q_{finger} using the coherence measure. (a) A good quality fingerprint image and (b) corresponding local quality map. (c) A poor quality fingerprint image and (d) corresponding local quality map. In (b) and (d), brighter blocks indicate higher quality regions. The values of Q_{finger} for the two images are 0.95 and 0.20, respectively.

quality of matching between the template and query images, $Q_{finger}(T_f, I_f)$, is then defined as follows.

$$Q_{finger}(T_f, I_f) = \left(\frac{r_1 + r_2}{m + n}\right)\left(\frac{2A_o}{A + A'}\right), \tag{17.4}$$

where

$$r_1 = \sum_{i=1}^{m} \gamma(x_i, y_i)\gamma'(t(x_i, y_i, \Delta)) \text{ and}$$

$$r_2 = \sum_{j=1}^{n} \gamma(t(x'_j, y'_j, -\Delta))\gamma'(x'_j, y'_j).$$

Here, $0 \leq Q_{finger}(T_f, I_f) \leq 1$. Note that if a minutia point in the template (query) falls outside the fingerprint region of the query (template) image, then the quality of that minutia is set to zero. Given good quality template and query fingerprint images with large overlap, $Q_{finger}(T_f, I_f) \approx 1$. In practical biometric systems, only the template minutiae set is stored in the database and the raw template image is not available during matching. Since user enrollment is usually done under human supervision, the enrollment images are generally of good quality. Therefore, the global quality of a query fingerprint image (given by equation (17.3)) may be sufficient to predict the matcher performance.

There have been several other researchers who have addressed the problem of fingerprint quality. Tabassi et al. [29] present a technique for assigning a quality label to a fingerprint image based on the discriminative ability of the extracted minutia features. This approach assumes that the feature extraction module is reliable, and that there is a strong correlation between the quality label assigned and the performance of the fingerprint matcher. Chen et al. [6] discuss a frequency domain approach for estimating the global quality of a fingerprint image. In March 2006, a NIST Workshop was convened to explore the topic of biometric image quality[3] thereby suggesting the significance of the problem and its implications in biometric system design.

17.2.2 Iris image quality

The quality of an iris image may be affected by factors such as occlusion due to eyelashes and eyelids, improper focus, motion blur, non-uniform illumination, large pupil area, off-angle acquisition, specular reflection, etc. Researchers have attempted to quantify these factors. Techniques for assessing the focus of iris images were proposed in [9] and [30]. Ma et al. [21] utilize the energy in the low, moderate and high frequency bands of the 2-dimensional Fourier power spectrum to classify the iris images based on their quality. However, Chen et al. [7] argue that since the Fourier transform does not localize well in the spatial domain, it (i.e., the Fourier transform) is not appropriate for deriving local quality measures. Hence, they propose a wavelet transform-based iris quality measurement algorithm.

The algorithm proposed by Chen et al. [7] consists of the following steps. The given iris image is segmented into iris and non-iris regions using Canny edge detection and Hough transform (for detecting circles). The detected iris and eye-lid boundaries for a good quality iris image and a poor quality iris image are shown in Figures 17.3(a) and 17.3(b), respectively. An intensity thresholding is applied to remove the eyelashes. Figures 17.3(c) and 17.3(d) show the extracted iris patterns after the removal of eyelashes. Once the iris region has been localized, a 2-dimensional isotropic Mexican hat wavelet filter [22] is applied to the extracted pattern. The Mexican hat filter is applied at

---

[3] http://www.itl.nist.gov/iad/894.03/quality/workshop/

three different scales and the product of the responses at the three scales is treated as the overall response of the filter. The quality of the local regions in the iris image is obtained by partitioning the iris region into concentric windows. Let the number of windows be N. The energy, E_t, of the tth window is defined as

$$E_t = \frac{1}{N_t} \sum_{i=1}^{N_t} |w_{t,i}|^2,$$ (17.5)

where $w_{t,i}$ is the ith wavelet response in the tth window, N_t is the total number of wavelet coefficients in the tth window and $t = 1, 2, \ldots, N$. Chen et al. [7] claim that the energy E_t is a good indicator of the quality of the iris features and hence, it is a reliable measure of local iris quality (high values of E_t indicate good quality regions and vice versa). Figures 17.3(e) and 17.3(f) show the local quality based on the energy concentration in the individual windows.

The global quality Q of the iris image is then estimated as a weighted average of the local quality measures. The global quality index Q is given by

$$Q_{iris} = \frac{1}{N} \sum_{t=1}^{N} (m_t \times \log E_t),$$ (17.6)

where m_t is the weight assigned to each window. Since the inner regions of the iris pattern which are close to the pupil contain richer texture information and are less occluded by eyelashes compared to the outer iris regions [28], higher weights can be assigned to windows near the pupil center. To account for the variations in the pupil dilation, iris size and rotation, the rubber sheet model proposed by Daugman [9] is used to normalize the iris texture and the local quality measures.

The wavelet-based iris image quality measure described above quantifies the quality of an individual iris image. When both the template (T_i) and query (I_i) iris images are available during matching, a pairwise quality index [25] can be computed to represent the quality of the match between the two images as follows. The responses obtained after applying the wavelet filter are sampled at R different radii and at S angles for each radius. Let $w_{r,s}$ be the wavelet response at the rth radius ($r = 1, \ldots, R$) and s^{th} angle ($s = 1, \ldots, S$) in T_i and let $w'_{r,s}$ be the corresponding wavelet response in I_i. The average wavelet response at each radius r is computed as w_r $(= \frac{1}{S} \sum_{s=1}^{S} w_{r,s})$ and w'_r $(= \frac{1}{S} \sum_{s=1}^{S} w'_{r,s})$ in T_i and I_i, respectively. The quality of match between the template and query iris images, $Q_{iris}(T_i, I_i)$, is defined as the correlation coefficient between the vectors $\boldsymbol{w} = [w_1, \ldots, w_R]$ and $\boldsymbol{w'} = [w'_1, \ldots, w'_R]$. Here, $-1 \leq Q_{iris}(T_i, I_i) \leq 1$ and the quality is good ($Q_{iris}(T_i, I_i) \approx 1$) when the template and query iris images are of similar quality.

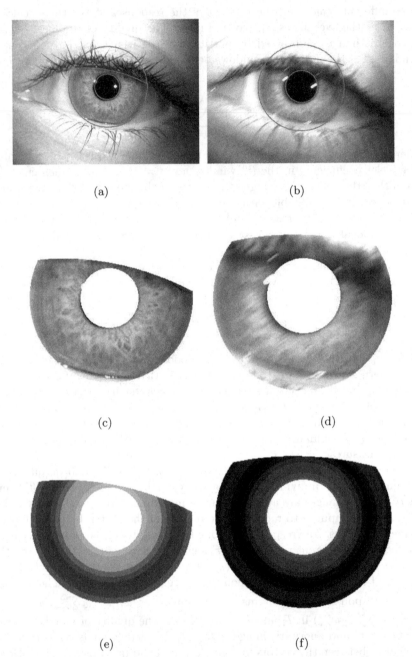

Fig. 17.3. Quality estimation for two iris images. (a) and (b) Detected iris boundaries and eyelids. (c) and (d) Extracted iris patterns after eyelash removal. (e) and (f) Local quality measures based on the energy concentration in the individual windows. The quality score for the good quality iris image on the left is 0.89, while the quality score for the poor quality iris image on the right is 0.58. Note that brighter pixel intensities indicate higher quality.

17.2.3 Quality-based fusion techniques

The quality information of a biometric signal can be utilized by any of the three match score fusion approaches, namely, density-based fusion, transformation-based fusion and classifier-based fusion. This section describes schemes for incorporating the estimated quality measures in each of the three score fusion techniques. Besides these techniques, other methods to incorporate quality measures in match score fusion have also been proposed in the literature. For example, Baker and Maurer [2] adopt a hybrid (density-based and classifier-based) score fusion approach in a multi-instance biometric system that uses fingerprints from all 10 fingers of a person. The fingerprint images are divided into five quality levels and the genuine and impostor score densities are estimated at each quality level. Based on the quality-dependent density estimates, a Bayesian Belief Network (BBN) classifier is used to decide whether the set of input fingerprints come from a "genuine user" or an "impostor".

Classifier-based fusion

The following methodology to incorporate the quality of the input biometric samples into a support vector machine (SVM) classifier, which determines the decision boundary between the genuine and impostor classes, was proposed in [11]. Let $s = [s_1, s_2, \ldots, s_R]^T$ be the vector of match scores output by R biometric matchers and $q = [q_1, q_2, \ldots, q_R]^T$ be the vector containing the corresponding quality measures of the biometric samples presented at the input of the R biometric matchers. Let us assume that we have N training samples of the form (s_i, q_i, y_i), where s_i and q_i represent the R-dimensional match score vector and the quality vector of the ith training sample, respectively, and $y_i \in \{-1, 1\}$ represents the corresponding class label (-1 if the sample belongs to the impostor class and $+1$ if the sample comes from the genuine class). The goal is to learn the fusion function $f_{sq}(s_t, q_t)$ that takes the match score and quality vectors (s_t and q_t, respectively) of the test sample as input and generates a fused score which helps in predicting the output label y_t as accurately as possible. A SVM is used to determine an initial fusion function $f_s(s) = ws + w_0$ by solving the following optimization problem.

$$\min_{s, w_0} \left(\frac{1}{2} ||w||^2 + \sum_{i=1}^{N} C_i \epsilon_i \right), \text{ such that} \tag{17.7}$$
$$y_i (ws_i + w_0) \geq 1 - \epsilon_i,$$
$$\epsilon_i \geq 0, \forall i, \ i = 1, 2, \ldots, N.$$

In Equation 17.7, ϵ_i represents the training error (distance between an incorrectly classified training sample and the decision boundary) and C_i represents the cost assigned to the training error. The weight vector $w = [w_1, w_2, \ldots, w_R]$ represents the weight assigned to each component of the match score vector s, which indicates the relative importance of the different biometric matchers. In a general SVM classifier, the cost C_i, $i = 1, \ldots, N$, is assigned a positive constant C and the value of C is a tradeoff between the training error rate and the generalization error rate. In [11], the authors argue that if a biometric sample is of good quality, then the cost of misclassifying this sample during training must be relatively high and vice versa. Hence, the cost C_i for each training sample is made to be proportional to the biometric signal quality. Further, R different SVMs were trained by leaving out one component from the vectors s_i at a time, i.e., f_s^j is trained using $s_i^j = \left[s_{i1}, \ldots, s_{i,(j-1)}, s_{i,(j+1)}, \ldots, s_{iR}\right]$.

During the authentication phase, the fused score provided by the SVM classifier is adaptively weighted based on the quality of each input biometric component. Experiments conducted on the MCYT database [26] containing fingerprint and online signature modalities show that the quality based fusion scheme results in a relative reduction of 20% in the Equal Error Rate (EER) over the case where no quality measures are used [11]. In these experiments the quality scores are manually assigned to the fingerprint images while the quality of all the signature samples is assumed to be the same.

Transformation-based fusion

A quality-weighted sum rule for score level fusion was proposed in [10]. The scores from minutiae-based and ridge-based fingerprint matchers were combined using a weighted sum rule, where the weights were determined based on the sensitivity of the two matchers to the quality of the fingerprint image. When the fingerprint image is of low quality, the ridge-based matcher is assigned a higher weight because it was found to be less sensitive to image quality. On the other hand, when the fingerprint image is of good quality, the minutiae-based matcher was found to be more accurate and hence, assigned a higher weight. The match scores from the minutiae-based and ridge-based fingerprint matchers were normalized using tanh and double-sigmoid methods of normalization, respectively, transforming them into similarity scores in the range $[0, 1]$. The fused score was obtained as

$$s_q = \frac{Q}{2} s_m + \left(1 - \frac{Q}{2}\right) s_r, \tag{17.8}$$

where s_m and s_r are the normalized match scores from the minutiae- and ridge-based matchers, respectively, and Q is the global quality of the input fingerprint image computed using the algorithm proposed in [6]. Experiments conducted on a subset of the MCYT database [26] containing 750 fingers with 10 impressions per finger, indicate that the combination of minutiae and texture-based matchers using the quality-weighted sum rule performs better than the two individual matchers and also the simple sum rule (without weights) as shown in Figure 17.4.

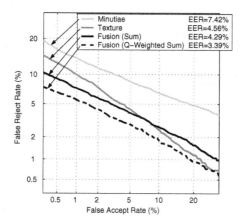

Fig. 17.4. DET plot demonstrating the improvement in the verification performance due to the quality-weighted sum rule.

Density-based fusion

Based on the likelihood ratio-based match score fusion approach described in [8], Nandakumar et al. [25] proposed the following quality-based likelihood ratio fusion scheme. This scheme is based on the following observation. When a poor quality sample is presented to a matcher, the matcher cannot reliably distinguish between genuine and impostor users and the likelihood ratio will be closer to 1. On the other hand, for good quality samples, the likelihood ratio will be greater than 1 for genuine users and less than 1 for impostors. Hence, if we estimate the joint density of the match score and the quality of the match for each matcher, the resulting likelihood ratios of the individual matchers will be implicitly weighted. Let q_r be the quality of the match provided by the rth matcher, for $r = 1, \ldots, R$, where R is the number of matchers to be fused. Let $f_{gen,r}(s_r, q_r)$ $((f_{imp,r}(s_r, q_r))$ be the joint density of the match score and the quality estimated from the genuine (impostor) template-query pairs of the rth matcher. The quality-based fusion score, $FS(s, q)$, is given by

$$FS(s, q) = \prod_{r=1}^{R} \frac{f_{gen,r}(s_r, q_r)}{f_{imp,r}(s_r, q_r)}. \tag{17.9}$$

The above quality-based fusion rule assumes independence between the R biometric matchers. However, within each matcher the match score and the quality measure can be correlated. Experiments on the West Virginia University multimodal database, which consists of 320 subjects with five samples each of fingerprint and iris modalities, demonstrate that quality-based fusion leads to significant improvement in the performance (see Figure 17.5).

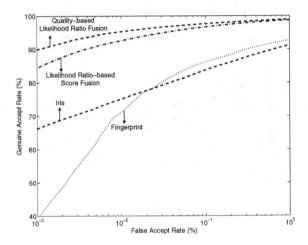

Fig. 17.5. ROC plots demonstrating the improvement in the verification performance due to the quality-based likelihood ratio fusion rule.

17.3 Soft biometrics

A multimodal biometric system that utilizes a combination of biometric identifiers like face, fingerprint, hand geometry and iris is more robust to noise and can alleviate problems such as non-universality and lack of distinctiveness, thereby reducing the error rates significantly. However, using multiple traits may increase the enrollment and verification times, cause more inconvenience to the users and increase the overall cost of the system. Hence, Jain et al. [17] propose another solution to reduce the error rates of the biometric system without causing any additional inconvenience to the user. Their solution is based on incorporating soft identifiers of human identity like gender, ethnicity, height, eye color, etc. into a (primary) biometric identification system. Figure 17.6 depicts a scenario where both primary (face) and soft (gender, ethnicity, height and eye color) biometric information can be automatically extracted and utilized to verify a user's identity. In this scenario, the height of the user can be estimated as he approaches the camera and his gender, ethnicity and eye color can be estimated from his face image. These additional attributes can be used along with the face biometric to accurately identify the person. Though soft biometric information is commonly collected in Automated Fingerprint Identification Systems (AFIS) used in the forensic community, it is not utilized during the automatic fingerprint matching phase. For example, the fingerprint card used by the Federal Bureau of Investigation (FBI) includes information on the gender, ethnicity, height, weight, eye color and hair color of the person along with the prints of all ten fingers.

Soft biometric traits have also been referred to as "meta-data" or "biographic information" in the literature.

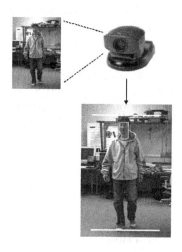

Height: 5.9 ft.

Eye color: Black

Gender: Male

Ethnicity: Asian

Face features: LDA Coefficients

Identity: Unsang

Fig. 17.6. A scenario where the primary biometric identifier (face) and the soft biometric attributes (gender, ethnicity, eye color and height) are automatically extracted and utilized to verify a person's identity.

17.3.1 Motivation

The usefulness of soft biometric traits can be illustrated by the following example. Consider three users A (1.8m tall, male), B (1.7m tall, female), and C (1.6m tall, male) who are enrolled in a fingerprint biometric system that works in the identification mode. Suppose user A presents his fingerprint sample X to the system. It is compared to the templates of all the three users stored in the database and the posteriori matching probabilities of all the three users given the sample X are calculated. Let us assume that the outputs of the fingerprint matcher are $P(A|X) = 0.42$, $P(B|X) = 0.43$, and $P(C|X) = 0.15$. In this case, user A will be falsely identified as user B based on the Bayesian decision rule. On the other hand, let us assume that as the user approaches the fingerprint sensor, there exists a secondary system that automatically identifies the gender of the user as male and measures the user's height as 1.78m. If we have this information in addition to the posteriori probabilities given by the fingerprint matcher, then a proper combination of these sources of information is likely to lead to a correct identification of the user as A.

The first biometric system developed by Alphonse Bertillon in 1883 used anthropometric features such as the length and breadth of the head and the ear, length of the middle finger and foot, height, etc. along with attributes like eye color, scars, and tatoo marks for ascertaining a person's identity [4].

Although each individual measurement in the Bertillonage system may exhibit some (intra-class) variability, a combination of several quantized (or binned) measurements was sufficient to manually identify a person with reasonable accuracy. Like the Bertillon system, Heckathorn et al. [14] use attributes such as gender, race, eye color, height, and other visible marks like scars and tattoos to recognize individuals for the purpose of welfare distribution. More recently, Ailisto et al. [1] showed that unobtrusive user identification can be performed in low security applications such as access to health clubs using a combination of "light" biometric identifiers like height, weight, and body fat percentage. While the biometric features used in the above mentioned systems provide some information about the identity of the user, they are not sufficient for accurately identifying the user. Hence, these attributes can be referred to as "soft biometric traits". The soft biometric information complements the identity information provided by traditional (primary) biometric identifiers such as fingerprint, iris, and voice. Thus, utilizing soft biometric traits can improve the recognition accuracy of primary biometric systems.

17.3.2 Automatic soft biometric feature extraction

Any trait that provides some information about the identity of a person, but does not provide sufficient evidence to precisely determine the identity can be referred to as soft biometric trait. Figure 17.7 shows some examples of soft biometric traits. Soft biometric traits are available and can be extracted in a number of practical biometric applications. For example, attributes like gender, ethnicity, age and eye color can be extracted with sufficient reliability from the face images [12, 24, 3, 20, 19]. Gender [27], speech accent [13], and perceptual age [23] of the speaker can be inferred from the speech signal.

The weight of a user can be measured by asking him to stand on a weight sensor while he is providing his primary biometric. The height of a person can be estimated from a real-time sequence of images as the user approaches the biometric system. For example, in [18], geometric features like vanishing points and vanishing lines were used to compute the height of an object. Jain et al. [17] implemented a real-time vision system for automatic extraction of gender, ethnicity, height, and eye color. The system was designed to extract the soft biometric attributes as the person approaches the primary biometric system to present his primary biometric identifier (face and fingerprint). Their soft biometric system is equipped with two pan/tilt/zoom cameras. Camera 1 monitors the scene for any human presence based on the motion segmentation image. Once camera 1 detects an approaching person, it measures the height of the person and then guides camera 2 to focus on the person's face.

17.3.3 Fusion of primary and soft biometric information

A Bayesian framework for fusion of soft and primary biometric information was proposed in [17]. The main advantage of this framework is that it does not

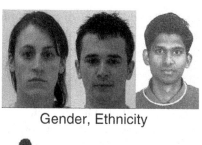

Gender, Ethnicity

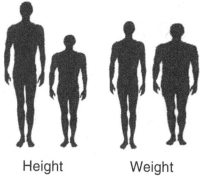

Height   Weight

Fig. 17.7. Examples of soft biometric traits.

require the soft biometric feature extractors to be perfect (100% accurate). Let us assume that the primary biometric system is based on R_p, $R_p \geq 1$ biometric identifiers like fingerprint, face, iris and hand geometry. Further, the soft biometric system is based on R_s, $R_s \geq 1$ attributes like age, gender, ethnicity, eye color and height. Let $\omega_1, \omega_2, \ldots, \omega_M$ represent the M users enrolled in the database. Let $\boldsymbol{x} = [\boldsymbol{x}_1, \boldsymbol{x}_2, \ldots, \boldsymbol{x}_{R_p}]$ be the collection of primary biometric feature vectors. Let $p(\boldsymbol{x}_j|\omega_k)$ be the likelihood of observing the primary biometric feature vector $\boldsymbol{x}_j$ given the user is ω_k. If the output of each individual modality in the primary biometric system is a set of match scores, $\boldsymbol{s}_k = [s_{1,k}, s_{2,k}, \ldots, s_{R_p,k}]$, one can approximate $p(\boldsymbol{x}_j|\omega_k)$ by $p(s_j|\omega_k)$, provided the genuine match score distribution of each modality is known.

Let $\boldsymbol{y} = [y_1, y_2, \ldots, y_{R_s}]$ be the soft biometric feature vector, where, for example, y_1 could be the gender, y_2 could be the eye color, etc. We require an estimate of the posteriori probability of user ω_k given both $\boldsymbol{x}$ and $\boldsymbol{y}$. This posteriori probability can be calculated by applying the Bayes rule as follows:

$$P(\omega_k|\boldsymbol{x}, \boldsymbol{y}) = \frac{p(\boldsymbol{x}, \boldsymbol{y}|\omega_k)P(\omega_k)}{p(\boldsymbol{x}, \boldsymbol{y})}. \qquad (17.10)$$

If all the users are equally likely to access the system, then $P(\omega_k) = \frac{1}{M}$, $\forall\, k$. Further, if we assume that all the primary biometric feature vectors $\boldsymbol{x}_1, \ldots, \boldsymbol{x}_{R_p}$ and all the soft biometric variables $y_1, y_2, \ldots, y_{R_s}$ are independent of each other given the user's identity ω_k, the posteriori probability in

Equation (17.10) can be expressed in terms of the product of the likelihoods as

$$P(\omega_k|\boldsymbol{x},\boldsymbol{y}) \propto \prod_{j=1}^{R_p} p(\boldsymbol{x}_j|\omega_k) \prod_{r=1}^{R_s} p(y_r|\omega_k). \qquad (17.11)$$

where $\propto$ is the proportionality symbol. The logarithm of the posteriori probability can be considered as the discriminant function, $g_k(\boldsymbol{x},\boldsymbol{y})$, for user ω_k.

$$g_k(\boldsymbol{x},\boldsymbol{y}) = \sum_{j=1}^{R_p} \log p(\boldsymbol{x}_j|\omega_k) + \sum_{r=1}^{R_s} \log p(y_r|\omega_k). \qquad (17.12)$$

During the identification phase, the input biometric sample is compared with the templates of all the M users enrolled in the database and the discriminant functions $g_1,\ldots,g_M$ are computed. The test user is identified as that user with the largest value of discriminant function among all the enrolled users. The above Bayesian framework can also be easily adapted for a biometric system operating in the verification mode [17].

Computation of soft biometric likelihoods

A simple method for computing the soft biometric likelihoods $p(y_r|\omega_k), r = 1,\ldots,R_s, k = 1,2,\ldots,M$ is to estimate them based on the accuracy of the soft biometric feature extractors. For example, if the accuracy of the gender classifier is α, we can estimate the likelihood for the gender attribute as

1. P(observed gender is male | true gender of the user is male) $= \alpha$,
2. P(observed gender is female | true gender of the user is female) $= \alpha$,
3. P(observed gender is male | true gender of the user is female) $= 1 - \alpha$,
4. P(observed gender is female | true gender of the user is male) $= 1 - \alpha$.

Similarly, if the average error made by the system in measuring the height of a person is μ_e and the standard deviation of the error is σ_e, then it is reasonable to assume that p(measured height$|\omega_k$) follows a Gaussian distribution with mean $(h(\omega_k) + \mu_e)$ and standard deviation σ_e, where $h(\omega_k)$ is the true height of user ω_k. When the error in height measurement (characterized by the parameters μ_e and σ_e) is small, the distribution of the measured height of a person is highly peaked around the true height of the person. As a result, the measured height can provide better discrimination between the users.

There is a potential problem when the likelihoods are estimated only based on the accuracy of the soft biometric feature extractors. The discriminant function in Equation (17.12) is dominated by the soft biometric terms due to the large dynamic range of the soft biometric log-likelihood values. For example, if the gender classifier is 98% accurate ($\alpha = 0.98$), the log-likelihood for the gender term in Equation (17.12) is -0.02 if the classification is correct and -3.91 in the case of a misclassification. This large difference in the log-likelihood values is due to the large variance of the soft biometric feature values compared to the primary biometric feature values. To offset this phenomenon, Jain et al. [17] introduced a scaling factor β, $0 \leq \beta \leq 1$, to flatten the likelihood distribution of each soft biometric trait. If $q_{r,k}$ is an estimate of the likelihood $p(y_r|\omega_k)$ based on the accuracy of the feature extractor for the rth soft biometric trait, the weighted likelihood $\hat{p}(y_r|\omega_k)$ is computed as,

$$\hat{p}(y_r|\omega_k) = \frac{(q_{r,k})^{\beta_r}}{\sum_{Y_r}(q_{r,k})^{\beta_r}}, \qquad (17.13)$$

where Y_r is the set of all possible values of the discrete soft biometric variable y_r and β_r is the weight assigned to the rth trait. If the feature y_r is continuous with deviation σ_r, the likelihood can be scaled by replacing σ_r with σ_r/β_r.

The above method of likelihood computation also has other implicit advantages. An impostor can easily circumvent the soft biometric feature extraction because it is relatively easy to modify/hide one's soft biometric attributes by applying cosmetics and wearing other accessories (like mask, shoes with high heels, etc.). In this scenario, the scaling factor β_r can act as a measure of the reliability of the rth soft biometric feature and its value can be set depending on the environment in which the system operates. If the environment is hostile (where many users are trying to circumvent the system), the value of β_r can be set close to 0. Finally, the discriminant function given in equation (17.12) is optimal only if the assumption of independence between all the biometric traits is true. If there is any dependence between the features, the discriminant function is sub-optimal. In this case, appropriate selection of the weights β_r, $r = 1, \ldots, R_s$, during training can result in better recognition rates.

17.3.4 Performance gain using soft biometrics

Experiments by Jain et al. [17] demonstrated the benefits of utilizing the gender, ethnicity, and height information of the user in addition to the face and fingerprint biometric identifiers. A subset of the Joint Multibiometric Database (JMD), collected at West Virginia University, containing 4 face images and 4 impressions of the left index finger obtained from 263 users was used in their experiments. The LDA-based classifier proposed in [20] was used for gender and ethnicity classification of each user. The accuracy of the ethnicity classifier for the problem of classifying the users in the JMD as "Asian" and "Non-Asian" was 96.3%. The accuracy of the gender classifier on the JMD was 89.6%. When the reject rate was fixed at 25%, the accuracy of the ethnicity and gender classifiers were 99% and 98%, respectively. In cases where the ethnicity or the gender classifier made a reject decision on a user, the corresponding information is not utilized for updating the discriminant function, i.e., if the label assigned to the rth soft biometric trait is "reject", then the log-likelihood term corresponding to the rth feature in Equation (17.12) is set to zero. Since no real-time height measurement was performed during recognition, Jain et al. [17] simulated values for the measured height of user ω_k, $k = 1, \ldots, 263$ from a normal distribution with mean $h(\omega_k) + \mu_e$ and standard deviation σ_e, where $h(\omega_k)$ is the true height of user ω_k recorded manually during the database collection, $\mu_e = 2$ cm and $\sigma_e = 5$ cm. Here, μ_e and σ_e are the average and standard deviation of the height measurement error.

Figure 17.8 depicts the performance gain obtained when the soft biometric identifiers were used along with both face and fingerprint modalities. We can observe that the rank-one recognition rate of the multimodal biometric system based on face and fingerprint modalities is approximately 97% (rank-one error rate is 3%) and the addition of soft biometric information improves the rank-one accuracy by about 1% (rank-one error rate is now 2%). Although the absolute improvement in the rank-one accuracy due to the additional soft biometric information is small, it must be noted that the relative reduction in the rank-one error rate is about 33%, which is significant.

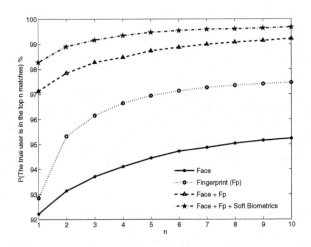

Fig. 17.8. Improvement in the performance of a multimodal (face and fingerprint) system after addition of soft biometric traits.

17.4 Summary

In addition to the match scores provided by the biometric matchers, ancillary information may also be available to a multibiometric system. Biometric signal quality and soft biometric information are two examples of such additional information that can be utilized to improve the accuracy of a multibiometric system. While biometric signal quality does not explicitly contain any information about the identity of the user, different matchers exhibit different levels of sensitivity to the quality of the acquired biometric sample. Therefore, the match scores can be appropriately weighted during fusion based on the quality of the input sample. Soft biometric characteristics like gender, ethnicity, height and weight directly provide information about the identity of the user. Although the soft biometric information alone is not sufficient for accurate recognition, they can be used to complement the information provided by the primary biometric identifiers like fingerprint, iris and face. Techniques for automatically extracting soft biometric information and estimating biometric signal quality have been developed only recently. Hence, fusion schemes that incorporate such ancillary information have not been thoroughly explored and there is tremendous scope for conducting more in-depth research in this area.

References

1. H. Aillisto, M. Lindholm, S. M. Makela, and E. Vildjiounaite. Unobtrusive User Identification with Light Biometrics. In *Proceedings of Nordic Conference on Human-Computer Interaction*, pages 327–330, Tampere, Finland, October 2004.
2. J. P. Baker and D. E. Maurer. Fusion of Biometric Data with Quality Estimates via a Bayesian Belief Network. In *Special Session on Research at The Biometric Consortium Conference (BC2005)*, pages 21–22, Arlington, USA, Sept. 2005.
3. K. Balci and V. Atalay. PCA for Gender Estimation: Which Eigenvectors Contribute? In *Proceedings of Sixteenth International Conference on Pattern Recognition (ICPR)*, volume 3, pages 363–366, Quebec City, Canada, August 2002.
4. A. Bertillon. *Signaletic Instructions including the Theory and Practice of Anthropometrical Identification, R.W. McClaughry Translation*. The Werner Company, 1896.
5. R. Bolle, S. Pankanti, and Y.-S. Yao. System and Method for Determining the Quality of Fingerprint Images. United States Patent Number US 5963656, 1999.
6. Y. Chen, S. C. Dass, and A. K. Jain. Fingerprint Quality Indices for Predicting Authentication Performance. In *Proceedings of Fifth International Conference on AVBPA*, pages 160–170, Rye Brook, USA, July 2005.
7. Y. Chen, S. C. Dass, and A. K. Jain. Localized Iris Image Quality Using 2-D Wavelets. In *IAPR International Conference on Biometrics (ICB)*, pages 373–381, Hong Kong, China, January 2006.
8. S. C. Dass, K. Nandakumar, and A. K. Jain. A Principled Approach to Score Level Fusion in Multimodal Biometric Systems. In *Proceedings of Fifth International Conference on AVBPA*, pages 1049–1058, Rye Brook, USA, July 2005.
9. J. Daugman. Statistical Richness of Visual Phase Information: Update on Recognizing Persons by Iris Patterns. *International Journal on Computer Vision*, 45(1):25–38, 2001.
10. J. Fierrez-Aguilar, Y. Chen, J. Ortega-Garcia, and A. K. Jain. Incorporating Image Quality in Multi-algorithm Fingerprint Verification. In *International Conference on Biometrics (ICB)*, pages 213–220, Hong Kong, January 2006.
11. J. Fierrez-Aguilar, J. Ortega-Garcia, J. Gonzalez-Rodriguez, and J. Bigun. Discriminative Multimodal Biometric Authentication based on Quality Measures. *Pattern Recognition*, 38(5):777–779, May 2005.
12. S. Gutta, J. R. J. Huang, P. J. Phillips, and H. Wechsler. Mixture of Experts for Classification of Gender, Ethnic Origin, and Pose of Human Faces. *IEEE Transactions on Neural Networks*, 11(4):948–960, July 2000.

13. J. H. L. Hansen and L. Arslan. Foreign Accent Classification using Source Generator based Prosodic Features. In *Proceedings of IEEE International Conference on Acoustics, Speech, and Signal Processing (ICASSP)*, pages 836–839, Detroit, USA, May 1995.

14. D. D. Heckathorn, R. S. Broadhead, and B. Sergeyev. A Methodology for Reducing Respondent Duplication and Impersonation in Samples of Hidden Populations. *Journal of Drug Issues*, 31:543–564, 2001.

15. L. Hong, Y. Wan, and A. K. Jain. Fingerprint Image Enhancement: Algorithms and Performance Evaluation. *IEEE Transactions on Pattern Analysis and Machine Intelligence*, 20(8):777–789, August 1998.

16. A. K. Jain, L. Hong, and R. Bolle. On-line Fingerprint Verification. *IEEE Trans. on Pattern Analysis and Machine Intelligence*, 19(4):302–314, April 1997.

17. A. K. Jain, K. Nandakumar, X. Lu, and U. Park. Integrating Faces, Fingerprints and Soft Biometric Traits for User Recognition. In *Proceedings of ECCV International Workshop on Biometric Authentication (BioAW)*, volume LNCS 3087, pages 259–269, Prague, Czech Republic, May 2004. Springer.

18. J.-S. Kim, D.-H. Hyeon, J.-S. Choi, J.-W. Kim, B.-H. Choi, and H.-K. Jung. Object Extraction for Superimposition and Height Measurement. In *Proceedings of Eighth Korea-Japan Joint Workshop On Frontiers of Computer Vision*, pages 7–12, Sapporo, Japan, January 2002.

19. A. Lanitis, C. Draganova, and C. Christodoulou. Comparing Different Classifiers for Automatic Age Estimation. *IEEE Transactions on Systems, Man, and Cybernetics, Part B: Cybernetics*, 34(1):621–628, February 2004.

20. X. Lu and A. K. Jain. Ethnicity Identification from Face Images. In *Proceedings of SPIE Conference on Biometric Technology for Human Identification*, volume 5404, pages 114–123, Orlando, USA, April 2004.

21. L. Ma, T. Tan, Y. Wang, and D. Zhang. Personal Identification Based on Iris Texture Analysis. *IEEE Transactions on Pattern Analysis and Machine Intelligence*, 25(12):1519–1533, December 2003.

22. S. Mallet. *A Wavelet Tour of Signal Processing*. Academic Press, 1998.

23. N. Minematsu, K. Yamauchi, and K. Hirose. Automatic Estimation of Perceptual Age Using Speaker Modeling Techniques. In *Proceedings of the Eighth European Conference on Speech Communication and Technology*, pages 3005–3008, Geneva, Switzerland, September 2003.

24. B. Moghaddam and M. H. Yang. Learning Gender with Support Faces. *IEEE Trans. on Pattern Analysis and Machine Intelligence*, 24(5):707–711, May 2002.

25. K. Nandakumar, Y. Chen, A. K. Jain, and S. Dass. Quality-based Score Level Fusion in Multibiometric Systems. In *Proceedings of International Conference on Pattern Recognition (ICPR)*, pages 473–476, Hong Kong, August 2006.

26. J. Ortega-Garcia, J. Fierrez-Aguilar, D. Simon, J. Gonzalez-Rodriguez, M. Faundez, V. Espinosa, A. Satue, I. Hernaez, J.-J. Igarza, C. Vivaracho, D. Escudero, and Q.-I. Moro. MCYT Baseline Corpus: A Bimodal Biometric Database. *IEE Proceedings on Vision, Image and Signal Processing, Special Issue on Biometrics on the Internet*, 150(6):395–401, December 2003.

27. E. S. Parris and M. J. Carey. Language Independent Gender Identification. In *Proceedings of IEEE International Conference on Acoustics, Speech, and Signal Processing (ICASSP)*, pages 685–688, Atlanta, USA, May 1996.

28. H. Sung, J. Lim, J Park, and Y. Lee. Iris Recognition Using Collarette Boundary Localization. In *Seventeenth International Conference on Pattern Recognition (ICPR)*, volume 4, pages 857–860, Cambridge, UK, August 2004.

29. E. Tabassi, C. Wilson, and C. Watson. Fingerprint Image Quality. Technical Report 7151, National Institute of Standards and Technology, August 2004.
30. G. Zhang and M. Salganicoff. Method of Measuring the Focus of Close-Up Image of Eyes. United States patent number US 5953440, 1999.

The Law and the Use of Biometrics

John D. Woodward, Jr.

Adjunct Professor, Elliott School of International Affairs, George Washington University, USA

18.1 Introduction

This chapter, based in part on my earlier work, *Biometrics: Identity Assurance in the Information Age*, (2003), provides an overview of legal considerations related to the use of biometrics. Although a densely-written, heavily footnoted tome would be required for a detailed treatment of this topic, the modest goal here is to offer enough information for the reader to gain an understanding of the many legal issues involved with, and implicated by, the use of biometrics.

We begin by first determining who is deploying the biometric program. Whether the actor is a government-sector entity or private-sector one informs the legal analysis because U.S. law makes a sharp distinction depending on who is deploying the biometric system. Accordingly, this chapter analyzes each of these government- and private-sector options in turn. It concludes with a "Biometric Hypothetical" to capture some of the issues implicated by biometric use.

18.2 The Law and Government-Sector Use of Biometrics

The public, or government, sector, particularly U.S. government agencies, is increasingly interested in using biometric technologies for a variety of applications. Since the terrorist attacks of September 11, 2001, both the Administration and the Congress have identified biometrics as a tool for improving homeland security. As the National Biometric Security Project reported in 2006, one of the most important programs relating to the use of biometrics is the United States Visitor and Immigrant Status Indicator Technology Program, administered by the Department of Homeland Security, in 2004. Known as US-VISIT, this program seeks to ensure the accurate tracking of foreign nationals entering and exiting the United States through the use of biometric technology. US-VISIT currently requires covered foreign nationals to submit digital photographs and two index fingerprints as a condition of their entry into the U.S. US-VISIT will soon expand to include more foreign nationalities and more biometric data - all ten fingerprints will be taken. However, the program has experienced difficulties in deploying a system to track the departure of foreign visitors at land borders, primarily due to the high costs and technical obstacles.

In light of this high-level interest, this section discusses the privacy protections afforded by law in the context of government-sector use of biometrics. What happens, for example, when an individual must provide a biometric identifier to receive an entitlement or benefit from the U.S. government? What legal rights, if any, does an individual providing a biometric have, and what legal responsibilities, if any, does the government agency collecting the biometric owe with respect to the data taken? Can a citizen refuse to provide a biometric identifier? To begin to answer these questions, we first must look to the United States Constitution.

18.3 Constitutional Law Considerations

Because the U.S. Constitution is the highest law of the land, there is something to be said for starting at the "top" with our legal discussion. The following text describes how biometrics and the U.S. Constitution interact. We start with analyzing what the right to privacy means based on the judiciary's interpretation of the Constitution.

18.3.1 The Right to Privacy

The American concept of privacy has changed over the centuries as America has changed – reflecting the idiom that law mirrors the society that creates it. Prior to the birth of the nation, the American colonists essentially recognized a strong right of physical privacy centered in the home, where a person could be free from contact with others. As early as 1761, James Otis, a leading Boston attorney and revolutionary, expressed this right when he said, "Now one of the most essential branches of English liberty is the freedom of one's house. A man's house is his castle; and while he is quiet, he is well guarded as a prince in his castle."

Since colonial times, jurists and legal scholars have grappled with defining privacy and explaining what the right to privacy should encompass. By the second half of the nineteenth century, the judiciary and academia focused more attention on privacy rights, moving beyond privacy of place to privacy of person. In 1879, Judge Thomas M. Cooley, in his classic treatise on torts, included "the right to be let alone" as a class of tort rights, contending that "the right to one's person may be said to be a right of complete immunity."

Echoing and popularizing Cooley's phrase, Samuel D. Warren and Louis D. Brandeis, in their landmark *Harvard Law Review* article, "The Right to Privacy," written in 1890, articulated their view of privacy as a "right to be let alone." Brandeis, as a Supreme Court Justice, later used this phrase in his dissent in *Olmstead v. United States*, 277 U.S. 438 (1928), where by a 5-4 vote the Court ruled that a law enforcement wiretap of a telephone line did not trigger the Fourth Amendment reasoning that "[s]ince the wiretap itself had not been made on Olmstead's premises, there was no physical trespass," and thus no Fourth Amendment violation occurred. He declared that the Founding Fathers "conferred, as against the Government, the right to be let alone – the most comprehensive of rights and the right most valued by civilized men."

Privacy as the "right to be let alone" has a positive appeal and commendable simplicity; however, privacy scholars such as Ellen Alderman and Caroline Kennedy criticize the phrase in that "legally, it offers no guidance at all. Coveting an indefinable right is one thing; enforcing it in a court of law is another." Even the Supreme Court may have a change of heart. For example, in *Katz v. United States*, 389 U.S. 347 (1967) the Court overturned *Olmstead* by finding that the Fourth Amendment protected individuals using a public telephone from wiretaps by authorities without a warrant.

Readers interested in learning more about privacy and biometrics should consult *Biometrics & Privacy: Building a Conceptual Foundation* (2006), prepared by the National Science and Technology Council's Subcommittee on Biometrics, available at `www.biometrics.gov`. For a provocative examination of technology and privacy, read David Brin, *The Transparent Society: Will Technology Force Us to Choose Between Privacy and Freedom?* (1998).

18.3.2 Constitutional Background

The Constitution regulates government-sector action; however, it generally provides no protection from actions taken by private individuals. As constitutional law scholar Laurence H. Tribe has explained, "The Constitution, with the sole exception of the Thirteenth Amendment prohibiting slavery, regulates action by the government rather than the conduct of private individuals and groups." Thus, the Constitution, in its essence, provides individuals with protections from actions taken by government.

The word *privacy*, like the word *biometrics*, is nowhere to be found in the text of the U.S. Constitution. An obvious point needs stating: Just because something is not in the text of the Constitution does not mean that it is outside the Constitution's authority or protection. After all, no one supposes that Congress is without power to fund and regulate the Air Force simply because the Constitution refers only to land and naval forces. Therefore, it makes sense that without making explicit reference to privacy, the Constitution can nonetheless protect certain privacy interests, or "zones of privacy," to use Justice William Douglas's term. Justice Douglas used "zones of privacy" in his opinion in *Griswold v. Connecticut*, 381 U.S. 479 (1965), a landmark Supreme Court case holding unconstitutional a state statute that criminalized the sale of contraceptives to married couples.

With the founding of the republic, the Constitution, without making explicit reference to privacy, protected privacy interests. The Bill of Rights, or the first ten amendments to the Constitution, reflects these "zones of privacy" protections in the First Amendment rights of freedom of speech, press, religion and association; the Third Amendment prohibition against the quartering of soldiers in one's home; the Fourth Amendment right to be free from unreasonable searches and seizures; the Fifth Amendment right against self-incrimination; the Ninth Amendment's provision that "the enumeration in the Constitution, of certain rights, shall not be construed to deny or disparage others retained by the people," and the Tenth Amendment's provision that "the powers not delegated to the United States by the Constitution, nor prohibited by it to the States, are reserved to the States respectively, or to the people."

What, then, is the constitutional right to privacy and how does it affect biometrics used in government mandated applications? The answer to the first part of the question is legally fuzzy. Although the federal courts have made it clear that there is a zone of privacy, they have not done such a thorough job of mapping it and drawing its legal boundaries.

The roots of many modern constitutional privacy interests are found in the Due Process Clause of the Fourteenth Amendment. This clause provides that no State shall "deprive any person of life, liberty, or property, without due process of law." For more than 100 years, the Supreme Court has interpreted these words as containing a substantive protection that "bar[s] certain government actions regardless of the fairness of the procedures used to implement them." In other words, the Due Process Clause bars the government from doing certain things to us.

18.3.3 Three Forms of Privacy under Law

The Supreme Court has emphasized "there is a realm of personal liberty which the government may not enter." This realm, or zone of privacy, consists of rights that are "fundamental" or "implicit in the concept of ordered liberty" as the Court phrased it in *Griswold*, or as the Court would later rephrase it, "deeply rooted in this Nation's history and tradition" in *Moore v. City of East Cleveland*, 431 U.S. 494 (1977).

These terms may read well, but they lack clarity. For example, Robert H. Bork, a former federal judge, believes "the judge-created phrases specify no particular freedom, but merely assure us, in sonorous phrases, that they, the judges, will know what freedoms are required when the time comes."

Accordingly, it is difficult to determine precisely what is protected. In what specific areas of the zone of privacy is the government forbidden entry? In its consideration of privacy interests, the Supreme Court has implicitly categorized privacy as taking three distinct forms. These three forms of privacy, or what can be viewed as three slices of the privacy pie, are physical, decisional, and information (or informational).

Physical Privacy

This form of privacy is also known as freedom from contact with other people or monitoring agents. Physical privacy enjoys its greatest constitutional protection under the Fourth Amendment, which governs searches and seizures conducted by government agents. The amendment provides that "the right of the people to be secure in their persons, houses, papers, and effects, against unreasonable searches and seizures, shall not be violated."

Decisional Privacy

This form of privacy is also known as the freedom of the individual to make private choices, without undue government interference, about the personal and intimate matters that affect him or her such as "personal decisions relating to marriage, procreation, contraception, family relationships, child rearing and education" as expressed in *Planned Parenthood of Southeastern Pennsylvania v. Casey*, 505 U.S. 833 (1992). One of the most controversial Supreme Court cases of the twentieth century, *Roe v. Wade*, concerning a woman's right to have an abortion, may be thought of as a decisional privacy case.

Information Privacy

This form of privacy is described as the freedom of the individual to limit access to certain personal information about him or herself. The Court of Appeals for the Ninth Circuit in *Doe v. Attorney General* has defined it as "the individual interest in avoiding disclosure of personal matters ..." In his classic 1967 study, *Privacy and Freedom*, scholar Alan Westin defines it as "the claim of individuals ... to determine for themselves when, how, and to what extent information about them is communicated to others." Similarly, Professor Lawrence Lessig, drawing heavily on the scholarship of Ethan Katsh, has defined privacy in this context as "the power to control what others can come to know about you." Readers interested in an in-depth treatment of this topic should consult Daniel Solove and Marc Rottenberg, *Information Privacy Law* (2003).

As Lessig goes on to explain in *Code and Other Laws of Cyberspace*, (1999) others can acquire information about you by monitoring and searching. Monitoring refers to that part of one's daily existence that others see, observe, and can respond to. Searching refers to that part of one's life that leaves a record that can later be scrutinized. Noting both quantity and quality aspects to information privacy, a federal appellate court has phrased it in terms of, "control over knowledge about oneself. But it is not simply control over the quantity of information abroad; there are modulations in the quality of knowledge as well."

U.S. government biometric programs could potentially require government personnel, along with many others, such as citizens, and taxpayers, to be compelled to provide biometric identification information to a government agency for collection, maintenance, use, and dissemination in government-controlled databases. Such government-sector use of biometrics implicates physical and information privacy concerns; on the other hand, decisional privacy concerns are not so much affected.

18.3.4 Physical Privacy and Biometrics

Public sector biometric applications could implicate Fourth Amendment considerations when biometrics, like fingerprints, are used in noncriminal contexts or when they are used in a criminal justice context. The courts have decided many Fourth Amendment cases involving individuals having to provide physical characteristics or personal traits, such as fingerprints or voice samples, to the government. Accordingly, analysis of the state of the law in the noncriminal and criminal justice areas is instructive.

Constitutional Challenges to Fingerprinting in Noncriminal Context

The overwhelming majority of government biometric applications will fall into the noncriminal context, for such matters as logical or physical access control, fraud prevention, and other business processes. Many decisions have established that an individual has minimal constitutional privileges concerning his fingerprints or similar physical characteristics and personal traits.

Moreover, the courts have upheld numerous federal, state, and municipal requirements mandating fingerprinting for employment and licensing purposes, provided that the government has a rational basis for requiring fingerprinting. In the federal context, the so-called *rational basis test* means that Congress must show that the fingerprinting requirement bears a rational relationship to a legitimate government objective or interest. The rational basis test is a lesser standard of judicial scrutiny than the compelling state interest test. Courts apply the compelling state interest test when state action affects the exercise of a fundamental right, such as political speech. Accordingly, using the rational basis test, courts have upheld government-mandated fingerprinting for employment and licensing purposes in connection with the taking of fingerprints for spouses of liquor licensees, male employees of alcoholic beverage wholesalers, taxi drivers, cabaret employees, bartenders, dealers in secondhand articles, all employees of member firms of national security exchanges registered with the Securities and Exchange Commission, and all individuals permitted unescorted access to nuclear power facilities.

For example, in *Utility Workers Union of America v. Nuclear Regulatory Commission*, decided in 1987, a union representing some 5,170 utility workers in nuclear power plants challenged as unconstitutional that part of a newly-enacted federal statute requiring that these workers be fingerprinted. The Utility Workers Union claimed the fingerprinting requirement violated the workers' Fourth Amendment and privacy rights. The federal district court in the Southern District of New York disagreed and upheld the fingerprinting requirement. Citing a long string of cases, the court noted that in noncriminal contexts, the judiciary has "regularly upheld fingerprinting of employees."

As for the workers' constitutional right to privacy claim, the court, quoting from a leading federal appellate court case, *Iacobucci v. City of Newport*, did not find decisional privacy interests implicated:

"Whatever the outer limits of the right to privacy, clearly it cannot be extended to apply to a procedure the Supreme Court regards as only minimally intrusive. Enhanced protection has been held to apply only to such fundamental decisions as contraception ... and family living arrangements. Fingerprints have not been held to merit the same level of constitutional concern."

Constitutional Challenges to Fingerprinting in Criminal Justice Context

What will happen when government authorities want a biometric identifier from someone whom they suspect has committed a crime? Capturing the biometric identifier in this context should not run afoul of the Constitution. The Fourth Amendment governs searchers and seizures conducted by government agents. The amendment makes clear that the Constitution does not forbid all searches and seizures, only "unreasonable" ones. The Supreme Court defines a search as an invasion of a person's reasonable expectations of privacy. To evaluate whether providing a biometric identifier in a criminal justice context constitutes a search, the judiciary focuses on two factors. First, the court examines the nature of the intrusion. Actual physical intrusions into the body, such as blood-drawing, breathalyzer testing, and urine analysis, can constitute Fourth Amendment searches. Second, the court examines the scope of the intrusiveness paying close attention to the "host of private medical facts" as explained in the Supreme Court case, *Skinner v. Railway Labor Executives' Ass'n*, 489 U.S. 602 (1989).

In the criminal justice context, the Supreme Court has examined the issue of whether acquiring information about an individual's personal characteristics constitutes a search. It has found that requiring a person to give voice exemplars is not a search because the physical characteristics of a person's voice, its tone and manner, as opposed to the content of a specific conversation, are constantly exposed to the public, such that no person can have a reasonable expectation that others will not know the sound of his voice, as discussed in *United States v. Dionisio*, 410 U.S. 1 (1973). For this reason, government-deployed facial recognition systems with surveillance cameras aimed at public spaces do not implicate U.S. constitutional privacy protections.

Using the same reasoning, the Supreme Court in *United States v. Mara*, 410 U.S. 19 (1973), has ruled that requiring a person to give handwriting exemplars is not a search. In *Cupp v. Murphy*, 412 U.S. 291 (1973), the Court has described fingerprinting as nothing more than obtaining physical characteristics constantly exposed to the public, and that fingerprinting involved none of the probing into an individual's private life and thoughts that marks an interrogation or search, per *Davis v. Mississippi*, 394 U.S. 721 (1969).

In cases where provision of a biometric identifier might be found to constitute a search (such as in the hypothetical case of a physically intrusive, DNA-based biometric that would reveal extensive private medical facts about the individual), the Supreme Court in *Vernonia Sch. Dist. 47J v. Acton*, 515 U.S. 646, (1995) has explained that "the ultimate measure of the constitutionality of a governmental search is 'reasonableness.' " To make this determination, a court must balance the "intrusion on the individual's Fourth Amendment interests against its promotion of legitimate governmental interests." In the criminal context, a search is "reasonable" only if the law enforcement agency has probable cause or reasonable suspicion of criminal activity.

18.3.5 Decisional Privacy

Decisional privacy involves a person's decisions relating to intimate matters such as marriage, procreation, contraception, and so on. Biometric applications will not likely involve decisional privacy.

18.3.6 Information Privacy - *Whalen v. Roe*

Why is a Supreme Court case decided 30 years ago required reading? Because while the Information Age and technological advances have drastically changed our lives since 1977, the Supreme Court's articulation of information privacy is still anchored to its 1977 decision in *Whalen v. Roe*, 429 U.S. 589 (1977).

Whalen involved the constitutional question of whether the state of New York could record and store, in a centralized computer database, "the names and addresses of all persons who have obtained, pursuant to a doctor's prescription, certain drugs." *Whalen* is instructive because it demonstrates the federal judiciary's approach to deciding some of the major constitutional law issues likely to be raised by government-mandated biometric applications. Accordingly, the facts of the case, the holding and the judicial reasoning deserve examination.

Facts: In 1970, the New York state legislature, disturbed about the growing drug problem, established a state commission to evaluate the state's drug control laws. After study, the commission made recommendations. Based on these recommendations, the state legislature amended the New York Public Health Law to require that all prescriptions for Schedule II drugs (defined as the most dangerous of legitimate drugs, to include opium, methadone, and amphetamines) had to be prepared by the physician on an official state-provided form. The completed form identified:

- The prescribing physician

- The dispensing pharmacy
- The prescribed drug and prescribed dosage
- The name, address, and age of the patient

The statute required that a copy of the completed form be forwarded to the New York State Department of Health in Albany. There the government agency recorded the information for computer processing. The legislature thought that these measures would help identify unscrupulous medical professionals and show the pattern of the state's drug flow.

Patients, doctors, and physician associations challenged the New York state statute in the federal courts. The evidence offered before the federal district court, where *Whalen v. Roe* was first heard, included testimony from:

- Two parents who "were concerned that their children would be stigmatized [as drug addicts] by the State's central filing system"
- Three adult patients who "feared disclosure of their names" to unauthorized third parties
- Four physicians who believed that the New York statute "entrenches on patients' privacy, and that each had observed a reaction of shock, fear and concern on the part of their patients"

The parties thus advanced two related privacy concerns that eventually reached the Supreme Court's consideration: "the nondisclosure of private information" or information privacy, and an individual's "interest in making important decisions independently" or decisional privacy.

Holding: In his opinion for the Court, Justice John Paul Stevens, joined by the Chief Justice and five other justices, found that "neither the immediate nor the threatened impact of the [statue's] patient-identification requirements...on either the reputation or the independence of patients...is sufficient to constitute an invasion of any right or liberty protected by the [Due Process Clause of the] Fourteenth Amendment." With these words, the Supreme Court rejected the privacy claim.

In sum, the nation's highest court ruled that a government's centralized, computerized database containing massive amounts of extremely sensitive medical information about citizens passed constitutional muster.

Judicial Reasoning: What factors influenced the Supreme Court's reasoning? First, the Court seemed impressed by the fact that the New York state legislature had created a specially appointed commission, which held numerous hearings and interviews. Put simply, a commission empowered by the legislature had done its homework in an attempt to help solve the menacing problem of drugs. The Court concluded that the statute was "manifestly the product of an orderly and rational legislative decision." In other words, there was a rational basis for the legislative action.

In its analysis of the information privacy concerns raised, the Court paid close attention to what specific steps the state agency had taken to prevent any unauthorized disclosures of information from the centralized database. In particular, the Court noted that:

- The forms and the records were kept in a physically secure facility.
- The computer system was secured by restricting the number of computer terminals that could access the database.
- Employee access to the database was strictly limited.
- There were criminal sanctions for unauthorized disclosure.

Thus, the *Whalen* court scrutinized the technical and procedural protections in place to safeguard the information. A lot has changed in 30 years. Perhaps a contemporary court will examine technical protections and look for such things as firewalls, encryption, and biometric access control. But it's safe to predict that even a contemporary court will be impressed with procedural safeguards in the form of criminal sanctions for unauthorized disclosure.

The Court took a somewhat practical approach to the way personal information is used in the contemporary age. It accepted the view that disclosure of such medical information to various government agencies and private sector organizations, such as insurance companies, is "often an essential part of modern medical practice even when the disclosure may reflect unfavorably on the character of the patient. Requiring such disclosures to representations of the State having responsibility for the health of the community does not automatically amount to an impermissible invasion of privacy."

In addressing decisional privacy issues, the Court acknowledged genuine concern that the very existence of the database will disturb some people so greatly that they will refuse to go to the doctor to get necessary medication. However, given the large number of prescriptions processed at Albany, approximately 100,000 prescription forms for Schedule II drugs monthly, the Court concluded that the "statute did not deprive the public of access to the [legal] drugs."

The Court's opinion concluded with a cautionary note that still echoes loudly today:

> "We are not unaware of the threat to privacy implicit in the accumulation of vast amounts of personal information in computerized data banks or other massive government files...The right to collect and use such data for public purposes is typically accompanied by a concomitant statutory or regulatory duty to avoid unwarranted disclosures."

The New York statute and its related implementation showed "a proper concern with, and protection of, the individual's interest in privacy." The Court, however, limited the effect of its decision by reserving for another day consideration of legal questions which could arise from unauthorized disclosures of information from a government database "by a system that did not contain comparable security provisions."

Cautionary Note: The *Whalen* Court expressed its concern about "unwarranted disclosures" from government databases. Moreover, the majority of the justices adopted a prospective approach. That is, by intensely focusing on the facts of *Whalen*, the Court left itself with ample judicial wiggle room to find that government-mandated use of new technologies combined with powerful computer systems might lack necessary constitutional safeguards. As Professor Steve Goldberg has explained, since the *Whalen* decision is tied so intimately to the specific facts of *Whalen*, a future Court could easily distinguish the facts of a future case from the facts of *Whalen* to reach a different result.

In sum, a lesson to take away from *Whalen* is that a future Court might find an information privacy right violated unless the government agency collecting the information had made clear its need and purpose in collecting the information and had taken strong and effective measures to prevent unwarranted disclosures from its databases. In other words, if the government agency ignores these steps, the Court's cautionary note of *Whalen* could turn into a clear-sounding constitutional alarm bell in the future.

Under the American system of federalism, the fifty states are free to provide greater privacy protections in their own state constitutions than those afforded in the U.S. Constitution. Therefore, when evaluating the use of a specific biometric system, its legality must be analyzed under state constitutional provisions as well.

18.3.7 Other Constitutionally Based Considerations of Biometrics

Some limited segments of American society have expressed religious objections to the use of biometrics. Although these religious-based concerns may not on the surface appear to implicate privacy issues, the constitutionally protected right to the free exercise of religion can be understood to vindicate privacy-related values. Some individuals oppose being compelled to participate in a government program that mandates the provision of a biometric identifier.

These religious-based refusals raise a sensitive issue, in which the intrusion on the free exercise of religion must be carefully weighed. Some "real-world" cases provide guidance as to how the law reacts to such refusals. For example, the New York Department of Social Services and the Connecticut Department of Social Services (DSS) have encountered legal challenges based on religious concerns from entitlement program recipients who refused to provide a biometric identifier. Based on these objections, other government agencies might encounter a similar legal challenge to its mandated use of biometrics. Accordingly, the New York DSS and Connecticut DSS experiences might offer useful insight to how the legal system reacts.

New York Experience

Liberty Buchanan, a New York resident, received Aid to Families with Dependent Children (ADC) and Food Stamps for herself and her four minor children.

In 1996, New York DSS informed her that she would be required to participate in an automated finger imaging system (AFIS). New York law required
participation in AFIS as a condition of eligibility for ADC and other entitle-
ments. Buchanan refused to participate in AFIS. She based her refusal on her
religious convictions, grounded in part on her interpretation of the "mark of
the beast" language in the Book of Revelation. Because she refused to provide
a fingerprint, DSS discontinued the Buchanans' entitlement benefits. After a
DSS agency hearing, the State Commissioner of Social Services affirmed the
DSS decision, finding that Buchanan did not demonstrate a good cause basis
for exemption from the finger imaging requirement. Buchanan then appealed
to the New York Supreme Court. After a hearing, in 1997, the New York
Supreme Court Appellate Division, Third Judicial Department, in *Buchanan
v. Wing*, found that Ms. Buchanan had failed to "set forth any competent
proof that the AFIS actually involved any invasive procedures marking them
in violation of [her] beliefs." Accordingly, the court upheld the DSS decision.

Connecticut Experience

Similarly, in Connecticut, John Doe, his wife and minor children, recipients
of Temporary Family Assistance (TFA), refused to submit to the Connecticut
DSS digital imaging requirement. ("John Doe" is an alias used to protect the
true identity of the individual out of respect for his and his family's privacy.)
Beginning in January 1996, DSS, pursuant to state law, began requiring all
TFA recipients to be biometrically enrolled for identification purposes by providing copies of the fingerprints of their two index fingers. In April 1996, Mr.
and Mrs. Doe objected based on their religious beliefs. DSS exempted them
from the requirement in April 1996 and October 1997. In July 1998, however,
DSS reviewed its policy and determined that the Does would have to comply
with the biometric enrollment. Doe requested a DSS hearing.

At the August 1998 hearing, he testified as to his objections to providing
a biometric identifier. He based these objections on his religious beliefs. He
therefore requested a "good cause" exception to the digital imaging requirement as provided in the DSS regulations.

In November 1998, the hearing officer ruled that Doe, "although having
strong religious beliefs, some of which he interprets as a barrier for him to be
digitally imaged, does not have as a result of this religious belief a circum-
stance beyond his control which prevents him from being digitally imaged."
Doe appealed from this final DSS decision to the Connecticut state court.
While his case was pending, the DSS Commissioner decided to vacate the
hearing decision and grant the Does an exception from the digital-imaging
requirement. Rather than fight the Does in state court, in a legal battle that
attracted the interest of civil liberties groups, the Commissioner took an easier way out - the Does got their exception from the biometric requirement;
the state of Connecticut avoided potentially controversial litigation, and we
are left wondering what the higher courts would have done.

18.3.8 Statutory and Administrative Law Concerns

In examining the privacy rights recognized by the Constitution, we see that information privacy is the one most likely implicated by government-mandated use of biometrics. The Court's decision in *Whalen v. Roe* provides a framework for how a future court might address such issues related to information privacy. We have also examined physical and decisional privacy as well as how the court would deal with religious-based objections to biometrics. With this constitutional basis thus established, we next have to examine statutory and administrative law protections. Congress is free to regulate government-mandated use of biometrics. Congress has already passed comprehensive legislation, known as the Privacy Act, affecting how U.S. government agencies must protect personal information. This act also applies to biometric records. For this reason, we next examine the Privacy Act.

18.3.9 The Privacy Act of 1974

The Privacy Act of 1974 (codified at 5 U.S.C. § 552a, as amended) regulates the collection, maintenance, use and dissemination of personal information by federal government agencies.

In broad terms, the Privacy Act gives certain rights to the "data subject," or the individual who provides personal information, and places certain responsibilities on the "data collector," or the agency collecting the personal information. The Privacy Act balances a federal agency's need to collect, use, and disseminate information about individuals with the privacy rights of those individuals. In particular, the act tries to protect the individual from unwarranted invasions of privacy stemming from a federal agency's collection, maintenance, use and dissemination of personal information.

There are several things the Privacy Act does not do. For example, the Privacy Act does not regulate the collection, maintenance, use, and dissemination of personal information by state and local government agencies. The Privacy Act does not regulate personal information held by private sector entities. The Privacy Act does not apply when the individual, or data subject, is a non-U.S. person, i.e., not a U.S. citizen or an alien lawfully admitted for permanent residence. Thus, the U.S. military, for example, can take biometric data such as fingerprints from foreigners it encounters in Iraq without running afoul of the Privacy Act.

The Privacy Act's basic provisions include the following:

- Restricting federal agencies from disclosing personally identifiable records maintained by the agencies
- Requiring federal agencies to maintain records with accuracy and diligence
- Granting individuals increased rights to access records about themselves maintained by federal agencies and to amend their records provided they show that the records are not accurate, relevant, timely, or complete

- Requiring federal agencies to establish administrative, technical, and policy safeguards to protect record security

As these basic provisions suggest, the Privacy Act sets forth a so-called "Code of Fair Information Practices" (CFIP) requiring federal agencies to adopt minimum standards for collection, maintenance, use and dissemination of records. It also required that agencies publish detailed descriptions of these standards and the procedures used to implement them.

Although the Privacy Act does not specifically mention "biometrics," there is little doubt that the Act can apply to biometrics. As the Act applies to a "record" that is "contained in a system of records," the threshold issue to resolve is whether biometric identification information, whether in the form of an image file or a template file, falls within the Act's broad definition of record.

18.3.10 Agency Responsibilities

The Privacy Act (U.S.C. § 552a(b)) places certain responsibilities on the government data collector. Some of these responsibilities include publishing information about the systems of records in the data collector's charge, giving notice to data subjects, and safeguarding data. The Privacy Act further prohibits a federal agency from disclos[ing] any record which is contained in a system of records by any means of communication to any person, or to another agency, except pursuant to a written request by, or with the prior written consent of, the individual to whom the record pertains..." This provision is known as the "No Disclosure Without Consent Rule." Although the "No Disclosure Without Consent Rule" applies, the Privacy Act contains twelve enumerated exceptions to this rule, to accommodate civil or criminal law enforcement activities, "routine use," and others. Detailed discussion of the Privacy Act is beyond the scope of this chapter; for more information, see, e.g., U.S. Department of Justice, *Overview of the Privacy Act of 1974*, available at http://www.usdoj.gov/oip/04_7_1.html.

18.3.11 Additional Legal Safeguards

The Computer Matching and Privacy Act of 1988 amended the Privacy Act by adding new provisions regulating federal agencies' computer matching practices and placing requirements on the agencies.

Administrative regulation is another safeguard. From the administrative regulatory perspective, Congress can follow two well-worn policy paths when dealing with a public policy issue involving a new technology such as biometrics. It can take the direct route and pass legislation regulating a government agency's use of the technology, or it can delegate its authority to the appropriate administrative agencies within government agency. The delegation route is the road most frequently traveled. However, even though the government agencies, in general, are well equipped with expertise, experience, and institutional memory, they still face enormous challenges in designing, formulating, and implementing government policy for biometric applications. In addition, numerous competing groups (many well-organized and some politically influential) will want to press their claims in this public policy process.

Congress, through the legislative process, can require a government agency to satisfy additional conditions related to its biometric applications. For example, Congress could go beyond the Privacy Act and place additional prohibitions on disclosure of biometric identification information and further restrict sharing. Moreover, the state governments can also provide be various legal protections as they see fit. Or biometric applications may be designed such that controversial legal or policy issues are not reached. For example, as related above, the Connecticut DSS Commissioner gave the Doe family an exemption from the biometric requirement even though she was on fairly solid legal ground. Similarly, some schools that use a touch fingerprint system for students to get free or reduced-price lunches provide an alternative means, such as a PIN, for the students to use.

18.4 The Law and Private-Sector Use of Biometrics

This section discusses the legal considerations related to private-sector, or non-governmental, use of biometrics. It focuses on two areas: how does the law enable private-sector use of biometrics, and how does the law regulate the private-sector use of biometrics with respect to privacy?

To answer the first question, we have to examine how biometrics can be used in commercial or business transactions, particularly in the digital world. In the information age, we are moving closer and closer to the complete transition from "sign on the dotted line" to "no paper, no problem." As the world goes increasingly digital, biometric authentication can play a more important role for transactions, based on contracts and other legal agreements. Ideally, whenever a signature is required on a piece of paper, we could provide our biometric data attached to an electronic document. However, before we replace a manually executed "John Hancock" with a camera-captured iris template, we need to determine the legal and policy concerns related to such use of biometrics.

To answer the second question, we must discuss regulations affecting the use of biometrics that stem from privacy concerns of the technology. If a private entity collects biometrics from individuals, does that private entity have any legal responsibilities or duties to the individuals from whom the biometrics have been collected? Or as information privacy lawyers and public policymakers might phrase it: Does the data collector have any legal duties to the data subject from whom the data is collected? To get these answers, explain how we got them, and add recommendations, the following section discusses law as an enabler for private-sector use of biometrics.

18.4.1 Law as an Enabler for Private-Sector Use of Biometrics

The broad topic discussed here is whether biometrics can play a role as an enabling technology for e-commerce and e-government. More specifically, the analysis focuses on one important aspect of this topic: Whether an electronic signature, in the form of a biometric, can be legally enforceable to the same extent as a conventional, manually executed paper-and-ink signature when the electronic signature is used to enter into agreements. In other words, can a biometric-based signature have legal equivalence to a conventional, hand-written signature?

For many transactions, an individual must provide a manually executed paper-and-ink signature to enter into an agreement. Replacing this paper-and-ink signature with a biometric-based electronic signature promises a more effective and convenient way of entering into agreements, particularly in the electronic world. So, instead of signing his name in ink on a piece of paper representing an agreement, an individual would simply be asked to place his fingerprint on a biometric sensor; his fingerprint would be captured and converted into a template unique to that individual; and that template would be attached to an electronic document representing the agreement. Something akin to this process occurs daily at commercial establishments like the Piggly Wiggly, Thriftway, and Kroger supermarket chains where shoppers can voluntarily use a fingerprint system to pay for their purchases in many stores. Some grocery stores use fingerprint systems to reduce check fraud. In general, the companies find that the biometric system speeds throughput (as it decreases the writing of paper checks), improves security (as it protects against identity theft), works accurately, and is popular with the customers.

Definitions

The term "electronic signature" refers to any means of "signing" an electronic document in digital form, in which the "signature" is represented in ones and zeroes. *See, e.g.*, Thomas J. Smedinghoff and Ruth Hill Bro, *Electronic Signature Legislation* (1999). Although the terms "electronic signatures" and "digital signature" have sometimes been used interchangeably, a digital signature is more accurately defined as one particular type of electronic signature; it uses a specific technology - public-key cryptography - to sign a message. An electronic signature, on the other hand, is a technology-neutral term and encompasses many methods of "signing" an electronic record, including the technology at issue here, the use of a biometric-based identifier. Thus, digital signatures are a subset of electronic signatures, which, in turn are a subset of signatures.

Attributes of a Conventional Signature

The legal enforceability of a transaction often depends on the parties' adherence to certain formalities. Many agreements must be "in writing" and "signed" by the parties to be enforceable. For example, the law has long forbidden the enforcement of certain types of agreements, such as contract for the sale of land, unless the agreement is in writing and is signed. Similarly, the Uniform Commercial Code (UCC), which seeks to make uniform the various state laws governing commercial transactions, requires a signed writing to enforce a contract for the sale of goods valued at $500 or more. This signed writing requirement is also contained in thousands of other federal, state, and local laws and regulations, covering transactions ranging from the execution of wills and other testamentary dispositions, to adoption and child custody agreements.

The signed writing requirement serves four useful functions:

- Evidentiary
- Cautionary
- Approval
- Efficiency

Let's briefly discuss each in turn: A signed writing serves an *evidentiary* function by providing some proof that the alleged agreement was actually made. Similarly, the act of signing a document serves a *cautionary* function by emphasizing to the parties the significance of entering into a binding agreement and thereby helping to minimize ill-considered or impulsive agreements. The *approval* function refers to the idea that a person's signature, in the context of the document to which it is appended, indicates the signer's approval or authorization of the contents of the document. Finally, a signed document lends *efficiency* to the contracting process by providing clarity and finality as to the scope and terms of the agreement.

From these principles, legal experts have deduced what general attributes an enforceable signature should have. The American Bar Association (ABA) identifies these attributes as "signer authentication" and "document authentication."

Signer authentication means that the signature should identify who signed the document and show that the signature should be difficult for another person to produce without authorization.

Document authentication means the signature should identify what is being signed, such that it would be impracticable to falsify or alter either the signed document or the signature without detection.

Accordingly, a signature should identify the person signing, the signature should be unique to the signer, and the signature should be associated with the document in such a way as to indicate the signer's intent and to make it difficult to falsify the document or the signature without detection.

Electronic Signatures

Does an electronic signature have the attributes of an enforceable signature? To satisfy a statute or regulation that requires a transaction to be "in writing" and "signed" required three elements: (1) a writing, (2) a signature, and (3) shows "intention to authenticate" the transaction. The first question, therefore, is whether an electronic signature contains these three elements.

Courts have recognized that many types of "writings" may satisfy this statutory requirement. For example, courts have recognized that a telegram constitutes a writing and have found that a facsimile (or "fax") satisfies the requirement. Courts have also found that data stored on a computer disk can constitute a writing. Provided that an electronic record of the transaction is retained on computer disk or hard drive, therefore, it appears likely that courts would find the writing requirement to be satisfied.

In accordance with the UCC definition that "any symbol" can constitute a signature, courts have recognized that letterhead, trademarks, stamped or printed symbols, or even an "X," can satisfy the signature requirement. Three examples drawn from New York legal history demonstrate that the state law adapted to recognize many signatures. In 1880, the New York courts accepted that any figure or mark may be used in lieu of one's proper name, a legal recognition of the fact that New York attracted many immigrants, not all of whom were literate. By 1911, the courts accepted that a handwritten signature was not required on an agreement, acknowledging that New York's many corporations and service industries could more efficiently use rubber stamps to signify their agreement for any of their standard language contracts, such as those commonly used in the insurance industry. After World War II, the New York state legislature captured what the New York courts had already, in effect, done when it modified the law by broadly defining a signature to include "any memorandum, mark or sign, printed, stamped, photographed, engraved, or otherwise placed on an instrument or writing." The point to remember is that the law adapts to changed circumstances to include demographic, technological, and business advances.

Thus, the restriction on what symbol may constitute a signature is not particularly rigorous because the nub of the requirement is that the signature demonstrate an intention to authenticate the writing. If one party to a transaction places an "X" at the bottom of a contract, the other part (and a court) can reasonably infer that the signer has agreed to be bound by the contract. It may be more difficult, however, to infer such intent in an electronic environment.

Providing a biometric-based electronic signature would seem to constitute a legally enforceable means of entering into a contract. A biometric identifier appended to an electronic record would meet the signature and writing requirements, and the requisite intent by the party to authenticate the transaction could be inferred from the context of the transaction. But such after-the-fact determinations may undermine the predictability that is necessary to foster effective and efficient transactions in the e-commerce and e-government arenas. Basically, it's important to know with relative certainty whether the transaction is enforceable before the transaction is performed. The difference in context between the execution of a paper-and-ink signature and an electronic signature raises some doubt about whether simply affixing any electronic symbol to an electronic record embodies sufficient attributes of authentication to warrant enforceability.

Accordingly, to ensure predictability in these transactions and to avoid after-the-fact reliance on proof of "intention to authenticate," lawmakers at both the federal and state levels have addressed the circumstances in which electronic signatures will be valid and enforceable.

18.4.2 Electronic Signature Legislation in the United States

Federal Law: Electronic Signatures in Global and National Commerce Act

A major piece of federal legislation dealing with electronic signatures is the Electronic Signatures in Global and National Commerce Act (E-SIGN Act), 15 U.S.C.A. § 7001 *et seq.* (2000) The E-SIGN Act promotes the use of electronic contract formation, signatures, and record keeping in private commerce by establishing legal equivalence between contracts written on paper and contracts in electronic form, and between pen-and-ink signatures and electronic signatures.

E-SIGN Act Summary

The heart of the E-SIGN law is summarized below:

- Legal validity of a transaction document is not denied "solely because it is in electronic form."
- "No paper; no problem."
- E-SIGN applies to biometrics:
  - Definition is broadly written to include biometric data.
  - Law is technology neutral, giving flexibility to the parties.
- E-SIGN is a pre-emptive rule:
  - Overrules old laws requiring signature in writing and on paper for certain transactions.
  - Establishes a uniform but voluntary standard.

Federal Law: Government Paperwork Elimination Act

The Government Paperwork Elimination Act (GPEA), codified at 44 U.S.C. § 3504 *et seq.*, which took effect in 1998, helps make e-government a reality. GPEA aims to improve the delivery of government services by charging executive agencies with developing procedures to use and accept electronic documents and signatures.

State Law

The rapid growth of e-commerce, as well as the desire to increase productivity and efficiency by moving to paperless environments, led many states to enact statutes and regulations governing electronic transactions. One approach, followed by almost one-third of the states, is to define electronic signatures in such a way that the definition itself would embody all the attributes of a valid, enforceable signature. Although the precise wording may differ in various state statutes, those states following this approach require that, to be legally enforceable, an electronic signature must be:

- Unique to the person using it
- Capable of verification
- Under the sole control of the person using it
- Linked to the electronic record to which it relates in such a manner that if the record were changed the electronic signature is invalidated

Other states provide a more general definition for electronic signatures and rely on the context of the transaction to establish the intention to authenticate. The Uniform Electronic Transaction Act (UETA) takes this approach.

UETA defines an electronic signature as "an electronic sound, symbol or process attached to or logically associated with a record and executed or adopted by a person with the intent to sign the record.

18.4.3 Law as a Regulator of Private-Sector Use of Biometrics: Privacy

When it comes to private-sector actions, the Constitution embodies what is essentially a laissez-faire, or "hands-off" spirit. With respect to the conduct of private individuals, the Supreme Court has not found a constitutional privacy right in personal information given voluntarily by an individual to private parties. This reluctance to find such a privacy right bears on private-sector use of biometrics because biometrics identifiers may be categorized as personal information that an individual, or the data subject, gives voluntarily to private parties, or the data collectors. Generally, as a matter of law, a private party in possession of information has the right to disclose it.

Accordingly, the private-sector enjoys great leeway as far as what it can do with an individual's information. As Marc Rotenberg, the executive director of the Electronic Privacy Information Center, and Emilio Cividanes, a privacy attorney, have concluded in *The Law of Information Privacy: Case and Commentary*, in 1997: "Except in isolated categories of data, an individual has nothing to say about the use of information that he has given about himself or that has been collected about him. In particular, an organization can acquire information for one purpose and use it for another...generally the private sector is not legislatively constrained."

18.5 International Law Considerations

Organizations increasingly operate globally. As a result, their overseas activities, international business partners, and foreign customers may be subject to different foreign laws and regulations. These organizations need to make certain that they are in full compliance with these non-U.S. legal norms, such as laws of a foreign nation-state or an institutional framework such as the European Union. These international law considerations are all the more important for organizations managing, processing, and using information across national boundaries. The European Union (E.U.) Privacy Directive deserves special attention. Based on this law, all E.U. member states have enacted comprehensive privacy legislation requiring organizations to implement personal data policies. The Directive applies to biometric data, and thus can implicate a wide array of biometric applications. In 2003, the Asia Pacific Economic Cooperation Forum (APEC) issued guidelines related to personal information, to include biometrics.

Individuals and businesses using biometrics will increasingly be using these systems in a global environment. When operating in an overseas environment, end users obviously do not want to do things that are in conflict with foreign law. Once an end user entity determines exactly what type of biometric application it wants to deploy in an overseas location, therefore, it must also take into account any applicable local laws to determine how best to proceed to ensure compliance with these laws.

18.6 Recommendations

Organizations considering the deployment of biometric applications may want to consider adopting a privacy enhancing biometric blueprint based on what is known as a Code of Fair Information Practices (CFIP). Such a CFIP-based approach merits considerations because it is arguably an effective way to balance privacy concerns with the benefits of biometrics. As a bedrock premise, a CFIP establishes rights for data subjects and places responsibilities on the data collectors.

18.6.1 Biometric Blueprint

The CFIP consists of five principles: notice, access, correction mechanism, informed consent, and reliability/safeguarding. The CFIP, as the name implies, is not unique to biometrics but can apply anytime information is at stake.

The CFIP-based biometric blueprint for private-sector use should consist of these same five basic principles, along with optional wording, to include:

- **Notice**: The capture of biometric identification information in the private-sector must be accompanied by prominent notice. A more privacy-protective principle would prohibit the clandestine capture of biometric identification information in the private sector; no secret databases should exist.

- **Access**: The individual (or data subject) has the right to access his information in the database. Specifically, the individual must be able to find out if his biometric identification information is in the database and how the data collector is using it. Accordingly, the data collector would be required to disclose its privacy practices.

- **Correction mechanism**: The individual must be able to correct or make changes to any biometric identification information in the database.

- **Informed consent**: Before any information can be disclosed to third parties, the individual must consent. The individual must voluntarily and knowingly provide his biometric identification information to the data collector in the primary market. Once in the possession of the data collector, this information would then be governed by a use limitation principle, which means that the individual has consented that the information she provided would be used in the primary market for a purpose defined by the data collector and known to the individual. The individual must knowingly consent to any exchange, such as buying and selling of his biometric identification information, before it could be traded in a secondary market. Reasonable exceptions can be accommodated as appropriate for academic research, national security, and law enforcement.

- **Reliability/safeguarding**: Any data collector that collects and stores biometric identification information must guarantee the reliability of the data for its intended use and must take precautions to safeguard the data. At its most basic level, appropriate managerial and technical controls must be used to protect the confidentiality and integrity of the information. The controls would include making the database and the computer system physically and virtually secure. (Perhaps, policymakers should consider providing criminal sanctions for willful disclosures, or consider providing for the recovery of civil damages when biometric identification information is disclosed without the consent of the individual.)

Assuming one decides to give this five-prong CFIP-based biometric blueprint or any other approach the force of law, one has to determine who should pass the law. Specifically, if "there oughta be a law," then should Congress or the various state legislatures take action? Federal legislation offers the advantage of providing a uniform standard of privacy protection across the United States. Any organization using biometrics would only need to look to the federal law and its implementing regulations to know what is needed to ensure legal compliance.

On the other hand, some states might move more quickly and provide more extensive privacy protection than Congress, while some states might do nothing. Thus, the various states might take widely divergent approaches to regulation of biometrics, which would require end-users to comply with many different state laws.

18.6.2 Forward-looking Approach

The biometric blueprint admittedly is a forward-looking approach to how the law can sensibly regulate this emerging technology. It presumes that privacy concerns related to biometrics can best be accommodated by legislative enactment of a limited, yet uniform biometric blueprint to provide a framework to address legal and policy issues related to the private-sector's use of biometrics. Not all will agree with this approach. Many will advise that it is not needed; others will claim the time is not right, as the technology is still relatively new. As biometric applications become more common, so too will the law and policy concerns of biometrics become more commonplace.

18.6.3 Biometric Hypothetical

I let my local sports club in Criglersville, Virginia take a photograph of my face and capture two of my fingerprints so I can access the club and keep better track of my workouts. I do this by presenting my face to a camera (and facial recognition system) whenever I enter and by touching my finger to the computer display on the treadmill and other sports equipment whenever I use them. I get a detailed monthly fitness report from the club. The sports club conveniently enrolled both of my index fingers so I do not even have to remember which pointer finger to use with the equipment. I was in a hurry to enroll and get started so I did not read the agreement very closely.

After a while, I start getting marketing information telling me to just show up at the local grocery store, retail outlet, etc. I am told that I am already pre-registered and biometrically enrolled in their customer service systems. That's because, along with my facial photograph, the sports club kept my raw data or file images, not just my fingerprint templates, so another party could get my raw biometric data and create a template of my fingerprint in their system.

Later, while shopping in the mall (that great American pastime), sales associates insist on trying to sell me athletic gear, protein supplements, diet aids, and Viagra because their stores' facial recognition systems identified me as a failed jock from the sports club.

Later, the Virginia State Police are confronted with the grisly homicide of the sports club manager in his office, where the only evidence is a single latent print left on a barbell - the murder weapon. The latent print is searched against the FBI's criminal master file but, alas, no matches are made. The Virginia State Police ask the sports club management to turn over the file images of the fingerprints of all its club members, including mine, so the latent print can be searched against them. Club management readily agrees.

Questions:

1. Have any of my legal rights to privacy under Virginia State or federal law been violated in the above hypothetical?
2. Has my privacy in any way been violated in the above hypothetical?

19

Biometric System Security

Andy Adler

Systems and Computer Engineering, Carleton University, Ottawa, Canada
adler@sce.carleton.ca

19.1 Introduction

Security is "freedom from risk or danger", while computer and data security is "the ability of a system to protect information and system resources with respect to confidentiality and integrity". Defining biometrics system security is difficult, because of the ways biometric systems differ from traditional computer and cryptographic security [39]. Implicit in all definitions is the concept of an attacker; however, biometrics should always be assumed to operate in an (at least somewhat) hostile environment – after all, why should one test identity if all can be trusted? The ability of a biometric system to stand up to "zero-effort" attackers is measured by the false accept rate (FAR). Attackers may then change makeup, facial hair and glasses, or abrade and cut fingerprints in order to avoid being recognized; attackers prepared to try harder may use spoofing. This chapter deals with attacks which are not spoofing, but those that target processing within the biometric system.

We define biometric system security by its absence. Since biometrics is "automated recognition of individuals based on their behavioral and biological characteristics", a vulnerability in biometric security results in incorrect recognition or failure to correctly recognize individuals. This definition includes methods to falsely accept an individual (template regeneration), impact overall system performance (denial of service), or to attack another system via leaked data (identity theft). Vulnerabilities are measured against explicit or implicit design claims.

19.2 Biometrics Security Overview

The key design challenge for biometric algorithms is that people's biometric features vary, both with changes in features themselves (cuts to fingers, facial wrinkles with age) and with the presentation and sensor environment (moisture on fingerprints, illumination and rotation of a presented iris). A biometric algorithm must reject "natural" and environmental changes to samples, while focusing on those which differ between individuals. This chapter concentrates on system vulnerabilities which are a consequence of this core biometric challenge. Since biometric systems are implemented on server computers, they are vulnerable to all cryptographic, virus and other attacks which plague modern computer systems [15]; we point out these issues, but do not cover them in detail.

Maltoni *et al.* [26], classify biometric system vulnerabilities as follows:

- *Circumvention* is an attack which gains access to the protected resources by a technical measure to subvert the biometric system. Such an attack may subvert the underlying computer systems (overriding matcher decisions, or replacing database templates) or may involve replay of valid data.
- *Covert acquisition (contamination)* is use of biometric information captured from legitimate users to access a system. Examples are spoofing via capture and playback of voice passwords, and lifting latent fingerprints to construct a mold. This category can also be considered to cover regenerated biometric images (Sec. 19.4). For example, a fingerprint image can be regenerated from the template stored in a database (and these data can be captured covertly [43]). Covert acquisition is worrisome for cross-application usage (eg. biometric records from a ticket for an amusement park used to access bank accounts).
- *Collusion and Coercion* are biometric system vulnerabilities from legitimate system users. The distinction is that, in collusion, the legitimate user is a willing (perhaps by bribe), while the coerced user is not (through a physical threat or blackmail). Such vulnerabilities bypass the computer security system, since the biometric features are legitimate. It may be possible to mitigate such threats by automatically detecting the unusual pattern of activity. Such attacks can be mounted from both administrator and user accounts on such a system; attacks from user accounts would first need to perform a privilege escalation attack [15].
- *Denial of Service (DoS)* is an attack which prevents legitimate use of the biometric system. This can take the form of slowing or stopping the system (via an overload of network requests) or by degrading performance. An example of the latter would be enrolling many noisy samples which can make a system automatically decrease its decision threshold and thus increase the FAR. The goal of DoS is often to force a fall back to another system (such as operator override) which can be more easily circumvented, but DoS may be used for extortion or political reasons.
- *Repudiation* is the case where the attacker denies accessing the system. A corrupt user may deny her actions by claiming that their biometric data were "stolen" (by covert acquisition or circumvention) or that an illegitimate user was able to perform the actions due to the biometric false accept. Interestingly, biometric systems are often presented as a solution to the repudiation problem in the computer security literature [15]. One

approach to help prevent repudiation would be to store presented images for later forensic analysis, however, this need must be balanced against user privacy concerns [7].

Another class of biometric vulnerabilities are those faced by the system user, which impact the user's privacy and can lead to identity theft or system compromise [34].

- *Biometrics are not secret:* Technology is readily available to image faces, fingerprints, irises and make recordings of voice or signature – without subject consent or knowledge [39][20]. From this perspective, biometrics are not secret. On the other hand, from a cryptography [6] or privacy [7] perspective, biometric data are often considered to be private and secret. This distinction is important, as our understanding of computer and network security is centered around the use of secret codes and tokens [15]. For this reason, cryptographic protocols which are not robust against disclosure of biometric samples are flawed. One proposed solution is revocable biometrics (Sec 19.5.1), although the vulnerability of such systems is not well understood.
- *Biometrics cannot be revoked:* A biometric feature is permanently associated with an individual, and a compromised biometric sample will compromise all applications that use that biometric. Such compromise may prevent a user from re-enrolling [39]. Note, however, that this concern implies that biometrics are secret, contradicting the previous consideration.
- *Biometrics have secondary uses:* If an individual uses the same biometric feature in multiple applications, then the user can be tracked if the organizations share biometric data. Another aspect to this problem is *secondary use* of ID cards. For example, a driver's license is designed with the requirements to prove identity and driver certification to a police officer, but it is used to prove age, name and even citizenship. Similarly, biometric applications will be designed with a narrow range of security concerns, but may be used in very different threat environments.

Biometric systems form part of larger security systems and their risks and vulnerabilities must be understood in the context of the larger system requirements. An excellent review of the security of biometric authentication systems is [20]. Each assurance level from "passwords and PINs" to "Hard crypto token" is analyzed to determine which biometric devices are suitable.

19.3 Vulnerabilities in Biometric Systems

In order to classify biometric security vulnerabilities, it is typical to study each subsystem and interconnection in a system diagram (Figure 19.1). Early work is presented in [33], with later contributions coming from [9, 44, 46]. We consider each system module in turn:

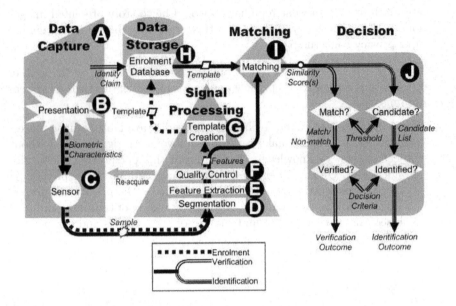

Fig. 19.1. Biometric System Block Diagram (from [22]). Steps A – H are analyzed in sec. 19.3. Each presented sample (B) is acquired by a sensor (C) processed via segmentation (D) and feature extraction (D) algorithms. If available, a sample quality (E) assessment algorithm is used to indicate a need to reacquire the sample. Biometric features are encoded into a template, which is stored (H) in a database, on an identity card or in secure hardware. For biometric encryption (Sec. 19.5.2) systems, a code or token is combined with the biometric features in the template. During enrollment, biometric samples are linked to a claimed identity (A), and during subsequent verification or identification, samples are tested against enrolled samples, using a matching algorithm (I) and an identity decision (J) is made, either automatically, or by a human agent reviewing biometric system outputs.

19.3.1 Identity Claim (A):

Identity claims are not biometric properties, but form an essential part of most biometric security systems An example of an exception is in verifying a season ticket holder; the person's identity doesn't matter, and long as he is the one who paid. Identity claims are primarily based on links to government issued identity documents, and are thus vulnerable to all forms of fraud of such documents. This is a problem even for highly secure documents, such as passports, which are often issued on the basis of less secure "breeder documents" [36] such as birth certificates issued by local government, hospital or even religious authorities.

19.3.2 Presentation (B):

An attack on the biometric sensor introduces a false biometric sample into the system. Such attacks are designed to either avoid detection (false negative) or masquerade as another (false positive). The latter attack is typically called spoofing. Clearly, avoiding detection is easier than masquerading, since features simply need to be changed enough to confuse the segmentation or feature extraction module. Changing makeup, facial hair and glasses or abrading or wetting fingers is often successful; although recent progress in biometric algorithms has dramatically reduced the effectiveness of such techniques. Knowledge of the details of algorithms can make such attacks easier; for example, rotating the head will confuse many iris algorithms that do not expect image rotation of more than a few degrees.

19.3.3 Sensor (C):

Attacks on the biometric sensor include any technique which subverts or replaces the sensor hardware. In some cases subverting the sensor allows complete bypassing of the biometric system. For example, in some biometric door locks, the sensor module includes the entire biometric system including a Wiegand output or relay output to activate the solenoid in a door lock. Subverting such a system may be as simple as physically bypassing the biometric system.

In many cases, an attack on the sensor would take the form of a replay. The connection between the biometric sensor and the biometric system is subverted to allow input of arbitrary signals, and images from legitimate users are input into the system. In order to obtain the signals, several strategies may be employed. Eavesdropping requires hiding the recording instruments and wiring of the sensor. For biometrics using contactless smart cards such eavesdropping becomes more feasible (see [43]). Another approach is to record signals from a sensor under the control of the attacker.

19.3.4 Segmentation (D):

Biometric segmentation extracts the image or signal of interest from the background, and a failure to segment means the system does not detect the presence of the appropriate biometric feature. Segmentation attacks may be used to escape surveillance or to generate a denial of service (DoS) attack. For example, consider a surveillance system in which the face detection algorithm assumes faces have two eyes. By covering an eye, a person is not detected in the biometric system. Another example would be where parts of a fingerprint core are damaged to cause a particular algorithm to mis-locate the core. Since the damaged area is small, it would not arouse the suspicion of an agent reviewing the images.

19.3.5 Feature Extraction (E):

Attacks of the feature extraction module can be used either to escape detection or to create impostors. The first category is similar to those of Sec. 19.3.4. Knowledge of the feature extraction algorithms can be used to design special features in presented biometric samples to cause incorrect features to be calculated.

Characterizing feature extraction algorithms:

In order to implement such an attack, it is necessary to discover the characteristics of the feature extraction algorithm. Are facial hair or glasses excluded (face recognition)? How are the eyelid/eyelash regions detected and cropped (iris recognition)? Most current high performing biometric recognition algorithms are proprietary, but are often based on published scientific literature, which may provide such information. Another approach is to obtain copies of the biometric software and conduct offline experiments. Biometric algorithms are likely susceptible to reverse engineering techniques. It would appear possible to automatically conduct such reverse engineering, but we are not aware of any published results.

Biometric "zoo":

There is great variability between individuals in terms of the accuracy and reliability of their calculated biometric features. Doddington *et al.* developed a taxonomy for different user classes [13]. *Sheep* are the dominant type, and biometric systems perform well for them. *Goats* are difficult to recognize. They adversely affect system performance, accounting for a significant fraction of the FRR. *Lambs* are easy to imitate – a randomly chosen individual is likely to be identified as a lamb. They account for a significant fraction of the FAR. *Wolves* are more likely to be identified as other individuals, and account for a large fraction of the FAR. The existence of lambs and wolves represents a vulnerability to biometric systems. If wolves can be identified, they may be recruited to defeat systems; similarly, if lambs can be identified in the legitimate user population, either through correlation or via directly observable characteristics, they may be targets of attacks.

19.3.6 Quality Control (F):

Evaluation of biometric sample quality is important to ensure low biometric error rates. Most systems, especially during enrollment, verify the quality of input images. Biometric quality assessment is an active area of research, and current approaches are almost exclusively algorithm specific. If the details of the quality assessment module can be measured (either though trial and error or through off-line analysis) it may be possible to create specific image features which force classification in either category. Quality assessment algorithms often look for high frequency noise content in images as evidence of poor quality, while line structures in images indicate higher quality. Attacks on the quality control algorithm are of two types: classifying a good image as poor, and classifying a low quality image as good. In the former case, the goal of the attack would be to evade detection, since poor images will not be used for matching. In the latter case, low quality images will be enrolled. Such images may force internal match thresholds to be lowered (either for that image, or in some cases, globally). Such a scenario will create "lambs" in the database and increase system FAR.

19.3.7 Template Creation (G):

Biometric features are encoded into a template, a (proprietary or standards-conforming) compact digital representation of the essential features of the sample image. One common claim is that, since template creation is a one-way function, it is impossible or infeasible to regenerate the image from the templates [17]. Recent research has shown regeneration of biometric samples from images to be feasible (see Sec. 19.4).

Interoperability:

Government applications of biometrics need to be concerned with interoperability. Biometric samples enrolled on one system must be usable on other vendor systems if a government is to allow cross-jurisdictional use, and to avoid vendor lock-in. However, recent work on interoperability has revealed it to be difficult, even when all vendors conform to standards. Tests of the International Labour Organization seafarer's ID card [21] showed incompatibilities with the use of the minutiae type "other" and incompatible ways to quantize minutiae angles. Such interoperability difficulties present biometric system vulnerabilities, which could be used to increase FRR or for a DoS attack.

19.3.8 Data Storage (H):

Enrolled biometric templates are stored for future verification or identification. Vulnerabilities of template storage concern modifying the storage (adding, modifying or removing templates), copying template data for secondary uses (identity theft), or modifying the identity to which the biometric is assigned.

Storage may take many forms, including databases (local or distributed), on ID documents (into a smart card [43] or 2D barcode [21]) or on electronic devices (a hardened token [20], laptop, mobile telephone, or door access module). Template data may be in plaintext, encrypted or digitally signed. In many government applications, it may be necessary to provide public information on the template format and encryption used, in order to reassure citizens about the nature of the data stored on their ID cards, but this may also increase the possibility of identity theft. Vulnerabilities of template storage are primarily those of the underlying computer infrastructure, and are not dealt with in detail here.

Template transmission:

The transmission medium between the template storage and matcher is similarly vulnerable to the template storage. In many cases, attacks against template data transmission may be easier than against the template storage. This is especially the case for passive eavesdropping and recording of data in transit for wireless transmission (such as contactless ID cards). Encrypted transmission is essential, but may still be vulnerable to key discovery [43].

19.3.9 Matching (I):

A biometric matcher calculates a similarity score related to the likelihood that two biometrics samples are from the same individual. Attacks against the matcher are somewhat obscure, but may be possible in certain cases. For biometric fusion systems, extreme scores in one biometric modality may override the inputs from other modalities. Biometric matchers which are based on Fisher discriminant strategies calculate global thresholds based on the between class covariance, which may be modified by enrolling specifically crafted biometric samples.

19.3.10 Decision (J):

Biometric decisions are often reviewed by a human operator (such as for most government applications). Such operators are well known to be susceptible to fatigue and boredom. One of the goals of DoS attacks can be to force operators to abandon a biometric system, or to mistrust its output (by causing it to produce a sufficiently large number of errors) [15].

19.3.11 Attack Trees

Complex systems are exposed to multiple possible vulnerabilities, and the ability to exploit a given vulnerability is dependent on a chain of requirements. Vulnerabilities vary in severity, and may be protected against by various countermeasures, such as: supervision of enrollment or verification, liveness detection, template anonymization, cryptographic storage and transport, and traditional network security measures. Countermeasures vary in maturity, cost, and cost-effectiveness. In order to analyze such a complex scenario, the factors may be organized into *attack trees*. This analysis methodology was developed by Schneier [38] and formalized by Moore *et al.* [28]. In [38], the example attack "Open Safe", is analyzed to occur due to "Pick Lock", "Learn Combo",

"Cut Open Safe" or "Install Improperly". "Learn Combo" may, in turn, occur due to "Eavesdrop", "Bribe" or other reasons, which in turn depend on further factors. The requirements for each factor can be assessed (Eavesdropping requires a technical skill, while Bribing requires an amount of money). Attack trees may be analyzed by assigning each node with a feasibility, the requirement for special equipment, or cost.

Attack tree techniques for biometric system security have been developed by Cukic and Bartlow [9]. Figure 19.2 shows a fraction of the attack tree of [9] for template regeneration [46].

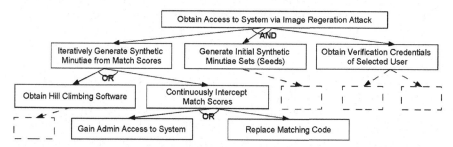

Fig. 19.2. Attack tree fraction adapted from [9] (dotted blocks represent removed tree portions) to implement the template regeneration attack of [46]. AND/OR nodes indicate that *all/one* of the sub-blocks are/is required, Further analysis of the attack tree may be performed by assigning each block a parameter (feasibility, required technical skill, expense) and calculating the cost for the overall attack.

19.4 Biometric Template Security

Biometric templates carry the most important biometric information, and thus present an important concern for privacy and security of systems. The basic concern is that templates may be used to spoof the owner of the document, or for identity theft to another system. Biometric algorithm vendors have largely claimed that it is impossible or infeasible to regenerate the image from the templates [17]; thus biometric templates are sometimes considered to be effectively non-identifiable data, much like a password hash. These claims are supported by: 1) the template records features (such as fingerprint minutiae) and not image primitives, 2) templates are typically calculated using only a small portion of the image, 3) templates are small – a few hundred bytes – much smaller than the sample image, and 4) the proprietary nature of the storage format makes templates infeasible to "hack". In this section, we consider two pathways to regenerate images from templates: 1) from the template directly, based on a knowledge of the features, and 2) from match score values from a biometric algorithm.

19.4.1 Image Regeneration from Templates

The goal of image regeneration from a biometric template is to compute an image which best matches the feature values in the template. In order to regenerate images in this way, it is necessary for templates to be available in unencrypted form. Thus, encryption of template data storage does impede this vulnerability; however, templates must be available in unencrypted form to perform matching, and are vulnerable at that point.

Published work on image regeneration from templates is for fingerprints, for the reason that regeneration is trivial for most iris and face recognition templates, in which the template features are based on subspace image transforms. If feature vector, $\mathbf{y}$, is computed from an image, $\mathbf{x}$ using a transform that can be approximated by $\mathbf{y} = \mathbf{Hx}$ for a convolution matrix, $\mathbf{H}$, then a reconstructed image, $\hat{\mathbf{x}}$, can be computed from $\hat{\mathbf{x}} = \mathbf{H}^{\dagger}\mathbf{y}$ using a pseudo-inverse $\mathbf{H}^{\dagger}$.

Hill [19] developed an ad-hoc approach to calculate an image from the template of an unspecified fingerprint system vendor. Software was designed to create line pattern images which had a sufficient resemblance to the underlying ridge pattern to be verified by the match software. This work also devised a simple scheme to predict the shape (class) of the fingerprint using the minutiae template. The algorithm iterated over each orientation, core and delta position keeping the image with the best match score. It is worth noting the line patterns do not visually resemble a fingerprint, although these images could be easily improved manually or automatically.

More recently, Ross *et al.* [35] have demonstrated a technique to reconstruct fingerprint images from a minutiae description, without using match score values. First, the orientation map and the class are inferred based on analysis of local minutiae triplets and a nearest neighbor classifier, trained with feature exemplars. Then, Gabor-like filters were used to reconstruct fingerprints using the orientation information. Correct classification of fingerprint class was obtained in 82% of cases, and regenerated images resembled the overall structure of the original, although the images were visually clearly synthetic and had gaps in regions which lacked minutiae. Another valuable contribution of this work is calculation of the probability density fields of minutiae; such information could be used to attack fingerprint based biometric encryption schemes (Sec. 19.5.2).

19.4.2 Image Regeneration from Match Scores

Image regeneration from match score values does not require access to the template, and, therefore, template encryption is not a countermeasure. Instead, the requirements are: the ability to present arbitrary images for matching against a target, and access to calculated match scores. The goal is to: 1) determine an image which matches against the target for the specific biometric algorithm, and 2) determine a good estimate of the original image. Clearly, if one can test arbitrary images, one could mount a brute force attack. Given a biometric database of sufficient quality and variety, it should be possible to attain the first goal in approximately 1/FAR attempts. A brute-force attack would be guaranteed to succeed in the second goal, but the size of image space is extremely large.

Brute force searches would only be necessary if biometric image space were random, and nothing could be learned from the output of previous tests. Soutar *et al.* [40] first proposed the possibility of "hill-climbing" in order to practically regenerate images from match score data. A hill-climbing algorithm functions as follows:

1. *Initial image selection*: Choose an initial image estimate (IM). Typically, a sample of initial biometric patterns are tested and the one with the largest match score, MS, is selected.
2. *Iterative estimate improvement*:
   a) Modify IM (to get IM_{test}) in a random, but biometrically reasonable way (details below).
   b) Calculate MS_{test} for IM_{test}.
   c) If $MS_{test} > MS$, set $IM = IM_{test}$ and $MS = MS_{test}$.
   d) End iterations if MS is no longer increasing.

The only difficulty to a practical implementation of this algorithm is to implement "biometrically reasonable" modifications. For face images, Adler [1] added a small factor times a PCA (eigenface) component to the face image. For fingerprint minutiae, Uludag and Jain [46] made modifications to perturb, add, replace, or delete an existing minutiae point at each step. The key constraint is that such modifications attempt to maintain "biometric feasibility" in the search space. Other image modifications, such as changing random pixels in the image, do not converge under hill-climbing.

In fact, "hill-climbing" algorithms are simply one type of multi-dimensional optimization algorithm. Other methods for unconstrained minimization (or maximization) such as the Nelder-Mead simplex perform equally or better than hill-climbing (unpublished observations).

In order to protect against regeneration of biometric images, Soutar *et al.* [40] suggested that match score output be quantized to a limited set of levels. The idea is that small image modifications are unlikely to push the MS up by one quantum, so that the hill-climbing algorithm will not see the effect of its changes. This recommendation is maintained in the BioAPI specification [5]. However, by an appropriate modification of the algorithm, Adler showed that hill-climbing could still function [3]. Each hill-climbing iteration is applied to a quadrant of IM. Before each calculation, noise is added to the image in the opposite quadrant, in order to force the match score to a value just below the quantization threshold. This means that the quantized match score is brought into a range where it provides useful information. Images were successfully regenerated for quantization levels equal to a 10% change in FAR.

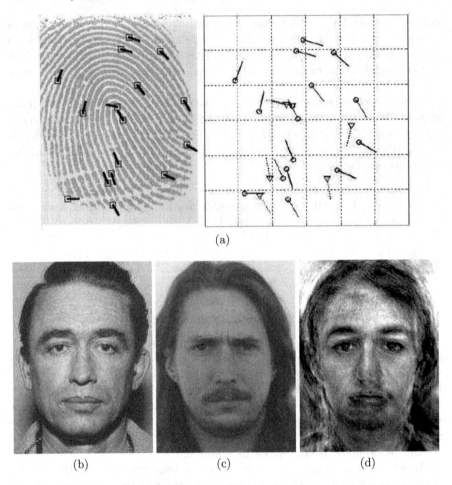

(a)

(b)   (c)   (d)

Fig. 19.3. Regenerated images using hill climbing techniques. (a) Regenerated fingerprint minutiae (from [46]). The target fingerprint with labeled minutiae (left), and regenerated minutiae positions (right). b – d: Regenerated face images (from [1]). The target face image (b); the initial selected image for hill climbing (c), and regenerated face image (d).

These results suggest that biometric images can generally be regenerated if: 1) arbitrary images can be input into the biometric system, and 2) raw or quantized match score values are output. The images calculated are of sufficient quality to masquerade to the algorithm as the target, and give a good visual impression of the biometric characteristics. In order to prevent this attack, it is necessary to either limit image input, or to provide only Match/Non-match decisions.

19.5   Encoded Biometric Schemes

Classical biometric systems require access to enrolled templates in uncoded form. This differs from traditional computer security systems, where a raw password need never be stored. Instead, a cryptographic hash (one-way function) of the password is stored, and each new test password is hashed and compared to the stored version. Since such cryptographic techniques provide important protections, there is great incentive to develop analogous methods for biometric systems. Encoded encryption techniques are designed to avoid these problems by embedding the secret code into the template, in a way that can be decrypted only with an image of the enrolled individual [11, 41]. Since the code is bound to the biometric template, an attacker should not be able to determine either the enrolled biometric image or secret code, even if they have access to the biometric software and hardware. Such technology would enable enhanced privacy protection, primarily against secondary use of biometric images [7, 45]. It would also reduce the vulnerability of network protocols based on biometrics [20]. Biometrically enabled computers and mobile phones currently must hide passwords and keys in software; biometric encryption would protect against this vulnerability. Another interesting application is for control of access to digital content with the aim of preventing copyright infringement. Biometrically encoded digital documents are subject to attacks, especially since both the documents and the software to access them will be widely distributed [24]. Currently, to the best of our knowledge, biometric encryption systems are not widely deployed; research systems still suffer from high error rates and slow processing speed. However, such systems offer some compelling benefits for many applications, and research is active (eg. [48, 18, 25, 34, 37]).

19.5.1   Revocable Biometrics

Revocable biometrics are encoded with a distortion scheme that varies for each application. The concept was developed by Ratha *et al.* [32] (and clarified in [33, 34]), to address the privacy and security concerns that biometrics are not secret and cannot be canceled. During enrollment, the input biometric image is subjected to a known distortion (Figure 19.4) controlled by a set of distortion parameters. The distorted biometric sample can then be processed with standard biometrics algorithms, which are unaware that the features presented to them are distorted. During matching, the live biometric sample must be distorted in exactly the same way, otherwise it cannot match the enrolled sample. This distortion must also satisfy the constraint that multiple different distortion profiles cannot match. Thus, the revocable nature of this scheme is provided by the distortion, in that it is not the user's "actual" biometric which is stored, but simply one of an arbitrarily large number of possible permutations. One key advantage of this scheme is that it is independent of the biometrics matching algorithm.

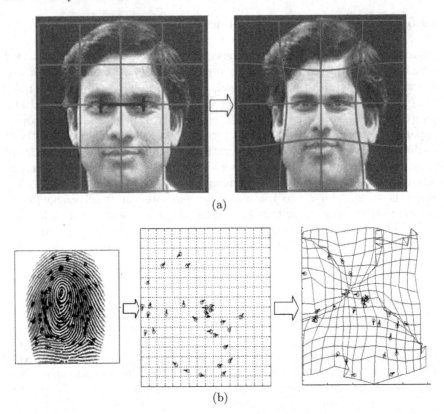

(a)

(b)

Fig. 19.4. Distortions of images to implement revocable biometrics. (a) A distorted face image centered at the eyes (from [33]), and (b) a fingerprint minutiae set distorted spatially and in minutiae angle (from [34]).

For faces, the distortion takes place in the raw image space [33], since face recognition feature sets are not standardized. This places tight constraints on the nature of the distortion, since severely distorted faces will not be recognized and properly encoded by the algorithms (note that the face image in Figure 19.4 was not part of an implemented system). A different approach is taken by Savvides *et al.* [37] in which the revocable distortion is tied to a face recognition algorithm based on correlation filters. Enrolled and test face images are distorted with a random kernel calculated from a key to generate an encrypted correlation filter. Since the same convolution kernel is present for both images, its effect is mathematically canceled in the correlation filter. This scheme is somewhat similar to the biometric encryption approach of Soutar *et al.* [41].

A theoretical approach to revocable biometrics uses shielding functions [25], to allow a verifier to check the authenticity of a prover (user wanting to be verified) without learning any biometric information, using proposed δ-contracting and ϵ-revealing functions. The proposed system was based on simple Gaussian noise models and not tested with an actual biometric system. Unfortunately, it is unclear how practical functions can be found which account for the inherent biometric feature variability.

The cancelable fingerprint templates of [34] use the minutiae rather than the raw image, since this allows both minutiae position and angle to be permuted (increasing the degrees of freedom of the transformation), and since distortion will interfere with the feature extraction process. The distortion is modeled on the electric field distribution for random charges. Results show a small impact on biometric errors (5% increase in FRR) over undistorted features.

While revocable biometrics represent a promising approach to address biometric security and privacy vulnerabilities, we are unaware of security analyses of such schemes, so the security strength of such a transformation is unclear. More significantly, it appears trivial to "undistort" the template given knowledge of the distortion key. Since such keys will presumably not be much better protected than current passwords and PINs, in many application scenarios there is no security advantage of such revocable schemes over an encrypted traditional template.

19.5.2 Biometrics Encryption

Biometric encryption seeks to use the biometric sample as a key to conduct cryptographic protocols. Normally the biometric template is bound to a secret key which is designed to only be recoverable with a biometric image from the enrolled individual. The primary difficulty in designing biometric encryption systems is the variability in the biometric image between measurements [14]. This means that the presented biometric image cannot itself be treated as a code, since it varies with each presentation. For biometric encryption systems, this variability becomes especially difficult. An algorithm must be designed which allows an image from the enrolled person, with significant differences from the original, to decode the complete secret code. At the same time, an image from another person – which may only be slightly more different from the enrolled image – must not only not decode the secret, it must not be allowed to decode (or "leak") any information at all.

The earliest biometric encryption system was proposed by Soutar [41, 42]. Enrollment requires several sample images and a secret code, and creates a template binding the code to the images. During enrollment, an average image f_0 is obtained (with 2D Fourier transform F_0) from multiple samples of the input fingerprint, after suitable alignment. In order to encode the secret, a random code is chosen and encoded as a phase-only function R_0. A Wiener inverse filter is calculated, $H_0 = (F_0^* R_0^*) / (F_0^* F_0 + N^2)$, where N^2 is the image noise power. As N increases, an image more dissimilar from the one enrolled can decrypt the code, at the expense of a smaller secret (in bits). In order for biometric encryption to allow for variability in the input image, the secret code must be robustly encoded, using an error correcting code (ECC); [41] uses Hamming distances and majority decision. During key release, a new image, f_1, is acquired. This image is deconvolved with the filter H_0 to calculate $R_1 = sign(imag(H_0F_1))$, an estimate of R_0. If F_1 is from the same individual as F_0, then R_1 should be a good estimate of R_0; but since $R_1 \neq R_0$, some phase elements will be incorrect. However, if R_1 is sufficiently close, the ECC should allow the correct value of the secret to be obtained.

A somewhat similar scheme was proposed for voice passwords by Monrose *et al.* [27], in which a vector of features is calculated. From this vector each value is used to select a fraction of the key bits from a table. A correct feature value during key release will select correct key bits while an incorrect value will select a table entry with random data. For features determined to be less reliable, correct key bits are put in all table positions. Reported error rates were FRR = 20%; however, it would seem that such a scheme could make better use of an ECC, since a single feature error will prevent code release.

Hao *et al.* recently proposed a biometric encryption scheme for Iris images based on similar techniques [18]. During enrollment, an encoded key is XORed with the 2048 bit iris code to produce an encrypted code. Variability in the iris is due to background random errors, and to burst errors from undetected eyelashes and specular reflections. The key is encoded with a Hadamard code to protect against background errors, and with a Reed-Solomon code to protect against burst errors. During key release, the encrypted code is XORed with a new iris code sample, and Hadamard and Reed-Solomon decoding are used to correct for errors in the key. Rotation of the iris is handled by iteratively shifting the observed iris codes and attempting decoding. Results show FRR = 0.47% for a key length of 140 bits. In terms of security, the authors note that iris images have significant spatial correlations, which will be preserved in such a linear cryptographic scheme.

Fig. 19.5. Schematic diagram of the biometric encryption scheme of [8]. *Left:* a raw fingerprint image is enrolled. *Middle:* minutiae points (circles) are used to encode the value of a polynomial representing the secret. *Right:* chaff points (squares), sufficiently far from minutiae, are used to encode random values of the polynomial.

More recent work in biometric encryption has been done in the cryptography community, with much based on the *fuzzy vault* construction of Juels and Sudan [23]. This scheme allows a cryptographic encoding with a variable number of un-ordered data points, which makes it suitable for fingerprint minutiae. This approach has been pursued by Dodis *et al.* [14], who develop the concept of a *fuzzy extractor* which extracts uniformly random and error-tolerant bits from its input, and a *secure sketch* which produces public output that does not reveal the input. Boyen *et al.* [6] further develop this scheme for secure remote authentication. Unfortunately, neither work clarifies how to use these frameworks in a practical biometric application. Not all biometric encryption schemes use a key; for example, in [12, 11], the biometric image forms a unique key, although the results of Linnartz *et al.* [25] suggest encryption schemes based on the biometric only are inherently vulnerable.

Based on [23], Clancy *et al.* [8] designed a fingerprint algorithm which encodes the secret as the coefficients of a Galois field polynomial (Figure 19.5). After alignment, minutiae points are encoded as pairs (x_i, y_i) where x_i is a minutiae point, and y_i is a point on the polynomial. Additionally, numerous "chaff" points are encoded, in which the value of y_i is random. During key release, the minutiae of the new fingerprint image are calculated, and the points x_i closest to the minutiae are chosen. The y_i corresponding to these points are used to estimate the polynomial, using a Reed-Solomon ECC framework. If enough legitimate points are identified (equal to the number selected at vault design), the correct polynomial will be obtained and the correct secret decrypted. An interesting generalization of this scheme is given by the "secure sketches" of [14].

Little work has been done to attack biometric encryption schemes, and their security is thus mostly unknown. In their analysis, Uludag *et al.* [48] note that most proposed biometric encryption systems only appear to account for a "limited amount of variability in the biometric representation." In order to quantify this notion, experiments were conducted to estimate the variability in fingerprint minutiae. Matched fingerprint pairs were imaged and minutiae locations identified by a human expert, which was assumed to give an upper bound on system performance. Using these data, the algorithm of [8] was analyzed to estimate the ROC curve during key generation and key release, with an equal error rate of approximately 6.3%. This suggests that biometric encryption systems can be attacked simply via the FAR, by presenting biometric samples from a representative population. A cryptographic attack of biometric encryption was developed by Adler [4], based on using any "leaked" information to attempt a "hill-climbing" of the biometric template, using the quantized *MS* hill-climbing algorithm. This approach was used to reconstruct a face image from a biometric encryption scheme based on [41, 42].

Based on the success of these early attacks, we feel that biometric encryption schemes have significant remaining vulnerabilities. Although some schemes offer security proofs (ie. [23, 14]) these depend on invalid models of the biometric data. Biometric data inherently has strong internal correlations, many of which cover the entire image. Another important area for attack is the requirement for segmentation and alignment of images before comparison can take place. In a practical system, such as that of Uludag *et al.* [47], carefully selected data are made available to permit alignment with a minimum of "leaked information". Thus, we feel that, in general, current biometric encryption schemes have unknown security value.

19.5.3 Measures of biometric information content

The information content of biometric samples (or biometric feature entropy) is related to many issues in biometric technology. For example, one of the most common biometric questions is that of uniqueness – "are fingerprints unique?" [30] Such a measure is important for biometric system vulnerabilities, especially as a measure of the strength of cryptosystems and for privacy measures. It also is relevant for applications such as biometric fusion, where one would like to quantify the biometric information in each system individually, and the potential gain from fusing the systems.

Several approaches have been taken to answer this question. Wayman [49] introduced a statistical approach to measure the separability of Gaussian feature distributions using a "cotton ball model". Daugman [10] developed the "discrimination entropy" to measure the information content of iris images. This value has the advantage that it is calculated directly from the match score distributions, but it is unclear how it relates to traditional measures of entropy. Golfarelli *et al.* [16] showed that the most commonly used feature representations of hand geometry and face biometrics have a limited number of distinguishable patterns, on the order of 10^5 and 10^3, respectively, as measured by a theoretical estimate of the equal error rate. Penev *et al.* [31] determined that the dimentionality of the PCA subspace necessary to characterize the identity information in faces is in the range 400–700. Biometric encryption studies calculate 46 bits in spoken passwords [27], and 69 bits in fingerprints [8]. Adler *et al.* [2] developed a measure of biometric information in terms of the relative entropy $D(p\|q)$ between the population (inter-class) feature distribution q and the individual (intra-class) distribution p, and calculated an information content for various face recognition feature representations to be between 37 and 45 bits. In this work, the term *biometric information* is defined as the "decrease in uncertainty about the identity of a person due to a set of biometric measurements". Biometric information content is still an open field, with no consensus on techniques used. All cited work measures the information content of a given feature representation, and not that of the biometric sample itself.

19.6 Discussion

Our understanding of biometrics system security is in its early stages – much more so than many aspects of biometric recognition algorithms. This is perhaps to be expected; people needed to be convinced the technology would work at all, before it was worth trying to understand when it failed.

It is also worth noting that many privacy issues associated with biometric systems are closely related to the security vulnerabilities. Thus, according to Cavoukian [7],

> The threat to privacy arises not from the positive identification that biometrics provide best, but the ability of third parties to access this data in identifiable form and link it to other information, resulting in secondary uses of the information, without the consent of the data subject.

Based on this understanding, a biometric requirement list was developed to include: original biometric image must be destroyed, biometrics must be encrypted, biometrics used only for verification, fingerprint image cannot be reconstructed, and finger cannot be used as a unique ID. The other significant privacy concern is that "we only have 10 fingers" – biometric data loss is catastrophic in the sense that it cannot be replaced [39]. While there are many promising developments that address these issues, such as biometric encryption (Sec. 19.5.2), revocable biometrics (Sec. 19.5.1), or work to de-identify images [29], unfortunately, our analysis in this chapter suggests that currently mature biometric technology is unable to properly address these privacy concerns in the way they are stated.

At the same time, biometric systems are being used in many scenarios with high security value. Vulnerabilities and attack scenarios have been carefully considered and well thought out recommendations are available (eg. [20]). Recent work in standards bodies has given much thought to security standards for biometrics. In summary, biometrics system security is challenged by many vulnerabilities, from the biometrics system, the computer infrastructure which supports it, and the users it identifies. However, biometrics can also provide (with careful use) the identity assurance that is foundational to systems security.

References

1. A. Adler. Sample Images can be Independently Restored from Face Recognition Templates. In *Proceedings of Canadian Conference on Electrical and Computer Engineering*, volume 2, pages 1163–1166, Montreal, Canada, May 2003.
2. A Adler, R Youmaran, and S Loyka. Information content of biometric features. In *Proceedings of Biometrics Consortium Conference*, Washington DC, USA, 2005.
3. Andy Adler. Images can be Regenerated from Quantized Biometric Match Score Data. In *Proceedings Canadian Conference on Electrical and Computer Engineering*, pages 469–472, Niagara Falls, Canada, May 2004.
4. Andy Adler. Vulnerabilities in biometric encryption systems. In *Proceedings of AVBPA*, volume 3546, pages 1100–1109, 2005.

5. BioAPI Consortium. Bioapi specification version 1.1, 2001.
6. X. Boyen, Y. Dodis, J. Katz, R. Ostrovsky, and A. Smith. Secure remote authentication using biometric data. In *Advances in Cryptology (EUROCRYPT)*, 2005.
7. A. Cavoukian. Privacy and Biometrics. In *Proceedings of International Conference on Privacy and Personal Data Protection*, Hong Kong, China, 1999.
8. T. Clancy, D. Lin, and N. Kiyavash. Secure Smartcard-Based Fingerprint Authentication. In *Proceedings of ACM SIGMM Workshop on Biometric Methods and Applications*, pages 45–52, Berkley, USA, November 2003.
9. B. Cukic and N. Bartlow. Threats and Countermeasures. In *Proceedings of Biometrics Consortium Conference*, Washington DC, USA, 2005.
10. J. Daugman. The importance of being random: Statistical principles of iris recognition. *Pattern Recognition*, 36:279–291, 2003.
11. G. I. Davida, Y. Frankel, B. J. Matt, and R. Peralta. On enabling secure applications through off-line biometric identification. In *Proceedings of the IEEE Symposium on Privacy and Security*, pages 148–157, 1998.
12. G. I. Davida, Y. Frankel, B. J. Matt, and R. Peralta. On the relation of error correction and cryptography to an offline biometric based identification scheme. In *Proceedings of International Workshop on Coding and Cryptography (WCC'99)*, pages 129–138, 1999.
13. G. Doddington, W. Liggett, A. Martin, N. Przybocki, and D. Reynolds. Sheep, Goats, Lambs and Wolves: An Analysis of Individual Differences in Speaker Recognition Performance. In *Proceedings of the International Conference on Auditory-Visual Speech Processing*, Sidney, Australia, 1998.
14. Y. Dodis, L. Reyzin, and A. Smith. Fuzzy Extractors and Cryptography, or How to Use Your Fingerprints. In *Proceedings of Eurocrypt'04*, 2004.
15. N. Ferguson and B. Schneier. *Practical Cryptography*. John Wiley & Sons, NJ, USA, 2003.
16. M. Golfarelli, D. Maio, and D. Maltoni. On the Error-Reject Tradeoff in Biometric Verification Systems. *IEEE Transactions on Pattern Analysis and Machine Intelligence*, 19(7):786–796, July 1997.
17. International Biometric Group. Generating images from templates, 2002.
18. F. Hao, R. Anderson, and J. Daugman. Combining cryptography with biometrics effectively. Technical Report UCAM-CL-TR-640, University of Cambridge, Cambridge, UK, 2005.
19. C. Hill. Risk of Masquerade Arising from the Storage of Biometrics. B.s. thesis, Austrailian National University, 2001.
20. InterNational Committee for Information Technology Standards (INCITS). Study report on biometrics in e-authentication. Technical Report Technical Report INCITS M1/06-0693, 2006.
21. International Labour Organization. Biometric testing campaign report (addendum to part i), 2005.
22. ISO. Standing document 2, version 5 – harmonized biometric vocabulary. Technical Report Technical Report ISO/IEC JTC 1/SC 37 N 1480, 2006.
23. A. Juels and M. Sudan. A fuzzy vault schem. In *Proceedings of the IEEE International Symposium on Information Theory*, page 408, 2002.
24. D. Kundur, C-Y. Lin, and H. Yu. Special Issue on Enabling Security Technologies for Digital Rights Management. In *Proceedings of IEEE*, volume 92, pages 879–882, 2004.

25. J-P. Linnartz and P. Tuyls. New shielding functions to enhance privacy and prevent misuse of biometric templates. In *Proceedings of the International Conference on Audio- and Video-Based Biometric Person Authentication (AVBPA) in LNCS*, volume 2688, pages 393–402, Guiford, UK, 2003.

26. D. Maltoni, D. Maio, A. K. Jain, and S. Prabhakar. *Handbook of Fingerprint Recognition*. Springer-Verlag, 2003.

27. F. Monrose, M.K. Reiter, Q. Li, and S. Wetzel. Cryptographic Key Generation from Voice. In *Proceedings of IEEE Symposium on Security and Privacy*, pages 202–213, Oakland, USA, May 2001.

28. A. P. Moore, R. J. Ellison, and R. C. Linger. Attack modeling for information security and survivability. Technical Report Technical Report CMU/SEI-2001-TN-001, Carnegie Mellon University, Pittsburgh, PA, USA, 2001.

29. E. M. Newton, L. Sweeney, and B. Malin. Preserving privacy by de-identifying face images. *IEEE Transactions on Knowledge Data Engineering*, 17:232–243, 2005.

30. S. Pankanti, S. Prabhakar, and A. K. Jain. On the Individuality of Fingerprints. *IEEE Transactions on Pattern Analysis and Machine Intelligence*, 24(8):1010–1025, August 2002.

31. P. S. Penev and L. Sirovich. The Global Dimensionality of Face Space. In *Proceedings of 4th IEEE International Conference on Automatic Face and Gesture Recognition*, pages 264–270, Grenoble, France, 2000.

32. N. K. Ratha, J. H. Connell, and R. M. Bolle. Cancelable Biometrics . In *Proceedings of Biometric Consortium Conference*, 2000.

33. N. K. Ratha, J. H. Connell, and R. M. Bolle. Enhancing security and privacy in biometrics-based authentication systems. *IBM Systems Journal*, 40:614–634, 2001.

34. N. K. Ratha, J. H. Connell, R. M. Bolle, and S. Chikkerur. Cancelable Biometrics: A Case Study in Fingerprints. In *Proceedings of IEEE International Conference Pattern Recognition*, volume 4, pages 370–373, Hong Kong, China, August 2006.

35. A. Ross, J. Shah, and A. K. Jain. Towards Reconstructing Fingerprints from Minutiae Points. In *Proceedings of SPIE Conference on Biometric Technology for Human Identification II*, volume 5779, pages 68–80, Orlando, USA, 2005.

36. M. B. Salter. Passports, Mobility, and Security: How smart can the border be? *International Studies Perspectives*, 5:71–91, 2004.

37. M. Savvides, B. V. K. Vijaya Kumar, and P. K. Khosla. Cancelable biometric filters for face recognition . In *Proceedings of the International Conference on Pattern Recognition*, pages 922–925, 2004.

38. B. Schneier. Attack Trees. *Dr. Dobb's Journal*, 1999.

39. B. Schneier. The Uses and Abuses of Biometrics. *Communications of the ACM*, 42(8), 1999.

40. C. Soutar, R. Gilroy, and A. Stoianov. Biometric System Performance and Security . In *Proceedings of the IEEE Workshop on Automatic Identification Advanced Technologies*, 1999.

41. C. Soutar, D. Roberge, A. Stoianov, R. Gilroy, and B. V. K. Vijaya Kumar. Biometric Encryption using image processing. In *Proceedings of SPIE, Optical Security and Counterfeit Deterrence Techniques II*, volume 3314, pages 178–188, 1998.

42. C. Soutar, D. Roberge, A. Stoianov, R. Gilroy, and B. V. K. Vijaya Kumar. Biometric Encryption: enrollment and verification procedures. In *Proceedings of SPIE, Optical Pattern Recognition IX*, volume 3386, pages 24–35, 1998.

43. The Guardian. Cracked it, 17 November 2006.

44. C. Tilton. Biometrics in E-Authentication: Threat Model. In *Proceedings of the Biometrics Consortium Conference*, Baltimore, MD, USA, 2006.

45. G. Tomko. Privacy Implications of Biometrics - A Solution in Biometric Encryption. In *Proceedings of the 8th Annual Conference on Computers, Freedom and Privacy*, Austin, TX, USA, 1998.

46. U. Uludag and A.K. Jain. Attacks on Biometric Systems: A Case Study in Fingerprints. In *Proceedings of SPIE Conference on Security, Seganography and Watermarking of Multimedia Contents VI*, pages 622–633, San Jose, USA, January 2004.

47. U. Uludag, S. Pankanti, and A. K. Jain. Fuzzy Vault for Fingerprints. In *Proceedings of Fifth International Conference on Audio- and Video-based Biometric Person Authentication*, pages 310–319, Rye Town, USA, July 2005.

48. U. Uludag, S. Pankanti, S. Prabhakar, and A. K. Jain. Biometric Cryptosystems: Issues and Challenges. *Proceedings of the IEEE, Special Issue on Multimedia Security for Digital Rights Management*, 92(6):948–960, June 2004.

49. J. Wayman. The cotton ball problem. In *Proceedings of Biometrics Consortium Conference*, Washington DC, USA, 2004.

Spoof Detection Schemes

Kristin Adair Nixon[1], Valerio Aimale, and Robert K. Rowe[1]

[1]Lumidigm, Inc., Albuquerque, New Mexico 87106, USA
KANixon@Lumidigm.com, Rob.Rowe@Lumidigm.com

20.1 Introduction

Biometrics is defined as an automated method of verifying or recognizing the identity of a living person based on physiological or behavioral characteristics [1]. While much research has been done both to determine which traits can differentiate humans and to optimize that differentiation, the problem of determining if the presented trait originates from a living person has received relatively less attention. Between acquiring biometric data and delivering a result, there are various points where the overall security of a biometric access system can be compromised.

The information flow of a biometric access system is simple (see Figure 20.1). First the biometric is presented to the sensor by the person requesting access. A camera may capture a face or iris, a sensor may capture a fingerprint, a microphone may capture a voice; in each case, the raw biometric information is acquired and sent to the biometric *feature extractor*. The extractor is generally software that extracts the features important for determining identity from the raw information. For a fingerprint, this might be the minutiae points and for a face this could be the distance between the eyes. This extracted feature information is called a *template*. The template is then sent to the *matcher*. The matcher compares the newly-presented biometric information to previously submitted template information to make a decision. Presented along with a pin number or access card, the template may be matched against that of a single enrolled user for verification. Alternatively, it may be compared to all enrolled users for identification.

One type of biometric sensor attack happens at the beginning of this process: fake biometric data may be presented to the sensor. Known as a *spoof attack*, this can take the form of an artificial finger, a mask over a face, or a contact lens on an eye. A *replay attack* intercepts the output flow of a sensor and puts previously stored genuine biometric information (either in raw or extracted form) into the proper place in the processing chain. An enrollment database used in the verification/identification process can also be altered to effectively enroll an unauthorized person or replace a person's information with someone else's. A *Trojan horse attack* replaces the original extractor with a fake extractor (the "Trojan horse") which outputs pre-determined biometric information. Similarly, the original matcher could be replaced with a fake matcher that always gives a specified result - match, no match, or a score. Buhan and Hartel have published a detailed review of vulnerability points [2].

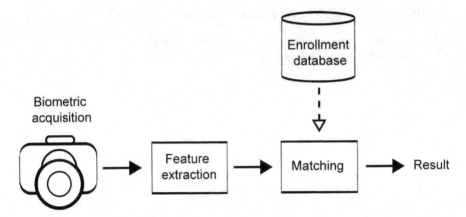

Fig. 20.1. An example of how biometric data travels to obtain a result.

While security vulnerabilities can be found at many points in the capture and processing of a biometric, the most susceptible point is the one that all people have access to: the presentation of the biometric trait at the sensor interface itself. Producing cloned biometric data is relatively simple, making the sensor an easy target for intruders.

An attack on a biometric system can occur for many reasons. First, a person may wish to disguise their own identity. A terrorist trying to enter a foreign country, for example, may try to modify their biometric information or conceal it by placing an alternate form of the biometric, such as an artificial fingerprint, mask, or contact lens, over their genuine biometric trait. As long as the modified or false biometric is not in the database being searched, the attack could be successful. Secondly, an attack on a biometric system can occur because a person wants to gain privileges that another person has. In this case, the individual might counterfeit an authorized user's biometric to try to access that person's bank account or gain physical access to a restricted area. Finally, an attack might occur because there is a benefit to sharing a biometric. For example, a person may create a new identity using an artificial biometric, enroll in a system, then share that identity with multiple people by sharing the artificial biometric. In this final case, it does not matter who the artificial biometric actually belongs to, only that it can be used in the enrollment process and later shared.

A *spoof* is a counterfeit biometric that is used in an attempt to circumvent a biometric sensor. In the case of fingerprints, this can be as simple as a latent print on a sensor, reactivated by breathing on it, or as sinister as using a dismembered finger. Differentiating a genuine biometric trait presented from a live person versus some other source is called *spoof detection*. The act of sensing vitality (*"liveness"*) signs such as pulse is one method of spoof detection. In some areas of research, the term liveness detection is synonymous with spoof detection. In other areas of research, liveness detection is the more limited problem of distinguishing a live human trait from a non-live human trait and in still others liveness detection is, very narrowly, defined as the sensing of vitality signs. For the purposes of this chapter, spoof detection will be broadly defined as correctly identifying when the biometric presented is from a live human versus any other material using any method.

Spoof detection can occur before biometric data is collected or during data processing. In a *decoupled system*, no biometric data is collected until the spoof detection method is satisfied that a live human is present. In an *integrated system*, spoof detection occurs along the processing chain after the biometric information is captured.

Spoof detection methods can be categorized using three different approaches: a) use only the data collected for biometric purposes; b) further process information already collected to generate discriminating information or collect additional biometric images over time; or c) use additional hardware and associated software to detect signals that have higher discriminating power than biometric data alone. In general, using only data collected for biometric purposes is hard to leverage for spoof detection; academic research and commercial solutions have focused on further processing or collection of biometric data, or on using additional hardware.

In spoof detection systems, the resistance to spoof attacks can be measured in the same manner as the biometric authentication performance. By generalizing the concept of Receiver Operator Characteristic (ROC) curves, and assuming that there exists a threshold for which a spoof decision is made, the probability of labeling fake biometric data as genuine ("false accept") or labeling genuine data as fake ("false reject") can be plotted with respect to each other at discrete threshold points. ROC plots offer a means to choose the operating threshold of the system with full knowledge of the probability of accepting fake biometric data as genuine and vice-versa. The ROC is also a good instrument for comparing heterogeneous approaches to spoof detection.

There are, however, irregularities to fake biometric data that are not revealed by ROC plots. To concentrate attention on securing systems against the most successful fake biometric attacks, it is important to derive knowledge of both the repeatability of a single example of a spoof and the ability to reproduce examples of a spoof. ROC curves aggregate all attacks under a single class. For example, if a gelatin spoof is able to successfully fool a fingerprint system but no other material is, the number of other materials sampled with respect to gelatin will skew the ROC curve. Also, if a specific sample of a gelatin spoof can fool the fingerprint sensor but the technique can not be replicated, that information is very important to the overall security of the system but is not adequately captured in a ROC curve alone.

Measuring the security of biometric systems against spoof attacks has received a lot of attention through publications in recent years; an industry- and technology-wide performance evaluation, however, has yet to be undertaken. The International Biometric Group (IBG) will conduct a trial to evaluate the anti-spoofing capabilities of biometric sensors currently available on the market. The IBG trial will focus on the integrated software/sensor solutions with respect to their spoof detection capabilities [3].

20.2 Historical Survey

20.2.1 Fingerprint

Sensor Attacks

The first attempt to compromise the security of fingerprint-based identification systems dates to the 1920s when Alert Wehde, then an inmate at a Kansas penitentiary, used his experience in photography and engraving to forge latent prints. A latent fingerprint was dusted to reveal and increase contrast, and a photograph was taken. The negative was used to etch the print onto a copper plate. Lightly greased, the plate could be used to leave counterfeit latent prints on objects [4, 5].

In more recent times, Putte and Keuning [6] and Mutsumoto et al. [7] independently showed how soft material artificial fingers could be falsely accepted as real fingers on widely available biometric fingerprint sensors. Their pioneering work prompted the development of a research area focused on probing sensor vulnerabilities and finding countermeasures to attacks.

When the goal of the spoof is to gain access that another person has, the first step is to retrieve the fingerprint of that person - i.e., a person that is already enrolled. There are two approaches to acquiring an enrolled subject's fingerprint: cooperative retrieval and non-cooperative retrieval.

In cooperative retrieval, the subject allows the collection of one or more fingerprints. The fingerprint is usually collected by pressing the finger in a small amount of suitable material such as wax or dental mold material; the impression creates a mold from which artificial fingers can be cast. A variety of materials have been used for casting such as silicone, moldable plastic, plaster, clay, and dental molding material [8-10].

In a real-world scenario, it is highly unlikely that a person would agree to produce a mold from a finger. For non-cooperative retrieval, the method devised by Albert Wehde [5, 11] is still in use: today, printed circuit board etching is a successful molding technique for producing 'gummy' and other soft material artificial fingers [4].

Sensors for Fingerprinting

There are three families of fingerprint acquisition technologies: optical, solid-state, and ultrasound [12]. Each technology has strengths and weaknesses with regard to preventing spoof attacks.

Many optical fingerprint sensors are based on frustrated total internal reflection (TIR). In TIR sensors, the fingerprint image is generated by the differential reflectivity of friction ridges - which are in contact with a glass platen and the valleys of the fingerprint (air). The finger surface is illuminated through one side of a prism and reflected through the opposite side. Ridges and valleys are imaged in contrast. Sensors based on this technology are susceptible to attack with artificial fingers made of material that has light reflectivity similar to that of skin. If the valleys of the artificial finger are similar in depth to those of a real finger, the resulting image will be indistinguishable from a real fingerprint. In some cases, an ink jet can print a fingerprint with enough relief to spoof an optical fingerprint reader [13].

Some TIR optical sensors are also highly vulnerable to being spoofed by latent prints. The palmar surface of fingertips is often covered with sebaceous secretions which find their way to the fingertips by normal everyday behavior like rubbing the face, combing, etc. These secretions, along with sweat and skin debris, can produce latent prints that are left on objects. (This is the basis of fingerprinting in forensic science.) When a real finger touches a glass platen of an optical sensor, a latent print may remain on the platen. The latent print can compromise an optical scanner when a light is directed onto the platen. The light incident on the latent print is optically scattered, causing a fingerprint image to be detected by the sensor [14].

Recently, an optical sensor based on multispectral imaging (MSI) has been introduced as a commercial product [15]. Sensors in this class image features of the tissue that lie below the surface of the skin as well as the usual surface features. Some of the subsurface features provide a second representation of the surface pattern, which enables the MSI sensor to collect a fingerprint even when the surface features are worn or the measurement is made under adverse sampling conditions. Importantly for spoof detection, the subsurface tissue features also represent a rich source of information about the material being imaged and provide a strong basis for discrimination between genuine fingers and other materials. The details of this means of spoof detection will be described in Section 20.3.

Solid-state sensors incorporate an array that measures physical character-istics of skin. The most common is the capacitive sensor, consisting of an array of capacitor plates. When a fingertip rests on the sensing surface, the ridges and valleys constitute the opposite plate of a virtual capacitor. Air lodged between the sensing surface and the valleys induces differential capacitance of valleys and ridges, creating the image acquired through the array. Thermal sensors, in this family, sense the difference in temperature between the surface of ridges, which are in direct contact to the sensor surface, and valleys, whose radiated heat reaches the sensor via air. Electric field sensors reveal the characteristic amplitude modulation of the skin derma on a sinusoid signal. The signal is generated by a drive ring inside the sensor and is received, when modulated, by an array of micro-antennae embedded in the sensor. Piezoelectric sensors generate images by differential mechanical stress of ridges and valleys when a finger is presented. Solid-state sensors are susceptible to soft artificial fingers (commonly, gelatin-based spoofs [6]) whose material mimics the single physical characteristic of the skin they are measuring.

Ultrasound sensors employ acoustic signals transmitted towards the fingertip surface. Acoustic waves travel at different speeds though ridges and air lodged under the skin. The reflected acoustic signal (echo) is captured by a receiver, which generates the fingerprint image. Ultrasound fingerprint scanners can be compromised by soft artificial materials whose material has the same echoing characteristics of fingers, such as gelatin.

Vulnerability of Fingerprint Sensors to Spoof Attacks

Sensor resilience to attacks undertaken with spoofing materials has been tested by several groups. Table 20.1 summarizes the published, aggregate results. Sensor devices tested were produced by BioLink Technologies, Biometric Access Corp, Biometrika, Compaq Computer Corporation, Crossmatch, Dermalog, Digital Persona, Ethentica Inc/Security First Corp, FingerMatrix, Fujitsu Microelectronics America, IdentAlink, Identix, Mitsubishi Electronic Corporation, NEC Corporation, Omron Corporation, Precise Biometrics, Siemens, Sony Corporation, Tacoma, Targus, TST, Ultra-Scan, Upek, and Veridicom. Data for aggregation were collected from heterogeneous sources [6, 7, 14, 16-27]. Some of the data presented was collected at the Lumidigm laboratories.

Measures to Minimize Sensor Vulnerability

Among the three different approaches for spoof detection in biometrics discussed in Section 20.1, namely, using only biometric data, collecting additional data or extra processing of collected data, and additional hardware, only further processing or additional collection of biometric data and additional hardware are represented in current fingerprint research and development. Due to the limited amount of information in fingerprint images and the ability to make high-resolution fingerprint spoofs, use of existing biometric fingerprint images has not proven useful for spoof detection.

Researchers at West Virginia University have used the collection of additional fingerprint images and processing to determine if the source is a live finger or a spoof [8-10, 13]. Attention has been focused on the perspiration from the skin surface. The presence of sweat on a finger surface enables both capacitive and optical scanners to discriminate against spoofs. The combination of skin and aqueous solution changes: when dry skin contacts a sensing surface, moisture is secreted over a short period of time. The West Virginia

Table 20.1. Published sensor vulnerability results from several studies. Tests performed at Lumidigm laboratories are marked with (*).

Sensor Type	Gelatin	Silicone	Wood-Glue	Wood Cement	Play-Doh	Clay	Rubber	Soft Plastic	Scotch Tape	Dismembered Finger
Optical A	(*)[23]	(*)[23]	(*)[23]		(*)[23]		(*)[23]		(*)	(*)
Optical B	[6, 14, 20, 27-29]	[6, 14, 20, 27-29]		[6, 14, 20, 27-29]	(*)					
Optical C		[17, 30]			[17, 30]					
Optical D	[6, 8, 14, 30, 31]	[6, 8, 14, 30, 31]							[6, 8, 14, 30, 31]	
Optical E	[7, 8, 29, 32]	[7, 8, 29, 32]	[7, 8, 29, 32]		[8-10]	[7, 8, 29, 32]	[7, 8, 29, 32]	[8-10]		[8-10]
Optical F	[7, 33]	[7, 33]								
Optical G	[26, 34]	[26, 34]								
Optical H	[26, 34]	[26, 34]								
Optical I	[32, 34]	[32, 34]								
Optical J		[6, 34]								
Optical K		[6, 31]								
Optical L		[17, 30]		[17, 30]						
Optical M	[29, 31]		[29, 31]				[29, 31]	[29, 31]		
Optical N	[33, 34]	[33, 34]								
Optical O		[26, 35]								
Optical P		[26, 35]								
Electro-Optical	[29, 31-33]	[29, 31-33]			[29, 31-33]	[29, 31-33]				[29, 31-33]
Capacitive A	[34, 35]	[17, 34, 35]		[17, 35]						
Capacitive B		[6, 36]			[28, 36]				[14, 36]	[28, 36]
Capacitive C		[6]							[6]	
Capacitive D	[7, 36]	[7, 36]							[7, 36]	
Capacitive E	(*)[23, 29, 31]				(*)[23, 29, 31]	(*)[23, 29, 31]				
Capacitive F	(*)[7]	(*)[7]								
Capacitive G	(*)[7]	(*)[7]								
RF Imaging	[7, 29, 31, 32]				[7, 29, 31, 32]	[7, 29, 31, 32]				[7, 29, 31, 32]
Thermal	[8, 9, 29, 32]	[8, 9, 29, 32]						[8, 9, 29, 32]		
Ultra-sound	[29]		[29]					[29]	[29]	
Piezoelectric	[29]		[29]				[29]			

approach employs frequency domain analysis of acquired images. Images are sliced into a number of one-dimensional quasi-sinusoidal time-bound waveforms. Each time-bound waveform corresponds to a row of the original image. The periodic signal derives from the interposition of ridges and valleys; the signal is prominent when the acquired image row is orthogonal to the local ridge orientation. Frequency domain analysis can be performed by Fourier or wavelet analysis [28, 37]. In either approach, the goal is to quantify waveform changes due to temporal changes in the quantity of sweat present of the finger surface. As the quantity of perspiration changes rapidly over time, both static and dynamic waveform changes are sought. The approach has proven to be viable in the testing performed at the Biomedical Signal Analysis Laboratory at West Virginia University.

Several spoof detection approaches based on additional hardware are currently being researched. Although few approaches have become commercial products, they all give positive results against some types of spoofs. (A commercially available spoof detection method is discussed in detail in Section 20.3 below.) One approach uses skin absorbance and reflection profiles [38]. Skin cells and red blood cells flowing through capillaries contain active dipoles. Although soft materials, like gelatin, might have reflectivity similar to skin, it is difficult to replicate the spectral absorption profile of living human skin. Skin temperature has also been used as a discriminating, though limited, property that can be used to detect a spoof [6]. Although most soft material artificial fingers can be worn on a real finger, the material interface between finger and sensor is enough to dissipate part of the surface heat and work as partial thermal insulator, resulting in lower-than-physiological temperature detected at the sensor [6]. The heartbeat is transmitted through the vascular system up to the capillary bed of vascular periphery; therefore pulse can be detected in fingertips and can be used as a sign of vitality. As with any other discriminating approach that uses physiological signs, pulse detection as spoof detection is limited by inter-personal variance in rest heart beat. Moreover, physiological and pathological conditions can significantly vary the heart rate of an individual or from person to person [39]. Related to pulse detection is the use of pulse oximetry. Hemoglobin has a differential absorbance, at particular wavelengths, as a function of its oxygen saturation. The absorption profile also has a pulsating component due to heartbeat [39]. Several other physiological characteristics have been proposed for spoof discrimination: skin electric resistance [6], dielectric permittivity [6, 7], and ultrasonic detection of dermal structures [6, 12]. Further studies are required to confirm that the above approaches have potential for introduction into the biometric market.

20.2.2 Iris

Iris recognition is based on discriminating the fine structure of the textured area of the eye that surrounds the pupil. Most commercial iris sensors collect a digital image of the eye using a silicon imager and near-infrared or visible illumination. One of the most common commercial implementations of an iris feature extractor and matcher generates binary templates based on the phase of a Gabor decomposition of a series of concentric annular rings within the iris [40, 41]. The degree of correspondence of two such binary templates forms the basis of the determination of biometric match.

A straightforward method that has been used to spoof an iris sensor is based on a high-quality photograph of the eye [14]. In one study [34], three different commercial iris sensors were examined for their ability to discriminate against such photographic spoofs. Images of an iris were generated from the data collected from one of the three sensors as well as from an image generated by a digital microscope. Both of these images were printed on mat paper using a standard laser jet printer. After the pupil regions of the images were cut out, each image was presented to each of the tested sensors in both enrollment and verification modes. Although the rate of spoof acceptance differed considerably by device and condition (enroll or verify, image from microscope or from an iris sensor), acceptance levels were significant and approached 100% under certain conditions. Another method used to successfully spoof some iris sensors is to use a contact lens on which an iris pattern is printed [42]. Even more sophisticated, multilayered and three-dimensional artificial irises may also be produced to spoof a sensor [43].

Iris spoof detection may be accomplished in a variety of ways. Mathematical interrogation of the fine texture of the iris image using Fourier analysis may be employed to detect and discriminate against the dot matrix pattern of many common printing processes [44]. Figure 20.2 shows images of a real and fake iris and their associated Fourier spectrum. The unique optical effects of the iris and/or other parts of the eye may be analyzed [45]. Involuntary motions of the pupil at rest ("hippus") or in reaction to changing ambient light conditions may be checked to determine if a live eye is in the sensor's field of view [46]. In addition, challenge-response transactions may be implemented wherein the person under test is asked to blink or move their eyes in a certain direction to ensure that the random instructions are carried out properly [47].

20.2.3 Face

Commercial facial recognition systems most often are based on digital images collected using visible or near-infrared light. These systems can be broadly divided into two categories: 2-dimensional (2D) and 3-dimensional (3D) facial recognition. 2D systems are those that collect and process a single two-dimensional image of the face. 3D facial recognition systems use various techniques such as patterned illumination light or paraxial viewing to develop a 3D representation of the face.

The form and degree of susceptibility to spoof attempts of facial recognition systems from different manufacturers varies widely. The 2D facial recognition systems with the simplest forms of spoof detection have been shown to be able to be spoofed using a simple photograph of the enrolled person's face,

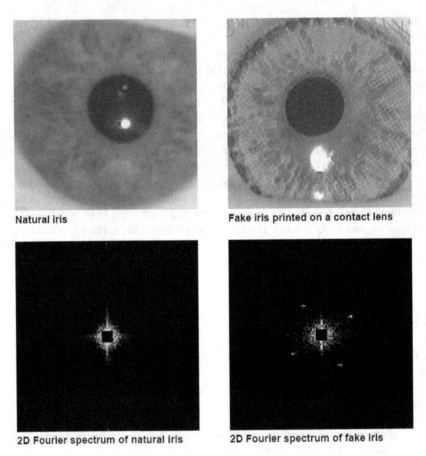

Natural iris

Fake iris printed on a contact lens

2D Fourier spectrum of natural iris

2D Fourier spectrum of fake iris

Fig. 20.2. Images of a real and fake iris and their associated Fourier spectra [44].

which may be displayed as a photographic hardcopy or on a laptop monitor [14]. Some poorly-designed facial recognition systems have even been shown to be susceptible to accepting very crude line drawings of a human face [16]. An effective means to guard against spoofs based on a static image of a face relies on the detection of motion of the facial image such as the blinking of eyes and the small, involuntary movements of parts of the face and head. However, this method of spoof detection is still subject to being fooled fairly easily by using a laptop to display a short video of the authentic user to the facial recognition system [14].

A very specific weakness is the potential for identical twins to be authorized interchangeably by a facial recognition system. One commercial vendor claims to be able to eliminate this ambiguity by performing an analysis of the random features associated with the surface texture of the skin [48]. Thermal images of the face are also reported to be able to provide sufficient information to distinguish between identical twins [49]. In a similar way, Fourier analysis has been shown to differentiate between live faces and certain types of spoofs based on the fine structure of the face [50].

Facial recognition systems based on 3D sensing have an additional protection against spoof attempts since the requisite spoof would have to be three dimensional and thereby somewhat more difficult to fabricate than a 2D spoof. However, such spoofs have been fabricated and successfully used to defeat commercial systems [51]. A variety of challenge-response methods have been described in the literature for facial spoof detection. One commercial system had a challenge-response method implemented that directed the user to blink, smile or frown while video images of the face were being collected [52]. The system analyzed the resulting video sequence to ensure that the proper response was provided at the proper time, ensuring the authenticity of the subject. Another form of challenge response incorporated in a commercial system relies on the user properly repeating a set of randomly generated phrases [13].

Finally, a number of different methods have been proposed to measure various optical qualities of skin to ensure that the object in front of the biometric sensor is a live human face [53]. These properties include optical absorption, reflection, scattering, and refraction under different illumination wavelengths.

20.3 Fingerprint Case Study

An optical fingerprint sensor based on multispectral imaging (MSI) has recently been introduced by Lumidigm as a commercial product called the J110. This sensor is configured to image both the surface and subsurface characteristics of the finger under a variety of optical conditions. The combination of surface and subsurface imaging ensures that usable biometric data can be taken across a wide range of environmental and physiological conditions. Bright ambient lighting, wetness, poor contact between the finger and sensor, dry skin, and various topical contaminants present little impediment to collecting usable MSI data. Moreover, the ability of the MSI sensor to measure the optical characteristics of the skin below the surface allows strong discrimination between living human skin and spoofs. An overview of skin histology, the MSI principles of operation, and procedures and results from a spoof study performed with the J110 follow.

20.3.1 Finger Skin Histology

Human skin is a complex organ that forms the interface between the person and the outside environment. The skin contains receptors for the nervous system, blood vessels to nourish the cells, sweat glands to aid thermal regulation, sebaceous glands for oil secretion, hair follicles, and many other elements. As well, the skin itself is not a single, homogeneous layer, but is made of different

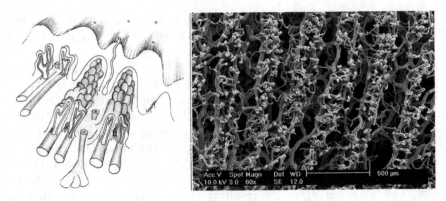

Fig. 20.3. Histology of the skin on the palmar surface of the fingertip. The sketch on the left shows the pattern of the capillary tufts and dermal papillae that lie below the fingerprint ridges. The scanning electron microscope (SEM) photo on the right side shows the rows of capillary tufts imaged from a portion of an excised thumb after the surrounding skin has been removed [56].

layers with different material properties. These layers can be broadly separated into the epidermis, which is the most superficial layer; the dermis, which is the blood-bearing layer; and the subcutaneous skin layer, which contains fat and other relatively inert components.

The skin on the palmar side of the finger tips contains dermatoglyphic patterns comprising the ridges and valleys commonly measured for fingerprint-based biometrics. Importantly, these patterns do not exist solely on the surface of the skin - many of the anatomical structures *below the surface* of the skin mimic the surface patterns. For example, the interface between the epidermal and dermal layers of skin is an undulating layer made of multiple protrusions of the dermis into the epidermis known as dermal papillae. These papillae follow the shape of the surface dermatoglyphic patterns [54] and thus represent an internal fingerprint in the same form as the external pattern. Small blood vessels known as capillaries protrude into the dermal papillae [55] as shown in Figure 20.3. These blood vessels form another representation of the external fingerprint pattern.

There are various methods that can be used to image the internal structure of the skin of the finger. One method is the use of optics. Recently published research demonstrated the use of optical coherence tomography to investigate features of the finger skin below the ridges and valleys [57]. This research showed that there is a distinct area of high reflectivity (at 850 nm) in the skin approximately 500 μm below each finger ridge and, furthermore, that this subsurface pattern continued to exist even when the surface pattern was deformed by application of pressure or obscured by a wrinkle in the skin. Multispectral imaging is another optical method that can be used to capture surface and subsurface features of the skin. The following section describes one optical configuration used in a commercial MSI sensor.

20.3.2 Multispectral Imaging Principles of Operation

In order to capture information-rich data about the surface and subsurface features of the skin of the finger, the MSI sensor collects multiple images of the finger under a variety of optical conditions. The raw images are captured using different wavelengths of illumination light, different polarization conditions, and different illumination orientations. In this manner, each of the raw images contains somewhat different and complementary information about the finger. The different wavelengths penetrate the skin to different depths and are absorbed differently by various chemical components of the skin. The different polarization conditions change the degree of contribution of surface and subsurface features to the raw image. Finally, different illumination orientations change the location and degree to which surface features are accentuated.

Figure 20.4 shows a simplified schematic of the major optical components of an MSI fingerprint sensor. Illumination for each of the multiple raw images is generated by one of the light emitting diodes (LEDs). The figure illustrates the case of polarized, direct illumination being used to collect a raw image. The light from the lower right LED passes through a linear polarizer before illuminating the finger as it rests on the sensor platen. Light interacts with the finger and a portion of the light is directed toward the imager through the imaging polarizer. The imaging polarizer is oriented with its optical axis to be orthogonal to the axis of the illumination polarizer, such that light with the same polarization as the illumination light is substantially attenuated by the polarizer. This severely reduces the influence of light reflected from the surface of the skin and emphasizes light that has undergone multiple optical scattering events after penetrating the skin.

A second direct illumination LED shown in Figure 20.4 does not have a polarizer placed in the illumination path. When this LED is illuminated, the light is randomly polarized. In this case the surface-reflected light and the deeply penetrating light are both able to pass through the imaging polarizer in equal proportions. As such, the image produced from this non-polarized LED contains a much stronger influence from surface features of the finger. Importantly, all of these direct illumination sources (both polarized and non-polarized) as well as the imaging system are arranged to avoid any critical-angle phenomena at the platen-air interfaces. In this way, each illuminator is certain to illuminate the finger and the imager is certain to image the finger regardless of whether the skin is dry, dirty or even in contact with the sensor. This aspect of the MSI imager is distinctly different from most other conventional fingerprint imaging technologies and is a key aspect of the robustness of the MSI methodology.

In addition to the direct illumination illustrated in Figure 20.4, the MSI sensor also integrates a form of TIR imaging, illustrated in Figure 20.5. In

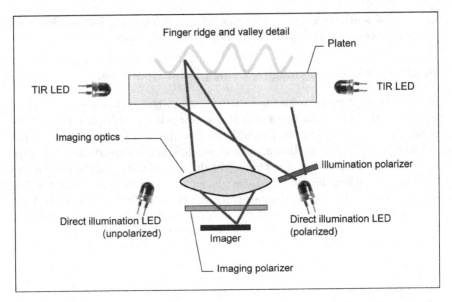

Fig. 20.4. Optical configuration of an MSI sensor. The thick lines illustrate the direct illumination of a finger by a polarized LED.

this illumination mode, one or more LEDs illuminate the side of the platen. A portion of the illumination light propagates through the platen by making multiple TIR reflections at the platen-air interfaces. At points where the TIR is broken by contact with the skin, light enters the skin and is diffusely reflected. A portion of this diffusely reflected light is directed toward the imaging system and passes through the imaging polarizer (since this light is randomly polarized), forming an image for this illumination state. Unlike all of the direct illumination states, the quality of the TIR image is critically dependent on having skin of sufficient moisture content and cleanliness making good optical contact with the platen, just as is the case with conventional TIR sensors. However, unlike conventional TIR sensors, the MSI sensor is able to form a useable representation of the fingerprint from the direct illumination images even when the TIR image is degraded or missing.

In practice, MSI sensors typically contain multiple direct-illumination LEDs of different wavelengths. For example, the Lumidigm J110 MSI sensor is an industrial-grade sensor that has four direct-illumination wavelength bands (430, 530, and 630 nm as well as a white light) in both polarized and unpolarized configurations. When a finger is placed on the sensor platen, 8 direct-illumination images are captured along with a single TIR image. The raw images are captured on a 640 x 480 image array with a pixel resolution of 525 ppi. All 9 images are captured in approximately 500 mSec. In addition to the optical system, the Lumidigm J110 comprises control electronics for the imager and illumination components, an embedded processor, memory,

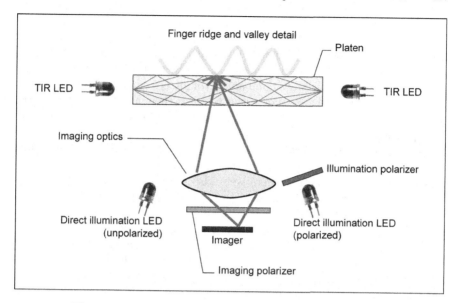

Fig. 20.5. MSI sensor schematic showing TIR illumination.

power conversion electronics, and interface circuitry. The embedded processor performs the capture and communicates to the rest of the biometric system through the interface circuitry. In addition to controlling the image acquisition process and communications, the embedded processor is capable of processing the 9 raw images to extract and synthesize a single 8-bit fingerprint image from the raw data. The embedded processor also analyzes the raw MSI data to ensure that the sample being imaged is a genuine human finger rather than an artificial or spoof material. Fingerprint image synthesis and spoof detection will be described in greater detail in the following sections. In some applications, the J110 is configured to perform on-board feature extraction and matching.

20.3.3 MSI Spoof Testing

To rigorously test the spoof detection abilities of the Lumidigm J110 multi-spectral imaging system, a large study was conducted using a representative population of human volunteers and a large assortment of spoof samples. Three Lumidigm J110 sensors were deployed in the study in which 118 people were recruited to participate. The study duration was three weeks long, during which time the volunteers made multiple visits. Volunteers were divided roughly evenly between males and females. The ages ranged between 18 and over 80 years old. Volunteers were not prescreened for any particular characteristic and the demographic distribution of the volunteers participating in the study generally reflected the local (Albuquerque, New Mexico) population.

All fingers (i.e., index, middle, ring, and little finger) of the right hand of each volunteer were measured multiple times throughout the study. The first three presentations of a particular finger on the first J110 sensor were used as enrollment data against which data taken on all other sensors and during subsequent visits were compared. Volunteers came "as they were" to each study session and were not asked to wash their hands or pre-treat the finger skin in any way. Spoof samples comprised all spoof types described in the open literature as well as some additional sample types. A total of 49 types of spoofs were collected. Latex, silicone, Play-Doh, clay, rubber, glue, resin, gelatin, and tape were used in various colors, concentrations, and thicknesses. Multiple prosthetic fingers were also used. Each of the transparent and semitransparent spoof samples were tested in conjunction with each of the volunteers' index fingers. The spoof sample was placed on top of the volunteer's finger prior to touching the sensor and collecting the MSI data. A total of 17,454 images were taken on the volunteers' real fingers and 27,486 spoof images were collected. For each class of spoof, between 40 and 1940 samples were collected. Transparent spoofs worn by the volunteers' fingers resulted in an order of magnitude more samples than opaque spoofs.

Each image was processed using wavelets to create features based on the spectral and textural information available. A variant of Fisher's linear discriminant was used to create eight features for classification. For testing, the difference between the squared Euclidian distance to the spoof and person class means was used to calculate the error trade-off of correctly classifying a subject and misclassifying a spoof. The results are shown in Figure 20.6, which is an ROC curve similar to those used to describe biometric matching performance over a range of operating points. In this case, the TAR is the rate at which a measurement taken on a genuine person is properly classified as a genuine sample. As such, this is a metric for the convenience of the spoof detection method as seen by an authorized user.

The FAR describes the rate at which a spoof is falsely classified as genuine. This rate provides a metric for the degree of security against spoofs provided by the system at a particular operating point. The security and convenience of this spoof detection system trade off in the same way as in the case of biometric matching: a greater TAR can be achieved at the expense of a reduction in spoof detection and vice versa. One possible operating point is where the decision criteria are set to provide a TAR of 99.5% and the resulting overall spoof FAR is approximately 0.9%. Further analysis showed that at this operating point many spoof samples were never accepted as genuine and no single class of spoof had an FAR greater than 15%. This demonstrates that a very strong form of spoof detection can be implemented with an MSI sensor with minimal adverse impact to the genuine user.

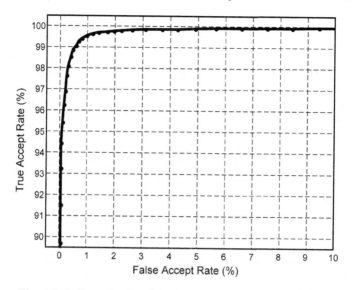

Fig. 20.6. Error trade-off for multispectral spoof detection.

20.4 Conclusion

From the pioneering fake biometric production attempts by Albert Wehde to the modern use of painted contact lenses and polymeric fake fingers, the art of attacking a biometric system has become more complex. In parallel, devising countermeasures to secure biometric systems has witnessed giant leaps in both academia and industry. Much has been learned from research work that has hypothesized how attacks can be performed. It is arguable that there is a significant imbalance in data derived from research work versus data from real world scenarios. Those who are entrusted with securing biometric systems lie awake at night wondering what the next attack methodology will be. What has been overlooked? Are systems adequately protected against yet unknown fake biometrics? How resilient are anti-spoofing approaches to attacks that significantly differ from the known methodologies? For the known fake biometric attacks, we can positively conclude that success has been achieved with various techniques. As shown in Section 20.3, multispectral imaging technology is a powerful instrument in the detection of known fingerprint spoofs and shows promising results in securing against yet unknown fake devices. As biometric access control permeates our everyday lives, spoofing attempts and anti-spoofing research will co-evolve. Further research is welcome in the area of anti-spoofing performance measurement, as is the development of vendor-independent measurement of performance.

References

1. J. Wayman, A. Jain, D. Maltoni, and D. Maio. Biometric Systems: Technology, Design and Performance Evaluation Springer. 2005.
2. I. R. Buhan, P. H. Hartel. The state of the art in abuse of biometrics: Centre for Telematics and Information Technology, University of Twente, Enschede. 2005.
3. International Biometric Group. Spoof 2007 - High-Level Test Plan. New York, NY. 2006.
4. M. Sandström. Liveness Detection in Fingerprint Recognition systems. Linköpings Universitet: Linköping, Sweden. 2004.
5. S. A. Cole. Suspect Identities - A History of Fingerprinting and Criminal Identification. Cambridge, MA: Harvard University Press. 2001.
6. T. Van der Putte, J. Keuning. Biometrical fingerprint recognition: don't get your fingers burned. IFIP TC8/WG88 Fourth Working Conference on Smart Card Research and Advanced Applications: Kluwer Academic; 2000. p. 289-303.
7. T. Matsumoto, H. Matsumoto, K. Yamada, S. Hoshino. Impact of artificial gummy fingers on fingerprint systems. Proc SPIE, 4677:275-89, 2002.
8. S. T. V. Parthasaradhi. Comparison of Classification methods for perspiration based liveness algorithm. West Virginia University: Morgantown, West Virginia. 2003.
9. S. Schuckers, R. Derakhshani, S. Parthasardhi, L. Hornak. Liveness Detection in Biometric Devices. Electrical Engineering Handbook. 3rd ed. CRC Press. 2005.
10. S. T. V. Parthasaradhi, R. Derakhshani, L. A. Hornak, S. A. C. Schuckers. Time-series detection of perspiration as a liveness test in fingerprint devices. Systems, Man and Cybernetics, Part C, IEEE Transactions on, 35(3):335-43, 2005.
11. A. Wehde, J. N. Beffel. Finger-Prints can be forged. Chicago: Tremonia Publish Co. 1924.
12. D. Maltoni, D. Maio, A. K. Jain, S. Prabhakar. Handbook of Fingerprint Recognition: Springer. 2003.
13. S. Schuckers. Spoofing and Anti-Spoofing Measures. Information Security Technical Report, 7(4):56-62, 2002.
14. L. Thalheim, J. Krissler, P.-M. Ziegler. Body Check: Biometric Access Protection Devices and their Programs Put to the Test. Heise Online. November 2002.
15. Lumidigm. J-Series Multispectral Fingerprint Sensors. Albuquerque, NM. 2006.
16. M. Lewis, P. Statham. CESG Biometric Security Capabilities Programme: Method, Results and Research Challenges. Biometrics Consortium Conference. Arlington, Virginia. 2004.
17. A. Wiehe, T. Søndrol, O. K. Olsen, F. Skarderud. Attacking Fingerprint Sensors. Gjøvik University College. 2004.

18. PhysOrg.com. Biometric expert shows an easy way to spoof fingerprint scanning devices. 2005.

19. J. Leyden. Biometric sensors beaten senseless in tests. The Register. May 23, 2002.

20. V. A. Grønland, H. Hasli, J. F. Pettersen. Challenging fingerprint scanner: NISLAB Authentication Laboratory, Gjøvik University College. 2005.

21. D. Rutter. Thinking Putty defeats Biometric Fingerprint Scanners! www.dansdata.com. 2007.

22. B. Schneier. Biometrics: Truths and Fictions. Crypto-Gram Newsletter. 1998.

23. A. Kaseva, A. Stén. Fooling Fingerprint Scanners: Biometric Vulnerabilities of the Precise Biometrics 100 SC Scanner. Helsinki University of Technology. 2003.

24. J. Leyden. Gummi bears defeat fingerprint sensors. The Register. May 16, 2002.

25. D. Rutter. Review: DigitalPersona U.are.U Personal fingerprint scanner. www.dansdata.com. 2002.

26. D. Willis, M. Lee. Six Biometric Devices Point The Finger At Security. Network Computing. 1998.

27. A. Ligon. An Investigation into the Vulnerability of the Siemens ID Mouse Professional Version 4. 2002.

28. R. Derakhshani, S. Schuckers, L. Hornak, L. O. Gorman. Determination of Vitality from A Non-Invasive Biomedical Measurement for Use in Fingerprint Scanners. Pattern Recognition Journal, 36(2):383-96, 2003.

29. FIDIS Consortium. Forensic Implications of Identity Management Systems. 2006.

30. H. Gravnås. Biometric Authentication: Is it a threat to take the end-users for granted? Gjøvik University College. 2005.

31. J. Blommé. Evaluation of biometric security systems against artificial fingers. Linköpings Universitet: Linköping, Sweden. 2003.

32. H. Kang, B. Lee, H. Kim, D. Shin, J. Kim. A Study on Performance Evaluation of the Liveness Detection for Various Fingerprint Sensor Modules. Lecture Notes in Computer Science, Volume 2774/2003:1245-53, 2003.

33. Chaos Computer Club. How to fake fingerprints? www.ccc.de. 2004.

34. T. Matsumoto. Gummy Fingers and Paper Iris: An Update. The 2004 Workshop on Information Security Research: Yokohama National University. 2004.

35. D. C. Hitchcock. Evaluation and Combination of Biometric Authentication Systems. University of Florida. 2003.

36. InterNational Committee for Information Technology Standards. Study Report on Biometrics in E-Authentication. Washington, DC: Information Technology Industry Council. 2006.

37. A. S. Abhyankar, S. C. Schuckers. A wavelet-based approach to detecting liveness in fingerprint scanners. A. K. Jain, N. K. Ratha, editors. SPIE. 2004. p. 278-86.

38. R. K. Rowe. Multispectral Fingerprint Sensors. Biometric Consortium Conference. Arlington, Virginia USA. 2005.
39. P. Lapsley, J. Less, J. DF Pare, N. Hoffman, inventors; SmartTouch, LLC, assignee. Anti-Fraud Biometric Sensor that Accurately Detects Blood Flow. 1998.
40. J. Daugman, inventor Biometric Personal Identification System Based on Iris Analysis. US patent 5,291,560. 1994.
41. J. Daugman. How Iris Recognition Works. IEEE Transactions on Circuits and Systems for Video Technology, 14(1):21-30, 2004.
42. U. C. von Seelen. Countermeasures Against Iris Spoofing with Contact Lenses. Biometrics Consortium Conference. Arlington, VA. 2005.
43. A. Lefohn, B. Budge, P. Shirley, R. Caruso, E. Reinhard. An ocularist's approach to human iris synthesis. Computer Graphics and Applications, IEEE, 23(6):70-5, 2003.
44. A. K. Jain, R. Bolle and S. Pankanti (Eds.), BIOMETRICS: Personal Identification in Networked society, Kluwer Academic Publishers, 1999.
45. findBiometrics.com. Interview with Dr. John Daugman, Cambridge University. 2004.
46. J. Daugman. Liveness Detection Countermeasures. University of Cambridge. 2005.
47. A. A. Ross, K. Nandakumar, A. K. Jain. Handbook of Multibiometrics Springer. 2006.
48. D. Sarkar. Identix integrating state-of-the-art skin and facial recognition technology. Federal Computer Week. 2004.
49. F. J. Prokoski, R. B. Riedel. Infrared identification of faces and body parts. A. K. Jain, R. Bolle, S. Pankanti, editors. Biometrics: Personal Identification in Networked Society, International Series in Engineering and Computer Science. Kluwer. 1999. p. 191-212.
50. J. Li, Y. Wang, T. Tan, A. K. Jain. Biometric Technology for Human Identification. In: A. K. Jain, N. K. Ratha, editors. SPIE; 2004. p. 296-303.
51. T. Fladsrud. Face Recognition in a Border Control Environment. Gjøvik University College. 2005.
52. European Commission BioSecure Project. Biometrics for Secure Authentication. 2005.
53. G. Parziale, J. Dittmann, M. Tistarelli. Analysis and evaluation of alternatives and advanced solutions for system elements: BioSecure. 2005.
54. H. Cummins, C. Midlo. Fingerprints, Palms and Soles: An Introduction to Dermatoglyphics. New York: Dover Publications Inc. 1961.
55. S. Sangiorgi, A. Manelli, T. Congiu, A. Bini, G. Pilato, M. Reguzzoni, et al. Microvascularization of the human digit as studied by corrosion casting. Journal of Anatomy, 204 (2):123-31, 2004.
56. S. Sangiorgi. Personal Communication with Matthew Ennis, PhD, Lumidigm. 2005.

57. A. Shiratsuki, E. Sano, M. Shikai, T. Nakashima, T. Takashima, M. Ohmi, et al. Novel optical fingerprint sensor utilizing optical characteristics of skin tissue under fingerprints. International Society for Optical Engineering, Proceedings of SPIE, 5686:80-7, 2005.

Linkages between Biometrics and Forensic Science

Damien Dessimoz and Christophe Champod

Forensic Science Institute, School of Criminal Sciences, Batochime - Quartier Sorge, University of Lausanne, 1015 Lausanne-Dorigny, Switzerland.
{damien.dessimoz, christophe.champod}@unil.ch

21.1 Forensic science and biometrics - a general contrast

Using biometric data for classification and/or identification in forensic science dates back to the turn of the 20th century. Biometrics as we know it today can be viewed as extension of Bertillon's anthropometric approach, benefiting from automation and the use of additional features. This chapter presents a historical and technical overview of the development and the evolution of forensic biometric systems, used initially manually and then in a semi-automatic way. Before focusing on specific forensic fields, we will define the area, its terminology and draw distinctions between forensic science and biometrics.

Forensic science refers to the applications of scientific principles and technical methods to an investigation in relation to criminal activities, in order to establish the existence of a crime, to determine the identity of its perpetrator(s) and their modus operandi. It is thus logical that this area was a fertile ground for the use of physiological or behavioral data to sort and potentially individualize protagonists involved in offences. Although manual classification of physical measures (anthropometry), and of physical traces left and recovered from crime scenes (fingermarks, earmarks,...) was largely successful, an automatic approach was needed to facilitate and to speed up the retrieval of promising candidates in large databases. Even if the term *biometrics* usually refers "to identifying an individual based on his or her distinguishing characteristics" [14], biometric systems in forensic science today aim at filtering potential candidates and putting forward candidates for further 1-to-1 verification by a forensic specialist trained in that discipline, in the following traditional typical *cases* (here exemplified using fingerprints):

Case 1: A biometric set of features in question coming from an unknown individual (living or dead), is searched against a reference set of known (or declared as such) individuals. In the fingerprint domain, we can think of a ten-print to ten-print search based on features obtained from a ten-print card (holding potentially both rolled and flap inked impression from fingers and palms), compared to a database of ten-print cards.

Case 2: An unknown biometric set of features left in circumstances of interest to an investigation, is searched against a reference set of known (or declared as such) individuals based on the features available. We can think of a fingermark recovered from a crime scene that will be searched against a database of ten-print cards. The converse is also possible, meaning the search of the features from a new ten-print card against the database of (unresolved) fingermarks.

Case 3: An unknown to unknown comparison resulting in the possible detection of series of relevant incidents. For fingerprints, it would mean comparing latent prints to latent prints.

Both *case 2* and *case 3* involve biometric features (in physical or other forms) that can be left on scenes relevant to an investigation. In forensic investigation, one of the main objectives is to find marks associating an offender to an event under investigation. These marks can be either left by the perpetrator during the event or found on the perpetrator after it. This mechanism of "exchange" of marks is known under the misnomer of "Locard's exchange principle" in reference to the French criminalist Edmond Locard [59]. Forensic information can be found either as *physical* marks, or as *digital* traces. Physical mark are made for example by the apposition of fingers, ears or feet on any kind of surfaces, while digital traces are analog or digital recordings typically from phone-tapping and security cameras. Face and speech biometrics, and to some extent modalities captured at distance such as ear, iris and gait can be used as digital traces in forensic science.

As a **first distinction** between biometrics and forensic science, it is important to stress that forensic biometric systems are used in practice as sorting devices without any embedded decision mechanism on the truthfulness of the identification (although we do see some developments in that direction). Indeed, the search algorithms are deployed as sorting devices. These ranking tools allow (at an average known rate of efficiency) presenting the user a short list (generally 15 to 20) containing potentially the right "candidate" to a defined query. Here the term "candidate" refers to the result of a search against biometric features originating from either individuals or marks (known or unknown). It is then the duty of the forensic specialist to examine each candidate from the list as if that candidate was submitted through the regular channels of a police inquiry. This first contrast shows that forensic biometric systems are considered by forensic scientists as external to the inferential process that will follow.

The **second distinction** lies in the terminology, performance measures and reported conclusions used in the processes. Although forensic biometric systems can be used in both *verification* (one to one) or *identification* modes (one to many), depending on the circumstances of the case, the identification mode can be seen as a series of verification tasks. The reported conclusion by the forensic specialist when comparing an unknown to a known entry can take different forms depending on the area considered.

In the fingerprint field, conclusions can take three states: *individualization, exclusion* or *inconclusive* (for a more detailed discussion see [20]). The first two are categorical conclusions accounting for all possible entities on the Earth. In other words an individualization of a finger mark is a statement that associates that mark to its designated source to the exclusion of all other fingers or more generally all other friction ridge skin formations. Individualization is often presented as the distinguishing factor between forensic science and other scientific classification and identification tasks [50].

In the fields of face or ear recognition carried out manually by skilled examniers, speaker verification based on phonetic/linguistic analysis, dental analysis or handwriting examination, the three conclusions described above will remain under the same definition, but probabilistic conclusions will also be allowed on a grading scale both in favor or against identity of sources with qualifiers such as: *possible, probable* or *very likely*. For a discussion of the adequacy of the scale in forensic decision making refer to [21].

The principles and protocols regarding how these conclusions (outside the DNA area) can be reached by a trained and competent examiner is outside our scope. However, the general principles of the inference of identity of sources are treated in detail by Kwan [55] or by Champod et al. (for fingerprints) [25]. In all these areas, based on different features, the expert subjectively weighs the similarities and dissimilarities to reach his/her conclusion. Nowadays the reliability of these so-called "subjective disciplines" are being increasingly challenged, especially because of (*i*) the development of evidence based on DNA profiles governed by hard data and (*ii*) the evolving requirements for the admissibility of evidence following the Daubert decision by the Supreme Court of the USA[1]. The absence of underpinning statistical data in the classic identification fields is viewed as a main pitfall that requires a paradigm shift [81].

In the field of DNA, the strength of evidence is indeed generally expressed statistically using case specific calculations [97] linked to a likelihood ratio (defined later). In essence the process is probabilistic although we do see some tendencies to remove uncertainty from the debate [18].

It is our opinion that inferences of sources across all forensic identification fields, when put forward to a factfinder in court for example, must be approached within a probabilistic framework even in areas that had been traditionally presented through categorical opinions such as fingerprints [20]. An approach based on the concept of *likelihood ratio* should be promoted. In-

---

[1] Daubert v Merrell Dow Pharmaceuticals 43 F 3d 1311; 125 L Ed (2d) 469; 509 US 579; 113 S Ct 2786 (1993).

deed, a likelihood ratio (LR) is a statistical measure that offers a balanced presentation of the strength of the evidence [78]. It is especially suitable for assessing the contribution of forensic findings in a fair and balanced way [2]. Note that we restrict our analysis to an evaluative context, meaning that the forensic findings may be used as evidence against a defendant in court. There is a wide scope of application of biometric systems in investigative mode (e.g. surveillance) that we will not cover.

Formally, the LR can be defined as follows:

$$LR = \frac{p(E \mid S, I)}{p(E \mid \bar{S}, I)} \tag{21.1}$$

Where:

E: Result of the comparison (set of concordances and discordances or a similarity measure such as a score) between the biometric data from the unknown source and the biometric data from the putative source.
S: The putative source is truly the source of the unknown biometric features observed (also known as the prosecution proposition).
$\bar{S}$: Someone else, from a relevant population of potential donors, is truly the source of the unknown biometric features observed (also known as the defense proposition).
I: Relevant background information about the case such as information about the selection of the putative source and the nature of the relevant population of potential donors.

This LR measure forces the scientist to focus on the relevant question (the forensic findings) and to consider them in the light of a set of competing propositions. The weight of forensic findings is essentially a relative and conditional measure that helps to progress a case in one direction or the other depending on the magnitude of the likelihood ratio. When the numerator is close to 1, the LR is simply the reverse of the random match probability (RMP) in a specified population. In these cases, reporting the evidence through the RMP is adequate. However most biometric features suffer from within individual variability facing an assessment of the numerator on a case by case basis.

The performance measures for forensic science are obtained from the analysis of the distributions of the LRs in simulated cases with given S and $\bar{S}$. These distributions are studied using a specific plot (called Tippett plot) that shows one minus the cumulative distribution for respectively the LRs computed under S and the LRs computed under $\bar{S}$. These plots also allow study and comparison of the proportions of misleading evidence: the percentage of $LR < 1$ when the prosecution proposition S is true and the percentage of $LR > 1$ when the defense proposition $\bar{S}$ is true. These two rates of misleading results are defined as follows [67]:

RMED: Rate of misleading evidence in favor of the defense: among all *LR*s computed under the prosecution proposition *S*, proportion of *LR* below 1.

RMEP: Rate of misleading evidence in favor of the prosecution: among all *LR*s computed under the defense proposition $\bar{S}$, proportion of *LR* above 1.

Whereas a *LR* is a case-specific measure of the contribution of the forensic findings to the identity of sources, the Tippett plot and the associated rates (*RMED, RMEP*) provide global measures of the efficiency of a forensic biometric system. *LR* based measures are now regularly used in the forensic areas of speaker recognition [26, 33, 76], fingerprints [67, 66], and DNA [37]. That constitutes a major difference compared to standard global measures of biometric performances based on type I and type II error rates (e.g. Receiver Operating Characteristic (ROC) or Detection Error Tradeoff (DET) curves). For a discussion on the limitations associated with these traditional measures when used in legal proceedings, see [26].

The concept of identity of sources is essential and needs to be distinguished from the determination of civil identity (e.g. assigning the name of a donor to a recovered mark), from guidance as to the activities of the individual or its further unlawful nature. Forensic comparisons aim initially at providing scientific evidence to help address issues of identity of sources of two sets of biometric data; whether these data are coupled with personal information (such as name, date of birth or social security number) is irrelevant for the comparison process. From the result of this comparison and depending on the availability and quality of personal information, then inference as to the civil identity can be made if needed. Likewise there is a progression of inferences between the issue of identity of sources towards their alleged activities and offences. It is a hierarchical system of issues as described by Cook et al. [29]. The forensic biometric comparison process aims at handling source level issues as its primary task: the whole process is not about names or identity, but in relation to source attribution between two submitted sets of features (respectively from a source 1 and a source 2).

A **third distinction** lies in the wide range of *selectivity* of the biometric data that can be submitted due to varying quality of the material. Selectivity here can be seen as the discrimination power of the features, meaning the ability to allow a differentiation when they are coming from distinct sources. Some of the main modalities will be reviewed in the next sections but there is an all-encompassing phenomenon that goes across modalities in varying degrees. In the commission of a crime, contrary to usual biometric systems (for access control e.g.), it may not be possible to obtain high quality input biometric features - either for the template or transaction data. These biometric data are limited by numerous factors such as: the availability of the person and his/her level of cooperation, the invasiveness of the acquisition, the various objects and positions one can take or touch while a crime is being committed. The subjects make no effort to present their biometric data to the system in an ideal and controlled way. Hence, whether the biometric data is acquired directly from individuals (living or dead), from images (of individuals, part thereof or X-rays) or marks left by them following criminal activities, the quality of the material available for the biometric comparison process, and thus its selectivity, may vary drastically from case to case and so will the within-person variability. This loss of selectivity is illustrated in Figure 21.1. The overall performance of the system is largely influenced by the quality of the input data conditioned by the acquisition and environmental conditions as summarized in Table 21.1. These factors are common in all biometric deployments, but forensic scenarios tend to maximize their variability.

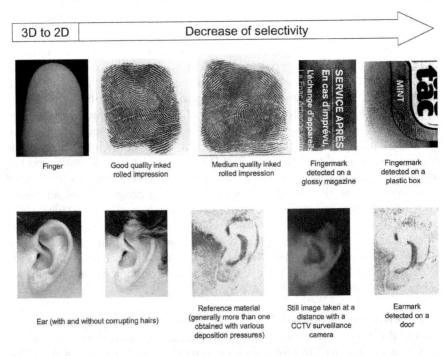

Fig. 21.1. Illustration of the diminishing selectivity of the biometric features as a function of the circumstances and conditions under which the biometric data are collected or obtained. Here is a clear relationship between selectivity and quality of the input information.

The **last distinction** we would like to stress upon is the range of comparisons that can be undertaken in the forensic environment depending on the circumstances of the cases. The three *cases* outlined initially all deal with

Acquisition conditions	Quality of the acquisition device (e.g. resolution). Amount of input information (e.g. a rolled inked fingerprint on a card versus a limited poorly developed fingermark on a curved surface). The availability of multiple templates (e.g. rolled and flap impressions of the same finger). The types of acquisition of both templates and transaction data (declared supervised versus covert). The acquisition at distance, the target size, the object movement, and the horizontal or vertical misalignments between the device and the subject. Presence of corrupting elements (e.g. glasses, beard, hair, clothes, or health condition - living or dead - of the subject). The time interval between the acquisitions of both sets of biometric material to be compared.
Environmental conditions	Background noise and uncontrolled conditions (e.g. illumination, noisy environment).
Data processing	The choice of the feature extraction algorithms and their level of automation (e.g. poor quality fingermarks may need to be manually processed by skilled operator in order to guide the system as to the relevant features). Efficiency of the detection and tracking algorithms (e.g. face detection and tracking). The matching algorithms in place and their hierarchy.
Operator	The operator interaction with the system at all stages (from acquisition to verification of candidates' lists).

Table 21.1. List of the factors affecting the selectivity of biometric information and thus the performances of biometric systems deployed in forensic applications.

comparisons of biometric information (with one side or the other being known) but at differing levels of selectivity. The driving force here is more the selectivity level associated with each compared biometric data sets, which can be similar (*case 1* and *case 3*) or largely different (*case 2*). The availability of known information, such as the name, the date of birth, the social security number (i.e. the *personal data* associated with each compared biometric data set), associated with the biometric features is not directly relevant to the comparison process. This information is although decisive to progress in the hierarchy, but has no impact on the decision of the identity of sources, which is driven by the selectivity of the compared biometric data. This progression is illustrated in Figure 21.2. The distinction between mark and reference material in a forensic case is that in general, marks are of lower quality than reference material (although the reverse could also be true). This concept of selectivity (Figures 21.1 and 21.2) that is driving the move from *case 1* to *case 3* is a continuum on both sides (source 1 and source 2). Essentially, we can expect performances to degrade as we move down in selectivity levels.

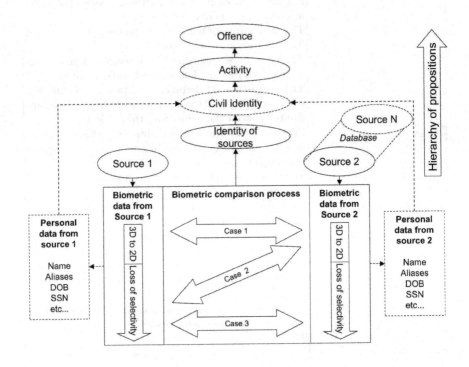

Fig. 21.2. General scheme of a forensic biometric system.

In the following sections we will cover the main forensic biometric modalities and then show how an automatic approach has and will change the conduct of forensic examinations.

21.2 Anthropometry

The abolition in 1832 of physical branding for habitual offenders in France resulted in legal authorities being incapable of recognizing them. The enforcement of new legislation allowing tougher sentences in cases of recidivism remained wishful thinking until the development of a proper identification system.

Some classifications, based on the declared name (not trustworthy) or the type of offence, were introduced, but without more than anecdotal success for obvious reasons. Identity documents or other official documents were not yet issued or, at the time, were prone to forgery. Even adding photography to the offender card did not solve the issue, because of the lack of standardization and the difficulty extracting commonly understood descriptors to include them in a manual retrieval system.

Facing this state of affairs, Bertillon proposed in 1881 a solution to the problem of the identification of recidivists based on anthropological methods developed by Quételet and Broca [12]. The principles were the following: (i) adult bone lengths remain constant, but (ii) vary from individuals to individuals and (iii) they can be measured with reasonable precision. A classification method was then required, in order to structure these distinctive characteristics. Indeed for Bertillon "The solution of the problem of forensic identification consisted less in the search for new distinctive elements of the individual than in the uncovering of a classification tool"[2]. He proposed the use of the description of the iris' color combined with eleven precise measurements.

These measurable characteristics (Figure 21.3) were divided into three classes (small, medium and large), defined arbitrarily by fixed intervals to ensure equal number of cards for each class, while the iris color was classified in seven classes (Figure 21.4).

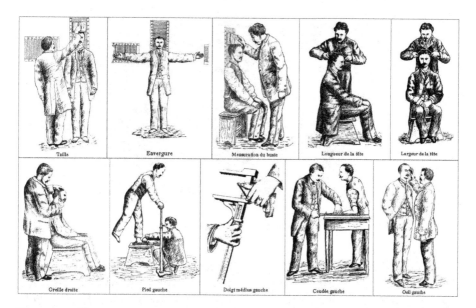

Fig. 21.3. Illustration of Bertillon's anthropometric measurements (adapted from [12]).

---

[2] Free translation from [12], for "La solution du problème de l'identification judiciaire consistait moins dans la recherche de nouveaux éléments caractéristiques de l'individu que dans la découverte d'un moyen de classification".

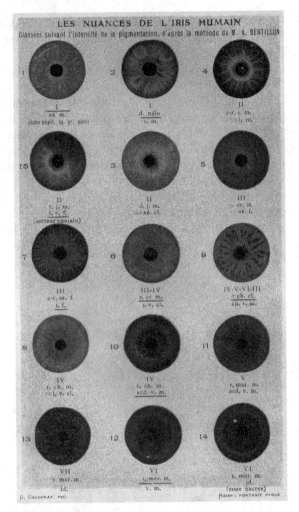

Fig. 21.4. Classification of the iris, classes are numbered I to VII (from [75]).

This classification method could allow theoretically up to 1,240,029 combinations ($3^{11} \times 7$). The measures taken on an arrested individual were registered onto an anthropometric card, together with the photograph, the name and a detailed description of peculiar marks, such as tattoos and scars. Each new card was then manually searched for one or more matches among the cards bearing identity (*case 1*). Bertillon established match criteria according to some tolerance values fixed by reference to variations recorded between operators. For instance, for ear measurements ±1mm was considered as an acceptable variation, ±2mm was a sign of divergence and ±4mm established non-identity (full criteria given in [58], p. 150-152).

It is important to stress that when among the known cards a match (within tolerance) with the unknown was found, the formal identification was only established following the examination of the photographs and the peculiar marks. In the same way that forensic biometric systems are used today, Bertillon's anthropometric approach was not an identification method per se. Indeed, Bertillon never claimed that the same set of measurements could not be shared by two different individuals [89]. It allowed the exclusion of potential candidates and acted as a powerful sorting system used to focus the attention of the investigators on a subset of cards deserving more attention, meaning a systematic analysis of the photographs and peculiar marks. Bertillon's approach was first deployed in 1882 and its efficiency proven by the considerable increase of the amount of habitual offenders identified through the assistance of the system: from 49 identifications in 1883, to 680 in 1892. This approach, recommended in 1885 for use in all French territory, attracted considerable attention abroad.

In parallel, Bertillon developed a standardized forensic photograph method, as well as a nomenclature for the description of the physiological features of the nose, the forehead and the ear, called "portrait parlé" or "spoken portrait" [11]. This standardized language offers description possibilities which can be used among police officers locally and internationally. Bertillon standardized photographic setup (focal distance, negative size, pose and illumination) and proposed taking two facial images, a frontal and a profile one, for each individual, noticing rightly that the profile image gave much more stable information for recognition than the frontal image [11]. Figure 21.5 presents the classification method for the ear, considered as the most identifying part of an individual, as proposed by Bertillon and taken up by Reiss [75]. The combination of the anthropometric method, the forensic photography and the spoken portrait was coined "Bertillonnage". Further bibliographical references to the work of Bertillon on anthropometry and its relationship with fingerprinting can be found in [24, 42].

A rapid spread of Bertillonnage was observed at the turn of the 20th Century across the police departments and penal institutions [28]. This deployment quickly highlighted the limitations of the technique: (i) uneven distributions of the measures in the population; (ii) the correlation between features; (iii) inter-operator variations due to lack of training, instrumentation or non-cooperative subjects and (iv) the need of the body and the absence of anthropometric "traces" left on crime scenes.

The deployment of forensic anthropometry was successful but carried out after careful, fit-for-purpose, evaluations. During the same period, fingerprinting started to gain recognition for the same purpose. Hence prominent individuals such as Galton in England, Vucetich in Argentina, or specific committees (Troup and Belper (England), Straton (India Colonial Gov.), Dastre (France)) were tasked to assess the merits of Bertillon's method and prepare

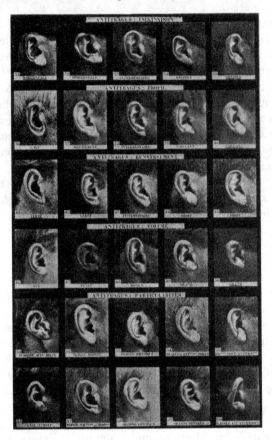

Fig. 21.5. Classification of the shapes of the ear, here the classification of the antitragus (from [75]).

recommendations for their government. The outcome of these assessments, although initially in favor of Anthropometry due to the lack of fully efficient large-scale classification systems for fingerprints, led to the progressive substitution of Bertillonnage by fingerprinting for the advantages that will be detailed in the next section. Even though Bertillon regarded fingerprints with skepticism as the right choice for classifying and searching individuals in large databases, he included them on his anthropometric cards in 1894, convinced of their value in identification as a complement to the individual distinctive marks (tatoos, scars, etc.) and was thrilled by the possibilities to identify offenders based on the fingermarks left at crime scenes. Bertillon is known for the first fingerprint identification in France (1902) based on fingermarks recovered on a murder scene [83].

21.3 Fingerprinting

21.3.1 Ten-print identification systems

Historically [10] the first classification attempt was proposed by Purkinje in 1823, who sorted the friction ridge flows into nine categories: *arch*, tented arch, two types of *loops*, four types of *whorl* and twinned *loop*, for description purposes and without realizing the identification potential of the friction ridge skin. Fifty years later, William Herschel, a colonial administrator in India, proposed fingerprints to identify individuals, while undertaking the first study of permanence (i.e. the fingerprint features do not change over time) [43]. At the same time, Henry Faulds, a medical missionary in Japan, proposed in 1880 to use fingerprints for investigative identification purposes, as fingermarks could be detected on crime scenes [35]. His important contribution remained largely undervalued by his peers.

The main forensic operational contribution came from the work of Galton [39]. He presented in 1892 the basic axioms of fingerprinting, which are the notion of permanence (based on Herschel's work and data), and uniqueness (Galton published the first statistical model on the fingerprint variability). He also mentioned the possibility to reliably classify fingerprints patterns into three basic patterns (*arches*, (inner and outer) *loops*, and *whorls*).

Note that the research on forensic fingerprinting concentrated first on its use as an identification system based on reasonable quality ten-print cards obtained from living or dead individuals (hence *case 1* only). The use of lower quality information (in *case 2* or *3*) from marks recovered on crime scenes, for example, was viewed as a beneficial side effect but without being approached systematically at the outset.

The first classification method proposed by Galton was judged unsuitable to handle large collections of individuals. The method was then drastically improved by Henry (helped by his Indian colleagues), who added a fourth group, called *composites* and refined ridge counting (for loops, the number of ridges crossed on an imaginary line between the core and the delta) and ridge tracing methods (relative positions - classified in three categories: inside, outside and meet - of the right delta relative to the core when ridges and furrows are followed from the left delta). The classification is achieved through a series of imbricated classifying features, namely primary, secondary and sub-secondary classifications and major and final divisions. The primary classification consists of a ratio: the numerator is related to the number of whorls and their position on the even numbered fingers, while the denominator is related to the whorls on the odd numbered fingers. The secondary classification is also a ratio giving the pattern type of the index fingers, as well as an indication of all tented arches, arches and radial loops in other fingers. The fingers of the right hand go into the numerator, while those of the left hand go into the denominator. The sub-secondary classification, the major and final divisions are subsidiary classifiers based on ridge counts or ridge tracing. This Galton-Henry classification largely gained acceptance for handling large databases such as the FBI central repository [91].

Almost simultaneously, Vucetich elaborated on Galton's proposal and offered a simpler method. General pattern main classification consisted of four basic patterns: *arches*, (internal and external) *loops* and *whorls*, organized in a ratio with a numerator devoted to the right hand and a denominator dealing with the left hand. As secondary classification, Vucetich divided each primary pattern into subclasses using ridge counts on loops and ridge tracing on whorls [96]. Vucetich's system proved very successful for small to medium sized databases.

Argentina adopted fingerprints (and Vucetich's classification method) as the sole method of identification of recidivists in 1896, while Great Britain (first in its overseas colonies) adopted Galton-Henry's system from 1897. In almost all agencies, fingerprint classifications were inspired from either one or the other original systems, but were adapted from country to country. Locard published an overview of the state of affairs in 1909 [58].

Standardization was a big issue already and had to wait until 1914 to see an uniform format for ten-prints cards: positioning of right hand fingers prints (from left to right beginning with the thumb) on a first line, left hand fingers (with the same fingers' order) on a second line, and controlled prints on the bottom of the ten-print card with two flat appositions of all the fingers (called *flaps*).

21.3.2 From ten-prints to single print manual searches

Telegraphic transmission of results of such classifications were not easy, hence 10 simple alphanumerical codes were developed for a 10-finger card. The most widely known is the codification of the National Crime Information Center (NCIC) dating back to 1967 based on the Galton-Henry classification. The NCIC code gives alphanumeric assignments from the right thumb (finger #1) to the left little finger (finger #10). This detailed NCIC fingerprint classification code was easily transferable between agencies and offered unprecedented efficiency to check if an unknown individual arrested in Washington DC could be known in Las Vegas (based on its NCIC classification).

These classification systems of fingerprints were above all, as the anthropometrical approach, sorting systems of full records obtained from the 10 fingers. These comparisons - known as ten-print to ten-print - were efficient only when the input data was complete (or almost). In other words, efficiency was achieved for *case 1*, but when input data consisted of, for example, a poor quality single mark recovered from a crime scene, the retrieval efficiency was more limited (when no suspect was available). Hence ten-print classification systems lacked efficiency for both *case 2* and *case 3*. The solution lay in the development of single-print classification systems (such as Battley [9]). They were very demanding in terms of manpower and "cold" searches against the database based on a single mark were still very costly in terms of time.

21.3.3 Development of AFIS systems

Automatic fingerprint processes are already presented in Chapter 2. This section will thus concentrate only on the first automation attempts as well as the specific standardization efforts in the area. The book by Komarinski serves as an introduction to forensic AFIS systems [52].

With the increase of ten-print card collections and the difficulties of single latent searches, the evolution of automatic (analogue or digital) retrieval processing systems took off in parallel with the technological advances. Manual systems were improved by the use of punch card retrieval systems, the addition of videofiles for images (Ampex bands) and in the late sixties the first efforts to digitize and automatically process fingerprint images were made. Several computer-based fingerprint comparison systems were developed concurrently in many countries and these initiatives laid down the basis of modern Automatic Fingerprint Identification Systems (AFIS). For example, in the United States, the Project SEARCH (System for Electronic Analysis and Retrieval of Criminal Histories) has been allowed to finance, coordinate, and supervise research projects in this area [36]. The National Bureau of Standards (now known as the National Institute of Standards and Technology NIST) and the FBI proposed in 1968 a computer matching fingerprint system, based on minutiae features. The work by Wegstein et al. still remains a cornerstone of the development of AFIS [64]. The development work towards the Printrak system (now owned by Motorola) also dates back to these early years [99]. In France, Thiebault presented in 1967 a first computer matching fingerprint system, based on minutiae features and their spatial relationship [90]. This approach led to the development of the Morpho system (now part of Sagem) [79]. Likewise, researchers in Japan proposed a computer matching fingerprint system based on minutiae features, that served as a basis for the NEC AFIS [8].

All forensic AFIS are largely based on minutiae matching. The extracted template encompasses mainly the x,y coordinates of detected minutiae, their orientation and, for some providers, the ridge counts between minutiae. The main advantages of an AFIS are the ability to compare a single print, as well as a ten-print card to the whole database, hence covering all types of *cases*. We recall that although an AFIS provides a list of best candidates (according to a scoring/ranking metric), the identification process is not completed by the system, but manually by an expert (through a dedicated user interface). Of course, advances in computer technologies have increased speed and efficiency of the encoding and retrieval. Computational power allows now the use of both rolled and flap impressions and the introduction of palm marks and prints in AFIS and above all with a very quick response time and high reliability. Operational efficiency has been monitored by law enforcement agencies [13, 51,

56, 74]. Benchmarking has allowed monitoring of progress and improvements in this field. The NIST is today a reference in this area[3].

Standardization of forensic AFIS technology gained large momentum when fierce competition between providers brought to the fore the difficulties of interoperability between systems both nationally and internationally. The ANSI/NIST ITL-1 2000 standard manages the interoperability between all proprietary minutiae classification methods [6]. It also includes recommendations regarding data interchange of facial, scar mark and tattoo (SMT) information. This standard proposes the classification in fourteen pattern types, four minutiae types, with a localization (x,y-coordinates) and a direction (angle). The standard is currently under review and additional features beyond minutiae will be added to the ANSI/NIST ITL-1 2006 standard for the next generation AFIS. The extended features proposed[4] are finer classification of general patterns, additional ridge path elements, ridge flow quality for detecting open fields (areas without minutiae) and a larger spectrum of features (dots, incipient ridges, creases, scars, ridge shapes and width,...).

Another driving force is the willingness to provide this specific market with devices of known and recognized qualities. For example the FBI recommendations on the image quality specifications [30] propose (for fingerprint scanners) specific characteristics on geometric image accuracy, modulation transfer function, signal-to-noise ratio, range of gray-scale, gray-scale accuracy and output gray level uniformity. Furthermore, to archive large fingerprint databases, an efficient compression algorithm was required. The FBI proposed the Wavelet Scalar Quantization (WSQ) image compression algorithm as a way to standardize the digitization and compression of gray-scale fingerprint images [17]. This algorithm, capable of compressing images in the recommended 15:1 ratio, is based on discrete wavelet transform decomposition, scalar quantization and Huffman entropy coding. It is expected that WSQ will be replaced by JPEG2000 in a very near future.

The last big shift in technology is the widespread provision of livescan devices for law enforcement agencies to acquire ten-print forms instead of using the traditional procedure of inking fingerprints on paper. The use of small livescan devices for border control or police control is increasing rapidly (in Switzerland e.g. [71]).

21.3.4 A snapshot on the Swiss national fingerprint identification database and processes

Table 21.2 presents the statistics of the Swiss fingerprint criminal justice database for 2005[5]. 694,788 ten-print (TP) cards, provided from Swiss can-

---

[3] http://fingerprint.nist.gov/

[4] http://fingerprint.nist.gov/standard/cdeffs/index.html

[5] The statistical data on the Swiss fingerprint criminal justice database were kindly provided by Dr Axel Glaeser, Managment AFIS DNA Services - Federal Office of Police.

tonal police departments and from asylum centers, as well as 28,107 two-fingerprint (2-FP) sets and 34,485 latent prints, are stored in the Swiss fingerprint database. The 2-FP sets are used for identification purposes for police, border controls or embassy visa requests based on livescan images of two fingers. Due to legal regulations, only a fraction of them can be kept in the national database. Furthermore, for each latent print, about three encoded searches are stored in the database, which corresponds to about 10,000 unsolved fingermarks. Most transactions have been requested through police investigation, either for TP searches (28,005 requests in 2005) or 2-FP searches (38,131 requests in 2005). The annual numbers of requests for asylum or border control transactions are smaller (8,907 TP searches and 23,747 2-FP searches respectively). 14,500 TP versus TP matches (*case 1*) have been obtained from these transactions during a year, as well as 1,444 identification of latent prints versus TP or TP versus latent prints (*case 2*). Around a quarter of these hits result from TP versus latent transactions. The number of latent identifications includes about 233 matches with palm prints. Until now, latent prints were not compared to other registered latent prints (*case 3*), but some tests are currently being conducted to evaluate the benefits of such comparison in a Swiss perspective [7]. 22,202 and 5,383 2-FP matches have been obtained from the police and border control/embassy transactions respectively.

The average response time is about 3 to 10 minutes for 2-FP transactions, maximum 4 hours for TP transactions, and about 4 working days for latent transactions (urgent cases are processed within a couple of hours). For reasons of quality control, two fingerprint experts work on each latent case independently.

Records		
TP	2-FP	LATENT
694,788	28,107	34,485
Transactions		
POLICE	ASYLUM	BORDER CONTROL
28,005 (TP) 38,131 (2-FP)	8,907 (TP)	23,747 (2-FP)
Hits		
TP-TP	LATENT-TP / TP-LATENT	2-FP
14,500	1,444	22,202 (Police) 5,383 (Border control / Embassy)

Table 21.2. Statistics for 2005 of the Swiss fingerprint criminal justice database.

21.3.5 Recent research on evidential value of fingerprints

The weaknesses of the statistical models developed to date in fingerprint identification have motivated recent research projects [87]. These have as main objective the assessment of the evidential contribution of fingermarks that can
be partial, distorted, and with a poor signal/noise ratio. Although conclusions
in the fingerprint area have traditionally been categorical, there is no obstacle
to treat that type of evidence from a probabilistic perspective as discussed by
Champod and Evett [22].

The strength of evidence is evaluated by a likelihood ratio according to the
within- and between-sources variability of three or more minutiae [66, 67]. The
feature set consists of the type of minutiae, their location, orientation and relative position, avoiding strong independence assumption. Fingerprint images
acquired under different distortion conditions and feature sets generated arti-
ficially using a distortion model, have been used to model the within-source
variability of the feature set. To model the between-sources variability of the
feature set, fingerprints from randomly selected individuals from a criminal
justice database have been used. The forensic qualities of the system have been
assessed by studying simulations of the distributions of the likelihood ratios.
This can be done considering the respective propositions of identity or non-
identity of sources, combined with the estimation of the rates of misleading
evidence ($RMEP$ and $RMED$). The results demonstrate that even partial
fingermarks with three minutiae can contribute significantly to the evaluation
of the strength of evidence for forensic cases. The performance increases with
the number of minutiae.

21.4 DNA

Deoxyribonucleic acid (DNA), a chain of nucleotides contained in the nucleus
of our cells, can be used as a biometric tool to classify and guide the identification of unknown individuals or biological samples left by them. The analysis
of the DNA molecule in forensic science is called forensic DNA profiling. The
book, "Forensic DNA Typing", by Butler [19], is an exhaustive and up to date
reference. The objective of this section is to introduce the concepts and highlight how DNA analysis differs from biometrics. We will concentrate on DNA
contained in the nucleus and the analytical processes that have led to large
forensic databases. For the use of mitochondrial DNA, mini-STRs, Y-specific
STRs and *single nucleotide polymorphisms* (SNPs), the reader should refer to
[19].

DNA contains in its coding parts the genetic instructions allowing the encoding of different biological functions. About 32,000 genes are part of the
human DNA. The nucleotide chain (about three million pairs of nucleotides)
enables the encoding of sequences of amino acids in all proteins required for

cellular life. The gene pool of each individual is transmitted by his/her biological parents: a half by the father and the other half by the mother.

Non-coding parts, which represent about 98% of the total DNA, contain at
different locations (*loci*) highly variable number of repetitive sequences, called
Short Tandem Repeat (STR) which have a large polymorphism. At a given
locus, one individual will show two specific numbers of repetitions of the given
sequence of nucleotides. These two numbers called (*alleles*) give the biometric
template for that locus. Note that one allele results from the genetic transmission from the biological father, while the biological mother transmits the
other. When both alleles are identical, the individual is *monozygote* (at that
locus), and when they are different, the individual is termed *heterozygote* (at
that locus). Currently, most forensic DNA profiling systems used for database
purposes are based on the analysis of STRs. The advantage of using STRs is
that they are stable within individuals, but vary greatly between individuals.
STR population genetics are well documented, and when located on different
chromosomes, STRs have shown robust independence from a statistical perspective. They can hence be combined to achieve a very high discrimination
power. The template for a DNA profile obtained with a STR profiling system
is then a simple string, as in Table 21.3.

D3		VWA		D16		D2		D8	
12	13	16	17	10	11	18	19	8	9

D21		D18		D19		THO1		FGA	
26	27	14	15	10	11	5	6	29	30

D3		VWA		D16		D5		D8		D7		TPOX	
14	15	20	21	10	13	6	7	15	16	10	10	10	12

D21		D18		D13		THO1		FGA		CSF1PO	
27	31	19	19	23	24	6	7	24	24	6	6

Table 21.3. Example of a DNA profile obtained with a 10-loci system (SGM Plus
10 loci system used for the UK national DNA database) at the top and, below, with
a 13-loci system (core STR markers for the US/FBI Combined DNA Index System
- CODIS). Note that both systems share the same 8 loci. Currently the number of
STRs used in commercial kits can amount to 16 loci.

Nuclear DNA can be extracted from all biological tissues. For living persons, a buccal swab is the easiest non-invasive way to obtain reference material. Profiles can be generated from biological stains or cells left behind at
crime scenes, typically stains of blood, saliva, urine or semen, from hairs (with
roots) and from skin cells (left by mere contact e.g. such as a fingermark).
Obtaining DNA samples from living or dead bodies generally does not constitute a difficulty. For traces left behind, the location and retrieval is done
manually, by visual examination (helped by the use of specialized light sources
and magnification), and using presumptive tests. Traces are also more prone

to DNA degradation and interference during the extraction or amplification process. It means that for low-quantity or degraded samples, the DNA profile obtained may be partial (not all loci allow allelic designation) and/or mixed (when more than one individual contributed DNA to the sample). In all cases, the template will maintain the same format with either limited information or more than two alleles detected at one or more locus.

The extracted DNA is amplified using a sensitive and selective DNA replication method known as the *Polymerase Chain Reaction* (PCR). It is used to amplify, through multiple thermal cycles (between 28 to 34), the selected STRs for all loci in a multiplex way. This amplification provides extraordinary sensitivity, theoretically, even down to the detection of a single DNA molecule. In practice, sensitivity to levels below 100 pg of DNA (a few cells) can be achieved. The benefit is evident: it allows obtaining profiles from very limited amounts of DNA, hence widening the investigative possibilities in difficult cases. The drawback lies in the technical capacity to amplify not only the relevant DNA but also background DNA left for reasons not linked to the alleged activities of forensic interest.

The detection of these amplified repetitive sequences is completed by *capillary electrophoresis* (CE) and fluorescence detection. CE is an analytical technique that separates charged DNA amplified fragments according to their size, by applying voltage across buffer-filled capillaries. The whole DNA profiling process requires specialist laboratory staff, costly analytical equipment and a minimum of 12 hours. Automation of most parts of this procedure is achievable with current technology, but still requires some hours of processing time.

DNA profiles can easily be arranged in databases for law enforcement purposes or the management of large disasters (such as the 9/11 terrorist acts or the 2005 tsunami). The American FBI CODIS now has more than 4 million profiles from individuals and 150,000 crime scene sample profiles[6]. The UK national DNA database reaches more than 3 million subjects and a yearly rate of crime scene submissions of about 50,000 profiles [65]. These are the two largest national DNA databases in use.

Seven STR loci were selected by the European Network of Forensic Science Institutes (ENFSI) and Interpol [47] to ensure a minimal consensus on databasing in Europe. The American FBI CODIS database is built on thirteen loci, including the seven selected by the ENFSI. This standardization ensures a relative interoperability between all countries, in order to enable collaborations between jurisdictions for forensic cases. Even if a consensus on a restricted set of loci has been adopted, the nature of the population registered on national DNA databases (i.e. the introduction criterion for profiles in these databases) differs greatly from state to state, especially in Europe [98]. Some member states incorporate in their databases all individuals suspected or arrested for any recordable offences, such as the United Kingdom,

---

[6] http://www.fbi.gov/hq/lab/codis/

while other states register only individuals convicted for crimes and offences sanctioned by imprisonment, such as Switzerland.

Table 21.4 gives the 2005 statistics of the Swiss DNA criminal justice database managed with the CODIS software (but based on the SGM Plus STR system)[7]. 69,019 DNA profiles from known individuals, with 11,125 unresolved stain profiles, provided by Swiss cantonal police departments are stored in the Swiss DNA criminal justice database. About 15,000 DNA profiles and 5,000 crime scene profiles have been compared to the database in one year, from which 2,800 crime scene to person and 2,100 crime scene to crime scene matches have been obtained.

Records	
PROFILES	CRIME SCENE
69,019	11,125
Transactions	
PROFILES	CRIME SCENE
15,000	5,000
Hits	
CRIME SCENE-PERSON	CRIME SCENE-CRIME SCENE
2,800	2,100

Table 21.4. 2005 statistics of the Swiss DNA criminal justice database.

When there is no need to consider relatives or mixtures, the matching process is straightforward: for a match to be declared, all alleles from the unknown profile should correspond to the profile from the known. Currently, most operational forensic DNA matching systems are based on the search for equalities. Research is currently under way to improve searches with degraded profiles, mixed profiles and when only relatives are available. Forensic applications of DNA are wide, as presented in Table 21.5.

It is important to stress that a match between two DNA profiles does not conclusively establish the identity of sources. Indeed, although the selectivity of DNA profiling is very high, there exists a probability for an adventitious association. The methods for computing match probabilities have received considerable attention among scholars and, after some initial controversies, gained general acceptance. A full account of these methods, including the use of likelihood ratios, is given in [37, 97]. In general terms, for a complete unmixed DNA profile, the predicted random match probability with unrelated individuals is in the order of 1 in a billion [38]. However, note that the match probabilities are of a complete different order of magnitude for relatives. For

---

[7] The statistical data on the Swiss DNA criminal justice database were kindly provided by Dr Axel Glaeser, Managment AFIS DNA Services - Federal Office of Police.

Activity	Levels of selectivity of the information
Comparison of the DNA profile of unknown individuals against profiles from known individuals.	*High* when the collected DNA is not degraded, (provides a full profile on all analyzed loci). *Lower* when part of the DNA available is degraded, hence giving a partial DNA profile.
Comparison of the DNA profile obtained from human remains (missing persons or disaster victims) against profiles from known missing persons or relatives thereof.	*High* as above when the comparison is made against DNA profiles from known missing persons. *Lower* when part of the DNA available is degraded or when the data used as reference are provided through blood relatives (at various levels).
Filiations testings (paternity, maternity and any types of blood relationship)	*High* when the direct putative genitors are available. *Lower* when the DNA profile from one or both putative genitors is informed from data collected among his/her blood relatives (ancestors or descendants).
Comparison of DNA profile obtained from biological stains, material or contact traces recovered in association with criminal activities against profiles from known individuals.	*High* when the recovered material is in large quantity and its analysis lead to a full unmixed DNA profile. *Lower* when the recovered material is of low quantity or degraded and consequently offers a partial DNA profile. Equally when the sample gave a mixed DNA profile of 2 or more contributors.
Forensic intelligence gathered through the systematic comparison of DNA profiles coming from various scenes. Familial searches on the DNA database.	Depending on the quality of the DNA information obtained.

Table 21.5. Inventories of the forensic applications of DNA profiles.

the SGM Plus system (10 loci), an average match probability for a potential brother/sister is 1 in 10'000.

For assigning statistical weights to relationships based on DNA mixtures or filiation cases, refer to [97]. As a general principle, when the quality of the information decreases, the weight of the DNA findings tends to decrease as well. Hence, the more the DNA is partial or distant in terms of genetic relationship, the higher the uncertainty. With DNA, the selectivity of the available information can be assessed by its extent (quantity of DNA and number of loci) and the amount of predicting information allowed by the profiles obtained from relatives.

21.5 Voice

Forensic speaker recognition is the process of determining if a specific individual is the source of a questioned occurrence. Typically, forensic speaker recognition by experts relies on a variety of techniques (used alone or in combination), such as aural comparison (careful listening), semi-automatic methods for extraction of certain parameters (e.g. formant frequencies, average fundamental frequencies, pitch contour, etc.), visual comparison of spectrograms, and automatic speaker recognition (computer-based) [53, 62, 76]. Three main processes can be used in forensic speaker recognition: the auditory (also known as aural perceptual), semi-automatic (also known as auditory instrumental) and the automatic analysis.

In *auditory* analysis, trained phoneticians carefully listen to recordings and use the perceived differences in the speech to form an opinion about their similarity [68]. They base their judgment on parameters such as the voice (e.g. timbre and pitch), speech (e.g. articulation and speech rate), language (e.g. prosody and style) and linguistic characteristics (e.g. syntax and breathing). This is a challenging task requiring training and a careful ear. Voice comparison by untrained (also called naive) listeners is not often used in forensic cases, although they have shown to perform well in certain conditions [5].

In *semi-automatic* analysis, the experts measure various acoustic parameters, such as average fundamental frequency, vowel formants, pitch contour, spectral energy, etc. They assess those characteristics either subjectively or objectively, using signal processing tools to quantify them. They can even combine approaches to formulate their conclusions, according to verbal probability equivalents [40]. One of the semi-automatic methods, which uses visual spectrographic comparison (popularly known as "voice printing"), has come under severe criticism in recent years. It consists of visually comparing graphical representations of spectrums of identical speech utterances. It was first proposed in 1962, and some weak points, such as the large variability of these spectrograms for a same individual and the fact that the visual representation of these spectrograms is not specifically speaker-dependent, were quickly highlighted. In 1976, the US National Academy of Sciences recommended that this approach should only be used in forensic cases with utmost caution [15]. A strong word of caution is certainly deserved [16].

In terms of *automatic* speaker recognition, two types of approaches are available, as mentioned in Chapter 8: the text-dependent and the text-independent (often required in forensic cases). Several feature characterizations and statistical modeling tools have been developed for automatic speaker recognition and have been successfully applied to forensic cases [33, 54]. Automatic methods perform well in similar recording conditions, but are sensitive to distortions due to recording and/or in transmission conditions. In forensic cases, the recording conditions of the trace and the reference materials are rarely similar and ideal, but rather recorded in different and unconstrained conditions [4], e.g. through mobile communications (GSM) transmission and with background noise. Due to these factors, the comparison is often under-taken under adverse conditions.

As with other forensic fields, a likelihood ratio-based approach was proposed for forensic speaker recognition [26] and gained acceptance among practitioners [76]. The proposed statistical-probabilistic methodology uses three different databases, in addition to the digital trace [33, 41, 63]: a suspect reference database (R), a suspect control database (C) and a potential population database (P). The P database is used to model the variability of the potential population. The R database is used to model the variability of the suspect's voice, according to the recording conditions of the P database. The C database is used to evaluate the variability of the suspect's voice, according to the recording conditions of the trace. The similarity scores, obtained by comparing the recordings of databases C and R, model the within-source variability, while those obtained by comparing the recordings of database P to the trace, model the between-sources variability. The score obtained by comparing the trace to the model of the suspect's voice, created with database R, gives the evidence E. The LR is computed by the ratios of the heights of the probability densities of the within- and between-sources distributions at a score of E. The LRs obtained with this methodology can assess the common origin of two speech signals in a specific forensic case. The readers can refer to [4, 32, 63, 76] and to Chapter 8 for further reading and additional bibliographical references on forensic and non-forensic speaker recognition.

21.6 Face and ear

As presented in Section 21.2, the face was already used at the end of the 19th century for forensic discrimination purposes. Bertillon standardized the lighting conditions, as well as the posture of the subject. He proposed that two facial images were taken for each individual, namely a frontal and a profile (with the latter considered as more reliable).

21.6.1 Non-automatic forensic face recognition

Forensic face recognition was until recently generally performed by human operators using different approaches [48, 100]: morphological analysis of facial structures, anthropometric measurements and superimposition of images.

The *morphological analysis-based* approach can be described as the scientific follow-on to Bertillon's spoken portrait (Section 21.2). It is based on a nomenclature for the description of the physiological aspects of the nose, the forehead and the ear. The morphological classification describes facial physiological characteristic, such as the facial shape, the hairline, the forehead height and width, the mouth and the chin shapes, the nose length, breadth and shape, and the ear size and form. These characteristics can be described, using the following sets of terms: "none, few, moderate, extreme; small, medium, large;

absent, slight medium, pronounced; thin, average, thick". In addition, information such as facial wrinkles, can also be used. As this description is rather subjective, variations were observed between the descriptions of a same set of photographs made by operators for some features [95]. According to these authors, other features were nevertheless proven to be invariant between operators and to have some discriminating power, without explicitly specifying these features. Additional limits of this approach are the variability of the features for an individual due to changes in expression, photographic angles and changes due to aging. It is difficult to determine if these features are statistically independent [48].

The *anthropometric-based* approach can be described as the quantification of physiological proportions between specific facial landmarks. This method is only used for the comparison of faces having the same orientation. These landmarks are for example the midpoint of the hairline, the most anterior point of the forehead, the deepest point of the nasal root, the most anterior point of the nose tip, the midpoint of the occlusal line between the lips, the most anterior and inferior points of the chin, the corners of the mouth and the most superior, inferior and posterior points of the ear [48]. Other landmarks can be chosen, as long as they are clearly visible on the facial images. In order to avoid any scale and absolute size differences between photographs, relative ratios should be calculated from these landmarks. The use of the maximum dimension as denominator for each of these ratios is recommended for linear measurements. Even if the quantifications of these proportions reduce subjectivity, some problems still remain. Lighting conditions, camera distortions, camera positioning, facial orientation, facial expressions and aging may result in different ratio values. However, the main problems are the high correlation between some measurements and the lack of statistical data to determine the relative contribution of these measurements in a specific population [60]. Anthropometric measurements could be used for forensic purposes if these problems were resolved.

The *image superimposition-based* approach is the juxtaposition or the superposition of facial images, taken under similar acquisition conditions (the orientation, pose and size) in order to verify the correspondence of the facial features. This approach is either represented by an image where both 2D facial photographs are vertically or horizontally juxtaposed, or by an animation where the first photograph appears and then disappears into the other. This latter demonstration tool should not be used to assess a correspondence between two facial images, because of the subjectivity generated by such visualization. Matches are not only based on a superimposition correspondence, but significant features matches need to be included as well, such as ears and scars [94]. However, the superimposition-based approach is considered as the least accurate facial comparison method [48]. The comparison between photographs can be reliably performed only if they were taken under the same conditions and with identical poses. A solution to these issues, a 2D/3D approach has been developed. It consists of modeling the 3D shape of the suspect's face and comparing it to the 2D questioned facial image [100]. The advantage of this method is that it is possible to adjust the pose and orientation of the suspect's face to the facial image. Furthermore, some objective computer-assisted matching criteria can be obtained with this approach.

21.6.2 Automatic forensic face recognition

The three main comparison approaches discussed in Section 21.6.1 do not consider automatic face recognition, except the 2D/3D superimposition approach described above. Automatic face recognition can be described as a visual pattern recognition problem, where selected facial features of a query image were compared to the features of a reference image or a database. As presented in [57], face recognition attempts to represent the complex multi-dimensional features extracted from the image of a face in simpler and more general representations using e.g. principal component analysis (PCA), shape and texture or Gabor wavelets, and to perform the classification between the different patterns using e.g. Bayes, linear discriminant analysis (LDA), independent component analysis (ICA) or Graph matching. The contribution of such systems in surveillance activities and access control (see Chapter 3), especially with the performance improvement highlighted recently with the Face Recognition Vendor Test (FRVT) 2006 [72], will gain more and more importance. However, we will only mention one attempt of using automatic face recognition in an evaluative and LR-based framework [70]. The experiments of this study were based on a small set of subjects, recorded under fixed constraints with passport type photographs. The conditions generating the most significant variations in facial images (i.e. illumination, pose, expression, age, image quality,...) in forensic scenarios were not explored in a large scale scenario.

As ruled by the UK Court of Appeal Criminal Division decision in *R. v. Gray* ([2003] EWCA Crim 1001), an adequate evaluation methodology for face recognition, based on reliable statistical data, is needed. Our view is that automatic face recognition systems will have a large role to play here. Before automatic face recognition is accepted in court, a full and systematic assessment of the technology must be conducted under realistic conditions using fit-for-purpose forensic efficiency measures.

21.6.3 Ear

The ear was considered by Bertillon as the most identifying part of an individual (see Section 21.2). This modality was then quickly used for identification purposes in forensic cases. This identification can be based on photographs (or still images from video recordings) or based on earmarks left at crime scenes (for example when a burglar presses his ear against a door or windowpane to listen into a room). Forensic ear comparison is traditionally performed by skilled examiners. The principles and protocols for ear and earprint examination can be found in [46, 92].

The identification is mainly demonstrated by overlaying transparent known and unknown images or by using a photomontage of various sections of the ears. There is a big difference in terms of selectivity between a well-taken photograph of an ear and its impression on a door (see Figure 21.1). However, to date there have not been sufficient systematic studies about forensic identification decision making using these impressions. Thus the evidential contribution of earmark to earprint comparisons has been criticized [23]. The large variability of the ear morphology has been covered well in the literature, but the variability of earmarks has been relatively poorly treated. This is also the same with within-subject variations. A recent Court of Appeal judgment[8] expressed some reservations as to the absolute strength of the earmark evidence presented. For the comparison between video recordings of ears, a recent study has shown how the quality of the video images determine to a large extent the ability to identify a person [44].

The first forensic earmark recognition proof of concept was presented in [23], it uses the antihelix area of the mark to extract some features, such as the width, the height and the inner and outer contours. Another concept system is presented in [80]. It uses as features manually annotated intersection points between a grid and the mark or the print. A maximum of four points on the inner side of the helix, and four points on the outer side of the antihelix are selected. A polygon matrix based on these tags is calculated. The only performance data presented in this article refers to a verification protocol where the earmarks tested were always identified at a 100% probability match (highest score) to the corresponding prints. The number of tests carried out and cases where marks were identified to non-corresponding prints at a 100% probability match were unfortunately not mentioned. The authors also propose alternatively the use of centroids for each separate earmark's part as features, in order to avoid the mark's variability due to pressure changes. The Forensic Ear IDentification (FearID) project (funded by the 6th EU research framework) proposed to use weighted width, angular development and anatomical annotation as distinctive features for their semi-automatic system [3]. Manual annotations on the prints and marks are performed before the matching process to facilitate the segmentation of the images and to locate anatomical points. With a set 7364 prints and 216 marks from 1229 donors, this approach reached an equal error rate (EER) of 3.9% for lab quality prints, and an EER of 9.3% for simulated marks against the prints database. At this stage of research, to our knowledge, no operational system has been deployed in forensic services. For further reading on automatic ear recognition, refer to Chapters 7 and 16.

---

[8] *R. v. Dallagher* No (2002) EWCA Crim 1903, July 25.

21.7 Dental features

Dental features are heavily used by forensic odontologists for the identification of human remains in cases of missing persons or mass disasters [88]. The features used range from the standard dental record (indications of missing teeth, restorations, crowns,...) to dental radiographs that provide information about teeth, including tooth contours, relative positions of neighboring teeth, and shapes of the dental work. These anatomical features have shown very good stability and variability and the teeth serve as a suitable repository of the history of man-made operations that left various marks and shape changes. The diversity of the dental record features and their use for identification have been recently documented [1]. Alphanumerical data can easily be organized in databases and such systems are used operationally in cases of mass disasters.

The use of radiographs recently received attention from the biometric community with promising results [34, 27, 49, 69, 101].

The area of bitemark identification is covered in [31]. To our knowledge, no automatic feature extraction and matching procedures have been proposed to handle these marks.

21.8 Handwriting

The principles and procedures used by forensic experts to assign questioned handwritten documents to known individual are described in [45]. The forensic expert tries to assess existing similarities and dissimilarities between control and recovered samples through a subjective estimation of the individuality and variability of the material at hand. Again, such a subjective approach has come under criticism and the profession has been urged to move towards more objective measures of selectivity [82].

In this context, a few embryonic methods for databasing and systematically analyzing handwriting have been presented: the computer-based measurement and retrieval of letter shapes of the WANDA-system [93], the use of Fourier descriptors to discriminate between writers [61], the automatic identification of a writer by the use of connected-component contours [84] and the CEDAR-FOX identification/verification system [85, 86]. The scope for development is important both to provide tools to assist the evaluation of forensic evidence but also to bring investigative possibilities based on handwriting. Gannon Technologies Group recently announced a breakthrough in the area following research at George Mason University and the FBI[9].

No forensic attempts towards automation are known for signatures despite the very large development of biometric systems based on this modality (see Chapter 10).

---

[9] http://gazette.gmu.edu/articles/8037/

21.9 Discussion and perspectives

As presented in Section 21.1, forensic science and biometrics are differentiated by four main distinctions. First, forensic biometric systems are mainly used as sorting devices, presenting to the forensic specialist a short list of candidates, while traditional biometric systems report their conclusions with binary decisions ("accepted" or "rejected"). Secondly, adequate global measures ($RMED$, $RMEP$) should complement the assessment of the efficiency of forensic biometric systems (in addition to the traditional biometric measures such as ROC and DET curves). Thirdly, forensic biometric applications are characterized by the wide range of selectivity of the biometric data that are submitted, while traditional biometric systems use data acquired in rather controlled conditions. Finally, the last distinction concerns the range of comparisons that can be undertaken in the forensic environment depending on the circumstances of the cases.

Despite these differences, the same scientific principles and technical methods are used for handling biometric data in non-forensic and forensic applications. The research efforts undertaken in the biometric community will help to address the issues of the selectivity decrease encounter in forensic applications. Furthermore, multimodal approaches (see Chapters 14 to 16 and [77]) may handle not only the limitations of each single modality (i.e. intra-class variability, distinctiveness, non-universality, etc.), but the selectivity decrease as well, which occurs in forensic biometrics at distance for example. The application of multimodal approaches on forensic data should increase the reliability of such biometric systems in unconstrained conditions, for investigative and evaluation purposes.

Recognition at distance, based on biometric data, will quickly be the major component of forthcoming forensic inquiries. The UK Police Information Technology Organization (PITO) recommends the development of more effective tools to handle the large amount of Closed-Circuit Television (CCTV) images, not only for human identification, but also for crime detection and prevention [73]. New kinds of digital traces will thus be used for law enforcement purposes. While face and voice are already used as digital traces for human identification, modalities such as ear, iris and gait may also be involved in forensic science. The increasing forensic needs and the advances in the biometric research community mean that forensic science and biometrics will be more intertwined in the future.

Acknowledgments

The authors are grateful to Dr Axel Glaeser for providing us with statistical data on the Swiss fingerprint and DNA criminal justice databases and to Dr Anil Alexander for his valuable remarks and suggestions.

References

1. B. J. Adams. The diversity of adult dental patterns in the united states and the implications for personal identification. *Journal of Forensic Sciences*, 48:497–503, 2003.
2. C. Aitken and F. Taroni. *Statistics and the Evaluation of Evidence for Forensic Scientists*. John Wiley & Sons, Ltd, 2004.
3. I. Alberink and A. Ruifrok. Performance of the FearID earprint identification system. *Forensic Science International*, 166:145–154, 2007.
4. A. Alexander. *Forensic Automatic Speaker Recognition using Bayesian Interpretation and Statistical Compensation for Mismatched Conditions*. PhD thesis, Swiss Federal Institute of Technology, Lausanne, 2005.
5. A. Alexander, D. Dessimoz, F. Botti, and A. Drygajlo. Aural and automatic forensic speaker recognition in mismatched conditions. *International Journal of Speech, Language and Law*, 12(2):214–234, 2005.
6. ANSI/NIST. *ANSI/NIST-ITL 1-2000 Data Format for the Interchange of Fingerprint, Facial, Scar Mark and Tattoo (SMT)*. American National Standard Institute - National Institute of Technology, 2000.
7. A. Anthonioz, A. Aguzzi, A. Girod, N. Egli, and O. Ribaux. Potential use of fingerprint in forensic intelligence: Crime scene linking. *Z Zagadnien Nauk Sadowych - Problems of Forensic Sciences*, 51:166–170, 2002.
8. K. Asai, Y. Kato, Y. Hoshino, and K. Kiji. Automatic fingerprint identification. In *SPIE - Imaging Applications for Automated Industrial Inspection and Assembly*, volume 182, pages 49–56, 1979.
9. H. Battley. *Single Finger Prints*. H. M. Stationery Office, London, 1930.
10. J. Berry and D. A. Stoney. The history and development of fingerprinting. In R. E. Gaensslen, editor, *Advances in Fingerprint Technology*, pages 1–40. CRC Press, Boca Raton, 2001.
11. A. Bertillon. *La Photographie Judiciaire*. Gauthier-Villars et fils, Paris, 1890.
12. A. Bertillon. *Identification Anthropométrique et Instructions Signalétiques*. Imprimerie administrative, Melun, 1893.
13. B. Blain. Automated palm identification. *Fingerprint Whorld*, 28:102–107, 2002.
14. R. M. Bolle, J. H. Connell, S. Pankanti, N. K. Ratha, and A. W. Senior. *Guide to Biometrics*. Springer-Verlag, New-York, 2003.
15. R. H. Bolt, F. S. Cooper, D. M. Green, S. L. Hamlet, J. G. McKnight, J. M. Pickett, O. Tosi, B. D. Underwood, and D. L. Hogan. *On the Theory and Practice of Voice Identification*. National Research Council, National Academy of Sciences, Washington D.C., 1979.
16. J. F. Bonastre, F. Bimbot, L. J. Boe, J. P. Campbell, D. A. Reynolds, and I. Magrin-Chagnolleau. Person authentication by voice: A need for caution. In *Proceedings of Eurospeech 2003*, pages 33–36, Geneva, Switzerland, 2003.
17. C. M. Brislawn, J. N. Bradley, R. J. Onyshczak, and T. Hopper. The FBI compression standard for digitized fingerprint images. In *Proceedings of the SPIE*, volume 2847, pages 344–355, 1996.
18. B. Budowle, R. Chakraborty, G. Carmody, and K. L. Monson. Source attribution of a forensic DNA profile. *Forensic Science Communications*, 2(3), 2000.
19. J. M. Butler. *Forensic DNA Typing*. Elsevier Academic Press, Burlington, MA, 2005.

20. C. Champod. Identification/Individualization: Overview and meaning of ID. In Jay M. Siegel, Geoffrey C. Knupfer, and Pekka J. Saukko, editors, *Encyclopedia of Forensic Sciences*, pages 1077–1084. Academic Press, London, 2000.

21. C. Champod and I. W. Evett. Commentary on: Broeders, A. P. A. (1999) 'Some observations on the use of probability scales in forensic identification', Forensic Linguistics, 6(2): 228-41. *Forensic Linguistics*, 7:238–243, 2000.

22. C. Champod and I. W. Evett. A probabilistic approach to fingerprint evidence. *Journal of Forensic Identification*, 51:101–122, 2001.

23. C. Champod, I. W. Evett, and B. Kuchler. Earmarks as evidence: A critical review. *Journal of Forensic Sciences*, 46(6):1275–1284, 2001.

24. C. Champod, C. Lennard, and P. Margot. Alphonse Bertillon and dactyloscopy. *Journal of Forensic Identification*, 43(6):604–625, 1993.

25. C. Champod, C. Lennard, P. Margot, and M. Stoilovic. *Fingerprints and Other Ridge Skin Impressions*. CRC Press, Boca Raton, 2004.

26. C. Champod and D. Meuwly. The inference of identity in forensic speaker recognition. *Speech Communication*, 31(2-3):193–203, 2000.

27. H. Chen and A. K. Jain. Dental biometrics: Alignment and matching of dental radiographs. *IEEE Transactions on Pattern Analysis and Machine Intelligence*, 27:1319–1326, 2005.

28. S. Cole. *Suspect Identities: A History of Fingerprinting and Criminal Identification*. Harvard University Press, 2001.

29. R. Cook, I. W. Evett, G. Jackson, P. J. Jones, and J. A. Lambert. A hierarchy of propositions: Deciding which level to address in casework. *Science & Justice*, 38:231–240, 1998.

30. Criminal Justice Information Services Division. *Electronic Fingerprint Transmission Specifications CJIS-RS-0010 (V7)*. Department of Justice, Federal Bureau of Investigation, Criminal Justice Information Services Division, Washington, D.C., 1999.

31. B. J. Dorion. *Bitemark Evidence*. Marcel Dekker, New York, 2005.

32. A. Drygajlo. Forensic speaker recognition. *IEEE Signal Processing Magazine*, 24(2):132–135, 2007.

33. A. Drygajlo, D. Meuwly, and A. Alexander. Statistical methods and bayesian interpretation of evidence in forensic automatic speaker recognition. In *Eurospeech*, pages 689–692, Geneva, 2003.

34. G. Fahmy, D. E. M. Nassar, E. Haj-Said, H. Chen, O. Nomir, J. Zhou, R. Howell, H. H. Ammar, M. Abdel-Mottaleb, and A. K. Jain. Toward an automated dental identification system. *Journal of Electronic Imaging*, 14(4):043018, 2005.

35. H. Faulds. On the skin-furrows on the hands. *Nature*, 22:605, 1880.

36. R. D. Foote. Fingerprint identification: A survey of present technology, automated applications and potential for future development. *Criminal Justice Monography*, V(2):1–33, 1974.

37. L. A. Foreman, C. Champod, I. W. Evett, J. A. Lambert, and S. Pope. Interpreting DNA evidence: A review. *International Statistical Review*, 71:473–495, 2003.

38. L. A. Foreman and I. W. Evett. Statistical analyses to support forensic interpretation for a new ten-locus STR profiling system. *International Journal of Legal Medicine*, 114:147–155, 2001.

39. F. Galton. *Finger Prints*. Macmillian and Co., London, 1892.

40. S. Gfroerer. Auditory instrumental forensic speaker recognition. In *Proceedings of Eurospeech 2003*, pages 705–708, Geneva, Switzerland, 2003.

41. J. Gonzalez-Rodriguez, A. Drygajlo, D. Ramos-Castro, M. Garcia-Gomar, and J. Garcia-Ortega. Robust estimation, interpretation and assessment of likelihood ratios in forensic speaker recognition. *Computer Speech and Language*, 20:331–355, 2006.

42. K. Hashimoto. *De la classification à l'identification: Alphonse Bertillon (1853-1914) et l'anthropométrie judiciaire*. Mémoire de DEA d'Epistémologie, Histoire des sciences et des techniques, Université de Nantes, 2003.

43. W. Herschel. Skin furrows on the hand. *Nature*, 23:76, 1880.

44. A. J. Hoogstrate, C. van den Heuvel, and E. Huyben. Ear identification based on surveillance camera images. *Science & Justice*, 41:167–172, 2001.

45. R. A. Huber and A. M. Headrick. *Handwriting Identification: Facts and Fundamentals*. CRC Press, Boca Raton, 1999.

46. A. V. Iannarelli. *Ear Identification*. Paramont Publishing Company, Fremont, CA, 1989.

47. Interpol DNA Monitoring Expert Group. *Interpol Handbook on DNA Data Exchange and Practice*. International Criminal Police Organization, Lyon, 2001.

48. M. Y. Iscan. Introduction of techniques for photographic comparison: Potential and problems. In M. Y. Iscan and R. P. Helmer, editors, *Forensic Analysis of the Skull: Craniofacial Analysis, Reconstruction, and Identification*, pages 57–70. Wiley-Liss, New York, 1993.

49. A. K. Jain and H. Chen. Matching of dental X-Ray images for human identification. *Pattern Recognition*, 37:1519–1532, 2004.

50. P. L. Kirk. The ontogeny of criminalistics. *Journal of Criminal Law, Criminology and Police Science*, 54:235–238, 1963.

51. D. Klug, J. L. Peterson, and D. A. Stoney. Automated fingerprint identification systems: Their acquisition, management, performance and organizational impact. Report, National Institute of Justice, 1992.

52. P. Komarinski. *Automated Fingerprint Identification Systems (AFIS)*. Elsevier Academic Press, New York, 2005.

53. H. J. Kunzel. Current approaches to forensic speaker recognition. In *Proceedings of the 1st ESCA Workshop on Speaker Recognition, Identification and Verification*, pages 135–141, Martigny, Switzerland, 1994.

54. H. J. Kunzel and J. Gonzalez-Rodriguez. Combining automatic and phonetic-acoustic speaker recognition techniques for forensic applications. In *Proceedings of the 15th International Congress of Phonetic Sciences*, pages 1619–1622, Barcelona, Spain, 2003.

55. Q. Y. Kwan. *Inference of Identity of Source*. Phd thesis, Department of Forensic Science - University of California, Berkeley, 1977.

56. M. J. Leadbetter. The use of automated fingerprint identification systems to process, search and identify palm prints and latent palm marks. *Journal of Forensic Identification*, 49:18–36, 1999.

57. C. Liu and H. Wechsler. Face recognition. In J. L. Wayman, A. K. Jain, D. Maltoni, and D. Maio, editors, *Biometric Systems: Technology, Design and Performance Evaluation*, pages 97–114. Springer-Verlag, London, 2005.

58. E. Locard. *L'Identification des Récidivistes*. A. Maloine, Paris, 1909.

59. E. Locard. *L'Enquête Criminelle et les Méthodes Scientifiques*. Ernst Flammarion, Paris, 1920.

60. K. V. Mardia, A. Coombes, J. Kirkbride, A. Linney, and J. L. Bowie. On statistical problems with face identification from photographs. *Journal of Applied Statistics*, 23(6):655–675, 1996.

61. R. Marquis, M. Schmittbuhl, W. D. Mazzella, and F. Taroni. Quantification of the shape of handwritten characters: A step to objective discrimination between writers based on the study of the capital character o. *Forensic Science International*, 150:23–32, 2005.

62. D. Meuwly. Voice analysis. In J. M. Siegel, G. C. Knupfer, and P. J. Saukko, editors, *Encyclopedia of Forensic Sciences*, pages 1413–1421. Academic Press, London, 2000.

63. D. Meuwly. *Reconnaissance de Locuteurs en Sciences Forensiques: l'Apport d'une Approche Automatique*. PhD thesis, Université de Lausanne, 2001.

64. R. T. Moore. Automatic fingerprint identification systems. In H. C. Lee and R. E. Gaensslen, editors, *Advances in Fingerprint Technology*, pages 163–191. Elsevier Science Publishing Co., Inc., New-York, 1991.

65. National DNA Database. The national DNA database, annual report 2004-2005. Annual report, ACPO, 2006.

66. C. Neumann, C. Champod, R. Puch-Solis, N. Egli, A. Anthonioz, and A. Bromage-Griffiths. Computation of likelihood ratios in fingerprint identification for configurations of any number of minutiae. *Journal of Forensic Sciences*, 52(1):54–64, 2007.

67. C. Neumann, C. Champod, R. Puch-Solis, N. Egli, A. Anthonioz, D. Meuwly, and A. Bromage-Griffiths. Computation of likelihood ratios in fingerprint identification for configurations of three minutiae. *Journal of Forensic Sciences*, 51(6):1255–1266, 2006.

68. F. Nolan. Speaker identification evidence: its forms, limitations, and roles. In *Proceedings of the conference "Law and Language: Prospect and Retrospect"*, Levi (Finnish Lapland), 2001.

69. O. Nomir and M. Abdel-Mottaleb. A system for human identification from X-ray dental radiographs. *Pattern Recognition*, 8:1295–1305, 2005.

70. C. Peacock, A. Goode, and A. Brett. Automatic forensic face recognition from digital images. *Science & Justice*, 44(1):29–34, 2004.

71. P. W. Pfefferli. Rapid - Response - AFIS. In J. Almog and E. Springer, editors, *Proceedings of the International Symposium on Fingerprint Detection and Identification*, pages 225–256, Ne'urim, Israel, 1996.

72. P. J. Phillips, W. T. Scruggs, A. J. O'Toole, P. J. Flynn, K. W. Bowyer, C. L. Schott, and M. Sharpe. FRVT 2006 and ICE 2006 large-scale results. Technical report, National Institute of Standards and Technology (NIST), March 29 2007.

73. Police IT Organisation. Part 1: Identification roadmap 2005-2020 - Biometrics technology roadmap for person identification within the police service. Report, Police IT Organisation, 2005.

74. J. A. Ratkovic. Increasing efficiency in the criminal justice system: the use of new technology for criminal identification and latent print processing. The rand paper series, The Rand Corporation, 1980.

75. R. A. Reiss. *Portrait Parlé*. Th. Sack, Lausanne, 2nd edition, 1914.

76. P. Rose. *Forensic Speaker Identification*. Taylor & Francis London, London, New-York, 2002.

77. A. A. Ross, K. Nandakumar, and A. K. Jain. *Handbook of Multibiometrics*. Springer, New York, 2006.

78. R. M. Royall. *Statistical Evidence - A Likelihood Paradigm*. Chapman Hall, London, 1997.

79. T. Ruggles, S. Thieme, and D. Elman. Automatic fingerprint identification systems I. North American Morpho System. In H. C. Lee and R. E. Gaensslen, editors, *Advances in Fingerprint Technology*, pages 211–226. Elsevier Science Publishing Co., Inc., New-York, 1991.

80. G. N. Rutty and A. Abbas. Could earprint identification be computerised? An illustrated proof of concept paper. *International Journal of Legal Medicine*, 119:335–343, 2005.

81. M. J. Saks and J. J. Koehler. The coming paradigm shift in forensic identification science. *Science*, 309:892–895, 2005.

82. M. J. Saks and D. M. Risinger. Science and nonscience in the courts: Daubert meets handwriting identification expertise. *Iowa Law Review*, 82:21–74, 1996.

83. C. Sannié. Alphonse Bertillon et la dactyloscopie. L'affaire Scheffer. *Revue Internationale de Police Criminelle*, 5(41):255–262, 1950.

84. L. Schomaker and M. Bulacu. Automatic writer identification using connected-component contours and edge-based features of upper-case western script. *IEEE Transactions on Pattern Analysis and Machine Intelligence (PAMI)*, 26:787–798, 2004.

85. S. N. Srihari, M. J. Beal, K. Bandi, V. Shah, and P. Krishnamurthy. A statistical model for writer verification. In *Proceeding of the International Conference on Document Analysis and Recognition*, pages 1105–1109, 2005.

86. S. N. Srihari, S.-H. Cha, H. Arora, and S. Lee. Individuality of handwriting. *Journal of Forensic Sciences*, 47:1–17, 2002.

87. D. A. Stoney. Measurement of fingerprint individuality. In H. C. Lee and R. E. Gaensslen, editors, *Advances in Fingerprint Technology*, pages 327–387. CRC Press, Boca Raton, 2001.

88. D. Sweet and I. A. Pretty. A look at forensic dentistry - part 1: The role of teeth in the determination of human identity. *British Dental Journal*, 190:359–366, 2001.

89. F. Taroni, C. Champod, and P. Margot. Forerunners of bayesianism in early forensic science. *Jurimetrics Journal*, 38:183–200, 1998.

90. R. Thiebault. Automatic process for automated fingerprint identification. In *Proceedings of the International Symposium on Automation of Population Register Systems*, volume 1, pages 207–226, 1967.

91. United States Department of Justice and Federal Bureau of Investigation. *The Science of Fingerprints*. U.S. Government Printing Office, Washington DC, 1984.

92. C. van der Lugt. *Earprint Identification*. Elsevier Bedrijfsinformatie, Gravenhage, 2001.

93. M. van Erp, L. Vuurpijl, K. Franke, and L. Schomaker. The WANDA measurement tool for forensic document examination. *Journal of Forensic Document Examination*, 16:103–118, 2004.

94. P. Vanezis and C. Brierley. Facial image comparison of crime suspects using video superimposition. *Science & Justice*, 36(1):27–34, 1996.

95. P. Vanezis, D. Lu, J. Cockburn, A. Gonzalez, G. McCombe, O. Trujillo, and M. Vanezis. Morphological classification of facial features in adult Caucasian males based on an assessment of photographs of 50 subjects. *Journal of Forensic Sciences*, 41(5):786–791, 1996.

96. J. Vucetich. *Dactyloscopia comparada: El nuevo sistema argentino*. Jacobo Peuser, La Plata, Argentina, 1904.

97. S. J. Walsh, C. M. Triggs, and J. S. Buckleton. *Forensic DNA Evidence Interpretation: Methods and Interpretation.* CRC Press, Boca Raton, 2004.
98. R. Williams and P. Johnson. Forensic DNA databasing : A european perspective. Interim report, School of Applied Social Sciences, University of Durham, June 2005.
99. F. G. Wood. Automatic fingerprint identification systems II. De La Rue Printrak system. Technical report, Elsevier Science Publishing Co., Inc., 1991.
100. M. Yoshino. Conventional and novels methods for facial-image identification. *Forensic Science Review*, 16(2):104–114, 2004.
101. J. Zhou and M. Abdel-Mottaleb. A content-based system for human identification based on bitewing dental X-ray images. *Pattern Recognition*, 38:2132–2142, 2005.

Biometrics in the Government Sector

R. Lazarick[1] and J. L. Cambier[2]

[1] Computer Sciences Corporation Identity Labs, West Trenton, NJ 08628, USA
rlazarick@csc.com
[2] Biometric Consultant, Medford, NJ 08055, USA
jlcambier@gmail.com

22.1 Introduction

This chapter addresses two case studies to illustrate the use of biometrics in Government-controlled applications. The first case study explores the on-going large scale border management application in the United Arab Emirates used to protect against the re-entry of expellees. The second case study examines the emerging United States application known as "Registered Traveler" used to expedite airport security screening.

22.2 Iris Deportation Tracking System

This case study will describe the application of iris biometric recognition for the UAE Deportation Tracking System, focusing on the capabilities of iris recognition to function effectively in a large-scale "watchlist" application requiring identification.

22.2.1 Description of the Application

The United Arab Emirates (UAE) instituted the Iris Deportation Tracking System (IDTS) in July 2001 to prevent re-entry of deportees into the country after they had been expelled [1]. The system is designed to address one of the most important problems that any country faces; that of enforcing a deportation order. In normal cases, the authorities decide to deport a certain individual, who is then processed for deportation. This processing usually involves placing the person's name, nationality, passport and other information on a deportees list, and then he or she is deported from the country. That same individual could request a new passport from his home country with a slightly different name and would be able to re-enter the country from which he was deported on new documentation. The problem with this situation is that the passport and visa are not a forgery; they are original documents issued by his government and hence counter-forgery tactics at the border point would not detect this case. The return of such a person to the country is compounded by his previous experience with the authorities, and he is most probably more confident in avoiding capture and will require the authorities to exact more efforts to catch him the second time. With iris recognition technology (IRT), the person's iris is imaged and the match is done based on a stored template collected before he was deported. This is something he cannot change or alter in any way, and is accomplished without any reference to his other documents. The IRT system has proven to be extremely effective in preventing re-entry of persons who have previously been deported, and has deterred many expellees from attempting re-entry. As of late 2006, the system has enrolled over 1,050,000 expellees, performed over 9,800,000 searches and prevented over 115,000 attempts at re-entry.

The system has three basic functions:

1. **Enrollment** – Enrollment stations are deployed in 22 deportation centers around the UAE, and employ a total of 49 iris cameras. The enrollment process includes the scanning of both of the enrollee's irises. Later recognition uses data from only one iris, but both are enrolled to prevent attempted avoidance of recognition by enrolling one eye then presenting the other for recognition.

2. **Central Storage** – The IrisCode® templates [2] that have been collected from the enrollment centers around the country are deposited into a Central Repository, which performs database management tasks such as linking with geographical- and time-based data, as well as performing updates and maintenance. The database searches conducted to identify expellees occur on the Iris Search Engine located at the Central IrisCode Repository.

3. **Border Screening** – Iris Finder Workstations are deployed at 35 border centers, including 7 international airports (multiple terminals), 3 land ports, and 7 sea ports. A total of 81 cameras are used to scan the irises of selected incoming travelers; iris data is then transmitted to the Central Repository where the enrollment database is searched for matches. The identification process uses exhaustive 1-to-N searching and does not rely on any demographic data. The total turn-around time range is a matter of seconds, allowing real-time processing. The workstations are designed to operate without input devices (keyboard or mouse) and have a very easy-to-understand universal user interface. The person approaches the camera, and the workstation automatically generates the IrisCode template and sends it to the Central Repository. If a match is found a STOP sign is displayed, otherwise a GO sign will be shown. In the case of a STOP sign, the operator directs the person to another station capable of producing a paper printout of the details associated with this person (expulsion data, crime, name etc.) The authorities then take action as appropriate.

22.2.2 Role of the Government

The Iris Biometric Deportation System is operated by the General Headquarters of Abu Dhabi Police, which is responsible for enforcement of the UAE's immigration laws. Originally championed by H.R.H. Sheikh Saif Bin Zayed, now Minister of Interior, the system enrolls the irises of inmates and expellees at geographically distributed deportation centers throughout the UAE into a central database at the General Headquarters of Abu Dhabi Police. A real-time, one-to-all iris check of arriving passengers with new visit or work visas at any UAE border point quickly reveals if that person has been previously expelled from the country. People are being enrolled at 22 enrollment centers, covering the entire United Arab Emirates, while simultaneous searches are taking place at border points, all without any interruptions or delays.

22.2.3 Biometrics in Use

Iris Recognition

At the heart of the border control system is the Iris Recognition Technology (IRT) invented by Daugman [3] and now solely owned by Iridian Technologies, Inc. a subsidiary of L-1 Identity Solutions [4]. The iris itself, being the only visible internal organ, is well protected behind the cornea and does not change through time. The individual to be recognized presents his or her eye to the iris camera, a specially formatted image is captured, the iris area is located, and the texture features within the iris are encoded in a binary IrisCode template. The IrisCode template is a very compact mathematical description of the iris pattern. In order to complete the recognition process the template generated from the presented image is compared against previously collected and stored templates and a match decision is made depending upon whether the person was previously enrolled or not.

System Architecture

The framework for the IDTS is the Iris Farm Architecture (IFA®), a scalable architecture designed to support geographically distributed Iris Enrollment Centers and Iris Finder Workstations. The IFA was developed by IrisGuard, Inc. [5], the company that originally designed the IDTS. This unique architecture is specifically designed to support the needs of large scale systems performing iris-based enrollments and searches. IrisGuard's products also include a very high quality iris camera, particularly suited to large deployments, that is being used in the IDTS.

The system consists of three main components as shown in Figure 22.1: an Enrollment Center, a Central Iris Repository and an Iris Finder Workstation. Each component is made up of one or more stand-alone applications designed to communicate with each other using a TCP/IP link. At the Enrollment Centers, persons are enrolled, which consists of capturing personal information (name, crime, date etc.) along with the person's two irises. This information is consolidated, at regular intervals, with the Central Iris Repository. At the main center, all irises coming in from different geographically dispersed locations are consolidated in such a way as to support extremely fast searching. At the border points, the Iris Finder Workstation component captures the presented iris, generates a template, and transmits it to the Central Iris Repository for matching against the expellee database. This enables the officer to scan and check a person's iris in real-time.

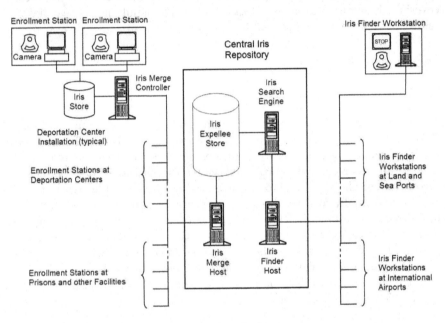

Fig. 22.1. System Architecture.

Location of Iris Search

Typically the iris search at the border point takes place before the traveler reaches passport control. At this point the person is technically still outside the country. Therefore, if a record exists on this person, he can be simply returned on the next plane home without excessive paperwork. The recommended approach is to set up a dedicated Iris Search room at a point before passport control. This room is equipped with a number of Iris Finder Workstations and inbound travelers are steered to this room and then continue on to regular passport control. The iris search has also been successfully implemented at the immigration counter using a handheld Iris device (IG-H100®).

22.2.4 System Platform and Components

The system is constructed from a variety of commercial off the shelf (COTS) components integrated with special Iris Technology cameras, interfaces and software. The databases of all irises are memory resident, offering search speeds reaching more than 650,000 Iris comparisons per second. The search speed can be increased by distributing the database among multiple parallel search engines and conducting parallel searches. The operating system upon which the system resides is Microsoft Windows 2000, which provides a most dependable and robust environment for such a demanding system. The system uses an existing TCP/IP telecommunication infrastructure, but could just as easily use a COTS solution from Microsoft, based on the Virtual Private Network (VPN) with DES encryption to secure all communication between the system components residing over geographically distributed locations. Note that all communication to and from the Central Database is encrypted.

22.2.5 Communication Requirements

All components of the system communicate using the TCP/IP protocol. Hence they can function with fast lines, leased lines and even dialup when dialup is the only solution. For border points, tests on a 33.6 KB dialup line resulted in the return of the search result against a database of 100,000 irises in less than 3 seconds. However, it is always preferable to have a leased line or fast area-wide networking capabilities. The recommended link between the Enrollment Centers and the Central Iris Repository is a leased line of at least 64KB in speed.

22.2.6 Ease of Use

The system is designed to be user-friendly. Screens for different applications in different system components are designed to be simple and focus the user's attention on the task at hand. Simple, self-explanatory error messages are provided. The results of searching are depicted in "traffic signs," those indicating STOP (meaning a record is found), GO (meaning no record is found and the person may proceed to passport control) and YIELD (meaning the camera could not capture the Iris and the person is to open his eyes a little wider). The system produces concise reports that are easy to read, and all the applications employ standard Graphical User Interface (GUI) components such as buttons, pull-down menus etc. The Components of the Enrollment Centers and the Iris Remote Workstations are available in both Arabic and English. The components of the Central Iris Repository are available in English only. However, where appropriate, and for information that is needed in both languages such as site names and system names, the Central Iris Repository offers bilingual entry and display capabilities.

22.2.7 External Interfaces

The system is designed with an external interface capable of consolidating information from external applications (such as the country's Criminal Investigation Department (CID) system). This interface automatically imports into the IRT system those fields supplied by the external system. The information can be defined at runtime and will be displayed at the border point when a match is found at an Iris Finder Workstation.

System Performance and Scalability

The overall search turn-around time from Iris Finder Workstations at border points does not exceed a few seconds. The Central Iris Repository can perform over 650,000 Iris searches per second using a single Iris Search Engine. The architecture of the system allows for significant growth in Central Iris Repository size without loss of performance. The built-in feature of multiple search engines sustains this scalability. The Central Iris Repository can be served by a large number of engines, each capable of searching with speeds exceeding 650,000 irises per second. Furthermore, the system can be extended to serve other functions in the future, such as tracking residents, driver license holders, narcotics users, pedophiles etc. At the Enrollment Centers, a full enrollment process of one person by a trained operator takes approximately 30-45 seconds. This includes enrollment of both irises and typing the associated information for this person. The system will not allow duplicate irises to be enrolled from the same center and alerts are issued to the operator of the fact that this same person, whose iris has just been scanned, already has a record in the Enrollment Center. For cases where a person has been enrolled in two Enrollment Centers (as is the case with having two residency records in two states within the same country) the system will merge the two IrisCode templates at the Central Iris Repository and maintain only one. However, an information record created during that merge process would hold all the information associated with this person in any other center.

22.2.8 Synchronization of the Central Database

As stated before, the Central Iris Repository synchronizes data from various Enrollment Centers. As the enrollment of persons takes place in various geographically detached enrollment centers, the central database polls each Enrollment Center and reads in the latest set of information that may have been acquired by that center since the last time it was polled. This efficient, regular and fully automatic procedure ensures that the central database is kept up to date. The System Administrator can set the frequency of these polls per day from the central database site. As information is obtained from each Enrollment Center, the central database merges this information with the information already present. This intelligent merge activity performs an iris search on each new iris to detect duplicates, resulting from a person having been enrolled in two centers. Information generated during duplicate detection is also used to enrich the information presented when a search is conducted from an Iris Finder Workstation. Should a match for the person's iris occur, the central database reports the existence of multiple enrollment data resulting from a duplicate detection. At the same time that the central database is performing its synchronization and merge functions, its database is available to Iris Finder Remote Workstations for screening new subjects. No interruption of service or any noticeable loss in performance occurs.

22.2.9 Application Security

While the system employs username and password security at the Enrollment Centers, it also allows operators to log on using their own iris template, which is stored locally and not with the templates of expellees. The enrollee data transmitted to the Central Iris Repository includes the username of the enrolling officer and the date the record was created. The same information is recorded for the most recent modification of the enrollee data. This lends accountability to the enrollment process. The Iris Finder Workstation at the border point is monitored by the Central Iris Repository, which maintains an audit trail for each workstation that includes records found, searches performed, and operator access records. Standard security and performance reports can be produced at the Central Iris Repository to monitor remote Iris Finder Workstations at any time.

22.2.10 Data Security

All IrisCode templates in the system are encrypted using the Triple Data Encryption Standard (Triple DES) with a 192-bit key. All transmissions to and from the central database are encrypted, as are templates stored in the database.

22.2.11 Fault Tolerance

The system is designed to handle a large number of Enrollment Centers and Iris Finder Workstations working simultaneously. If an enrollment center loses its connection to the Central Iris Repository, it can continue performing enrollments without any loss of functionality, simply storing the enrollment data it collects locally. When communication is restored, stored enrollment data is automatically transmitted to the Central Iris Repository. At border points, each Iris Finder Workstation must be connected directly to the Central Iris Repository. Therefore, a telecommunications failure will result in loss of service. However, the configuration includes a secondary (backup) Central Iris Repository that is automatically synchronized with the Primary Repository.

Iris Finder Workstations are programmed to automatically switch over to the secondary site if the connection to the primary site is lost. This changeover is completed within 30 seconds.

22.2.12 Backup Procedures

The system performs automatic backup procedures that operate without user intervention where backups are performed for the iris information at the Enrollment Centers and the Central Iris Repository onto hard disks and tapes. The system is temporarily not available while the backup procedure executes but automatically becomes available when the backup is concluded. The total down time for each backup session does not exceed a few minutes. During the backup time, the Remote Iris Workstations will advise the user that the system is temporarily down and will connect back automatically when the backup at the center is concluded. No user intervention is required at any location for the backup to be carried out. The client can request the backup procedure to occur multiple times within one day if that is desired. The system supports a frequency setting of 0 (no backup) up to 24 (once every hour).

22.2.13 Rapid Deployment

As previously mentioned, the IDTS is constructed from a variety of COTS components integrated with special iris technology cameras, interfaces and software. The system components are installed in indoor locations, such as in prisons and deportation centers. The system is sensitive to ambient light and special care is taken to limit light reflections from nearby windows. Overhead ambient (fluorescent) lighting does not affect system operation. The Iris Cameras are wall mounted to preserve floor space and Iris Workstations, used for processing and data entry, are typically several meters away.

The Iris Cameras have operated with very high MTBF (Mean Time Between Failure). They do not require any special maintenance or care other than that normally expected for computer devices.

22.2.14 Biometrics related findings

The accuracy and speed of the IDTS has met all of the expectations of the UAE government. The system handles on average 9,000 and at times up to 12,000 searches per day, stopping dozens of previously expelled persons from re-entering the country each day. Iris recognition is ideally suited to this large-scale identity management task. Its ability to quickly and accurately identify a large number of people in real-time against large databases is impressive and not easy to achieve with other biometric technologies.

No Failure to Enroll (FTE) or Failure to Acquire (FTA) events have been reported. There is no limit on the number of attempts allowed for image capture, and to date no subject has been encountered that could not be acquired, although some certainly require more attempts than others. No false accepts have been reported. Since this is a "watch list" or "negative authentication" application, false rejects are not reported. False rejects are minimized by requiring that eyeglasses be removed for enrollment, and also for recognition if the system encounters difficulty capturing an image with eyeglasses on. False rejects are also minimized by checking for unusually large pupil diameters, which might indicate an attempt to avoid detection through use of eye drops that cause the pupil to dilate, reducing the iris area and increasing the false reject rate. A number of other criteria, such as visible iris area and number of usable template bits, are used to assure excellent image quality and a low false reject rate. Independent performance tests of commercial iris recognition systems have reported that the false reject rate with commercially available cameras and multiple attempts is well under 1 percent. If a usable image cannot be captured at the border crossing, the arriving traveler must submit to an interview and manual check against a computer blacklist.

22.3 Registered Traveler Program Case Study

This case study will describe the application of biometrics to the Registered Traveler Program in the United States with particular focus on the approach to achieving interoperability with a standards-based approach.

22.3.1 Description of the application

The Registered Traveler (RT) program is an airport traveler facilitation initiative for outbound passengers at the security screening checkpoint. RT is an opt-in or voluntary program geared toward frequent air travelers. An individual seeking the privileges of the RT program will enroll (with an Enrollment Provider) and pay a fixed annual fee for membership. Upon successful completion of a security background check, the traveler is granted privileged access to security checkpoints at participating US airports. The benefits to the traveler may include a shorter and more predictable time to reach the TSA passenger screening checkpoint, and fewer secondary screening procedures.

The program establishes competition in the private sector for the business of the Enrollment Provider and the Verification Provider, which are selected by US airports wishing to participate in the program. The key requirement for **interoperability** across both airport locations and Service Providers spawned the development of the technical specification, known as the RTIC Technical Interoperability Specification, version 1 [6]. This document, developed by the industry participants and approved by the TSA, provides the technical framework for all aspects of the program, with particular emphasis on Information System Security, Enrollment/Verification Process and Ongoing Compliance with RT Standards.

22.3.2 Role of Government

The US Department of Homeland Security (DHS) Transportation Security Administration (TSA) participates in the RT program. TSAs role includes both active participation in the operations of RT, as well as having regulatory control and oversight of the program. RT can be termed a "public-private partnership" with a clearly defined delineation of roles and responsibilities.

As shown in Figure 22.2 below, the TSA performs traveler risk analysis and background checks as a service to the Enrollment Service Providers via the CIMS (Central Information Management System). In addition to establishing and maintaining the eligibility status for RT Participants, the TSA has the on-going responsibility to perform all passenger screening at the airport prior to allowing passengers access to the airport sterile area and aircraft boarding. Membership in the RT program does not allow RT Participants to by-pass this TSA screening.

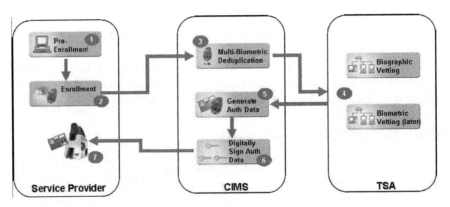

Fig. 22.2. Basic Enrollment Process Flow Diagram.

22.3.3 Enrollment

Biometrics is used to support two distinctly different processes in the RT Program: risk assessment and identity verification. At the time of enrollment, each applicant submits a full set of 10 fingerprints. The fingerprint acquisition uses a "slap" style capture, resulting in three images: 4 left hand fingers, 4 right hand fingers and two thumbs. Fingerprint quality is determined during enrollment using the NFIQ (NIST Fingerprint Image Quality) scale. Applicants unable to provide at least 4 quality fingerprint images fail to enroll and are ineligible for the program. The applicant also has the option to enroll with iris image capture. If so, then the enrollment will include two iris images (left and right). In addition, a face image is captured for all RT applicants (but is not currently used for identification).

22.3.4 Standardized Data Formats

For an interoperable, open, standards-based system design, one critical factor is the precise technical specification of standards. In the RT Program, the biometric standards and usage of these standards are defined in the RTIC Technical Interoperability Specification, version 1. Table 22.1 contains the specific standards references for the fingerprint and iris data interchanges. Note that due to the participation of multiple Enrollment Providers, the CIMS must receive biometric enrollment data in a consistent and standardized format, as dictated in the "Enrollment Data Standards" column of the table. To support interoperability at the point of verification, the CIMS employs the standards as defined in the "RT Card Data Standards" to develop the biometric payload (the data record to be loaded onto the card) which can then be read and used by all Verification Providers.

Biometric	Enrollment Data Standards	RT Card Data Standards
Fingerprint	**EFTS 7.1 Type-14** 3 Type-14 records, represented as XML	**INCITS 378-2004** 1 to 2 CBEFF records, each containing 1 INCITS 378 record - The first INCITS 378-2004 record contains 2 fingerprint templates - The second INCITS 378-2004 record, if used, contains 1 to 2 fingerprint templates
Iris	**ISO/IEC 19794-6:2005** 0 to 2 CBEFF records, each containing 1 ISO/IEC 19794-6:2005 record - Each ISO/IEC 19794-6:2005 record contains 1 iris rectilinear image, compressed using a compression ratio no higher than 6:1	**ISO/IEC 19794-6:2005** 0 to 2 CBEFF records, each containing 1 ISO/IEC 19794-6:2005 record - Each ISO/IEC 19794-6:2005 record contains 1 iris polar image, compressed - Compression ratio is arbitrary, provided resulting record fits within the specified iris container size on the RT card.

Table 22.1. Applicable Data Interchange Standards.

Electronic Fingerprint Transmission Specification (EFTS)

The U.S. Department of Justice has defined an implementation (profile) of the ANSI/NIST-ITL 1-2000 standard, for use by law-enforcement agencies: the Electronic Fingerprint Transmission Specification (EFTS) [7]. As part of fingerprint enrollment, the Enrollment Provider will format fingerprint slap impressions using an XML representation of EFTS Type-14 records.

INCITS 378-2004

INCITS 378-2004 is the US national standard defining methods for representing fingerprint information using the concept of minutiae. It defines the placement of the minutiae on a fingerprint, a record format for containing the minutiae data, and optional extensions for ridge count and core/delta information. It is intended to be used within a CBEFF-compliant structure in the CBEFF Biometric Data Block (BDB) as specified in INCITS 398-2005. This standard applies to fingerprint templates, as opposed to fingerprint images, and allows processed fingerprint data to be exchanged. The basic INCITS 378-2004 format (with no extended data) consists of minutia type, location (X,Y in pixels), angle (in two degree increments), and quality (0-100).

RT utilizes one or two CBEFF records. The first CBEFF record contains one INCITS 378-2004 record with two fingerprint templates. The second CBEFF record, if used, contains one INCITS 378-2004 record with one or two fingerprint templates. Note that the CIMS will always attempt to generate four fingerprint templates. If the CIMS cannot generate four fingerprint templates (e.g., due to poor fingerprint quality or technical error), then the second CBEFF record will not be provided by CIMS.

Several manufacturers of fingerprint processing software (algorithms) that generate minutiae templates, and/or perform minutiae template matching have adopted this standard, and testing for interoperability using this standard has been performed by NIST (MINEX test) [8], and similar testing has been conducted for the ILO Seafarer Identification Card program [9].

Common Biometric Exchange Formats Framework (CBEFF)

The Common Biometric Exchange Formats Framework is described in INCITS 398-2005. CBEFF describes a set of data elements necessary to support biometric technologies in a common way. These data can be placed in a single file used to exchange biometric information between different system components or between systems. The result promotes interoperability of biometric-based application programs and systems developed by different vendors by facilitating biometric data interchange.

ISO/IEC 19794-6:2005

ISO/IEC 19794-6:2005 specifies two alternative image interchange formats for biometric authentication systems that utilize iris recognition. The first is based on a rectilinear image storage format that may be a raw, uncompressed array of intensity values or a compressed format. The second format is based on a polar image specification that requires certain pre-processing steps, but produces a much more compact data structure. Iris image data is intended to be embedded in a CBEFF-compliant structure in the CBEFF Biometric Data Block (BDB) as specified in INCITS 398-2005. Note that unlike fingerprint minutiae, this standard does not specify a template format (because of their diverse and proprietary nature) but rather facilitates the interchange of iris image data.

The primary intended use for iris data within the RT program is for verification of RT Participants at the verification station. For this purpose, iris enrollment data is stored on the RT card in polar format to assure compact data size and interoperability. Other potential uses exist, including checking for duplicate traveler enrollments, search of iris watch lists using data records presented for enrollment, and archival storage of iris enrollments to enable future technology upgrades.

In order to achieve the highest level of performance and interoperability, it is appropriate to specify a number of parameters and options that are defined in the ISO/IEC 19794-6:2005 standard. The RT Program provides specifications (in Table 3-3 of RTIC Technical Interoperability Specification, version 1 [6]). Rectilinear iris images are compressed using JPEG, with a compression ratio no higher than 6:1. For the RT card, RT utilizes up to two CBEFF records, each containing one ISO/IEC 19794-6:2005 record with one iris image in polar format. The polar iris image may be compressed using JPEG 2000, with a compression ratio that produces the best fit to the allocated memory space on the RT card.

22.3.5 Duplicate Enrollment Check

Enrollment Providers collect the biometric data for all RT applicants and forward the collected biometric data to the CIMS. To maintain the integrity of the RT system, it is important that RT cards not be issued to the same person under different identities. The only way to ensure this is to perform a 1:N biometric check against a central database at the CIMS. The individual may be able to obtain identity documents under different names, but cannot change his intrinsic biometrics. The CIMS is responsible for detecting any instance of duplicate enrollments and the biometric data is used at that point to enable duplicate identification.

Both fingerprint and iris technologies are able to support 1:N searches of very large databases with acceptable accuracy. The identification must be done against a single (logical) database of biometric records. However, since iris enrollment is optional for the RT Applicant, iris technology is not used as the primary basis for a duplicate check. Therefore, the CIMS provides a 1:N matching capability for fingerprint data. Iris data is used as a secondary means of duplicate identification in the event such information is available.

If an applicant is detected as having been previously enrolled, decisions of eligibility will be performed. If the applicant is matched with a previous enrollee with the same claim of identity, and the previous enrollment was not revoked, then the application is valid and proceeds. An application can be denied further processing if the applicant had previously been denied, had his RT privilege revoked or the applicant was detected as enrolling under an alias (false identity). The deduplication process (also called database scrubbing) is performed within the CIMS, using only RT biometric data retained within the CIMS.

22.3.6 Background Check - Risk Determination

Applicants' fingerprint information is sent from the CIMS via the TSA to the FBI IAFIS (Federal Bureau of Investigation, Integrated Automated Fingerprint Identification System) for background checking (criminal history). TSA uses the results of the FBI search and makes a final risk determination of applicant eligibility for enrollment in the RT Program.

22.3.7 Biometric Storage on the RT Card

To support biometric verification at the verification station, the RT Participant's biometric authentication data is securely stored (digitally) on the RT card. The RT card contains the following biometric authentication data:

- Four distinct fingerprint templates (left and right index and middle fingers preferred, but any can be used, at least two are required).
- Two iris images in polar format (if provided).

In order to maximize interoperability and ensure the chain of trust, the CIMS has been assigned the responsibility for generating the standards-based fingerprint templates and the iris polar images for storage on the RT card. This concept of centralizing the creation of the biometric data used for verification (known as the "biometric payload") is the key ingredient for achieving an efficient and simplified approach to interoperability. Once created at the CIMS, this data is transmitted back to the Enrollment Provider for use in RT card production.

Iris Polar Image Form

One particular note of special interest concerns the specification of the polar image format. In the detailed specifications table, the parameter "Boundary Extraction (6.5.1)" includes the comment "For polar: **pupil and iris boundaries shall not be extracted**". It was determined that use of the more compact version of the iris format, which includes iris image data only (based on the determination of the pupil and iris boundaries), may cause interoperability or performance difficulties. The precise method of boundary localization and iris region extraction could be variable across service providers (depending upon the iris recognition software in current or future use). Therefore, for the assurance of the highest levels of performance and interoperability, the specification requires no boundary extraction. This results in a storage size (on the card) increase from 5KB (for polar images with boundary extraction) to 8KB.

Fingerprint Enrollment Selection

For fingerprint templates, the Enrollment Provider may indicate which fingers from the fingerprint enrollment data should be included on the RT card. If these preferences are provided, and the prints meet the minimum NFIQ quality requirements, the CIMS attempts to generate fingerprint templates for the preferred fingers. If no preferences are provided, the CIMS attempts to generate fingerprint templates for the left index, right index, left middle, and right middle fingers. If the CIMS cannot generate a fingerprint template (e.g., due to poor fingerprint quality or technical error), then the CIMS selects an alternate finger. The CIMS notifies the Enrollment Provider which fingerprint templates were generated. If the full four fingerprint templates can not be generated, then a minimum of two are generated for storage on the RT card. If at least two fingerprint templates can not be generated, then the enrollment application will be rejected and new fingerprint samples will need to be captured from the RT Applicant.

Centralized Biometric Payload Creation

The design of the RT biometric information flow was based on the concept of having a centralized fingerprint template and iris polar image conversion function within the CIMS. The individual fingerprint images are obtained from the segmented slap fingerprint enrollment images, and minutiae templates are generated using a single (CIMS selected) extraction algorithm. Similarly, the iris image polar conversion is performed centrally using one (CIMS selected) polar image localization and transformation algorithm.

The major benefit of this approach is the drastic simplification of the biometric interoperability testing requirements. At the time a new (or revised) product is qualified as being interoperable with the legacy deployed equipment, the testing will be significantly less complex, since it will be limited to verifying the end-to-end performance of verification stations all using a common enrollment template or iris image.

22.3.8 Biometric decision logic

At the verification station, the identity of the RT Participant must be verified to ensure that he/she is the person to whom the RT card was issued. (Other checks are also performed to ensure that the card is still valid and privileges have not been revoked, but these do not involve biometrics.) Figure 22.3 shows the basic steps in the verification process.

Upon authentication and verification of a valid RT card, the Verification Provider matches the presented biometrics from the RT Participant against the enrolled biometrics stored on the RT card. This involves the following steps:

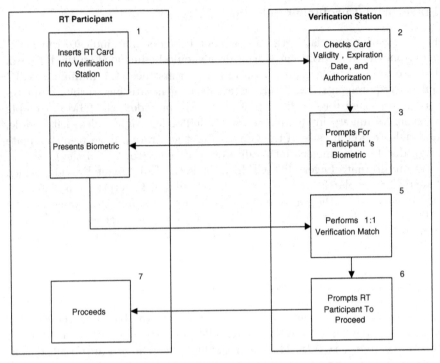

Fig. 22.3. Basic Verification Process Steps [6].

- The RT Participant's preferred biometric option and selected biometric data are read off of the RT card.
- The RT Participant is prompted to interact with the biometric capture device on the verification station.
- The RT Participant presents their biometric to the sensor, and the data is captured.
- The presented biometric data is processed for matching.
- 1:1 matching is performed on the verification station between the enrolled biometric data obtained from the RT card and the processed presented sample obtained from the RT Participant.
- Throughout the process, strict data security and integrity practices are present to protect the biometric template data.

If the match to the preferred biometric is successful, then the RT Participant is permitted to proceed forward in the security checkpoint process. If the match is not successful, the Verification Provider may recapture biometric data from the RT Participant and try the match again, up to three verification attempts. If a match to the preferred biometric is not made, the Verification Provider shall attempt to match to a secondary biometric stored on the RT card. The Verification Provider may make up to three verification attempts using the secondary biometric. If the match is still unsuccessful, the RT Participant is redirected to a non-RT airport checkpoint screening lane.

For the RT Program biometric verification process, the required false reject rate may not exceed 1% (1 in 100) at a fixed 1% false accept rate operating point. Verification Providers are not precluded from using more stringent false accept rate criteria. (Note that the TSA has established verification and validation procedures to enforce these performance criteria.)

A Verification Provider may choose to use more than one biometric in either a layered/cascaded fashion or with true multi-biometric fusion, as long as the above false reject rate and false accept rate requirements are still met.

22.3.9 The operating environment

The RT Program components are typically placed within the public areas of US airport terminals. The verification station is of necessity located in immediate proximity to the entry point for the TSA screening checkpoint, so that flow control of the verified traveler can be enforced. The enrollment station is usually nearby, or in another more central location in the airport terminal (or occasionally elsewhere entirely). In general the operating environment can be characterized as indoor, with controlled climate conditions and variable lighting conditions.

With regard to the biometric devices operating in the environment, the fingerprint devices should be expected to have no adverse effects. Capture of the enrollment face image may be adversely affected by lighting and background conditions. Iris image capture may be adversely affected by lighting conditions, particularly in the presence of direct sunlight (or possibly also the close proximity of fluorescent lighting sources).

22.3.10 Biometrics related findings

The RT Program (at the time of this writing) is in the early stages of deployment, so real-world findings relative to the operation of the biometrics will be a subject for future consideration. However, the establishment of the detailed technical specifications for a truly open and interoperable, multiple biometric, standards-based and distributed large scale application presented a significant challenge to the TSA and its industry partners. Achieving both industry and government consensus on these specifications revealed the following interesting points.

This may be (probably is) the very first initiative using iris recognition in an open system configuration. The iris recognition field is evolving, due in part to the expiration of the concept patent, and the emergence of new devices and software. In order to ensure that the RT Program can transition, if desired, to future iris technologies and techniques, the standards-based polar form iris image (without boundary extraction) was specified, despite its sub-optimal card storage requirement. This zealous effort to achieve immediate and long term interoperability and open architecture deserves acknowledgement and astute observation of its outcome. There will be lessons learned.

The choice of interoperable minutiae templates for on-card storage and verification may be an indication of a trend. Prior to the RT decision, the ILO Seafarer Identity Card Program, and notably the US FIPS-201 Personal Identity Verification (PIV) initiatives chose the same approach. Not long ago, prior to the creation of ISO Subcommittee 37 (2002) and the US INCITS M1 standards committees, there were no biometric standards addressing interoperability. Now these standards are published, frequently referenced and specified, and deployments based on these standards are flourishing. Through the continued efforts of these standards bodies and the support of government (and other) programs utilizing these standards, the biometrics community will gain the long awaited status of a fully adopted and embraced technology.

References

1. J. Daugman and I. Malhas, Iris recognition border-crossing system in the UAE, International Airport Review, 2004(2): p. 49-53.
2. J. Daugman, High confidence visual recognition of persons by a test of statistical independence, IEEE Transactions on Pattern Analysis and Machine Intelligence, 15(11):1148-1161, 1993.
3. J. Daugman, US Patent No. 5,291,560, Biometric Personal Identification System Based on Iris Analysis, 1 March 1994.
4. L-1 Identity Solutions, wwww.l1id.com
5. IrisGuard Incorporated, www.irisguard.com
6. Registered Traveler Interoperability Consortium (2006), RTIC Technical Interoperability Specification, version 1.
7. U.S Department of Justice, Federal Bureau of Investigations, Criminal Justice Information Services, Electronic Fingerprint Transmission Specification (EFTS), version 7.1, 2 May 2005.
8. U.S. Department of Commerce, National Institute of Standards and Technology (NIST), Minutiae Interoperability (MINEX) Test (on-going), http://fingerprint.nist.gov/minex/index.html.
9. J. Campbell, and M. Madden, International Labour Office (ILO), ILO Seafarers' Identity Documents Biometric Interoperability Test (ISBIT-3) Report, 15 August 2006.

Biometrics in the Commercial Sector

Salil Prabhakar[1] and Vance Bjorn[1]

DigitalPersona Inc, 720 Bay Road, Suite 100, Redwood City, CA 94063, USA
salilp@digitalpersona.com,vanceb@digitalpersona.com

23.1 Introduction

Biometrics systems have long captured people's imagination as the inevitable way people will authenticate their identity in the future. Sometimes such a world is depicted as sinister Big Brother, other times it is with the cool sex appeal of James Bond. The reality is much more mundane: commercial organizations are driven by a desire to improve their bottom-line. They do so by improving efficiency and customer service as well as reducing fraud and risk. Biometrics technology has matured into a viable tool to solve many business problems. In this chapter, we will give you a glimpse of some of the business problems that biometric systems are solving in the commercial sector.

23.1.1 Opportunities for biometrics in the commercial sector

There are primarily three unmet business needs that are creating an urgency for enterprises to adopt biometrics:

- *Reduce Fraud:* Businesses are losing billions of U.S. dollars annually due to fraudulent activities. The amount of fraud has reached epidemic proportions in our global electronically interconnected society. No longer is it the case that a business deal is done with a handshake and signature on paper; business transactions conducted fully automatically from remote locations are the norm. This makes it easier for hackers to commit fraud from remote location without the risk of getting caught. Surrogate representations of identity such as passwords and tokens have proven deficient in keeping fraud down to acceptable levels. When the fraud is committed by a single person by faking multiple identities, no technology other than biometrics can address it (for example, a single person availing certain benefits multiple times under multiple identities). Strong tools to link a person to their digital identity is imperatively needed to check fraud.

- *Improve convenience of security:* Traditional technologies used for authentication such as passwords and tokens are not only expensive to maintain but they are also inconvenient to use. Businesses enforce strong password policies to improve security but people disdain them because remembering several different, long, random, passwords that have to be changed every so often is frustrating. To overcome this nuisance, people write their passwords down on post-it notes or in a computer file, defeating their purpose. Otherwise, people forget their passwords and call the business's helpdesk for a reset, which is expensive to the businesses. For example, SC magazine reported in 2002 that organizations spend $150 on an average per employee/per year on helpdesk costs driven by forgotten and expired passwords. In addition, productivity is lost when people are "locked out". Tokens cause similar problems to businesses - people lose them or forget to carry them. A more convenient method of providing strong user authentication is needed.
- *Provide increased security and non-repudiation:* Passwords and tokens provide inadequate security and privacy and are ineffective in providing audit trails and regulatory compliance. Passwords and tokens can be shared and cannot ascertain that the person begin authenticated was physically present at the point of authentication. A stronger method of security and accountability is needed.

Businesses understand that foolproof personal recognition and security systems do not exist and perhaps never will. Security is a risk management strategy that identifies, controls, eliminates, or minimizes uncertain events that may adversely affect system resources, information assets, and a business's bottom-line. The security requirements of a system depend on the threat model of a commercial application and a cost-benefit analysis. When businesses conduct such an analysis, an assessment of security risks, and an evaluation of available systems and products, they often find out that biometric systems provide a *layer of security* that alleviates threats that other technologies don't.

23.1.2 Benefits of biometrics in the commercial sector

Traditional technologies used in the commercial sector for achieving a positive recognition primarily include knowledge-based methods (for example, personal identification numbers (PIN) and passwords) and token-based methods (for example, keys and cards). Earlier we alluded to their deficiencies. Let us elaborate:

- *Weak passwords are easy to crack.* Most people set their passwords to words or digits they can easily remember, for example, names and birthdays of family members, favorite movie or music stars, and dictionary words. In 2001, a survey of 1,200 British office workers conducted by CentralNic found that almost half chose their own name, a pet's name, or a family member's name as a password. Others based their passwords on celebrity or movie character names, such as "Darth Vader" and "Homer Simpson". Such passwords are easy to crack by guessing or by simple brute-force dictionary attacks. Although it is possible, and even advisable, to keep different passwords for different applications and to change them frequently, most people use the same password across different applications and never change it. Compromising a single password can thus cause a break in security in many applications. For example, a hacker might create a bogus Web site enticing users with freebies if they register with a login name and password. The hacker could then have a good chance of success in using the same login name and password to attack the users' corporate accounts.

- *Strong passwords are difficult to remember.* In an effort to address weak passwords, businesses often enforce policies to make passwords strong, for example, a business may require that a password is at least 8 characters long, contains at least one digit and one special character, and must be changed every couple of weeks. Such policies backfire. Certainly, longer complex random passwords are more secure, but they are so much harder to remember, that they prompt users to write them down in accessible locations such as Post-it notes hidden under the keyboard, an unprotected electronic file on their computer, or other electronic devices such as cellular phones or personal digital assistants (PDAs), creating a security vulnerability. Else, people forget their passwords, which creates a financial nightmare to businesses as they have to employ helpdesk support staff to reset forgotten or expired passwords. Cryptographic techniques can provide very long passwords (encryption keys) that the users need not remember; however, these are in turn protected by weak passwords, which defeats their purpose.

- *Password cracking is scalable.* In a password-based network authentication application, a hacker may launch an attack remotely against all the user accounts without knowing any of the users. It costs the hacker almost the same amount of time, effort, and money to attack millions of accounts as it costs to attack one. In fact, the same password (for example, a dictionary word) can be used to launch an attack against (a dictionary of) user accounts. Given that a hacker needs to break only one password among those of all the employees to gain access to a company's intranet, a single weak password compromises the overall security of every system that user has access to. Thus, the entire system's security is only as good as the weakest password.

- *Password and tokens do not provide non-repudiation.* When a user shares a password with a colleague, there is no way for the system to know who the actual user is. Similarly, tokens can be lost, stolen, shared, duplicated or a hacker could make a master key that opens many locks. Only biometrics can provide a guarantee of authentication that cannot subsequently be refused by a user. It is very hard for the user to deny having accessed a biometric-based system.

In the case of negative recognition (to find if a single person has multiple identities in a commercial application/database), any other useful technology simply does not exist. For example, passwords and tokens cannot be used to find out duplicate identities in a database. Either the businesses have to trust that the government has not issued multiple identity documents (such as driver licenses and passports) to a single person and that the issued documents are unforgeable (for example, by using anti-counterfeiting technologies) or the businesses have to depend on biometrics technology to find the duplicates themselves. Even in the case when the businesses rely on the government-issued identification documents, they are merely transferring a function that only biometric technology can provide from the commercial sector to the government sector.

It is significantly more difficult to copy, share, or distribute biometrics than passwords and tokens. Biometrics cannot be lost or forgotten, and biometrics-based recognition systems require the person being recognized to be present at the point of recognition. Biometrics strongly links an identity to a physical human being. Biometrics are difficult for attackers to forge and for users to repudiate. Furthermore, the security level is relatively equal for all users in a system, which means that one account is not much easier to break than any other (for example, through social engineering methods). The main advantage of a biometric system in the commercial applications is that it gives users greater convenience (they no longer have to remember multiple, long and complex, frequently changing passwords or carry multiple keys) while maintaining sufficiently high accuracy and ensuring that the user is present at the point and time of recognition and later cannot deny having accessed the system. Biometrics addresses the human factor of authentication and used together with standard cryptographic techniques to guard against Trojan horse and replay attacks, provides a good balance of convenience, security, privacy, and accountability.

23.1.3 Barriers to biometrics adoption in the commercial sector

While there is no doubt in our minds that biometric systems address an important security function in the commercial sector applications and that its adoption is increasing, the rate of adoption has been somewhat slower than expected. We believe that this is primarily because of lack of education and awareness about the benefits and capabilities of biometric technologies. Secondarily, it may be because the business case for biometrics has often proven to be somewhat difficult due to the following reasons:

- The business value of "security" and "deterrence" has always been difficult to quantify in terms of return on investment, regardless of the technology.

- Fraud rates and costs of long standing business systems (for example, tokens and passwords) are not well understood, quantified, and documented.
- Biometrics, being an emerging technology is sometimes confronted with unrealistic performance expectations and not fairly compared with existing alternatives (for example, tokens and passwords), whose inconvenience and high cost businesses have resigned to tolerate. A successful biometric solution does not have to be 100% accurate and 100% secure. A particular application demands a *satisfactory* performance justifying the additional investments needed for the biometric system. The system designer can exploit the application context to engineer the system to achieve the target performance levels.
- The "quality" of biometric technology varies quite dramatically from one biometric characteristic to another (for example, from fingerprint to gait) and from one vendor to another. Businesses cannot easily access credible reports on vendor comparisons because of a dearth of standardized scenario testing of biometric systems. Vendor's own claims of performance could sometimes be misleading due to vast differences in their testing protocols and demographics of test subjects. Certain biometrics vendors have, unfortunately at times, even made bogus performance claims. This leaves businesses to either perform their own evaluation (which delays deployment) or rely on references (which could be difficult to obtain because of unique operational scenarios). If a business has a poor experience with a certain specific vendor/system whose claim of high performance could not be substantiated in a pilot, unfortunately they are inclined to incorrectly dismiss all of biometrics as a premature technology.
- Several biometric system vendors are not financially stable, leaving businesses with concerns over continued product and support availability.

23.1.4 Biometrics technology adoption in the commercial sector

In the past, the most concrete return on investment estimation for businesses has come from taking people out of business processes and transactions. For example, forgotten passwords result in helpdesk calls which are expensive to businesses. It is abundantly clear and widely documented in popular press that biometric systems can significantly reduce the spending on helpdesk calls much beyond the cost of investment. In many commercial applications, the use of biometrics can facilitate businesses to move to a user-friendly self-service model of service and support while providing the same or even higher level of security as the attended model, thus lowering their expenses. It is slowly but surely becoming apparent to businesses that they do indeed lose significant amounts of money due to fraudulent activities against their data systems and centers often conducted over electronic medium by uncatchable remote hackers. A reduction of fraud alone provides businesses significant savings that often more than justify the investment in appropriate biometrics technology.

Biometrics technology, when properly implemented, provides more security, convenience, and efficiency than other means. No other technology has the capability to provide non-repudiation or ensure that the person being authenticated is physically present at the point of authentication. We believe that any system assuring reliable person recognition must necessarily involve a biometric component. Because of the unique person recognition capability provided by biometrics, biometric systems have and will continue to offer useful value by providing convenience, deterring crime, identifying criminals, and eliminating fraud. We believe that as businesses become more educated on biometric technologies and their strengths and weaknesses in the context of their business problems, the adoption rate will accelerate further.

23.2 Biometric system functions and trade-offs

Biometrics provides two main functions for businesses: *positive recognition* (to prevent multiple people from using the same identity) and *negative recognition* (to prevent a single person from using multiple identities). In positive recognition, the claim of identity could be explicit, leading to a system deployed in *verification* mode (also called *authentication* mode or *1-to-1 matching* mode) or implicit, leading to a system deployed in *identification* mode (also called *1-to-many matching* mode). The positive recognition function can be subdivided into logical access control, physical access control, time and attendance, transactional authentication, wireless device security, etc. functions based on the differences in an application's requirements. Negative recognition systems are always deployed in the identification mode. Notably, negative recognition can not be accomplished without the use of biometrics.

In other words, when a biometric system is deployed by a business for positive recognition, for example to authenticate a user's identity for logical or physical access control, it is typically done as a better alternative over other types of credentials such as passwords and tokens. If the claim of identity is explicit, the user types in her username and presents her biometric as the means of confirmation that she indeed is that person. The biometric itself could also be used to identify the user, eliminating the need to enter a username and make the transaction more efficient as well. In this case, the claim of identity is implicit. The user's account is already enrolled in the system and the biometric is a more convenient and secure approach for that user to verify her identity. The goal is to allow enrolled users a better way to access their accounts.

In the case of negative recognition, the goal is to detect if a person attempting to enroll is already present in the system, for example under a different name. In other words, identification during enrollment solves account fraud, where a person attempts to take out multiple accounts under different identities. Commercial applications can be found to take advantage of either or both positive and negative recognition functions of biometric systems for different aspects of their business problems.

Each commercial application presents its own opportunities and challenges and each one has a different threat model and thus different requirements for the biometric system. For example, requirements of a nuclear facility physical access control application may differ quite a bit from the requirements of a health club physical access control application. Each biometric has its own strengths and weaknesses and no single biometric is suitable for all commercial applications. Table 23.1 shows Frost & Sullivan's estimate of the market adoption trend for the most widely used biometric technologies in the commercial and the government applications (forensic applications are excluded).

Table 23.1. Total Biometrics Market: Application Markets Adoption Trends (World), World Biometrics Markets report, 2006. Table courtesy of Frost & Sullivan. Key: T&A = Time and Attendance; PC = Personal Computer; Govnt/LE = Government and Law enforcement; TA = Transactional Authentication.

Biometric Technology	Physical Access Control / T&A	PC / Network Security	Govnt/LE	TA	Wireless Device Security
Finger-scan	Dominant	Dominant	Dominant	Dominant	Dominant
Face	Niche applications	Limited activity	Gaining traction	Limited activity	Limited activity
Iris	Niche applications	Limited activity	Gaining traction	None	None
Hand Geometry	Significant activity	None	Limited activity	None	None
Voice Verification	None	Limited activity	Limited activity	Limited activity	None

Fingerprint is the most mature technology that is dominant in almost all areas of the commercial applications. Fingerprint readers are available in various sizes and many mature products and solutions are available for a wide variety of commercial applications. Face recognition has been primarily used in the government applications such as airport security and border control. Usage of face recognition technology in the commercial sector are emerging in some niche applications such as casino surveillance and user authentication at Automatic Teller Machines (ATMs). Iris recognition technology is being deployed in high security government applications such as airport security and passport issuance, especially where identification is needed against large databases. Iris technology is also gaining some traction in physical access control, time and attendance, commercial surveillance, and ATM applications. Hand geometry technology is primarily deployed in physical access control and time and attendance applications, especially in harsh physical environments (hand geometry readers are very rugged). Voice verification is primarily being used by financial institutions to authenticate the identity of remote users over telecommunication channels.

Given the scenario and goals of a commercial application, there are a number of trade-offs that the vendors of biometric systems must take into account during design. These trade-off may include recognition reliability, system integrity, complexity, cost (component price as well as integration and support costs), privacy, government standards, liveness detection, ease of integration, durability, modality of usage, etc. For example, a commercial application that requires the biometric system to work for all the people all the time demands a high recognition reliability which may come at an expense of requiring high computation/memory power or specialized capture equipment (for example, large-area fingerprint readers or face recognition booths with controlled lighting). In another example, compliance with certain government standards may facilitate inter-operability but may decrease recognition reliability.

The biometric system vendors spend a great deal of effort in optimizing and balancing the various trade-offs for the commercial applications they target. They try to find a sweet-spot of the trade-offs that satisfies a majority of their target applications. For example, a vendor who targets large-scale government applications may make a trade-off on cost to provide high recognition reliability or compliance with government standards. A vendor who targets commercial applications may make the trade-off on government standards to provide low cost and high recognition reliability. Similarly, within the commercial applications, a vendor who targets mission-critical enterprise applications may make the trade-off on reader size to provide high recognition reliability. Another vendor who targets the commercial application of access control to miniature personal computing devices may make the trade-off on recognition reliability to provide low reader cost and small size. Trade-offs in the commercial applications typically include reader size, reader cost, reader ruggedness, accuracy reliability, template size, memory and cache size, security issues, system design, etc. In general, all commercial applications are typically cost sensitive with a strong incentive for being user-friendly.

In this chapter, when we discuss a commercial application and the benefits of using biometrics in it, we assume that the biometric system vendor has addressed the trade-offs and has achieved a satisfactory balance/sweet-spot. Use of an inappropriate biometric system can of course make matters worse instead of improving them. And depending on the application, a biometric system may not be the best choice - other technologies, with their own strengths and weaknesses, or a layered approach may be a better fit. Finally, a vendor may have gone too far with some of their trade-offs rendering their product stunted. Therefore, businesses must perform due diligence in selecting the technology and the vendor.

It is not possible to divide the infinite number of commercial applications of biometrics into any meaningful categories. Each application has different requirements and desires different trade-offs from the biometric system. We have categorized the commercial applications into sections below based on a few primary functions and a few vertical industries. First, we cover the four broad functional categories: logical access control, physical access control, time and attendance, and negative recognition, that have wide applicability across all industries. Thereafter we delve into some of the business problems that various functions of biometrics solve in three specific industries - healthcare, finance, and retail. While this classification is somewhat artificial and certainly non-exhaustive, we hope that it provides some orderliness to the readers in browsing the vast landscape of commercial biometric applications.

23.3 Commercial Function: Logical Access Control

The key to opening almost any door in the digital realm has traditionally been a password. This was a natural consequence of the fact that at any place where someone manipulated data, from a desktop personal computer (PC) to a cellular phone, a keypad was already available. Furthermore, from a theoretical standpoint, a password can offer extremely strong security since the only place a password needs to be stored un-encrypted is in the user's mind. In practice however, the mind is a terrible place to store complex secrets; people cannot easily remember complex passwords so they write them down or tell them to others, and most people end up using the same password everywhere. Exploiting these human factors that affect security are increasingly the quickest path for hackers to break into computer systems. In addition, there are many automated points of attacks on password-based security systems. For instance, a user's password can be compromised via insertion of a hardware or software-based key-logger to trap the keystrokes as they are being entered. As computers gain speed, it has become easy to reverse a cryptographic hash, or any other cryptographic representation of a password stored in the computer, even if the password is very complex.

End users do not want to be encumbered with complexities and inconveniences that slow them down while doing their job. On the other hand, businesses increasingly find out that they must implement strong authentication to satisfy industry and government auditors. It is fairly straightforward for a system administrator to patch a piece of software or install a firewall, but it is not trivial to tackle the human factors of security. A secure password policy, such as requiring users to change their passwords every month enforces complexity in construction but in reality makes it more likely that users will find ways to simplify and recall, such as by writing their passwords down on a note under their keyboard. Information technology support costs also go up as more people forget their passwords and need to call the helpdesk. In the end, since passwords are chosen not by the system administrator in a corporation, but by the end users, the system administrator must rely on each user to follow the policy. This typically becomes the weakest link in network security. Other methods, such as tokens and smartcards, succumb to the same challenge - it remains the end user who bears the responsibility of maintaining the security of the credential. Biometrics provide the only credential that does not rely on the end user to maintain its security. Furthermore, biometric systems are potentially cheaper to support and easier to use since the end user does not need to remember complex secrets.

Shrink-wrapped packaged software solutions are available today to enable the use of biometric-based authentication to logon to virtually any consumer and enterprise application, including Microsoft Windows networks, websites, web services, and virtual private networks. Since few applications implement biometric authentication natively, the role of many such software solutions is to map a successful biometric authentication to a long and complex password, which is then used by the application for logon. The end user, however, will likely not need to know her underlying password or be able to enter it, and thus, a biometric solution effectively eliminates passwords for the user. Similarly, a user's biometric credential can be bound to the private key associated with a digital certificate, to facilitate digital signing of data, such as financial transactions, email, forms, and documents. In addition, to aid compliance, the system administrator can access an event log to confirm that a biometric match was performed for access and whether the match was successful or not.

Fingerprint-based solutions, in particular, have emerged as the most common method for logical access control with biometrics (see Table 23.1). The use of a fingerprint requires the user to declare their credential with a definitive action, such as a finger press or swipe, for authentication. Fingerprint readers have attained the size, price, and performance necessary to be integrated in a range of logical access devices, including notebooks, keyboards, mice, and smartphones.

Fig. 23.1. A swipe fingerprint reader is embedded into an IBM notebook to prevent anyone other than the owner from accessing data on it.

It is typical for the logical access control applications to have only one user per biometric reader, a reader that may be attached to the user's PC or embedded in her notebook or smartphone (see Figure 23.1). This is unlike most other commercial applications such as physical access control, time and attendance, or authentication at point of sale terminals, where the biometric reader would be shared among many users. Certain logical access control application deployments may offer the biometric authentication as a choice to the users. A user could chose to use the biometric system or chose to continue using the passwords. In such deployments, the intention of the enterprise is to provide maximum end user convenience while still availing cost savings by reducing helpdesk calls. The above properties of logical access control deployments drive fundamentally different requirements for the single-user biometric reader in terms of accuracy, ease of use, cost, size, and security, as compared to the requirements for the shared-use biometric readers. Shared-use biometric readers traditionally focus on ease of use, durability, and accuracy over a wide demographic population. Single-use biometric readers prioritize low cost, small size, and cryptographic security. For fingerprint-based readers, this trend has manifested itself through the use of placement-based readers for shared-use applications, and swipe-based readers for individual use applications.

Most platforms and peripherals that come with embedded fingerprint readers include software to access the local PC and applications. These applications may include biometric-based access to the PC, pre-boot authentication, full disk encryption, Windows logon, and a general password manager application to facilitate the use of biometrics for other applications and websites. Such a suite of applications protects the specific PC on which it is deployed and makes personal access to data more secure, convenient, and fun. Companies such as Dell, Lenovo, Microsoft, and Hewlett-Packard ship platforms and peripherals pre-loaded with such capability. However, these are end user utilities with the scope of use only on the local PC. As a result, they may be challenging and costly to manage if deployed widely in an enterprise since each user will need to setup, enroll her biometric, and configure the appropriate policy, all by herself. Usually the user is given the option to use the biometric system as a cool individual convenience, rather than enforced by an enterprise-wide authentication policy.

The other major class of logical access control biometric application for the enterprise network are server-based solutions. These solutions typically limit the flexibility given to the end user and instead focus on the needs of the organization and the system administrator to deploy, enroll users' biometric credentials into the enterprise directory, and centrally configure enterprise-wide policies. An enterprise-wide policy, however, drives stronger requirements for the reliability, security, and inter-operability of the biometric authentication. If it is a business policy that everyone in the organization must use the biometric system for authentication, the reliability of the biometric system must be higher than a client-side-only solution where the user can opt-in to use the biometric system just for convenience. A server-based logical access control solution generally needs to be inter-operable with data coming from many different biometric readers since not every platform in the organization will use the same model of the biometric reader. Inter-operability can be accomplished at either the enrollment template level or the biometric image level. Lastly, since a server-based solution typically stores biometric credentials in a central database, the security model of the whole chain from the reader to the server must be considered to protect against hackers and maintain user privacy. However, unlike government deployments that store the user's actual biometric image(s) for archival purposes, a biometric solution used for enterprise authentication typically stores only the biometric enrollment templates.

Biometric systems remove the responsibility of managing credentials from the hands of the end users and therefore resolve the human factors affecting the system security. However, the flip-side is that the biometric capture and match process must be trustworthy. Logical access control for users is typically accomplished through a client device, such as a notebook or a desktop PC, by authenticating the user to a trusted, managed server. The root challenge of protecting the biometric match process is to remove all means by which a hacker could affect the user authentication by tampering with the client operating system. This can be accomplished by carefully monitoring the health of the client operating system with adequate virus and spyware software, and in the future, with the use of trusted computing. Or, if operating from an untrusted client, by removing the client operating system entirely from the system security equation. The practical means to accomplish this is by either performing the biometric match in a secure co-processor, or by encrypting/digitally-signing the raw biometric data on the biometric reader itself so that the biometric data is trusted by the server. Of course, depending on the threats present in a given environment, some deployments of logical access control may need to resolve more than just the human factors of security and will need to use multiple factors of authentication, such as two-factor (biometric plus password) or even three-factor (biometric, smartcard, and PIN) to protect against active adversaries.

After many years of fits and starts as a niche technology, the use of biometrics for logical access control has gained a foothold in protecting corporate assets and networks as the cost of solutions has gone down, and the security and reliability has gone up. Use of biometric authentication for logical access control resolves threats that other secret-based methods such as passwords and tokens cannot, the main threat being the human factors that lower security and are costly and difficult to manage. No security method is a magic bullet, but biometric solutions for logical access control can be a reliable tool/layer to add to a holistic approach to enterprise security.

23.4 Commercial Function: Physical Access Control

In the same manner that a password is a universal unlocking mechanism in the digital realm, almost any application that uses a physical lock opens with a token (key, proximity card, access card, etc.) and is an application where access to some physical space or property such as building, hall, room, office, cabinet, car, house, garage, locker, mailbox, safety deposit box, etc. is being controlled. Only authorized users are allowed access to the physical locations. Tokens do not provide sufficient security (since they can be stolen or shared), convenience (since they need to be carried around and can be lost or misplaced), or non-repudiation (since an employee may claim that his key had been lost or stolen). Stronger physical access control is provided by either replacing the older system with a biometric system or layering the token and/or PIN-based system with a biometric system.

As an example, a biometric physical access control system may be used at schools and daycare centers. For children's safety, it is important that only authorized parents and staff is allowed to enter a school or a daycare center. It is important to record who dropped off and who picked up a child and to record staff hours. A biometric system archives this very effectively by offering security and providing convenience. It is a deterrent to criminals and gives peace of mind to the parents. Some other examples of biometric physical access control commercial applications are shown in Figures 23.2, 23.3, and 23.4.

Fig. 23.2. Rental lockers at an Airport. These lockers, manufactured by Smarte Carte, use biometrics for locker access control.

A biometric physical access control system may be a stand-alone system. A stand-alone system is not networked and usually does not have access to large amounts of memory, computational power, and disk storage. In general, these stand-alone *embedded systems* tend to have a very small footprint and require the biometric reader to be of very small size. Limited resources and small size of the reader puts significant strain on the recognition reliability since small

Fig. 23.3. The first picture shows a biometric-enabled stand-alone physical access control system for room entry. The second picture shows a biometric-enabled stand-alone door lock.

readers are not very accurate and high performance biometric matching algorithms tend to be very computationally intensive. Stand-alone physical access control biometric systems typically perform the user biometric enrollment on the self-contained device, store the enrolled templates on the device, conduct feature extraction and matching on the device, and have a controller on board to control the external locking mechanism. Upon a successful biometric verification, the system may accentuate a door locking mechanism without any external means to grant access. Often, these systems are used by a single user (or very few users such as members of a family). They cannot be connected to a printer for printing audit logs and do not have network connections, displays, and input/output interfaces, with the exception of perhaps a keypad that can often be found on such systems. Although the lock and the biometric systems may be physically separated (just electronically connected), there is a trend to integrate such stand-alone biometric systems onto the lock itself (see figure 23.3).

Networked biometric physical access control systems are desirable in commercial applications where access to a physical location is controlled through multiple doors. For example, large enterprises usually have several buildings and each building has several doors. Authorized employees may enter any of the buildings through any of the doors. Further, certain employees may have special privileges to enter selected areas of the building. Networked biometric physical access control systems offer many advantages over stand-alone systems. A more powerful computer (with more memory, processing power, and disk storage) can be used as a server. Enrollment templates of a large number of users can be stored here and the biometric matching and/or feature extraction can be performed more accurately. A networked system provides better administration since all the doors can be managed from a central location. Functions such as user enrollment, deleting a user record, changing user access privileges, etc. can be performed by the system administrator from a single location. The server typically has other resources such as displays,

Fig. 23.4. The first picture shows a biometric physical access control system based on iris recognition used in Tokyo to gain entry into a condominium building. The elevator is automatically called and programmed to bring the residents to their residential floor. Picture courtesy of Dr. John Daugman. The second picture shows an iris recognition system from LG Iris being used for physical access control at Equinox Health Club in New York. Picture courtesy of LG Iris.

input/outout interfaces, and printers to print audit logs, and if needed, can even relay the authentication information to other information systems over the network. Such networked physical access control systems use biometric readers that are typically larger, more expensive, and more accurate than those used in stand-alone systems.

Finally, large enterprises are expressing a need to integrate their physical and logical access control systems into a single homogeneous seamless system such that both types of access controls can be centrally managed from a single place. The advantage of such an integrated system is rooted in manageability – a user needs to be enrolled only once for both physical and logical access, the enrollment can occur at one or more central locations, the system administrator can delete a user record or change access control rights for a user for both physical and logical access from a central place, and so on. Such requirements translate into a number of trade-offs that the vendor of the system must balance to provide an effective solution at a reasonable price.

23.5 Commercial Function: Time and Attendance

The objective of an automated time and attendance system is to keep track of working hours for employee pay computation and payroll processing, avoid unauthorized overtime, enforce company policies (for example, store open and close times), and so forth. Time and attendance systems that are based on badges, cards, or PIN numbers are plagued with *buddy-punching* fraud (unauthorized person serving as a proxy for a worker) because cards and PIN numbers can be shared. American Payroll Association reported in its January 2002 issue of PayTech Magazine that over 5% of gross payroll in the U.S. is fraudulent. A biometric system can eliminate buddy-punching fraud and the costs associated with badges/cards. As a result of the efficiency of a biometric system, businesses also save money by quicker and more accurate payroll processing. Workers do not need to carry cards or remember and punch in PINs and thus biometric systems are more convenient to them as well.

Fig. 23.5. A hand-geometry biometric time and attendance system being used in a factory environment. Picture courtesy of Ingersoll Rand.

There is another type of time and attendance fraud/inefficiency that is quite prevalent, called *lollygagging* (when workers get distracted and take a long time to get from the time and attendance station to the location of their work). For example, in a department store, time and attendance stations may be attended and the workers may need to go to a manager's office to clock-in. They then may take half an hour to get to their point-of-sale (POS) station, which may be on a different floor or a different area of a departmental store, without the knowledge of the manager that so much time was wasted. The reason why many traditional time and attendance systems are operated in an attended mode is to reduce buddy-punching. However, this increases lollygagging. By integrating biometrics-based time and attendance into the point-of-sale terminal itself, the time and attendance can be made unattended and lollygagging can be significantly reduced together with buddy-punching.

Biometrically-enabled time and attendance systems are used today in school and colleges for students and in factories (see Figure 23.5), retail stores, offices, hospitals, health clubs, and many other places of work for employees. They are especially useful in places and industries where workers are paid on an hourly basis, work in shifts, and the employee turn-over rate is high.

A biometric system may be used either exclusively for time and attendance purposes or could provide time and attendance function in the background while being actively used for some other purpose such as logical access to work computer/network, physical access into a factory, or employee authentication at the POS terminal.

An interesting example of a biometric time and attendance system is in the area of distance learning. In traditional class-room based learning, an instructor is present during learning, and especially during testing. In a departure from this, in distance learning, the learning occurs in the absence of an instructor in any location such as home or office. The students can take tests remotely often over the Internet in the absence of an instructor/proctor. Since passwords and tokens can be shared, it would be impossible to detect if a student has enlisted a proxy for taking the test. A biometric system can solve this problem. For example, a face-based biometric system could use a video camera mounted on the top of the student's computer screen and continually verify the student every few minutes or even on every frame of the video. If high-stake tests (and certifications) are conducted over the Internet (for example, for airplane pilots) it is imperative that the student is authenticated by strong means.

23.6 Commercial Function: Negative Recognition

The above three functions of biometrics: logical access control, physical access control, and time and attendance, are primarily positive recognition functions. In such positive recognition functions, biometric systems provide better balance of convenience and security over traditional authentication methods such as passwords and tokens. There is no alternative technology that can provide negative recognition function. A biometric system used for negative recognition function must necessarily work in the identification (that is, 1-to-many matching) mode. Negative recognition biometric systems have been used extensively in government applications such as criminal identification, background checks, welfare disbursement, border control, etc. with tremendous success. Such negative recognition biometric systems are increasingly being deployed in many employee-facing as well as and customer-facing commercial applications.

In order to reduce fraud and increase security, enterprises like to avoid doing business with known cheats, criminals, and terrorists. If enterprises could prepare a "blacklist" or a "watchlist" of such undesirable individuals (for example, card counters in casinos, shoplifters in stores, criminals/terrorists at sports events, etc.), they could use a biometric system to achieve their objective. However, they must do so without inconveniencing their legitimate customers. Therefore, a non-intrusive biometric system is desirable. Since many businesses such as casinos and retail stores already have cameras mounted in the gaming and shopping areas, they have been drawn by face recognition technology to achieve non-intrusive surveillance and negative recognition. Businesses may share their watchlist databases with each other to bar the undesirable individuals from entering each other's casinos or stores. The biometric system may be fully automated or may raise a flag and inform a security personnel when it finds a match.

Negative recognition biometric systems are now being used by financial institutions to deny access to new accounts or lines of credit to recidivists listed in their blacklist. Further, the biometric system may be used before a new account or credit line is approved to find out if the user already has an account under a different name/identity. In such an application, the biometric database size could grow over time and become quite large. For example, a bank may have millions of customers. Matching a new enrollment against such a large database puts a heavy strain on recognition accuracy and throughput of the biometric system. High-end servers or specialized hardware may be used to improve throughput. To improve the recognition accuracy, there is a trend to use multi-biometric systems in such large scale applications. A multi-biometric system may combine, for example, multiple fingers of a person or multiple biometrics such as fingerprint and iris. Multi-biometric systems may also improve the throughput. In some of these applications, the biometric system can be used in an off-line batch mode, for example, in processing a loan application.

So far we have covered four primary functions of biometric systems. Next, we will cover three vertical commercial sectors: healthcare, financial, and retail. We will cover a few other functions of biometric systems such as financial transaction authentication in the context of these vertical commercial sectors.

23.7 Commercial Sector: Healthcare

Compliance with the security requirements of the Health Insurance Portability and Accountability Act (HIPAA) of 1996 accelerated the adoption of biometric systems in the U.S. healthcare industry. This regulation does not specify the use of biometrics explicitly, but it states that access to any healthcare data must be restricted through strong user authentication. Such a requirement made access to healthcare information technology systems and patient data more burdensome. The healthcare industry turned to the biometric systems to get a good balance of convenience, security, and compliance. The Joint Commission on Accreditation of Healthcare Organizations (JCAHO) auditing requirements also contributed to the adoption rate. Once the healthcare industry was educated on the biometric technologies, it adopted biometric systems for other applications as well. Today the healthcare industry uses biometric systems in many different applications to reduce fraud that is prevalent in the industry and to provide convenience to medical professional without compromising their need for quick and easy access to critical health data.

The majority of initial adoption in the healthcare industry was in the employee-facing applications. Customer-facing applications have started getting some traction recently. Some examples of business objectives in the healthcare industry that are being successfully met with biometrics deployments are given below.

Restrict logical access to medical information systems.

Medical records are private and government regulations such as HIPAA require that access to them is controlled. No one other than the authorized doctors, nurses, administrative personal in hospitals and testing laboratories, and the patient herself, may have access to them. Further, an auditable record of access instances must be maintained. Doctors and nurses may not use computers very often and therefore are likely to forget their passwords frequently. With the use of a biometric logical access control system, there is no need to remember the passwords and the medical records are readily available to them with a quick and easy biometric authentication. Such biometric systems often record the access instances transparently in the background and provide efficient government regulation compliance to the enterprise.

Improve hospital efficiency and compliance.

When a doctor orders a drug for a hospitalized patient, the drug is typically sent over from a centralized hospital pharmacy. To improve the efficiency of drug dispensing, hospitals are now using smart networked medicine cabinets can work like an ATM. These cabinets decentralize drug dispensing in hospitals to nursing floors. Medicines are more easily accessible on each floor or area of a hospital instead of being sent every time from the central pharmacy.

These medicine cabinets often use biometric systems to restrict access to sensitive drugs such as narcotics, reduce opportunities for medication errors, and provide government regulatory compliance. Scrubs worth thousands of U.S. dollars are lost every year creating unnecessary expense for the hospitals. A biometrically-enabled scrub dispensing and return unit limits scrub access to only authorized people by providing a secure station for scrub management and thus improves hospital operational efficiency as well as cost of scrub management (see Figure 23.6).

Fig. 23.6. A biometrically-enabled scrub management station manufactured by Cardinal Health.

Improve pharmacy efficiency and compliance.

In U.S. pharmacies, a pharmacist needs to personally sign out each bottle of prescription drug dispensed. There may be many pharmacist in a single pharmacy and each pharmacist needs to record each dispensed prescription in a computer that is shared with other pharmacists. A pharmacist needs to first logout the previous pharmacist from the system and then login to her own account. Given that each pharmacist may need to sign out hundred of bottles each day and maintain records and audit trails, entering long and frequently changing passwords that are compliant with high security policies/requirements of government privacy regulations can be very tedious and slow. Replacing the authentication mechanism with biometric authentication replaces the tedious authentication method with the ease of a simple biometric authentication, raises the bar of security, provides compliance with regulations, provides audit trails, and promotes prescription accuracy and customer privacy.

Reduce medical benefits fraud.

Hospitals and insurance agencies are facing growing medical benefits fraud, especially in developing countries. Fraud occurs when a single person purchases a health insurance policy that is then used by many people. Usually the proof of health coverage is provided by a benefits card. The card often does not have even a photograph of the insured person printed on it. Such cards can be easily shared with family members and friends to defraud the hospitals and insurance agencies. Hospitals are successfully reducing this type of fraud by implementing a biometric solution. When a patient presents her card to avail a medical benefit, the system retrieves the patient record from the hospital's database. If the patient does not have a record (that is, this is a new patient), the patient is required to enroll in the hospital's biometric system as the rightful owner of the card. At subsequent visits, the patient verifies at the hospital that she is the person authorized to use that benefits card. A problem still remains that the same card may be used by different people at different hospitals. However, this can be solved if insurance agencies and hospitals cooperate and combine their biometrics enrollment and card issuance operations.

Patient verification.

There have been a few cases in hospitals where a surgery was performed on a wrong patient. Such cases, even though very few, are obviously traumatic to the patient and very embarrassing for the hospital. Biometrics can come in handy for solving this problem. A patient can be quickly verified using her biometric just before a procedure is performed to assure the nurses and the doctors that they are performing the correct procedure on the correct patient. Biometric systems can be used to correctly match the patient with the prescribed procedure even when the patient may not be in a condition to answer questions.

23.8 Commercial Sector: Financial

In the U.S., Financial Services Modernization Act of 1999, also known as Gramm-Leach-Bliley Act of 1999 mandates high standards of safeguarding financial transactions, data, and assets. The U.S. Sarbanes-Oxley (SOX) Act of 2002 requires higher security standards for data that is financial or confidential. According to this act, any public company may be liable if it has not taken adequate steps to protect financial records and data. The government considers financial records to be confidential and private. It is imperative that they are secure and access is allowed only to authorized users. Many existing password and security policies would not be considered sufficient under SOX. Compliance with these two acts is contributing to an increase in the rate of adoption of biometrics in the financial sector applications. In this respect the financial industry is somewhat similar to the healthcare industry - adoption of biometric systems in both these industries is being accelerated by government regulations.

Financial institutions are using biometric systems for logical access control as well as physical access control both in employee-facing and customer-facing applications. They are using biometrics systems for employee time and attendance as well as background checks for new hires. Biometric systems are beginning to be used by financial institutions in customer-facing negative recognition applications to reduce fraud. Some of the interesting and emerging applications are described below.

Improve financial service efficiency.

Banks and credit unions are increasingly becoming automated. Employees need to constantly use a number of different computer and database systems to provide service to customers for various banking functions. When a financial service is being provided at a teller or over the phone, the bank employee must access many databases and accounts, all of which could have different complex passwords that are required to change frequently by the bank's information technology security policy. In order to switch databases, an employee must logout of one system and login to the next one. Customers must wait at the teller or at the phone as employees recall and enter the correct username and password for each system. It is difficult for a bank employee to provide quick, personalized, and friendly service when burdened with this cumbersome authentication process. In fact, a forgotten password could severely impact a service call. If the employees use a biometric-based single sign-on solution, they can quickly, easily, and safely access information from several different databases in a fraction of the time previously required. If audit trails are required for regulation compliance, the biometric system can provide a secure way of doing so in the background. Thus, the use of biometric systems delivers not only convenience to the bank employees but also a pleasant experience to their customers during financial services.

Reduce new-account fraud.

A significant amount of new-account fraud is committed by repeat offenders – people who have defrauded the bank before. Financial institutions that have been using biometric systems for other functions have started to use the system to reduce this type of fraud. When a bank determines that a certain account holder has committed fraud, they put the biometric enrollment template associated with the account from customer database into a "blacklist database" (or a "watchlist database"). When a person goes to a bank branch to open a new account, the teller requires the customer to provide a sample of her biometric, which is then matched against the blacklist database. If the biometric system finds a match, the customer's new-account application is

Fig. 23.7. A customer authenticating her account using a fingerprint reader at a Banco Azteca bank teller.

denied. If a match is not found, a new account is opened and the customer's biometric enrollment is put into the customer database. Depending on the policies adopted by the bank, the bank may make other similar databases. For example, a bank may have a policy that it does not extend credit to its own employees. In this case, a similar biometric identification may be performed against an "employee database" and new account application may be denied if a match is found against this database. Such applications often require attended use since users may appoint a proxy or provide corrupted biometric signal at remote unattended locations.

A blacklist database is useful in preventing repeat fraud once the first instance of the fraud has been detected through some other means. Financial institutions would benefit by going one step further and detect the first time offenders. They can find some of these cases by detecting if a single person is trying to open more than one account under different identities. In this case, the bank can extend the concept of the blacklist database to their entire "customer database" (all the people who already have an account at the bank). A new account application is denied if the biometric sample of the account opener results in a successful match against the customer database. A financial institution may have millions of customers and an identification against millions of identities presents challenges to the biometric system in terms of both response time and matching accuracy. By designing a system where the processing is done off-line (for example, a new application is approved after a few hours or the next day) and more biometric information is used (for example, several fingers of a person), the bank can achieve significant reduction in new account fraud. Such financial applications are witnessing a rapid adoption of biometrics in developing countries that do not have an identity infrastructure (such as social security numbers and driver licenses in the U.S.) and the banks must reply on biometrics in the absence of other reliable identity documents.

Reduce transaction fraud.

Most people in developed countries have accounts in several banks and possess several debit and credit cards. They often carry all their cards in a single wallet or purse and often use the same PIN number for all their cards since remembering many different PINs is hard. Else, people write down the PIN on the card itself. Loss or theft of a single wallet or purse puts all of their accounts at risk of fraud. Banks and credit unions have now begun to biometrically authenticate the rightful owner of the card each time it is used at an in-branch teller or an ATM. The bank enrolls the customer into the biometric system at the time a new account is opened or a new debit/credit card is issued. When the customer uses the debit/credit card, or performs an in-branch cash withdrawal, or accesses a bank safe-deposit box, etc., the customer verifies through the biometric system that she is the rightful owner of the account number or the card, thus reducing transaction fraud. The biometric system eliminates the need to remember several PINs and thus improves customer convenience. Such user-friendly service distinguishes a bank from other financial institutions (see Figure 23.7).

A significant fraction of financial transactions are now being conducted remotely either over the Internet or over the phone. Traditionally, customers have been required to provide either a password or some "secret information" (such as social security number, street address, and mother's maiden name) to verify their identity. Passwords are hard to remember, easy to guess, and the secret information is not really very secret! While digital certificates can authenticate the involved computers and public key infrastructure can ascertain that the electronic messages have not been read or modified, only biometrics can reliably authenticate the users in a remote financial transaction conducted over the Internet. Adoption of fingerprint-based authentication for transactions over the Internet and voice-based authentication for transactions over the phone is resulting in reduced fraud and increased security for the enterprises and increased convenience for the customers.

23.9 Commercial Sector: Retail

In the retail industry, biometrics systems are primarily used at the point-of-sale. The phrase point-of-sale (POS) describes a wide range of applications where payment is exchanged for some good or service. POS could be a self-service kiosk (such as a vending machine or an ATM) or attended (such as a checkout lane in a store). POS typically have high volume of transaction and thus experience very heavy shared usage of the deployed biometric readers. Depending on the deployment, a POS terminal could be a resource constraint computing device or a high-end computer, stand-alone or networked, wired or wireless, mobile or stationary, and so forth. There is a large variety of POS terminals that are used today in restaurants, night clubs, bars, delivery and quick service restaurants, hotels, stadiums, retailers, casinos, tanning salons, fitness and health clubs, and any number of other places where goods or services are sold. Below we give some examples of employee-facing and customer-facing POS applications benefiting from a deployment of the biometric systems.

Improve service efficiency.

POS terminals are often shared kiosks. For example, in a restaurant environment, a few POS terminals are shared by many waiters. A waiter has to logout the previous waiter and authenticate herself to the POS station in order to record meal orders for a table. Waiters are often very busy at peak meal times. Biometric systems provide a quick and easy method of authentication and bring efficiency to the restaurant. The speed of authentication process results in faster service and savings for the restaurant owners.

Reduce cash register fraud.

Employees sometimes steal from cash drawers of POS terminals. This results in losses to the businesses. According to the University of Florida's annual National Retail Security Survey, 2004, retailers lost U.S. $31 billion or about 1.6% of annual sales, to employee theft, shoplifting, fraud, and error. The supermarket industry provides an even more compelling evidence of cash register vulnerability. The National Supermarket Research Groups 2003/2004 Shrink Survey reported that supermarket shrinkage was 2.32% of sales in 2002. Due to this, retailers often require store manager's approval for high risk POS functions such as merchandise returns or discounts. The store managers have traditionally used either PIN numbers or tokens to perform the overrides. Due to the weaknesses of these methods described in earlier sections, significant fraud continues to occur at the POS terminals. Use of biometric systems for verifying employees and managers as well as keeping an audit trail of the authentications is reducing the fraud at the POS terminals.

Businesses using a biometrically enabled POS system can use the same biometric system (with additional solution software) to perform employee time and attendance and thus further save money by reducing buddy-punching and improving efficiency.

Reduce lunch benefits fraud.

In the U.S., about 30 million eligible school children receive subsidized or free lunch through federal government funded programs. An estimated 10-20% of government funds go towards purchase of lunches by ineligible children, some of whom are non-students who sneak into school dining halls at lunch times. Eligible children receive a lunch card but children often forget their card or they share it with their friends or the cards get stolen. Many schools are now using biometric systems to successfully reduce this type of benefits fraud.

Reduce payment fraud.

A significant number of merchants accept credit and debit cards from their customers for payment of the purchased goods and services. Credit and debit cards are tokens that can be lost or stolen. These lost or stolen cards are used by criminals to purchase merchandise against the owner's account. At the POS register, card holder's identity is either not checked at all or checked with just a cursory manual inspection of signature. Therefore, it is quite easy for the criminals to commit payment fraud. While a victim cardholder may be liable only for a small amount (for example $50 per U.S. Federal law), the victim merchant is often held responsible for the full amount plus research and investigation fees levied by the banks. Merchants loose not only their merchandise and services but also have to pay the research and investigative fees to the banks. Merchants anticipate a certain amount of credit card fraud and set prices accordingly, passing the cost to their customers. To remain competitive on pricing, merchants must reduce the credit card fraud to a minimum. Financial institutions that issue the credit cards may not always cooperate with the merchants since they do not bear the brunt of the fraud. As a result, merchants are implementing biometric systems to reduce credit card payment fraud. Merchants often issue their own credit and loyalty card to customers and link them to the customer's bank account or credit history. During a transaction at the POS terminal, the rightful owner of the card is authenticated using biometrics. Merchants not only lower their losses from fraud but also have to pay less to banks in credit card transaction fees. Some of these savings are eventually passed on to the customers in the form of lower prices.

Merchants face similar losses from check fraud. A very large number of "non-sufficient funds" checks (that is, the issuer of a check does not have enough money in the account to honor payment of the check), valued at billions of U.S. dollars are written to merchants and retailers annually. Merchants issue the merchandise to the customers with a hope that their check will clear. Later when the check does not clear, the merchants are left with losses as they cannot track down the offending customers. These costs translate to as much as 5-12% in lost revenues for the merchant and are eventually passed on to the customers as higher merchandise prices. Biometrics systems are now being used by merchants to reduce check fraud.

Fig. 23.8. A Point-Of-Sale terminal with integrated fingerprint reader. In this commercial application, the customers do not need to carry a credit/loyalty card to make payment for merchandise; they are authenticated by fingerprints against their account number entered through the keypad.

Improve customer convenience.

Biometric system at the POS terminals brings advantage of not only lower prices but also convenience to the customers by not requiring them to carry a card or remember a PIN. Instead of presenting a credit/debit card, a customer can pay at the POS by entering her account number on a keypad to claim an identity and providing a quick biometric sample to verify the claimed identify (see Figure 23.8). The transaction is more secure and more convenient.

Most card-based systems can be replaced by biometric systems to provide more security and convenience. For example, customers may need to present a store loyalty card to receive discounts in stores, to purchase goods in stores such the Costco and Sam's club in the U.S., to rent videos, to receive health clubs services, to checkout books from libraries (see Figure 23.9), to receive frequent flier miles from airlines, and so on. Customers may use gift cards and stored value cards instead of making payment by cash or credit card. They may have to provide identity card for age verification when purchasing tobacco or alcohol. It is very inconvenient for customers to manage so many different cards and remember to take a certain card before visiting that store/library. If the card(s) are lost, customers can loose many discounts. Merchants will need to reissue new cards, which is expensive. Biometric systems make it easier and faster to conduct POS transactions and reduce fraud at the same time.

Fig. 23.9. Children using a biometric-enabled library management system from Micro Librarian Systems to check out books from the library. The children do not need to worry about lost or damaged library cards and cannot share them with other borrowers. Picture courtesy of Micro Librarian Systems.

23.10 Summary

In this chapter we covered some of the most significant commercial applications of biometrics by classifying them under four major functions (logical access control, physical access control, time and attendance, and negative recognition) and three major sectors (healthcare, financial, and retail). There are so many commercial applications of biometrics that it is not possible to list them all exhaustively. Let us name just a few that are emerging in the commercial sector to give you a flavor of the vastness of the landscape. Biometric devices may be embedded on automobile doors and dashboards for keyless entry and ignition. Guests at hotels may have the convenience of biometrically-enabled keyless entry to their rooms after they enroll their biometric at the front desk at the time of check-in. Residential apartment complexes may use biometrics to control access to the main entrance, swimming pool, or gymnasium areas. Biometrics may also be used for personalization. For example, an elevator may be programmed to take residents to their floor in a condominium (see Figure 23.4). In an automobile, the driver seat position, mirrors, and climate control may be set to the personal preference of the driver. Different fingers of a user may serve as "hot keys" in a PC application.

While biometric systems may not be foolproof (no security systems are) and may not solve all security problems, businesses today are adopting them because they address the human component of security, produce measurable cost savings over passwords and tokens, and result in a significant reduction in fraud. Plus they are extremely convenient to use. The dollar value of such convenience may be difficult for businesses to quantify today but we think not having to carry around a credit card in a nudist colony is just priceless!

Biometrics Standards

Patrick Grother

National Institute of Standards and Technology, Gaithersburg, Maryland, USA
`patrick.grother@nist.gov`

24.1 Role of Standards

This chapter is intended as an introduction to biometric standards, and as a survey of the major efforts in the field. Published consensus standards in a wide range of fields have existed for many years. Biometric standards, however, have been developed only recently as biometric technologies have matured to offer a reliable additional factor for personal authentication and, crucially, as large-scale deployment involving multiple organizations and suppliers has been rolled out.

In virtually all cases, standards are developed in response to a need for interoperability. This creates a foundation for a marketplace of off-the-shelf products, and is a necessary condition to achieve supplier independence, and to avoid vendor lock-in. Interoperability allows modular integration of products without compromising architectural scope, and it facilitates the upgrade process and thereby mitigates against obsolescence.

The business implications of these benefits are many. A good standard, well implemented, may create entirely new markets (e.g. smartcards). On the other hand, robust standards tend to lead to competition and reduced profit margins. This process, commoditization, is an inhibitory factor for many technology companies that balance the promise of new or expanded marketplaces against reduced barriers to entry for competitors. The decision is determined by the amount of intellectual property that a standard allows suppliers to hide behind its implementation. From the user perspective, standards may serve to enhance competition and performance. For example, fingerprint minutiae standards (primarily ISO/IEC 19794-2), which are currently being mandated in a number of large government and international programs (see sec. 24.7.4), specify containers for minutiae without requiring particular extraction or matching algorithms.

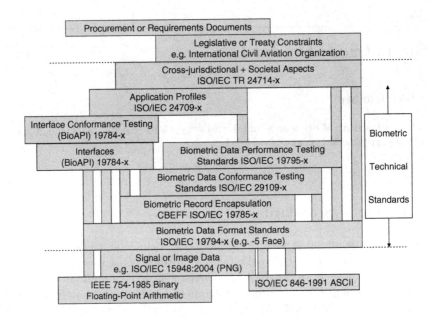

Fig. 24.1. The layers of the standards "cake".

Standards do not in and of themselves assure interoperability. Specifically, when a standard is not fully prescriptive, or it allows for optional content, then two implementations that are both exactly conformant to the standard may still not interoperate. This situation may be averted by applying further constraints on the application of the standard. This is done by means of "application profile" standards which formally call out the needed base standards and refine their optional content and interpretation.

Figure 24.1 depicts this layering of biometrics standards. The lowest levels establish data representations, the higher levels are concerned with applications, the application programming interfaces (APIs) they call, and assurance tests they may require. From top to bottom, a large scale program may rest on legal aspects, policy questions, and on an application profile which in turn calls out certain performance targets and interoperable data formats. The intent of the figure is not to suggest a definitive and complete exposition of the standards hierarchy, but instead to show the context for their development. The figure is a variation on a famous onion model of standards [7, 9, 8], in which the upper layers completely wrap the lower ones.

24.2 Standards Development Organizations

Standards are developed by a multitude of standards development organizations (SDOs) operating in a great variety of technical disciplines. SDO's exist within companies and governments, and underneath trade associations and international body umbrellas. International standards promise to regulate larger marketplaces and the development process involves more diverse and thorough review and so consensus is more difficult to achieve. With stakes often high, development processes are conducted according to definitive sets of rules. These are intended to achieve consensus standards that are legally defensible, implementable, and effective.

The following sub-sections give an overview of the relevant SDOs. These precede a more complete overview of the major standards in sections 24.3 through 24.8. The reader is cautioned that standards under development, or revision, are subject to change - the documents are owned by the respective working groups and their content can shift as a result of technical difficulties, the level of support, the need to gain consensus, or simple re-prioritization. Also note that standards drafts are only sometimes available to the public - the usual case is that interested parties must participate in the appropriate committees. Further, published standards are usually copyrighted documents and available only by purchase.

24.2.1 ISO JTC 1 SC 37

Although biometric standardization is underway within a number of SDOs, by far the most work is conducted in the main international forum, SubCommittee 37 (SC 37) *Biometrics*. This body was established in mid 2002 as the newest of seventeen active subcommittees beneath Joint Technical Committee 1 (JTC 1) and its parent the International Organization for Standardization (ISO)[1]. Although its focus is development of standards in support of generic identity management and security applications, its establishment was substantially motivated by a need for improved international border crossing mechanisms.

Its portfolio is divided into six working groups (WGs) addressing respectively, a biometric vocabulary (WG 1), data exchange infrastructure and application programming interfaces (WG 2), data interchange formats (WG 3), related applications profiles (WG 4), performance evaluation (WG 5), and cross jurisdictional and societal aspects (WG 6). These areas are covered in more detail in sections 24.3 through 24.8 respectively.

---

[1] ISO maintains a catalog of its standards development efforts at
http://www.iso.org/iso/en/CatalogueListPage.CatalogueList

24.2.2 M1

M1 is the United States Technical Advisory Group (TAG) to SC 37. It was established in June 2002 and is responsible for formulating U.S. positions in SC 37 where it holds the U.S. vote. Staff from its member organizations represent these positions in SC 37. It is notable because it is a standards development organization in its own right - its standards are published in the US as INCITS[2] standards, but may be purchased worldwide. M1's work has often been contributed to SC 37 as base documents for its development activities.

24.2.3 Other SDOs

JTC 1/SC 27, IT Security Techniques, develops many standards for security in the information technology arena, including three related to biometrics (see sec. 24.9). SC 27 maintains formal liaisons with SC 37.

JTC 1/SC 17, Cards and Personal Identification, develops smartcard standards. On the biometric side, it has codified the International Civil Aviation Organization (ICAO) passport specification as ISO/IEC 7501-1:2005 Machine Readable Passports. More recently, it has started work on ISO/IEC NP 24787, On-Card Fingerprint Matching.

ISO TC 68, Financial Services, develops Financial Services standards one of which addresses biometrics (see sec. 24.9).

The U.S. National Institute of Standards and Technology (NIST) is also a SDO. It develops biometric standards for law enforcement (see sec. 24.5.12).

24.3 Biometric Vocabulary

Vocabularies are frequently developed in standards bodies and SC 37 is developing ISO/IEC JTC1/SC 37 Standing Document 2, its Harmonized Biometric Vocabulary. The document systematically describes biometric concepts, and attempts to reconcile the variant terms of pre-existing biometric standards against the preferred terms, thereby clarifying the use of terms in this field.

24.4 Interface Standardization

Table 24.1 gives the program of work of Working Group 2 of SC 37. The group's primary activity is to refine interface specifications that date back to the late 1990s. The work items are detailed in the following subsections.

---

[2] INCITS, which stands for International Committee for Information Technology Standards, is the SDO arm of the Information Technology Industry Council based in Washington DC.

ISO/IEC Project	Pub. Date or Stage	Title
19784-1	2006	BioAPI specification
	Amend	BioGUI
19784-2	2007	Biometric archive function provider interface
19784-3	NP	BioAPI Lite
19784-4	NP	Biometric sensor function provider interface
24708	WD	BioAPI Interworking Protocol (BIP)
19785-1	2006	CBEFF Data element specification
19785-2	2006	CBEFF Procedures for the operation of the Biometric Registration Authority
19785-3	FCD	CBEFF Patron format specifications
24709-1	FDIS	BioAPI Conformance Testing Methods and procedures
24709-2	FDIS	BioAPI Conformance Test assertions for biometric service providers
24709-3	NP	BioAPI Conformance Test assertions for BioAPI frameworks
24709-4		BioAPI Conformance Test assertions for biometric applications
24741	TR	Technical Report for a Biometrics Tutorial
24722	TR	Multi-modal and other multibiometric fusion

Table 24.1. Standardization within SC 37's Working Group 2 - Application Programming Interfaces.

24.4.1 ISO/IEC 19784 BioAPI

ISO/IEC 19784 is a multipart standard defining application programming interfaces for biometric products. The first part, published in 2006, defines a ISO/IEC 9899 C language API known as BioAPI. Its data structures and function calls allow the components of a biometric system to be provided by different vendors in support of a high-level and modality-independent authentication model. At the top level, a BioAPI Framework supports calls by one or more application components (provided by different vendors, and potentially running concurrently). The BioAPI Framework provides this support by invoking (through a Service Provider Interface) one or more biometric service provider (BSP) components (provided by different vendors, and potentially running concurrently) which can be dynamically loaded and invoked.

At the lowest level BioAPI consists of "units" which may be pieces of hardware or software and which perform biometric functions such as capture, sample comparison, or storage. These units may be integral to a BSP or supplied as a separate BioAPI Function Provider (BFP) component. Interactions can occur between BSPs via the BioAPI Framework. Between vendors these will be mediated by standardized data records such as those defined by ISO/IEC 19794-x. An amendment to the standard defines a graphical user interface, BioGUI. Two other parts, ISO/IEC 19784-2 and -4, define, respectively, the archive and sensor function provider interfaces. The ISO/IEC 19784-3 standard will define a lightweight version known as BioAPI Lite.

An application may call BioAPI's high level functions: *BioAPI_Enrol*, *BioAPI_Verify*, and *BioAPI_Identify* which embed the necessary capture, template generation, feature extraction and comparison phases. Alternatively, in order to support, for example, client-server deployments, an application can more finely control when and where the core activities are conducted by calling the primitive functions: *BioAPI_Capture*, *BioAPI_CreateTemplate*,

BioAPI_Process, *BioAPI_VerifyMatch*, and *BioAPI_IdentifyMatch*. Although BioAPI does not explicitly support fusion, multimodal biometrics could be handled if the various components are capable of generating and consuming complex biometric information records. (e.g. bundled ISO 19794-5 face and 19794-6 iris samples).

24.4.2 ISO/IEC 24709 BioAPI Conformance Testing

This suite of standards is currently under development. The documents establish procedures for testing the conformance of ISO/IEC 19784-x BioAPI implementations. Conformance standards generally define a list of testing assertions that establish a very procedural means of determining the correctness of the implementation to the underlying standard, in this case BioAPI.

24.4.3 ISO/IEC 19785 CBEFF

The Common Biometric Exchange Formats Framework (CBEFF) standard establishes a means of defining standard structures for biometric information records (BIRs). A BIR is depicted in Figure 24.2 - it has at least two parts: a standard biometric header (SBH) and one or more biometric data blocks (BDBs). It may also have a third part called the security block (SB). CBEFF places no requirements on BDB content and encoding except that its length shall be an integral number of octets. The ISO/IEC 19794 data interchange standards (see sec. 24.5) define BDBs. CBEFF defines abstract data elements and defined abstract values for the SBH. The elements are expected to be of general utility - one example is the "creation date" of the biometric data. CBEFF itself does not establish datatypes for these values. Instead it conceives of Patron Formats, authored by Patrons (i.e. SDOs), that specify which fields must be present, and what their datatypes are. The standard also allows nested BIR structures to support, for example, multimodal encapsulation.

The standard has three parts: 19785-1 defines the data elements; 19785-2 gives procedures for the establishment and operation of a registration authority (to maintain BDB identifiers), and 19785-3 which defines several patron formats, including a Tag-Length-Value smartcard format.

24.4.4 ISO/IEC 24741 Biometrics Tutorial

This project is developing a technical report (i.e. a similarly drafted document but without the normative requirements of a standard) that will cover the properties of a biometric, the history of biometrics, the major modalities and technologies, a component-level functional view of systems, descriptions of the enrollment, verification and identification processes, and additional material on standards, applications, testing and privacy.

Standard Biometric Header (SBH)	Biometric Data Block (BDB) An ISO/IEC 19794-x biometric data block, or another standard Interchange format, or proprietary data					Security Block (SB)
CBEFF Header Formatted according to a Patron Format	BDB Header	1	View Header	View Data	Extended Data	CBEFF Security Block (optional)
		2	... (zero or more additional views) ...			
		3	View Header	View Data	Extended Data	

Fig. 24.2. CBEFF encapsulation of biometric data blocks.

24.4.5 ISO/IEC 24742 Multimodal and Other Biometric Fusion

This technical report articulates the concepts peculiar to fusion in biometrics. It describes the various levels of fusion (sample, feature, score, rank and decision), and includes material on correlation, score-normalization, characterization data (see section 24.5.11). It also discusses the future standardization of various data elements or functions in support of fusion, and notes that score-level fusion is likely to be the most immediate area of activity.

24.5 Data Format Standards

Standardization of data structures for interoperable use of biometric data between organizations is in many respects the largest and most important part of biometric standardization efforts. Activity is centered in two arenas: the ANSI-NIST process for law enforcement data (section 24.5.12), and SC 37 for all other applications. The goal is the same in both cases: seamless, correct and effective exchange of data between multiple vendors' products.

SC 37's Working Group 3 develops biometric data interchange format standards. It is the largest WG in SC 37 and is developing the standards with the highest profile adoption in the marketplace. For example, the ISO/IEC 19794-5 face image data standard has been specified by the International Civil Aviation Organization (ICAO) as the mandatory biometric in the electronic Passports now being issued in many developed nations.

Thus far the group has developed, or is developing, the thirteen standards of ISO/IEC 19794 shown in Table 24.2. Although all parts are developed independently, with different editors and interested experts, they all normatively cite the Part 1 Framework document.

In addition, the records defined by the standards all have (more or less) a similar design and structure. As depicted in Figure 24.2, each BDB holds one or more biometric samples of the same modality captured from a single individual. Each sample may be accompanied by "extended data" which would most often be proprietary feature information. The figure shows the record embedded within a ISO/IEC 19785-1 Common Biometric Exchange Formats Framework structure which may aid interoperability in applications

ISO/IEC Project	Pub. Date or Stage	Title of Standard or Amendment
19794-1	2007	Framework
19794-2	2005	Finger minutiae data
19794-3	2006	Finger pattern spectral data
19794-4	2005	Finger image data
19794-5	2005	Face image data
	Amend 1	Conditions for Taking Photographs for Face Image Data
	Amend 2	3 Dimensional Face Image Data Interchange Format
19794-6	2005	Iris image data
19794-7	2007	Signature/sign time series data
19794-8	2006	Finger pattern skeletal data
19794-9	2007	Vascular image data
19794-10	2007	Hand geometry silhouette data
19794-11	WD	Signature/sign processed dynamic data
19794-12	WD	Face identity data
19794-13	WD	Speaker recognition data

Table 24.2. Standardization within SC 37 Working Group 3.

involving multiple biometrics. The standards are intended to be application independent so they do not usually mandate, for example, minimum image resolutions. Some, however, contain informative "best-practice" annexes reflecting the common goal of high performance and interoperability. In addition, the common approach is to define a format without specifying how it is to be instantiated. For example, medial axis thinning algorithms for fingerprint minutiae extraction are not given in ISO/IEC 19795-2.

24.5.1 ISO/IEC 19794-1 Framework

ISO/IEC 19794-1 serves as a framework for the subsequent parts of the 19794 suite of biometric data interchange format standards. It establishes the purpose and role of those standards, it defines basic terms such as biometric type and biometric template, and addresses the common aspects associated with sample acquisition, processing and use. In so doing, it advances a generic architectural model of a biometric application. It enumerates conditions for proposed future data format standards: that kind of data should already be in use; the standard should enhance interoperability; reduce record size; offer low recognition error rates and define a format that is not already standardized yet is suitable for standardization. The standard also regulates format owner and type information so that 19794-x records can be embedded in CBEFF structures.

24.5.2 ISO/IEC 19794-2 Finger Minutiae Data

This standard defines a BDB container for minutiae points. As shown in Figure 24.3, three encodings are permitted, a default "record" format and two "card" formats for smartcards (e.g. ISO/IEC 7816-11) and other credentials. The minutiae type field has three possible values: unknown, ridge ending, and

Name	Fields and size in bits							Total in bytes
Record	type 2	x-coord 14	reserved 2	y-coord 14		angle 8	quality 8	6
Card Normal	type 2	x-coord 14	reserved 2	y-coord 14		angle 8		5
Card Compact		x-coord 8		y-coord 8	type 2	angle 6		3

Table 24.3. Minutia encoding alternatives in ISO/IEC 19794-2.

ridge bifurcation. The standard also defines structures for recording ridge count information. The standard does not specify image processing algorithms - for example while it defines a ridge skeleton, it does not specify, nor require, morphological operators for their preparation. For the "card" formats the standard allows a ridge ending to be encoded as the "center point of the ending ridge" or as "the point of forking of the medial skeleton of the valley area immediately in front of the ridge ending". Although this distinction is recorded within an optional enclosing ISO/IEC 19785-1 CBEFF header, it will lead to a displacement of the reported minutiae point and this is likely to degrade interoperable matching accuracy.

The performance available from templates conforming to the simpler U.S. variant of this standard, INCITS 378, has been compared with existing fully proprietary technologies in the MINEX evaluation [2]. That test also conducted interoperability trials, comparing one-to-one verification performance available when single vs. multiple vendors execute the template extraction and matching steps. Both the international and U.S. standards are being revised to include more extensive guidance on which minutiae may be included in the record, and on how angles should be computed.

24.5.3 ISO/IEC 19794-3 Finger Pattern Spectral Data

This standard encodes fingerprint ridge data by applying a spectral decomposition to each cell of an array. The cells may overlap and be rectangular. Three decomposition methods are permitted: co-sinusoidal triplets, discrete Fourier transform (DFT), and Gabor filters. The co-sinusoidal format encodes, in each cell, the propagation angle, ridge spacing, and a phase offset. The DFT representation allows the storage of the magnitude and phase values at all, or an arbitrary set of, the frequencies obtained from the 2D DFT of the possibly windowed cell data. The Gabor representation records in the header a single global wavelet width, and an enumerated set of frequencies and orientations. Then, in each cell, the record allows the highest magnitude value to be reported, or the magnitude, and optionally the phase, values of the Gabor wavelet at those frequencies and orientations. The standard does not support hierarchical multiscale decomposition of the image. The issue of whether the three encodings are interoperable (i.e. whether DFT-encoded templates can be compared with Gabor-encoded templates, for example) is an open question. Such interoperability would be mediated by an image reconstruction.

The use of this standard, therefore, probably rests on the existence of a robust governing application profile which would mandate, for example, the use of co-sinusoidal triplets. Indeed a U.S. variant, INCITS 377, encodes only the co-sinusoidal format.

24.5.4 ISO/IEC 19794-4 Finger Image Data

This standard defines a container for 2D raster images of greyscale fingers and palms. The record includes fields to indicate the finger position (index, ring etc), impression type (rolled, plain, latent, swipe etc), scanning and stored resolution, and certification status of the acquisition device. Precision may be 1-16 bits, and images may be either uncompressed (bit packed or byte aligned), or encoded using JPEG [4], JPEG 2000 [5], PNG [6], or WSQ [1]. The standard encodes essentially the same content as its law enforcement parent, the ANSI/NIST standard [3], and it directly inherits content such as enumerated values for impression type and finger position from it.

24.5.5 ISO/IEC 19794-5 Face Image Data

This standard defines a data structure for the storage of face images. The record includes fields for expression, eye-color, hair color, and gender. It optionally allows the inclusion of ISO/IEC 14496-2 MPEG 4 feature points. The standard includes various quality related requirements. For example the pose angle is required to be ± 5 deg, and there must be at least 7 bits of greylevel information on the face. Conformance to these requirements will elevate face recognition performance. Testing of conformance to such specifications requires application of non-trivial image analyses.

The standard establishes requirements for each image in an object oriented hierarchy of face images. A "basic" image, with few normative requirements on its semantic content is accompanied by an abstract frontal image from which two more regulated image types are derived. As shown in Figure 24.3, these differ geometrically: the Token image requires the eyes to be at predefined coordinates specified parametrically on the width of the image, while the Full Frontal image relaxes this[3]. The Token image will require the use of an eye-detection algorithm (or trained operator) to drive an affine transformation of the raw data. The intention is that face recognition products can be expedited if they are handed a Token image. However, successful interoperability may depend on the uniformity of eye-placement algorithms.

The standard is currently being amended to include fields for storage of co-temporal uncompressed 3D data, and to establish best practices for taking photographs in photo studios and automated photo booths.

---

[3] Note, however, the standard requires Full Frontal images to have a width of at least 180 pixels, implying about 90 pixels between the eyes.

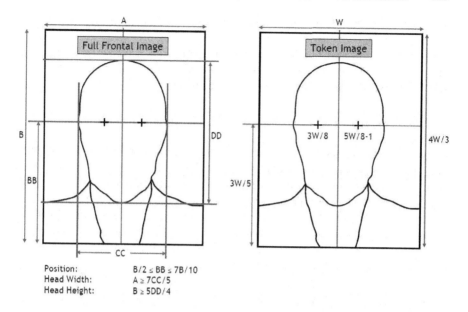

Fig. 24.3. Geometries of the ISO/IEC 19794-5 Frontal Face Images

24.5.6 ISO/IEC 19794-6 Iris Image Data

This standard defines a data structure for the storage of either a conventional rectilinear 2D raster image of an eye, or a polar coordinate representation of the iris data[4]. The polar format uses the region delimited by the inner iris-pupil and outer iris-sclera boundaries that are assumed to be circular but not necessarily concentric. The polar image, obtained by bilinear interpolation of the rectilinear image data, is considerably smaller than its parent. The standard does not regulate the sensor nor the illumination - the resulting images may be monochrome or color, but must have at least 8 bits per channel. A best-practice annex suggests quality values based solely on the optical resolution of the scan, and regards irides of greater than 200 pixels diameter to be of highest quality. This implies a scanner requirement of 16.7 lines pairs per mm.

24.5.7 ISO/IEC 19794-7 Signature/Sign Time Series Data

This standard defines a container for recording data captured when a person writes a signature or a personal sign on a digitizing tablet or with an advanced pen system. The standard does not regulate the capture device other than

---

[4] Some implementations are including more than just the iris itself in the polar format; This is an example of how an otherwise well-written standard can be re-interpreted yet remain conformant.

to require generation of pen location time series data (x, y, t). It optionally allows recording of thirteen other variables including pressure exerted, velocity and acceleration, and pen orientation. This comprehensive set is designed to support generic applications, and the standard acknowledges that a profile is needed to restrict these for a specific application.

24.5.8 ISO/IEC 19794-8 Finger Pattern Skeletal Data

This standard defines a container for the skeletal structure of a fingerprint's ridges and its minutiae points. The ridge skeletons are regarded as a sequence of line elements, and encoded using arbitrary precision location and angle information. The result is that the standard supports both minutiae and spectrally-based matching algorithms, and further, it claims to support the proliferation of low-cost commercial fingerprint sensors with limited coverage, dynamic range, or resolution. The standard also provides for recording of sweat-pore locations.

24.5.9 ISO/IEC 19794-9 Vascular Image Data

This standard establishes a simple record format for conventional 2D raster images of the front and back of fingers or hands. The record includes a field for indicating the use of transparency or reflectance imaging. A bitfield is provided to record whether the illuminant was visible, near IR, or midrange IR. Mixed illumination is allowed.

24.5.10 ISO/IEC 19794-10 Hand Geometry Silhouette Data

This standard establishes a container for silhouette information extracted from images of hands. The data is represented by a Freeman chain encoding of the outline of the binary hand silhouette viewed from the top and from the side. The result is a compact representation that supports perimeter image reconstruction and thereby any number of feature extraction algorithms. The record has fields for view direction, the subset of the fingers that are represented, the (isotropic) imaging resolution, a measure of (symmetric) distortion, quality, camera and hand position, chain code starting point coordinates, and boolean indicators of 4 or 8 way encoding, and optical or linear scanning array sensor class. This compact encoding supports reconstruction of the perimeter of the silhouette and this affords interoperability at the image level.

24.5.11 FIF - Fusion Information Format

Within the U.S, M1 is developing a standard to support score-level fusion [12]. The intent is to facilitate applications in which samples from one or more modalities are compared using two or more matching algorithms and the respective similarity scores are fused. The fusion process itself is not regulated. Accordingly the standard defines a container for either the location and scale parameters, or for the full cumulative distribution function, of the genuine and/or impostor scores. Operationally, score-level fusion is attractive because the clearly defined modularity of separately-supplied matching algorithms maps well to a large-scale systems integration paradigm: each matching algorithm supplier would contribute an appropriate record to an integrator or a third party fusion specialist. This concept means that the standard does not attempt to record joint score distributions. This limitation is minor if different modalities can be assumed independent.

24.5.12 ANSI/NIST ITL 1-2007

Initiated in 1986 as a minutiae transmission format, this standard [3] is the earliest [11], most widely deployed, and probably the most important biometric standard. It establishes formats for the markup and transmission of textual, minutiae, and image data between law enforcement agencies, both within the United States and internationally. The standard was developed at NIST by many collaborating parties in response to the Federal Bureau of Investigation's need to establish a consistent encoding for the data sent to it for criminal searches. It's maturity has led to its adoption by, among others, U.S. Department of Homeland Security for its internal applications, most notably those relating to border crossing, and for interoperability with the FBI.

The FBI formally leverages the ANSI/NIST standard in its Electronic Biometric Transmission Standard (EBTS)[5] which defines the interface between the FBI's biometric matching facility (known as IAFIS) and other agencies' systems. The standard is needed when a local law enforcement agency, equipped with its own sensors and workstations, collects and stores fingerprints for forwarding to State, and then FBI, search facilities. This entails the production (and storage) of a transaction consisting of mandatory Type 1 and 2 metadata records, optional Type 10 facial mugshots, and fourteen Type 4 fingerprint records (ten rolled fingers, two four-finger flat "slap" impressions, and two flat thumbs).

The standard has been revised three times (ANSI mandates a five year update cycle) and is more widely deployed than other, more recent, biometric standards. In its latest version [3], the standard now defines the sixteen record types shown in Table 24.4. Some material from recent ISO standardization efforts on face and iris have been introduced.

The standard is unique among biometric data formats standards in that it makes use of tag-delimited fields. A XML-based analogue of the sixteen typed records is under development.

---

[5] EBTS was for many years the Electronic Fingerprint Transmission Specification, or EFTS. The change reflects a migration toward multimodal biometrics.

Type	Contents or Purpose
1	Transaction information
2	User-defined descriptive text
3	Low resolution grayscale fingerprint image
4	High resolution grayscale fingerprint image - Most common submission to FBI
5	Low resolution binary fingerprint image
6	High resolution binary fingerprint image
7	User-defined image
8	Signature image
9	Minutiae data
10	Facial, Scar, Mark and Tattoo image (identified by tags)
13	Variable-resolution latent image
14	Variable-resolution fingerprint image - This is an improved Type 4
15	Variable-resolution palmprint image
16	User-defined variable-resolution testing image
17	Iris rectilinear image - Essentially the ISO/IEC 19794-6 rectilinear format image must be transmitted in the Type 99 record
99	CBEFF wrapped biometric data - Any other kind of biometric not already supported by Types 1-17. ISO/IEC 19794-x could reside here.

Table 24.4. The defined Types of the ANSI-NIST ITL 1-2007 standard.

24.6 Performance Testing

24.6.1 ISO/IEC 19795-1 Principles and Framework

Published in 2006, this standard provides a wealth of material on biometric testing and reporting. It is an evolution of a seminal biometric evaluation Best Practices document [10]. It serves as a definitive guide to the development of all "technical performance" evaluations of biometric systems and devices. The aim is to estimate error and throughput rates, with the goal of understanding and predicting the real-world performance of a biometric system. The standard addresses verification and identification, online and offline testing, crew recruitment and use, and statistical aspects. It establishes and differentiates core matching error rates from transactional rates and also defines failure-to-enroll and failure-to-acquire rates.

24.6.2 ISO/IEC 19795-2 Technology and Scenario Evaluation

Published in 2007, this standard regulates two mostly distinct kinds of biometric tests - technology tests (with offline test corpora) of core algorithmic capability of components, and scenario tests (with a live population) of products intended to be predictive of deployed operation. For scenario tests the standard defines the interaction of a person with a system in terms of placements, attempts and transactions and guides data collection activities for impostors and genuine users. The standard also establishes extensive requirements for what must be reported in an evaluation report.

24.6.3 ISO/IEC 19795-3 Modality-specific Testing

This technical report is under development to cover modality-specific aspects of biometric testing. It includes guidance on the unique aspects of composition of the test population, data collection, formulation of impostor transactions, and reporting requirements. It gives detailed enumeration of the influential factors for each modality (e.g. pose for face).

24.6.4 ISO/IEC 19795-4 Interoperability Performance Testing

This standard is under development to address interoperability evaluation of modular biometric components. It was initiated after completion of data interchange standards (most prominently the ISO/IEC 19794-2,3,8 fingerprint templates and 19794-6 iris image standards) and the question arose of just how interoperable conformant samples are. For example, if standard minutiae templates enrolled using product A are authenticated against templates from product B, using a matching algorithm C, is there an accuracy penalty with respect to single-supplier execution of the same tasks. The standard mandates an offline matching phase due to the polynomial cost of cross-vendor testing. The standard considers interoperability at all stages (acquisition, feature extraction, etc) in terms of recognition error rates. This departs from a conformance-only approach in which interoperability is assumed to follow if products can be certified in a standalone manner (by validating the optical properties of a fingerprint sensor, for example).

24.6.5 ISO/IEC 19795-5 Performance of Biometric Access Control Systems

This standard is under development to establish a definitive procedure for the testing of biometric access control products. It mandates a specific crew size, and regulates the minimum and maximum time periods for subject revisit. It guides on measurement and reporting of habituation effects. The standard is likely to include procedures to map receiver operating characteristic (Type I vs. Type II error rates) performance statements to ordered achievement indicators.

24.6.6 ISO/IEC 19795-6 Performance of Operational Systems

This standard is under development to address evaluation of fielded systems. It is intended to give a snapshot estimate of performance. It will enumerate aspects that are specific to live operations. For example, it allows a population to have been enrolled before the test. One peculiar aspect is that the presence of an impostor is usually not known operationally. To this end the standard is likely to include guidance on the instrumentation of various components to support interception of otherwise temporary data. Such activity could be of value if offline impostor comparisons can be executed.

24.7 Profiles

As indicated in Figure 24.1, application profiles are standards that tailor one or more underlying standards for a specific activity or operation. Profiles usually call out specific values for the optional content of standards, and for parameter values. For example, an application profile for iris-based verification of system administrators might specify that two ISO/IEC 19794-6 polar iris images must accompany a 19794-5 token face image on an identity credential. The following subsections give SC 37's activity in this area, while the final subsection describes a U.S. government application profile.

24.7.1 ISO/IEC 24713-1 Biometric System Reference Architecture

This standard enumerates the functional components of generic biometric systems, and identifies the nature of each. It also advances a biometric reference architecture that embeds the SC 37 base standards and shows their role in support of interoperability and data exchange.

24.7.2 ISO/IEC 24713-2 Physical Access Control for Employees at Airports

This standard describes a token-based role for biometrics in airport environments. It defines the environment as: the relevant parties (employees, authorities etc.), the token they carry, the physical infrastructure, and the token management and command systems. It defines enrollment, issuance, activation and usage processes. It includes profiles of Parts 2 to 8 of ISO/IEC 19794, and of BioAPI, ISO/IEC 19784-1.

24.7.3 ISO/IEC 24713-3 Biometric Based Verification and Identification of Seafarers

This standard is under development essentially as a codification of the biometric requirements of the International Labour Organization's Convention No. 185 (2003) that establishes specifications for an identity document that must be issued to seafarers from ratifying nations. This standard refers to Parts 2, 5 and 7 of ISO/IEC 19794.

24.7.4 NIST SP 800-76 Personal Identity Verification

In August 2004, Homeland Security Presidential Directive 12 directed the executive branch of the U.S. government to establish a highly secure credentialing mechanism and universally interoperable identification token for its employees and contractors. Under the legislative authority given to it by the 2002 Federal Information Security Management Act (FISMA), NIST authored

Federal Information Processing Standard 201, *Personal Identity Verification*, in January 2005. That standard mandated a smart-card credential containing fingerprint data from two fingers. The exact biometric specifications were subsequently published in NIST Special Publication 800-76 [13] which, serving essentially as an application profile, requires two INCITS 378 (the U.S. precursor to ISO/IEC 19794-2) fingerprint minutiae templates to be stored on the card. Further, the standard requires authentication processes involving those templates to use products certified as being interoperable under ISO/IEC 19795-4 testing procedures.

NIST SP 800-76 also rigidly specifies standardized face and fingerprint records, and requires FBI certified scanners. All biometric data must be digitally signed.

24.8 Societal and Cross-Jurisdictional Aspects

SC 37 Working Group 6 is developing two technical reports in the technical policy arena. The first, ISO/IEC 24714-1, Guide to the Accessibility, Privacy and Health and Safety Issues in the Deployment of Biometric Systems for Commercial Application, guides the design of systems using biometric technologies and recording biometric information with regards to: societal norms and legal requirements; privacy protection applicable to identifiable individuals; an individuals access to and use of recorded information provided by systems; and, health, safety and legal issues associated with capture of biometric data.

ISO/IEC 24714-2, Practical Application to Specific Contexts, is likely to list for many biometric modalities their individual jurisdictional accessibility, health and safety, usability, acceptance, and societal, cultural and ethical issues. Two examples: The possible need to re-enroll cataract surgery patients in iris systems is listed as an accessibility issue; the capture of a face photo is regarded as intrusive in some cultures.

24.9 Security Standards

24.9.1 ISO/IEC 19792 Security Evaluation of Biometrics

This standard is under development in SC 27. It considers active attacks and is distinct from SC 37's testing standards described in section 24.6 for which active attacks are out of scope. The standard differentiates between biometric components, systems, and applications and it quantifies security in terms of error rates, including the error rate encountered given specific active impostor attempts. It includes requirements on testing of vulnerability and on privacy (i.e. protection of enrolled data).

24.9.2 ISO/IEC 24761 Authentication Context for Biometrics

This standard is under development in SC 27 to enable organizations who receive results of users' biometric authentications over an open network to ascertain whether the circumstances of the remote authentication satisfied their requirements. It conceives of six "biometric processing units" (capture, intermediate and final signal processing, storage, comparison and decision) which may be tamper-proof. Each unit signs its standardized output data records (known as an AcBio) with its own private key.

24.9.3 ISO/IEC 24745 Biometric Template Protection

This standard is under development in SC 27 to guide the protection of biometric templates with respect to confidentiality, integrity and availability. It also discusses various techniques for binding the template with other user data and how the binding impacts confidentiality, integrity, availability and privacy concerns. In that context, the standard may discuss biometric templates for key generation.

24.9.4 ISO/IEC 19092-1 Security Framework

Published in 2006, this international standard was developed in ISO's TC 68. It establishes a security framework for biometric-based authentication of individuals in the financial services arena. It requires integrity protection (digital signature, for example) for biometric data and authentication results when these are transmitted between components. It also requires mutual authentication of the source and destination in such transactions. This standard originated as X9.84, X9 being the U.S. TAG to TC 68.

References

1. Criminal Justice Information Services Division, Federal Bureau of Investigation. *WSQ Gray-Scale Fingerprint Image Compression Specification, IAFIS-IC-0110 (V3)*, 1997.
2. P. J. Grother et al. MINEX - Performance and Interoperability of the INCITS 378 Fingerprint Template. NISTIR 7296, National Institute of Standards and Technology, Gaithersburg, Maryland, 2006. Available at http://fingerprint.nist.gov/minex04.
3. R. M. McCabe et al. *Data Format for the Interchange of Fingerprint, Facial, and Other Biometric Information.* ANSI/NIST, 2007.
4. JTC 1, SC29 Coding of audio, picture, multimedia and hypermedia information. *ISO/IEC 10918-1 Digital compression and coding of continuous-tone still images: Requirements and guidelines*, international standard edition, 1994.
5. JTC 1, SC29 Coding of audio, picture, multimedia and hypermedia information. *ISO/IEC 15444-1 JPEG 2000 image coding system: Core coding system*, international standard edition, 2004.

6. JTC 1, SC29 Coding of audio, picture, multimedia and hypermedia information. *ISO/IEC 15948 Computer graphics and image processing – Portable Network Graphics (PNG): Functional specification*, international standard edition, 2004.

7. JTC 1, SC37 Biometrics, Working Group 2. *ISO/IEC 24741 A Biometrics Tutorial*, dtr edition, 2007.

8. JTC 1, SC37 Biometrics, Working Group 3. *ISO/IEC FCD 24713-1 Biometric Reference Architecture*, 2005.

9. JTC 1, SC37 Biometrics, Working Group 3. *ISO/IEC 19794-1:2007 Framework*, international standard edition, 2007.

10. A. J. Mansfield and J. L. Wayman. *Best Practices in Testing and Reporting Performance of Biometric Devices*. National Physical Laboratory and San Jose State University, 2.01 edition, 2002.

11. R. M. McCabe. Fingerprint interoperability standards. In N. K. Ratha and R. Bolle, editors, *Automatic Fingerprint Recognition Systems*, chapter 21, pages 433–451. Springer, New York, 2004.

12. A. A. Ross, K. Nandakumar, and A. K. Jain. *Handbook of Multibiometrics*. Springer, New York, 2006.

13. C. Wilson, P. Grother, and R. Chandramouli. *Special Publication 800-76 - Biometric Data Specification for Personal Identity Verification*. National Institute of Standards and Technology, 1 edition, February 2006.

25

Biometrics databases

Patrick J. Flynn

Dept. of Computer Science and Engineering, University of Notre Dame, 384
Fitzpatrick Hall, Notre Dame, IN 46556 USA
flynn@nd.edu

25.1 Introduction

Biometric recognition systems are beginning to see broad deployment. The general trend in system use includes an increase in number of subjects sensed and an increase in number of samples acquired per subject and per mode. Anticipating the increase in deployment and driven by the desire for objective performance comparisons, a number of evaluation efforts have been mounted by governmental agencies, consortia, and by industrial groups [12, 13, 1]. Credible evaluations require statistical rigor, and hence require data of sufficient quantity and quality to underpin the performance claims made. Toward this end, a number of databases of biometric samples have been collected at research organizations across the world in support of evaluation efforts and are made available to researchers under a variety of conditions.

This chapter provides motivations for the assembly of biometric samples, notes desirable features of such collections of data, summarizes the most prominent databases available to research organizations and the terms of collection and distribution, and comments on potential future directions as well as challenges. Some of the issues raised here reflect the experiences of the author's research group in its multiple-year efforts to assemble data sets for several US Government sponsored biometrics data collections [12, 13], but the comments in this paper represent the conclusions and opinions of the author.

25.2 Motivation for biometric databases

Many biometric identification techniques are demonstrating excellent performance according to developers and vendors. The data used to make such claims is often proprietary, and the characteristics of the data set (*e.g.*, demographic distributions, type of sensor used, *etc.*) may not be provided. Opaque performance statements of this sort are difficult to assess comparatively, which is essential in a procurement context, assuming solutions from multiple vendors are available. These issues motivate vendor tests, of which several have been conducted since the advent of biometrics products.

The notable advances in the performance of commercial biometrics products has been driven by sustained research efforts in industry and academia. Many of these research accomplishments have been documented in the archival literature, which serves as the institutional memory (albeit incomplete and noisy) of the advancing science of biometrics. The use of custom or proprietary data sets (typically small) was common in years past, since the number of research groups was small, sensors were locally constructed and/or expensive, and computing facilities available at research groups often did not allow large-scale processing.

The emergence of a commercial market for biometrics, the maturation of research activity, and the increase in computer power have jointly driven efforts to perform comparable assessments of biometrics techniques. As the results of such assessments have been publicized, subsequent research can employ the data used in the assessment (if available) in order to show where a new technique stands relative to those tested in the prior assessment. Documented advances can, in the aggregate, motivate subsequent assessments. One example of this is the sequence of US government sponsored evaluations: FERET (1993 and 1997), FRVT (2000, 2002, 2006) and FRGC (2004). Another example is the sequence of fingerprint verification competitions (FVC 2000, 2002, 2004, 2006) organized by The University of Bologne and Michigan State University.

Lest the impression be given that custom or proprietary databases have no value, it must be noted that public data sets are not always appropriate for some products or some new techniques arising from basic research. One example would be a biometric systems product that tightly couples a matching technique to a novel sensor design. In such cases, it may be impossible, or at least inappropriate, to substitute the public data for the optimized data from the local sensor. The data from a new sensor design might, after suitable intellectual property protection is in place, be made available in response to broad interest.

25.2.1 Desiderata for biometrics databases

Having established the value of biometrics databases both to foster advanced research and to compare existing techniques, we next consider the properties of such databases.

1. Relevance – While it is impossible to predict every use to which a database may be put, the biometric applications area is dominated by three canonical tasks: 1-to-1 matching (verification), 1-to-many matching (identification), and 1-to-many matching plus rejection (watch list). Performance in each domain is characterized differently.

- In a verification scenario, accurate estimation of error rates militates a sufficiently large number of true positives to support the applicable statistical claims (*e.g.*, confidence intervals on the false reject rate).
- In an identification scenario, correct recognition rate (perhaps averaged across subjects) is typically the performance number of interest, in which case the number of samples per subject should be sufficiently large.
- In the watch list scenario, assuming a simple sequential classifier first performs identification and then rejects candidate matches based on a threshold, features of both scenarios apply. The number of true positives must be large enough to estimate the FRR on rejections from the watch list, and the number of samples per subject must be large enough to allow averaging to estimate the correct recognition rate for watch list matches.

Without proposing a solution, we note the existence of a chicken-and-egg problem in balancing sample size across subjects. It is sensible to assume that some subjects are more valuable than others in defining the decision regions for correct identification. It is necessary, however, to perform matching experiments to determine which subjects have this property.

2. Database size – The number of human subjects used in a collection and the number of samples collected from each subject are database design parameters and may be strictly controlled, weakly controlled, or completely uncontrolled. As noted earlier, a key requirement is that the number of samples and subjects be large enough to support the analyses and performance estimates made. Within this requirement, considerable flexibility is available. For a fixed desired number of match scores, there is a tradeoff between number of subjects and number of sessions of acquisition. Many biometric databases consist of two subject-sessions with a fixed or variable time-lapse between acquisitions. These are relatively easy to collect: all that must be done is to make sure subjects return for a second acquisition. Some databases (*e.g.*, the FRGC, ICE and FRVT database components collected at Notre Dame) contain multiple sessions per subject. Logistically, these are more difficult to construct.

An error rate (performance) target may dictate the number of samples in the database. For example, the FRGC program was designed to spur research that would cause the false reject rate at a fixed false accept rate of 0.1% to decrease from 20% (the rate achieved in FRVT 2002) to 2%. One thousand false rejects would be expected from 50,000 match scores at that error rate. A minimal number of subject sessions to permit that number of errors to be measured would be roughly $\sqrt{50,000}$, or about 225. This equates to 113 subjects at two sessions each, two subjects at 113 acquisition sessions each, or any intermediate values that yield or exceed this product. This minimal number arises from a "rule of thumb" for estimation of equal-error-rate ellipses. Realistically, several times this number is necessary. Guyon *et al.* [8] and Dass *et al.* [4] document thorough studies of validation sample set size that take into account factors that may be common in biometric systems (*e.g.*, the correlation in matching scores from the same user, from the same sensor, *etc.*).

All of the performance constraints and evaluation preferences argue in favor of the largest logistically possible number of subject-sessions. Once that number is established, practitioners should be careful not to make empirical or predictive claims that are not supported by the amount of data collected.

3. Demographic distribution – The variety in gender, ethnicity, age, and other demographic properties of the subject set is sometimes controllable and sometimes not easily controlled without post-acquisition editing. The acquisition location will sometimes determine the diversity of the pool. At Notre Dame, our acquisition subjects are composed of three broad "occupational" groups. One group contains undergraduate students who are primarily engineering majors. This group is predominantly Caucasian and all subjects are between 18 and 22 years of age. The second group contains graduate students, and is dominated by students with Asian ethnicity between 22 and 30 years of age. The third group consists of faculty and staff members and is balanced in gender, largely Caucasian in ethnicity, and between 30 and 65 years of age. When grouped, these subjects are 57% male/43% female, 68% Caucasian/22% Asian/10% other ethnicity, 65% 18-22 years old/18% 23-27 years old/17% 28 or more years old.

   In situations where the demographic balance cannot be controlled, it is in the database team's interest to note any imbalance so that it may be taken into account in analysis. If a specified demographic mix is needed, the gathering organization must be prepared to over-acquire in order to capture a correctly-sized sample from the most infrequent demographic combination.

4. Sensor type(s), models, *etc.* – There are many biometric sensing modalities (*e.g.*, grayscale or color photometry (still or video), long-, medium-, or short-wave infrared, structured light or stereo for 3D sensing, and other specialized or esoteric types) and biometric sensing sites (face, ear, iris, finger, hand, gait, *etc.*). Irrespective of whether the data is being collected to enable a vendor comparison or to further a research program, the choice of modes and sites is likely to be highly constrained. Generally, the context of evaluations and research programs leaves open only the choice of sensor model and capabilities. The natural choices in such a case are: (a) choose a vendor-specified model, or (b) choose the "best" sensor available, where sensors are ranked according to age, price, resolution, acquisition speed, or other criteria.

5. Metadata recording – It is highly useful to record enough information about each biometric sample to allow the database to be segmented by subject, date of acquisition, mode, site, sensor, and demographic characteristics. Rich metadata associated with samples is not burdensome to collect if an appropriate enrollment and registration is developed. For

large-scale acquisitions, metadata should be stored in a back-end database and accessible through standard SQL queries. The baseline matching software distributed with the biometric sample database in the FRGC and ICE programs uses an XML dialect to store data descriptors as well as experiments and software configurations.

6. Elapsed time – The dependency of face recognition performance on time elapsed between enrollment and trial was noted in the FRVT 2002 report [11]. The stability of biometrics over significant elapsed time (years) has not been well studied, except in the domain of fingerprint recognition and potentially iris recognition. In addition to the physical effects of aging (which would take years to manifest), there are physicological changes such as weight gain or loss and illness that can potentially affect some biometrics over shorter time scales. Acquisition plans with multiple sampling opportunities spaced in time are the obvious approach to capturing short- and long-range changes in the same batch of subjects. The circumstances of acquisition can affect a group's ability to capture multiple samples from a subject set of sufficient size. For example, in a university setting where many samples come from students, the largest lapse that can be realistically captured is a few years, due to graduation of students. Conversely, biometric sampling of a stable employee pool over a period of many years is feasible.

7. Data editing – Ideally, biometric samples captured should be distributed without editing of any kind. In practice, editing of various sorts is common and may be essential. The most common type of post-acquisition editing is likely the omission of samples that are judged to be useless because of poor quality. Such samples can be omitted without qualm if they arise from subject factors (e.g., an iris acquisition subject blinking at the wrong time) or operator error (although the fact that such edits were made and the reason they were made should be noted). Errors attributable to subject processing (*e.g.*, an incorrect subject identifier on an image, or an incorrect site attribute such as labeling a left iris as a right iris) should be repaired before the data is distributed, or noted and repaired via a database update after the initial release. However, there is value in preserving and distributing data of poorer quality from a sensor that is being operated correctly, or instances of lower-quality samples from a subject who also provided good quality samples. For example, the ICE 2005 data corpus [13] contains iris 12 iris images per subject session, organized as two three-image "shots" from the left iris and two shots from the right iris. The sensor used for these acquisition is varying focus during these shots and assigns quality metrics to all images, ultimately labeling one image in each shot as "best" and preserving its quality metrics. A conscious decision was made to distribute all twelve images, including the eight not labeled as "best", to preserve a spectrum of iris image quality in the database made available to ICE project participants.

While the preceding paragraph provides examples of situations where complete biometric samples can be omitted from distribution based on post-acquisition analysis, the editing of the contents of samples is more problematic. Such edits *must*, without exception, be justified and documented precisely. Examples of this sort of editing are not common in the biometrics community. One common form of sample content editing is the distortion that accompanies lossy compression of image files. Lossy compression is often motivated by the need to save storage space and/or reduce download times and bandwidth requirements. Of course, if a sensor produces image files that are stored in a lossy format (*e.g., JPEG*, a very common format used by digital cameras), preserving this data is not an instance of data editing. Subsequent additional compression would constitute editing and would require documentation. The need to carefully document data editing performed on samples in widely distributed data sets cannot be overemphasized.

25.3 Collecting Biometric Samples

The assembly of a biometrics database of significant size entails requirements and issues as well as logistical challenges. The following remarks are offered to researchers and practitioners interested in collecting and distributing data but curious about the housekeeping and other issues that may be unfamiliar.

25.3.1 Issues Surrounding the use of Human Subjects

Biometrics samples are collected from humans; hence, legal requirements for the protection and safety of experimental subjects are applicable in most jurisdictions. In the United States, experiments involving human subjects are governed by experimental protocols that are to be approved by a competent local authority. Subjects are generally required to read and sign an informed-consent form before data is collected and used, every time they are used as a subject. US universities have a human subjects review committee that periodically reviews and approves protocol documents. No data collections should occur in the absence of such approvals. While the safety issues for biometrics data collection are much less significant than in medical experiments (for example), there are privacy concerns that are unique and may represent a challenge to researchers intending to mount a collection effort. Researchers should contact the chair of the relevant committee and discuss the research project and its context prior to submission of a protocol for approval.

The consent form that must be completed by every subject used in acquisition should be written to clearly describe the general purpose of the research project. It must describe the data that will be taken, the qualifications for participation, the reason it is being collected, and the benefits and risks of such collection (including the privacy risks). It should also describe the disposition of the data after collection, the compensation (if any) for participation, and the names of the investigators. Subjects should indicate consent for participation and for publication of sample data if such publication is contemplated (by the researcher or by any party licensed to use the data). Subjects should also be given the opportunity to revoke consent within a grace period and to obtain their biometric sample data by request.

Demographic information on the subject is most easily gathered by self-reporting. In our acquisitions at Notre Dame, the subject's gender, age, height, weight, presence or absence of contact lenses, and eye color are requested. Subjects may decline to provide any or all of this information.

The issue of personal data protection with biometric sampling in Europe is discussed comprehensively by Rejman-Greene [15].

25.3.2 Anonymizing Samples and Privacy Risks

Researchers involved in a collection effort should be sensitive to the privacy issues associated with biometric sampling. It is impossible to remove identifying information from biometric sample data. However, some modes (e.g., face images) are much more revealing than others (e.g., fingerprints or iris images). Moreover, researchers collecting multibiometric data should consider the benefits and risks of releasing *linked* samples collected from one subject at multiple sites and/or in multiple modes. Multibiometric databases are not numerous; yet, they are essential to proper empirical evaluation of multibiometric recognition systems. At a minimum, personal identifiers not inherent in biometric samples must be removed from collected data prior to distribution. Under no circumstances should a subject name or government-issued ID number of any sort be distributed along with the data. An unique "subject ID" should be associated with each subject and all samples labeled with that ID, perhaps as part of the name of the file containing the sample.

25.3.3 Pre-collection and Post-collection tasks

The acquisition of images may be the most important component of a collection effort, but if a large-scale effort (hundreds of subjects and/or repeat collections) is envisioned, appropriate pre-acquisition and post-acquisition work can facilitate smooth operation of the collection process. While most of these tasks are rather mundane, they can affect the quality of the process and its output.

1. Personnel – An appropriate number of workers must be present for biometric acquisition sessions. We routinely use one trained sensor operator per sensor in our acquisitions, and often have a spare person available to handle the "check-in" process, where new subjects are enrolled in the subject database and existing subjects are logged. In our experience, talented students (undergraduate or graduate) are easily trained to use even

the most complicated sensors and so we rely exclusively on student work. Each sensor must have a key operator who trains every other operator in its proper use. In some cases, two key operators may be called for. The key operator should back up data collected on "their" sensor at the end of each acquisition session. It is also useful to designate a supervisor of the acquisition process, who is responsible for scheduling operators, publicizing the acquisition sessions to the human subjects and prospective recruits, and ensuring that staffing is present. We have used postdoctoral scholars, hourly staff, and students in this role.

2. Communications – When several hundred human subjects are to be used in acquisitions, there must be an effective communications medium. We use an email list to communicate with subjects. This list is constantly updated as new subjects join and existing subjects become unavailable due to graduation, loss of interest, and other reasons.

3. Compensation – When multiple repeat acquisitions are desired, an incentive should be provided to bring subjects back for each new acquisition session (curiosity generally wears off after the first session!). Some research groups provide a small food and/or drink item to participants. The acquisitions at Notre Dame carry a small cash award. We do not manage actual cash due to the security risk, but simply supply the list of participants to the University's food services office, which adds the award amount to the balance on their student account. In the past we have also used gift certificates to the campus bookstore, which was workable but more difficult logistically.

4. Acquisition error checking and prevention – Any large-scale data collection effort will produce errors of various sorts. Some are easily detected. For example, we have had data lost due to incorrect camera settings, lack of backup, lost consent forms, and the like. In other cases, errors are more difficult to detect, such as out-of-order acquisitions. When several subjects are being processed, they generally proceed pipeline-fashion from sensor to sensor. If they arrive at a sensor in a different order than when they checked in, the data sequencing may be incorrect (a package of samples ostensibly collected from one subject may in fact contain samples from two or more subjects). Occasionally, we have had subjects leave acquisition before all samples have been collected, or skip a sensor entirely. These problems are easily detected for face images, but considerably more difficult for non-face images and nonvisual modes. On occasion, sequencing errors are detected by running matching experiments and looking forensically at the errors. Untangling this sort of error strongly motivates the use of an acquisition log (who arrived when?), as well as collection of a token from the subjects. We have experimented with different token-passing strategies. Sometimes we have subjects carry their enrollment form with them, and the operator records their daily ID from the form. More recently, we have experimented with using a card reader at every acquisition station. Students are required to swipe their student ID card through

the reader to begin acquisition, and swipe again at every station. This provides per-station sequencing.

5. Ground-truthing acquired data – In some cases, it is useful to have a human operator mark features on each collected image. We marked every face image acquired between 2002 and Spring 2005 with the locations of the subjects' eyes. When several hundred images are collected per week, this is a nontrivial task, requiring hours of effort from lab personnel as well as custom software to facilitate the marking.

25.3.4 Distribution

If a research group plans to distribute biometric samples to others, some policy and operational decisions are required. A key question is *to whom shall data be provided?*. Generally, databases of biometric samples are distributed under nontrivial restrictions and license agreements. At Notre Dame, we have developed a license agreement that every organization must execute (by signature of an authorized party such as a legal officer) prior to the delivery of download instructions. This license motivates the reason for the database, states the qualifications for recipients, forbids redistribution, claims a collection copyright on the data, forbids modification and commercial use (beyond use in product development) of the data, imposes a citation requirement on publications using the data, and requires indemnification by the licensee for any claims or litigation arising from improper use of the data by the licensee.

The other key question is *how shall the data be delivered?* This question is of some importance since biometrics databases tend to be very large (our databases range from gigabytes to terabytes in size). During the first few years of our collection activity, we required licensees to ship us a hard drive upon which we placed the data and shipped it back to the licensee. Since 2005, however, we have delivered all of our data over the Internet using rsync, a bulk data transfer protocol with security and restart features (so that data transfers interrupted by network problems can be restarted where they stopped).

25.4 Extant Unimodal, single-site databases

This section describes some available unimodal databases for biometrics research and evaluation. The list of databases here is not intended to be exhaustive, but instead is designed to note those databases that have been used in significant numbers of papers since their introduction. For each database, a URL containing information about the database is listed along with some of its key descriptors including mode, size of image, number of images, and number of subjects.

Some of the databases listed here are components of multimodal databases noted later in this chapter.

25.4.1 Face Image Databases

MIT face database

(URL: `ftp://whitechapel.media.mit.edu/pub/images`)[1]

- Size: 432 images; 16 subjects, 27 images per subject.
- Notes: variety of lighting conditions and head poses. This database was one of the first released and is not large enough to support strong claims about face recognition system performance. Its use is not recommended.

Olivetti/AT&T face database

(`http://www.cl.cam.ac.uk/research/dtg/attarchive/facedatabase.html`)

- Size: 400 images; 40 subjects, 10 images per subject.
- Notes: various lighting and expression combinations, with and without glasses. This database was one of the first released and is not large enough to support strong claims about face recognition system performance. Its use is not recommended.

FERET and Color FERET

(URL: `http://www.itl.nist.gov/iad/humanid/feret/`)

- Size: 14,051 images; 1204 subjects, variable number of images per subject.
- Notes: varying lighting, face pose, facial expressions. Pose and illumination prompted. License agreement required.

PIE

(URL: `http://www.ri.cmu.edu/projects/project_418_text.html`)

- Size: 41,368 images; 68 subjects, variable number of images per subject.
- Notes: varying and tightly controlled lighting, head pose, and facial expression. Includes descriptive metadata.

FRGC2.0

(URL: `http://face.nist.gov/FRGC`)

- Size: Training partition contains 12,776 images; 275 subjects, variable number of sessions per subject, 6 images per session.
- Size: Testing partition contains 24,042 images; 466 subjects, variable number of sessions per subject, 6 images per session.

---

[1] Link was dead as of February 3, 2007.

- Notes: varying lighting and facial expression. Accompanied by the FRGC software infrastructure (Biometric Experimentation Environment). Additional color images were acquired from a 3D scanner but are not counted as 2D face images here. Subject ID encoded in file names; consistent with Notre Dame biometrics database file names.

Figure 25.1 shows a pair of images from the FRGC 2.0 database. Part (a) shows an image captured under ambient light in a hallway, and (b) contains a controlled-illumination image.

Fig. 25.1. FRGC 2.0 data samples: (a) Image 02463d254 from the FRGC 2.0 image database, depicting a human subject photographed under uncontrolled illumination. (b): Image 02463d256 from the FRGC 2.0 image database, containing a human subject photographed under controlled illumination.

Notre Dame face data

(URL: http://www.nd.edu/%7Ecvrl/UNDBiometricsDatabase.html)

- Size: two databases of face images excluding 3D images.
- Size: Collection B contains 33,247 2D color images; 487 subjects, variable number of images per subject.
- Size: Collection C contains 2,492 infrared images; 241 subjects, variable number of images per subject.
- Notes: Collection B contains ground truth and session encodings.

Figure 25.1 contains examples of images in Collection B (some images are common to both the Notre Dame collection and to the FRGC database). Figure 25.2 shows an infrared image of a human subject in database C.

AR face database

(URL: http://cobweb.ecn.purdue.edu/%7Ealeix/aleix_face_DB.html)

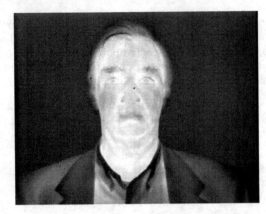

Fig. 25.2. Image 02463d349 from the Notre Dame Collection C, depicting a long-wave infrared image of a human subject.

- Size: 1534 images; 126 subjects, variable number of images per subject. Two sessions per subject.
- Notes: varying expression, lighting, glasses, head coverings.

BANCA

(URL: http://www.ee.surrey.ac.uk/Research/VSSP/banca/)

- Size: Four databases of stills.
- Database C (cooperative): 2,080 images, 52 subjects, 4 sessions, 10 images per session per subject.
- Database D (degraded): 2,080 images, 52 subjects, 4 sessions, 10 images per session per subject.
- Database A (adversarial): 2,080 images, 52 subjects, 4 sessions, 10 images per session per subject.
- WorldModel: 200 images; 40 subjects, 10 images per subject.

Yale face database B

(URL: http://cvc.yale.edu/projects/yalefacesB/yalefacesB.html)

- Size: 5,850 images; 10 subjects, 585 pose/illumination combinations per subject.
- Some metadata available.

CAS-PEAL database

(URL: http://www.jdl.ac.cn/peal/index.html)

- Size: 30,900 images; 1,040 subjects, varying number of images per subject.
- Notes: 21 pose variations per subject, plus lighting, expression, time-lapse, and other variations; subjects are all ethnic Chinese.

25.4.2 Iris Image Databases

CASIA 1.0, 2.0, 3.0 databases

(URLs:http://www.nlpr.ia.ac.cn/english/irds/irisdatabase.htm (CASIA 1.0); no URL for CASIA 2.0 (details provided when CASIA 1.0 download is authorized); http://www.cbsr.ia.ac.cn/Databases.htm (CASIA 3.0))

- CASIA 1.0 Size: 756 images; 108 eyes, 7 images per eye.
- Note: The CASIA 1.0 database images have been edited to suppress illuminant specularities in the pupil. The CASIA 3.0 database contains all of the CASIA 1.0 images in unedited form.
- CASIA 2 size: 2,400 images; 60 eyes, 20 images per eye, 2 sensors.
- CASIA 3.0 size: 22,051 images organized as three databases with largely disjoint subject groups. The "Interval" subset contains 2,655 images from 396 irises and is an unedited superset of the CASIA 1.0 database; images were acquired with a CASIA-developed sensor. The "Lamp" subset contains 16,213 images from 819 irises and an OKI Irispass camera was used to acquire images. The "Twins" database contains 3,183 images from 100 pairs of twins, and images were acquired using an OKI Irispass camera.

UPOL iris database

(URL: http://phoenix.inf.upol.cz/iris/)

- Size: 384 images; 3 images per eye, 64 subjects, both eyes. Images were acquired with a Sony DXC-950P camera.

UBIRIS database [14]

(URL: http://iris.di.ubi.pt/)

- Size: 1877 images; 241 subjects, 2 sessions.
- Note: includes controlled noise levels. Image were acquired from a Nikon E5700 camera.

Bath University iris database

(URL: http://www.bath.ac.uk/elec-eng/research/sipg/irisweb/database.htm)

- Size: 8,000 images (1,000 available free of charge); 800 irises, 400 subjects.
- Notes: images are high-resolution and stored in a proprietary compressed format. Camera type not specified.

ICE 2005 data set

(URL: http://iris.nist.gov/ICE)

- Size: 2,953 iris images; 132 individuals, varying number of images per subject.
- Note: collected from an LG 2200 iris camera.

Figure 25.3 contains an iris image from the ICE 2005 database.

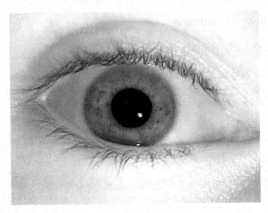

Fig. 25.3. Image 239320 from the ICE 2005 image database, containing an iris image of a cooperative human subject photographed by an LG 2200 EOU iris sensor.

25.4.3 Fingerprint Databases

NIST Fingerprint databases

(URL: http://www.itl.nist.gov/iad/894.03/databases/defs/dbases.html)

The US National Institute of Standards and Technology is to be credited for the earliest broad releases of biometrics data to the research and development community.

- Special Database 4: 2,000 fingerprint image pairs; 400 pairs from each of five classes (arch, left loop, right loop, tented arch, whorl). 8-bit grayscale images, scanned at 19.7 pixels per mm and stored in a variant of the lossless JPEG format. Cost: US$90.
- Special Database 9: five volumes with 2,700 matched tenprint card pairs in each volume. 8-bit grayscale images, scanned at 19.7 pixels per mm and stored in a variant of the lossless JPEG format. Cost: US$90 per volume.
- Special Database 10: Supplemental fingerprint data set containing samples of low-frequency and transitional fingerprints. 5,520 images, scanned at 19.7 pixels per mm and stored in a variant of the lossless JPEG format. Cost: US$90.
- Special Database 14: 27,000 mated image pairs (half are also contained in Special Database 9), scanned at 19.7 pixels per mm and stored in the wavelet scalar quantization (WSQ) fingerprint image compression format. Cost: US$90.
- Special Database 24: 200 MPEG-2 video files depicting live fingerprint scanning situations (*e.g.*, plastic distortions of the print). Cost: US$90.
- Special Database 27: 258 latent fingerprint matching cases, each consisting of a latent print, a matching tenprint image, and minutiae from the latent and matching prints (minutiae are validated by professional examiners). Data are scanned at 19.7 pixels per mm and encoded using the ANSI/NIST-ITL 1-2000 standard format. Cost: US$90.
- Special Database 29: 216 tenprint card images scanned at 19.7 pixels per mm and scored in WSQ format. Some images are repeated from Special Database 4. Cost: US$90.

- Special Database 30: 36 tenprint cards containing rolled and plain prints scanned at two resolutions (19.7 pixels per mm and 39.4 pixels per mm). Images are stored in 8-bit grayscale lossless JPEG format. Cost: US$90.

FVC Databases

Fingerprint image databases were made available for the Fingerprint Verification Competitions organized by the University of Bologna, Michigan State University, and San Jose State University in 2000, 2002, and 2004 [9, 3].

- FVC2000:   URL: http://bias.csr.unibo.it/fvc2000/default.asp. 3,520 images (four sensors, 110 fingers, 8 impressions each). Image resolutions are approximately 500 pixels per inch and image sizes vary. The data files are available as a DVD supplement to [9].
- FVC2002:   URL: http://bias.csr.unibo.it/fvc2002/default.asp. 3,520 images (four sensors, 110 fingers, 8 impressions each). Image resolutions are approximately 500 pixels per inch and image sizes vary. The data files are available as a DVD supplement to [9].
- FVC2004:   URL: http://bias.csr.unibo.it/fvc2004/default.asp. 3,520 images (four sensors, 110 fingers, 8 impressions each). The subject sets for the four sensor were almost completely disjoint. Image resolutions were about 500 pixels per inch and image sizes range from 328x364 to 260x480. Subjects were primed to vary finger moisture and placement on the sensor. The data files are available online at the URL above.
- FVC2006:   URL: http://bias.csr.unibo.it/fvc2006/default.asp. The competition is currently in progress as of this writing. Fingerprint data in this case come from the BioSec multimodal database [6], and will be made available by the organizers during 2007.

MCYT fingerprint corpus

(URL: http://atvs.ii.uam.es/bbdd_EN.html)

The fingerprint portion of the MCYT bimodal database [10] contains 79,200 fingerprint images collected from 330 subjects with two sensors (one optical and one capacitive, 12 impressions per finger, all 10 fingers per subject). A subset of 24,000 images (all images from 100 subjects) is freely. This data is available by license.

25.4.4 Speech Databases

There is a variety of digitized speech available on the Internet. Descriptions of several archives of such data in a variety of languages can be found. The YOHO database, described in [2] and available from the Linguistic Data Consortium (URL: http://www.ldc.upenn.edu), contains speech samples from 180 males and 30 females with 14 sessions of data collection each. Each session employed 24 test phrases (number-phrases that would be used to describe the setting of a combination lock). Speech samples were digitized at 8 kHz. The cost of this data depends on the profit status of the requesting institution and its status as a member of LDC. NIST has sponsored evaluations of speaker recognition systems yearly since 1996. The data for these evaluations is obtained from LDC. The corpus assembled for the DARPA TIMIT project is also a well-known speech data set (http://www.ldc.upenn.edu/Catalog/CatalogEntry.jsp?catalogId=LDC93S1).

25.4.5 Gait video

(URL: http://www.gaitchallenge.org)

Sarkar *et al.* [16] describe a baseline challenge problem assembled for gait recognition as part of the HumanID research program sponsored by the US Government. The data available to researchers interested in this challenge problem consists of 1,870 video sequences captured from 122 subjects in a variety of conditions (shoes worn, unloaded or carrying a briefcase, surface, viewpoint, and time of acquisition).

25.4.6 Other Unimodal databases

On-line signature data

As noted in [7], signature data is not routinely distributed outside of research groups. While the peripherals that capture handwriting (either as images, or as time-series data recording pen position and perhaps pressure and pen angle as a function of time) are quite affordable, meaningful comparisons require shared data. There was data assembled for the 2004 Signature Verification Competition [17] (URL: http://www.cs.ust.hk/svc2004/) which is available to researchers. The available data consists of two tasks, with 1,600 time-series captures in each task (40 subjects, 40 signatures each, half of them forgeries). The MCYT bimodal biometrics database [10] (URL: http://atvs.ii.uam.es/bbdd_EN.html) includes two corpora of signature data: an on-line collection containing 25 authentic signatures and 25 forged signatures from 330 users (all signatures from 100 users freely available by license), and an off-line collection obtained from 75 subjects with 2,250 signatures including both forgeries and genuine signatures, scanned at 600 pixels per inch. (all of them available by license).

Palmprint database

(URL: http://www.comp.polyu.edu.hk/~biometrics/)

Hong Kong Polytechnic University has developed a sensor for palmprint sensing and assembled a database to foster research in the area [18]. It contains 7,752 images captured from 386 palms, with about 10 samples captured in each of two capture sessions.

25.5 Multimodal databases

Databases assembled to support research in multimodal biometric applications have begun to appear over the last several years. A key requirement for such databases is that they represent real multimodal samples. The early practice of "chimeric" multimodal databases containing synthetic subjects (face images from one subject in one database, fingerprint images from another subject in another database, aligned so that the "subject" identity determined the identity of the source unimodal subjects) is no longer necessary in many application areas. The additional burden of collecting multimodal samples as part of a data collection effort has these aspects:

- More time is generally required for acquisition; if not well managed, subjects may react negatively to the need to wait longer for processing.
- More sensors are needed to acquire the new samples. If some modes are to be collected using rare and/or expensive sensors, sensor procurement issues may be complex, and exacerbated by the understandable desire to have a backup sensor available in case of primary sensor failure. This is easily and cheaply done in the case of a consumer-grade digital camera, but significantly more difficult in the case of commercial-grade fingerprint sensors, infrared cameras, and the like.

25.5.1 FRGC database

(URL: http://face.nist.gov/FRGC)

The FRGC/FRVT2006 technology evaluation and vendor test program conducted by the US National Institute of Standards and Technology was designed to assess commercial and research systems for multimodal face recognition. The FRGC and FRVT data corpus was collected at Notre Dame in the 2003-2004 and 2004-2005 academic years. A detailed description of the FRVT2006 data corpus will be published in the project reports, which are not available as of this writing. The color face image component of the FRGC corpus was described in Section 25.4.1. Accompanying each of the intensity image bundles in a subject-session was one 3D face image of the same subject taken within five minutes (usually within 30 seconds) of the color face images' acquisition. The 3D image was captured using a Minolta Vivid 900/910 range camera (which was chosen after a length evaluation of 3D cameras to provide the best overall data quality and resolution). The 3D image contained a 3D polygonal mesh capturing the shape of the face with a 640x480 rectangular sampling grid in the row and column coordinates and a measured depth value along the camera's optical direction. Accompanying this 3D mesh image was a color image captured a second or two after the 3D data was acquired. In the absence of subject motion, the color and 3D images were registered and the range data could be viewed as an image with a six-dimensional measurement at each pixel (except that some range pixels had no valid measurements due to shadowing of the structured light source). In practice, the images are often treated separately. The FRGC 2.0 data contains 4,960 of these 3D images (4,007 test images and 953 training images). Thus, the FRGC 2.0 data set enables research in 2D, 3D, and 2D+3D face recognition. FRGC2.0 data is available by permission of the NIST office that organized the program.

25.5.2 XM2VTS

(URL: `http://www.ee.surrey.ac.uk/Research/VSSP/xm2vtsdb/`)

The XM2VTS database was collected to support 2D and 3D face recognition, voice recognition, face recognition in video sequences, and various combinations of these modes. The data was collected at the University of Surrey and is available by license for a nominal fee to bona fide research groups. The data is distributed in multiple volumes.

- There are two volumes of face images. Each contains 1 frontal view for 295 human subjects at four acquisition sessions. The four sessions are common to the two volumes; they differ in the image retrieved from a session-specific video sequence of the head rotating.
- There is one volume of audio samples containing 7,080 16-bit 32kHz monophonic recordings obtained during the acquisition sessions of the 295 subjects. Audio has been segmented into sentences.
- One volume contains a polygonal mesh 3D head model for each of the 295 subjects.
- One volume contains profile face images and darkened face images (one of each) for the 295 subjects in 8 acquisition sessions, for a total of 2,360 images.
- One volume contains 4 frontal images of each subject present at the last of four acquisition sessions, captured under four lighting combinations.
- There are four volumes of video data available. One contains an audio/video clip from each subject speaking the same sentence at each of the four acquisition sessions. Another volume contains a video clip of the head being rotated by the subject. An additional volume contains two audio/video clips for 200 of the 295 subjects speaking two sentences containing numerical digits at four different sessions. Another volume contains two sequences per subject for 95 subjects (some posing as impostors) across four acquisition sessions.

25.5.3 BANCA database

URL: `http://www.ee.surrey.ac.uk/banca/`

The BANCA database and an associated experimental protocol were developed at a set of European Universities [1]. The BANCA database is a bimodal database containing face video and speech samples (captured simultaneously). 208 subjects were captured (52 subjects in each of four European languages). Each subject participated in 12 sessions, of which four represented a controlled (cooperative) scenario, four a degraded scenario, and four an adversarial scenario. A high-quality camera was used in the controlled and adversarial scenario, and a webcam was used in the degraded scenario. Each session contained both a genuine identity claim and an impostor claim.

25.5.4 MyIDea database

(URL: `http://diuf.unifr.ch/diva/biometrics/MyIdea/en/institutions.html`)

The MyIDea database [5] is relatively new and sponsored by the European BioSecure initiative. As of this writing, a signature + voice portion of its corpus has been made available. It contains data collected from 70 subjects and three acquisition sessions. At each session, subjects produced data representing true and false identity claims, yielding hundreds of genuine tests and thousands of impostor tests.

25.5.5 MCYT, BIOSEC, BIOSECUR-ID, and BIOSECURE databases

(URL: `http://atvs.ii.uam.es/bbdd_EN.html`)

The MCYT multimodal database bimodal database distributed by the University Autonoma de Madrid consists of fingerprint and signature data as noted above.

Although not yet available as of this writing, the European BioSec IP research project collected a multimodal database called BIOSEC with a baseline experimental component containing 19,200 fingerprint images, 1,600 face images, 11,200 speech utterances, and 3,200 iris images [6]. Additional multimodal databases (BIOSECUR-ID and BIOSECURE) will also be made available in 2007 and 2008 from other European research consortia.

25.6 Conclusions

The distribution of data by a research group may be mandated by research contract requirements, a gesture of goodwill to the research community, a promotional exercise, or some combination of these. All such efforts should be applauded and encouraged because the entire community benefits from contributions of useful data. Groups using such data have an obligation to protect it in keeping with the terms under which the data was provided, and the provider has an obligation to monitor its use and control unauthorized spread of the data. In the area of biometric data, there are special concerns associated with the implicit disclosure of identifying information in presentations and publications. The terms of distribution should be designed to protect the interests of human subject participants.

References

1. E. Bailly-Baillire, S. Bengio, F. Bimbot, M. Hamouz, J. Kittler, J. Marithoz, J. Matas, K. Messer, V. Popovici, F. Pore, B. Ruz, and J.-P. Thiran. The BANCA database and evaluation protocol. In *Proc. AVBPA 2003*, pages 625–638, Surrey, UK, 2003.
2. J. Campbell. Testing with the YOHO CD-ROM voice verification corpus. In *Proc. ICASSP*, pages 341–344, Detroit, 1995.
3. R. Cappelli, D. Maio, D. Maltoni, J.L. Wayman, and A.K. Jain. Performance evaluation of fingerprint verification systems. *IEEE Transactions on Pattern Analysis and Machine Intelligence*, 28(1):3–18, 2006.
4. S.C. Dass, Y. Zhu, and A.K. Jain. Validating a biometric authentication system: sample size requirements. *IEEE Transactions on Pattern Analysis and Machine Intelligence*, 28(12):1902–1913, 2006.

5. B. Dumas, C. Pugin, J. Hennebert, D. Petrovska-Delacrtaz, A. Humm, F. Evquoz, R. Ingold, and D. Von Rotz. MyIdea - multimodal biometrics database, description of acquisition protocols. In *Proc. of Third COST 275 Workshop (COST 275)*, pages 59–62, Hatfield (UK), October 2005.

6. Julian Fierrez, Javier Ortega-Garcia, Doroteo Torre Toledano, and Joaquin Gonzalez-Rodriguez. Biosec baseline corpus: A multimodal biometric database. *Pattern Recognition*, 40(4):1389–1392, 2007.

7. J. Fierrez-Aguilar, S. Krawczyk, J. Ortega-Garcia, and A. K. Jain. Fusion of local and regional approaches for on-line signature verification. In *Proc. International Workshop on Biometric Recognition Systems (IWBRS)*, pages 188–196, Beijing, 2005.

8. I. Guyon, J. Mokhoul, R. Schwartz, and V. Vapnik. What size test gives good error rate estimates? *IEEE Transactions on Pattern Analysis and Machine Intelligence*, 20(1):52–64, 1998.

9. D. Maltoni, D. Maio, A.K. Jain, and S. Prabhakar. *Handbook of Fingerprint Recognition*. Springer, 2003.

10. J. Ortega-Garcia, J. Fierrez-Aguilar, D. Simon, J. Gonzalez, M. Faundez-Zanuy, V. Espinoza, A. Satue, I. Hernaez, J.-J. Igarza, C. Vivaracho, D. Escudero, and Q.-I. Moro. MCYT baseline corpus: a bimodal biometric database. *IEE Proceedings–Vision, Speech and Signal Processing*, 150(6):395–401, December 2003.

11. P. J. Phillips, P. Grother, R. Micheals, D. Blackburn, E. Tabassi, and M. Bone. Face recognition vendor test 2002: Overview and summary. Technical Report 6965, National Institute of Standards and Technology, 2003.

12. P. Jonathon Phillips, Patrick J. Flynn, Todd Scruggs, Kevin W. Bowyer, Jin Chang, Kevin Hoffman, Joe Marques, Jaesik Min, and William Worek. Overview of the face recognition grand challenge. In *Proc. CVPR*, pages I:947–954, 2005.

13. P.J. Phillips. ICE2006 presentation. http://iris.nist.gov/ICE/.

14. Hugo Proena and Lus A. Alexandre. UBIRIS: A noisy iris image database. In *Proceed. of ICIAP 2005 - Intern. Confer. on Image Analysis and Processing*, volume 1, pages 970–977, 2005.

15. M. Rejman-Greene. *Privacy issues in the application of biometrics: a European perspective (Wayman, Jain, Maltoni and Maio, eds.)*, chapter 12. Springer, 2005.

16. S. Sarkar, P. Jonathon Phillips, Z. Liu, I. Robledo, P. Grother, and K. W. Bowyer. The Human ID Gait Challenge problem: Data sets, performance, and analysis. *IEEE Transactions on Pattern Analysis and Machine Intelligence*, 27(2):162–177, 2005.

17. Dit-Yan Yeung, Hong Chang, Yimin Xiong, Susan George, Ramanujan Kashi, Takashi Matsumoto, and Gerhard Rigoll. SVC2004: First international signature verification competition. In *Proceedings of the International Conference on Biometric Authentication (ICBA)*, pages 16–22, Hong Kong, 2004.

18. David Zhang, Wai-Kin Kong, Jane You, and Michael Wong. On-line palmprint identification. *IEEE Transactions on Pattern Analysis and Machine Intelligence*, 25(9):1041–1050, 2003.

Index